Oswald Chambers

OSWALD CHAMBERS

THE BEST FROM ALL HIS BOOKS

Chosen and Edited by Harry Verploegh

OLIVER NELSON

A Division of Thomas Nelson Publishers
Nashville • Atlanta • Camden • Kansas City

For
Our Children
Virginia and Case
"Our Legacy from the Lord"

RUTH AND HARRY VERPLOEGH

Published in Nashville, Tennessee, by Oliver-Nelson Books, a division of Thomas Nelson, Inc., Publishers, and distributed in Canada by Lawson Falle, Ltd., Cambridge, Ontario.

Printed in the United States.

Library of Congress Cataloging-in-Publication Data

Chambers, Oswald, 1874-1917.
    Oswald Chambers : the best from all his books.

    Includes index.
    2. Theology—Quotations, maxims, etc. 2. Chambers,
Oswald, 1874-1917—Quotations. I. Verploegh, Harry.
II. Title
BR96.C452   1987   240   87-1674
ISBN 0-8407-9007-4

1 2 3 4 5 6 7 8—92 91 90 89 88 87

Contents

Foreword

"One individual life may be of priceless value to God's purposes, and yours may be that life."

How unforgettably true these words were in my parents' lives— the spoken words became books as God's purposes were fulfilled. All my father's messages were *spoken* and the printed pages come from my mother's shorthand notes of those messages.

May God bless all those who gave of their time and prayer in preparing this anthology, and may the voice of God's love and power speak out of every page.

KATHLEEN M. CHAMBERS

Introduction

Oswald Chambers was remembered as a child for his readiness to pray and his confidence that God would answer his prayers, but it was not until his teenage years that prayer became the working of the miracle of Redemption in him. Chambers was born on July 24, 1874, in Aberdeen, the fourth son of Clarence and Hannah Chambers. Hannah had been raised an Irvingite but became a Baptist under Spurgeon. Oswald's father was pastor of the Crown Terrace Baptist Church in Aberdeen, and later ministered in Stoke-on-Trent, Perth, and London.

As a boy Chambers studied drawing at Sharp's Institute in Perth. After hearing Spurgeon preach in Dulwich, the city where his father retired, Chambers asked to be baptised and began visiting men in the YMCA lodging house. He won an arts scholarship to study abroad from the Art School in South Kensington, but instead took the Arts Course at the University of Edinburgh until he decided at twenty-three to follow the counsel of a number of Scottish men of God, who were aware of his spiritual gifts and encouraged him to accept God's call to the ministry.

He attended the Dunoon Training School, founded by Duncan MacGregor, and within a year became a tutor in philosophy and psychology, taught art, and formed a Browning Society. Chambers became known at Dunoon as a man of prayer who relied unequivocally on God to supply his needs. He was admired for his love of art and poetry, his radiant disposition, and his generosity to others. At this time he began to speak in open air meetings. He worked in city missions and taught Sunday school.

After seven years of study and teaching, Chambers left Dunoon in 1905. In that same year he met Bishop Juji Nakada, the Japanese evangelist, at a Pentecostal League meeting in Perth. Together these two men, Chambers, long "like a poker," and Nakada, "short like a shovel," planned to stir up the Spirit of God among the Holiness people in an evangelistic tour of America and Japan. Of this tour in 1906 1907, Chambers wrote in his diary that he felt a perfect sense of God's call and leading as one of "the Lord's spoilt bairns" who was being introduced in Brooklyn, Providence, Cincinnati, and Seattle to "choice souls." In considering the evangelist's work he wrote,

> The goodness of God strikes me. People don't know Him, but it is not
> a wicked ignoring, it is ignorance. The full compassionate love of the
> Holy Ghost for the crowd is a precious, though intolerable compas-
> sion.

During his tour of Japan, Chambers visited the Oriental Mission Bible
Society in Tokyo and several interior mission stations. He preached
and witnessed the mighty preaching of Nakada.

Upon returning to London via Hong Kong, the Suez, Rome, and Paris,
Chambers continued evangelistic work with the League of Prayer and
made the acquaintance of the family of the Reverend David Lambert,
then a junior minister in Sunderland. Lambert became one of the circle
around Gertrude Chambers who later helped publish Chambers' messages, lectures, and prayers and who in the 1970s published a valuable
account of Chambers' life and works, *Oswald Chambers: An Unbribed Soul*. David Lambert wrote of the Chambers of this period of
evangelistic preaching that

> at the big London meetings he would find an odd corner to be alone
> with God before speaking in public. Now I know how much prepara-
> tion there had been in years of discipline, and Christ-following, and
> strenuous thinking. I did not know it then, yet felt that there was
> insight and authority and spiritual power far above that of the average
> minister or missioner.

In the years 1911–1915 preceding his principleship of the Bible Training School near Clapham Common, London, Chambers preached and
taught many missions for the League of Prayer in England, Scotland,
and Ireland. He began to develop some of the characteristic emphases
of his ministry. He stressed the artificiality of man-made religion. He
insisted on God's high intention of blessing toward the lowliest and
most ordinary Christian who abandons himself or herself in faith to
Jesus Christ and makes an absolute commitment to the Word of God.
He believed in disciplined study of the humanities as well as of the
Bible lest the student learn no method to study God's Word and be
forced, in Chambers' terms, to wander aimlessly in it as in a cultivated
park. He stressed the importance of seeking a means of applying the
experience of sanctification in practical Christian service.

Chambers' own characteristic readiness for God's use is demon-
strated in a comment he made to H. Stark upon arriving in Plymouth
for meetings: "I hope we shall have a very blessed week-end, Mr.
Chambers," said Stark. Chambers replied, "If we behave ourselves, the
Lord will help Himself to all He wants from us."

In the spring of 1910 Chambers married Gertrude Hobbs ("Biddy"), the woman who would later use her language skills to publish Oswald Chambers' manuscripts and her notes of his lectures, sermons, and talks after his death, including the devotional classic, *My Utmost for His Highest,* which she compiled.

After their marriage, Mrs. Chambers accompanied Chambers on a four-month mission to the United States. On their return, Chambers settled into his work as Principal of the new nondenominational Bible Training College for the education of home and foreign workers founded in Battersea, London, the center of the League of Prayer. After Chambers' death, student after student wrote of the special features of Chambers' leadership of the school in the five years before he went to the Eastern front as a chaplain for the YMCA. As a teacher Chambers knew instinctively which students could not be forced to change their pet theories and required only his listening ear and patience to develop new understanding and which students needed a devastating but salutary blow to their prejudices and pettinesses. Chambers was a beloved example to them of child like trust in God and self-discipline ("Get out of bed and think about it afterwards" he would advise) and of a rare balance between flexibility and strength in both spiritual and practical matters.

At the outbreak of World War I, Chambers felt a deep and urgent need to exercise his ministry among the British forces but waited patiently for almost nine months for the details to fall into place. Between the fall of 1915 and his death in November 1917, Chambers established two desert mission camps for British troops in Egypt at Zeitoun, nine miles from Cairo and at Ismailia, on the banks of the Suez Canal.

These places of peace in the midst of war preparation were built of native rush mats. The Zeitoun camp included a refreshment marquee for soldiers, a devotional hut for worship services, a smaller hut where Chambers and his assistants conducted Bible classes, a tiny "items" hut where stationery and books were sold, and a dugout. The Chambers family, which now included the tiny Kathleen and their devoted helper, Mary Riley, lived in a bungalow built for them. There they entertained a constant stream of guests. Former students from the Bible Training College assisted Chambers with the administration of the camp activities and the care of souls.

During his two-year ministry in Egypt, Chambers kept a diary where he recorded his early morning thoughts, activities of the day, plans for Bible studies or talks, the responses of his audiences, and encounters with individuals. Sixteen years after his death, extracts from this diary were published with many tributes to his influence on the Mediterranean Expeditionary Forces in *Oswald Chambers: His Life and Work*. With a painter's eye, Chambers repeatedly described the sunrise on the desert, sublime and dazzling with praise to God, a "sealing witness of peace," and at other times a scene of desperate turmoil about which he could be equally delighted:

> This morning is thick with Khamseen wind. As I write, the sky is a most formidable colour, dense lurid copper, and the wind is rampaging with the old antique heat of leagues of desert, not a heat like the sun's heat, but the heat of blinding devastation. . . .

Chambers found his work among the men and the activity of the desert camps constantly invigorating. Of the sunrise near the Suez, he wrote:

> The splendor of these sunrises is unique. . . . All the noises of the camp are stirring and fine, the men are astir at 4 A.M., the stir, the movement of horses, the bugles, the whirr of aeroplanes, all makes this life a real delight to me somehow.

And of an Egyptian noon in July, Chambers noted:

> Sun! I have been considering it. One cannot conceive of such sun unless one has summered in Egypt. It is the only power that makes this land possibly habitable. It is fierce, appallingly so, but fascinating; my own experience is that desert life is productive of intense vitality and energy, not of languor.

Boundless energy and vitality is precisely what Chambers gave to thousands of soldiers from all parts of the Commonwealth who passed through the YMCA mission camps. Living in the discomfort of military bases, their futures uncertain, many afterwards gave tribute to the eloquence and spiritual influence of this gifted man of God. Douglas Downes described Chambers at work in Egypt:

> One of my early memories of Oswald Chambers is that of a lithe figure in khaki, with the eyes of a prophet and the profile of a Savaronola, seated with a group of younger men at a table in the Central YMCA in Cairo. He is telling them in his delightful, sparkling, humorous way that he cannot see the need of so much entertainment stuff to keep the men together of an evening. Out there in his hut at Zeitoun he can get a crowd of Australians night after night attracted by nothing but the message of Redemption.
> I went over to Zeitoun, and found the unheard-of thing had come to

pass. Men whom no one could accuse of being religious turned up in large numbers on a week-night to hear a religious talk. But it is no ordinary talk, and the man who gives it is no ordinary man. There is no appeal to the emotions, no cant religious phrases, no anecdotes, just a flow of clear convincing reasoning—stark sincerity, speaking with the authority of deep personal experience; you are brought to the point where the natural man breaks down and where the supernatural must come in to carry you with its confidence right into the presence of God.

Men who visited the mission huts used similar words to describe Chambers' discernment of biblical truth as well as of human need. They mentioned his "penetrating gaze," his keen and alert face, his "canny" understanding of individual men. Many remembered the personal words of comfort Chambers gave them on their departure for front lines in Palestine or France. Others were visited by him while laid aside in hot canvas hospitals. He was for more than one soldier a "detective of the soul, one who has been in intimate fellowship with the unseen." With others who have written of the heightened intensity that war brings to the experience of life, Chambers knew that with many men bound for the front, irresponsible pleasure-seeking would end and stern issues would confront them. He relished the opportunity to speak to them at a time when they would be more open to talk about God and the soul, when the faith of many would be strained. He insisted that in the midst of life-threatening circumstances, a soldier could maintain an unchanging relationship to God through the redemptive work of Christ.

Throughout the period of his chaplaincy Chambers would not allow the disruption, devastation, and death that impinged on his consciousness and crippled many spirits working near the front to undermine his natural buoyancy and confidence in God's sovereignty. He was steadfast in his belief that "the lack of ability and master-mindedness to conduct the war" was an occasion for men to cast themselves on God and find His order in the "haphazard" of ordinary experience or in the midst of an appalling war when hundreds of thousands of men would be battered into eternity.

Chambers was aware, however, that his confidence in God's ends could seem like indifference to the senses of others assaulted by the horror and the contradictions of war. Together with the soldiers who visited the YMCA camps, he probed the meaning of war to men of faith, lecturing boldly on such topics as "Religious Problems Raised by War," "Is Human Sacrifice Redemptive?", "Has History Disproved the

Song of the Angels?" (a Christmas talk), and "Does War Create or Reveal Wickedness?" Chambers read other men's attempts to sustain a Christian hope in wartime and was particularly helped by Denny's *War and the Fear of God* and Forsyth's *The Christian Ethics of War.*

At one point in his diary, Chambers recorded his mistaken intuition that the war would end by late 1916. Chambers found that his miscalculation was an indication that "the Holy Spirit must be recognized as the sagacious Ruler in all affairs, and not our astute common sense." In his own experience and in his detailed study of the Old Testament prophets in the last months of his life, Chambers found God's ways inscrutable, but that in the mystery of Redemption.

> God is prepared to run the risk of evil, so to speak, and the Cross is the proof that He Himself has taken the responsibility of its removal.

With many Christians of the Great War period, Chambers looked with amazement, wonder, and tears at the great bravery of the young men who, made of "grand human stuff," withstood the wrath and chaos of war. He prayed that their sacrifices would be acts of worship mirroring the obedience of Christ's painful sacrifice as the means of God's redeeming work. In the last weeks of his life, Chambers meditated on Israel's history as seen through the eyes of the prophets Hosea, Joel, and Amos and considered the spectacle of human evil in his own time. He noted that Amos ascribes to God the power to effect "blasting and mildew and disease and pestilence and error and wrong." He concluded with Amos that all these occurrences are beyond the control of man, that all the consequences are in the "powerful hand of God, and not of blind cause and effect." Again and again Chambers recorded his "joyful detection of God's ruling in the haphazard" in his diary. A month before his death, on a glorious morning when the East was "like a celestial scheme of shot silk" Chambers' heart sprang up to the call of the prophet Amos:

> Seek him that maketh the Pleiades and Orion, and maketh the day dark with night, and turneth the shadow of death into the morning. (Amos 4:8)

In the entries for October 1917, one senses that Chambers had extended himself to the limit of God's requirement. Twice he had to lump diary entries together for lack of opportunity to write. He persuaded Swan, a colleague in the YMCA mission, to lecture on Islam for him. Then in preparation for a mission to Palestine to minister to the wounded and dying for General Allenby, he asked Mrs. Chambers to conduct services and rejoiced in the "lift" of inspiration he felt at those she led. By November 15, 1917, Oswald Chambers was at rest from the intense labor of biblical interpretation and spiritual counsel he fulfilled for the church in the period of the Great War.

It is hoped that this new anthology of excerpts from the Chambers publications will introduce a rising generation of Christians to the profound themes this gifted and faithful teacher explored during his vital ministry in God's joy and under His hand in the second decade of this century.

VIRGINIA VERPLOEGH STEINMETZ

Key to Sources

Quotations are followed by letter codes with numbers that indicate the title of the work from which the extract is taken and the page number on which it appears. For example,

> The way our heart is hardened is by sticking to our convictions instead of to Christ. GW. 38

The letters GW indicate the quotation is taken from *God's Workmanship*; the number 38 indicates the quotation is found on page 38 of that work.

Following are the letter codes used in this collection to refer to the works of Oswald Chambers. All the books were first published by Christian Literature Crusade in Fort Washington, Pennsylvania. The copyright year follows each title.

AUG	*Approved unto God*, 1946
BE	*Biblical Ethics*, 1947
BFB	*Baffled to Fight Better*, 1931
BP	*Biblical Psychology*, 1962
BSG	*Bringing Sons unto Glory*, 1943
CD. VOL. 1	*Christian Discipline*, Vol. 1, 1936
CD. VOL. 2	*Christian Discipline*, Vol. 2, 1936
CHI	*Conformed to His Image*, 1950
DI	*Disciples Indeed*, 1955
GW	*God's Workmanship*, 1953
HG	*The Highest Good*, 1938
HGM	*He Shall Glorify Me*, 1946
IWP	*If Thou Wilt Be Perfect*, 1941
IYA	*If Ye Shall Ask*, 1958
LG	*The Love of God*, 1938
MFL	*The Moral Foundations of Life*, 1966
NKW	*Not Knowing Whither*, 1934
OBH	*Our Brilliant Heritage*, 1929
OPG	*Our Portrait in Genesis*, 1957

A

ABANDONMENT

Abandon to the love of Christ is the one thing that bears fruit. Personal holiness may easily step over into sanctified Pharisaism, but abandon to the love of God will always leave the impression of the holiness and the power of God. AUG. 31

When God's voice will come you do not know, but whenever the realization of God comes again in the faintest way imaginable, recklessly abandon. It is only by abandon that you find Him. GW. 58

There are pietistic movements started by certain forms of vision which are characterized by fasting and times of prayer and devotion, but they are the antipodes of everything Jesus Christ taught. Jesus Christ taught absolute abandonment to Himself and identification with His aims. The test of all spiritual vision is, 'That I may know Him.' GW. 133

The great aim of the Holy Spirit is to get us abandoned to God. HGM. 78

When a soul abandons to God, God will not abandon it. NKW. 145

Abandon to God is of more value than personal holiness. Personal holiness focuses our eyes on our own whiteness; when we are abandoned to God, He works through us all the time. PH. 142

Assurance of faith is never gained by reserve but only by abandonment. PH. 209

We must abandon to God at all costs. Abandon is of infinitely more value than self-scrutiny. PR. 94

The weakest saint can experience the power of the Deity of the Son of God if he is willing to 'let go.' PR. 116

The characteristic of the saintly life is abandon to God, not a settling down on our own whiteness. God is not making hot-house plants, but sons and daughters of God, men and women with a strong family likeness to Jesus Christ. PR. 116

What is needed in spiritual matters is reckless abandonment to the Lord Jesus Christ, reckless and uncalculating abandonment, with no reserve anywhere about it; not sad, you cannot be sad if you are abandoned absolutely. PS. 23

No man can abandon to Jesus Christ without an amazing humiliation to his own self-importance. We are all tremendously important until the Holy Ghost takes us in hand, then we cease to be important and God becomes all-important. SHL. 80

God can do what He likes with the man who is abandoned to Him. SSM. 73

Many of us are subtly serving our own ends, and Jesus Christ cannot help Himself to our lives; if I am abandoned to Jesus, I have no ends of my own to serve. SSY. 22

ABIDING

Our Lord did not say, 'Ask God that you may abide in Me;' He said "Abide in Me," it is something we have to do. Abiding in Jesus embraces physical, mental and moral phases as well as spiritual. MFL. 38

We have to form the habit of abiding until we come into the relationship with God where we rely upon Him almost unconsciously in every particular. MFL. 39

The secret of bringing forth fruit is to abide in Jesus. "Abide in Me," says Jesus, in spiritual matters, in intellectual matters, in money matters, in every one of the matters that make human life what it is. OBH. 107

Begin to abide *now!* In the initial stage abiding is a continual effort until it becomes so much of the law of our lives that we abide in Him unconsciously. OBH. 107

We must get into the habit of constantly realizing the Atonement, of centralizing everything there. To concentrate causes consciousness of effort to begin with. *"Abide in Me,"* says Jesus. It is imperative on our part that we abide in Jesus. OBH. 121

If we are abiding in Jesus, we shall ask what He wants us to ask whether we are conscious of doing so or not. "Ye shall ask what ye *will,*" i.e., what your will is in. OBH. 122

The disciple who is in the condition of abiding in Jesus *is* the will of God, and his apparent free choices are God's foreordained decrees. Mysterious? Logically absurd? But a glorious truth to a saint. OBH. 122

ABILITY

It is folly to think that because a man has natural ability, he must make a good Christian. People with the best natural equipment may make the worst disciples because they will 'boss' themselves. PH. 180

It is not a question of our equipment, but of our poverty; not what we bring with us, but what He puts in us; not our natural virtues, our strength of character, our knowledge, our experience; all that is of no avail in this matter; the only thing that is of avail is that we are taken up into the big compelling of God and made His comrade. His comradeship is made out of men who know their poverty. God can do nothing with the men who think they will be of use to Him. PH. 180

When it is a question of God's Almighty Spirit, never say "I can't". Never let the limitation of natural ability come in. If we have received the Holy Spirit, God expects the work of the Holy Spirit to be manifested in us. RTR. 89

ACTION

We are never justified in taking any line of action other than that indicated by the teaching of Jesus and made possible for us by the grace of God. DI. 71

The most unwholesome people spiritually are those who like to have their emotions stirred by prayer meetings and devotional readings, but they never act them out. GW. 142

Frequently God has to say to us—'Say no more to Me on this matter; don't everlastingly cry to Me about this thing, do it yourself, keep your forces together and go forward.' God is for you, the Spirit of God is in you, and every place that the sole of your foot shall tread upon, shall be yours. MFL. 41

God does what we cannot do: He alters the mainspring and plants in us a totally new disposition; then begins our work, we must work out what God works in. The practising is ours, not God's. MFL. 52

If God tells us to awake, we must get into the habit of awakening. We have to wake up physically before we can wake up spiritually. When God tells us to do a thing He empowers us to do it, only we must do the doing. MFL. 76

. . . in Christian work we are suffering from a phase of spiritual dyspepsia that emphasises *doing*. The great thing *to do* is *to be* a believer in Jesus. With Jesus it is never *"Do, do"* but *"Be, be* and I will do through you." OBH. 55

Don't let the sense of failure corrupt your new action. RTR. 48

The next best thing to do is to ask, if you have not received; to seek, if you have not found; to knock if the door is not opened to you. RTR. 68

So many people are obsessed with this idea—'What are you going to *do*?' I hope none of us are going to *do* anything: I hope we are going to *be* what He wants us to be. SSY. 135

ACTIVITY

It is not what a man *does* that is of final importance, but what he *is* in what he does. The atmosphere produced by a man, much more than his activities, has the lasting influence. BFB. 20

Beware of Christian *activities* instead of Christian *being*. The reason workers come to stupendous collapses is that their work is the evidence of a heart that evades facing the truth of God for itself—'I have no time for prayer, for Bible study, I must be always at it'. DI. 87

The measure of the worth of our public activity to God is the private, profound communion we have with Him. NKW. 19

The people who are always desperately active are a nuisance; it is through the saints who are one with Him that God is doing things all the time. The broken and the jaded and the twisted are being ministered to by God through the saints who are not overcome by their own panic, who because of their oneness with Him are absolutely at rest, consequently He can work through them. PH. 41

In the Christian life it is never 'Do, do but 'Be, be, and I will do through you. PH. 67

. . . through an overplus of Christian activities, Jesus Christ is being dethroned in hearts and Christian wits and wisdom are taking His place . . . PR. 70

We may be taken up with the activities of a denomination, or be giving ourselves up to this committee and that, whilst all about us people are ripe unto harvest and we do not reap one of them, but waste our Lord's time in over-energized activities for furthering some cause or denomination. SSY. 128

3

ADAM

Adam was not afraid of God; he was not afraid of the beasts of the field, or of anything, because there was no consciousness of himself apart from God. Immediately he disobeyed, he became conscious of himself and he felt afraid . . . BE. 82

It is impossible for us to conceive what Adam was like as God made him—his material body instinct with spiritual light, his flesh in the likeness of God, his soul in absolute harmony with God, and his spirit in the image of God. BP. 15

There is quite sufficient to indicate that when Adam's spirit, soul and body were united in perfect faith and love to God, his soul was the medium through which the marvellous life of the Spirit of God was brought down. The very image of God was brought down into his material body and it was clothed in an inconceivable splendour of light until the whole man was in the likeness of God. The moment he disobeyed, the connection with God was shut off, and spirit, soul and body tumbled into death that instant. The fact of dissolving into dust in a few years' time is nothing more than death visible. BP. 25

God turned man out of the garden of Eden into destitution, but in turning him out He put him on the way to become an infinitely grander and nobler being than even Adam was at the first. The whole Bible, from Genesis to Revelation, instead of being a picture of despair is the very opposite. The worst is always 'bettered' by God. God as it were, took His hand off man and let Satan do the very worst that diabolical spiritual genius could do. Satan knew what would happen, he knew that God would have to punish man, and God did punish him, but with the perfect certainty that the being that was to come out of the ordeal of the fall would be greater than the first Adam. BP. 26

When Adam sinned his union with God was cut off, and God turned him out of the garden and guarded the way to the tree of life, that is to say, God prevented Adam from getting back as a fallen being. If Adam had got back to the tree of life as a fallen being, he would have become an incarnate devil, and God would have been finally thwarted with man; but when Adam was driven out, God placed Cherubims and a gleaming sword to keep the way of the tree of life. BP. 27

It is impossible for us to conceive what Adam was like before the Fall; his body must have been dazzling with light through his spiritual communion with God. When he took his rule over himself he not only lost his communion with God, lost the covering of glory and light inconceivable to us, he lost the dominion God intended him to have had—"Thou madest him to have dominion over the works of Thy hands." CHI. 13

Adam switched off from God's design, instead of maintaining his dependence on God he took his rule over himself, and thereby introduced sin into the world. Sin is not wrong doing, it is wrong *being*, deliberate and emphatic independence of God. CHI. 16

God intended that Adam should develop, not from evil to good, but from the natural to the spiritual, by obedience; it was to be a natural progress; but Adam stopped short, and sin entered in by his stopping short. GW. 83

Adam represented what Jesus Christ represents, viz., the whole human race, and if Adam had obeyed and transformed his innocence into holiness by a series of moral choices, the transfiguration of the human race would have happened in due course. But Adam disobeyed, and there entered in the disposition of sin, the disposition of self-realisation—I am my own God. PR. 75

Adam was created to be the friend and companion of God; he was to have dominion over all the life in the air and earth and sea, but one thing he was not to have dominion over, and that was himself. SA. 115

ADAM AND EVE

Adam and Eve are both needed before the image of God can be perfectly presented. God is, as it were, all that the best manhood presents us with, and all that the best womanhood presents us with. BP. 6

In thinking of man and woman as they were first created, it is extremely difficult, especially nowadays, to present the subject without introducing small, petty and disreputable ideas relative to the distinctions between man and woman. In Adam and Eve we are dealing with the primal creations of God. Adam was created immediately by the hand of God; Eve was created mediately. Eve stands for the soul side, the psychic side, of the human creation; all her sympathies and affinities were with the other creations of God around. Adam stands for the spirit side, the kingly, Godward side. Adam and Eve together are the likeness of God, "And God said, Let us make man in our image, . . . male and female, created He them." The revelation made here is not that woman stands as inferior to man, but that she

stands in quite a different relation to all things, and that both man and woman are required for the complete creation of God referred to by the big general term 'Man.' BP. 18

The Bible says that Eve was deceived, it does not say that Adam was deceived; consequently Adam is far more responsible than Eve because he sinned deliberately. There was no conscious intention to disobey in Eve's heart, she was deceived by the subtle wisdom of Satan *via* the serpent. Adam, however, was not deceived, he sinned with a deliberate understanding of what he was doing; so the Bible associates 'sin' with Adam and 'transgression' with Eve. BP. 19

It is a familiar revelation fact to us that there was no rebellion in Adam and Eve. They did not fight against God, they simply went out of the garden covered with fear and shame. Satan was the originator of sin; Adam was not. Adam accepted the way Eve had been deceived and sinned with his eyes open, and instantly an extraordinary thing happened: "they knew that they were naked." BP. 25

Satan was part of God's natural creation, he spoke to the woman first, who represented all we understand by the affinities of a human soul for the natural life, unsuspecting, unsuspicious, sympathetic and curious. PS. 11

ADAM, First and Second

Jesus Christ, the last Adam, did what the first Adam failed to do; He transformed innocence into holy character. The law of God was incarnated in Jesus Christ, He walked this earth in human guise and lived the perfect life which God desired. Never think of Jesus

Christ as an individual, He is the Federal Head of the race; He not only fulfilled all God's demands, but He made the way for every imperfect son of man to live the same kind of life. Jesus Christ does not put us back where Adam was, He puts us where Adam never was: He puts us where He is Himself; He presences us with Divinity, viz., the Holy Spirit. BE. 15

Adam was created a son of God, that is, he was innocent in relation to God, and God intended him to take part in his own development by a series of moral choices whereby he was to sacrifice the natural life to the spiritual. If Adam had done this there would have been no death, but transfiguration, as in Jesus Christ, the last Adam. But Adam refused to let God be his Ruler; he took his right to himself and became his own god, thereby cutting himself off from the domain of God. BE. 44

We are not the sons of God by natural generation. Adam did not come into the world as we do; neither did Adam come into the world as Jesus Christ came. Adam was not 'begotten'; Jesus Christ was. Adam was 'created.' God created Adam, He did not beget him. We are all generated, we are not created beings. Adam was the "son of God," and God created him as well as everything else that was created. BP. 6

The first Adam and the last Adam came direct from the hand of God. BSG. 10

Adam was intended by God to partake in his own development by sacrificing the life of nature to the will of God, and in that way to transform innocence into holiness. Our Lord came on the same plane as Adam and He did all that Adam failed to do; He transformed innocence into holy character, and when He had reached the full purpose of His Manhood He was transfigured. BSG. 36

A saint is "a new creation", made by the Last Adam out of the progeny of the first Adam no matter how degraded. DI. 63

The Son of God came to alter the basis of human life: the first Adam put it on a wrong basis, the basis of self-realization; Jesus Christ makes the basis Redemptive. The Redemption means that God paid the price of sin. GW. 83

The first Adam came in the flesh, not in sinful flesh: Jesus Christ, the last Adam, came on the plane of the first Adam; He partook of our nature but not of our sin. MFL. 105

The Bible only mentions two men— Adam and Jesus Christ, and it is the last Adam Who rehabilitates the human race. SA. 15

The Bible states that God made man, i.e., the Federal Head of the race, in His own image. The only other Being in the image of God is Jesus Christ, the Second Adam. By eating of the fruit of the tree of knowledge of good and evil, Adam knew evil positively and good negatively. The Second Adam never ate of the fruit of the tree; He knew evil negatively by positively knowing good, and when a man is reborn of the Spirit of God he finds that that is the order God intended. Until we are born again we know good only by contrast with evil. The bias of the human heart is to find out the bad things first. SHH. 110

Jesus Christ carried out all that Adam failed to do, and He did it in the simple way of obedience to His Father. SHL. 67

6

ADVENT, Second

In Bible revelation there is always a Coming Age, a Coming Day, a Coming Prophet, a Coming One—a perennial Coming. GW. 88

Ages will fade into foolish fancies beside the wonder of that blessed Age, that blessed period of Christ's reign among men. We have to remain stedfastly certain in Him, not go out of Him to see when He is coming; it is to be prophetic *living* as well as prophetic study. To the saint everything is instinct with the purpose of God. History is fulfilling prophecy all the time. GW. 89

If we dwell much on the Second Coming without having a right spiritual relationship to God, it will make us ignore the need for spiritual tenacity. GW. 136

When our Lord does come, He will come quickly, and we will find He has been there all the time. One of the greatest strains in life is the strain of waiting for God. GW. 136

The only way to wait for the Second Coming is to watch that you do what you should do so that *when* He comes is a matter of indifference. It is the attitude of a child, certain that God knows what He is about. When the Lord does come it will be as natural as breathing. God never does anything hysterical, and He never produces hysterics. OPG. 23

AFFECTATION

If we are not concentrated we affect a great many attitudes; but when we 'set our faces unto the Lord God' all affectation is gone—the religious pose, the devout pose, the pious pose, all go instantly when we determine to con-

centrate; our attention is so concentrated that we have no time to wonder how we look. HGM. 71

Beware of affectation spiritually, it is the very paw of the devil over the saint. HGM. 133

AFFLICTION

The actual things in life are sordid and decaying and wrong and twisted, but we do not look at them, we look at the eternal things beyond, and the consequence is that in the actual tribulations and circumstances of the moment, pain works for us an eternal hope. We have all had the experience that it is only in the days of affliction that our true interests are furthered. PH. 155

"Our light affliction . . ."—To escape affliction is a cowardly thing to do; to sink under it is natural; to get at God through it is a spiritual thing. Most of us have tried the first, a good many of us have known the second, and the Spirit of God in us knows the third, getting through into the weight of glory. PH. 156

There are disasters to be faced by the one who is in real fellowship with the Lord Jesus Christ. God has never promised to keep us immune from trouble; He says "I will be with him in trouble", which is a very different thing. RTR. 39

On the top of those very billows, which look as if they would overwhelm us, walks the Son of God. RTR. 43

If God has made your cup sweet, drink it with grace; if He has made it bitter, drink it in communion with Him. RTR. 49

God will put you through many mills that are not meant for you, mills you

7

would not be put through but that He wants to make you good bread for His little ones to eat. You can see now the meaning of that hard place you have been in. RTR. 80

The afflictions after sanctification are not meant to purify us, but to make us broken bread in the Hands of our Lord to nourish others. RTR. 82

AGNOSTICISM

Agnosticism is not always the deplorable thing it is imagined to be. An acknowledged intellectual agnosticism is a healthy thing; the difficulty arises when agnosticism is not acknowledged. To be an agnostic means I recognize that there is more than I know, and that if I am ever to know more, it must be by revelation. BFB. 37

ALONENESS

The friendship of a soul who walks alone with God is as abiding as God Himself, and, in degree, as terrible. CD. VOL. 2, 65

Loneliness marks the child of God. CD. VOL. 2, 67

You cannot become a disciple of Jesus Christ as a rich man, or as a landed proprietor, or as a man of splendid reputation, or as a man of good name and family. The only road to Jesus is ALONE. CD. VOL. 2, 74

The sad eyes of the Son of God lure us into the wilderness alone, and these questions ring in our hearts. From all desire for position, place, power, from every pedestal of devotion, or dedication, or deed, He draws and separates us; and suddenly we discern what He wants, deeper than tongue can express,

and obedience to the heavenly vision, arising from an abandonment of love to Himself, leads us to heaven. Not as faithful friends, or as moral men, or as devout souls, or as righteous men— Jesus separates us from all these positions by an unbridgeable distance when He is making clear to us that we must leave ALL. These lonely moments are given to each of us. CD. VOL. 2, 80

Alone with God! It is there that what is hid with God is made known—God's ideals, God's hopes, God's doings. The intense individual responsibility of walking amongst men from the standpoint of being alone with the real God, is never guessed until we do stand alone with God. It is a hidden thing, so hidden that it seems not only untenable but a wild quixotic thing to do, and so it would be if God were not known to be real. CD. VOL. 2, 120

It is one thing to go through a crisis grandly, and another thing to go through every day glorifying God when nobody is paying any attention to you. RTR. 51

AMBITION

The natural reaction of ambition in a man or woman saved by God's grace is that they will not be beaten by anything the world, the flesh or the devil can put in the way of their fulfilling God's idea for them. MFL. 73

In our natural life our ambitions are our own. In the Christian life we have no aim of our own, and God's aim looks like missing the mark because we are too short-sighted to see what He is aiming at. PH. 177

Don't make the ambition of your life in accordance with your old human nature, but be the children of the Highest—put your concentration on the things of God. Jesus Christ is not simply making fine characters or virtuous men; His end and aim is that we may be the children of our Father in heaven (Matthew v. 48). PR. 46

My worth to God in public is what I am in private. Is my master ambition to please Him and be acceptable to Him, or is it something else, no matter how noble? RTR. 36

ANARCHY

The Bible reveals that there is anarchy somewhere, real thorough-going anarchy in the heart of men against God; therefore the need is strong that something should come into us from the outside to readjust us, to reconcile us, to turn us round, to put us right with God. The doctrine of the Atonement is the explanation of how God does that. The doctrine of the Atonement is that "while we were yet sinners, Christ died for us". BE. 119

In the New Testament this spirit of anarchy is called "the old man," "the carnal mind," which, until it is crucified by identification with the Cross of Christ, will continually rebel and vex His Holy Spirit. It is this spirit of anarchy that has confused the interpretation of God's dealings with men. CD. VOL. 2, 136

Every other view of sin, saving the Bible view, looks on sin as a disease, a weakness, a blunder, an infirmity; the Bible revelation shows sin to be an anarchy, not a missing of the mark merely, but a refusal to aim at the mark. CD. VOL. 2, 137

When you get the nature of sin revealed by the Holy Spirit, you know that this phrase is not too strong—red-handed anarchy against God. GW. 83

None of us is conscious of this spirit of anarchy against God; the devil is the only being in whom sin is absolute, conscious anarchy. GW. 83

The great element in sin is defiance against God. SA. 105

This is the result in civilization of Adam's sin. Sin is red-handed anarchy against God. Not one in a thousand understands *sin*; we understand only about sins on the physical line, which are external weaknesses. In the common-sense domain sin does not amount to much; sin belongs to the real domain. The sin the Bible refers to is a terrific and powerful thing, a deliberate and emphatic independence of God and His claim to me, *self-realization*. SA. 116

Anarchy is the very nature of sin as the Bible reveals it. SA. 116

ANGELS

The phrase "sons of God" in the Old Testament always refers to angels, and we have to find out from the context whether they are fallen angels or not. Angels have no physical frame, they are not like man, and they are not manifested after this order of things; since, however, they are called "sons of God," the inference is clear that they bear the image of God. BP. 11

Angels can come and go through rocks and doors, can appear and disappear in a way we cannot understand. Their consciousness is above ours, different from it. When anyone tries to explain to you how an angel sees and knows things, say to yourself, 'private speculation.' You will always find that God's Book puts the barrier clearly, 'Thus far and no farther.' BP. 198

Jesus Christ did not take on Him the consciousness of an angel; He came down to where man was, into the world we live in, and He took on Him a body and a nervous system like our own. Jesus Christ saw the world as we see it, and He came in contact with it as we do. BP. 198

When God came into this order of things, He did not come as an angel, He came as a Man, He took upon Him our human nature. This is the marvel of the Incarnation. BP. 216

An angel next in power to God is revealed to be the originator of sin. PS. 10

God's programme for a man is Now, not what he is going to do presently but what he is now . . . your attitude to life as it actually is now, is to remember you are a man or woman, and that you have to live on the earth as a human being and not try to be an angel. SHH. 120

ANIMALS

There is nothing said in the Bible about the immortality of animals. The Bible says that there will be animals in the regenerated earth, but nowhere does it say that the animals which we see now are immortal and that when they die they are raised again. BP. 45

ANTICHRIST

Every spirit that dissolves Jesus by analysis is antichrist. SA. 117

Where did the Christ come from historically? From the people called the Jews. The blasphemy of a Gentile like Voltaire is futile; no Gentile can blaspheme, because no Gentile knows God in the way the Jew does. It takes the race that produced Jesus to produce Judas;

and it will take the race that produced Christ to produce the anti-Christ. We are on the verge of this discovery. We are insular and closed in, and are looking in the wrong direction for the great big thing to come, instead of taking the Bible revelation. SHH. 33

ANXIETY

The centre of true anguish is in the heart, and when God puts our hearts right, He brings us into fellowship with Jesus Christ and we enter into fellowship with His sufferings. BP. 129

If your heart is troubled you are not living up to your belief. GW. 25

When once I realize that everything is in Jesus Christ, I will never allow any questions that spring from without to trouble my heart. GW. 26

We do get troubled when we do not remember the amazing power of God. LG. 144

Jesus says, 'Be anxious for nothing, fix your mind on Me, be carefully careless about everything saving your relationship to Me.' PR. 46

When we know the love of Christ, which passeth knowledge, it means we are free from anxiety, free from carefulness, so that, during the twenty-four hours of the day, we do what we ought to do all the time, with the strength of life bubbling up with real spontaneous joy. RTR. 86

APOCALYPSE

Apocalyptic literature is never easy to understand, its language is either a revelation or fantastic nonsense. We study it and worry over it and never begin to make head or tail of it, while obedience will put us on the line of understanding. HGM. 78

ARGUMENT

You can never argue anyone into the Kingdom of heaven, you cannot argue anyone anywhere. The only result of arguing is to prove to your own mind that you are right and the other fellow wrong. MFL. 10

You cannot argue for truth; but immediately Incarnate Truth is presented, a want awakens in the soul which only God can meet. MFL. 10

ARMOUR

Put on the whole armour of God and keep continuously practising, then the wiles of the devil cannot get you unawares. IYA. 33

The devil is a bully, but when we stand in the armour of God, he cannot harm us; if we tackle him in our own strength we are soon done for; but if we stand with the strength and courage of God, he cannot gain one inch of way at all. OBH. 55

The armour God gives us is not the armour of prayer, but the armour of Himself, the armour *of God*. OBH. 55

The armour is for the battle of prayer. 'Take up the whole armour of God, . . . Stand therefore . . . ,' and then pray. The armour is not to fight in, but to shield us while we pray. Prayer is the battle. SSY. 127

ASCENSION

The Ascension placed Jesus Christ back in the glory which He had with the Father before the world was. The Ascension, not the Resurrection, is the completion of the Transfiguration. BSG. 56

By His Ascension Our Lord raises Himself to glory, He becomes omnipotent, omniscient and omnipresent. All the splendid power, so circumscribed in His earthly life, becomes omnipotence; all the wisdom and insight, so precious but so limited during His life on earth, becomes omniscience; all the unspeakable comfort of the presence of Jesus, so confined to a few in His earthly life, becomes omnipresence, He is with us all the days. BSG. 59

At His Ascension our Lord entered Heaven, and He keeps the door open for humanity to enter. LG. 130

Because of His Resurrection our Lord has the right to give eternal life to every individual man; and by His Ascension He becomes the possessor of all power in heaven and in earth. PR. 118

On the Mount of Ascension the Transfiguration is completed. There is a similarity in the details of the two scenes, because the Ascension is the consummation of the Transfiguration. Our Lord does now, without any hesitation, go back into His primal glory; He does now go straight to the fulfilment of all the Transfiguration promised. But He does not go back simply as Son of God: He goes back to God as *Son of Man* as well as Son of God. The barriers are broken down, sin is done away with, death is destroyed, the power of the enemy is paralysed, and there is now freedom of access for any one straight to the very

11

throne of God by the Ascension of the Son of Man. PR. 120

for the whole human race to be atheistic. PS. 71

ASCETICISM

Asceticism is the passion of giving up things, and is recognizable in a life not born again of the Spirit of God. It is all very well if it ends in giving up the one thing God wants us to give up, viz. our right to ourselves, but if it does not end there, it will do endless damage to the life. PS. 36

. . . a man cannot shut out what is inside by cutting himself off from the outside. Jesus Christ was not a solitary man . . . SHH. 47

ATHEISM

We are all atheists at heart, and the whole world is but a gigantic palace of mirrors wherein we see ourselves reflected, and we call the reflection, God. CD. VOL. 2, 136

There are elements in human nature that are the same in everybody, and if once the human mind succeeded in obliterating God, the whole of the human race would become one vast phalanx of atheism. PS. 71

What encumbers and embarrasses humanity is an uncomfortable feeling that God is laughing at them all the time, and in the history of men up to the present time the hindrance to perfectly organized atheism has been the saints who represent the derision of God: if they were removed, we should find perfectly organized atheism. PS. 71

The solidarity of sin forms the basis of the power of Satan, and it runs all through humanity, making it possible

ATONEMENT

The marvel of the Atonement is that Jesus Christ can create endlessly in lives the oneness which He had with the Father. BE. 87

. . . the whole meaning of the Atonement is to destroy the idolatry of self-love, to extract the pernicious poison of self-interest, and presence us with the Divinity which enables us to love God with all our heart, and soul, and mind, and strength. BE. 105

The modern view of the Atonement is that it simply reveals the oneness of God and man; immediately we turn to the New Testament we find that the doctrine of the Atonement is that God can readjust man to Himself, indicating that there is something wrong, something out of joint, something that has to be put right. BE. 119

Jesus Christ became identified not only with the disposition of sin, but with the very body of sin. He Who had no sin, no connection in Himself with the body of sin, became identified with sin, 'Him who knew no sin, He made to be sin.' Language can hardly bear the strain put upon it, but it may nevertheless convey the thought that Jesus Christ went straight through identification with sin in order that every man and woman on earth might be freed from sin through the Atonement. He went through the depths of damnation, through the deepest depths of death and hell, and came out more than conqueror; consequently anyone and everyone who is willing to be identified with Him will find that he is freed from the disposition of sin, freed from his connection with the body of sin, and that he too can come out 'more than conqueror' because of what Jesus Christ has done. BP. 35

There are two sides to the Atonement—it is not only the life of Christ *for* me but His life *in* me for my life; no Christ *for* me if I do not have Christ *in* me. All through there is to be this strenuous, glorious practising in our bodily life of the changes which God has wrought in our soul through His Spirit, and the only proof that we are in earnest is that we work out what God works in. BP. 71

We have to be solemnly careful that we do not travesty and belittle the work of God and the Atonement of the Lord Jesus Christ. If we belittle it in the tiniest degree, although we may do it in ignorance, we shall surely suffer. The first thing which will make us belittle the Atonement is getting out of sympathy with God into sympathy with human beings, because when we do this we begin to drag down the tremendous revelation that the essential nature of God is Will and Love and Light, and that it is these characteristics which are imparted to us by the Holy Ghost. BP. 218

If God cannot cleanse us from all sin and make us "holy and without blame" in His sight, then Jesus Christ has totally misled us, and the Atonement is not what it claims to be. BP. 222

The meaning of the Atonement is that man's spirit can be restored into harmony with God. BSG. 76

If our best obedience, our most spotless moral walking, our most earnest prayers, are offered to God in the very least measure as the ground of our acceptance by Him, it is a fatal denial of the Atonement. CHI. 80

Until we have become spiritual by new birth the Atonement of Jesus has no meaning for us; it only begins to get meaning when we live "in heavenly places in Christ Jesus". DI. 56

Our Lord came to make atonement for the sin of the world, not by any impulse of a noble nature, but by the perfect conscious Self-sacrifice whereby alone God could redeem man. DI. 56

The understanding of the Atonement depends not on Bible study, not on praying, but on spiritual growth. MFL. 25

The best gift the Son of God had was His Holy Manhood, and He gave that as a love-gift to God that He might use it as an Atonement for the world. He poured out His soul unto death, and that is to be the characteristic of our lives. God is at perfect liberty to waste us if He chooses. MFL. 108

The Atonement of the Lord alone touches sin. We must not tamper with it for one second. We can do nothing with sin; we must leave God's Redemption to deal with it. NKW. 149

If we make the Atonement of the Lord Jesus Christ the great exerting influence of our life, every phase of our life will bear fruit for God. Take time and get to know whether the Atonement is the central point of all power for you, and remember that Satan's aim is to keep you away from that point of power. OBH. 123

The Bible deals with the worst tragedy that human nature and the devil could concoct. We seem to have forgotten this nowadays. The Atonement has been made a kind of moral "lavatory" wherein a man can wash and go out and get dirty again. SHH. 102

AUTHORITY

There is always a tendency to produce an absolute authority; we accept the authority of the Church, or of the Bible, or of a creed, and often refuse to do any more thinking on the matter; and in so doing we ignore the essential nature of Christianity which is based on a personal relationship to Jesus Christ, and works on the basis of our responsibility. BFB. 91

The authority we blindly grope after is God Himself, not a tendency making for righteousness, not a set of principles. Behind Reality is God Himself, and the final authority is a personal relationship. BFB. 94

. . . Our Lord never taught dogma, He declared. There is no argument or discussion in what He says, it is not a question of the insight of a marvellous man, but a question of speaking with authority. IWP. 124

Self-chosen authority is an impertinence. Jesus said that the great ones in this world exercise authority but that in His Kingdom it is not so; no one exercises authority over another because in His Kingdom the King is Servant of all. If a saint tries to exercise authority it is a proof that he is not rightly related to Jesus Christ. MFL. 128

B

BACKSLIDING

Backsliding is turning away from what we know to be best to what we know is second-best. If you have known God better than you know Him to-day and are deliberately settling down to something less than the best—watch, for you will not escape, God will bring embarrassments out against you, in your private life, in your domestic life, He will enmesh you on the right hand and on the left. PH. 228

It is no use to tell the backslider to receive the Holy Spirit, he cannot; the Holy Spirit will not be received by him; he has to come back to God in desolation. SHL. 75

The statement is frequently made that in dealing with a backslider, the worker has to bring him to being born again of the Spirit. A backslider has not to be born again, he is in a much worse condition than a man not born again: he has to have his backslidings healed and be restored. WG. 42

A backslider is a man who does know what God's grace is, who does know what sin is, and who does know what deliverance is, but who has deliberately forsaken God and gone back because he loved something else better. WG. 42

The backsliders are the most dangerous class under Heaven to touch, and no one but a man or woman who knows how to live bathed moment by moment in the love of God, who knows how to prevail in prayer, ought to touch the case of a backslider. WG. 49

BAPTISM

The experience of Jesus at His Baptism is as foreign to us as His Incarnation. Read the so-called 'Lives' of Jesus and see how little is made of His baptism, the reason being that most of the writers take the Baptism to be something to teach us, or as an illustration of the rite of baptism. In the New Testament the Baptism of Jesus is not taken as an illustration of anything which we experience, it is recorded as a manifestation of Who Jesus was. BSG. 23

At His baptism Jesus took on Him His vocation; it was the public manifestation that He became part of fallen humanity; that is why He was baptised with John's baptism of repentance. BSG. 26

"Christ did not send me to baptise"—to put religious rites in the front—"but to preach the gospel." PH. 135

For thirty years our Lord had done nothing in public, then at the preaching of John the Baptist He emerged and was baptised with the baptism of John, which is a baptism of repentance from sin. Our Lord's baptism is not an illustration of the Christian rite of baptism, nor of the baptism of the Holy Ghost. At His baptism our Lord accepted His vocation, which was to bear away the sin of the world. PR. 48

Our Lord knew what He had come to do, and His baptism is the first public manifestation of His identification with sin with a conscious understanding of what He was doing. At His baptism He visibly and distinctly and historically took upon Him His vocation. PR. 49

Jesus Christ is the true Baptiser; He baptises with the Holy Ghost. He is the Lamb of God which taketh away the sin of the world, *my* sin. He is the One Who can make me like Himself; the baptism of John could not do that. PR. 49

John's baptism was a baptism of repentance from sin, and that was the baptism with which Jesus was baptised. He was baptised into sin, *made to be sin*, and that is why His Father was well pleased with Him. PR. 52

The Cross of Jesus Christ and His baptism express the same thing. Our Lord was not a martyr; He was not merely a good man; He was God Incarnate. PR. 52

The vocation of our Lord was His identification with sin; He became absolutely and entirely identified with sin, and His baptism is the sign before the whole world of the acceptance of His vocation 'This is what I am here for.' It was not a baptism into power and dominion, but a baptism into identification with sin. PR. 57

BELIEF/UNBELIEF

We begin our religious life by believing our beliefs, we accept what we are taught without questioning; but when we come up against things we begin to be critical, and find out that the beliefs, however right, are not right for us be-

cause we have not bought them by suffering. What we take for granted is never ours until we have bought it by pain. A thing is worth just what it costs. AUG. 78

It is absurd to tell a man he must believe this and that; in the meantime he can't! Scepticism is produced by telling men what to believe. We are in danger of putting the cart before the horse and saying a man must believe certain things before he can be a Christian; his beliefs are the effect of his being a Christian, not the cause of it. Our Lord's word 'believe' does not refer to an intellectual act, but to a moral act. With Him 'to believe' means 'to commit'. AUG. 78

To believe in Jesus means much more than the experience of salvation in any form, it entails a mental and moral commitment to our Lord Jesus Christ's view of God and man, of sin and the devil, and of the Scriptures. AUG. 104

According to the New Testament, belief arises from intellectual conviction and goes through moral self-surrender to identification with the Lord Jesus Christ. AUG. 110

The one thing that tells is the great fundamental rock: "Believe also in Me." Many know a good deal about salvation, but not much about this intense patience of 'hanging in' in perfect certainty to the fact that what Jesus Christ says is true. AUG. 117

If we believe in Jesus Christ we will determine to make our relationship to men what Jesus Christ's was to us. He believed that He could save every man irrespective of his condition. AUG. 117

The reason people disbelieve God is not because they do not understand with their heads—we understand very few things with our heads, but because they have turned their hearts in another direction. BP. 144

. . . if we would only get into the way of bringing our limitations before God and telling Him He cannot do these things, we should begin to see the awful wickedness of unbelief, and why our Lord was so vigorous against it, and why the Apostle John places fearfulness and unbelief at the head of all the most awful sins. BP. 222

Belief is a wholesale committal, it means making things inevitable, cutting off every possible retreat. Belief is as irrevocable as bereavement. DI. 1

Belief is the abandonment of all claim to merit. That is why it is so difficult to believe. DI. 1

The further we get away from Jesus the more dogmatic we become over what we call our religious beliefs, while the nearer we live to Jesus the less we have of certitude and the more of confidence in Him. DI. 2

Watch the things you say you can't believe, and then recall the things you accept without thinking, e.g., your own existence. DI. 3

The great paralysis of our heart is unbelief. Immediately I view anything as inevitable about any human being, I am an unbeliever. DI. 5

It is easy to say we believe in God as long as we remain in the little world we choose to live in; but get out into the great world of facts, the noisy world where people are absolutely indifferent to you, where your message is nothing more than a crazy tale belonging to a bygone age, can you believe God there? GW. 92

Anything Jesus Christ revealed may be missed. The disbelief of the human mind always wastes itself in the sentimental idea that God would never let us miss the greatest good. Jesus says He will, that is why we don't like Him, and that is why the teaching of to-day is not the teaching of the Jesus Christ of the New Testament. HG. 18

To introduce the idea of merit into belief, i.e. that I have done something by believing, is to annul my belief and make it blasphemous. Belief is the abandonment of all claim to desert; that is why it is so difficult to believe in Jesus. HG. 120

A man's beliefs are the effect of his being a Christian, not the cause of it. HGM. 28

Unless I receive a totally new Spirit, all the believing and correct doctrine in the world will never alter me; it is not a question of believing, but of *receiving*. HGM. 34

Belief is not that God can do the thing, but belief *in God*. HGM. 71

We blunder when we tell people they must believe certain things about Jesus Christ; a man cannot believe until he knows Him, then belief is spontaneous and natural. HGM. 98

Un-belief is the most active thing on earth; it is negative on God's side, not on ours. Un-belief is a fretful, worrying, questioning, annoying, self-centred spirit. To believe is to stop all this and let God work. IWP. 62

If we really believed some phases of our Lord's teaching it would make us a laughing stock in the eyes of the world. It requires the miracle of God's grace for us to believe as Jesus taught us to. OBH. 118

It is heroism to believe in God. PH. 44

It is easy to *say* God reigns, and then to see Satan, suffering and sin reigning, and God apparently powerless. Belief in God must be tried before it is of value to God or to a child of His. PH. 73

To believe is literally to commit. Belief is a moral act, and Jesus makes an enormous demand of a man when He asks him to believe in Him. PH. 222

Belief must be the *will* to believe. There must be a surrender of the will, not a surrender to persuasive power, but a deliberate launching forth on God, and on what He says, until I am no longer confident in what I have done, I am confident only in God. The hindrance is that I will not trust God, but only my mental understanding. RTR. 29

Never run away with the idea that it doesn't matter much what we believe or think; it does. What we believe and think, we are; not what we say we believe and think, but what we really do believe and think, we are; there is no divorce at all. RTR. 33

When we have a certain belief, we kill God in our lives, because we do not believe Him, we believe our beliefs about Him and do what Job's friends did— bring God and human life to the standard of our beliefs and not to the standard of God. RTR. 85

One of the dangers of denominational teaching is that we are told that before

we can be Christians we must believe that Jesus Christ is the son of God, and that the Bible is the Word of God from Genesis to Revelation. Creeds are the effect of our belief, not the cause of it. I do not have to believe all that before I can be a Christian. SA. 35

A moral preparation is necessary before we can believe; truth is a moral vision, and does not exist for a man until he sees it. SA. 122

If you do not believe practically in your heart that the Lord Jesus Christ can alter and save the man you are talking to, you limit Jesus Christ in that life. WG. 25

BELIEVER

We do not now use the old evangelical phrase 'a believer', we are apt to think we have something better, but we cannot have. 'A believer in Jesus Christ' is a phrase that embraces the whole of Christianity. AUG. 104

It is a great thing to be a believer, but easy to misunderstand what the New Testament means by it. It is not that we believe Jesus Christ can *do* things, or that we believe in a plan of salvation; it is that we believe *Him*; whatever happens we will hang in to the fact that He is true. If we say, 'I am going to believe He will put things right', we shall lose our confidence when we see things go wrong. AUG. 114

The problems of life get hold of a man and make it difficult for him to know whether in the face of these things he really is confident in Jesus Christ. The attitude of a believer must be, 'Things do look black, but I believe Him; and when the whole thing is told I am confident my belief will be justified and

18

God will be revealed as a God of love and justice.' It does not mean that we won't have problems, but it does mean that our problems will never come in between us and our faith in Him. AUG. 114

To be 'a believer in Jesus Christ' means we are committed to His way of looking at everything, not that we are open to discuss what people say He taught; that is the way difficulties have arisen with regard to Christian faith. AUG. 116

I have no right to say I believe in God unless I order my life as under His all-seeing Eye. DI. 1

A believer is one whose whole being is based on the finished work of Redemption. DI. 1

Believe what you do believe and stick to it, but don't profess to believe more than you intend to stick to. If you say you believe God is love, stick to it, though all Providence becomes a pandemonium shouting that God is cruel to allow what He does. DI. 12

So as long as we live in a religious compartment, make our own theology, wear doctrinal 'blinkers,' and live only amongst those who agree with us, we shall not see where the shame comes in; but let God shift us and bring us into contact with those who are indifferent to what we believe, and we shall realize soon the truth of what our Lord said— "therefore the world hateth you." OBH. 118

The test of a Christian, according to the New Testament, is not that a man believes aright, but that he lives as he believes, i.e., he is able to manifest that he has a power which, apart from his personal relationship to Jesus Christ, he would not have. We all know about the

power that spoils our sin, but does not take away our appetite for it. SA. 69

BIBLE

The mere reading of the Word of God has power to communicate the life of God to us mentally, morally and spiritually. God makes the words of the Bible a sacrament, i.e., the means whereby we partake of His life, it is one of His secret doors for the communication of His life to us. AUG. 13

Immediately a man becomes spiritual by being born from above, the Bible becomes his authority, because he discerns a law in his conscience that has no objective resting place save in the Bible; and when the Bible is quoted, instantly his intuition says, 'Yes, that must be the truth'; not because the Bible says so, but because he discerns what the Bible says to be the word of God for him. When a man is born from above he has a new internal standard, and the only objective standard that agrees with it is the word of God as expressed in the Bible. AUG. 16

The way to become complete for the Master's service is to be well soaked in the Bible, some of us only exploit certain passages. Our Lord wants to give us continuous instruction out of His word; continuous instruction turns hearers into disciples. Beware of 'spooned meat' spirituality, of using the Bible for the sake of getting messages; use it to nourish your own soul. Be a continuous learner, don't stop short, and the truth will open to you on the right hand and on the left until you find there is no problem in human life with which the Bible does not deal. AUG. 34

The key to my understanding of the Bible is not my intelligence, but personal relationship to Jesus Christ. I begin my theories after I have got on the inside. AUG. 79

You may believe the Bible is the Word of God from Genesis to Revelation and not be a Christian at all. AUG. 79

The mystery of the Bible is that its inspiration was direct from God, not verbally inspired, but the inspired Word of God—the Final Word of God; not that God is not saying anything now, but He is not saying anything different from the Final Word, Jesus Christ. All God says is expounding that Word. The Final Word and the only Word are very different. Be reverent with the Bible explanation of itself. AUG. 79

We can prove anything we choose from the Bible once we forget the message Jesus says it contains. 'The test that you know the Bible is that you understand what it is driving at, it is expounding Me, giving the exposition of what I am after.' AUG. 80

The Bible instructs us in righteousness, in the rightness of practical living; its meaning is to keep us living right. Most people like to use the Bible for anything other than that, for a kind of jugglery to prove special doctrines. AUG. 80

The New Testament is not written to prove that Jesus Christ was the Son of God, but written for those who believe He is. AUG. 80

How much intellectual impertinence there is to-day among many Christians relative to the Scriptures, because they forget that to "believe also" in Jesus means that they are committed beforehand to His attitude to the Bible. He

said that He was the context of the Scriptures, ". . . they are they which testify of me." AUG. 104

We hear much about 'key words' to the Scriptures, but there is only one 'key word' to the Scriptures for a believer, and that is our Lord Jesus Christ Himself. AUG. 104

One !

(How one wishes that people who read books about the Bible would read the Bible itself! BE. 115)

The only interpreter of the Scriptures is the Holy Spirit, and when we have received the Holy Spirit we learn the first golden lesson of spiritual life, which is that God reveals His will according to the state of our character. BE. 123

The only way to understand the Scriptures is not to accept them blindly, but to read them in the light of a personal relationship to Jesus Christ. BFB. 91

If the Bible agreed with modern science, it would soon be out of date, because, in the very nature of things, modern science is bound to change. BP. 5

What is revealed in God's Book is for us; what is not revealed is not for us. Speculation is searching into what is not revealed. The subject of pre-existence as it is popularly taught is not revealed in God's Book; it is a speculation based on certain things said in God's Book. BP. 83

. . . do not belittle the Bible and say that it has only to do with man's salvation. The Bible is a universe of revelation facts which explains the world in which we live, and it is simply 'giving a sop to Satan' to say, as some modern teachers do, that the Bible does not pretend to tell us how the world came into existence. The Bible claims to be the only exposition of how the world came into being and how it keeps going, and the only Book which tells us how we may understand the world. BP. 225

If I have not the Spirit of God, I shall never interpret the world of Nature in the way God does; the Bible will be to me simply an Oriental tradition, a 'cunningly devised fable.' If I am to understand the Bible, I must have the Spirit of God. BP. 228

There is a context to the Bible, and Jesus Christ is that Context. The right order is personal relationship to Him first, then the interpretation of the Scriptures according to His Spirit. Difficulties come because beliefs and creeds are put in the place of Jesus Christ. BSG. 63

The Bible is the Word of God only to those who are born from above and who walk in the light. Our Lord Jesus Christ, the *Word* of God, and the Bible, the *words* of God, stand or fall together, they can never be separated without fatal results. CD. VOL. 1, 14

Profoundly speaking, it is not sufficient to say, 'Because God says it', or, 'Because the Bible says it', unless you are talking to people who know God and know the Bible to be His Word. If you appeal from the authority of God or of the Bible to a man not born again, he will pay no attention to you because he does not stand on the same platform. You have to find a provisional platform on which he can stand with you, and in the majority of cases you will find that the platform is that of moral worth. DI. 7

Beware of bartering the Word of God for a more suitable conception of your own. DI. 7

There is no true illumination apart from the written Word. Spiritual impressions generated from my own experience are of no importance, and if I pay attention to them I will pay no attention to the words of Jesus. DI. 7

The statements of Scripture apart from the Holy Spirit's illumination are dull; it needs no spiritual insight to regard Jesus Christ as a Man who lived beyond His time, but when I am born again I have insight into the Person of Jesus, an insight that comes through communion with God by means of the Bible. DI. 8

It is what the Bible imparts to us that is of value. DI. 8

The Bible does not thrill, the Bible nourishes. Give time to the reading of the Bible and the recreating effect is as real as that of fresh air physically. DI. 8

The reason some of us are not healthy spiritually is because we don't use the Bible as the Word of God but only as a text-book. DI. 8

Beware of reasoning about God's Word, obey it. DI. 9

We are to be servants and handmaids of the Gospel, not devotees of the Bible, then God can make us living mediums whereby His Word becomes a sacrament to others. DI. 9

Don't go to your Bible in a yawning mood. DI. 50

The words of the Bible apart from being interpreted by the Word of God, are worse than lifeless, they kill. GW. 34

. . . when a soul is born from above and lifted to the atmosphere of the domain where our Lord lives, the Bible becomes its native air, its words become the storehouse of omnipotence, its commands and prophecies become alive, its limitless horizons brace the heart and mind to a new consciousness, its comforts in Psalms and prayers and exhortations delight the whole man. And better than all, the Lord Jesus Christ becomes the altogether Lovely One, it is in His light that we see light, it is in Him that we become new creatures. He who is the Word of God unfolds to us the revelation of God until we say in sacred rapture, 'I hold in my hands the Thought of God'. GW. 34

The Bible is a whole library of literature giving us the final interpretation of the Truth, and to take the Bible apart from that one supreme purpose is to have a book and nothing more; and further, to take our Lord Jesus Christ away from the revelation of Him given in the Bible is to be left with one who is open to all the irreverent slanders of unbelief. GW. 35

The research of specialists, both in the natural world and in the revelation world, is of the very greatest value, but remember, it is essential to be born of the Spirit before we can enter the domain of Bible revelation. The only method of Bible study is to 'prove all things', not by intellect, but by personal experience. GW. 70

The Bible is not a book containing communications from God, it is God's revelation of Himself, in the interests of grace; God's giving of Himself in the limitation of words. The Bible is not a faery romance to beguile us for a while from the sordid realities of life, it is the Divine complement of the laws of Nature, of Conscience and of Humanity, it introduces us to a new universe of revelation facts not known to unregenerate commonsense. GW. 70

The Bible not only tests experience, it tests truth. GW. 70

In the Bible there is nothing altogether minor; nothing, that is, of the nature of despair. The Bible deals with terrors and upsets, with people who have got into despair—in fact, the Bible deals with all that the devil can do, and yet all through there is the uncrushable certainty that in the end everything will be all right. HG. 7

The test of regeneration is that the Bible instantly becomes the Book of books to us. HG. 97

To use the New Testament as a book of proof is nonsense. If you do not believe that Jesus Christ is the Son of God, the New Testament will not convince you that He is; if you do not believe in the Resurrection, the New Testament will not convince you of it. The New Testament is written for those who do not need convincing. HGM. 35

In the Bible there is no twilight, but intense light and intense darkness. HGM. 39

The Bible never deals with the domains our human minds delight to deal with. The Bible deals with heaven and hell, good and bad, God and the devil, right and wrong, salvation and damnation; we like to deal with the things in between. HGM. 39

If we are ever going to understand the Book of the Revelation we have to remember that it gives the programme of God, not the guess of a man. HGM. 78

God's Book is packed full of overwhelming riches, they are unsearchable, the more we have the more there is to have. IWP. 76

There are tremendous thoughts expressed in God's Book, and unless we have learned to rely on the Holy Spirit we shall say, 'Oh, I shall never understand that,' but the Holy Spirit in us understands it, and as we recognise and rely on Him, He will work it out, whether we consciously understand or not. IYA. 104

The Bible does not deal with the domain of common-sense facts, we get at those by our senses; the Bible deals with the world of revelation facts which we only get at by faith in God. LG. 23

The Bible is like life and deals with facts, not with principles, and life is not logical. OBH. 92

Read the Bible, whether you understand it or not, and the Holy Spirit will bring back some word of Jesus to you in a particular set of circumstances and make it living; the point is—will you be loyal to that word? OBH. 121

There are people who vagabond through the Bible, taking sufficient only out of it for the making of sermons, they never let the word of God walk out of the Bible and talk to them. Beware of living from hand to mouth in spiritual matters; do not be a spiritual mendicant. OBH. 127

We cannot know the Holy Scriptures by intellectual exercises. The key to our understanding of the Bible is not our intelligence, but our personal relationship to Jesus Christ OBH. 127

The Bible treats us as human life does—roughly. OBH. 128

The Bible never argues or debates, it states revelation facts, and in order to understand these facts we are dependent entirely, not on intellectual curiosity, but on a relationship of faith. OPG. 1

The Scriptures do not give us life unless Jesus speaks them to us. Jesus Christ makes His words "spirit and life" to us if we will obey them. If we are not born again the Word of God is nothing to us. When men tear this Book of God to pieces it reveals how blind they are. To the saint this Book of God is a sacrament, it conveys the real Presence of God. God by His providence puts needs in our actual life which drive us to search the Scriptures, and as we search them, the sacrament of God's Presence comes to us through the words of His Book. PH. 138

The context of the Bible is the Lord Jesus Christ. PH. 138

The Bible is the only Book that tells us anything about the originator of sin. PS. 9

To people who are satisfied on too shallow a level the Bible is a book of impertinences, but whenever human nature is driven to the end of things, then the Bible becomes the only Book and God the only Being in the world. PS. 9

As long as we live on the surface of things merely as splendid animals, we shall find the Bible nonsense. PS. 13

Bible facts are either revelation facts or nonsense. It depends on me which they are to me. RTR. 41

Beware of interpreting Scripture in order to make it suit a pre-arranged doctrine of your own. RTR. 41

Our attitude to the Bible is a stupid one, we come to the Bible for proof of God's existence: the Bible has no meaning for us unless we know that God *does* exist. The Bible states and affirms facts for the benefit of those who believe in God, those who don't believe in God can tear it to bits if they like. RTR. 80

If you sow vows, resolutions, aspirations, emotions, you will reap nothing but exhaustion, but sow the Word of God, and, as sure as God is God, it will bring forth fruit. RTR. 82

The context of the Bible is Jesus Christ, and a personal relationship with Him interprets the Bible in a man's life. SA. 63

The Bible is neither obsolete nonsense nor poetic blether: it is a universe of revelation facts. SHH. 50

The Bible has no sympathy with saying things ought not to be as they are. The practical thing is to look at things as they are. SHH. 58

The Bible attitude to things is absolutely robust, there is not the tiniest whine about it; there is no possibility of lying like a limp jellyfish on God's providence, it is never allowed for a second. There is always a sting and a kick all through the Bible. SHH. 60

The Bible is a relation of facts, the truth of which must be tested. SHH. 87

The Bible is a universe of revelation facts which have no meaning for us until we are born from above; when we are born again we see in it what we never saw before. We are lifted into the realm where Jesus lives and we begin to see what He sees. SSM. 25

There are bald shocking statements in the Bible, but from cover to cover the Bible will do nothing in the shape of harm to the pure in heart, it is to the impure in heart that these things are corrupting. SSM. 33

God's spiritual open air is the Bible. SSM. 103

The Bible is the universe of revelation facts; if we live there our roots will be healthy and our lives right. SSM. 103

Jesus says that the way to put foundations under spiritual castles is by hearing and doing "these sayings of Mine." Pay attention to His words, and give time to doing it. Try five minutes a day with your Bible. SSM. 108

BLAMELESSNESS

Blameless does not mean perfection, but undeserving of censure in God's sight. That is the full meaning of being baptized with the Holy Ghost. Then, and only then, does Jesus become our Example. GW. 31

We never can be faultless in this life, but God's Book brings out that we must be blameless, that is, undeserving of censure from God's standpoint, and remember what His standpoint is. He can see into every crook and cranny of my spirit and soul and body, and He demands that I be blameless in all my relationships so that He Himself can see nothing worthy of censure. LG. 137

The seal of sanctification in the practical life is that it is blameless, undeserving of censure before God. Blamelessness is not faultlessness; faultlessness was the condition of the Lord Jesus Christ. We never can be faultless in this life, we are in impaired human bodies; but by sanctification we can be blameless. LG. 138

If we are sanctified by the power of the God of peace, our self life is blameless before Him, there is nothing to hide; and the more we bring our soul under the searchlight of God the more we realize the ineffable comfort of the supernatural work He has done. LG. 139

Of ourselves we can never be any of the things God says we must be. We can never be blameless by thinking about it, or by praying about it, but only by being sanctified, and that is God's absolute sovereign work of grace. LG. 140

If God has not sanctified us and made us blameless, there is only one reason why He has not—we do not want Him to. *"This is the will of God, even your sanctification."* We have not to urge God to do it, it is His will; is it our will? Sanctification is the work of the supernatural power of God. LG. 141

BLESSING

It appears as if God were sometimes most unnatural, we ask Him to bless our lives and bring benedictions and what immediately follows turns everything into actual ruin. The reason is that before God can make the heart into a garden of the Lord, He has to plough it, and that will take away a great deal of natural beauty. CD. VOL. 2, 48

All the great blessings of God in salvation and sanctification, all the Holy Spirit's illumination, are ours not because we obey, they are ours because we have put ourselves into a right relationship with God by receiving Christ Jesus the Lord, and we obey spontaneously. GW. 15

As we look back we find that every time we have been blessed it was not through mechanical obedience, but by receiving from Jesus something that enabled us to obey without knowing it and life was flooded with the power of God. GW. 15

. . . God's blessings fall, like His rain, on evil and good alike. The great blessings of health, genius, prosperity, all come from His overflowing grace, and not from the condition of the character of the recipients. GW. 50

If God is going to bless me, He must condemn and blast out of my being what He cannot bless. "Our God is a consuming fire." HG. 16

The only way to peace and salvation and power, and to all that God has in the way of benedictions and blessings for us individually and for the whole world, is in the Son of Man. HGM. 10

The notion has grown almost imperceptibly that God is simply a blessing machine for men—'If I link myself on to God He will see me through'; instead, the human race is meant to be the servant of God, a different thing altogether. HGM. 79

The greatest blessing we ever get from God is to know that we are destitute spiritually. LG. 115

When we no longer seek God for His blessings, we have time to seek Him for Himself. MFL. 114

The greatest benefits God has conferred on human life, e.g., fatherhood, motherhood, childhood, home, become the greatest curse if Jesus Christ is not the Head. PH. 37

Moral and spiritual integrity cannot be measured by God's blessings. God sends His favours on good and bad alike. The blessings of God are an indication that God is overflowing in grace and bendiction irrespective of a man's relationship to Him. Men may partake of the blessings of God and yet never come into relationship with Him. PH. 75

We worship Man, and God is looked upon as a blessing machine for humanity. SHL. 95

BLOOD

When Jesus Christ shed His blood on the Cross it was not the blood of a martyr, or the blood of one man for another; it was the life of God poured out to redeem the world. BE. 60

God redeemed the world by shedding His blood, by putting the whole passion of the Godhead into it. He did not become interested and put one arm in to help the human race up, He went into the Redemption absolutely, there was nothing of Himself left out. BE. 63

Jesus Christ insists on the fact that if we are His disciples it will be revealed in the blood, i.e., the physical life. The old soul tyranny and disposition, the old selfish determination to seek our own ends, manifests itself in our body, through our blood; and when that disposition of soul is altered, the alteration shows itself at once in the blood also. Instead of the old tempers and the old passions being manifested in our physical blood, the good temper reveals itself. It never does to remove Jesus Christ's spiritual teaching into the domain of the inane and vague, it must come right down where the devil works; and just as the devil works not in vague ways but through flesh and blood, so

does the Lord, and the characteristics of the soul for better or worse are shown in the blood. BP. 70

'Blood' was, and is, the offence. GW. 117

'Blood', the vital life-stream—offensive! Is there nothing offensive in sin, that devastating thing which poisons the very fountain of life, which makes the world a howling wilderness and our cities unendurable to thought—a defect! GW. 117

Sin has alienated man from God, and the story of the ages is an accumulation of wrongdoing and of judgement days; there is an utter hopelessness in any attempt to meet the righteousness of God; but let a man begin to realize what sin is, then, *'the blood of Jesus Christ His Son cleanseth us from all sin'*, will be a holy word to his soul. GW. 117

'The Cross' and 'the blood of Jesus' are indeed names for profound mysteries, but when a soul shattered by the crushing sense of his guilt believes that through the blood of Jesus there is forgiveness for sins, he receives a new life-energy, he is purged from his old sins, and with the Spirit of Jesus in him, he begins to work out his own salvation. Then begins the true evolution of a man's soul. GW. 117

'Blood' is an offence not only at the beginning of the Christian career, but in the midst of it. GW. 118

The word 'blood', which offends so many, speaks of forgiveness of sins. GW. 119

When we speak of the blood of Jesus Christ cleansing us from all sin, we do not mean the physical blood shed on Calvary, but the whole life of the Son of

God which was poured out to redeem the world. All the perfections of the essential nature of God were in that blood, and all the holiest attainments of mankind as well. It was the life of the perfection of Deity that has poured out on Calvary, ". . . the church of God, which He purchased with His own blood." PH. 162

We are apt to look upon the blood of Jesus Christ as a magic-working power instead of its being the very life of the Son of God poured forth for men. PH. 162

The whole meaning of our being identified with the death of Jesus is that His blood may flow through our mortal bodies. PH. 162

Identification with the death of Jesus Christ means identification with Him to the death of everything that never was in Him, and it is the blood of Christ, in the sense of the whole personal life of the Son of God, that comes into us and "cleanseth us from all sin." PH. 162

BODY

The best I have is my claim to my right to myself, my body. If I am born again of the Spirit of God, I will give up that body to Jesus Christ. AUG. 88

We have to treat the body as the servant of Jesus Christ: when the body says 'Sit', and He says 'Go', go! When the body says 'Eat', and He says 'Fast', fast! When the body says 'Yawn', and He says 'Pray', pray! BE. 57

Man's body before he degenerated must have been dazzling with light. BP. 11

Thank God we are not going to be angels, we are going to be something tenfold better. By the Redemption of Jesus Christ there is a time coming when our bodies will be in the image of God. The "body of our humiliation" is to be "conformed to the body of His glory," and our body will bear the image of God as our spirit does. BP. 42

Man's body and the earth on which he treads are to partake in the final restitution. Our soul's history is not furthered 'in spite of our bodies,' but because of our bodies. BP. 50

Jesus Christ had a fleshly body as we have, but He was never tempted by lust, because lust resides in the ruling disposition, not in the body. When God changes the ruling disposition, the same body that was used as the instrument of sin to work all manner of uncleanness and unrighteousness, can now be used as the slave of the new disposition. It is not a different body; it is the same body, with a new disposition. BP. 77

The Bible has a great deal to tell us about our bodies. The main point to emphasize is that the Bible reveals that our body is the medium through which we develop our spiritual life. BP. 166

Instead of our body being a hindrance to our development, it is only through our body that we are developed. BP. 167

We express our character through our body: you cannot express a character without a body. When we speak of character, we think of a flesh and blood thing; when we speak of disposition, we think of something that is not flesh and blood. Through the Atonement God gives us the right disposition; that disposition is inside our body, and we have to manifest it in character through our body and by means of our body. BP. 167

The meaning of bodily control is that the body is the obedient medium for expressing the right disposition. BP. 167

The Bible, instead of ignoring the fact that we have a body, exalts it. BP. 167

Our body is to be the temple of the Holy Ghost, the medium for manifesting the marvellous disposition of Jesus Christ all through. BP. 167

The Bible never says any thing so vague as 'present your "all," ' but 'present your "bodies." ' There is nothing ambiguous or indefinite about that statement, it is definite and clear. The body means only one thing to us all, viz., this flesh and blood body. BP. 167

The marvellous power which the glorified resurrection body will have is pictured in the Lord Jesus Christ. He could materialize whenever He chose, He proved that He could, and He could disappear whenever He chose; and we shall do exactly the same. BP. 256

Just think of the time when our thinking will be in language as soon as we think it! If we have the idea that we are to be penned up for ever in a little physical temple, we are twisted away from the Bible revelation. Just now in this order of things we are confined in this bodily temple for a particular reason, but at any second, in the "twinkling of an eye," God can change this body into a glorified body. BP. 257

When I am born again my human nature is not different, it is the same as before, I am related to life in the same way, I have the same bodily organs, but the mainspring is different, and I have to see now that all my members are dominated by the new disposition. CHI. 21

Once let it dawn on your mind that your body is the temple of the Holy Ghost and instantly the impossible becomes possible; the things you used to pray about, you no longer pray about, but *do*. HGM. 24

Because man's body and his earthly setting have been affected by sin, we are apt to think that being made of the dust of the ground is his shame; the Bible implies that it is his chief glory, because it is in that body that the Son of God was manifested. HGM. 86

Our spiritual life does not grow *in spite of* the body, but *because* of the body. "Of the earth, earthy," is man's glory, not his shame; and it is in the "earth, earthy" that the full regenerating work of Jesus Christ has its ultimate reach. MFL. 39

If our body has been the slave of wrong habits physically, mentally and morally, we must get hold of a power big enough to re-make our habits and that power lies in the word 'Regeneration.' MFL. 41

Have I ever realised that the most wonderful thing in the world is the thing that is nearest to me, viz., my body? Who made it? Almighty God. Do I pay the remotest attention to my body as being the temple of the Holy Ghost? Remember our Lord lived in a body like ours. The next reality that I come in contact with by my body is other people's bodies. All our relationships in life, all the joys and all the miseries, all the hells and all the heavens, are based on bodies; and the reality of Jesus Christ's salvation brings us down to the Mother Earth we live on, and makes us see by the regenerating power of God's grace how amazingly precious are the ordinary things that are always with us. Master that, and you have mastered everything. We imagine that our bodies are a hindrance to our development, whereas it is only through our bodies that we develop. We cannot express a character without a body. MFL. 62

When we are saved God does not alter the construction of our bodily life, but He does expect us to manifest in our bodily life the alteration He has made. We express ourselves naturally through our bodies, and we express the supernatural life of God in the same way, but it can only be done by the sacrifice of the natural. MFL. 68

God always locates His spiritual revelations in a physical body. The great God became Incarnate in flesh and blood; the great thoughts of God became crystallized in words. MFL. 78

Beware of being side-tracked by the idea that you can develop a spiritual life apart from physical accompaniments. It is a desperately dangerous thing to allow the spiritual vision to go ahead of physical obedience.
Do some practical obeying. MFL. 80

It is not sinful to have a body and a natural life; if it were, it would be untrue to say that Jesus Christ was sinless, because He had a body and was placed in a natural life; but He continually sacrificed His natural life to the word and the will of His Father and made it a spiritual life, and we have to form the same habit. It is the discipline of a lifetime; we cannot do it all at once. MFL. 104

We have to remember that we have a bodily machine which we must regulate, God does not regulate it for us. Until we learn to bring the bodily machine into harmony with God's Will, there will be friction, and the friction is a warning that part of the machine is not in working order. As we bring our bodily

life into line bit by bit we shall find that we have God's marvellous grace on the inside enabling us to work out what He has worked in. MFL. 121

The only way in which we can have God as our Guest is by receiving from Him the Holy Spirit Who will turn our bodies into His house. It is not that we prepare a palace for God, but that He comes into our mortal flesh and we do our ordinary work, in an ordinary setting, amongst ordinary people, as for Him. NKW. 74

It is one thing to have the body in subjection, but another thing to be able to command it. When I command my body, I make it an ally, the means by which my spiritual life is furthered. OBH. 116

If I am to serve Jesus Christ, I have to remember that my body is the temple of the Holy Ghost. Talk about it being a 'soft' thing to be a follower of Jesus Christ! It is about the sternest and most heroic thing a man ever 'struck' in his life to keep himself absolutely undefiled, one who by chastity maintains his integrity. It is a discipline, and thank God for the discipline. PH. 148

It is not a sin to have a body, to have natural appetites, but it is a sin to refuse to sacrifice them at the word of God. PS. 12

The life of nature is neither moral nor immoral; our bodies are neither moral nor immoral, we make them moral or immoral. PS. 12

The dust of a man's body is his glory, not his shame. Jesus Christ manifested Himself in that dust, and He claims that He can presence any man with His own divinity. SHH. 57

The Bible teaches that the body is the temple of the Holy Ghost, it was moulded by God of the dust of the ground and is man's chief glory, not his shame. When God became Incarnate "He took not on Him the nature of angels," but was made "in the likeness of men," and it is man's body that is yet to manifest the glory of God on earth. Material things are going to be translucent with the light of God. SHH, 67

God does not give a man a new body when he is saved: his body is the same, but he is given a new disposition. God alters the mainspring; He puts love in the place of lust. SSM. 34

BODY/SOUL/SPIRIT

A common mistake is to infer that the soul was made along with the body; the Bible says that the body was created prior to the soul. Man's body was formed by God "of the dust of the ground"; which means that man is constituted to have affinity with everything on this earth. This is not man's calamity but his peculiar dignity. We do not further our spiritual life in spite of our bodies, but in and by means of our bodies. Then we read that God "breathed into his nostrils the breath of life; and man became a living soul," i.e., a soul-enlivened nature. BP. 13

God's inbreathing into man's nostrils the breath of life called into actual existence his soul, which was potentially in the body, i.e., existing in possibility. Man's soul is neither his body nor his spirit, it is that creation which holds his spirit and his body together, and is the medium of expressing his spirit in his body. It is not true to state that man's soul moulds his body; it is his spirit that moulds his body, and soul is the medium his spirit uses to express itself. BP. 15

The marvellous revelation is that in and through Jesus Christ, our personality in its three aspects of body, soul and spirit, is sanctified and preserved blameless in this dispensation; and in another dispensation, body, soul and spirit will be instinct with the glory of God. BP. 15

The Bible reveals that every part of man's physical life is closely connected with sin or with salvation, and that anything that sin has put wrong, Jesus Christ can put right. We are dealing with soul as it expresses itself through the body. The organs of the body are used as indicators of the state of the spiritual life. BP. 73

. . . our body is the most gracious gift God has given us, and that if we hand over the mainspring of our life to God we can work out in our bodily life all that He works in. It is through our bodily lives that Satan works and, thank God, it is through our bodily lives that God's Spirit works. God gives us His grace and His Spirit; He puts right all that was wrong, He does not suppress it nor counteract it, but readjusts the whole thing; then begins our work. BP. 132

Soul and body depend upon each other, spirit does not, spirit is immortal. Soul is simply the spirit expressing itself in the body. Immediately the body goes, the soul is gone, but the moment the body is brought back, soul is brought back, and spirit, soul and body will again be together. Spirit has never died, can never die, in the sense in which the body dies; the spirit is immortal, either in immortal life or in immortal death. There is no such thing as annihilation taught in the Bible. The separation of spirit from body and soul is temporary. The resurrection is the resurrection of the body. BP. 259

Soul is the expression of spirit in the body; soul has no existence apart from spirit and body. Immediately body goes, the spirit returns to God who gave it, and soul is not. The resurrection is of body, not of spirit or soul. Spirit is the immortal, indestructible part of a man, and it goes back to God who gave it, with all the characteristics that marked it while it was on this earth. BSG. 74

Never run away with the idea that you are a person who has a spirit, has a soul, and has a body; you are a person that *is* spirit, soul and body. Man is one; body, soul and spirit are terms of definition. My body is the manifest "me." CHI. 38

When we are filled with the Holy Spirit He unites us body, soul and spirit with God until we are one with God even as Jesus was. This is the meaning of the Atonement—at-one-ment with God. IWP. 16

God never develops one part of our being at the expense of the other; spirit, soul and body are kept in harmony. IWP. 33

Beware of dividing man up into body, soul and spirit. Man *is* body, soul and spirit. Soul is the expression of man's personal spirit in his body. Spirit means I, myself, the incalculable being that is 'me,' the essence that expresses itself in the soul. The immortal part of a man is not his soul, but his spirit. Man's spirit is as indestructible as Almighty God; the expression of his spirit in the soul depends on the body. In the Bible the soul is always referred to in connection with the body. The soul is the holder of the body and spirit together, and when

the body disappears, the soul disappears, but the essential personality of the man remains. PR. 10

There are two entrances into the soul, viz., the body and the spirit. The body is within our control, the spirit is not, and if our spirit is not under the control of God there is nothing to prevent other spirits communicating through it to the soul and body. It is impossible to guard our spirit, the only One who can guard its entrances is God. SHL. 57

We cannot play the fool with our bodies and souls and hoodwink God. Certain kinds of moral disobedience produce sicknesses which no physical remedy can touch, the only cure is obedience to Jesus Christ. SHL. 56

BOOKS

. . . if you are religious, it is easier to read some pious book than the Bible. The Bible treats you like human life does—roughly. AUG. 77

We are always more willing to get ideas from books and from other people, which is simply an indication that we are not willing to attend but prefer to have our natural interest awakened. We scoop other people's brains either in books or in conversation in order to avoid attending ourselves. MFL. 58

The books and the men who help us most are not those who teach us, but those who can express for us what we feel inarticulate about. PH. 154

We should always choose our books as God chooses our friends, just a bit beyond us, so that we have to do our level best to keep up with them. If we choose our own friends, we choose those we can lord it over. SHH. 66

BORN AGAIN

In the natural world it is impossible to be made all over again, but in the spiritual world it is exactly what Jesus Christ makes possible. "Verily, verily, I say unto you, Except a man be born again, he cannot see the kingdom of God." BFB. 35

If ever we are to see the domain where Jesus lives and enter into it, we must be born again, become regenerated by receiving the Holy Spirit; then we shall find that Truth is not in a creed or a logical statement, but in Life and Personality. BFB. 102

Jesus Christ's salvation works first at the centre, not at the circumference. No one is capable of thinking about being born, or of how they will live when they are born, until they are born; we have to be born into this world first before we can think about it. "Marvel not that I said unto thee, Ye must be born again,"—'you must be born into a new world first, and if you want to know My doctrine, do My will' said Jesus. A right relation to God first is essential. BP. 144

No man ought to need to be born again; the fact that he does indicates that something has gone wrong with the human race. CHI. 19

Human earnestness and vowing cannot make a man a disciple of Jesus Christ any more than it can turn him into an angel; a man must receive something, and that is the meaning of being born again. When once a man is struck by his need of the Holy Spirit, God will put the Holy Spirit into his spirit. LG. 113

When we are born again we become natural for the first time; as long as we are in sin we are abnormal, because sin is not normal. MFL. 72

The whole meaning of being born again and becoming identified with the death of Christ is that His life might be manifested in our mortal flesh. When we are born from above the life of the Son of God is born in us, and the perfection of that life enables us not only to 'make out' what the will of God is, but to carry out His will in our natural human life. OPG. 5

Unless we are born again, we will always be 'natural' men. PR. 11

If I am a Christian, to whom is my appeal? To none but to those God sends you to. You can't get men to come; nobody could get you to come till you came. "The wind bloweth where it listeth . . . so is everyone that is born of the Spirit." RTR. 75

Nothing has any power to alter a man save the incoming of the life of Jesus, and that is the only sign that he is born again. RTR. 76

Education will never alter the "want to," neither will high ideals nor vowing; that is where the great fundamental mistake in dealing with human problems has been made. It is only when a man is born from above of the Spirit of God that he finds the "want to" is altered. God does not take away the capacity to go wrong; if He did, we should not be worth anything. It is never impossible to go wrong. SHH. 106

If we say we are right with God, the world has a perfect right to watch our private life and see if we are so. If we say we are born again, we are put under scrutiny, and rightly so. SSM. 101

BROTHERHOOD

Remember, each life has a solitary way alone with God. Be reverent with His ways in dealing with other souls because you have no notion, any more than Job had, why things are as they are. Most of us are much too desirous of getting hold of a line which will vindicate us in our view of God. DI. 13

All men are brothers, but they are not the brothers of Christ until they have become so by a moral likeness of disposition. LG. 128

Men who are not the servants of God may have a right vision in view for the human race, a vision of the time when men shall live as brothers. The difference does not lie in the vision, because the source of the vision is the Spirit of God; it lies in the way the vision is to be fulfilled. LG. 128

BURDEN

We must strenuously cast our ways and our burdens on Him and wait for Him in all haphazard and topsy-turvy moments. RTR. 42

We must distinguish between the burden-bearing that is right and the burden-bearing that is wrong. We ought never to bear the burden of sin or doubt, but there are burdens placed on us by God which He does not intend to lift off. He wants us to roll them back on Him. "Cast that He hath given thee upon the Lord" (Psalm 1v, 22 R.V.). RTR. 50

BUSINESS

It is a foolish and a shameful thing to be a saint in business. To be a saint may be to be outcast and ridiculed. Try it. CD. VOL. 2, 87

". . . not slothful in business," i.e., the Lord's business. Don't exhaust yourself with other things. DI. 47

C

CALLING

It is an erroneous notion that you have to wait for the call of God: see that you are in such a condition that you can realize it. DI. 10

Call is the inner motive of having been gripped by God—spoilt for every aim in life saving that of disciplining men to Jesus. DI. 10

No experience on earth is sufficient to be taken as a call of God; you must know that the call is from God for whom you care more than for all your experiences; then nothing can daunt you. DI. 10

If I hear the call of God and refuse to obey, I become the dullest, most common-place of Christians because I have seen and heard and refused to obey. DI. 10

We need no call of God to help our fellow men, that is the natural call of humanity; but we do need the supernatural work of God's grace before we are fit for God to help Himself through us. DI. 11

The call of God only becomes clear as we obey, never as we weigh the *pros* and *cons* and try to reason it out. NKW. 12

One man or woman called of God is worth a hundred who have elected to work for God. RTR. 41

CALVARY

We hear it said that if God created everything that was created, then He is responsible for the presence of sin. The Bible reveals all through that God has taken the responsibility for sin. What is the proof that He has? Calvary! BP. 228

If it cost God Calvary to deal with sin, we have no business to make light of it. CHI. 16

'Calvary' means 'the place of a skull,' and that is where our Lord is always crucified, in the culture and intellect of men who will not have self-knowledge given by the light of Jesus Christ. HG. 36

At the back of all the condemnation of God put 'Calvary'. OPG. 17

The sin of the world upon the Son of God rent the Holy Ghost from Him on the Cross, and the cry on Calvary is the cry of the Holy Ghost to Jesus Christ— "My God, My God, why hast Thou forsaken Me?" It was not the cry of Jesus Christ to His Father. Jesus never spoke to God as 'God'; He spoke to Him always as "Father." PR. 86

If any human life can stand before God on its own basis, Calvary is much ado about nothing. If it can be proved that rationalism is the basis of human life, then the New Testament is nonsense; instead of its being a revelation, it is a cunningly devised fable. PR. 95

34

If we can stand before God apart from Jesus Christ, we have proved that Calvary is not needed. PR. 95

Be careful how you picture our Lord when you read His terrible utterances. Read His denunciations with Calvary in your mind. SSM. 92

CAUSE

I have no right to identify myself with a cause unless it represents that for which Jesus Christ died. PH. 36

We are not out for our cause at all as Christians, we are out for the cause of God, which can never be our cause. It is not that God is on our side, we must see that we are on God's side, which is a different matter. PH. 180

CHANCE

If once we accept the Lord Jesus Christ and the domination of His Lordship, then nothing happens by chance, because we know that God is ordering and engineering circumstances, the fuss has gone, the amateur providence has gone, the amateur disposer has gone, and we know that "all things work together for good to them that love God." IYA. 20

Things look as if they happen by chance, but behind all is the purpose of God, and the New Testament reveals what that purpose is. PH. 38

The fact that history fulfils prophecy is a small matter compared to our maintenance of a right relationship to God Who is working out His purposes. The things that happen do not happen by chance at all, they happen entirely in the decrees of God. PH. 181

Who of us can see, behind chance and in chance, God? Who of us can see the finger of God in the weather? When we are in living touch with God we begin to discern that nothing happens by chance. RTR. 88

CHARACTER

Manners refer to Christian character, and we are responsible for our manners. BP. 42

Character is the whole trend of a man's life, not isolated acts here and there, and God deals with us on the line of character building. BP. 109

Character in a saint means the disposition of Jesus Christ persistently manifested. BP. 205

Character is the sum total of a man's actions. You cannot judge a man by the good things he does at times; you must take all the times together, and if in the greater number of times he does bad things, he is a bad character, in spite of the noble things he does intermittently. BP. 205

God Himself, our Lord Jesus Christ, and the saints, are examples of contradiction judged by every standard saving one, viz., the standard of personal responsibility to God on the basis of personal character. CD. VOL. 1, 5

God alters our disposition, but He does not make our character. When God alters my disposition the first thing the new disposition will do is to stir up my brain to think along God's line. As I begin to think, begin to work out what God has worked in, it will become character. Character is consolidated thought. God makes me pure in heart; I must make myself pure in conduct. CHI. 58

Crises reveal character. When we are put to the test the hidden resources of our character are revealed exactly. DI. 30

In this life we must forgo much in order that we might develop a spiritual character which can be a glory to God for Time and Eternity. DI. 33

It is an appalling fact that our features tell our moral character unmistakably to those who can read them, and we may be very thankful there are few who can; our safety is in other people's ignorance. In spite of the disguise of refinement, sensuality, selfishness and self-indulgence speak in our features as loud as a thunder-clap. Our inner spirit tells with an indelible mark on every feature, no matter how beautiful or how ugly the features may be. Let us remember that that is how God sees us. DI. 33

God is no respecter of persons with regard to salvation, but He has a tremendous respect for Christian character. There are degrees in glory which are determined by our obedience. DI. 55

We have to develop a saintly character by fight. Jesus Christ fits us to be overcomers. GW. 102

The one thing God is after is character. HG. 27

If there is anything hidden from us as disciples to-day it is because we are not in a fit state to understand it. As soon as we become fit in spiritual character the thing is revealed, it is concealed at God's discretion until the life is developed sufficiently. IWP. 123

The revelation of God to me is determined by my character, not by God's. If I am mean, that is how God will appear to me.

> 'Tis because I am mean,
> Thy ways so oft
> Look mean to me.' NKW. 127

God does not supply us with character, He gives us the life of His Son and we can either ignore Him and refuse to obey Him, or we can so obey Him, so bring every thought and imagination into captivity, that the life of Jesus is manifested in our mortal flesh. It is not a question of being saved from hell, but of being saved in order to manifest the Son of God in our mortal flesh. Our responsibility is to keep ourselves fit to manifest Him. OBH. 73

Character is the way we have grown to act with our hands and our feet, our eyes and our tongue, and the character we make always reveals the ruling disposition within. If any man is in Christ, there is a new creation. OBH. 81

We must never put character in the place of faith, there is a great danger of doing so. Our character can never be meritorious before God: we stand before God on the basis of His grace. Character is the evidence that we are built on the right foundation. OBH. 120

The way I will discern God's character is determined by my own character. God remains true to His character, and as I grow in integrity I discern Him. OPG. 53

. . . a crisis does not make character; a crisis reveals character. PS. 42

A man's character is what he habitually is. SA. 50

Character must be attained, it is never given to us. SA. 94

If I receive the Spirit of God and become a son of God by right of regeneration, God does not give me my Christian character, I have to make that. He gives me the disposition of His Son; He puts Holy Spirit into me, then He says— Now, breast and back as they should be, and work it out. SA. 109

We make character out of our disposition. Character is what we make, disposition is what we are born with; and when we are born again we are given a new disposition. A man must make his own character, but he cannot make his disposition; that is a gift. Our natural disposition is gifted to us by heredity; by regeneration God gives us the disposition of His Son. SSM. 29

If the Holy Spirit has transformed us within, we will not exhibit good human characteristics, but Divine characteristics in our human nature. SSM. 53

No man is born with character; we make our own character. When a man is born from above a new disposition is given to him, but not a new character; neither naturally nor supernaturally are we born with character. Character is what a man makes out of his disposition as it comes in contact with external things. A man's character cannot be summed up by what he does in spots, but only by what he is in the main trend of his existence. When we describe a man we fix on the exceptional things, but it is the steady trend of a man's life that tells. Character is that which steadily prevails, not something that occasionally manifests itself. SSM. 76

CHASTENING

The chief ingredient in chastening is that it is meant to develop us, and is a means of expression. BFB. 23

If we are despising the chastening of the Lord and fainting when rebuked of Him, it is because we do not understand what God is doing; He is weaning us from creatures to Himself, from the things we have been united to instead of being united to Him only. IWP. 15

We say, 'sorrow, disaster, calamity'; God says, 'chastening,' and it sounds sweet to Him though it is a discord in our ears. Don't faint when you are rebuked, and don't despise the chastenings of the Lord. "In your patience possess ye your souls." If God has given you a time of rest, then lie curled up in His leaves of healing. LG. 74

CHASTITY

Our Lord requires not only chastity of body, He requires chastity of thought. NKW. 87

Personal chastity is an impregnable barrier against evil. Like virtue, chastity is not a gift, but an attainment of determined integrity. Unsoiledness may be nothing more than necessity, the result of a shielded life, and is no more chastity than innocence is purity. Virtue and chastity are forged by me, not by God. OPG. 71

Gain a moral victory in chastity or in your emotional life, it may be known to no one but yourself, and you are an untold benefit to everyone else; but if you refuse to struggle everyone else is enervated. This is a recognised psychological law, although little known. PH. 79

One ounce of chastity is worth fifty years of intellect in moral discernment. SHH. 88

The one thing Jesus Christ insists on in my bodily life is chastity. As individuals we must not desecrate the temple of God by tampering with anything we ought not to tamper with; if we do, the scourge of God will come. SHL. 71

Chastity is strong and fierce, and the man who is going to be chaste for Jesus Christ's sake has a gloriously sterling job in front of him. SSM. 36

CHILD

When we are rightly related to God as Jesus was, the spiritual life becomes as natural as the life of a child. BSG. 14

When a little child becomes conscious of being a little child, the child-likeness is gone; and when a saint becomes conscious of being a saint, something has gone wrong. OBH. 66

The religion of Jesus Christ is the religion of a little child. There is no affectation about a disciple of Jesus, he is as a little child, amazingly simple but unfathomably deep. Many of us are not childlike enough, we are childish. Jesus said—"Except ye become *as little children. . . .*" OBH. 97

Jesus Christ uses the child-spirit as a touchstone for the character of a disciple. He did not put up a child before His disciples as an ideal, but as an expression of the simple-hearted life they would live when they were born again. The life of a little child is expectant, full of wonder, and free from self-consciousness, and Jesus said, "Except ye turn, and become as little children, ye

shall in no wise enter into the kingdom of heaven." PH. 185

The Spirit of God creates the intuitions of a child in a man and keeps him in touch with the elemental and real, and the miracle of Christianity is that a man can be made young in heart and mind and spirit. PH. 186

Jesus Christ says, "Except ye become as little children. . . ." A little child is certain of its parents, but uncertain about everything else, therefore it lives a perfectly delightful healthy life. RTR. 85

Jesus Christ founded His Kingdom on the weakest link of all—a Baby. SHH. 46

When once we are related to Jesus Christ, our relation to actual life is that of a child, perfectly simple and marvellous. SHH. 74

. . . If I never correct my child I am making a nice mess for other folks by and by. SHH. 116

We are so built that in childhood we can more easily come to a knowledge of God in simplicity than in later years. And in those formative years the personal life can be shaped and fitted to God's standard more surely than later on. SHH. 149

Profoundly speaking, a child is not pure, and yet the innocence of a child charms us because it makes visible all that we understand by purity. SHL. 67

CHOICE

. . . in your practical life you come to a crisis where there are two distinct ways before you, one the way of ordinary, strong, moral, common sense and the other the way of waiting on God until the mind is formed which can understand His will. Any amount of backing will be given you for the first line, the backing of worldly people and of semi-Christian people, but you will feel the warning, the drawing back of the Spirit of God, and if you wait on God, study His Word, and watch Him at work in your circumstances, you will be brought to a decision along God's line, and your worldly 'backers' and your semi-Christian 'backers' will fall away from you with disgust and say, 'It is absurd, you are getting fanatical.' BP. 242

The one great enemy of discipleship to Jesus Christ is spiritual obstinacy, the emphatic 'I won't' which runs all through. Jesus says, 'If you are to be My disciple this and that must go'; we are at liberty to say, 'No, thank you,' and to go away like the rich young ruler with fallen countenances and sorrowful because we have great possessions, we are somebodies, we have opinions of our own, we know exactly what we intend to do. HG. 8

When we pray in the Holy Ghost we begin to have a more intimate conception of God; the Holy Ghost brings all through us the sense of His resources. For instance, we may be called to a definite purpose for our life which the Holy Ghost reveals and we know that it means a decision, a reckless fling over on to God, a burning of our bridges behind us; and there is not a soul to advise us when we take that step saving the Holy Ghost. Our clingings come in this way—we put one foot on God's side and one on the side of human reasoning; then God widens the space until we either drop down in between or jump on to one side or the other. We have to take a leap, a reckless leap, and if we have learned to rely on the Holy Ghost, it will be a reckless leap on to God's side. IYA. 62

The freedom man has is not that of power but of choice, consequently he is accountable for choosing the course he takes. For instance, we can choose whether or not we will accept the proposition of salvation which God puts before us; whether or not we will let God rule our lives; but we have not the power to do exactly what we like. MFL. 27

I am at liberty if I choose to try every independent plan of my own, but I shall find in the end (whether too late or not is another matter), that what God said I had better do at the beginning was the right thing, if only I had listened to Him. NKW. 56

The power of individual choice is the secret of human responsibility. I can choose which line I will go on, but I have no power to alter the destination of that line once I have taken it—yet I always have the power to get off one line on to the other. OPG. 50

A man must believe in Jesus Christ by a deliberate determination of his own choice. PR. 67

"Many are called, but few chosen," i.e. few prove themselves the chosen ones. PS. 46

CHRIST, Teaching of

Try to apply the teachings of Jesus to your life without an understanding of His Death and you will find it cannot be done; it would either make you commit suicide or take you to the Cross and give you an understanding of why it was necessary for Him to die. BSG. 13

. . . we have got away from Jesus Christ's teaching. We bring in all kinds of things, we talk about salvation and sanctification and forgiveness of sins; Jesus did not mention these things to Nicodemus HG. 7

When we try to understand Jesus Christ's teaching with our heads we get into a fog. What Jesus Christ taught is only explainable to the personality of the mind in relation to the personality of Jesus Christ. It is a relationship of life, not of intellect. HG. 9

If He is a Teacher only, then He is a most cruel Teacher, for He puts ideals before us that blanch us white to the lips and lead us to a hell of despair. But if He came to do something else as well as teach—if He came to re-make us on the inside and put within us His own disposition of unsullied holiness, then we can understand why He taught like He did. HG. 14

Jesus Christ will not water down His teaching to suit our weakness in any shape or form; He will not allow us to cringe in the tiniest degree. Whenever there is a trace of cringing or whining, or wanting something different from what He wants, it is the stern front of the Son of God uncloaking sin every time we look at Him; but if we come as paupers, what happens? Exactly the opposite. He will lift us up and wash us whiter than snow, and put the Holy Ghost in us and place us before the Throne of God, undeserving of censure, by the sheer omnipotence of His Atonement. HG. 32

Jesus Christ bases all His teaching on the fundamental fact that God can do for a man what he cannot do for himself. HGM. 100

Jesus Christ's teaching never beats about the bush. OPG. 15

Jesus Christ did not come to teach man to be what he cannot be, but to reveal that He can put into him a totally new heredity; and all He requires a man to say is—"I need it"—no shibboleth, but a recognition of his need. SA. 38

If Jesus Christ is only a Teacher, then all He can do is to tantalize us, to erect a standard we cannot attain to; but when we are born again of the Spirit of God, we know that He did not come only to teach us, *He came to make us what He teaches we should be.* SA. 85

Whenever Jesus Christ applied His teaching to actual life He focussed it round two points—marriage and money. If the religion of Jesus Christ and the indwelling of the Spirit of God cannot deal with these things and keep a man and woman as God wants them to be, His religion is useless. SHH. 48

. . . the teaching of Jesus Christ does not appear at first to be what it is. At first it appears to be beautiful and pious and lukewarm; but before long it becomes a ripping and tearing torpedo which splits to atoms every preconceived notion a man ever had. SSM. 51

Unless Jesus Christ can remake us within, His teaching is the biggest mockery human ears ever listened to. SSM. 52

CHRISTIAN

The supreme test of a Christian is that he has the Spirit of Jesus Christ in his actual life. AUG. 78

As long as a Christian complies with the standards of this world, the world recognizes him; but when he works from the real standard, which is God, the world cannot understand him, and consequently it either ignores or ridicules him. BP. 187

I am not here to be a specimen of what God can do; I am here to live the life so hid with Christ in God that what Jesus said will be true, 'Men will see your good works, and glorify your Father which is in heaven.' BSG. 45

A Christian is a sanctified man in his business, or legal or civic affairs, or artistic and literary affairs. CD. VOL. 2, 86

In every age it has always been the despised crowd that have been called Christians. CD. VOL. 2, 146

Unless Christians are facing up to God's commands there is no use pushing forward to meet the life of our time. Jesus wants us to face the life of our time in the power of the Holy Ghost. CHI. 54

We should make less excuses for the weaknesses of a Christian than for any other man. A Christian has God's honour at stake. DI. 72

When a man is regenerated and bears the Name of Christ the Spirit of God will see to it that he is scrutinized by the world, and the more we are able to meet that scrutiny the healthier will we be as Christians. DI. 73

The men with God's 'go' in them have these three characteristics—a saving experience; the evidence of supernatural power at work, and the spiritual efficacy of success in prayer. GW. 47

It is impossible for a man to become a Christian by natural reasoning effort, which is simply the working of his own mind; a man becomes a Christian by there being wrought in him 'a new creation', and that new creation is 'the forming of the Son of God' in him. 'The old things are passed away; behold, they are become new': God does not discard the old, He creates that in the old which makes the old and the new one. GW. 63

No Christian has any right to be un-enthusiastic. 'And be not drunk with wine, wherein is excess; but be filled with the Spirit.' It is easy for many men to obey the first part of this injunction while they disobey the latter. GW. 68

Our conception of things has to be torn to shreds until we realize that what makes a man a Christian is a simple heart-relationship to Jesus Christ, not intellectual conceptions. HG. 9

A Christian is an impossible being unless a man can be made all over again. HGM. 14

When I become a Christian Jesus Christ exhibits the character of His own Name in me. HGM. 97

If you are trying to be a Christian it is a sure sign you are not one. IWP. 83

The New Testament view of a Christian is that he is one in whom the Son of God has been revealed, and prayer deals with the nourishment of that life. One way it is nourished is by refusing to worry over anything, for worry means there is something over which we cannot have our own way, and is in reality personal irritation with God. Jesus Christ says, 'Don't worry about your life, don't fear them which kill the body; be afraid only of not doing what the Spirit of God indicates to you.' IYA. 13

A Christian's duty is not to himself or to others, but to Christ. IYA. 83

There are a great many people trying to be Christians; they pray and long and fast and consecrate, but it is nothing but imitation, it has no life in it. MFL. 21

. . . you cannot be a Christian by trying; you must be born into the life before you can live it. MFL. 21

We are apt to think of a Christian as a civilised individual; a Christian is one who is identified with Jesus and who has learned the lesson that the servant is not greater than his Lord. OBH. 61

The one essential thing which makes a man a Christian is not what he believes in his head but what he is in disposition. PH. 61

A Christian is not consistent to hard and fast creeds, he is consistent only to the life of the Son of God in him. PH. 62

The Christian is one who trusts the wisdom of God, not his own wits. The astute mind behind the saint's life is the mind of God, not his own mind. PH. 182

The characteristic of a man who has come to God is that you cannot get him to take anyone seriously but God. PH. 185

If we have been trying to be holy, it is a sure sign we are not. Christians are born, not made. They are not produced by imitation, nor by praying and vowing; they are produced by new birth. PR. 35

The Baptism and the Transfiguration reveal Who our Lord is, and the secret of the Christian is that he knows the absolute Deity of Jesus Christ. PR. 73

"For we are unto God a sweet savour of Christ." We are enwheeled with the odour of Jesus, and wherever we go we are a wonderful refreshment to God. RTR. 46

That a Christian can smilingly do a smart trick is a staggering thing. Destruction of conscientiousness means we have lost the fierce purity of the Holy Ghost and taken on the pattern and print of the age. RTR. 71

For one man who can introduce another to Jesus Christ by the way he lives and by the atmosphere of his life, there are a thousand who can only talk jargon about Him. RTR. 76

It is not necessary for a man to understand things before he can be a Christian. The understanding of the mystery of life is a secondary thing; the main thing is to be alive. SA. 21

The Christian aspect of God represents the One Who has been in the very thick of it; and whenever a man through Nature or through conviction of sin touches the moral frontiers, then the work of Jesus Christ begins. SA. 29

A Christian is a disciple of Jesus Christ's by the possession of a new heredity, one who has been brought into personal relationship with Jesus Christ by the indwelling Spirit of God, not one with certain forms of creed or doctrine; these are the effects of his relationship, not the ground of it. SA. 68

God made man of the dust of the ground, and that dust can express either Deity or devilishness. Remember we are to be not numbskulls, but holy men, full-blooded and holy to the last degree, not anæmic creatures without enough strength to be bad. SHH. 99

A Christian is an avowed agnostic. I cannot find God out by my reason, therefore I have to accept the revelation given of Him by Jesus Christ. SHH. 144

The Christian life is drawn from first to last, and all in between, from the Resurrection life of the Lord Jesus. SHL. 18

CHRISTIANITY

Christianity is a society based on the brotherhood of men who have been lifted into a right relationship with God by regeneration. AUG. 17

Christianity is in its essence social. When once we begin to live from the otherworldly standpoint, as Jesus Christ wants us to live, we shall need all the fellowship with other Christians we can get. Some of us can do without Church fellowship because we are not Christians of the otherworldly order. Immediately a man dares to live on Jesus Christ's line, the world, the flesh and the devil are dead against him in every particular. 'The only virtue you will have in the eyes of the world as My disciples,' says Jesus, 'is that you will be hated.' That is why we need to be knit together with those of like faith; and that is the meaning of the Christian Church. AUG. 17

The essence of Christianity is not a creed or a doctrine, but an illumination that emancipates me—'I see who Jesus Christ is'. It is always a surprise, never an intellectual conception. AUG. 83

If . . . Jesus Christ is not a humbug, and not a dreamer, but what He claims to be, then Christianity is the grandest fact that ever was introduced to any man. AUG. 84

Christianity is personal, passionate devotion to Jesus Christ as God manifest in the flesh. AUG. 115

Christianity is drawing on the overflowing favour of God in the second of trial. AUG. 124

The Christian revelation is not that Jesus Christ stands to us as the Representative of God, but that He *is* God. If He is not, then we have no God. ". . . *God was in Christ*, reconciling the world unto Himself." We do not worship an austere, remote God, He is here in the thick of it. BE. 61

There is a presentation of Christianity which is sentimental and weak and unworthy of God; the Christianity of the New Testament is something "angels desire to look into". BE. 65

Christianity is not consistency to conscience or to convictions; Christianity is being true to Jesus Christ. BE. 66

Wherever Christianity has ceased to be vigorous it is because it has become Christian *ethics* instead of the Christian *evangel*. BE. 66

It is absurd to call Christianity a system of non-resistance; the great doctrine of Christianity is resistance 'unto blood' against sin. BE. 67

The Christian faith affirms the existence of a personal God Who reveals Himself. Pseudo-Christianity departs from this, we are told we cannot know anything at all about God, we do not know whether He is a personal Being, we cannot know whether He is good. The Christian revelation is that God is a personal Being and He is good. By 'good', I mean morally good. BE. 102

The central citadel of Christianity is the Person of our Lord Jesus Christ. The final standard for the Christian is given at the outset—"to be conformed to the image of His Son." BE. 108

Christianity is a personal relationship to a personal God on the ground of the Redemption. The reason Jesus Christ is our Lord and Master is not first because He is God Incarnate, but because He is easily first in the human domain. BFB. 94

The test of Christianity is that a man lives better than he preaches. BFB. 104

Christianity does not consist in telling the truth, or walking in a conscientious way, or adhering to principles; Christianity is something other than all that, it is adhering in absolute surrender to a Person, the Lord Jesus Christ. BFB. 106

God has loved me to the end of all my sinfulness, the end of all my self-will, all my selfishness, all my stiff-necked-ness, all my pride, all my self-interest; now He says—"love one another; as I have loved you." I am to show to my fellow-men the same love that God showed to me. That is Christianity in practical working order. BP. 192

Christianity is based on heroism and manifested in martyrdom; and the prep-aration for being a Christian is drastic, definite and destructive. CD. VOL. 2, 73

In Christianity the Kingdom and its laws and principles must be put first, and everything else second, and if the holy calling demands it, there must be instant and military obedience, leaving all and rallying round the standard of Jesus Christ. CD. VOL. 2, 86

The greatest test of Christianity is the wear and tear of daily life, it is like the shining of silver, the more it is rubbed the brighter it grows. DI. 30

Christianity is not service for Jesus Christ, not winning souls, it is nothing less than the life of Jesus being man-ifested more and more in my mortal flesh. DI. 37

In our modern conception of Chris-tianity there is no miracle, the empha-sis is put not on the regenerating power of the Cross, but on individual con-secrations, individual fasting and prayer, individual devotion. It is simply individualism veneered over with re-ligious phraseology. There is no need for the Cross of Christ for all that kind of thing. GW. 55

If Jesus Christ cannot produce a meek-ness and lowliness of heart like His own, Christianity is nonsense from be-ginning to end, and His teaching had better be blotted out. HG. 16

We have, as Christian disciples, to con-tinually recognize that much of what is called Christianity to-day is not the Christianity of the New Testament; it is distinctly different in generation and manifestation. Jesus is not the fountain-head of modern Christianity; He is scarcely thought about. Christian preachers, Sunday School teachers, re-ligious books, all without any apology patronize Jesus Christ and put Him on one side. We have to learn that to stand true to Jesus Christ's point of view means ostracism, the ostracism that was brought on Him; most of us know nothing whatever about it. The modern view looks upon human nature as pa-thetic: men and women are poor igno-rant babes in the wood who have lost themselves. Jesus Christ's view is totally different, He does not look on men and women as babes in the wood, but as sinners who need saving, and the modern mind detests His view. Our Lord's teaching is based on something we violently hate, viz. His doctrine of sin; we do not believe it unless we have had a radical dealing with God on the line of His teaching. HG. 19

. . . Christianity, if it is not a supernatural miracle, is a sham. HG. 26

Christianity is a complete sham or a supernatural miracle from beginning to end; immediately we admit it is a miracle we are responsible for walking in the light of what we know Jesus Christ to be. HG. 30

People have the idea that Christianity and Stoicism are alike; the writings of the stoics sound so like the teaching of Jesus Christ, but just at the point where they seem most alike, they are most divergent. A stoic overcomes the world by making himself indifferent, by passionlessness; the saint overcomes the world by passionateness, by the passion of his love for Jesus Christ. HG. 34

The bedrock of Christianity is not decision for Christ, for a man who decides banks on his decision, not on God. It is the inability to decide—'I have no power to get hold of God, no power to be what I know He wants me to be.' Then, says Jesus, "Blessed are you." "Blessed are the poor in spirit: for theirs is the kingdom of heaven." HGM. 28

Christianity is a personal relationship to Jesus Christ made efficacious by the indwelling Holy Spirit. HGM. 76

It looks as if we had to give up everything, lose all we have, and instead of Christianity bringing joy and simplicity, it makes us miserable; until suddenly we realize what God's aim is, viz., that we have to take part in our own moral development, and we do this through the sacrifice of the natural to the spiritual by obedience, not denying the natural, but sacrificing it. HGM. 76

The presentation of Christianity which is not based on the New Testament produces an abortion—that a man's main aim is to get saved and put right for heaven; New Testament Christianity produces a strong family likeness to Jesus Christ and a man's notions are not centred on himself. HGM. 78

Christianity is not devotion to work, or to a cause, or a doctrine, but devotion to a Person, the Lord Jesus Christ. HGM. 113

The passion of Christianity is that I deliberately sign away my own rights and become a bondslave of Jesus Christ. HGM. 130

Christianity is not a thing of times and seasons, but of God and faith. LG. 15

Both nations and individuals have tried Christianity and abandoned it, because it has been found too difficult; but no man has ever gone through the crisis of deliberately making Jesus Lord and found Him to be a failure. LG. 127

"The expulsive power of a new affection"—that is what Christianity supplies. The Spirit of God on the basis of Redemption gives us something else to think about. MFL. 63

The danger in the modern form of Christianity is its departure more and more from the great central Figure of the Lord Jesus Christ. PH. 30

The essence of Christianity is that we give the Son of God a chance to live and move and have His being in us, and the meaning of all spiritual growth is that He has an increasing opportunity to manifest Himself in our mortal flesh. PH. 35

If Christianity does not affect my money and my marriage relationships, it is not worth anything. PH. 62

Christianity is not my consciousness of God, but God's consciousness of me. We must build our faith on the reality that we are taken up into God's consciousness in Christ, not that we take God into our consciousness. PH. 111

Christianity is not devotion to a cause or to a set of principles, but devotion to a Person, and the great watchword of a Christian is not a passion for souls, but a passion for Christ. PH. 166

The main thing about Christianity is not the work we do, but the relationship we maintain. The only things God asks us to look after are the atmosphere of our life and our relationships, these are the only things that preserve us from priggishness, from impertinence and from worry, and it is these things that are assailed all through. PH. 178

The Christianity of Jesus Christ refuses to be careworn. Our Lord is indicating that we have to be carefully careless about everything saving our relationship to Him. PH. 185

Christianity is the vital realisation of the unsearchable riches of Christ. PH. 223

Christianity means staking ourselves on the honour of Jesus; His honour means that He will see us through time, death and eternity. PH. 226

Christianity has always been a forlorn hope because the saints are in alien territory; but it is all right, God is working out His tremendous purpose for the overthrow of everything Satan and sin can do. PS. 75

Christianity makes no allowance for heroic moods. It is easy to feel heroic in an armchair, when everything goes well, but Christianity deals with God's standard in the common days when you are out of your arm-chair, and when things are not going well. RTR. 14

Christianity is not service for Jesus Christ, not winning souls; it is nothing less than the life of Jesus being manifested more and more in my mortal flesh. RTR. 39

The essence of Christianity is that we give the Son of God a chance to live and move and have His being in us. RTR. 70

The revelation of Christianity is that God, in order to be of use in human affairs, had to become a typical Man. That is the great revelation of Christianity, that God Himself became human; became incarnate in the weakest side of His own creation. SA. 59

Our Christianity has been as powerless as dish-water with regard to things as they are; consequently the net result of Christianity is judged to be a failure. But Christianity, according to Jesus Christ, has never been tried and failed; it has been tried and abandoned in individual cases because it has been found a bit too hard, too definite and emphatic, and for the same reason it has been abandoned in nations and in Churches; but Christianity has never been tried and gone through with honourably and found to fail. SA. 88

The moral miracle of Christianity is that when I know my limitations, when I reach the frontiers by weakness not by will, Jesus Christ says, Blessed are you, I will do the rest. But I have to get there; it is not that God will not do anything for me until I do, but that He cannot. God cannot put into me, a moral being, the disposition that is in Jesus Christ unless I am conscious I need it. I cannot receive that which I do not believe I need; but when I am struck by an agony, or the sense of helplessness with regard to Jesus Christ's teaching, I am ready then to receive the donation of Deity. SA. 109

The Christian religion founds everything on the radical, positive nature of sin. Sin is self-realization, self-sufficiency, entire and complete mastership of myself—gain that, and you lose control of everything over which God intended you to have dominion. SA. 116

Christianity is based on another universe of facts than the universe we get at by our common sense; it is based on the universe of revelation facts which we only get at by faith born of the Spirit of God. The revelation which Christianity makes is that the essential nature of Deity is holiness, and the might of God is shown in that He became the weakest thing in His own creation. Jesus Christ claims that, on the basis of Redemption, He has put the whole of the human race back to where God designed it to be, and individuals begin to see this when they are awakened by their own agony. SA. 118

The Christian faith is exhibited by the man who has the spiritual courage to say that that is the God he trusts in, and

it takes some moral backbone to do it. SHH. 44

The basis of Christianity is not primarily virtue and honesty and goodness, not even holiness, but a personal relationship to God in Jesus Christ which works out all the time by "spontaneous moral originality." SHH. 124

Christianity is not a 'sanctified' anything; it is the life of Jesus manifested in our mortal flesh by the miracle of His Redemption, and that will mean that whenever a crisis comes, Jesus is instantly seen to be Master without a moment's hesitation; there is no debate. SSY. 87

CHRISTIAN LIFE

Always now is the secret of the Christian life. AUG. 128

The Christian life does not take its pattern from good men, but from God Himself, that is why it is an absolutely supernormal life all through. BE. 80

There is a great snare especially in evangelical circles of knowing the will of God as expressed in the Bible without the slightest practical working of it out in the life. The Christian religion is the most practical thing on earth. CHI. 58

The Christian life is stamped all through with impossibility, human nature cannot come anywhere near what Jesus Christ demands, and any rational being facing His demands honestly, says, 'It can't be done, apart from a miracle'. Exactly. GW. 55

The great simplicity of the Christian life is the relationship to the Highest.

Reckless confidence in God is of far more value than personal holiness, if personal holiness is looked upon as an end in itself. GW. 106

The Christian life is not a bandbox life. We must live where we can be tested by the whole of life. OBH. 107

The Christian life is the simplest, the gayest, the most regardless-of-consequences life, lived as it is taught by Jesus. The plan of our life comes through the haphazard moments, but behind it is the order of God. RTR. 9

The Christian life is stamped by "moral spontaneous originality", consequently the disciple is open to the same charge that Jesus Christ was, viz: that of inconsistency. But Jesus Christ was always consistent to God. RTR. 64

. . . there is nothing more heroic or more grand than the Christian life. SSM. 36

The Christian life is a holy life; never substitute the word 'happy' for 'holy.' We certainly will have happiness, but as a consequence of holiness. SSM. 97

In the Christian life there are stages of experience that are exalted; times when we know what it is to live in the heavenly places in Christ Jesus, when we seem to be more on the mount than anywhere else. But we are not made for the mountain, we are made for the valley; we are made for the actual world, not for the ideal world; but to be so in communion with the ideal that we can work it out in the actual and make it real. SSY. 94

CHRISTIAN SCIENCE

There is no objection to what Christian Science does to people's bodies, but there is a tremendous objection to its effect on people's minds. Its effect on people's minds is to make them intolerably indifferent to physical suffering, and in time it produces the antipodes of the Christian character, viz., a hardness and callousness of heart. BP. 115

The Christian Science theory says there are no such facts as pain or suffering or death, they are all imaginations; it has forgotten that there are bad facts as well as good. AUG. 77

CHURCH

The Church confronts the world with a message the world craves for but resents because it comes through the Cross of Christ. AUG. 39

When the world gets in a bad way, she refers to the Church; when she is prosperous, she hates it. If men could blot out the standard of the Christian Church they would do so: but in a crisis they find a need in their own heart. AUG. 39

The Church does not lead the world nor echo it; she confronts it. Her note is the supernatural note. AUG. 39

The Church owns a mastery the world can neither ignore nor do without, the mastery of the Lord Jesus Christ. AUG. 40

The bedrock of membership of the Christian Church is that we know Who Jesus Christ is by a personal revelation of Him by the Spirit of God. AUG. 83

The institutions of Churchianity are not Christianity. AUG. 83

The Christian Church should not be a secret society of specialists, but a public manifestation of believers in Jesus.

The one right thing to be is a believer in Jesus. AUG. 107

Our Lord said that His Church would be so completely taken up with its precedents and preconceptions that when He came it would be "as a thief in the night"; they would not see Him because they were taken up with another point of view. BFB. 22

The Church is a separated band of people who are united to God by the regenerating power of the Spirit, and the bedrock of membership in the Church is that we know who Jesus is by a personal revelation of Him. The indwelling Spirit is the supreme Guide, and He keeps us absorbed with our Lord. The emphasis to-day is placed on the furtherance of an organisation; the note is, "We must keep this thing going." If we are in God's order the thing will go; if we are not in His order, it won't. CHI. 50

The Church is called to deliver God's message and to be for the praise of His glory, not to be a socialistic institution under the patronage of God. GW. 73

All our Lord succeeded in doing during His life on earth was to gather together a group of fishermen—the whole Church of God and the enterprise of our Lord on earth in a fishing boat! PH. 180

The Church of Jesus Christ is built on these two things: the Divine revelation of Who Jesus Christ is, and the public confession of it. PR. 76

There is only one thing as futile as the Roman Catholic Church and that is Protestantism. In Roman Catholicism the great dominating authority is Churchianity, the Church is vested with all authority. In Protestantism it is what the Book says that is the supreme authority, and a man gets rest when he decides for either. "I am going to give up all the turmoil and let my Church do my thinking for me." SA. 63

The divisions of the churches are to be deplored, and denominationalism is to be deplored, but we must not forget that denominations have reared up the best men we know. SA. 76

The Church of Jesus Christ is an organism; we are built up into Him, baptized by one Spirit into one body. Churchianity is an organization; Christianity is an organism. Organization is an enormous benefit until it is mistaken for the life. God has no concern about our organizations. When their purpose is finished He allows them to be swept aside, and if we are attached to the organization, we shall go with it. Organization is a great necessity, but not an end in itself, and to live for any organization is a spiritual disaster. SA. 118

Our word "Church" is connected with civilized organizations of religious people; Our Lord's attitude to the Church is different. He says it is composed of those who have had a personal revelation from God as to Who Jesus Christ is, and have made a public declaration of the same. SA. 119

According to Our Lord, there is not a home church and a foreign church, it is all one great work, beginning at home and then going elsewhere, 'beginning from Jerusalem.' SSY. 79

CIRCUMCISION

Circumcision, or sanctification which it symbolizes, is the decision to cut away all self-idolatry and abandon to God entirely. The old nature and the new have to be made one, and the sign that they are one is circumcision in the Old Testament and sanctification in the New. NKW. 66

Circumcision is the Old Testament symbol for New Testament sanctification. SSY. 170

CIRCUMSTANCES

It is never the big things that disturb us, but the trivial things. Do I believe in the circumstances that are apt to bother me just now, that Jesus Christ is not perplexed at all? If I do, His peace is mine. If I try to worry it out, I obliterate Him and deserve what I get. CD. VOL. 1, 153

When we know that nothing can separate us from the love of Christ, it does not matter what calamities may occur, we are as unshakeable as God's throne. CD. VOL. 1, 157

That God engineers our circumstances for us if we accept His purpose in Christ Jesus is a thought of great practical moment. CD. VOL. 2, 55

We are not responsible for the circumstances we are in, but we are responsible for the way we allow those circumstances to affect us; we can either allow them to get on top of us, or we can allow them to transform us into what God wants us to be. CHI. 40

If we go under in circumstances we are held responsible because God has promised an absolutely overcoming Spirit to any man who will receive Him. If you are at a loss to know how to get at what God wants you to be, listen to the Lord Jesus. He says, "If you ask God He will

plant in you the very Spirit that is in Me". CHI. 40

If you receive the Holy Spirit you find that circumstances will never have power to do anything but give you the chance of sacrificing the natural to the spiritual and proving you are a son or daughter of God. CHI. 40

God will bring us into circumstances and make us learn the particular lessons He wants us to learn, and slowly and surely we will work out all that He works in. CHI. 55

If I recognize Jesus as my Lord, I have no business with where He engineers my circumstances. GW. 57

Recognize Jesus as Lord, obey Him, and let the next thing happen as He wills. GW. 58

One of the last things we learn is that God engineers our circumstances; we do not believe He does, we say we do. Never look for second causes; if you do, you will go wrong. We blunder when we look at circumstances as secondary, 'And we know that all things work together for good to them that love God, to them who are the called according to His purpose.' GW. 59

God engineers circumstances to see what we will do. HG. 16

It is only the loyal saint who believes that God engineers circumstances. HGM. 131

The things we are going through are either making us sweeter, better, nobler men and women, or they are making us more captious and fault-finding, more insistent on our own way. We are either getting more like our Father in heaven, or we are getting more mean and intensely selfish. IYA. 55

The circumstances of a saint's life are ordained by God, and not by happy-go-lucky chance. IYA. 107

We have an idea that we have to alter things, we have not; we have to remain true to God in the midst of things as they are, to allow things as they are to transmute us. 'Things as they are' are the very means God uses to make us into the praise of His glory. LG. 9

It is in the ordinary commonplace circumstances that the unconscious light of God is seen. LG. 44

God engineers our circumstances as He did those of His Son; all we have to do is to follow where He places us. The majority of us are busy trying to place ourselves. God alters things while we wait for Him. LG. 65

A Christian is one who can live in the midst of the trouble and turmoil with the glory of God indwelling him, while he stedfastly looks not at the things which are seen, but at the things which are not seen. We have to learn to think only of things which are seen as a glorious chance of enabling us to concentrate on the things which are not seen. LG. 89

If you are a child of God and there is some part of your circumstances which is tearing you, if you are living in the heavenly places you will thank God for the tearing things; if you are not in the heavenly places you cry to God over and over again—'O Lord, remove this thing from me. If only I could live in golden streets and be surrounded with angels, and have the Spirit of God consciously indwelling me all the time and have

everything wonderfully sweet, then I think I might be a Christian'. That is not being a Christian! LG. 89

God engineers external things for the purpose of revealing to us whether we are living in this imperturbable place of unutterable strength and glory, viz., the life hid with Christ in God. If we are, then let the troubles and difficulties work as they may on the outside, we are confident that they are working out a grander weight of glory in the heavenlies. LG. 89

It is misleading to imagine that we are developed in spite of our circumstances, we are developed because of them. It is mastery *in* circumstances that is needed, not mastery over them. We have to manifest the graces of the Spirit amongst things as they are, not to wait for the Millennium. LG. 98

Watch when God shifts your circumstances and see whether you are going with Jesus or siding with the world, the flesh and the devil. LG. 153

No matter what your circumstances may be, don't try to shield yourself from things God is bringing into your life. We have the idea sometimes that we ought to shield ourselves from some of the circumstances God brings round us. Never! God engineers circumstances; we have to see that we face them abiding continually with Him in His temptations. They are *His* temptations, they are not temptations to us, but to the Son of God in us. LG. 156

We talk about 'circumstances over which we have no control.' None of us have control over our circumstances, but we are responsible for the way we pilot ourselves in the midst of things as they are. MFL. 95

It is only by living in the presence of God that we cease to act in an ungodlike manner in perplexing circumstances. NKW. 22

God engineers our circumstances and He brings across our paths some extraordinary people, viz., embodiments of ourselves in so many forms, and it is part of the humour of the situation that we recognize ourselves. Now, God says, exhibit the attitude to them that I showed to you. This is the one way of keeping a conscience void of offence towards God and man. OBH. 70

No matter how difficult the circumstances may be, if we will let Jesus Christ manifest Himself in them, it will prove to be a new means of exhibiting the wonderful perfection and extraordinary purity of the Son of God. This keen enthusiasm of letting the Son of God manifest Himself in us is the only thing that will keep us enjoying the discipline of the disagreeable. OBH. 75

When once the saint begins to realize that God engineers circumstances, there will be no more whine, but only a reckless abandon to Jesus. OBH. 104

We are not to be changing and arranging our circumstances ourselves. Our Lord and Master never chose His own circumstances, He was meek towards His Father's dispensation for Him; He was at home with His Father wherever His body was placed. OBH. 107

When you are brought face to face with something in God's word, watch your circumstances: the tyranny of things will either imperil your faith or increase it. RTR. 9

Circumstances make a man reveal what spirit he is of. Crises reveal character more quickly than anything else. SA. 101

. . . you cannot locate yourself, you are placed in circumstances over which you have no control. You do not choose your own heredity or your own disposition, these things are beyond your control, and yet these are the things which influence you. You may rake the bottom of the universe, but you cannot explain things; they are wild, there is nothing rational about them. We cannot get to the bottom of things; we cannot get behind the before of birth or the after of death; therefore the wise man is the one who trusts the wisdom of God, not his own wits. SHH. 121

No one understands your circumstances but God, and He has given you the fighting chance to prove you can be more than conqueror in all these things. Let God lift you out of the broken place, out of the bedraggled place. Let Him put within you the Holy Spirit so that you can face the music of life and become more than conqueror in every place where you have been defeated. SHL. 17

The proof that God has altered our disposition is not that we persuade ourselves He has, but that we prove He has when circumstances put us to the test. SSM. 30

No matter how complicated the circumstances may be, one moment of contact with Jesus and the fuss is gone, the panic is gone, all the shallow emptiness is gone, and His peace is put in, absolute tranquillity, because of what He says—'All power is given unto me.' SSY. 134

We have to be entirely His, to exhibit His Spirit no matter what circumstances we are in. It is extraordinary to watch God alter things. SSY. 171

We have to worship God in the difficult circumstances, and when He chooses, He will alter them in two seconds. SSY. 171

CIVILIZATION

"Seek ye first the kingdom of God"—and apply it to modern life and you will find its statements are either those of a madman or of God Incarnate. AUG. 63

We have the idea that our civilization is God-ordained, whereas it has been built up by ourselves. We have made a thousand and one necessities until our system of civilized life is as cast iron, and then we apologize to the Lord for not following Him. AUG. 63

To follow Jesus Christ to-day is to follow a madman according to the ideals of present-day civilization. AUG. 63

One thing we are realising to-day is that to the majority of us civilised life is an elaborate way of doing without God. We have not been living a life hid with Christ in God, we have been living in the abundance of the things which we possess. CD. VOL. 1, 131

Over-refinement in civilization turns God's order upside down. DI. 15

God has no respect for our civilizations because He did not found them. While civilization is not God's, it is His providential protection for men, generally restraining the bad, and affording His children the means of developing their life in Him. DI. 15

In a time of calamity God appears to pay scant courtesy to all our art and culture, He sweeps the whole thing aside till civilization rages at Him. It is 'the babe' and 'the fool' who get through in the day of God's visitation. DI. 15

Have I ever had a glimpse of this—that God would not be altered if all our civilized life went to pieces? DI. 15

The whole teaching of Jesus is opposed to the idea of civilization, viz., possessing things for myself—'This is mine'. GW. 78

Epochs and civilizations appear after a time to be flung on the scrap-heap by God in a strangely careless manner. The remarkable thing in the record of the Ages that have been, and that are, and that are going to be, is that each Age ends in apparent disaster. GW. 88

Civilization was started by a murderer, and the whole of our civilized life is based on competition. GW. 136

Our present-day communities are man's attempt at building up the city of God; man is confident that if only God will give him time enough he will build not only a holy city, but a holy community and establish peace on earth, and God is allowing him ample opportunity to try, until he is satisfied that God's way is the only way. HG. 14

If we try and live the life Jesus Christ lived, modern civilization will fling us out like waste material; we are no good, we do not add anything to the hard cash of the times we live in, and the sooner we are flung out the better. HG. 28

Jesus knew He was here for His Father's purpose and He never allowed the cares of civilization to bother Him. He did nothing to add to the wealth of the civilization in which He lived, He earned nothing, modern civilization would not have tolerated Him for two minutes. HG. 28

. . . civilizations are despatched at a minute's notice, armies come together and annihilate one another and God seems to pay no attention. His attitude is one which makes us blaspheme and say that He does not care an atom for human beings. Jesus Christ says He does, He says He is a Father, and that He, Jesus, is exactly like His Father. The point is that Jesus saw life from God's standpoint, we don't. We won't accept the responsibility of life as God gives it to us, we only accept responsibility as we wish to take it, and the responsibility we wish to take is to save our own skins, make comfortable positions for ourselves and those we are related to, exert ourselves a little to keep ourselves clean and vigorous and upright; but when it comes to following out what Jesus says, His sayings are nothing but jargon. We name the Name of Christ but we are not based on His one issue of life, and Jesus says, "What shall it profit a man, if he shall gain the whole world,"—and he can easily do it—"and lose his own soul?" HG. 29

The kingdoms of this world are founded on strong men, consequently they go. Jesus Christ founds His kingdom on the weakest link, a Baby. God made His own Son a Babe. We must base our thinking on the rugged facts of life according to God's Book, and not according to the finesse of modern civilization. Let us not be so careful as to how we offend or please human ears, but let us never offend God's ears. HG. 41

What we are trying to do to-day is to Christianize civilization, and our social problems exist because Jesus Christ's teaching is being ruled out. HG. 42

Civilization is based on principles which imply that the passing moment is permanent. The only permanent thing is God, and if I put anyting else as permanent, I become atheistic. HG. 116

. . . if civilized life is right and the best we can know, Christianity is a profound mistake; but if you turn back to the Bible you find that its diagnosis of civilization is not that it is the best we know, it is on an entirely wrong basis. Civilized life is based on the *reason* at the heart of things; Jesus Christ's teaching is based on the *tragedy* at the heart of things, and consequently the position of true spiritual life is that of the forlorn hope. HGM. 69

The great scheme is the scheme of civilized life upon this earth. The apostle says, "Seeing that these things are all to be dissolved, . . ." he does not say 'destroyed', but 'dissolved'. What men have built upon the earth without any regard for God will be destroyed. The great scheme is that the physical universe which we see will be transfigured, i.e., become translucent with light. HGM. 83

When civilized life goes into the crucible, as it is doing just now, men lose their wits, Jesus said they would; but to His disciples He said, "When ye hear of wars and rumours of wars: *see that ye be not troubled.*" HGM. 84

There are grand ingredients in civilisation, it is full of shelter and protection, but its basis is not good. LG. 29

How much of our security and peace is the outcome of the civilized life we live, and how much of it is built up in faith in God? RTR. 63

Our civilisation is based on the foundation of murder—the first civilisation was founded by Cain; and civilised life is a vast, complicated, more or less gilded-over system of murder. SHH. 40

At the basis of trade and civilised life lie oppression and tyranny. Whether you are king or subject, says Solomon, you cannot find joy in any system of civilised life, or in trade and commerce; for underneath there is a rivalry that stings and bites, and the kindest man will put his heel on his greatest friend. These are not the blind statements of a disappointed man, but statements of facts discerned by the wisest man that ever lived. SHH. 45

There is a rivalry between men, and we have made it a good thing; we have made ambition and competition the very essence of civilised life. No wonder there is no room for Jesus Christ, and no room for the Bible. We are all so scientifically orthodox nowadays, so materialistic and certain that rationalism is the basis of things, that we make the Bible out to be the most revolutionary, unorthodox and heretical of books. SHH. 45

The curious things about civilisation is that it tends to take men away from the soil, and makes them develop an artificial existence away from the elemental. Civilisation has become an elaborate way of doing without God, and when civilised life is hit a smashing blow by any order of tyranny, most of us have not a leg to stand on. SHH. 62

Society is based on play-acting, it must be. You cannot say what you really think; if you do, other people will too,

and if everyone were absolutely frank there would be no room for us! SHH. 113

The saint has to remain loyal to God in the midst of the machinery of successful civilization, in the midst of worldly prosperity, and in the face of crushing defeat. SHL. 96

The idea of the 'missionary' class, the 'ministerial' class, the 'Christian worker' class has arisen out of our ideas of civilized life, not out of the New Testament faith and order. SSY. 142

What is needed to-day is *Christian sociology*, not *sociology Christianized*. One way in which God will re-introduce the emphasis on the Gospel is by bringing into His service men and women who not only understand the problems, but who have learned that the secret of the whole thing is supernatural regeneration, that is, personal holiness wrought by the grace of God. SSY. 154

CLOUDS

In the Bible clouds are always connected with God. Clouds are those sorrows or sufferings or providences without or within our personal lives which seem to dispute the empire of God. If there were no clouds we would not need faith. Seen apart from God, the clouds or difficulties are accidents, but by those very clouds the Spirit of God teaches us to walk by faith. GW. 127

It is not true to say that God wants to teach us something in our trials. In every cloud He brings, God wants us to *un*-learn something. God's purpose in the cloud is to simplify our belief until our relationship to Him is exactly that of a child. God uses every cloud which comes in our physical life, in our moral or spiritual life, or in our circumstances, to bring us nearer to Him, until we come to the place where our Lord Jesus Christ lived, and we do not allow our hearts to be troubled. GW. 127

We ought to interpret all the clouds and mysteries of life in the light of our knowledge of God. In everything that happens, we should be un-learning that which keeps us from a simple relationship to God. GW. 128

"They feared as they entered the cloud." Is there anyone "save Jesus only" in your cloud? If so, it will get darker; you must get into the place where there is "no one save Jesus only". RTR. 27

"Why does God bring thunderclouds and disasters when we want green pastures and still waters?" Bit by bit we find, behind the clouds, the Father's feet; behind the lightning, an abiding day that has no night; behind the thunder, "a still small voice" that comforts with a comfort that is unspeakable. RTR. 40

COERCION

Jesus Christ never coerced anyone; He never used the apparatus of sacerdotalism or of supernatural powers, or what we understand by revivals; He faced men on the ground on which all men stood, and refused to stagger human wits into submission to Himself. BFB. 95

God never coerces, neither does He ever accommodate His demands to human compromise, and we are disloyal to Him if we do. DI. 14

The word of God through the Spirit is creative, not persuasive. It hinders the work of the Spirit when we try and persuade people, it puts the basis not on Redemptive Reality but on our ingenious reasoning. GW. 18

Our Lord never made a fuss over anyone, and the reason He didn't could not have been that He was callous or indifferent, or that He was not tenderhearted, or that He did not understand every detail, but the fact remains that He did not make a fuss over anyone. He never pleaded, He never cajoled, He never entrapped; He simply spoke the sternest words mortal ears ever heard, and then left it alone. GW. 76

We are apt to make the mistake of thinking that God is going to coerce men; He never does. God is giving men ample time to do exactly what they like, both as individuals and as nations; He allows us to develop as we choose, but in the end we will come to agree with Him. HGM. 96

Our Lord never says 'you *must*', but if we are to be His disciples we know we must. SSY. 87

Obedience to Jesus Christ is essential, but not compulsory; He never insists on being Master. We feel that if only He would insist, we should obey Him. But Our Lord never enforces His 'thou shalt's' and 'thou shalt not's'; He never takes means to force us to do what He says; He never coerces. In certain moods we wish He would *make* us do the thing, but He will not; and in other moods we wish He would leave us alone altogether, but He will not. If we do not keep His commandments, He does not come and tell us we are wrong, we know it, we cannot get away from it. SSY. 87

COMMANDMENTS

The commandments were given with the inexorable awfulness of Almighty God; and the subsequent history of the people is the record of how they could not keep them. BE. 7

. . . the commandments were given irrespective of human ability or inability to keep them; then when Jesus Christ came, instead of doing what we all too glibly say He did—put something easier before men, He made it a hundredfold more difficult, because He goes behind the law to the disposition. BE. 9

Our Lord did not say, 'If a man *obeys* Me, he will keep My commandments'; but, "If ye *love* Me, ye will keep My commandments." MFL. 53

God's commands are made to the life of His Son in us, not to our human nature; consequently all that God tells us to do is always humanly difficult; but it becomes divinely easy immediately we obey because our obedience has behind it all the omnipotent power of the grace of God. OBH. 73

It sounds the right thing to say that Jesus Christ came here to help mankind: but His great desire was to do the will of His Father, and our Lord was misunderstood because He would not put the needs of men first. He said the first commandment is "Thou shalt love the Lord thy God with all thy heart, and with all thy soul, and with all thy mind, and with all thy strength." PH. 146

If the old commandments were difficult, our Lord's principles are unfathomably more difficult. Our Lord goes behind the old law to the disposition. Everything He teaches is impossible unless He can put into us His Spirit and remake us from within. SSM. 21

COMMITMENT

'Commit yourself to Me', He says, and it takes a man all he is worth to believe in Jesus Christ. AUG. 78

If we commit ourselves to Jesus He says, 'Stake your all on Me and I will see you through, don't worry about anything but your relationship to Me.' "The Best is yet to be." AUG. 117

To commit his life and reasoning to Jesus Christ's attitude takes a man right out of himself and into Jesus Christ. This is not rational, it is redemptive. AUG. 118

When a man has entered into a personal relationship with Jesus by means of the reception of the Holy Spirit, the first characteristic of that relationship is the nourishing of those who believe in Jesus. 'Lovest thou Me?' 'Feed My sheep.' That is what we are saved for, not to feed our converts, or to promulgate our explanation of things, but to be sent out by Christ, possessed of His Spirit, to feed His sheep. There is no release from that commission. LG. 123

Be simply and directly and unmistakably His to-day. RTR. 52

COMMONPLACE

What we call crises, God ignores, and what God reveals as the great critical moments of a man's life we look on as humdrum commonplaces. When we become spiritual we discern that God was in the humdrum commonplace and we never knew it. RTR. 14

57

One of the most amazing revelations of God comes when we learn that it is in the commonplace things that the Deity of Jesus Christ is realized. RTR. 31

COMMON SENSE

There is no such thing as sin to common-sense reasoning, therefore no meaning in the Cross because that view rules out what the Bible bases everything on, viz., the hiatus between God and man produced by sin, and the Cross where sin is dealt with. When common-sense reasoning comes to the Cross it is embarrassed, it looks at the death of Jesus as the death of a martyr, One who lived beyond His dispensation. According to the New Testament, the Cross is the Cross of God, not of a man. CHI. 114

The majority of us do not enthrone God, we enthrone common-sense. We make our decisions and then ask the real God to bless our god's decision. HG. 29

Watch the difference between the faces marred by sin and those marred by coming in contact with the Sadducees, who have all their inner shrines destroyed and nothing given in their place; the latter have a look of withered, mean sanity. Sin does not produce it, it is the effect of the presence of this monster—the rational, healthy-minded Sadducee; this 'monster' has been inside the Christian Church for the past twenty centuries, and is one of the problems that has to be faced. There are comparatively few Pharisees to-day, the greater number are Sadducees, who back up their little bits of common sense against all that Jesus Christ said and against everything anyone says who has had a vision of things differing from common sense. HG. 37

We never turn to God unless we are desperate, we turn to common sense, to one another, to helps and means and assistances, but when we do turn to the Lord it is always in desperation. The desperation of consecration is reached when we realize our indolence and our reluctance in coming to God. HGM. 71

To debate with God and trust common sense is moral blasphemy against God. NKW. 11

We cling to the certainty that the rational common-sense life is the right one; Jesus Christ stands for the fact that a life based on the Redemption is the only right one, consequently when a man shifts from the one to the other there is a period of desolation. OPG. 41

Never let common sense obtrude and push the Son of God on one side. Common sense is a gift which God gave to human nature; but it is not the gift of His Son; never enthrone common sense. The Son detects the Father common sense never yet detected the Father and never will. RTR. 18

The reason we know so little about God's wisdom is that we will only trust Him as far as we can work things out according to our own reasonable common sense. RTR. 63

Every time you venture out in the life of faith you will find something in your common sense cares that flatly contradicts your faith. RTR. 68

It is appalling to find spiritual people when they come into a crisis taking an ordinary common-sense standpoint as if Jesus Christ had never lived or died. SHH. 65

We hear it said that Jesus Christ taught nothing contrary to common sense: everything Jesus Christ taught was contrary to common sense. Not one thing in the Sermon on the Mount is common sense. The basis of Christianity is neither common sense nor rationalism, it springs from another centre, viz. a personal relationship to God in Christ Jesus in which everything is ventured on from a basis that is not seen. We are told that God expects us to use our "sanctified common sense"; but if we mean that that is Christianity, we will have to come to the conclusion that Jesus Christ was mad. SHH. 141

If you listen to the talk of the day in which we live you find it is sagacious common sense that rules, the spiritual standpoint is taboo, like a fairy-story. SHL. 94

We live in two universes: the universe of common-sense in which we come in contact with things by our senses, and the universe of revelation with which we come in contact by faith. The wisdom of God fits the two universes exactly, the one interprets the other. SSM. 48

. . . when we come to the domain which Jesus Christ reveals, no amount of studying or curiosity will avail an atom, our ordinary comon-sense faculties are of no use, we cannot see God or taste God, we can dispute with Him, but we cannot get at Him by our senses at all, and common-sense is apt to say there is nothing other than this universe. SSM. 49

To have faith tests a man for all he is worth, he has to stand in the common-sense universe in the midst of things which conflict with his faith, and place his confidence in the God Whose character is revealed in Jesus Christ. SSM. 66

Faith is our personal confidence in a Being Whose character we know, but Whose ways we cannot trace by common-sense. SSM. 66

Common-sense is mathematical; faith is not mathematical, faith works on illogical lines. SSM. 66

If a man is going to do anything worth while, there are times when he has to risk everything on a leap, and in the spiritual world Jesus Christ demands that we risk everything we hold by our common-sense and leap into what He says. Immediately we do, we find that what He says fits on as solidly as our common-sense. SSM. 71

Jesus sums up common-sense carefulness in a man indwelt by the Spirit of God as infidelity. SSM. 72

At the bar of common-sense Jesus Christ's statements are those of a fool; but bring them to the bar of faith and the Word of God, and you begin to find with awestruck spirit that they are the words of God. SSM. 74

COMMUNION WITH GOD

There are three ways in which we can responsibly receive communications from God: by giving deliberate thoughtful attention to the Incarnation; by identifying ourselves with the Church, and by means of Bible revelation. God gave Himself in the Incarnation; He gives Himself to the Church; and He gives Himself in His Word; and these are the ways He has ordained for conveying His life to us. AUG. 13

Every saint of God knows those times when in closest communion with God nothing is articulated, and yet there seems to be an absolute intimacy not so much between God's mind and their mind as between God's Spirit and their spirit. CD. VOL. 2, 53

The enemy goes all he can against our communion with God, against our solitude with God, he tries to prevent us from 'drawing our breath in the fear of the Lord'. DI. 41

Put communion with God on the throne, and then ask God to direct your common sense to choose according to His will. Worship first and wits after. NKW. 86

The only Being in whom communication with God was never broken is the Lord Jesus Christ, and His claim is that through the Redemption He can put every one of us in the place where communication with God can be re-established. OPG. 40

There is nothing more wearying to the eye than perpetual sunshine, and the same is true spiritually. The valley of the shadow gives us time to reflect, and we learn to praise God for the valley because in it our soul was restored in its communion with God. PH. 84

CONCEIT

Conceit means to have a point of view; a point of view takes the wonder out of life. BSG. 16

A sense of personal unworthiness is frequently the reaction of overweening conceit; genuine unworthiness has no conscious interest in itself. OPG. 53

The greatest cure for spiritual conceit is for God to give us a dose of the 'plague of our own heart.' PH. 121

Shyness is often unmitigated conceit, an unconscious over-estimate of your own worth; you are not prepared to speak until you have a proper audience. If you talk in the wrong mood, you will remain in the wrong mood and put the 'bastard self' on the throne; but if you talk in the mood which comes from revelation, emancipation will be yours. PH. 210

If we are going to have a sympathetic understanding of the Bible, we must rid ourselves of the abominable conceit that we are the wisest people that have ever been on the earth; we must stop our patronage of Jesus Christ and of the Bible, and have a bigger respect for the fundamental conception of life as it is. SHH. 76

CONCENTRATION

By a 'disciple' we mean one who continues to be concentrated on our Lord. Concentration is of much more value than consecration, because consecration is apt to end in mere religious sentiment. AUG. 119

When I set my face and determine to concentrate I am not devoted to creeds or forms of belief or to any phase of truth, not to prayer or to holiness, or to the spreading of any propaganda, but unto God. HGM. 71

Prayer and fasting means concentration on God. LG. 57

Concentration is the law of life mentally, morally and spiritually. MFL. 101

Seek, concentrate, and you will find. To concentrate is to fast from every other thing. OBH. 94

It is concentration on God that keeps us free from moral and spiritual panic. PH. 75

To-day we are evading concentration on God and devoting ourselves to the cause of Christian work. The busy-ness of duties will knock us out of relationship to God more quickly than the devil. PH. 75

Soul is my personal spirit as it reasons, and thinks, and looks at things; I have to call my powers together and concentrate on God. It is possible to concentrate and yet not concentrate on God. We may have a dead set about our lives, but it may be a dead set on comfort or on money, not a dead set on God and on the wonder and majesty of His dealings. PH. 92

Rouse your soul out of its drowsiness to consider God. Fix your attention on God, on the great themes of His Redemption and His holiness, on the great and glorious outlines of His character, be silent to Him there; then be as busy as you like in the ordinary affairs of life. PH. 94

Not *consecrated* service, but *concentrated*. Consecration would soon be changed into sanctification if we would only concentrate on what God wants. Concentration means pinning down the four corners of the mind until it is settled on what God wants. SSM. 18

Do not make the ruling factor of your life what you shall eat, or what you shall drink, but make zealous concentration on God the one point of your life. SSM. 67

God saves us and sanctifies us, then He expects us to concentrate on Him in every circumstance we are in. SSM. 73

Concentration on God is of more value than personal holiness. SSM. 73

CONDEMNATION

A man gets the seal of condemnation when he sees the light, and prefers darkness. CHI. 11

If, when we realize that Jesus Christ came to deliver us from the wrong disposition by putting in a right one, we refuse to allow Him to do it, that is the moment when condemnation begins. SA. 106

It is easy to condemn a state of things we know nothing about while we make excuses for the condition of things we ourselves live in. SHH. 115

Jesus Christ never says that a man is damned because he is a sinner; the condemnation is when a man sees what Jesus Christ came to do and will not let Him do it. That is the critical moment, 'the judgment', in a man's life. SHL. 60

CONDUCT

There are a great many things that are quite legitimate, but if they are not on our way to Jerusalem, we do not do them. AUG. 120

To do what we like always ends in immorality; to do what God would have us do always ends in growth in grace. BSG. 16

The matter of behaviour is ours, not God's. God does not make our character; character is formed by the reaction of our inner disposition to outer things through our nervous system. MFL. 52

The mighty work of God is done by His sovereign grace, then we have to work it out in our behaviour. MFL. 56

Don't waste time asking God to keep you from doing things—don't do them! RTR. 23

All I do ought to be founded on a perfect oneness with Him, not a self-willed determination to be godly. RTR. 30

Every man has, implicit within himself, a standard of conduct which he accepts for life. There is an intuitive certainty in every man that there are some things that he ought not to do, and the talk about innocence is nonsense. SA. 48

CONFESSION

Never allow anyone to confess to you unless it is for his own soul's sake, make him tell God. The habit of confessing tends to make one person dependent on another, and the one who confesses becomes a spiritual sponge, mopping up sympathy. DI. 89

Watch the difference between *confessing* and *admitting*; the majority of us are quite ready to admit, it is the rarest thing to get to the place where we will confess—confess to God, not to man. It is much more difficult to confess to God than we are apt to think. It is not confessing in order to be forgiven; confession is the evidence that I am forgiven. HGM. 132

God does not forgive me because I confess; I realize by my confession that I am forgiven. HGM. 132

"If we confess our sins, He is faithful and just to forgive us our sins, and to cleanse us from all unrighteousness."

To *admit* instead of *confess* is to trample the blood of the Son of God under foot, but immediately we allow the Holy Spirit to give us the gift of repentance, the shed blood of Christ will purge our conscience from dead works and send us into heart-spending service for God with a passionate devotion. OBH. 71

Many of us believe, but we will not confess to what we believe, consequently we are assured of nothing. 'I did ask God for the Holy Spirit, but I do not feel sure of anything.' Confess what you believe for, and instantly the assurance of that for which you believe will be made yours. We are so terribly afraid to venture on what God says. OBH. 125

Confession is not for the sake of other people, but for our own sake. Confession means we have trusted God for this thing and we believe on the ground of His word that the work is done. We realize by confessing that we have no one saving God to stand by us. OBH. 126

Emancipation comes through the "say so"; immediately we confess, the door opens, and life rushes on to a higher platform. PH. 209

If you want to encourage your own life in spiritual things, talk about them. Beware of the reserve that keeps to itself, that wants to develop spirituality alone; spirituality must be developed in the open. PH. 210

Some of us are living on too low a level, and remember, the door is shut on our side, not on God's. Immediately we will "say so," the door opens and the salvation for which we believe is ours in actual possession. Things only become clear as we say them. Too often we are like the child who will not do anything but murmur. We grouse and refuse to say the emancipating word which is within our reach all the time. Immediately we say the emancipating word, we undo the door and there rushes into us a higher and better life, and the revelation becomes real. PH. 211

When a man is able to state that he believes in God, it reacts on all his relationships. PH. 211

A man may betray Jesus Christ by speaking too many words, and he may betray Him through keeping his mouth shut. The revelation that perceives is that which recklessly states what it believes. When you stand up before your fellow-men and confess something about Jesus Christ, you feel you have no one to support you in the matter, but as you testify you begin to find the reality of your spiritual possessions, and there rushes into you the realisation of a totally new life. PH. 211

The disadvantage of a saint in the present order of things is that his confession of Jesus Christ is not to be in secret, but glaringly public. It would doubtless be to our advantage from the standpoint of self-realisation to keep quiet, and nowadays the tendency to say—'Be a Christian, live a holy life, but don't talk about it'—is growing stronger. Our Lord uses in illustration the most conspicuous things known to men, viz., salt, light, and a city set on a hill, and He says—'Be like that in your home, in your business, in your church; be conspicuously a Christian for ridicule or respect according to the mood of the people you are with.' SSM. 18

CONFIDENCE

When once a saint puts his confidence in the election of God, no tribulation or affliction can ever touch that confidence. When we realise that there is no hope of deliverance in human wisdom, or in human rectitude, or in anything that we can do . . . accept the justification of God and . . . stand true to the election of God in Christ Jesus. This is the finest cure for spiritual degeneration or for spiritual sulks. CD. VOL. 1, 156

The one thing Satan tries to shake is our confidence in God. HG. 28

Confidence in the natural world is self-reliance, in the spiritual world it is God-reliance. IYA. 32

A great point is reached spiritually when we stop worrying God over personal matters or over any matter. God expects of us the one thing that glorifies Him—and that is to remain absolutely confident in Him, remembering what He has said beforehand, and sure that His purpose will be fulfilled. RTR. 67

CONFUSION

At times in spiritual life there is confusion, and the usual way out is to say there ought to be no confusion. Some of us are inclined to be fanatical, we won't pay any attention to things that are not black or white, right or wrong. There are very few things that are black or white, right or wrong, and until we recognise this we are apt to be insolent or indifferent towards anything in between. A fog is as real as clear sunshine; if we don't pay any attention to the fog, we shall come to disaster. There are things in the spiritual life which are confused, not because we have disobeyed, but owing to the very nature of things. The confusion arises from being unschooled spiritually. PH. 95

The experience of being baffled is common to us all, and the more religious and thoughtful a man is, the more intensely is he baffled. With regard to your own baffling, recognise it and state it, but don't state it dishonestly to yourself. Don't say you are not baffled if you are, and don't tell a lie in order to justify your belief in God. PH. 106

CONSCIENCE

The most universal thing among men is conscience, and the Cross is God's conscience in supreme energy. AUG. 59

Conscience is a constituent in a natural man, but a Christian is judged by his personal relationship to God, not by his conscience. BFB. 27

The only way we get at God is through conscience, because through conscience we get at the moral relation to things. BFB. 94

Conscience is the innate law in human nature whereby man knows he is known. BP. 194

The phrase, 'Conscience can be educated,' is a truth that is half error. Strictly speaking, conscience cannot be educated. What is altered and educated is a man's reasoning. A man reasons not only on what his senses bring him, but on what the record of his conscience brings him. Immediately you face a man with the 'white light' of Jesus Christ (white is pure, true light, and embraces all shades of colour), his conscience records exactly what he sees, his reason is startled and amazed, and his conscience condemns him from every standpoint. BP. 196

The Gentiles knew nothing about Jesus Christ or about the law of God as an external standard, and they were judged according to their conscience. Take the grossest case you can think of—nowhere is there any record of a cannibal tribe thinking it right to eat a man; they always try to conceal it. BP. 200

Conscience is the standard by which men and women are to be judged until they are brought into contact with the Lord Jesus Christ. BP. 202

It is not sufficient for a Christian to live up to the light of his conscience; he must live in a sterner light, the light of the Lord Jesus Christ. BP. 202

Conscience will always record God when once it has been faced by God. BP. 202

My conscience makes me know what I ought to do, but it does not empower me to do it. DI. 26

Once conscience begins to be aroused it is aroused more and more till it reaches the terrible conviction that I am responsible before God for the breaking of His law; I know that God cannot forgive me and remain God; if He did I should have a clearer sense of justice than He has. There is nothing in my spirit to deliver me from sin, I am powerless—'sold under sin.' Conviction of sin brings a man to this hopeless, helpless condition; until he gets there the Cross of Christ has no meaning for him. GW. 84

Conscience is not peculiarly a Christian thing, it is a natural asset, it is the faculty in a man that fits on to the highest he knows. HGM. 76

Never go contrary to your conscience, no matter how absurd it may be in the eyes of others. MFL. 37

The refinement of conscience in a Christian means learning to walk in accordance with the life of the Lord Jesus, drawing from God as He did. It is a life of absolute largeness and freedom. MFL. 122

There is a difference between a refined conscience towards God and the fussy conscience of a hyper-conscientious person without the Spirit of God. Hyperconscientious people are an absolute plague to live with, they are morally and spiritually nervous, always in terror expecting something to happen, always expecting trials, and they always come. Jesus Christ was never morally or spiritually nervous any more than He was physically nervous. MFL. 122

Conscience is the faculty of the spirit that fits itself on to the highest a man knows, whether he be an agnostic or a Christian; every man has a conscience, although every man does not know God. OBH. 67

When conscience has been enlightened by the Son of God being formed in me, I have to make an effort to keep my conscience so sensitive that I obey that which I perceive to be God's will. I have to be so keen in the scent of the Lord, so sensitive to the tiniest touch of His Spirit, that I know what I should do. If I keep my soul inwardly open to God, then when I come in contact with the affairs of life outside, I know immediately what I should do; if I do not, I am to blame. OBH. 68

The one thing that keeps the conscience sensitive is the continual habit of seeing that I am open to God within. Whenever there is debate, quit. OBH. 68

When conscience speaks there must be no debate whatever. In a crisis human nature is put on the strain, and we usually know what to do; but the sensitive conscience of the Christian is realised in the ordinary things of life, the humdrum things. We are apt to think of conscience only in connection with something outrageous. OBH. 69

The sensitiveness of conscience is maintained by the habit of always being open towards God. At the peril of your soul you allow one thing to obscure your inner communion with God. Drop it whatever it is and see that you keep your inner vision clear. OBH. 69

Conscience is the eye of the soul recording what it looks at, but if what Ruskin calls "the innocence of the eye" is lost, then the recording of conscience may be distorted. If I continually twist the organ of my soul's recording, it will become perverted. If I do a wrong thing often enough, I cease to realise the wrong in it. A bad man can be perfectly happy in his badness. That is what a seared conscience means. OBH. 69

. . . conscience may be damaged by tampering with the occult side of things, giving too much time to speculation; then when we turn to human life we are as blind as bats. It may be all right for angels to spend their time in visions and meditation, but if I am a Christian I find God in the ordinary occurrences of my life. OBH. 70

The clearing house for a guilty conscience is that by our intercession Jesus repairs the damage done to other lives, and the consolation to our conscience is amazing. The saintly conscience means that I maintain an open scrutiny before God, and that I carry out the sensitiveness gained there all through my life. OBH. 72

When Our Lord is presented to the conscience, the first thing conscience does is to rouse the will, and the will agrees with God always. You say—'I do not know whether my will is in agreement with God'—look to Jesus, and you will find that your will and your conscience are in agreement with God every time. OBH. 129

Before a man is rightly related to God, his conscience may be a source of torture and distress to him, but when he is born again it becomes a source of joy and delight because he realizes that not only are his will and his conscience in agreement with God, but that God's will *is* his will, and the life is as natural as breathing, it is a life of proving, or making out, what is "the good, and acceptable, and perfect will of God." OBH. 130

The man who has done wrong has such a guilty conscience that he imagines everything is against him: everything *is* against him—God is against him, every bit of earth is against him; he stands absolutely alone. OPG. 11

Some of us have a social conscience, we are shocked at moral crime; some of us have a religious conscience, we are shocked at the things that go against our creeds. The conscience formed in us by the Holy Spirit makes us amazingly sensitive to the things that tell against the honour of God. PS. 23

Conscience is that innate faculty in a man's spirit that attaches itself to the highest the man knows, whether he be an atheist or a Christian. The highest the Christian knows is God: the highest the atheist knows is his principles. PS. 61

That "Conscience is the voice of God" is easily proved to be absurd. If conscience were the voice of God, it would be the same in everyone. PS. 61

The eye in the body records exactly what it looks at. The eye simply records, and the record is according to the light thrown on what it looks at. Conscience in the eye of the soul which looks out on what it is taught is God, and how conscience records depends entirely upon what light is thrown upon God. Our Lord Jesus Christ is the only true light on God. When a man sees Jesus Christ he does not get a new conscience, but a totally new light is thrown upon God, and conscience records accordingly, with the result that he is absolutely upset by conviction of sin. PS. 61

One effect of the disturbance caused by the light of conscience is to drive us into the outside hubbub of things. In the early days of Christianity men brooded on their sins, nowadays psychologists tell us the more wholesome way is to forget all about sin—fling yourself into the work of the world. Rushing into work in order to deaden conscience is characteristic of the life we live to-day. 'Live the simple life; keep a healthy body; never let your conscience be disturbed; for any sake keep away from religious meetings; don't bring before us the morbid tendency of things.' We shall find that the morbid tendency of things is the conviction of the Holy Ghost. PS. 63

When conscience begins to be awakened by God, we either become subtle hypocrites or saints, that is, either we let God's law working through conscience bring us to the place where we can be put right, or we begin to hoodwink ourselves, to affect a religious pose, not before other people, but before ourselves, in order to appease conscience—anything to be kept out of the real presence of God because wherever He comes, He disturbs. PS. 63

. . . when conscience is illuminated by the Holy Ghost, these three amazing articles—God is Love, God is Holy, God is Near—are brought straight down to our inner life and we can neither look up nor down for terror. PS. 66

Conscience is best thought of as the eye of the soul recording what it looks at; it will always record exactly what it is turned towards. SA. 44

Conscience and character in the saint, then, means the disposition of Jesus Christ persistently manifested. SA. 51

If we keep our individual consciences open towards God as He is revealed in Jesus Christ, God will bring hundreds of other souls into oneness with Himself through us. SA. 53

Sin is a wrong element, an element that has to be dealt with by God in Redemption through man's conscience. SA. 60

Jesus Christ always appeals to men's consciences,—why? Because He is Incarnate Righteousness. WG. 25

CONSCIOUSNESS

Transgression is nearly always an unconscious act, there is no conscious determination to do wrong. Sin is never an unconscious act, as far as culpability is concerned, it is always a conscious determination. Adam was the introducer of sin into this order of things. BP. 20

It is a snare to want to be conscious of God; you cannot be conscious of your consciousness and remain sane. GW. 25

Many of us are on the borders of consciousness—consciously serving, consciously devoted to God; all that is immature, it is not the life yet. The first stages of spiritual life are passed in conscientious carefulness; the mature life is lived in unconscious consecration. MFL. 54

Redemption does infinitely more than alter our conscious life; it safeguards the unconscious realm which we cannot touch. Our conscious experience is simply the doorway into the only Reality there is, viz., the Redemption. We are not only 'presenced with Divinity', but protected by Deity in the depths of personality below the conscious realm. SHL. 53

Part of our personal life is conscious, but the greater part is unconscious, and every now and again the unconscious part emerges into the conscious and upsets us because we do not know where it comes from or where it leads to, and we get afraid of ourselves. There is a great deal more of 'me' I do not know than that I do know. SHL. 53

Below the threshold of consciousness is the subconscious part of our personality which is full of mystery. There are forces in this realm which may interfere with us and we cannot control them, it is with this realm that the Spirit of God deals. SHL. 54

If we estimate our life by the abundance of things which we possess consciously, there will come a drastic awakening one day because we shall have to leave it all at death. We shall have to leave this body, which keeps the personal spirit in conscious life, and go clean through the threshold of consciousness to where we do not know. It is a desperate thing to die if we have only been living in the conscious realm. SHL. 60

We imagine that we have to take God into our consciousness, whereas God takes us into His consciousness; consequently we are rarely conscious of Him. SSY. 159

CONSECRATION

Consecration is not the giving over of the calling in life to God, but the separation from all other callings and the giving over of ourselves to God, letting His providence place us where He will—in business, or law, or science; in workshop, in politics, or in drudgery. CD. VOL. 2, 86

Consecration is the narrow, lonely way to over-flooding love. We are not called upon to live long on this planet, but we are called upon to be holy at any and every cost. If obedience costs you your life, then pay it. CD. VOL. 2, 87

The teaching that presents consecration as giving to God our gifts, our possessions, our comrades, is a profound error. These are all abandoned, and we give up for ever *our right to ourselves*. A sanctified soul may be an artist, or a musician; but he is not a sanctified artist or musician: he is one who expresses the message of God through a particular medium. As long as the artist or musician imagines he can consecrate his artistic gifts to God, he is deluded. Abandonment of ourselves is the kernel of consecration, not presenting our gifts, but presenting ourselves without reserve. CD. VOL. 2, 89

Every expansion of brain and heart that God gives in meetings or in private reading of the Bible must be paid for inevitably and inexorably by concentration on our part, not by consecration. God will continually bring us into circumstances to make us prove whether we will work out with determined concentration what He has worked in. CHI. 54

We use the word 'consecration' before sanctification, it should be used after sanctification. The fundamental meaning of consecration is the separating of a holy thing to God, not the separating of an un-holy thing to be made holy. DI. 58

CONVICTION

Christianity is not walking in the light of our convictions but walking in the light of the Lord, a very different thing. Convictions are necessary, but only as stepping stones to all that God wants us to be. BSG. 62

The way our heart is hardened is by sticking to our convictions instead of to Christ. GW. 38

Convictions and creeds are always about God; eternal life is to know Him. GW. 38

It is easier to be true to convictions formed in a vivid religious experience than to be true to Jesus Christ, because if we are going true to Jesus Christ our convictions have to be altered. MFL. 123

Some of us are no good unless we are placed in the circumstances in which our convictions were formed; but God continually stirs up our circumstances and flings us out to make us know that the only simplicity is not the simplicity of a logical belief, but of a maintained relationship with Jesus Christ, and that is never altered in any circumstances. MFL. 124

The essence of true religious faith is devotion to a Person. Beware of sticking to convictions instead of to Christ; convictions are simply the clothes of your growing life. NKW. 123

Never object to the intense sensitiveness of the Holy Spirit in you when He is educating you down to the scruple; and never discard a conviction. If it is important enough for the Holy Spirit to have brought it to your mind, that is the thing He is detecting. SSM. 31

The only way I can begin to fulfil the call of God is by keeping my convictions out of the way, my convictions as to what I imagine I am fitted for. The fitting goes much deeper down than the natural equipment of a man. SSY. 16

COVETOUSNESS

Covetousness is called idolatry because every drop of blood in the life of a covetous man is drawn away from God spiritually. BP. 101

CREATION

"Wherefore if any man is in Christ, there is a new creation"! We do not sufficiently realise the wonder of it. Those of us who are in the experience of God's mighty salvation do not give ourselves half enough prayerful time, and wondering time, and studying time to allow the Spirit of God to bring this marvellous truth home to us. OBH. 25

The fullest and most gracious meaning of regeneration and sanctification is that in Christ Jesus we can be made a new creation. Sanctification is not being given a new start, not that God

wipes out the past and says it is forgiven, but something inconceivably grander, viz., that Jesus Christ has the power to create in us the image of God as it was in Himself. OBH. 26

God lays down His life in the very creation we utilise for our own selfish ends: God lays down His life in His long-suffering patience with the civilised worlds which men have erected on God's earth in defiance of all He has revealed. PH. 27

If a man is terrified by the vastness of creation, he has never been touched by the moral problem. When he has, he knows that God created the universe for him. God created man to be master of the life in the earth and sea and sky, and the reason he is not is because he took the law into his own hands, and became master of himself, but of nothing else. SA. 29

CREATOR

Satan was the means of the ruin of the first created order, and now God begins to create another order out of the confusion of ruin. BP. 4

The Bible says that God created the world "by the breath of His mouth." Meditate for a moment on the word 'creation,' and see what a supernatural word it is. No philosopher ever thought of it, no expounder of natural history ever imagined such a word. We can understand 'evolution' and 'emanation,' but we simply do not know what 'creation' means. There is only one Being Who knows, and that is God Himself, and the Bible says that God *created* the heavens and the earth. BP. 225

What God created is a satisfaction to God, but to no one less than God, consequently until we come to know Him there is a great deal in His creation we shrug our shoulders over; but when we come to understand God we are as delighted with His creation as He is Himself. GW. 44

If the only aspect of God is that of Creator, to talk about a moral or spiritual life is nonsense; but the Creator aspect is not the complete Christian aspect; it is only one ingredient in it. SA. 24

CREED

A creed is necessary, but it is not essential. If I am a devotee of a creed, I cannot see God unless He comes along that line. AUG. 83

The man who rests in a creed is apt to be a coward and refuse to come into a personal relationship with God. BFB. 40

It is quite possible to have an intellectual appreciation of the Redemption without any experience of supernatural grace; an experience of supernatural grace comes by committing myself to a Person, not to a creed or a conviction. CHI. 29

Men worship an intellectual creed, and you can't dispute it because it is logically correct, but it does not produce saints; it produces stalwarts and stoics but not New Testament saints, because it is based on adherence to the literal words rather than on a vital relationship to God, who is the one abiding Reality. CHI. 29

No man begins his Christian life by believing a creed. The man with a dogmatic creed says, "You must believe this and that." Jesus "Do the will," i.e., "commit yourself to Me." CHI. 46

Immediately you lose sight of the central, majestic Figure of Jesus Christ you are swept off your feet by all kinds of doctrine, and when big things hit you find your religion does not stand you in good stead because your creed does not agree with the Truth. CHI. 46

It is ridiculous to pin our faith to a creed about God. The experience of Job is a proof that creeds must go. Every now and again we have to outgrow our creeds. Morally it is better to be an atheist than to believe in a God whom "to be God is not fit." SHH. 38

CRITICISM

Beware of looking to see where other people come short. God expects us to be exactly what we know the other person should be—when we realise that, we will stop criticising and having a measuring rod for other people. PH. 67

The criticism of Christians is not wrong, it is absolutely right. When a man says he is born again, he is put under scrutiny, and rightly so. If we are born again of the Holy Ghost and have the life of Jesus in us by means of His Cross, we must show it in the way we walk and talk and transact all our business. SSM. 30

Watch the thing that makes you snort morally. SSM. 32

'As a disciple, cultivate the uncritical temper.' In the spiritual domain, criticism is love turned sour. In a wholesome spiritual life there is no room for criticism. The critical faculty is an intellectual one, not a moral one. If criticism becomes a habit it will destroy the moral energy of the life and paralyse spiritual force. SSM. 76

The only Person who can criticise human beings is the Holy Spirit. SSM. 76

Criticism is deadly in its effect because it divides a man's powers and prevents his being a force for anything. SSM. 77

The Holy Ghost alone is in the true position of a critic; He is able to show what is wrong without wounding and hurting. SSM. 77

The Holy Spirit does reveal what is wrong in others, but His discernment is never for purposes of cricitism, but for purposes of intercession. SSM. 77

Whenever you are in a critical temper, it is impossible to enter into communion with God. Criticism makes you hard and vindictive and cruel, and leaves you with the flattering unction that you are a superior person. It is impossible to develop the characteristics of a saint and maintain a critical attitude. SSM. 78

CROSS

The central keystone for all Time and Eternity on which the whole purpose of God depends is the Cross. AUG. 39

The aspect of the cross in discipleship is lost altogether in the present-day view of following Jesus. The cross is looked upon as something beautiful and simple instead of a stern heroism. Our Lord never said it was easy to be a Christian; He warned men that they would have to face a variety of hardships, which He termed 'bearing the cross.' AUG. 49

The Cross of Christ stands unique and alone; we are never called upon to carry His Cross. Our cross is something that comes only with the peculiar relationship of a disciple to Jesus Christ, it

is the evidence that we have denied the right to ourselves. AUG. 50

The Cross of Jesus Christ is a revelation; our cross is an experience. AUG. 51

What the Cross was to our Lord such also in measure was it to be to those who followed Him. The cross is the pain involved in doing the will of God. AUG. 51

Most of our emphasis to-day is on what Our Lord's death means to us: the thing that is of importance is that we understand what God means in the Cross. AUG. 56

Study the Cross for no other sake than God's sake, and you will be holy without knowing it. AUG. 56

The cross Jesus asks us to take up cannot be suffering for conviction's sake, because a man will suffer for conviction's sake whether he is a Christian or not. Neither can it be suffering for conscience sake, because a man will go to martyrdom for his principles without having one spark of the grace of God in his heart. AUG. 97

Our cross is something that comes only with the peculiar relationship of a disciple to Jesus. It is the sign that we have denied our right to ourselves and are determined to manifest that we are no longer our own, we have given away for ever our right to ourselves to Jesus Christ. AUG. 97

We may be clean and upright and religious, we may be Christian workers and have been mightily used of God; but if the bedrock of self-realization has not been blasted out by our own free choice at the Cross of Christ, shipwreck is the only thing in the end. AUG. 98

The characteristic of the cross we carry daily is that we have been 'crucified with Christ'. AUG. 98

The Cross is a Reality, not a symbol—at the wall of the world stands God with His arms outstretched. BE. 61

Either the Cross is the only way there is of explaining God, the only way of explaining Jesus Christ, and of explaining the human race, or there is nothing in it at all. BE. 61

There is nothing more certain in Time or Eternity than what Jesus Christ did on the Cross: He switched the whole human race back into right relationship to God and made the basis of human life Redemptive, consequently any member of the human race can get into touch with God *now*. BE. 61

If the human race apart from the Cross is all right, then the Redemption was a useless waste. BE. 61

The Cross is not the cross of a martyr: it is the mirror of the nature of God focussed in one point of history. If I want to know what God is like, I see it in the Cross. Jesus Christ is not Someone who leads me to God: either He is God, or I have none. BE. 65

The conscience of the race, i.e., the standard whereby men are judged, is the Cross. I do not make my own conscience the standard, or the Sermon on the Mount the standard; the Cross of Christ, not His teaching, is the central thing, and what God condemns in the Cross is His standard for me. BE. 66

All heaven is interested in the Cross of Christ, all hell terribly afraid of it, while men are the only beings who more or less ignore its meaning. BE. 119

The Cross did not *happen* to Jesus: He came on purpose for it. BSG. 40

The Cross of Christ means that the salvation of God goes deeper down than the deepest depths of iniquity man can commit. No man can get beyond the reach of Jesus: He made a way back to the throne of God from the very heart of hell by His tremendous Atonement. BSG. 51

The Cross is a tragedy to man, but a tremendous triumph to God, an absolute triumph. BSG. 52

To ignore the Cross in either living or thinking is to become a traitor to Jesus Christ. BSG. 67

The Cross is the symbol of Christian living and it is also the symbol of Christian thinking. BSG. 67

We are never called upon to carry Christ's Cross: His Cross is the centre of Time and Eternity; the answer to the enigmas of both. CD. VOL. 1, 90

The Cross of Jesus Christ stands unique and alone. His Cross is not our cross. Our cross is that we manifest before the world the fact that we are sanctified to do nothing but the will of God. By means of His Cross, our cross becomes our divinely appointed privilege. CD. VOL. 1, 90

One great characteristic in the life of a man whose life is hid with Christ in God is that he has received the gift Jesus Christ gives. What gift does Jesus Christ give to those who are identified with him? The gift His Father gave him, The Father gave Him the Cross, and He gives us our cross: *"If any man will come after Me, let him deny himself, and take up his cross daily, and follow Me."* 'Let him relinquish, give up his right to himself'—distinguished by one thing, "... *ye are not your own? For ye are bought with a price."* To take up our cross daily means that we take now what otherwise would go on to Jesus Christ. CD. VOL. 1. 133

Probably in the Cross more than in any other aspect of our Lord's life do we see the stumbling-block presented to the wisdom of the world. Wise men of intelligence after the flesh cannot understand why God does not speak, and misunderstanding, prejudices, and unbelief prevail among all men until by receiving the Spirit of God as babes they perceive that our Lord Jesus Christ from the Cradle to the Cross is God's great Eternal Word. CD. VOL. 2, 146

The Bible says that God Himself accepted the responsibility for sin; the Cross is the proof that He did. It cost Jesus Christ to the last drop of blood to deal with "the vast evil of the world." CHI. 45

The true portrayal is that the Cross is not the cross of a man, but the Cross of God. The tragedy of the Cross is the hurt to God. In the Cross God and sinful man merge; consequently the Cross is of more importance than all the world's civilisations. CHI. 45

By the Cross of Christ I am saved from sin; by the Cross of Christ I am sanctified; but I never am a sacramental disciple until I deliberately lay myself on the altar of the Cross, and give myself over emphatically and entirely to be actually what I am potentially in the sight of God, viz., a member of the Body of Christ. When I swing clear of myself and my own consciousness and give myself over to Jesus Christ, He can use

me as a sacrament to nourish other lives. CHI. 92

What the enemies of the cross so strenuously oppose is identification on the part of the believer with what the death of Christ on the Cross represents, viz., death to sin in every shape and form. CHI. 108

The Cross of Christ is God's last and endless Word. There the prince of this world is judged, there sin is killed, and pride is done to death, there lust is frozen, and self-interest slaughtered, not one can get through. DI. 66

I cannot save a soul, or sanctify a soul, but if I will preach the Cross with all the mighty emphasis of God's Spirit on it, instantly the Holy Spirit creates the very thing which the Redemption has made possible—the miracle of God in human souls, not by magic, but by surrender. GW. 18

Through His death on the Cross Jesus Christ not only readjusts a man in conscience and heart to God, He does something grander, He imparts to him the power to do all God wants, He presences him with Divinity, i.e., the Holy Spirit, so that he is garrisoned from within, and enabled to live without blame before God. GW. 31

The Cross of Christ alone makes me holy, and it does so the second I am willing to let it. GW. 54

We are not always in the condition to understand the Cross, but it is of vital importance that we let God bring us at times where every commonplace mood is stripped off, and we take the shoes from off our feet and stand alone for one moment while God spells out to us the

A B C of what the Cross of Christ means. GW. 86

. . . our human life viewed from a moral standpoint is a tragedy, and that preaching precepts while we ignore the Cross of Jesus Christ is like giving "a pill to cure an earthquake," or a poultice for a cancer. HG. 12

The reason we are so shallow and flippant in our presentation of the Cross is that we have never seen ourselves for one second in the light of God. When we do see ourselves in the light of God, there is only one of two refuges—suicide or the Cross of Christ. HG. 98

The Cross is the crystallized point in history where Eternity merges with Time. HG. 98

The Cross of Christ is not the cross of a martyr, it has become the symbol of the martyr; it is the revelation of Redemption. HG. 98

The Cross is the secret of the heart of God, the secret of the Person of the Son of God, the secret of the Holy Ghost's work. HGM. 22

It is the Cross alone that made it possible for God to give us the gift of eternal life, and to usher in the great era in which we live—the dispensation of the Holy Ghost. HGM. 22

We talk about the joys and comforts of salvation; Jesus Christ talks about taking up the cross and following Him. HGM. 129

. . . it was not the 'offscouring' that crucified Jesus, it was the highest reach of natural morality crucified Him. It is the refined, cultured, religious, moral people who refuse to sacrifice the natural

for the spiritual. When once you get that thought, you understand the inveterate detestation of the Cross of Christ. IWP. 102

The Cross is the supreme moment in Time and Eternity, and it is the concentrated essence of the very nature of the Divine love. PH. 27

The Cross of Christ reveals that the blazing centre of the love of God is the holiness of God, not His kindness and compassion. If the Divine love pretends I am all right when I am all wrong, then I have a keener sense of justice than the Almighty. PH. 65

In the Cross we may see the dimensions of Divine love. The Cross is not the cross of a man, but the exhibition of the heart of God. At the back of the wall of the world stands God with His arms outstretched, and every man driven there is driven into the arms of God. The Cross of Jesus is the supreme evidence of the love of God. PH. 65

In the Cross God is revealed not as One reigning in calm disdain above all the squalors of earth, but as One Who suffers more keenly than the keenest sufferer—"a man of sorrows, and acquainted with grief." PH. 137

The death of Jesus goes away down underneath the deepest, vilest sin that human nature ever committed. Every pious mood must be stripped off when we stand before the Cross. PH. 137

The Cross in actual history is the point where the real Presence of God enters human history; and the point where the real Presence of God enters human life is the moment of absolute surrender, not of religious sentiment. PH. 137

It is only when a man gets to his wits' end and is stabbed wide awake that he realises for the first time the meaning of the Cross—'I thought that He was stricken, smitten by God and afflicted; now I see that He was wounded for my transgression.' PH. 137

The Cross of Jesus Christ is not the cross of a martyr, but the door whereby God keeps open house for the universe. Anyone can go in through that door. PR. 25

It is one thing to recognise what God is doing with us, but another thing to deliberately accept it as His appointment. We can never accept the appointment of Jesus Christ and bear away the sin of the world, that was His work; but He does ask us to accept our cross. What is my cross? The manifestation of the fact that I have given up my right to myself to Him for ever. PR. 57

Through His Cross He prepared a place for us to "sit with Him in the heavenly places, in Christ Jesus" *now*, not by and bye. PR. 82

No man can carry the cross of God. The Cross of God is the Redemption of the world. PR. 92

The cross we have to carry is that we have deliberately given up our right to ourselves to Jesus Christ. PR. 92

The Cross of Jesus Christ is a revelation; our cross is an experience. If we neglect for one moment the basal revelation of the Cross, we will make shipwreck of our faith, no matter what our experience is. The test of our spiritual life is our understanding of the Cross. PR. 100

We have so hallowed the Cross by twenty centuries of emotion and sentiment that it sounds a very beautiful and pathetic thing to talk about carrying our cross. But a wooden cross with iron nails in it is a clumsy thing to carry. The real cross was like that, and do we imagine that the external cross was more ugly than our actual one? Or that the thing that tore our Lord's hands and feet was not really so terrible as our imagination of it? PR. 100

We cannot be saved by consecration, or by praying, or by giving ourselves up to God. We can only be saved by the Cross of Jesus Christ. PR. 107

The Cross is the point where God and sinful man merge with a crash, and the way to life is opened, but the crash is on the heart of God. God is always the sufferer. PR. 107

It is through the Cross of Jesus Christ that we begin to fulfil all that we are created for, and the great aim of the life is for the fame of God, not for the needs of men. PR. 133

Thank God for salvation through the Cross, for sanctification through the Cross; but thank God also for insight into what it cost God to make that salvation and sanctification possible. God grant that the pulsing power of identification with the death of Jesus may come again into our testimony and make it glow with devotion to Him for His unspeakable salvation. PS. 19

Our cross is the steady exhibition of the fact that we are not our own but Christ's, and we know it, and are determined to be unenticed from living a life of dedication to Him. This is the beginning of the emergence of the real life of faith. PS. 38

Our Lord makes no allowance for not attaining because by means of His Cross we have all the marvellous grace of God to draw upon, all the mighty life of the Lord Jesus Christ to enable us to attain. PS. 51

When a so-called rationalist points out sin and iniquity and disease and death, and he says "How does God answer that?" you have always a fathomless answer—the Cross of Christ. RTR. 87

If Jesus Christ were only a martyr, His cross would be of no significance; but if the cross of Jesus Christ is the expression of the secret heart of God, the lever by which God lifts back the human race to what it was designed to be, then there is a new attitude to things. SA. 12

To ten men who talk about the character of Jesus there is only one who will talk about His Cross. SA. 35

The Cross is the presentation of God having done His "bit," that which man could never do. SA. 38

The basis of human life according to Jesus Christ is His Cross, and it is by His Cross that His conscience is manifested. SA. 41

In the Cross of Jesus Christ, God redeemed the whole human race from the possibility of damnation through the heredity of sin. SA. 106

The cross is the deliberate recognition of what my personal life is for, viz., to be given to Jesus Christ; I have to take up that cross daily and prove that I am no longer my own. Individual independence has gone, and all that is left is personal passionate devotion to Jesus Christ through identification with His Cross. SHL. 79

The cross is the deliberate recognition of what our personal self is for, viz., to be given to Jesus, and we take up that cross daily and prove we are no longer our own. SHL. 85

CRUCIFIXION

The death of Jesus Christ holds the secret of the mind of God. BSG. 49

The death of Jesus Christ was not the death of a martyr; it was the death of God. BSG. 50

"I am crucified with Christ"—it is a real definite personal experience. CD. VOL. 1, 132

To "crucify the flesh with the affections and lusts" is not God's business, it is man's. CHI. 42

The Bible makes more of the death of Jesus than of His life and His teaching, because the teaching of Jesus does not apply to you and me unless we have received His Spirit. CHI. 45

. . . the Death of Jesus looms all through the Bible! It is through His death that we are made partakers of His life and can have gifted to us a pure heart, which He says is the condition for seeing God. CHI. 120

On the Cross men crucified the Son of God—and God forgave them while they did it. GW. 85

If once a man has heard the appeal of Jesus from the Cross, he begins to find there is something there that answers the cry of the human heart and the problem of the whole world. What we have to do as God's servants is to lift up Christ crucified. IWP. 61

No sinner can get right with God on any other ground than the ground that Christ died *in his stead*, not *instead of him*. NKW. 125

That Christ is the substitute for me and therefore I go scot free, is never taught in the New Testament. If I say that Christ suffered instead of me, I knock the bottom board out of His sacrifice. *Christ died in the stead of me.* I, a guilty sinner, can never get right with God, it is impossible. I can only be brought into union with God by identification with the One Who died in my stead. No sinner can get right with God on any other ground than the ground that Christ died *in his stead*, not *instead of him*. NKW. 125

When we tell God that we want at all costs to be identified with the death of Jesus Christ, at that instant a supernatural identification with His death takes place, and we know with a knowledge that passes knowledge that our 'old man' is crucified with Christ, and we prove it for ever after by the amazing ease with which the supernatural life of God in us enables us to do His will. That is why the bed-rock of Christianity is personal, passionate devotion to the Lord Jesus. PH. 164

The death of Jesus is the only entrance into the life He lived. We cannot get into His life by admiring Him, or by saying what a beautiful life His was, so pure and holy. To dwell only on His life would drive us to despair. We enter into His life by means of His death. Until the Holy Spirit has had His way with us spiritually, the death of Jesus Christ is an insignificant thing, and we are amazed that the New Testament should make so much of it. PR. 79

The death of our Lord was not the death of a martyr, but the exhibition of the heart of God, and the gateway whereby any member of the human race can enter into union with God. PR. 99

. . . the death of Jesus was the death of God Incarnate. PS. 19

There is something infinitely profounder than pathos in the death of Jesus; there is a mystery we cannot begin to touch. PS. 20

The death of Jesus is the death of God, at the hands of man, inspired by the devil. He gathered round Him the raging hate of humanity, and was crucified. He offered Himself through the Eternal Spirit—He died in the Spirit in which He lived. PS. 20

The death of Jesus Christ is God's verdict on self-realization and every form of sin there is. If self-realization is to be the goal and end of the human race, then damned be God; if Jesus Christ is to be God, then damned be self-realization— the two cannot exist together. "If you would be My disciple, give up your right to yourself." GA. 89

CURIOSITY

In natural life we grow by means of curiosity, and spiritually we grow by the same power. The Spirit of God uses the natural reaction of curiosity to enable us to know more about the One Who is precious. The instinct is not denied, but lifted on to a different platform and turned towards knowing Jesus Christ. As saints our curiosity must not be all abroad; we become insatiably curious about Jesus Christ; He is the One Who rivets our attention. MFL. 70

One word of warning—we must guard the life where the Spirit of God warns we should guard it, and the first thing to be guarded against is inordinate curiosity. OBH. 38

Curiosity in the natural world is right, not wrong, and if we are not intellectually curious we shall never know anything, God never encourages laziness. PR. 20

In the common-sense universe the faculty required is intellectual curiosity, but when we enter into the domain from which Jesus Christ talks, intellectual curiosity is ruled out and moral obedience takes the absolute place. SSM. 49

CYNICISM

Jesus Christ never trusted human nature, yet He was never cynical, never in despair about any man, because He trusted absolutely in what the grace of God could do in human nature. PH. 187

When we are hurt we are apt to become cynical; cynicism is a sign that the hurt is recent. A mature mind is never cynical. SHH. 21

D

DEATH

"Let not your heart be troubled: ye believe in God, believe also in Me." Jesus Christ is talking here about what no man knows but Himself, viz. the day after death, and He says, 'Don't be troubled about it.' AUG. 116

. . . death has an amazing power of altering what a man desires, because death profoundly affects his outlook . . . BE. 18

If I am going to decide for the Spirit, I will crucify the flesh; God cannot do it, I must do it myself. To 'crucify' means to put to death, not counteract, not sit on, not whitewash, but kill. If I do not put to death the things in me which are not of God, they will put to death the things that are of God. BE. 79

Death is not annihilation: we exist in a kingdom of death. BSG. 76

Death is the inheritance of the whole human race; since Adam, no man has ever been alive to God saving by the supernatural act of re-birth. Do not get the idea that because man did not die suddenly physically, he is not dead. The manifestation of death in the body is simply a matter of time, "For *in the day that thou eatest thereof* thou shalt surely die." The birth of death was in that moment; not the birth of death for one man, but the birth of the death of the whole human race. God's attitude revealed in the Bible towards men is that they are "dead in trespasses and sins"; no touch with God, not alive towards God at all, they are quite indifferent to God's claims. IWP. 24

Death to us has become natural, but the Bible reveals it to be abnormal. PR. 11

. . . we all die. It is humiliating for our predications to remember that although the spirit of man is indestructible, the phase of life which we bank on naturally passes. We may have labour in it, and delight and satisfaction in it, but it will all pass. When a beast dies, his body disappears and his soul goes downwards into entire nature; the spirit of a man goes straight back to God Who made it; it is never absorbed into God. SHH. 38

The Bible never allows us to waste time over the departed. It does not mean that the fact of human grief is ignored, but the worship of reminiscence is never allowed. SHH. 125

Instead of death being the introduction to a second chance, it is the confirmation of the first chance. SHH. 142

There is no possibility of saying a word in favour of a man after death if he did not do things before his death. SHH. 144

It is the physical calamity of death *plus* the thing behind which no man can grasp, that makes death so terrible. SHL. 24

Death is a great dread. SHL. 24

Death has no terror for the man who is rightly related to God through Jesus Christ. SHL. 26

Our Lord makes little of physical death, but He makes much of moral and spiritual death. SSY. 97

DEBATE

Whenever I want to debate about doing what I know to be supremely right, I am not in touch with God. NKW. 114

It is extraordinary how we debate with right. We know a thing is right but we try to seek excuses for not doing it now. NKW. 115

DECEIT

It is one thing to deceive other people, but you have to get up very early if you want to take in God! OPG. 48

DECISION

Many of us do believe in Jesus, we have received the Holy Spirit and know we are children of God, and yet we won't make the moral decision about sin, viz., that it must be killed right out in us. It is the great moment of our lives when we decide that sin must die right out, not be curbed or suppressed or counteracted, but crucified. It is not done easily; it is only done by a moral wrench. CHI. 61

A moral decision is not a decision that takes time, one second is sufficient; what takes time is my stubborn refusal to come to the point of morally deciding. Here, where we sit, we can decide whether or not the Redemption shall take its full course in us. Once I decide that it shall, the great inrush of the Redemption takes efficacious effect immediately. CHI. 62

The phrase 'Decide for Christ' which we so frequently hear is too often an emphasis on the thing Our Lord never trusted. Our Lord never asks us to *decide for Him:* He asks us to *yield to Him*—a very different matter. LG. 36

Decisions for Christ fail not because men are not in earnest, but because the bedrock of Christianity is ignored. The bedrock of Christianity does not lie in vowing or in strength of will; to begin with it is not ethical at all, but simply the recognition of the fact that I have not the power within me to do what my spirit longs to do. 'Come unto Me,' said Jesus, not 'Decide for Me.' LG. 111

The modern phrase we hear so often, 'Decide for Christ', is most misleading, because it puts the emphasis on the wrong thing, and is apt to present Jesus Christ in a false way as Someone in need of our allegiance. A decision cannot hold for ever, because a man is the same after making it as before, and there will be a reaction sooner or later. Whenever a man fails in personal experience it is because he has never *received* anything. There is always a positive difference in a man when he has received something— new powers begin to manifest themselves. Nothing has any power to alter a man save the incoming of the life of Jesus, and that is the only sign that he is born again. LG. 111

Never postpone a moral decision. Second thoughts in moral matters are always deflections. Give as many second thoughts as you like to matters of prudence, but in the presence of God never think twice—*act*. MFL. 15

There is so much talk about our decision for Christ, our determination to be Christians, our decisions for this and for that. When we come to the New Testament we find that the other aspect, God's choosing of us, is the one that is brought out the oftenest. "Ye did not choose me, but I chose you . . ." PH. 177

Men are told to "decide for Christ"; no man can do it; what a man has to do is deliberately to commit himself to Jesus Christ. SHH. 91

DESIRE

When a man is born again he stops desiring the things he used to desire, not gradually, but suddenly; things begin to matter that did not matter before, and the things that used to matter no longer do so. BE. 18

If our desires are distorted we are apt to say that God gave us a stone when we asked for bread, whereas God always hears our prayers, but He answers them according to His own nature. BE. 49

Desire is what we determine in outline in our minds and plan and settle in our hearts; that is the desire which God will fulfil as we delight ourselves in Him. BP. 109

You can present morality, good principles, the duty of loving your neighbour, and never arouse a man's conscience to want anything; but when you present Jesus Christ, instantly there is a dumb awakening; a want to be what He would like me to be. It is not conviction of sin, but an awakening out of the sleep of indifference into a want. MFL. 10

. . . to be told that God will give us the Holy Spirit if we ask Him, may be a dead proposition; but when we come in contact with a person filled with the Spirit of God we instantly awaken to a want. MFL. 10

The desire at the heart of true spiritual life is for union with God; the tendency to rest in anything less than the realization of his desire becomes the arrest of desire. PS. 47

The Spirit of God alters my dominating desires; He alters the thing that matters, and a universe of desires I had never known before, suddenly comes on the horizon. RTR. 7

The best is always yet to be with God. Everything you have ever dreamed or longed for, will be. RTR. 51

When we are right with God, He gives us our desires and aspirations. Our Lord had only one desire, and that was to do the will of His Father, and to have this desire is the characteristic of a disciple. SSY. 58

DESPAIR

When a man gets to despair he knows that all his thinking will never get him out, he will only get out by the sheer creative effort of God, consequently he is in the right attitude to receive from God that which he cannot gain for himself. BFB. 12

. . . despair is the basis of human life unless a man accepts a revelation from God and enters into the Kingdom of Jesus Christ. BFB. 16

DESTINY

Soul destiny began with the human race, not before it. Take any passage which deals with individual destiny and you will find that destiny is determined in the lifetime of the individual soul. All speculations regarding the transmigration of soul are alien to the teaching of the Bible. BP. 86

No man's destiny is made for him, each man makes his own. OPG. 50

Our destiny is determined by our disposition. Our Lord's destiny was determined by His disposition. Our destiny is preordained, but we are free to choose which disposition we will be ruled by. We cannot alter our disposition, but we can choose to let God alter it. If our disposition is to be altered, it must be altered by the Creator, and He will introduce us into a totally new realm by the miracle of His sovereign grace. PR. 88

Our destiny is something fixed by God, but determined by our disposition. We are all born with a disposition, i.e., the peculiar bent of our personal life, and it is that which determines our destiny. Praying won't alter it, nor science, nor reasoning; if the destiny of a man is going to be altered it must be altered by the Creator. SA. 103

Our destiny is as eternal and as certain as God's throne; it is an unalterable decree of God; but I am free to choose by what disposition I am to be ruled. I cannot alter my disposition, but I can choose to let God alter it, and Redemption means that in my practical experience Jesus Christ can give me a new heredity, a new disposition. SA. 103

Jesus Christ makes human destiny depend absolutely on Who men say He is. Membership of His Church is based on that one thing only, a recognition of Who Jesus is and the public confession of it. SSY. 56

The destiny of every human being depends on his relationship to Jesus Christ, it is not on his relationship to life, or on his service or his usefulness, but simply and solely on his relationship to Jesus Christ. SSY. 157

DEVIL

The devil is the adversary of God in the rule of man and Satan is his representative. BFB. 8

The modern attitude to demon possession is very instructive; so many take the attitude that there is no such thing as demon possession, and infer that Jesus Christ Himself knew quite well that there was no such thing, not seeing that by such an attitude they put themselves in the place of the superior person, and claim to know all the private opinions of the Almighty about iniquity. Jesus unquestionably did believe in the fact of demon possession. The New Testament is full of the supernatural; Jesus Christ continually looked on scenery we do not see, and saw supernatural forces at work. BP. 91

The devil has an absolute detestation of God, an immortal hatred of God. BP. 117

The man who criticizes Jesus Christ's statements about demon possession does not realize what he is doing. BP. 156

Everything the devil does, God overreaches to serve His own purpose. DI. 15

We cannot stand against the wiles of the devil by our wits. The devil only comes along the lines that God understands, not along the lines we understand, and the only way we can be prepared for him is to do what God tells us, stand complete in His armour, indwelt by His Spirit, in complete obedience to Him. IYA. 33

The first sign of the dethronement of Jesus is the apparent absence of the devil, and the peaceful propaganda that is spread after he has withdrawn. PR. 68

Don't put things down to the devil, but to your own undisciplined nervous system. RTR. 53

The devil is a bully, but when we stand in the armour of God, he cannot harm us; if we tackle him in our own strength we are soon done for; but if we stand with the strength and courage of God, he cannot gain one inch of way at all. RTR. 55

The devil would like us to believe that we are in a losing battle; nothing of the sort! We are "more than conquerors", hilariously more than victors, "through Him that loved us". RTR. 64

DEVOTION

There is a difference between devotion to principles and devotion to a person. Hundreds of people to-day are devoting themselves to phases of truth, to causes. Jesus Christ never asks us to devote ourselves to a cause or a creed; He asks us to devote ourselves to Him, to sign away the right to ourselves and yield to Him absolutely, and take up that cross daily. AUG. 18

Devotion to a cause is the great mark of our day, and in religion it means being devoted to the application of religious principles. A disciple of Jesus Christ is devoted to a Person, not to principles. BFB. 72

Devotion to Jesus is the expression of the Holy Spirit's work in me. DI. 21

All my devotion is an insult to God unless every bit of my practical life squares with Jesus Christ's demands. DI. 72

Jesus Christ never blinds us into devotion to Himself, never startles and staggers us. Satan as an angel of light uses the things that captivate men against their will, he uses ecstasies, visions, excitement, the things that make for unholiness, for the aggrandizement of self, for insanity; but Jesus never does. GW. 114

Let Him make our lives narrow; let Him make them intense; let Him make them absolutely His! GW. 115

If we make devotional habits the source from which we draw our life, God will put us through the discipline of upsetting those times. IWP. 34

Anywhere the man who is devoted to Jesus Christ goes, Jesus Christ is there with him. PH. 146

Devotion and piety are apt to be the greatest opponents of Jesus Christ, because we devote ourselves to devotion instead of to Him. PR. 23

Fearless devotion to Jesus Christ ought to mark the saint today, but more often it is devotion to our set that marks us. We are more concerned about being in agreement with Christians than about being in agreement with God. RTR. 15

The true nature of devotion to Jesus Christ must be extravagance. SHH. 142

The one mainspring of the life is to be personal, passionate devotion to Jesus Christ. SHL. 123

Many of us who call ourselves Christians are not devoted to Jesus Christ. SSM. 29

The men who say—'Lord, Lord,' are not the ones Jesus takes on His enterprises;

He takes only those men in whom He has done everything, they are the ones upon whom He can rely. Many devote themselves to work for God in whom Jesus Christ has done nothing; consequently they bungle His business, run up the white flag to the prince of this world and compromise with him. Jesus says that the only ones He will take on His building and battling enterprises are those who are devoted to Him because He has altered their disposition. SSY. 168

DIFFICULTY

The God revealed in Jesus Christ is grand enough for every problem of life. "I am the Way, the Truth, and the Life." AUG. 118

When we confer with Jesus Christ over other lives all the perplexity goes, because He has no perplexity; and our concern is to abide in Him. The reason we get disturbed is that we have not been considering Him. Lay it all out before Him, and in the face of difficulties, bereavement and sorrow, hear Him say, "*Let not your heart be troubled.*" Let us be confident in His wisdom and His certainty that all will be well. CD. VOL. 1, 153

Too often we imagine that God lives in a place where He only repairs our broken treasures, but Jesus reveals that it is quite otherwise; He discerns all our difficulties and solves them before us. CD. VOL. 2, 37

Christianity does not add to our difficulties, it brings them to a focus, and in the difficulties we find Jesus Himself. We must get out of the habit of misinterpreting God by saying He wants to teach us something, it is not a New Testament idea, but an idea that is as unlike the God whom Jesus revealed as could

be. God is all the time bringing us to the place where we *un*-learn things. GW. 127

Our attempts to face the problems of human life apart from Jesus Christ are futile. HG. 12

The bigger the difficulty, the more amazing is your profit to Jesus Christ as you draw on His supernatural grace. MFL. 74

God is the Master Engineer. He allows difficulties to come to see if we can vault over them properly. OBH. 82

Where we go in the time of trial proves what the great underlying power in our lives is. OBH. 122

If I am to be identified with Jesus Christ in this life, I must lay my account with the fact that I am going to be troubled in the flesh in a way I would not be if I were not so related to Him, because the last stake of the enemy is in the flesh. PH. 213

God never gives strength for tomorrow, or for the next hour, but only for the strain of the moment. . . . The saint is hilarious when he is crushed with difficulties because the thing is so ludicrously impossible to anyone but God. RTR. 36

God does not do what false Christianity makes out—keep a man immune from trouble, there is no promise of that; God says, '*I will be with him in trouble.*' SHL. 98

The conflict for the Christian is not a conflict with sin, but a conflict over the natural life being turned into the spiritual life. SSM. 63

DILIGENCE

We are apt to be busy about everything but that which concerns our spiritual progress, and at the end of a profitless day we snatch up a Bible or Daily Light and read a few verses, and it does us good for precisely three-quarters of a second. We have to take time to be diligent. MFL. 65

If God is diligent, surely we ought to be diligent in doing our duty to Him. Think how patient and how diligent God has been with us! Over and over again God gets us near the point, and then by some petty individual sulk we spoil it all, and He patiently begins all over again. NKW. 118

DISCERNMENT

Beware of allowing the discernment of wrong in another to blind you to the fact that you are what you are by the grace of God. DI. 84

Never pray for the gift of discernment, live so much in contact with God that the Holy Spirit can point out through you to others where they are wrong. DI. 84

It is so easy to attend to the thing every one else is attending to, but it is difficult to attend to what no one is attending to. MFL. 60

If a man wants scientific knowledge, intellectual curiosity is his guide; but if he wants insight into what Jesus Christ teaches, he can only get it by obedience. SSM. 67

Discernment in the spiritual world is never gained by intellect; in the common-sense world it is. SSM. 67

Never ask God for discernment, because discernment increases your responsibility terrifically; and you cannot get out of it by talking, but only by bearing up the life in intercession before God until God puts him right. SSM. 77

DISCIPLE

'If you are My disciple, you will insist only on your right to give up your rights.' BP. 205

Discipleship and salvation are two different things: a disciple is one who, realizing the meaning of the Atonement, deliberately gives himself up to Jesus Christ in unspeakable gratitude. DI. 34

A disciple is one who not only proclaims God's truth, but one who manifests that he is no longer his own, he has been "bought with a price." DI. 35

I can be so rich in poverty, so rich in the consciousness that I am nobody, that I will never be a disciple of Jesus Christ; and I can be so rich in the consciousness that I am somebody that I will never be a disciple. GW. 79

'I will make the place of My feet glorious'—among the poor, the devil-possessed, the mean, the decrepit, the selfish, the sinful, the misunderstanding—that is where Jesus went, and that is exactly where He will take you if you are His disciple. GW. 97

Men do not care a bit for Jesus Christ's notion of their lives, and Jesus does not care for our notions. There is the antagonism. If we were to estimate ourselves from our Lord's standpoint, very few of us would be considered disciples. HG. 27

"If any man would come after Me . . ." 'If' means, 'You don't need to unless you like, but you won't be of any account to Me in this life unless you do.' HGM. 140

Those of us who have entered into a conscious experience of the salvation of Jesus by the grace of God, whose whole inner life is drawn towards God, have the privilege of being disciples, if we will. IWP. 110

The great stumbling-block in the way of some people being simple disciples is that they are gifted, so gifted that they won't trust God. So clear away all those things from the thought of discipleship; we all have absolutely equal privileges, and there is no limit to what God can do in and through us. IWP. 111

The disciple's Lord is in absolute harmony with the highest man knows and with the highest God has revealed. The Bible is not the authority, the Church is not the authority, the Lord Jesus Christ alone is the Authority. IWP. 122

We shall not always be respected if we are disciples of Jesus. OBH. 60

If you want a good time in this world, do not become a disciple of Jesus. OBH. 61

Not what the disciple says in public prayer, not what he preaches from pulpit or platform, not what he writes on paper or in letters, but what he is in his heart which God alone knows, determines God's revelation of Himself to him. Character determines revelation. PH. 11

The secret of a disciple's life is devotion to Jesus Christ, and the very nature of the life is that it is unobtrusive; it falls into the ground and dies: but presently it springs up and alters the whole landscape. PH. 145

A man may be saved without being a disciple, and it is the point of discipleship that is always kicked against. Our Lord is not talking of eternal salvation, but of the possibility of our being of temporal worth to Himself. PR. 103

Jesus Christ always said, "*If* any man will be My disciple"—He did not clamour for him, or button-hole him. He never took a man off his guard, or used a revivalistic meeting to get a man out of his wits and then say, "Believe in Me," but, "Take time and consider what you are doing; if you would be My disciple, you must lose your 'soul,' i.e., your way of reasoning about things." SA. 87

The romance of the life of a disciple is not an external fascination but an inner martyrdom. SHH. 43

If we are to be disciples of Jesus Christ, our independent right to our individual self must go, and go altogether. SHL. 84

It never cost a disciple anything to follow Jesus; to talk about cost when you are in love with anyone is an insult. SHL. 109

The motive of a disciple is to be well-pleasing to God. SSM. 16

If I let God alter my heredity, I will become devoted to Him, and Jesus Christ will have gained a disciple. SSM. 29

The Example of a disciple is God Almighty and no one less; not the best man you know, nor the finest saint you ever read about, but God Himself. SSM. 51

The characteristic of Jesus in a disciple is much deeper down than doing good things, it is goodness in motive because the disciple has been made good by the supernatural grace of God. SSM. 57

We have to do our utmost as disciples to prove that we appreciate God's utmost for us, and to learn never to allow 'I can't' to creep in. 'Oh, I am not a saint, I can't do that.' If that thought comes in, we are a disgrace to Jesus Christ. God's salvation is a glad thing, but it is a holy, difficult thing that tests us for all we are worth. SSM. 96

The walk of a disciple is gloriously difficult, but gloriously certain. SSM. 104

In our Lord's calling of a disciple He never puts personal holiness in the front, He puts in the front absolute annihilation of my right to myself and unconditional identification with Himself—such a relationship with Him that there is no other relationship on earth in comparison. SSY. 56

As long as we have the endeavour and the strain and the dead-set purpose of being disciples, it is almost certain we are not. Our Lord's making of a disciple is supernatural; He does not build on any natural capacity. SSY. 64

We are called to be unobtrusive disciples, not heroes. When we are right with God, the tiniest thing done out of love to Him is more precious to Him than any eloquent preaching of a sermon. We have introduced into our conception of Christianity heroic notions that come from paganism and not from the teaching of Our Lord. SSY. 68

Jesus warned His disciples that they would be treated as nobodies; He never said they would be brilliant or marvellous. We all have a lurking desire to be exhibitions for God, to be put, as it were, in His show room. Jesus does not want us to be specimens, He wants us to be so taken up with Him that we never think about ourselves, and the only impression left on others by our life is that Jesus Christ is having unhindered way. SSY. 68

A disciple is one who minds neither his own business nor any one else's business, but looks steadfastly to Jesus and goes on following Him. SSY. 70

Many of us want to be disciples, but we do not want to come by way of His atoning Death; we do not want to be compelled to be orthodox to the Cross of Christ, to drink the cup that He drank. But there is no other way. We must be regenerated, supernaturally made all over again, before we can be His disciples. SSY. 72

It is easy to talk, easy to have fine thoughts; but none of that means being a disciple. Being a disciple is to be something that is an infinite satisfaction to Jesus every minute, whether in secret or in public. SSY. 72

DISCIPLESHIP

We need to remind ourselves of the stern, heroic stuff Jesus Christ always spoke when He talked about discipleship. "If any man would come after Me, let him deny himself, and take up his cross daily, and follow Me." CD. VOL. 1, 145

In His teaching about discipleship Jesus Christ bases everything on the complete annihilation of individuality and the emancipation of personality. Until this is understood all our talk about discipleship passes into thin air. DI. 33

The one mark of discipleship is the mastership of Jesus—His right to me from the crown of my head to the sole of my foot. DI. 34

The one essential element in all our Lord's teaching about discipleship is abandon, no calculation, no trace of self-interest. DI. 35

In the initial stages of discipleship you get 'stormy weather', then you lose the nightmare of your own separate individuality and become part of the Personality of Christ, and the thought of yourself never bothers you any more because you are taken up with your relationship to God. HGM. 77

Jesus Christ always talked about discipleship with an 'If.' We are at perfect liberty to toss our spiritual head and say, 'No, thank you, that is a bit too stern for me,' and the Lord will never say a word, we can do exactly what we like. He will never plead, but the opportunity is there, 'If . . .' IWP. 61

Our Lord always prefaced His talks about discipleship with an 'if'; it has no reference whatever to a soul's salvation or condemnation, but to the discipleship of the personality. IWP. 95

Discipleship must always be a personal matter; we can never become disciples in crowds, or even in twos. It is so easy to talk about what 'we' mean to do— 'we' are going to do marvellous things, and it ends in none of us doing anything. The great element of discipleship is the personal one. IWP. 104

Discipleship is based on devotion to Jesus Christ, not on adherence to a doctrine. IWP. 105

The following in the steps of Jesus in discipleship is so great a mystery that few enter into it. IWP. 106

Our Lord's conception of discipleship is not that we work for God, but that God works through us; He uses us as He likes; He allots our work where He chooses, and we learn obedience as our Master did. IWP. 111

There is always an IF in connection with discipleship, and it implies that we need not unless we like. There is never any compulsion, Jesus does not coerce us. There is only one way of being a disciple, and that is by being devoted to Jesus. OBH. 61

The secret of sacramental discipleship is to be so abandoned to the disposition of God in us that He can use us as broken bread and poured out wine for His purpose in the world, even as He broke the life of His own Son to redeem us. PH. 139

The great privilege of discipleship is that I can sign on under His Cross—and that means death to sin. PH. 164

In laying down His conditions for discipleship in Luke xiv. 26–33, our Lord implies—'the only men I will use in My enterprises, are those of whom I have taken charge.' PH. 179

The cross of discipleship is that I daily and hourly delight to tell my human nature that I am not my own, I no longer claim my right to myself. RTR. 17

Discipleship is based not on devotion to abstract ideals, but on devotion to a Person, the Lord Jesus Christ, consequently the whole of the Christian life is stamped by originality. SSM. 16

Following Jesus Christ is a risk absolutely; we must yield right over to Him, and that is where our infidelity comes in, we will not trust what we cannot see, we will not believe what we cannot trace, then it is all up with our discipleship. SSM. 71

There is a difference between salvation and discipleship. A man can be saved by God's grace without becoming a disciple of Jesus Christ. Discipleship means a personal dedication of the life to Jesus Christ. Men are 'saved so as by fire' who have not been worth anything to God in their actual lives. SSM. 93

We have become so taken up with the idea of being prepared for something in the future that that is the conception we have of discipleship. It is true, but it is also untrue. The attitude of the Christian life is that we must be prepared *now*, this second; this is the time. SSY. 72

Our Lord never takes measures to make us obey Him. Our obedience is the outcome of a oneness of spirit with Him through His Redemption. That is why, whenever Our Lord talked about discipleship, He prefaced it with an 'IF'—'you do not need to unless you like'; but—'If any man will be my disciple, let him deny himself,' i.e., 'deny his independence, give up his right to himself to Me.' SSY. 86

We are all based on a conception of importance, either our own importance, or the importance of someone else; Jesus tells us to go and teach based on the revelation of *His* importance. 'All power is given unto *Me* . . . Go *ye* therefore . . .' SSY. 132

Jesus Christ is the only One Who has the right to tell us what it means to be His, and in Luke xiv. 26–33 He is laying down the conditions of discipleship. These conditions are summed up in one astounding word—'*hate*'. 'If any man cometh unto me, and hateth not . . .' (i.e., a hatred of every good thing that divides the heart from loyalty to Jesus) 'he cannot be my disciple.' SSY. 167

DISCIPLINE

A disciplined life means three things—a supreme aim incorporated into the life itself; an external law binding on the life from its Commander, and absolute loyalty to God and His word as the ingrained attitude of heart and mind. There must be no insubordination; every impulse, every emotion, every illumination must be rigorously handled and checked if it is not in accordance with God and His word. AUG. 65

When we depend on someone who has had no discipline, we both degenerate. We are always in danger of depending on people who are undisciplined, and the consequence is that in the actual strain of life they break down and we do too. We have to be actually dependable. AUG. 123

If we keep practising, what we practise becomes our second nature, then in a crisis and in the details of life we shall find that not only will the grace of God stand by us, but also our own nature. Whereas if we refuse to practise, it is not God's grace but our own nature that fails when the crisis comes, because we have not been practising in actual life. We may ask God to help us but He cannot, unless we have made our nature our ally. The practising is ours, not God's. He puts the Holy Spirit into us, He regenerates us, and puts us in contact with all His Divine resources, but He cannot make us walk and decide in the way He wants; we must do that ourselves. AUG. 123

The day we live in is a day of wild imaginations everywhere, unchecked imaginations in music, in literature, and, worst of all, in the interpretation of Scripture. People are going off on wild speculations, they get hold of one line and run clean off at a tangent and try to explain everything on that line, then they go off on another line: none of it is in accordance with the Spirit of God. There is no royal road for bringing our brains into harmony with the Spirit God has put in our hearts; we do not get there all at once, but only by steady discipline. BP. 237

Beware of saying, 'I do not need any discipline, I am saved and sanctified, therefore everything I think is right.' Nothing we think is right, only what God thinks in us is right. CD. VOL. 1, 148

The culture of the entirely sanctified life is often misunderstood. The discipline of that life consists of Suffering, Loneliness, Patience and Prayer. How many who started with the high ecstasy of vision have ended in the disasters of shallowness! Time, the world, and God fire out the fools. CD. VOL. 2, 68

Beware of saying, 'I haven't time to read the Bible, or to pray'; say rather, 'I haven't disciplined myself to do these things.' DI. 69

We must be willing to do in the spiritual domain what we have to do in the natural domain if we want to develop, viz., discipline ourselves. DI. 70

The element of discipline in the life of faith must never be lost sight of, because only by means of the discipline are we taught the difference between the natural interpretation of what we call good and what God means by 'good'. NKW. 22

The only way to keep yourself fit is by the discipline of the disagreeable. It is the disagreeable things which make us exhibit whether we are manifesting the life of the Son of God, or living a life which is antagonistic to Him. OBH. 75

We say many things which we believe, but they have never been tested. Discipline has to come through all the things we believe in order to turn them into real spiritual possessions. PH. 44

God takes deliberate time with us, He does not hurry, because we can only appreciate His point of view by a long discipline. The grace of God abides always the same. By His grace we stand on the basis of His Redemption; but we ought to be making headway in the development of our personal sonship. PH. 102

The resentment of discipline of any kind will warp the whole life away from God's purpose. RTR. 11

There are many things that are perfectly legitimate, but if you are going to concentrate on God you cannot do them. Your right hand is one of the best things you have, but Jesus says if it hinders you in following His precepts, cut it off. This line of discipline is the sternest one that ever struck mankind. RTR. 91

No amount of determination can give me the new life of God, that is a gift; where the determination comes in is in letting that new life work itself out according to Christ's standard. SSM. 94

God puts us through discipline, not for our own sake, but for the sake of His purpose and His call. Never debate about anything God is putting you through, and never try to find out why you are going through it. Keep right with God and let Him do what He likes in your circumstances, and you will find He is producing the kind of bread and wine that will be a benefit to others. SSY. 20

The one thing for which we are all being disciplined is to know that God is real. As soon as God becomes real, other people become shadows. Nothing that other saints do or say can ever perturb the one who is built on the real God. 'In all the world, my God, there is none but thee, there is none but thee.' SSY. 28

Let God put you on His wheel and whirl you as He likes, and as sure as God is God and you are you, you will turn out exactly in accordance with the vision He gave you. Don't lose heart in the process. SSY. 32

. . . nothing and no one can detect us saving God. We are in the quarry now and God is hewing us out. God's Spirit gathers and marks the stones, then they have to be blasted out of their holdings by the dynamite of the Holy Ghost, to be chiselled and shaped, and then lifted into the heavenly places. SSY. 41

The stern discipline that looks like distress and chastisement turns out to be the biggest benediction; it is the shadow of God's hand that keeps us perfectly fitted in Him. SSY. 109

DISCIPLING

There is a method of making disciples which is not sanctioned by Our Lord. It is an excessive pressing of people to be reconciled to God in a way that is unworthy of the dignity of the Gospel. The pleading is on the line of: Jesus has done so much for us, cannot we do something out of gratitude to Him? This method of getting people into relationship to God out of pity for Jesus is never recognized by Our Lord. It does not put sin in its right place, nor does it put the more serious aspect of the Gospel in its right place. Our Lord never pressed anyone to follow Him unconditionally; nor did He wish to be followed merely out of an impulse of enthusiasm. He never pleaded, He never entrapped; He made discipleship intensely narrow, and pointed out certain things which could never be in those who followed Him. Today there is a tendency to take the harshness out of Our Lord's statements. What Jesus says *is* hard; it is only easy when it comes to those who are His disciples. AUG. 49

Jesus did not say, 'Go and discourse about making disciples,' but 'Go and *make* disciples.' The making of converts is a Satanic perversion of this strenuous workmanlike product. How many make followers of their own convictions, and how few make disciples! CD. VOL. 2, 109

God Almighty regenerates men's souls; we make disciples. CD. VOL. 2, 110

God is apparently not very careful whom He uses or what He uses for the work of regeneration; but none but the master workmen, that is, the saints, can make disciples. CD. VOL. 2, 110

To make disciples, then, we must have been made disciples ourselves. There is no royal road to sainthood and discipleship. The way of the Cross is the only way. We see God only from a pure heart, never from an able intellect. CD. VOL. 2, 113

Jesus Christ did not send out the disciples to save souls, but to 'make disciples', men and women who manifest a life in accordance with the life of their Redeemer. DI. 55

When a worker has led a soul to Christ his work has only just begun. Our attitude is apt to be—So many saved; so many sanctified, and then we shout 'Hallelujah'. But it is only then that the true work of the worker begins. It is then that we have to be held in God's hand and let the word of God be driven through us. It is then that we have to be put under the millstone and ground, put into the kneading trough and be mixed properly, and then baked—all in order to be made broken bread to feed God's children. "Go ye therefore, and make disciples." LG. 91

Jesus Christ's last command to His disciples was not to go and save the world, the saving is done; He told them to go and make disciples. OBH. 61

Jesus Christ is engaged in making disciples in the internal sense, consequently He never entrances a man by rapture, or enamours him out of his wits by fascination. Instead, He puts Himself before a man in the baldest light conceivable, 'If you would be My disciple, these are the conditions'. PR. 66

As disciples of Jesus, we are to identify ourselves with God's interests in other people, to show to the other man what God has shown us, and God will give us ample opportunity in our actual lives to prove that we are perfect as our Father in heaven is perfect. SSM. 51

The salvation of souls comes about through the ministry of God's word and the proclaiming of the Redemption by God's servants; but the command to the missionary is to disciple those who are saved. Every now and again the Church becomes content with seeing people saved. When men get saved, then the disciple's work begins, and the great point about discipling is that you can never make a disciple unless you are one yourself. SSY. 75

Jesus Christ did not say—Go and save souls; the salvation of souls is God's work. Jesus told the disciples to go and teach, disciple, all nations. SSY. 75

The evangelical emphasis has too often been: 'So many souls saved, thank God, now they are all right,' the idea being that we have done this thing for God. It is God who saves men; we have to do the discipling after they are saved. SSY. 127

The disciple is Christ's own, and the disciple is not above his Master. He tells us to pray, His Spirit is abroad, and the fields are white already to harvest, but the eyes of all saving His disciples are holden. SSY. 129

DISCOURAGEMENT

The things that discourage and hurt us show from whence we get our succour. Jesus Christ was never discouraged because He was succoured by the Highest. Until a worker knows the succour of God he is in danger of becoming a stumbling-block to other souls. GW. 109

Our discouragement arises from egotism. Discouragement is 'disenchanted egotism'—the heart knocked out of what I want. PH. 73

A saint cannot be discouraged any more than Jesus Christ could be. PH. 73

We become discouraged because we do not like being told the truth; we look only for those things that will quicken and enliven us. PH. 73

"He shall not fail nor be discouraged." Why? Because He never wanted anything but His Father's will. PH. 73

It does not matter what happens, there may be disasters or calamities, or wars or bereavements and heartbreaks, but the marvelous thing in the man who is rightly related to Jesus Christ is that he is not discouraged. That is supernatural, no human being can stand these shocks and not be discouraged unless he is upheld by the supernatural grace of God. PH. 153

God grant we may get to the place where discouragement is as impossible to us as it was to the Lord Jesus. The one dominant note of His life was the doing of His Father's will. RTR 25

Discouragement always comes when we insist on having our own way. SSY. 170

DISPOSITION

What is imperatively needed is that emotional impressionisms and intellectual and moral interest be violently made by each individual into a moral verdict against our self-interest, our right to ourselves, determinedly letting go of all and signing the death warrant of the disposition of sin in us. AUG. 94

What counts in a man's life is the disposition that rules him. AUG. 115

Our temperament is not our disposition, temperament is the tone our nature has taken from the ruling disposition. When we had the disposition of sin our temperament took its tone from that disposition; when God alters the disposition the temperament begins to take its tone from the disposition He puts in, and that disposition is like Jesus Christ's. AUG. 128

Jesus Christ is merciless to self-realization, to self-indulgence, pride, unchastity, to everything that has to do with the disposition you did not know you had till you met Him. The Redemption does not tinker with the externals of a man's life; it deals with the disposition. BE. 79

No man can be forgiven for a disposition, we are forgiven for acts of sin; the disposition of sin must be cleansed by the miracle of God's grace. GW. 83

The reason man is not free is that within his personality there is a disposition which has been allowed to enslave his will, the disposition of sin. Man's destiny is determined by his disposition; he cannot alter his disposition, but he can choose to let God alter it. MFL. 28

The reason anything is a mystery and is coming in between yourself and God, is in the disposition, not in the intellect. When once the disposition is willingly submitted to the life of Jesus, the understanding becomes perfectly clear. "If any man *willeth* to do His will, he shall *know* of the teaching." PH. 117

If the disposition of the Son of God is in me, then heaven and God are my destination; if the disposition in me is not the disposition of God, my home is as obviously certain with the devil. SA. 103

Our destiny is determined by our disposition; pre-ordination in regard to individual life depends entirely on the disposition of the individual. SA. 103

The average preaching of Redemption deals mainly with the "scenic" cases. The message of Jesus Christ is different; He went straight to the disposition, and always said, "IF—you need not unless you like, but—IF any man will follow Me, let him give up his right to himself." SA. 116

I can make my domestic life, my bodily life, and my agricultural life a priestess of sorrow or delight if I watch my disposition. SHH. 26

Jesus says our disposition must be right to its depths, not only our conscious motives but our unconscious motives. SSM. 23

DOCTRINE

Christian doctrines are the explanation of how Jesus Christ makes us saints, but all the doctrine under heaven will never make a saint. The only thing that will make a saint is the Holy Ghost working in us what Jesus Christ did in the Atonement. Jesus Christ demands absolute devotion to Himself personally, then the application of His principles to our lives. BSG. 64

It is vastly important to remember that our duty is to fit our doctrines to our Lord Jesus Christ and not to fit our Lord into our doctrines. Our Lord is God-Man, not half God and half man, but a unique Being revealed from heaven, and the Holy Spirit alone can expound Him. CD. VOL. 2, 147

We are not sent to specialize in doctrine, but to lift up Jesus, and He will do the work of saving and sanctifying souls. When we become doctrine-mongers God's power is not known, only the passionateness of an individual appeal. DI. 2

God has a way of bringing in facts which upset a man's doctrines if these stand in the way of God getting at his soul. DI. 2

Doctrine is never the guide into Christian experience; doctrine is the exposition of Christian experience. DI. 2

Doctrine is the mere statement of the life of God for the purposes of teaching. Always beware of following your own convictions in doctrine instead of following the life of God. LG. 67

If we make sin a theological question and not a question of actual deliverance, we become adherents to doctrine, and if we put doctrine first, we shall be hoodwinked before we know where we are; or if we take an actual experience and deposit that as a truth on which we rest our souls, we go wrong at once. In stating holiness doctrinally we are apt to make it appear harsh and vindictive; it is technically right, but without the love of God in it. LG. 70

If we divorce what Jesus says from Himself, it leads to secret self-indulgence spiritually; the soul is swayed by a form of doctrine that has never been assimilated and the life is twisted away from the centre, Jesus Christ Himself. OBH. 80

. . . your life with God is more precious than proving you are right doctrinally. It is at the peril of your communion with God that you contend about a doctrine. OPG. 30

Belief of doctrine does not make a man a Christian. There are those who emphasise doctrine, they would go to martyrdom for the faith; whilst others emphasise experience, and take everything revealed in the Bible as picturing our experience. Either of these views is likely to become a dangerous side track. PR. 99

If we are only true to a doctrine of Christianity instead of to Jesus Christ, we drive our ideas home with sledge-hammer blows, and the people who listen to us say, 'Well, that may be true'; but they resent the way it is presented. SSM. 83

DOUBT

Doubt is not always a sign that a man is wrong; it may be a sign that he is thinking. DI. 82

Christ is our entire life. When once we realise this, certain forms of doubt and perplexity vanish for ever. If we set our affection on things above, those perplexities will never trouble us any more because we know the Lord Jesus, and He is not distracted by these present perplexities. The things that are obscure to the natural man become clear to the penetration of the mind that sets itself on the things above. PR. 117

Whenever there is the tiniest element of doubt, quit. Never say: "Why shouldn't I? There's no harm in it." RTR. 42

Every man ought to be intellectually sceptical, but that is different from moral doubt which springs from a moral twist. SA. 13

When in doubt physically, dare; when in moral doubt, stop; when in spiritual doubt, pray; and when in personal doubt, be guided by your life with God.

Base all on God, and slowly and surely the actual life will be educated along the particular line of your relationship to Him. SHH. 41

For a man to have doubts is not a sign that he is a bad man. SHH. 96

DRUNKENNESS

There are two ways of inspiration possible—being drunk with wine, and being filled with the Spirit. We have no business to be nondescript, drunk neither one way nor the other. A man may be sober and incapable as well as drunk and incapable. Watch human nature; we are so built that if we do not get thrilled in the right way, we will get thrilled in the wrong. If we are without the thrill of communion with God, we will try to get thrilled by the devil, or by some concoction of human ingenuity. MFL. 82

The Bible talks about drinking wine when we are glad; this is different from the modern view. It is bad to drink wine when you are in the dumps.

. . . a man should enjoy the pleasant things, remembering that that is why they are here. The universe is meant for enjoyment. ". . . God, who giveth us richly all things to enjoy." "Whatsoever ye do whether ye eat or drink, do all to the glory of God." We argue on the rational line—Don't do this or that because it is wrong.

. . . Don't do it, not because it is wrong, but because the man who follows you will stumble if he does it, therefore cut it out, never let him see you do it any more. Solomon's attitude is a safe and sane one, that when a man is rightly related to God he has to see that he enjoys his own life and that others do too. SHH. 145

DUST

These two things, dust and Divinity, make up man. That he is made of the dust is man's glory, not his shame; it has been the scene of his shame, but it was designed to be his glory. MFL. 42

Dust is the finest element in man, because in it the glory of God is to be manifested. SHH. 67

DUTY

The duty of every Christian, and it is the last lesson we learn, is to make room for God to deal with other people direct; we will try and limit others and make them into our mould. MFL. 123

Always go the second mile with God. It is never our duty to do it, but if we make duty our god we cease to be Christians in that particular. It is never our duty to go the second mile, to turn the other cheek, but it is what we will do if we are saints. OBH. 83

The tiniest detail in which we obey has all the omnipotent power of the grace of God behind it. When we do our duty, not for duty's sake, but because we believe that God is engineering our circumstances in that way, then at the very point of our obedience the whole superb grace of God is ours. OBH. 108

How often we have faced difficulties that never came, and every time we faced them we unfitted ourselves for the duty that lay before us. I have no business to be thinking about something else, my duty is always the duty that lies nearest. RTR. 16

"Trust in the Lord with all thine heart." It is this state of mind and heart which is absolutely free to do the duty that lies nearest without any flutter. RTR. 17

To go the second mile means always do your duty, and a great deal more than your duty, in a spirit of loving devotion that does not even know you have done it. If you are a saint the Lord will tax your walking capacity to the limit. The supreme difficulty is to go the second mile *with God*, because no one understands why you are being such a fool. SSY. 63

E

EARNESTNESS

Do not rely on your earnestness as the ground for being heard. This is a much-needed caution because it is so subtle a thing, this thing called earnestness. CD. VOL. 2, 20

Earnestness is not by any means everything; it is very often a subtle form of pious self-idolatry, because it is obsessed with the method and not with the Master. CD. VOL. 2, 20

The phrase 'pray through' often means working ourselves up into a frenzy of earnestness in which perspiration is taken for inspiration. It is a mistake to think we are heard on the ground of our earnestness; we are heard on the ground of the evangelical basis, "Having therefore, brethren, boldness to enter into the holiest by the blood of Jesus." CD. VOL. 2, 21

God is never impressed with our earnestness, He promises to answer us when we pray on one ground only, viz., the ground of the Redemption. The Redemption of the Lord Jesus provides me with a place for intercession. DI. 39

Prayer that is not saturated in the New Testament is apt to be based on human earnestness. God never hears prayer because a man is in earnest; He hears and answers prayer that is on the right platform—we have 'boldness to enter into the holy place *by the blood of Jesus*', and by no other way. It is not our agony and our distress, but our childlike confidence in God. GW. 47

It is not our earnestness that brings us into touch with God, not our stated times of prayer, but the vitalising death of our Lord Jesus Christ. PH. 224

Earnestness is not everything; I may be an earnest lunatic. SHH. 137

We are so tremendously in earnest that we are blinded by our earnestness and never see that God is more in earnest than we are. SSM. 30

Overmuch earnestness blinds the life to reality, earnestness becomes our god. SSM. 88

God is not impressed by our earnestness, He nowhere promises to answer prayer because of our agony in intercession, but only on the ground of Redemption. SSY. 126

EARTH

The establishment of men's rights on the earth is limited by the rights of the earth itself. BE. 24

Man was intended to replenish the earth by looking after it, being its lord not its tyrant; sin has made man its tyrant. BE. 24

The rights of the land will probably only be fully realized in the Millennium, because in this dispensation men ignore obedience to God's laws. BE. 24

The material earth is God's, and the way men treat it is a marvellous picture of the long-suffering of God. BE. 25

God created the earth and the life on the earth in order to fit the world for man. BP. 5

Man . . . is the head and the purpose of the six days' creation. Man's body has in it those constituents that connect it with the earth; it has fire and water and all the elements of animal life, consequently God keeps us here. The earth is man's domain, and we are going to be here again after the terrestrial cremation. 'Here-after,' without the devil, without sin and wrong. We are going to be here, marvellously redeemed in this wonderful place which God made very beautiful, and with which sin has played havoc, and creation itself is waiting "for the manifestation of the sons of God." BP. 8

Man's chief glory and dignity is that he was made "of the earth, earthy" to manifest the image of God in that substance. We are apt to think that to be made of the earth is our humiliation, but it is the very point of which God's Word makes most. God "formed man of the dust of the ground," and the Redemption is for the dust of the ground as well as for man's spirit. BP. 11

Jesus Christ took on Him the nature of the 'earthen vessel,' not the nature of the angels. "Of the earth, earthy," is man's glory, not his shame, and it is in the earth, earthy, that Jesus Christ's full regenerating work is to have its ultimate reach. BP. 50

The sin of man has polluted the material earth, and it will have to go through a cremation, out of which will emerge 'new heavens and a new earth, wherein dwelleth righteousness'. GW. 44

Sin has not only infected material things, it is the common inheritance of the human race; but the time is coming when it will be impossible for sin to be on the earth any more, when the very material earth will be shot through with the glory of God's presence, and when man himself will be 'conformed to the image of His Son'. Meantime there is the confusion and the agony which make men say, 'There is no God'. These things are the evidence that God is. GW. 45

There is a time coming when this earth will be the habitation of God, at present it is usurped by the world systems of men; when these disappear, then God's "new heaven and new earth" will emerge. HGM. 27

The sin of man has polluted the material earth and it will have to be disinfected and there will be "a new heaven and a new earth." HGM. 61

God's earth is like the earth we are on now; we can do what we like with it, shovel rubbish on it, mine it and turn it into trenches; we can score it, and make it the foundation for the erections of human pride; but Jesus Christ says, "the meek shall inherit *the earth.*" HGM. 69

"The meek shall inherit *the earth,*" not the 'world,' because the world, according to the Bible, is the system of civilized things that men place on God's earth. HGM. 69

There is a time coming when the earth itself shall be the very garment of God, when the systems of the world and those that represent them shall call on the mountains and the rocks to hide them, but at that time the earth won't shelter them. HGM. 70

We are shut up to this physical world; other planets may be inhabited, we are shut up to this one—shut up to our five senses and to this earth. Some minds are un-made when they realize this seclusion, other minds are made because they see God's purpose in it. HGM. 81

The earth is always spoken of in the Bible as God's. HGM. 95

The laws given in the Bible include a scheme for the treatment of the earth and they insist on proper rest being given to the land, and make it clear that that alone will bring profit in actual existence. Leviticus xxv. is the great classic on the rights of the earth. SHH. 62

The object of a man's life is not to hoard; he has to get enough for his brute life and no more; the best of his life is to be spent in confidence in God. Man is meant to utilise the earth and its product for food and the nourishment of his body, but he must not live in order to make his existence. If the children of Israel gathered more manna than they needed, it turned into dry rot, and that law still holds good. SHH. 73

. . . the way a man treats the soil will also prove whether or not he is a son of God. SHH. 99

ECSTASY

The state of ecstasy, something that lifts a man right out of his ordinary setting, and the transportation at times of body as well as spirit, then is revealed in the Bible. A miracle? Yes, but not more of a miracle than the fact that I am alive. BP. 257

Whenever ecstasies or visions of God unfit us for practical life they are danger signals that the life is on the wrong track. DI. 17

The best measure of a spiritual life is not its ecstasies, but its obedience. 'To obey is better than sacrifice.' NKW. 126

There is a real peril in being enchanted but unchanged. I may be enchanted by the truth Jesus presents, but when it comes to my life being marked in all its secular details with the disposition of the Holy Spirit, then I am out of it; I prove spiritually inefficient, of no worth at all to Jesus Christ. PH. 174

Experiences are good, enchantment is good, but it all makes for spiritual inefficiency unless the experience is turned into the expression of a strong family likeness to Jesus, and the enchantment is transformed into the energy of the Holy Spirit. PH. 175

EDUCATION

The meaning of education is not to pack in something alien, but the drawing out of what is in for the purpose of expression. BP. 246

Education and scholarship may enable a man to put things well, but they will never give him insight. Insight only comes from a pure-heartedness in working out the will of God. MFL. 23

In natural education everything is built up on difficulty, there is always something to overcome. And this is true in the spiritual world. If the world, the flesh and the devil have knocked you out once, get up and face them again, and again, until you have done with them. That is how character is made in the spiritual domain as well as in the natural. MFL. 73

Education is a bringing out of what is there and giving it the power of expression, not packing in what does not belong; and spiritual education means learning how to give expression to the Divine life that is in us when we are born from above. PH. 64

The first thing we need to be educated in spiritually is a knowledge of the dimensions of Divine love, its length and depth and breadth and height. PH. 64

It is a great thing to tell yourself the truth. These are some of the lines of spiritual education: learning the dimensions of Divine Love, that the centre of that love is holiness; that the direction of Divine living is a deliberate surrender of our own point of view in order to learn Jesus Christ's point of view, and seeing that men and women are nourished in the knowledge of Jesus. The only way that can be done is by being loyal to Jesus myself. PH. 68

EGOTISM

Egotism is a conceited insistence on my own particular ways and manners and customs. It is an easily discernible characteristic, and fortunately is condemned straightway by right thinking people. We are inclined to overlook egotism in young people and in ignorant people, but even in them it is of the detestable, vicious order. BP. 151

ELECTION

'Many are called, but few prove the choice ones', that is, few of us take up the cross and follow Jesus, the reason being not that we are irreligious and bad, but we don't prefer that Jesus should be Lord. HGM. 140

To ratify is to make sure of. I have to form the habit of assuring myself of my election, to bend the whole energy of my Christian powers to realise my calling, and to do that I must remember what I am saved for, viz., that the Son of God might be manifested in my mortal flesh. OBH. 80

Deliverance from sin is not a question of God's election, but of an experience in human life which God demands. The effective working of the new birth life in us is that we do not commit sin, not merely that we have the power not to sin, but that we have stopped sinning— a much more practical thing. PR. 35

"I have chosen you". Keep that note of greatness in your creed. It is not that you have got God, but that He has got you. Why is God at work in me, bending, breaking, moulding, doing just as He chooses?—for one purpose only— that He may be able to say, "This is My man, My woman". RTR. 21

When this election to God in Christ Jesus is realized by us individually, God begins to destroy our prejudices and our parochial notions and to turn us into the servants of His own purpose. The experience of salvation in individual lives means the incoming of this realization of the election of God. SSY. 101

If we have been living much in the presence of God, the first thing that strikes us is the smallness of the lives of men and women who do not recognize God. It did not occur to us before, their lives seemed to be broad and generous; but now there seems such a fuss of interests that have nothing whatever to do with God's purpose, and are altogether unrelated to the election of God. SSY. 103

The realization by regeneration of the election of God, and of being made thereby perfectly fit for Him, is the most joyful realization on earth. When we are born from above we *realize* the election of God, our being regenerated does not *create* it. When once we realize that through the salvation of Jesus we are made perfectly fit for God, we understand why Jesus is apparently so ruthless in His claims why He demands such absolute rectitude from the saint: He has given him the very nature of God. SSY. 105

"Ye have not chosen Me, but I have chosen you." Jesus turned away everyone who came to Him and said, 'I want to be Your disciple.' Jesus Christ knows the men and women He wants. WG. 85

EMOTIONS

The Christian is one who bases his whole confidence in God and His work of grace, then the emotions become the beautiful ornament of the life, not the source of it. BE. 70

Beware of the luxury of spiritual emotions unless you are prepared to work them out. God does the unseen, but we have to do the seen. MFL. 41

Beware of not worshipping God in your emotional history. Watch your fancies and your friends, heed who you love and who loves you, and you will be saved from many a pitfall. OPG. 44

You have no business to harbour an emotion the conclusion of which you see to be wrong. Grip it on the threshold of your mind in a vice of blood and allow it no more way. SSM. 34

ENEMY

It is never wise to under-estimate an enemy. We look upon the enemy of our souls as a conquered foe, so he is, but only to God, not to us. HG. 23

The Bible reveals God to be the Lover of His enemies. HG. 121

God laid down His life for His enemies, a thing no man can do. The fundamental revelation made in the New Testament is that God redeemed the human race when we were spitting in His face, as it were. HGM. 63

The greatest enemy of the life with God is not sin, but the good that is not good enough. NKW. 32

When a man does love his enemies, he knows that God has done a tremendous work in him, and every one else knows it too. SSM. 53

ETERNITY

The whole of Eternity will be taken up with understanding and knowing God, and, thank God, we may begin to know Him down here. OBH. 43

EUCHARIST

The real meaning of the word 'sacrament' is that the Presence of God comes through the common elements of the bread and the wine. If you are of a religious nature you will be inclined to put store on the symbol, but beware lest you put the symbol in the place of the thing symbolized; it is easy to do it, but once you mistake the symbol for what it symbolizes, you are off the track. HGM. 32

The ordinance of the Lord's Supper is a symbol of what we should be doing all the time. It is not a memorial of One Who has gone, but of One Who is always here. NKW. 74

EVANGELISM

Present-day Evangelism is inclined to go much more strongly on the line of the 'passion for souls' than 'the passion for sanctification'; everyone has gone a-slumming to save the lost; it suits our religious passion to help the men and women who are down and out. Saving souls is God's work, man's work is disciplining those souls. BE. 63

The pseudo-evangelical line is that you must be on the watch all the time and lose no opportunity of speaking to people, and this attitude is apt to produce the superior person. It may be a noble enough point of view, but it produces the wrong kind of character. It does not produce a disciple of Jesus, but too often the kind of person who smells of gunpowder and people are afraid of meeting him. According to Jesus Christ, what we have to do is to watch the Source and He will look after the outflow: 'He that believeth on Me, out of him shall flow rivers of living water.' BFB. 23

Pseudo-evangelism has twisted the revelation and made it mean—'Now that God has saved me, I do not need to do anything'. The New Testament revelation is that now I am saved by God's grace, I must work on that basis and keep myself clean. BFB. 103

The first appeal of present-day evangelism is apt to be, not on the line of how to get rid of sin, but how to be put right for heaven, consequently men are not convicted of sin, but left with a feeling of something; insufficient in life. DI. 64

One of the greatest snares of modern evangelism is this apotheosis of commercialism manifested in the soul saving craze. I do not mean God does not save souls, but I do believe the watchword 'A passion for souls' is a snare. The watchword of the saint is 'A passion for Christ.' HGM. 68

In listening to some evangelical addresses the practical conclusion one is driven to is that we have to be great sinners before we can be saved; and the majority of men are not great sinners. IWP. 116

The old systems of religion were distinctly ordained of God. All the ordinances to which the Pharisees held had been given by God, but the Pharisees had become second editions of the Almighty, they had usurped the place of God. There is always a danger of Phariseeism cropping up. In our own day its form is evangelical, man becomes a little god over his own crowd doctrinally. OBH. 99

Pseudo-evangelism has gone wildly off the track in that it has made salvation a bag of tricks whereby if I believe a certain shibboleth, I am tricked out of hell and made right for heaven—a travesty of the most tremendous revelation of the Redemption of the human race by Jesus Christ. SA. 108

One of the dangers in modern evangelism is that it lays the emphasis on decision for Christ instead of on surrender to Jesus Christ. That to me is a grave blunder. When a man decides for Christ he usually puts his confidence in his own honour, not in Christ at all. No man can keep himself a Christian, it is impossible; it is God Who keeps a man a Christian. SHH. 55

The insinuation of putting men's needs first, success first, has entered into the very domain of evangelism, and has substituted 'the passion for souls' for 'the passion for Christ', and we experience shame when we realize how completely we have muddled the whole thing by not maintaining steadfast loyalty to Jesus Christ. SHL. 97

Modern evangelism makes the mistake of thinking that a worker must plough his field, sow the seed, and reap the harvest in half-an-hour. Our Lord was never in a hurry with the disciples, He kept on sowing the seed and paid no attention to whether they understood Him or not. He spoke the truth of God, and by His own life produced the right atmosphere for it to grow, and then left it alone, because He knew well that the seed had in it all the germinating power of God and would bring forth fruit after its kind once it was put in the right soil. SHL. 114

Beware of the books that tell you how to catch men. Go to Calvary, and let God Almighty deal with you until you understand the meaning of the tremendous cost to our Lord Jesus Christ, and then go out to catch men. God grant we may get away from the instructors on how to catch fish and get out into the fishing business! WG. 84

EVIDENCES

There is no evidence of God outside the moral domain. PH. 204

The New Testament is not written to prove that Jesus Christ is God Incarnate; the New Testament does not prove anything; it simply confirms the faith of those who believe beforehand. Christian evidences don't amount to anything; you can't convince a man against his will. SA. 32

EVOLUTION

The Bible nowhere says that God set processes to work and out of those processes evolved the things which now appear. The Bible says that God created things by a distinct act. BP. 5

Evolution is a fact both scientific and scriptural, that is, if we mean by Evolution that there is growth in every species; but not growth from one species into another. BP. 68

Evolution is the characteristic of man's work, never of God's. God works by creation. GW. 88

Evolution is simply a working way of explaining the growth and development of anything. When evolution is made a fetish and taken to mean God, then call it 'bosh'; but evolution in a species, in an idea, in teaching, is exactly what our Lord taught: born of the Spirit and going on "till we all attain . . . , unto the measure of the stature of the fulness of Christ." HG. 5

Sooner or later every human heart flings away as chaff the idea that we are developing and growing better. HG. 21

The Bible does not look forward to an evolution of mankind: the Bible talks of a revolution—"Ye must be born again." PH. 78

The world to-day is obsessed with the idea of evolution, we hear speculations about the superman, we are told we are getting better and better; but we are tending towards we don't know what. The remarkable thing about the spiritual evolution represented by Jesus Christ is that the goal is given to us at the start, viz., Jesus Christ Himself. PH. 78

The evolutionist looks at man and says, What a glorious promise of what he is going to be! The New Testament looks at man's body and moral life and intelligence and says, What a ruin of what God designed him to be! SA. 115

Evolution, like Christian Science, is a hasty conclusion. There may be nine facts which seem to make a thing clear and conclusive, and one fact that contradicts. There is always something that swerves away from the explainable. The only explanation lies in a personal knowledge of God through Jesus Christ, not on the basis of philosophy or of thinking, but on the basis of a vital relationship to Him which works in the actual condition of things as they are. "I am the Way, the Truth, and the Life." SHH. 132

The Bible does not look forward to an evolution of mankind; the Bible talks of a *revolution*—'Marvel not that I said unto thee, Ye must be born anew.' We have to get back to the preaching of the Cross, and the remission of sins through the death of Our Lord. SSY. 77

EXAMPLE

The only way in which Our Lord does become our Example is when His life has been imparted to us. When we partake of His life through the experience of regeneration we are put into a state of innocence towards God, and we have then to do what Jesus did, viz., transform that innocence into holy character by a series of moral choices. BSG. 39

We look upon Jesus Christ as the best Example of the Christian life; we do not conceive of Him as Almighty God Incarnate, with all power in heaven and on earth. We make Him a comrade, One who in the battle of life has more breath than the rest of us and He turns round to lend a hand. We deal with Him as if He were one of ourselves; we do not take off the shoes from our feet when He speaks. Jesus Christ is Saviour, and He saves us into His own absolute and holy lordship. HGM. 129

If Jesus Christ came to be an Example only, He is the greatest torturer of the human race. But our Lord did not come primarily to teach us and give us an example; He came to lift us into a totally new kingdom, and to impart a new life to which His teachings would apply. PR. 78

The Bible reveals all through that Our Lord bore the sin of the world by *identification*, not by *sympathy*. He came here for one purpose only—to bear away the sin of the world in His own Person on the Cross. He came to redeem men, not to set them a wonderful example. SSY. 145

EXPERIENCE

If we have faith only in what we experience of salvation, we will get depressed and morbid; but to be a believer in Jesus Christ is to have an irrepressible belief and a life of uncrushable gaiety. AUG. 116

If when an experience is recorded, I say it is nonsense because I have never had it, I put myself in the place of the superior person, an attitude I have no business to take. BP. 257

Experience is never the ground of my faith; experience is the evidence of my faith. CHI. 52

Many of us have had a marvellous experience of deliverance from sin and of the baptism of the Holy Ghost, not a fictional experience, but a real experience whereby we prove to our amazement every day that God has delivered us, then comes the danger that we pin our faith to our experience instead of to Jesus Christ, and if we do, faith becomes distorted. CHI. 53

Our experience is the proof that our faith is right. Jesus Christ is always infinitely mightier than our faith, mightier than our experience, but our experience will be along the line of the faith we have in Him. CHI. 53

The great factor in Christian experience is the one our Lord continually brought out, viz., the reception of the Holy Spirit who does *in* us what He did *for* us, and slowly and surely our natural life is transformed into a spiritual life through obedience. CHI. 63

If your experience is not worthy of the Risen, Ascended Christ, then fling is overboard. DI. 17

Experience as an end in itself is a disease; experience as a result of the life being based on God is health. DI. 18

Spiritual famine and dearth, if it does not start from sin, starts from dwelling entirely on the experience God gave me instead of on God who gave me the experience. DI. 18

When I plant my faith on the Lord Jesus my experiences don't make me conscious of them, they produce in me the life of a child. DI. 18

If my experience makes anyone wish to emulate me, I am decoying that one away from God. DI. 18

Whenever we get light from God on a particular phase we incline to limit God's working to that phase, forgetting that we cannot tie up Almighty God to anything built up out of our own experience. DI. 19

One man's experience is as valuable as another's, but experience has nothing to do with facts. Facts pay no attention to us, facts have to be accepted, they are the real autocrats in life. DI. 19

In spiritual experience it is not your intellect that guides you; intellect illuminates what is yours, and you get a thrill of delight because you recognize what you have been going through but could not state. DI. 19

Whenever the Bible refers to facts of human experience, look to your experience for the answer; when the Bible refers to standards of revelation, look to God, not to your experience. DI. 19

What is the personal history between Jesus Christ and myself? Is there anything of the nature of 'the new creation' in me? or is what I call my 'experience' sentimental rubbish placed on top of 'me' as I am? DI. 35

The judicious weighing of what you should allow other people to tell you and what not to allow them to tell you, depends on two things: your experience of life among men, and your experience of life with God. DI. 89

In the early stages of our Christian experience we are inclined to hunt in an overplus of delight for the commandments of our Lord in order to obey them out of our love for Him, but when that conscious obedience is assimilated and we begin to mature in our life with God, we obey His commandments unconsciously, until in the maturest stage of all we are simply chidren of God through whom God does His will, for the most part unconsciously to us. GW. 10

God has not said that the relating of my experiences, of my insight into the truth, will not return to Him void; He says '*My word* shall not return unto Me void.' GW. 94

Never forget that the Almighty is a great deal bigger than our experience of Him; that the Lord Jesus Christ is a great deal bigger than our experience of Him. GW. 104

Our help is not in what God has done, but in God Himself. There is a danger of banking our faith and our testimony on our experience, whereas our experience is the gateway to a closer intimacy with God. HG. 27

It is not difficult for our confidence to be shaken if we build on our experience; but if we realize that all we experience is but the doorway leading to the knowledge of God, Satan may shake that as much as he likes, but he cannot shake the fact that God remains faithful, and we must not cast away our confidence in Him. HG. 28

Beware of any experience that is not built absolutely on the atoning merit of Jesus Christ; and remember, the measure of your freedom from sin is the measure of your sense of what sin is. HG. 46

The snare of experiences is that we keep coming back to the shore when God wants to get us out into the deeps. HGM. 19

The one great thing about the salvation of Jesus is that the more you experience it the less you know what you experience; it is only in the initial stages that you know what you experience. The danger is lest we mistake the shores of our experience for the ocean. HGM. 19

All we need to *experience* is that we have "passed out of death into life": what we need to *know* takes all Time and Eternity. HGM. 24

If we take the extraordinary experiences as a model for the Christian life, we erect a wrong standard without knowing it, and in the passing of the years we produce that worst abortion, the spiritual prig—an intolerant un-likeness to Jesus Christ. The man or woman who becomes a spiritual prig does so by imperceptible degrees, but the starting-point is a departure from the evangel of the New Testament and a building up on the evangel of Protestantism. LG. 35

Experience is never the ground of our trust, it is the gateway to the One Whom we trust. NKW. 17

We never can *experience* Jesus Christ, that is, we can never hold Him within the compass of our own hearts. Jesus Christ must always be greater than our experience of Him, but our experience will be along the line of the faith we have in Him. OBH. 86

Experience is not what a man *thinks* through, but what he *lives* through. OBH. 92

Christian experience means that we go to the whole of life open-eyed, wearing no doctrinal or denominational 'blinkers' which shut off whole areas of unwelcome fact. Our faith has to be applied in every domain of our lives. OBH. 92

There are definite stages of conscious experience, but never pin your faith to any experience; look to the Lord Who gives you the experience. Be ruthless with yourself if you are given to talking about the experiences you have had. Your experiences are not worth anything unless they keep you at the Source, viz., Jesus Christ. It is tremendously strengthening to meet a mature saint, a man or woman with a full orbed experience, whose faith is built in strong emphatic confidence in the One from Whom their experience springs. OBH. 93

Christian experience must be applied to the facts of life as they are, not to our fancies. We can live beautifully inside our own particular religious compartment as long as God does not disturb us; but God has a most uncomfortable way of stirring up our nests and of bringing in facts that have to be faced. It is actualities that produce the difficulty—the actual people we come in contact with, the actual circumstances of our lives, the actual things we discover in ourselves; and until we have been through the trial of faith in connection with actualities and have transfigured the actual into the real, we have no Christian experience. Experience is what is *lived* through. OBH. 95

We have to build in faith on the presupposition of the perfect Atonement of Jesus Christ, not build on an experience. If we construct our faith on our experience, we produce that most unscriptural type of holiness, an isolated life, with our eyes fixed on our own whiteness. OBH. 110

In all Christian experience there must be the presupposition of the Atonement; we have to build in faith on the great work which God has performed through Christ. We cannot save ourselves, or sanctify ourselves; we cannot atone for sin; we cannot redeem the world; we cannot make right what is wrong, pure what is impure, holy what is unholy—all that is the sovereign work of God. OBH. 120

Christian experience does not mean we have thought through the way God works in human lives by His grace, or that we are able to state theologically that God gives the Holy Ghost to them that ask Him—that may be Christian thinking, but it is not Christian experience. Christian experience is living through all this by the marvellous power of the Holy Ghost. PH. 30

In sanctification the one reality is the Lord Himself; if you know Him, you will pay no attention to experiences. Experiences are only a doorway to lead us into the awe and wonder of the revelation of God. Let experiences come and go; bank on the Lord. PH. 86

We so continually run down the revelations of the New Testament to the level of our own experience. That is wrong; we must let God lift up our experience to the standard of His word. PR. 52

Jesus Christ is either all that the New Testament claims Him to be—the Redeemer of the human race, or else a futile dreamer, and the only proof is in personal experience. PR. 92

There is a difference between revelation and experience. As Christians we must have an experience, but we must believe a great deal more than we can experience. For instance, no Christian can experience the Cross of Christ; but he can experience salvation through the Cross. No Christian can experience God becoming Incarnate; but he can experience the incoming of the life of God by regeneration. No Christian can experience the personal advent of the Holy Ghost on to this earth; but he can experience the indwelling of the Holy Ghost. PR. 98

We cannot experience Jesus Christ rising from the dead; we cannot experience His Destiny or His Deity, but we must understand where the regenerating forces in our lives come from. PR. 110

. . . we must have Christian experience, but we must have more. Many of us are kindly interested in Christianity and in being devoted to Jesus Christ, but we have never received anything from Him. If we told ourselves the truth, we could not say that God had regenerated us experimentally. If we are not to be merely sentimental Christians, we must know what it is to be born into the Kingdom of God and to find out that God has altered the thing that matters to us. PR. 129

If you put your faith in your experience anything that happens—toothache, indigestion, an east wind, uncongenial work—is likely to upset the experience, but nothing that happens can ever upset God or the almighty reality of the Re-demption; once based on that, you are as eternally sure as God Himself. RTR. 88

The man who has power over another may hurt himself by the exercise of that power unless he himself is ruled by a greater power. If I have had a vivid religious experience and have power over people by means of that experience, the danger is that I usurp the place of God and say, "You must come my way; you must have this experience." This may damage you, but it damages me more, because my spirit is far removed from the spirit of Jesus Christ, it is the spirit of a spiritual prig. Whenever I exercise will power without at the same time being dominated myself, I damage something or someone. SHH. 117

Personal experience is a mere illustration that explains the wonderful difference the Gospel has made in us. Our experience is the gateway into the Gospel for us; but it is not the Gospel. This is the Gospel: 'that repentance and remission of sins should be preached in his name. SSY. 149

EXTRAVAGANCE

We are economically drunk nowadays, everybody is an economist, consequently we imagine that God is economical. Think of God in Creation! Think of the number of trees and blades of grass and flowers, the extravagant wealth of beauty no one ever sees! Think of the sunrises and sunsets we never look at! God is lavish in every degree. For God's sake, don't be economical, be God's child. OPG. 55

To-day we enthrone insurance and economy, but it is striking to recall that the one thing Jesus Christ commended was extravagance. SHH. 73

It is possible to be so economical that you venture nothing. We have deified economy, placed insurance and economy on the throne, consequently we will do nothing on the line of adventure or extravagance. To use the word "economy" in connection with God is to belittle and misunderstand Him. Where is the economy of God in His sunsets and sunrises, in the grass and flowers and trees. God has made a super-abounding number of things that are of no *use* to anyone. How many of us bother our heads about the sunrises and sunsets? Yet they go on just the same. Lavish extravagance to an extraordinary degree is the characteristic of God, never economy. Grace is the overflowing favour of God. Imagine a man who is in love being economical!

SHH. 143

F

FACT

There are two domains of Fact: common-sense facts and revelation facts. It is impossible to prove a fact; a fact must be accepted. We accept common-sense facts on the ground of our senses, and we accept revelation facts on the ground of our faith in God. AUG. 77

There are two ways of dealing with facts—one is to shut your eyes and say that they are not there, the other is to open your eyes and look at them, and let them mould you. AUG. 77

It is impossible to prove a fact, facts have to be swallowed, and the man who swallows revelation facts is no more of a fool than the man who swallows common-sense facts on the evidence of his senses. Face facts, and play the sceptic with explanations. DI. 3

Never blink facts because they don't agree with your theory. RTR. 27

FAITH

Faith is not a conscious thing, it springs from a personal relationship and is the unconscious result of believing someone. AUG. 84

Our faith is in a Person Who is not deceived in anything He says or in the way He looks at things. AUG. 115

'The faith' is faith in the Redemption and in the indwelling Spirit of God;

faith that God is love, and that He will see after us if we stand steadfast to our confidence in Him. It is easy to stand fast in the big things, but very difficult in the small things. If we do stand fast in faith in Him we shall become irresistible disciples. AUG. 121

Faith in God is a terrific venture in the dark; I have to believe that God is good in spite of all that contradicts it in my experience. BFB. 100

Faith does not become its own object, that produces fanaticism; but it becomes the means whereby God unveils His purposes to us. CD. VOL. 2, 47

When we say we have no faith, we simply betray our own case, viz. that we have no confidence in God at all, for faith is born of confidence in Him. CD. VOL. 2, 49

Faith is built on heroism. CD. VOL. 2, 87

The life of faith is the life of a soul who has given over every other life but the life of faith. Faith is not an action of the mind, nor of the heart, nor of the will, nor of the sentiment, it is the centering of the entire man in God. CD. VOL. 2, 149

The heroes of faith catalogued in the eleventh chapter of Hebrews were not men who vaguely trusted that "somehow good would be the final goal of ill," they were heroes who died "*according to faith*", not faith in a principle, but faith in a Person Who promises. CD. VOL. 2, 149

The conception of faith given in the New Testament is that it must embrace the whole man. Faith is not a faculty, faith is the whole man rightly related to God by the power of the Spirit of Jesus. We are apt to apply faith to certain domains of our lives only—we have faith in God when we ask Him to save us, or ask Him for the Holy Spirit, but we trust something other than God in the actual details of our lives. CHI. 51

The proof that we have a healthy vigorous faith is that we are expressing it in our lives, and bearing testimony with our lips as to how it came about. CHI. 55

There is no end to the life of faith; sanctification itself is only the ABC of the Christian life. CHI. 55

The business of faith is to convert Truth into reality. CHI. 58

You can't pump up faith out of your own heart. Whenever faith is starved in your soul it is because you are not in contact with Jesus; get in contact with Him and lack of faith will go in two seconds. CHI. 60

Faith is implicit confidence in Jesus and in His faith. It is one thing to have faith in Jesus and another thing to have faith about everything for which He has faith. CHI. 61

Beware of worshipping Jesus as the Son of God, and professing your faith in Him as the Saviour of the world, while you blaspheme Him by the complete evidence in your daily life that He is powerless to do anything in and through you. DI. 5

We have to get out of the old pagan way of guiding ourselves by our heads and get into the Christian way of being guided by faith in a personal God, whose methods are a perpetual contradiction to our every preconceived notion. DI. 14

. . . our faith must be in the reality of the Redemption and never in what God has done in us and for us. GW. 7

To be able to state explicitly in words what you know by faith is an impossibility; if you can state it in words, it is not faith. GW. 108

There are times in your life when Redemption and rationalism come into conflict, and your faith in God seems the most feeble and ludicrous thing there is. GW. 123

Faith must have an autobiography; until we know God, we have no faith. Faith is the spontaneous outgoing of my person to another person whom I know. GW. 127

We all have faith in good principles, in good management, in good common sense, but who amongst us has faith in Jesus Christ? Physical courage is grand, moral courage is grander, but the man who trusts Jesus Christ in the face of the terrific problems of life is worth a whole crowd of heroes. HG. 17

It is not easy to have faith in God, and it is not meant to be easy because we have to make character. HG. 18

Faith is never defined; it is described, as in Hebrews xi. 1, but never defined. HGM. 143

Faith cannot be intellectually defined; faith is the inborn capacity to see God behind everything, the wonder that keeps you an eternal child. HGM. 143

Faith is the indefinable certainty of God behind everything, and is the one thing the Spirit of God makes clearer and clearer as we go on. HGM. 143

As you go on in the life of faith you find everything is becoming so simple that you are afraid it can't be true, it is so unlike what you had been taught. HGM. 145

Faith means keeping absolutely speck-lessly right with God, He does all the rest. LG. 73

Our Lord did not rebuke His disciples for making mistakes, but for not having faith. The two things that astonished Him were 'little faith' and 'great faith'. Faith is not in what Jesus Christ can do, but in Himself, and anything He can do is less than Himself. LG. 150

We have to learn how to 'go out' of everything, out of convictions, out of creeds, out of experiences, out of everything, until so far as our faith is concerned, there is nothing between us and God. LG. 151

Faith is not resignation to a power we do not know; faith is committal to One Whose character we do know because it has been revealed to us in Jesus Christ. NKW. 13

The whole discipline of the life of faith is to mix together the light of heaven and the sordid actuality of earth. NKW. 45

Faith is not that I see God, but that I know God sees me; that is good enough for me, I will run out and play—a life of absolute freedom. NKW. 60

It is the height of madness from common-sense standpoints to have faith in God. Faith is not a bargain with God—I will trust You if You give me money, but not if You don't. We have to trust in God whether He sends us money or not, whether He gives us health or not. We must have faith in God, not in His gifts. NKW. 61

Faith is not the means whereby we take God to ourselves for our select coterie; faith is the gift of God whereby He expresses His purposes through us. NKW. 65

Faith does not give us a feeling of eternal life upon which we draw; faith is a fountain of living water overflowing. NKW. 69

There is only one way to live the life of faith, and that is to *live it*. NKW. 69

It is never our merit God looks at but our faith. If there is only one strand of faith amongst all the corruption within us, God will take hold of that one strand. NKW. 80

Faith according to the Bible is confidence in God when He is inscrutable and apparently contradictory in His providences. NKW. 117

The turning points in the spiral ascent of faith are, first, obedience to the effectual call of God; and second, the culmination of unreserved resignation to God. NKW. 121

As long as the soul realises in the simplicity of faith that all that Jesus was and is, is his, then the very life, the very faith, the very holiness of Jesus is imparted to him. OBH. 15

Our idea of faith has a good deal to do with the harmful way faith is often spoken of. Faith is looked upon as an attitude of mind whereby we assent to a testimony on the authority of the one who testifies. We say that because Jesus says these things, we believe in Him. The faith of the New Testament is infinitely more than that; it is the means by which sanctification is manifested, the means of introducing the life of God into us, not the effect of our understanding only. OBH. 20

Just as we take food into our bodies and assimilate it, so, Jesus says, we must take Him into our souls. Faith is not seeing food and drink on the table; faith is taking it. OBH. 22

Faith in God does not mean that He presents me as a museum specimen, but it does mean that however ignoble I may feel, I remain true to God's character no matter what perplexities may rage. OPG. 55

It is a great thing to meet a man who believes in God, one who has not only retained his faith in God, but is continually getting a bigger faith. PH. 204

Faith is not credulity; faith is my personal spirit obeying God. PR. 20

There are certain tempers of mind in which we never dare indulge. If we find they have distracted us from faith in God, then until we get back to the quiet mood before God, our faith in Him is nil, and our confidence in the flesh and human ingenuity is the thing that rules. RTR. 30

You can shut the mouth of the man who has faith in God, but you cannot get away from the fact that he is being kept by God. SHL. 104

FAITH AND WORKS

If you have faith, prove it by your life. CHI. 52

Do something; the test of faith lies in *not* doing. NKW. 48

FAITHFULNESS

Faith is deliberate confidence in the character of God Whose ways you cannot understand at the time. 'I don't know why God allows what He does, but I will stick to my faith in His character no matter how contradictory things look.' AUG. 84

My faith is manifested in what I do, and I am able to explain slowly where I put my confidence. AUG. 84

Faith means implicit confidence in Jesus, and that requires not intellect only but a moral giving over of myself to Him. AUG. 111

We have to be so faithful to God that through us may come the awakening of those who have not yet realised that they are redeemed. CHI. 9

We do not need to mind how the wicked bluster and say, 'If you don't do this and that, you will starve.' Be faithful, make holiness your aim, holiness in every relationship—money, food, clothes, friendship—then you will see the Lord in all these domains. HG. 31

Faith is unbreakable confidence in the Personality of God, not in His power. There are some things over which we may lose faith if we have confidence in God's power only. There is so much that looks like the mighty power of God that is not. We must have confidence in God over and above everything He may do, and stand in confidence that His character is unsullied. IYA. 34

Faith in God is a terrific venture in the dark, we have to believe that God is love in spite of all that contradicts it. Every soul represents some kind of battlefield. The great point for the Christian is to remain perfectly confident in God. LG. 32

Watch where Jesus went. The one dominant note in His life was to do His Father's will. His is not the way of wisdom or of success, but the way of faithfulness. LG. 156

The work of faith is not an explanation to our minds, but a determination on our part to obey God and to make a concession of our faith in His character; immediately we do what God says, we discern what He means. NKW. 17

Beware of pronouncing any verdict on the life of faith if you are not living it. NKW. 116

The life of faith does not consist of acts of worship or of great self-denial and heroic virtues, but of all the daily conscious acts of our lives. NKW. 135

Faith is more than an attitude of the mind; faith is the complete, passionate, earnest trust of our whole nature in the Gospel of God's grace as it is presented in the Life and Death and Resurrection of our Lord Jesus Christ. OBH. 20

If we have faith at all it must be faith in Almighty God; when He has said a thing, He will perform it; we have to remain steadfastly obedient to Him. PH. 41

Faith for my deliverance is not faith in God. Faith means, whether I am visibly delivered or not, I will stick to my belief that God is love. There are some things only learned in a fiery furnace. RTR. 8

Faith is not intelligent understanding; faith is deliberate commitment to a Person where I see no way. RTR. 35

Faith is trust in a God Whose ways you cannot trace, but whose character you know, and the man of faith hangs on to the fact that he is a God of honor. Fatalism means "my number's up," I have to bow to the power whether I like it or not; I do not know the character of the power, but it is greater than I am and I must submit. SHH. 121

FAITH, TRIAL OF

It is the trial of our faith that is precious. If we go through the trial, there is so much wealth laid up in our heavenly banking account to draw upon when the next test comes. HG. 18

We have no faith at all until it is proved, proved through conflict and in no other way. HGM. 58

Faith is confidence in God before you see God emerging, therefore the nature of faith is that it must be tried. HGM. 70

The very nature of faith is that it must be tried; faith untried is only ideally real, not actually real. Faith is not rational, therefore it cannot be worked out on the basis of logical reason; it can only be worked out on the implicit line by living obedience. NKW. 112

Faith is not a mathematical problem, the nature of faith is that it must be tried. OBH. 103

Every time our programme of belief is clear to our minds we come across something that contradicts it. Faith, before it is real, must be tried. As we dispose ourselves to believe, we see God all the time, not in spasms. We see His arm behind all the facts in individual life and in history. OBH. 118

You cannot state definitely what the call of God is to; it is to be in comradeship with God for His own purposes, and the test of faith is to believe God knows what He is after. PH. 181

Jesus Christ places the strongest emphasis on faith, and especially on the faith that has been tried. SSM. 66

It is the trial of our faith that makes us wealthy in heaven. We want the treasure on earth all the time. We interpret answers to prayer on the material plane only, and if God does not answer there, we say He does not answer at all. SSY. 61

FALL, THE

The fundamental basis of the life of man was the life of God and communion with God, and until he fell Adam's spirit and soul and body were in absolute harmony with God. What do we mean by the Fall? God intended man to progress from innocence to holiness by a series of deliberate moral choices in which he was to sacrifice the life of nature to the will of God. Adam refused to do this, and that constitutes the Fall. When Adam fell the Spirit of God was withdrawn instantly, not after a time. The real seat of death is in man's spirit, the dissolution of the body is a mere incident; the point God's Book emphasises is the instant withdrawal of life, the withdrawal of the Spirit which held man's spirit, soul and body in living communion with God. BSG. 74

Up to the time of the Fall man drew all his sustenance from God; when he fell, he lost that harmony completely; and the danger now is that although man's spirit is as immortal as God, it receives no sustenance from God. The first thing that happened was that man became his own god, exactly what the devil said would happen. BSG. 75

. . . the knowledge of evil that came through the Fall gives a man a broad mind, but paralyses his action. SA. 51

FANATICISM

A fanatic sees God's point of view but not man's. He says God ought not to allow the devil, or war, or sin. We are in the whirlwind of things that are, what is the use of wasting time and saying things ought not to be? They *are!* SA. 58

If we do obey the words of Jesus Christ, we are sure to be called fanatics. The New Testament associates shame with the gospel. SSM. 108

FASTING

To fast is not to give up food, but to cut off the right arm, and pluck out the right eye. IIGM. 112

'Tarry ye . . . until . . .' This is the New Testament conception of fasting, not from food only but from everything, until the particular thing we have been told to expect is fulfilled. Fasting means concentration in order that the purpose of God may be developed in our lives. LG. 121

Fasting from food is an easy business, but fasting in its true nature means to fast from everything that is good until the appointments of God in my soul are accepted. PR. 58

When you fast, fast to your Father in secret, not before men. Do not make a cheap martyr of yourself, and never ask for pity. If you are going through a time of discipline, pretend you are not going through it—"appear not unto men to fast." SSM. 61

Ostensible external fasts are of no use, it is the internal fasting that counts. Fasting from food may be difficult for some, but it is child's play compared with fasting for the development of God's purpose in your life. Fasting means concentration. SSM. 61

Fasting is much more than doing without food, that is the least part, it is fasting from everything that manifests self-indulgence. SSM. 100

FATALISM

Fatalism is the deification of moral cowardice which arises from a refusal to accept the responsibility for choosing either of the two destined ends for the human race—salvation or damnation. OPG. 50

Fatalism means I am the sport of a force about which I know nothing; faith is trust in a God Whose ways I do not know, but Whose character I do know. The Bible point of view is that God is ruling and reigning, and that His character is holy. SHH. 24

FATHERHOOD

What men and women need is the 'Fathering' of God, so that from all affright and fear they may be held steady by the gentleness of God, and that is only realised in Christ. CD. VOL. 1, 139

Our Lord did not say, 'No man cometh unto God, but by Me.' There are many ways of coming to God other than by the Lord Jesus Christ, but no man ever came to *the Father*, but by Jesus Christ. He is the Exclusive Way there, the constant active medium to our intercourse with the Father. CD. VOL. 1, 141

Our Lord Jesus Christ is the Exclusive Way to the Father. By His Cross alone a man enters into the adoption of a son of God. CD. VOL. 1, 141

We are apt to talk sentimental nonsense about the Universal Fatherhood of God; to knock the bottom board out of Redemption by saying that God is love and of course He will forgive sin. When the Holy Spirit comes, He makes us know that God is *holy* love, and therefore He cannot forgive sin apart from the Atonement; He would contradict His own nature if He did. SSY. 144

FEAR

Fear resides in the heart. Take it physically, if you take a deep breath, you cause your heart to pump the blood faster through your veins, and physical fear goes; and it is the same with the spirit. God expels the old fear by putting in a new Spirit and a new concern. BP. 128

The greatest fear in life is not personal fear for myself, but fear that after all God will be worsted. HGM. 66

When once fear is taken out, the world is humiliated at the feet of the humblest of saints, it can do nothing, it cannot touch the amazing supremacy that comes through the Divine imperialism of the saint's Lord and Master. IWP. 125

There is never any fear for the life that is "hid with Christ in God", but there is not only fear, but terrible danger, for the life unguarded by God. "He that dwelleth in the secret place of the Most High"—once *there*, and although God's providence should take you to hell itself, you are as safe and secure as Almighty God can make you. RTR. 32

The remarkable thing about fearing God is that when you fear God you fear nothing else, whereas if you do not fear God you fear everything else. "Blessed is everyone that feareth the Lord." RTR. 59

It is the most natural thing in the world to be scared, and the clearest evidence that God's grace is at work in our hearts is when we do not get into panics. SA. 55

FELLOWSHIP

There are disasters to be faced by the one who is in real fellowship with the Lord Jesus Christ. God has never promised to keep us immune from trouble; He says "I will be with him in trouble," which is a very different thing. PH. 43

Human fellowship can go to great lengths, but not all the way. Fellowship with God can go all lengths. PH. 43

If I am in fellowship with Jesus Christ and am indwelt by Him, I have the answer of death in myself, and nothing the world, the flesh or the devil can do can touch me. PH. 44

If you are experiencing the disasters of fellowship, don't get into despair, remain unswervingly and unhesitatingly faithful to the Lord Jesus Christ and refuse to compromise for one second. Don't say 'it can't be done' because you see a thing is going to crush your physical life. Calculate on the disaster of fellowship, because through it God is going to bring you into fellowship with His Son. PH. 44

Most of us are surrounded with Christian fellowship and live such sheltered lives that we forget there are those who have to live a life of unspotted holiness in the midst of moral abominations, and God does not take them out of it. PH. 75

FOLLOWING

The one striking thing about following is we must not find our own way, for when we take the initiative we cease to follow. In the natural world everything depends upon our taking the initiative, but if we are followers of God, we cannot take the initiative, we cannot choose our own work or say what we will do; we have not to find out at all, we have just to follow. LG. 61

Everything Our Lord asks us to do is naturally frankly impossible to us. It is impossible for us to be the children of God naturally, to love our enemies, to forgive, to be holy, to be pure, and it is certainly impossible to us to follow God naturally; consequently the fundamental fact to recognize is that we must be born again. We recognize it fundamentally, but we must recognize it actually, that in spiritual matters we must not take the initiative. We must not make decisions of our own, we must "follow the Lamb whithersoever He goeth," and when He does not go anywhere, then we do not. LG. 61

FORGIVENESS

If I am forgiven without being altered, forgiveness is not only damaging to me, but a sign of unmitigated weakness in God. BFB. 42

Unless it is possible for God's forgiveness to establish an order of holiness and rectitude, forgiveness is a mean and abominable thing. BFB. 42

We know nothing about the Redemption or about forgiveness until we are enmeshed by the personal problem; then we begin to understand why we need to turn to God, and when we do turn to Him He becomes a Refuge and a Shelter and a complete Rest. BFB. 42

I have no right to say that I believe in forgiveness as an attribute of God if in my own heart I cherish an unforgiving temper. The forgiveness of God is the test by which I myself am judged. DI. 1

The bedrock permanent thing about Christianity is the forgiveness of God, not sanctification and personal holiness—the great abiding thing underneath is infinitely more rugged than that; it is all the New Testament means by that terrific word *'forgiveness'*. "In whom we have our redemption through His blood, the forgiveness of sins."
DI. 55

The forgiveness of God penetrates to the very heart of His nature and to the very heart of man's nature. That is why God cannot forgive until a man realizes what sin is. DI. 64

Think what God's forgiveness means: it means that He forgets away every sin. GW. 11

We take the forgiveness of sins to mean something we can understand, it is such a tremendous thing that it takes the Holy Spirit to enable us to begin to understand what is made ours through the grace of God. The forgiveness of God means that we are forgiven into a new relationship with God in Christ so that the forgiven man is the holy man. GW. 11

Forgiveness is a miracle, because in forgiving a man God imparts to him the power to be exactly the opposite of what he has been: God transmutes the sinner who sinned into the saint who does not sin, consequently the only true repentant man is the holy man. GW. 53

Unless God can alter me He dare not forgive me; if He did I should have a keener sense of justice and right than He has. HG. 105

When we have experienced the unfathomable forgiveness of God for all our wrong, we must exhibit that same forgiveness to others. HGM. 47

Forgiveness is the great message of the Gospel, and it satisfies a man's sense of justice completely. The fundamental factor of Christianity is "the forgiveness of sins." HGM. 100

According to the Bible the basis of things is tragic, and the way out is the way Jesus Christ made in the Redemption. Any man, whether he be Cain or Judas, or you or I, can receive absolute forgiveness from God the moment he knows he needs it: but God cannot forgive a man unless he repents. HGM. 101

We may talk as much as we like about forgiveness, but it will never make any difference to us unless we realize that we need it. HGM. 101

God can never forgive the man who does not want to be forgiven. HGM. 101

The background of the forgiveness of God is His holiness. If God were not holy, there would be nothing in His forgiveness. The conscience of God means that He has to completely forgive and finally redeem the whole human race. HGM. 101

We are apt to say glibly that God will forgive us, but when we come up against the thing we know He dare not; if He did, He would cease to be God. HGM. 102

There is no such thing as God overlooking sin. That is where people make a great mistake with regard to God's love; they say 'God is love and of course He will forgive sin': God is *holy* love and of course He cannot forgive sin. Therefore if God does forgive, there must be a reason that justifies Him in doing it. HGM. 102

Unless there is a possibility of forgiveness establishing an order of holiness and rectitude in a man, it would be a mean and abominable thing to be forgiven. If I am forgiven without being altered by the forgiveness, forgiveness is a damage to me and a sign of unmitigated weakness on the part of God. HGM. 102

A man has to clear God's character in forgiving him. The revelation of forgiveness in the Bible is not that God puts snow over a rubbish heap, but that He turns a man into the standard of Himself, the Forgiver. If I receive forgiveness and yet go on being bad, I prove that God is not justified in forgiving me. HGM. 102

The reason my sins are forgiven so easily is because the Redemption cost God so much. HGM. 102

The most marvellous ingredient in the forgiveness of God is that He also forgets, the one thing a human being can never do. Forgetting with God is a divine attribute; God's forgiveness forgets. We can never forget saving by the sovereign grace of God. HGM. 103

God exhausts metaphors to show what His forgiveness means—"I, even I, am He that blotteth out thy transgressions for Mine own sake, and will not remember thy sins"; "I have blotted out, as a thick cloud, thy transgressions, and as a cloud, thy sins"; "As far as the east is from the west, so far hath He removed our transgressions from us"; "For Thou has cast all my sins behind Thy back", "For I will forgive their iniquity, and I will remember their sin no more." HGM. 103

When we turn to God and say we are sorry, Jesus Christ has pledged His word that we will be forgiven, but the forgiveness is not operative unless we turn, because our turning is the proof that we know we need forgiveness. HGM. 104

The distinctive thing about Christianity is forgiveness, not sanctification or my holiness, but forgiveness—the greatest miracle God ever performs through the Redemption. HGM. 105

The forgiveness of God is a bigger miracle than we are apt to think. It is impossible for a human being to forgive; and it is because this is not realised that we fail to understand that the forgiveness of God is a miracle of Divine grace. PH. 183

Forgiveness, which is so easy for us to accept, cost God the agony of Calvary. PH. 184

When Jesus Christ says "Sin no more," He conveys the power that enables a man not to sin any more, and that power comes by right of what He did on the

Cross. That is the unspeakable wonder of the forgiveness of God. PH. 184

Divine forgiveness is part of the unsearchable riches that is ours through the Redemption, and it is because we do not realise the miracle of God's forgiveness that spiritual malingering results, that is, we remain feeble and weak in Christian faith in order to evade the enormous demands that our faith makes on us. We talk glibly about forgiving when we have never been injured; when we are injured we know that it is not possible, apart from God's grace, for one human being to forgive another. PH. 223

The forgiveness of God means that we are forgiven into a new relationship, viz., into identification with God in Christ, so that the forgiven man is the holy man. The only explanation of the forgiveness of God and of the unfathomable depth of His forgetting is the blood of Jesus. We trample the blood of the Son of God under foot if we think we are forgiven in any other way. Forgiveness is the Divine miracle of grace. PH. 224

There is a lot of sentimental talk about God forgiving because He is love: God is so holy that He cannot forgive. God can only destroy for ever the thing that is unlike Himself. The Atonement does not mean that God forgives a sinner and allows him to go on sinning and receiving forgiveness; it means that God saves the sinner and turns him into a saint, i.e. destroys the sinner out of him, and through his conscience he realizes that by the Atonement God has done what He never could have done apart from it. PS. 65

God, in forgiving a man, gives him the heredity of His own Son, i.e., He turns him into the standard of the Forgiver. Forgiveness is a revelation—hope for the hopeless; that is the message of the Gospel. SA. 19

God's forgiveness is a bigger miracle than we are apt to think. He will not only restore to us the years the cankerworm hath eaten; not only deliver us from hell; not only make a clearing house for conscience; but He will give a totally new heredity; and many a man who has shut himself down in despair need not despair any more. God can forgive a man anything but despair that He can forgive him. SA. 19

If I receive forgiveness and continue to be bad, I prove that God is immoral in forgiving me, and make a travesty of Redemption. When I accept Jesus Christ's way He transfigures me from within. "Jesus did it all," refers to Redemption; the thing is done; and if I step into it I will find the moral magic of the Redemption at work in me. SA. 42

There is a difference between sin and sins; sin is a disposition and is never spoken of as being forgiven; sins are acts for which we are responsible. SA. 105

A man cannot be forgiven for what he is not to blame, but God holds a man responsible for refusing to receive a new heredity when he sees that Jesus Christ can give it to him. SA. 105

The only ground on which God can forgive sin and reinstate us in His favour, is through the Cross of Christ, and in no other way. SSY. 144

FREE WILL

God has so constituted us that there must be a free willingness on our part.

This power is at once the most fearful and the most glorious power. BP. 58

The first fundamental characteristic of God the Father, or God Almighty, is that of pure free will. There is no such thing as pure free will in man; God Almighty is the only Being Who has the power of pure free will. By His will He created what His breath sustains. The Bible revelation is that the essential nature of God is this power of free will. BP. 214

The subject of human free will is nearly always either overstated or understated. There is a pre-determination in man's spirit which makes him will along certain lines; but no man has the power to make an act of pure free will. BP. 215

Our destiny is not determined for us, but it is determined by us. Man's free will is part of God's sovereign will. We have freedom to take which course we choose, but not freedom to determine the end of that choice. God makes clear what He desires, we must choose, and the result of the choice is not the inevitableness of law, but the inevitableness of God. CHI. 66

It is nonsense to talk about a man's free will, a man's will is only fundamentally free in God, that is, he is only free when the law of God and the Spirit of God are actively working in his will by his own choice. CHI. 104

God has so constituted man that it is not possible to convince him against his will; you can compel him and crush him, but you cannot convince him against his will. Only God could exercise constraint over a man which would compel him to do what in the moment of doing it is not his own will; but that God steadily refuses to do. MFL. 27

We are only free when the Son sets us free; but we are free to choose whether or not we will be made free. MFL. 28

Human free will is God's sovereign work, and God not only respects it in man but He delights to posit it in him. I have perfect power not to do God's will, and I have that power by the sovereign will of God; but I can never thwart God's will ultimately. NKW. 55

God is the only Being Who can act with absolute free will, and when His Spirit comes into us, He makes us free in will, consequently our obedience becomes of value. PR. 89

Every art, every healing, and every good, can be used for an opposite purpose. Every possibility I have of producing a fine character in time, I can use to produce the opposite; I have that liberty from the Creator. God will not prevent my disobeying Him; if He did, my obedience would not be worth anything. Some of us complain that God should have made the universe and human life like a foolproof machine, so simple that there would be no possibility of going wrong. If He had, we would have been like jelly-fish. If there is no possibility of being damned, there is no need for salvation. SHH. 25

There is always a point where I have the power to choose. I have no power to choose whether or not I will take the consequences of my choice; no power to say whether or not I will be born; no power to choose my "cage"; but within the cage I have power to choose which perch I will sit on. I cannot rule out the fact that between birth and death I have to choose. I have no power to act an act of pure will; to choose whether I will be born or not; but I have power to choose which way I will use the times as they come. SHH. 26

In certain moods we are inclined to criticize God for not having made the world like a foolproof machine whereby it would be impossible to go wrong. If God had made men and women like that we would have been of no worth to Him. SHL. 14

When we begin our life with God, we wish He would make it impossible for us to go wrong. If God did, our obedience would cease to be of value. When God created man, He put into his hands the free choice of good or evil, and that choice is there still, and the very test develops the character. The basis of life is antagonism in every domain, physical, mental, moral and spiritual, we only maintain health by fighting. SHL. 68

FRETTING

Fretfulness springs from a determination to get my own way. GW. 81

Fretting is sinful if you are a child of God. Get back to God and tell Him with shame that you have been bolstering up that stupid soul of yours with the idea that your circumstances are too much for Him. GW. 81

FRIEND

A friend is one who makes me do my best. HG. 12

Friendship with God means that there is now something of the nature of God in a man on which God can base His friendship. NKW. 72

God created man to be His friend. If we are the friends of Jesus we have deliber-ately and carefully to lay down our life for Him. OBH. 108

"Greater love hath no man than this, that a man lay down his life for his friends." If I am a friend of Jesus Christ, I lay down my life for Him. That does not mean that I go through the big crisis of death; it means that I lay down my life deliberately as I would lay out a pound note. I have this to lay out and expend; I have a day before me, and I am going to lay it out for Jesus Christ; I have my duty to perform, but I am going to lay it out in devotion to Jesus Christ all through. It is difficult, and thank God it is difficult. Salvation is easy because it cost God so much, but the manifestation of it in my life is difficult. God does expect a man to be a man. God saves a man and endues him with His Holy Spirit, and says in effect, 'Now it is up to you to prove it, work it out; be loyal to Me while the nature of things round about you would make you disloyal. I have called you friends, now stand loyal to your Friend.' His honour is at stake in our bodily life. PH. 147

FRUIT

Fruit is not the salvation of souls, that is God's work; fruit is "the fruit of the Spirit," love, joy, peace, etc. LG. 46

FUTURE

The atheist, or socialist, or Christian—all who look to the future and express a view of what ought to be, see the same vision. They see the brotherhood of man, a time of peace on earth when there will be no more war, but a state of goodwill and perfect liberty, at present inconceivable. There is nothing wrong with the vision, and there is no difference in the vision because its source is the Spirit of God; the difference is in the way it is to be reached. The vision is of the nature of a castle in the air. That is where a castle should be; who ever heard of a castle underground! SA. 62

G

GETHSEMANE

We can never fathom the agony in Gethsemane, but at least we need not *mis*understand. This is not the agony of a man: this is the distress of God in Man, or rather the distress of God as Man. It is not human in any phase, it is fathomless to a human mind, but we have got several lines to go on so as not to *mis*understand. Always beware of the tendency to think of our Lord as an extraordinary human being; He was not, He was God Incarnate. IYA. 18

Our Lord's object in becoming Deity Incarnate was to redeem mankind, and Satan's final onslaught in the Garden of Gethsemane was against our Lord *as Son of Man*, viz., that the purpose of His Incarnation would fail. The profundity of His agony has to do with the fulfilling of His destiny. MFL. 106

We can never fathom the agony in Gethsemane. . . . It is the agony of God and Man in one, face to face with sin. PR. 84

The agony of our Lord in Gethsemane is not typical of what we go through, any more than His Cross is typical of our cross. We know nothing about Gethsemane in personal experience. Gethsemane and Calvary stand for something unique; they are the gateway into Life for us. PR. 84

Put away the reverential blasphemy that what Jesus Christ feared in Gethsemane was death on the cross. There was no element of fear in His mind about it; He stated most emphatically that He came on purpose for the Cross. His fear in Gethsemane was that He might not get through as Son of Man. Satan's onslaught was that although He would get through as Son of God, it would only be as an isolated Figure; and this would mean that He could be no Saviour. PR. 85

The Garden of Gethsemane is the agony of Almighty God: the Cross of Christ is one terrific triumph, a triumph for the *Son of Man.* PR. 88

Gethsemane is the agony of the Son of God fulfilling His destiny as the Saviour of the world, and the veil is taken aside to show us what it cost Him to make it easy for us to become sons of God. PR. 88

Our Lord's dread in Gethsemane was born of the knowledge that if He did not get through as Son of Man, the redemption of mankind was hopeless; we could only then have imitated Him, we could never have known Him as Saviour. PR. 91

GIFTS/GIVING

The gifts of the Spirit are built on God's sovereignty, not on our temperament. AUG. 23

The Holy Spirit is a gift, remission of sins is a gift, eternal life is a gift, on the ground of the Cross of our Lord and Saviour Jesus Christ. Ignore that, and life is a wayless wilderness, where all our ideals fade and falter, leaving us only a grey, uncertain outlook, gathering to an eternal night. AUG. 93

We must not dictate to Jesus as to where we are going to serve Him. There is a theory abroad to-day that we have to consecrate our gifts to God. We cannot, they are not ours to consecrate; every gift we have has been given to us. Jesus Christ does not take my gifts and use them; He takes me and turns me right about face, and realizes Himself in me for His glory. AUG. 99

We never get credit spiritually for impulsive giving. If suddenly we feel we should give a shilling to a poor man, we get no credit from God for giving it, there is no virtue in it whatever. As a rule, that sort of giving is a relief to our feelings; it is not an indication of a generous character, but rather an indication of a lack of generosity. God never estimates what we give from impulse. We are given credit for what we determine in our hearts to give; for the giving that is governed by a fixed determination. The Spirit of God revolutionizes our philanthropic instincts. Much of our philanthropy is simply the impulse to save ourselves an uncomfortable feeling. The Spirit of God alters all that. As saints our attitude towards giving is that we give for Jesus Christ's sake, and from no other motive. God holds us responsible for the way we use this power of voluntary choice. BP. 108

It requires the greatest effort, and produces the greatest humility, to receive anything from God, we would much sooner earn it. CHI. 30

As Chrisians our giving is to be proportionate to all we have received of the infinite giving of God. "Freely ye have received, freely give." Not how much we give, but what we do not give, is the test of our Christianity. When we speak of giving we nearly always think only of money. Money is the life-blood of most of us. We have a remarkable trick—when we give money we don't give sympathy; and when we give sympathy we don't give money. CHI. 77

The only sign that a particular gift is from the Ascended Christ is that it edifies the Church. Much of our Christian work to-day is built on what the Apostle pleads it should not be built on, viz., the excellencies of the natural virtues. DI. 23

We cannot earn things from God, we can only take what is given us. Salvation, sanctification, eternal life, are all gifts wrought out in us through the Atonement. DI. 58

We are measured by what we do according to what we have. Some people only give to the deserving, because they imagine they deserve all they have. Our Lord says, Give, not because they deserve it, but because I tell you to. HG. 38

We cannot earn or win anything from God, we must receive it as a gift, like a pauper, or do without it. HGM. 14

We are never told to consecrate our gifts to God, but we are told to dedicate ourselves. LG. 63

The nature of love is to give, not to receive. Talk to a lover about giving up anything, and he doesn't begin to understand you! OPG. 45

We do not consecrate our gifts to God, they are not ours to give; we consecrate ourselves to God, that is, we give up the right to ourselves to Him. PH. 14

Forgiveness of sins is the gift of God; entrance into the holiest is the gift of God; sanctification is the gift of God. PH. 225

Salvation is an absolutely free, unmerited gift of God. We would a hundred times rather that God told us to do something than we would accept His salvation as a gift. PR. 107

Beware of the sentiment that we consecrate natural gifts to God; we cannot, we can only consecrate to God the holy disposition He gives us. RTR. 75

Don't be careful whether men receive what you give in the right way or the wrong way, see to it that you don't withhold your hand. As long as you have something to give, give, let the consequences be what they may. SHH. 144

. . . the spring of giving is not impulse nor inclination, but the inspiration of the Holy Spirit, I give because Jesus tells me to. SSM. 46

We enthrone common-sense as God and say, 'It is absurd; if I give to everyone that asks, every beggar in the place will be at my door.' Try it. I have yet to find the man who obeyed Jesus Christ's command and did not realise that God restrains those who beg. SSM. 47

Have no other motive in giving than to please God. In modern philanthropy we are 'egged on' with other motives—It will do them good; they need the help; they deserve it. Jesus Christ never brings out that aspect in His teaching; He allows no other motive in giving than to please God. SSM. 57

GOD

It is a great thing to have a God big enough to believe in. AUG. 118

To say 'Of course God is omniscient and knows everything' makes no effect on me, I don't care whether God is 'omni' anything; but when by the reception of the Holy Spirit I begin to realize that God knows all the deepest possibilities there are in me, knows all the eccentricities of my being, I find that the mystery of myself is solved by this besetting God. BE. 85

Give God 'elbow room'; let Him come into His universe as He pleases. If we confine God in His working to religious people or to certain ways, we place ourselves on an equality with God. BFB. 20

God Himself is the key to the riddle of the universe, and the basis of things is to be found only in Him. BFB. 100

I have never seen God; to call Him omnipotent and omnipresent and omniscient means nothing to me; I do not care one bit for an Almighty Incomprehensibile First Cause. To speak the thing which is right about God, I must be in living personal relationship with Him. BFB. 107

God is not after satisfying us and glorifying us; He wants to manifest in us what His Son can do. BP. 42

The characteristics of God Almighty are mirrored for us in Jesus Christ; therefore if we want to know what God is like, we must study Jesus Christ. BP. 216

God is not a supernatural interferer; God is the everlasting portion of His people. When a man "born from above" begins his new life he meets God at every turn, hears Him in every sound, sleeps at His feet, and wakes to find Him there. CD. VOL. 1, 5

When all religions and philosophies and philologies have tried to define God, one and all sink inane and pass, while the Bible statements stand like eternal monuments, shrouded in ineffable glory: "GOD IS LIGHT"; "GOD IS LOVE"; "GOD IS HOLY." Every attempted definition of God other than these sublime inspirations negates God, and we find ourselves possessed of our own ideas with never a glimpse of the living God. CD. VOL. 1, 11

The great point of the Bible revelation of God is not only that God was *in* Christ, but that Jesus Christ *is* God. If Jesus Christ is not God, then the only God we have is an abstraction of our own minds. CHI. 46

God is so almightily simple that it is impossible to complicate Him, impossible to put evil into Him or bring evil out of Him; impossible to alter His light and His love, and the nature of the faith born in me by the Holy Ghost will take me back to the Source and enable me to see what God is like, and until I am all light and all love in Him, the things in me which are not of that character will have to pass. CHI. 84

If you take all the manifestations of God in the Old Testament you find them a mass of contradictions: now God is pictured as a Man, now as a Woman, now as a lonely Hero, now as a suffering Servant, and until we come to the revelation in the New Testament these conflicting characteristics but add confusion to our conception of God. But immediately we see Jesus Christ, we find all the apparent contradictions blended in one unique Person. CHI. 117

The vindication of God to our intelligence is the most difficult process. Only when we see righteousness and justice exhibited in the Person of Jesus Christ can we vindicate God. DI. 12

Never accept an explanation that travesties God's character. DI. 12

Beware lest your attitude to God's truth reminds Him that He is very unwise. Everything worth while in life is dangerous, and yet we would have God such a tepid Being that He runs no risks! DI. 13

We only see another in the light of what we think he is, it takes an amount of surgery on the inside to make us see other people as they really are, and it is the same with what we think about God; we take the facts revealed in the Bible and try to fit them into our own ideas of what God is like. DI. 14

God is true to the laws of His own nature, not to my way of expounding how He works. DI. 14

God cannot come to me in any way but His own way, and His way is often insignificant and unobtrusive. DI. 15

God does not act according to His own precedents, therefore logic or a vivid past experience can never take the place of a personal faith in a personal God. DI. 16

We say that God foresaw sin, and made provision for it: the Bible revelation is that "the Lamb that hath been slain from the foundation of the world" is the exact expression of the nature of God. DI. 16

If we are in Christ the whole basis of our goings is God, not conceptions of God, not ideas of God, but God Himself. We do not need any more ideas about God, the world is full of ideas about God, they are all worthless, because the ideas of God in anyone's head are of no more use than our own ideas. What we need is a real God, not more ideas about Him. IWP. 68

God is never in a panic, nothing can be done that He is not absolute Master of, and no one in earth or heaven can shut a door He has opened, nor open a door He has shut. God alters the inevitable when we get in touch with Him. IWP. 127

We may say what we like, but God does allow the devil, He does allow sin, He does allow bad men to triumph and tyrants to rule, and these things either make us fiends or they make us saints, it depends entirely on the relationship we are in towards God. IYA. 55

Thou art the God of the early mornings, the God of the late-at-nights, the God of the mountain peaks, the God of the sea; but, my God, my soul has further horizons than the early mornings, deeper darkness than the nights of earth, higher peaks than any mountain, greater depths than any sea can know. My God, Thou art the God of these, be my God! I cannot reach to the heights or depths, there are motives I cannot touch, dreams I cannot fathom, God search me, winnow out my way. IYA. 72

God is the only Being Who can afford to be misunderstood; He deliberately stands aside and lets Himself be slandered and misrepresented; He never vindicates Himself. LG. 24

God does not tell us what He is going to do, He reveals to you who He is. LG. 149

God is a perplexing Being to man because He is never in the wrong, and through the process of allowing every bit of man's wrongdoing to appear right at the time, He proves Himself right ultimately. NKW. 55

God is never in a hurry. NKW. 119

Love, joy, peace, these things are not seen, yet they are eternal, and God's nature is made up of these things. PH. 155

The symbol of God's nature is the Cross, whose arms stretch out to limitless reaches. PR. 100

There is only one God for the Christian, and He is Jesus Christ. SA. 15

A God who did not know the last depth of sorrow and suffering, would be a God "whom to be God is not fit". RTR. 23

We impoverish God's ministry to us the moment we forget He is Almighty; the impoverishment is in us, not in Him. We will come to Jesus as Comforter or as Sympathizer, but we will not come to Him as Almighty. RTR. 32

The majority of us make the character of God out of our own heads; therefore He does not amount to anything at all. That God is called an omnipresent, omniscient, omnipotent Being who rules the universe does not matter one iota to me. But the New Testament reveals the essential nature of God to be not omnipotence, omnipresence, and omniscience, but holiness. God became the weakest thing in His own creation, viz., a Baby; He entered human history on that line. He was so ordinary that the folks of His day paid no attention to Him, and the religious people said He was making a farce of religion. SA. 34

If I . . . say that the essential nature of God can be defined as omnipotence, omniscience, and omnipresence, I shall end by proving that Jesus Christ is a liar, for He was not omnipotent and omniscient and omnipresent when He was on earth; yet He claimed to be the complete revelation of God— SA. 68

Who is God? I have never seen God, or spoken to Him. An omnipresent, omniscient, omnipotent Being does not amount to anything to me; He is an abstract finding of a man's intellect. Can God take on hands and foot and man's ways of doing things, and manifest Himself on the plane on which we live? The Bible says that that is what God did do. Jesus Christ lived a human life on this earth, and He exhibited a disposition not yours and not mine. SHH. 36

The natural mind of man thinks of God in a circle, everything is going to evolve and develop in a plain simple way. According to the Bible, things do not go as we expect them to, either in individual life or in history, but always at cross purposes. SSY. 76

The symbol of the nature of God is not a circle, complete and self-centred; the symbol of God's nature is the Cross. SSY. 77

GOD AND MAN

"God is a Spirit." Apart from the Spirit of God we cannot think about anything that has not its basis in space and time, consequently when people without the Spirit think of God, they think of a Being sitting somewhere or ruling somewhere. We cannot think about God until we have received the Spirit, our natural hearts are atheistic. BE. 100

All we can know about God is that His character is what Jesus Christ has manifested; and all we know about our fellow men presents an enigma which precludes the possibility of the final judgment being with us. BFB. 21

We have the idea that prosperity, or happiness, or morality, is the end of a man's existence; according to the Bible it is something other, viz., 'to glorify God and enjoy Him for ever.' When a man is right with God, God puts His honour in that man's keeping. BFB. 29

The Bible reveals that we are earth and spirit, a combination of the two. The devil is spirit, just as God is; the angels are spirit; but when we come to man, man is earth and spirit. BP. 6

In its primary reference the image of God in man is to the hidden or interior life of man. The image of God in man is primarily spiritual, yet it has to be manifested in his body also. BP. 11

Man's spirit is as immortal as God's Spirit; God can no more annihilate man's spirit than He can annihilate Himself. BSG. 74

"And the Lord God . . . breathed into his nostrils the breath of life", i.e., God breathed into man that which became man's spirit, that is the indestructible factor in every human being. Man is, and he will never be un-created. Man has kinship with God as no other creation of God has; his true kinship is with God and nowhere else. CHI. 40

Jesus Christ reveals, not an embarrassed God, not a confused God, not a God who stands apart from the problems, but One who stands in the thick of the whole thing with man. DI. 12

. . . life is the opportunity God gives to man to do his life work; that means that God has no respect whatever for our programmes and machinery. Our Lord insists on one thing only, God's purpose for him; He pays not the remotest attention to civilized forces, He estimates nothing but one standard. HG. 26

God pays not the remotest attention to our civilized cultures and our attitude to things, because that is not what we are here for. We are here for one thing—to glorify God. HG. 31

We are not built for ourselves, but for God, not for service for God, but for God; that explains the submission of life. IYA. 54

Every man carries his kingdom within, and no one knows what is taking place in another's kingdom. 'No one understands me!' Of course they don't, each one of us is a mystery. There is only One Who understands you, and that is God. Hand yourself over to Him. IYA. 56

How haphazard God seems, not sometimes but always. God's ways turn man's thinking upside down. NKW. 100

What an imperturbable certainty there is about the man who is in contact with the real God! NKW. 129

God is not an almighty sultan reigning aloof, He is right in the throes of life, and it is there that emotion shows itself. OPG. 16

God and man as God created him were at one, but severance came with the introduction of sin; then Jesus Christ came, and in Him God and man are again made at one. PH. 78

The natural view and the Bible view of man are different;—the natural point of view is that man is a great being in the making, his achievements are a wonderful promise of what he is going to be; the Bible point of view is that man is a magnificent ruin of what God designed him to be. PH. 78

The highest standard God has is Himself, and it is up to God to make a man as good as He is Himself; and it is up to me to let Him do it. If God is not just, the only honourable thing for a man to be is a blatant atheist. SA. 23

Is it not illuminating how God knows where we are, and the kennels we crawl into, no matter how much straw we hide under! He will hunt us up like a lightning flash. No human being knows human beings as God does. SSY. 30

Think of the enormous leisure of God! He never is in a hurry. We are in such a frantic hurry. We get down before God and pray, then we get up and say, 'It is all done now,' and in the light of the glory of the vision we go forth to do the thing. But it is not real, and God has to take us into the valley and put us through fires and floods to batter us into shape, until we get into the condition in which He can trust us with the reality of His recognition of us. SSY. 31

The purpose of God for man is that he should 'glorify God and enjoy Him for ever.' Sin has switched the human race off on to another line, but it has not altered God's purpose for the human race in the tiniest degree. SSY. 107

GOD, LOVE OF

If the love of God were presented as having no hatred of wrong and of sin and the devil, it would simply mean that God's love is not so strong as our love. The stronger and higher and more emphatic the love, the more intense is its obverse, hate. God loves the world so much that He hates with a perfect hatred the thing that is twisting men away from Him. To put it crudely, the two antagonists are God and the devil. BP. 120

"Keep yourselves in the love of God". That does not mean keep on trying to love God, it means something infinitely profounder, viz., 'Keep the windows of your soul open to the fact that God loves you'; then His love will continually flow through you to others. BP. 189

God's love is wrath towards wrong; He is never tender to that which hates goodness. CHI. 67

The presentation Jesus gives of the father is that he makes no conditions when the prodigal returns, neither does he bring home to him any remembrance of the far country—the elder brother does that. It is the revelation of the unfathomable, unalterable, amazing love of God. We would feel much happier in our backslidden condition if only we knew it had altered God towards us, but we know that immediately we do come back we will find Him the same, and this is one of the things that keeps men from coming back. If God would only be angry and demand an apology, it would be a gratification to our pride. When we have done wrong we like to be lashed for it. God never lashes. CHI. 115

A false idea of God's honour ends in misinterpreting His ways. It is the orthodox type of Christian who by sticking to a crude idea of God's character, presents the teaching which says, "God loves you when you are good, but not when you are bad." God

loves us whether we are good or bad. That is the marvel of His love. CHI. 115

The love of God is spelt on the Cross and nowhere else; there His conscience is satisfied. GW. 86

God loves the un-lovely, and it broke His heart to do it. The depth of the love of God is revealed by that wonderful word, 'whosoever.' HG. 120

To love God with all my heart means to be weaned from the dominance of earthly things as a guide; there is only one dominant passion in the deepest centre of the personality, and that is the love of God. IWP. 84

. . . God is Love, not, God is loving. God and love are synonymous. Love is not an attribute of God, it is God; whatever God is, love is. If your conception of love does not agree with justice and judgment and purity and holiness, then your idea of love is wrong. It is not love you conceive of in your mind, but some vague infinite foolishness, all tears and softness and of infinite weakness. LG. 9

The revelation of God's love is that He loved us when He could not possibly respect us—He loved us "while we were yet sinners"; "when we were enemies." OBH. 58

When we receive the nature of God into us, the first thing that happens is that God takes away all pretence and pious pose; and He does it by revealing that He loved us, not because we were lovable, but because it is His nature to love. "*God is love.*" OBH. 58

The curious thing about the love of God is that it is the cruellest thing on earth to everything that is not of Him. God hurts desperately when I am far away from Him; but when I am close to Him, He is unutterably tender. OBH. 58

The supreme moment of the Cross in actual history is but the concentrated essence of the very nature of the Divine love. God lays down His life for the very creation which men utilise for their own selfish ends. The Self-expenditure of the love of God exhibited in the life and death of our Lord becomes a bridge over the gulf of sin; whereby human love can be imbued by Divine love, the love that never fails. OBH. 60

The Holy Spirit sheds abroad in our hearts the love of God, a love which breaks all confines of body, soul and spirit. PH. 38

No one who faces facts as they are could ever prove that God is love unless he accepts the revelation of His love made by Jesus Christ. PH. 65

When we preach the love of God there is a danger of forgetting that the Bible reveals not first the love of God but the intense, blazing holiness of God, with His love as the centre of that holiness. PS. 20

To know that God is love, God is holy, God is near, is pure delight to man in his innocent relationship to God, but a terror extreme since the fall. God can never leave a man until He has burned him as pure as He is Himself. It is God's love that forbids He should let him go. PS. 61

The springs of love are in God, not in us. It is absurd to look for the love of God in our hearts naturally, it is only there when it has been shed abroad in our hearts by the Holy Spirit. RTR. 82

In the Cross we may see the dimensions of Divine love. The Cross is not the cross of a man, but an exhibition of the heart of God. At the back of the wall of the world stands God with His arms outstretched, and every man driven there is driven into the arms of God. The Cross of Jesus is the supreme evidence of the love of God. RTR. 88

The love of God is not like the love of a father or a mother, it is the love *of God*. SSM. 51

The love of God is wrought in us by the Holy Ghost. He sheds abroad the love of God, the nature of God, in our hearts, and that love works efficaciously through us as we come in contact with others. The test of love for Jesus Christ is the practical one, all the rest is sentimental jargon. SSY. 160

GOD, PRESENCE OF

No one can tell you where the shadow of the Almighty is, you must find that out for yourself. When you have found out where it is, stay there; under that shadow no evil can ever befall you. AUG. 27

God is never far enough away from His saints to think about them: He *thinks* them, we are taken up into His consciousness. BE. 87

We can never get away from God geographically, but we can get away from Him morally. HG. 29

One of the greatest evidences that we are born again of God is that we perceive the kingdom of God. When I am born from above I countenance God; the arm of the Lord is revealed and I see God as the Architect, as the One Who is doing all things. God is never away off some-where else; He is always *there*. HG. 37

The mystery of God is now, this minute, not in what is going to be; we look for it presently, in some cataclysmic happen-ing. GW. 26

'Show me Thy face'; there it is! 'Show me the Father'; there He is! always just here or nowhere; He is here *now*. Once realize that and the emancipation is im-mediate. GW. 26

Stand steadfastly true to God, and God will bring His truth out in a way that will make your life a sacrament, i.e., the abiding presence of God will come through the simple elements of your life, but you must wait for Him. GW. 123

"In everything give thanks," . . . not— Give thanks *for* everything, but give thanks that in everything that trans-pires there abides the real Presence of God. God is more real than the actual things—"therefore will we not fear, though the earth be removed." PH. 135

On the threshold of every new experi-ence of life we are conscious of it, and this is true in regard to our life with God. When we are born from above we are conscious of God until we get into the life of God, then we are no longer conscious of Him because our life is "hid with Christ in God." 'I don't feel God's presence,' you say; how can you when you are in God and God is in you? By asking God to give you 'feelings' you are pressing back to the entrance into life again. PH. 165

God is so immediately near and so im-mensely strong that I get more and more gay in my confidence in Him and less and less careful how I feel. RTR. 7

Unless in the first waking moment of the day you learn to fling the door wide back and let God in, you will work on a wrong level all day; but swing the door wide open and pray to your Father in secret, and every public thing will be stamped with the presence of God. RTR. 26

GOD, RELATIONSHIP TO

In the Christian life we are not being used for our own designs at all, but for the fulfillment of the prayer of Jesus Christ. He has prayed that we might be 'one with Him as He is one with the Father', consequently God is concerned only about one thing, and He never says 'By your leave'. BFB. 28

The basis of things must always be found in a personal relationship to a per-sonal God, never in thinking or feel-ing. BFB. 100

'Don't let your heart be troubled out of its relationship with Me.' It is never the big things that disturb us, but the trivial things. CD. VOL. 1, 153

My relationship to God embraces every faculty, I am to love Him with *all* my heart, *all* my soul, *all* my mind, *all* my strength, every detail is instinct with devotion to Him; if it is not I am dis-jointed somewhere. GW. 9

If God hurts it is because we are not liv-ing rightly related to Him, and if we say 'the devil' instead of 'God', it is evi-dence that we are living a sequestered life of our own apart from God. GW. 29

God not only requires us to have a right attitude to Him, He requires us to allow His truth to so react in us that we are actively related to Him. GW. 90

The value of a life can only be estimated by its spiritual relationship to God. GW. 126

Screw your attention with all your effort on the one reality, your relationship to God, and be an example on that all through. MFL. 60

Once we come into simple relationship with God, He can put us where He pleases and we are not even conscious of where He put us. All we are conscious of is an amazing simplicity of life that seems to be a haphazard life externally. OBH. 65

We do not know what God is after, but we have to maintain our relationship to Him whatever happens. Never allow anything to injure your relationship to God, cut it out at once; if you are getting out of touch with God, take time and get it right. PH. 181

A fanatic is one who takes the statements of Jesus and tries to live up to the standard of them while he ignores the necessity of a personal relationship with God through new birth. PR. 34

The thing that preserves a man from panic is his relationship to God; if he is only related to himself and to his own courage, there may come a moment when his courage gives out. RTR. 40

Be carefully careless about everything saving your relationship to God. Refuse to be swamped by the cares of this life. RTR. 42

I have to get to the implicit relationship that takes everything as it comes from God. He never guides presently, but always now. Realize that the Lord is here now, and the emancipation is immediate. RTR. 70

The only simple thing in human life is our relationship to God in Christ. SA. 58

When you come to your wits' end, remember there is a way out, viz., personal relationship to God through the Redemption of Jesus Christ. SA. 123

To serve God in order to gain heaven, is not the teaching of Christianity. Satisfaction cannot be found in gain, but only in a personal relationship to God. The presentation made by a false evangelism is that Jesus Christ taught a man must have his own soul saved, be delivered from hell and get a pass for heaven, and when one is taken and the other left, he must look out that he is the one taken. Could anything be more diametrically opposed to what Jesus Christ did teach, or more unlike the revelation of God given in the Bible? A man is not to serve God for the sake of gain, but to get to the place where the whole of his life is seen as a personal relationship to God. SHH. 17

. . . when I have discovered that the only thing that will last is a personal relationship to God; then it will be time for me to solve the problems round about me. SHH. 19

Whenever we put theology or a plan of salvation or any line of explanation before a man's personal relationship to God, we depart from the Bible line, because religion in the Bible is not faith in the rule of God, but faith in the God Who rules. SHH. 22

The man who is banked on a real relationship to a personal God will reap not the distress that works death, but the joy of life. SHH. 28

By the incarnate power of the Son of God, God rebuilds by degree the whole relationship of things, bringing everything back into oneness with Himself. That is the meaning of Redemption—God has done His "bit." Sin is man's "bit." God's plan and design is not altered, but in the meantime man is countering it by his own design—We can bring it out in our own way. God is infinitely patient. He says over and over again—Not that way. My son, this is the way for you, a moral relationship to Myself. SHH. 31

. . . whether you are wise or foolish, upright or not, a king or tyrannised over by a king, successful or a failure, in society or solitary, stubborn or sagacious, all alike ends the same way. All is passing, and we cannot find our lasting joy in any element we like to touch. It is disastrous for a man to try and find his true joy in any phase of truth, or in the fulfilment of ambition, or in physical or intellectual solitariness, or in society; he will find his joy only in a personal relationship to God. SHH. 49

If we try to find lasting joy in any human relationship it will end in vanity, something that passes like a morning cloud. The true joy of a man's life is in his relationship to God, and the great point of the Hebrew confidence in God is that it does not unfit a man for his actual life. That is always the test of a false religion. SHH. 51

When we are related to God, He guards from dangers seen and unseen. The man who fears God has nothing else to fear, he is guarded in his conscious and unconscious life, in his waking and his sleeping moments. SHH. 56

Our Lord taught that a man ought to be carefully careless about everything saving his relationship to Himself. We who call ourselves Christians are tremen-

dously far, almost opposingly far, from that central point of Christianity; it is not even intimate to us. Generation after generation of civilised life have been opposed to it, and as long as we are on the line of economy and insurance, Jesus Christ cannot have His innings. In personal life, in Church life and in national life, we try Jesus Christ's teaching, but as soon as it becomes difficult we abandon it, or else we compromise. SHH. 73

It takes a tremendous amount of relationship to God for a man to *be* what he is. SIII. 82

It is your relationship to God which fits you to live on the earth in the right way, not necessarily the successful way. Sometimes you will have the worst of it for doing right. SHH. 120

. . . food, sex, money and mother earth, must always have their place in the life of any man of God, and they either make men and women devils or make them what they should be. The man of God uses these things to express his relationship to God; whereas the man who does not know God tries to find his lasting good in the things themselves. SHH. 128

All things are permitted by God, but all things are not appointed by God, they appoint themselves; but God's order abides, and if I maintain my relationship to Him He will make everything that happens work for my good. God on the one hand, myself on the other, and the rush of the haphazard in between will work toward the best. SHH. 130

True enjoyment is not in what we do but in our relationships. If a man is true to God, everything between birth and death will work out on the line of joy. If we bank on what we do, whether it is good or bad, we are off the track; the one thing that matters is personal relationship. SSH. 39

. . . the great care of the life is to put the relationship to God first and everything else second. SSM. 67

When we are rightly related to God, life is full of spontaneous joyful uncertainty and expectancy—we do not know what God is going to do next; and He packs our life with surprises all the time. SSY. 35

GOD, WILL OF

We need to remember that we cannot train ourselves to be Christians; we cannot discipline ourselves to be saints; we cannot bend ourselves to the will of God: we have to be broken to the will of God. There must be a break with the dominant ruler. AUG. 98

There is a distinct period in our experience when we cease to say—'Lord, show me Thy will,' and the realization begins to dawn that we *are* God's will, and He can do with us what He likes. We wake up to the knowledge that we have the privilege of giving ourselves over to God's will. It is a question of being yielded to God. AUG. 108

Some people mature into an understanding of God's will more quickly than others because they obey more readily, they more readily sacrifice the life of nature to the will of God, they more easily swing clear of little determined opinions. It is these little determined opinions, convictions of our own that won't budge, that hinder growth in grace and makes us bitter and dogmatic, intolerant, and utterly un-Christlike. BSG. 16

Supernatural voices, dreams, ecstasies, visions and manifestations, may or may not be an indication of the will of God. The words of Scripture, the advice of the saints, strong impressions during prayer, may or may not be an indication of the will of God. The one test given in the Bible is discernment of a personal God and a personal relationship to Him, witnessed to ever after in walk and conversation. CD. VOL. 1, 9

To be 'in the will of God' is not a matter of intellectual discernment, but a state of heart. To a sanctified soul the will of God is its implicit life, as natural as breathing. It is the sick man who knows intellectually what health is, and a sinful man knows intellectually what the will of God is; but a sanctified heart is the expression of the will of God. CD. VOL. 1, 83

God's eternal purposes will be fulfilled, but His permissive will allows Satan, sin and strife to produce all kinds of misconceptions and false confidences until we all, individually as well as collectively, realise that His order is best. CD. VOL. 1, 120

God will never change His character to please anyone's pleading or petulance if they have deliberately spurned His counsel. CHI. 66

God's order is clearly marked out in the first and the last; His permissive will is seen in the process in between where everything is disorganized because of sin. The Christian is one who by the power of the indwelling Spirit sees the final issue. DI. 13

Learn to give honour to God when good works are done, but also learn to discern whether or not they are done by God's servants. The most outrageous moment for the devil will be when he finds that in spite of himself he has done God's will; and the same with the man who has been serving his own ends. DI. 15

Don't say—'Thy will be done,' but see it is done. GW. 59

When I am dwelling under the shadow of the Almighty, my life *is* the will of God; it is only through disobedience that I begin to ask what is the will of God. HG. 114

The will of God is the gladdest, brightest, most bountiful thing possible to conceive, and yet some of us talk of the will of God with a terrific sigh—'Oh well, I suppose it is the will of God,' as if His will were the most calamitous thing that could befall us. IWP. 19

A healthy man does not know what health is: a sick man knows what health is, because he has lost it; and a saint rightly related to God does not know what the will of God is because he *is* the will of God. A disobedient soul knows what the will of God is because he has disobeyed. IWP. 46

. . . there is a difference between God's order and God's permissive will. God's *order* reveals His character; His *permissive will* applies to what He permits. For instance, it is God's order that there should be no sin, no suffering, no sickness, no limitation and no death; His permissive will is all these things. God has so arranged matters that we are born into His permissive will, and we have to get at His order by an effort of our own, viz., by prayer. IYA. 11

If we say, "Thy will be done," we get the tremendous consolation of knowing that our Father is working everything according to His own wisdom. If we understand what God is after, we shall be saved from being mean and cynical. IYA. 55

You cannot teach another what is the will of God. A knowledge of the will of God comes only by insight into God through acting on the right intention. MFL. 23

How are we going to find out the will of God? 'God will communicate it to us.' He will not. His will is there all the time, but we have to discover it by being renewed in our minds, by taking heed to His word and obeying it. MFL. 80

. . . at first we pray "Teach me Thy way, O Lord;" then we pray, "Teach me to do Thy will," and step by step God teaches us what is His will; then comes a great burst of joy, 'I delight to do Thy will! There is nothing on earth I delight in more than in Thy will.' MFL. 127

When we become rightly related to God we *are* the will of God in disposition, and we have to work out God's will; it is the freest, most natural life imaginable. MFL. 127

The joy of Jesus lay in knowing that every power of His nature was in such harmony with His Father that He did His Father's will with delight. Some of us are slow to do God's will; we do it as if our shoes were iron and lead; we do it with a great sigh and with the corners of our mouths down, as if His will were the most arduous thing on earth. But when our wills are rectified and brought into harmony with God, it is a delight, a superabounding joy, to do God's will. MFL. 127

The knowledge of God's will is not in the nature of a mathematical problem; as we obey, we make out what is His will, it becomes as clear as daylight. NKW. 16

Our Lord's life is the exhibition of *the will of God,* not of *doing* the will of God. NKW. 27

Always beware of being more eager to do God's will than God is for you to do it. NKW. 49

How am I going to find out what the will of God is? In one way only, by not trying to find out. If you are born again of the Spirit of God, you *are* the will of God, and your ordinary common-sense decisions are God's will for you unless He gives an inner check. When He does, call a halt immediately and wait on Him. Be renewed in the spirit of your mind that you may make out His will, not in your mind, but in practical living. NKW. 108

God's will in my common-sense life is not for me to *accept* conditions and say—'Oh well, it is the will of God', but to *apprehend* them for Him, and that means conflict, and it is of God that we conflict. Doing the will of God is an active thing in my common-sense life. NKW. 108

By sanctification we are placed in the will of God. We have not to ask what the will of God is, we *are* the will of God, and as we keep in the light as He is in the light, the decisions of the mind and the natural progress of the life go on like a law, and when the decision is likely to be wrong the Spirit checks. OBH. 45

The disciple who is in the condition of abiding in Jesus *is* the will of God, and his apparent free choices are God's fore-ordained decrees. Mysterious? Logically absurd? But a glorious truth to a saint. OBH. 122

Do God's will. God not only expects me to do His will, but He is in me to do it. OBH. 130

Doing God's will is never hard. The only thing that is hard is *not* doing His will. All the forces of nature and of grace are at the back of the man who does God's will because in obedience we let God have His amazing way with us. OBH. 130

We ought to be superabounding with joy and delight because God is working in us to will and to do of His good pleasure. The 'goodest' thing there is is the will of God. God's will is hard only when it comes up against our stubbornness, then it is as cruel as a ploughshare and as devastating as an earthquake. God is merciless with the thing that tells against the relationship of a man to Himself. When once God does have His way, we are emancipated into the very life of God, i.e., into the life that Jesus lived. The only estimate of a consistent Christian character is that the life of the Son of God is being manifested in the bodily life. OBH. 130

God regenerates us and puts us in contact with all His divine resources, but He cannot make us walk according to His will. PR. 27

It is easy to get lost in mists when we talk about the will of God, but if we don't know what it is, we are to blame. RTR. 24

Notion your mind with the idea that God is there. Nothing happens in any particular unless God's will is behind it, therefore you can rest in perfect confidence in Him. RTR. 30

"I suppose it's God's will"—where is the joy of the Lord about that? The conception Jesus had of the will of God was that of glad, leaping obedience to it as the most glorious thing conceivable. RTR. 63

God will never begin to teach me His will in other matters until I do what I know. Theoretic knowledge becomes our condemnation—"If ye know these things blessed are ye if ye do them." RTR. 77

All through the Bible the difference between God's order and God's permissive will is brought out. God's permissive will is the things that are now, whether they are right or wrong. If you are looking for justice, you will come to the conclusion that God is the devil; and if the providential order of things to-ay were God's order, then that conclusion would be right. But if the order of things to-day is God's permissive will, that is quite another matter. God's order is no sin, no Satan, no wrong, no suffering, no pain, no death, no sickness and no limitation: God's providential will is every one of these things—sin, sickness, death, the devil, you and me, and things as they are. God's permissive will is the haphazard things that are on just now in which we have to fight and make character in, or else be damned by. We may kick and yell and say God is unjust, but we are all "in the soup." It is no use saying things are not as they are; it is no use being amazed at the providential order of tyranny, it is there. SHH. 59

In this dispensation we do know the character of God, although we do not know why His providential will should be as it is. . . . the only thing to do in the present condition of things is to remain true to God, and God will not only see us through but will see the whole thing

out to a perfect explanation. That is the faith of a Christian, and it takes some sticking to. SHH. 121

GOOD AND EVIL

An unemotional love is inconceivable. Love for the good must involve displeasure and grief for the evil. OPG. 16

Until we are born again we know good only by contrast with evil. SHH. 110

There are some things of which we must be ignorant, because knowledge of them comes in no other way than by disobedience to God. In the life originally designed for Adam it was not intended that he should be ignorant of evil, but that he should know evil through understanding good. Instead, he ate of the fruit of the tree of knowledge of good and evil and thereby knew evil positively and good negatively; consequently none of us knows the order God intended. The knowledge of evil that comes through the Fall has given human nature a bias of insatiable curiosity about the bad, and only when we have been introduced into the Kingdom of God do we know good and evil in the way God constituted man to know them. SHL. 61, 62

When a man knows good and evil in the way God intended he should he becomes intolerant of evil, and this intolerance shows itself in an intense activity against evil. SHL. 65

GOODNESS

. . . all morality, all goodness, all religion, and all spirituality that is not Christ-centred is drawing away from Jesus Christ all the time. BP. 191

Human beings know human beings too well to mistake where goodness comes from; when they see certain characteristics they will know they come only from the indwelling of Jesus. It is not the manifestation of noble human traits, but of a real family likeness to Jesus. It is *His* gentleness, *His* patience, *His* purity, never mine. CHI. 21

The whole meaning of life is that a man discovers God for himself. It is not sin that keeps us away from Jesus, but our own goodness. CHI. 46

It has been a favourite belief in all ages that if only men were taught what good is, everyone would choose it; but history and human experience prove that that is not so. To know what good *is* is not to *be* good. DI. 26

God does not ask us to be good men and women: He asks us to understand that we are not good; to believe that "none is good save one, even God," and that the grace of God was manifested in the Redemption that it might cover the incompleteness of man. DI. 54

The craze to-day is that the highest good is what a man has to live on: feed him, keep his body healthy, and his moral and religious life will be all right. That is the highest good according to the standard of many. As Christians it is more important to know how to live than what to live on. The attitude of the Christian is not, "I'm but a stranger here, heaven is my home," but rather 'I'm *not* a stranger here.' A stranger is exonerated from many things for which God holds us responsible. HG. 6

To experience the loss of my own goodness is the only way to enter into communion with God in Christ. HG. 108

When you are good you never try to be. MFL. 71

No man is so bad but that he is good enough to know he is bad. OPG. 51

Beware every time you notice yourself doing a good thing because you ruin it by the notice. RTR. 26

The test of a nature is the atmosphere it produces. When we are in contact with a good nature we are uplifted by it. We do not get anything we can state articulately, but the horizon is enlarged, the pressure is removed from the mind and heart and we see things differently. SHH. 79

I do not know anything about God, things look as if He were not good, and yet the revelation given by Jesus Christ is that He is good, and I have to hang in to that revelation in spite of appearances. SHH. 144

God cannot accept goodness from me. He can only accept my badness, and He will give me the solid goodness of the Lord Jesus in exchange for it. SSM. 28

Christian character is not expressed by good doing, but by God-likeness. It is not sufficient to do good, to do the right thing, we must have our goodness stamped by the image and superscription of God, it is supernatural all through. SSM. 53

Our Lord makes the test of goodness not only goodness in intention, but the active carrying out of God's will. Beware of confounding appearance and reality, of judging only by external evidence. SSM. 103

GOSPEL

We have no right to preach unless we present the Gospel; we have not to advocate a cause or a creed or an experience, but to present the Gospel, and we cannot do that unless we have a personal testimony based on the Gospel. That is why so many preach what is merely the outcome of a higher form of culture. Until men get into a right relationship with God the Gospel is always in bad taste. There is a feeling of silent resentment, 'Don't talk about being born again and being sanctified; be vague.' 'Do remember the people you are talking to.' 'Preach the simple Gospel, the thing that keeps us sound asleep.' If you take the people as a standard, you will never preach the Gospel, it is too positive. Our obligation to the Gospel is to preach it. AUG. 39

God or sin must die in me. The one elementary Bible truth we are in danger of forgetting is that the Gospel of God is addressed to men as sinners, and nothing else. AUG. 100

The Gospels were not written to prove anything, they were written to confirm in belief those who were already Christians by means of the death and resurrection of our Lord Jesus Christ, and their theological meaning. AUG. 106

Until we realize that God cannot make allowances, the Gospel has no meaning for us; if God made allowances He would cease to be God. BE. 15

The aspect of the Gospel that awakens desire in a man is the message of peace and goodwill—but I must give up my right to myself to get there. BE. 53

There is nothing attractive about the Gospel to the natural man; the only man who finds the Gospel attractive is the man who is convicted of sin. BE. 76

The gospel of Jesus Christ does not present what men want, it presents exactly what they need. As long as you talk about being happy and peaceful, men like to listen to you; but talk about having the disposition of the soul altered, and that the garden of the soul has first of all to be turned into a wilderness and afterwards into a garden of the Lord, and you will find opposition right away. BP. 80

When the Gospel is presented to an unsaved, healthy, happy, hilarious person, there is violent opposition straight away. BP. 80

Numbers of people to-day preach the gospel of temperament, the gospel of 'cheer up.' BP. 116

The essence of the Gospel of God working through conscience and conduct is that it shows itself at once in action. God can make simple, guileless people out of cunning, crafty people; that is the marvel of the grace of God. It can take the strands of evil and twistedness out of a man's mind and imagination and make him simple towards God, so that his life becomes radiantly beautiful by the miracle of God's grace. BP. 205

In listening to some presentations of the Gospel you get the impression that a man has to be a blackguard before Jesus Christ can do anything for him. It is true that Jesus Christ can make a saint out of any material, but the man down-and-out in sin is not the only crisis He deals with. CHI. 20

The appeal of the Gospel is not that it should be preached in order that men might be saved and put right for heaven, but that they might enter into a personal relationship with Jesus Christ here and now. DI. 34

Sermons may weary, the Gospel never does. DI. 49

By the preaching of the Gospel God creates what was never there before, viz., faith in Himself on the ground of the Redemption. DI. 49

Wherever there is true teaching of the Gospel there will be both salvation and sanctification taking place. DI. 60

We are apt to put the superb blessings of the Gospel as something for a special few, they are for sinners saved by grace. DI. 63

The Gospel of God awakens an intense craving in men and an equally intense resentment, and the tendency is to do away with the resentment. Jesus Christ claims that He can remove the disposition of sin from every man; the only testimony worthy of the Name of Jesus is that He can make a sinner a saint. The most marvellous testimony to the Gospel is a holy man, one whose living experience reveals what God can do. GW. 61

Thank God for the deep profound note of the glorious Gospel of God, that Jesus Christ as Saviour can justify ungodly men, can set them free from their sin; and as Sanctifier He can make them into sons and daughters of God, able to love others as God has loved them, able to show others the same unconditioned mercy He has showed them. GW. 73

If the Gospel is made to mean merely that 'it is better being good than bad', men like to listen to it, but immediately it shows me that sin, self-realization,

self-interest, must be put to death, I resent it. GW. 85

You cannot argue men into coming to Jesus, or socialize them into coming; only one thing will do it, and that is the power of the Gospel drawing men by the constraint of God's grace. GW. 109

The blessedness of the gospel of the kingdom of God in this dispensation is that a man is born from above while he is below, and he actually sees with the eyes of his spirit the rule of God in the devil's territory. HG. 7

Whenever the Gospel of Jesus loses the note of unutterable gladness, it is like salt that has lost its savour. HG. 7

The Bible never gives definitions, the Bible states facts, and the Gospel that Jesus brought of good news about God is the most astounding thing the world ever heard, but it must be the Gospel that Jesus brought. HG. 7

Preaching what we call the Gospel, i.e. salvation from hell does not appeal to men; but once get Jesus Christ to preach His own Gospel and the Spirit of God to expound it, then men are hauled up at once. HG. 8

Try and imagine what Jesus meant when He said, "Preach the gospel to every creature"; He keeps 'an open house' for the whole universe. It is a conception impossible of human comprehension. HG. 41

We are not here to woo and win men to God; we are here to present the Gospel which in individual cases will mean condemnation or salvation. HG. 102

The message of the Gospel is not that God gives a man a clean heart, but that He gives him a pure heart. HGM. 34

The Gospel is not good news to men, but good news about God, viz., that God has accepted the responsibility for creating a race that sinned, and the Cross is the proof that He has done so. The basis of human life is the Redemption. HGM. 65

When once a man's conscience is roused he knows God dare not forgive him and it awakens a sense of hopelessness. Forgiveness is a revelation—hope for the hopeless; that is the message of the Gospel. HGM. 101

It is not the gospel of being saved from hell and enjoying heaven that attracts men, saving in a very shallow mood; it is Christ crucified that attracts men; Jesus said so—"I, if I be lifted up from the earth, will draw all men unto Me." IWP. 61

The gospel gives access into privileges which no man can reach by any other way than the way Jesus Christ has appointed. Unsaved human nature resents this and tries to make out that Jesus Christ will bow in submissive weakness to the way it wants to go. IWP. 127

The preaching of the gospel awakens an intense craving and an equally intense resentment. IWP. 127

. . . if ever I am to be holy, I must be made holy by God's sovereign grace.

That is the Gospel. We receive it by faith; and the Spirit of God is the One Who makes the simple act of faith the supernatural work of God. To those outside Christian experience it sounds foolish; to those inside it is wonderfully real. OBH. 22

We say that Jesus preached the Gospel, but He did more: He came that there might be a Gospel to preach. PH. 70

Angels cannot preach the Gospel, only beings such as Paul and you and I can preach the Gospel. PH. 70

The Gospel can never be preached by sinless lips, but only by the lips of those who have been saved from sin by the Atonement. PH. 70

The Gospel of Jesus always forces an issue of will. PH. 164

The call to preach the Gospel to the heathen is not the frenzied doctrine that the heathen who have never known Jesus Christ, and never had the chance of knowing Him, are going to be eternally lost, but the command of Jesus Christ—"Go ye into all the world, and preach the gospel to every creature." PS. 43

. . . the essence of the Gospel of Jesus Christ working in conscience and conduct is that it shows itself at once in action. SA. 51

The first thing Jesus Christ faced in men was this heredity of sin, and it is because we have ignored it in our presentation of the Gospel that the message of the Gospel has lost its sting, its blasting power; we have drivelled it into insurance tickets for heaven, and made it deal only with the wastrel element of mankind. SA. 116

Let Jesus Christ proclaim His Gospel: we can have the very disposition of Jesus imparted to us, and if we have not got it we will have to tell God the reason why. We have to tell God we don't believe He can do it—there are details of our lives He cannot put right, back tracks He cannot clear up, ramifications of evil He cannot touch. Thank God that is a lie! He can. If God cannot do that we have 'followed cunningly devised fables'. That is where the fight has to be fought—along the line of what Jesus Christ can do in the human soul. Unless God has searched us and cleansed us and filled us with the Holy Spirit so that we are undeserving of censure in His sight, the Atonement has not been applied to our personal experience. SHL. 51

The words of our Lord, 'Think not that I came to cast peace on the earth: I came not to cast peace, but a sword', are a description of what happens when the Gospel is preached—upset, conviction, concern and confusion. SHL. 112

The Gospel of God is not that Jesus died for my sins only, but that He gave Himself for me that I might give myself to Him. SSM. 28

This is the age of the gospel of cheerfulness. We are told to ignore sin, ignore the gloomy people, and yet more than half the human race is gloomy. WG. 64

GOSSIP

Don't be a busybody in other men's matters. A gossip is not always the bad person he is made out to be, those who listen and don't talk are the dangerous folk. SHH. 101

Scandal should be treated as you treat mud on your clothes. If you try and deal with it while it is wet, you rub the mud into the texture, but if you leave it till it is dry you can flick it off with a touch, it is gone without a trace. Leave scandal alone, never touch it. SSM. 41

GOVERNMENT

God's government of the world is not for material prosperity, but for moral ends, for the production of moral characters, in the sense of holy characters. Time is nothing to God. CHI. 112

The Bible point of view about government is that God compels man to govern man for Him, whether he likes it or not. The ordinance of government, whether it is a bad or good government, does not lie with men, but is entirely in God's hands; the king or the government will have to answer to God. The conservative attitude—My king, right or wrong—is a degeneration from the one great central point of the government of man by man. SHH. 113

GRACE

The grace we had yesterday won't do for to-day. "The grace of God"—the overflowing favour of God; we can always reckon it is there to draw on if we don't trust our own merits. AUG. 124

Whenever you are going through any tribulation that tears, don't pray about it, but draw on the grace of God now. The exercise of prayer is the work of drawing now. AUG. 125

As we draw on the grace of God He increases voluntary poverty all along the line. Always give the best you have got every time; never think about who you are giving it to, let other people take it or leave it as they choose. Pour out the best you have, and always be poor. Never reserve anything, never be diplomatic and careful about the treasure God gives. AUG. 128

One of the greatest proofs that we are drawing on the grace of God is that we can be humiliated without the slightest trace of anything but the grace of God in us. Draw on the grace of God *now,* not presently. The one word in the spiritual vocabulary is 'NOW'. AUG. 128

The surest sign that God has done a work of grace in my heart is that I love Jesus Christ best, not weakly and faintly, not intellectually, but passionately, personally and devotedly, overwhelming every other love of my life. BP. 134

All the great prevailing grace of God is ours for the drawing on, and it scarcely needs any drawing on, take out the 'stopper' and it comes out in torrents; and yet we just manage to squeeze out enough grace for the day—'sinning in thought, word and deed every day'! You don't find that note in the New Testament. GW. 12

'Grace' is a theological word and is unfortunately used, because we usually mean by theology something remote that has to do with controversy, something whereby our mind is tied up in knots and our practical life left alone. In the Bible theology is immensely practical. 'Grace' means the overflowing nature of God; we see it in Nature, we have no words to describe the lavishness of God. "The grace of our Lord Jesus Christ" is the overflowing of God's nature in entire and absolute forgiveness through His own sacrifice. BSG. 47

If we know that we have received the unmerited favour of God and we do not give unmerited favour to other people, we are damned in that degree. HG. 38

To be saved by God's grace is not a beautifully pathetic thing; it is a desperately tragic thing. HG. 99

The grace of God is absolute, but your obedience must prove that you do not receive it in vain. OBH. 111

The phrase 'a sinner saved by grace' means that a man is no longer a sinner; if he is, he is not saved. PS. 25

It requires the Almighty grace of God to take the next step when there is no vision and no spectator. RTR. 40

The basis of panic is always cowardice. The clearest evidence that God's grace is at work in our hearts is that we do not get into panics. RTR. 50

"Grace"—the overflowing favour of God. SA. 15

GROWTH

We grow in this Great Life by making room for Jesus Christ in our outlook on everything. Before you seal your opinion on any matter, find out what He has said about it—about God, about life, about death. Men discuss matters of heaven and hell, of life and death, and leave Jesus Christ out altogether; He says, 'Before you finally seal your mind, Believe *also* in Me.' If the bit we do know about Jesus Christ is so full of light, why cannot we leave the matters of heaven and hell, of life and death, in His hand and stake our confidence in Him? "God is Light," and one day everything will be seen in that light. "I am the Light of the world, he that followeth Me shall not walk in darkness, but shall have the light of life." AUG. 116

There is nothing simpler under heaven than to become a Christian, but after that it is not easy; we have to "leave the word of the beginning of Christ and press on unto full growth." CHI. 19

The way the life of the Son of God is nourished in me is by prayer and Bible revelation, and by obedience when a crisis comes. CHI. 21

Watch God's way in your life, you will find He is developing you as He does the trees and flowers, a deep silent working of the God of Creation. DI. 41

If our spiritual life does not grow where we are, it will grow nowhere. HGM. 33

We learn through chastisement, because God is supplying heaven with sons and daughters, not with precious stones. Sons and daughters must grow, and God is never in a hurry with us. HGM. 145

It is never God's will for us to be dummies or babies spiritually, it is God's will for us to be sons and daughters of God, but He does not prevent us paying the price of being sons and daughters. He makes us sons and daughters potentially, and then sends us out to be sons and daughters actually. IYA. 89

Any man, every man, we ourselves, may partake of this marvellous raising up whereby God puts us into the wonderful life of His Son, and the very qualities of Jesus Christ are imparted to us. There is plenty of room to grow in the heavenly places; room for the head to grow, for the heart to grow, for the bodily relationships to grow, for the spirit to grow—plenty of room for every phase of us to grow into the realisation of what a marvellous Being our Lord Jesus Christ is. OBH. 32

If we build to please ourselves, we are building on the sand; if we build for the love of God, we are building on the rock. OBH. 53

If we grow in grace a little more every day, it is a sign that the destructive power of God has been at work, and that we have been delivered from the thing that hindered us growing. PS. 25

Measure your growth in grace by your sensitiveness to sin. RTR. 53

"Consider the lilies of the field, how they grow". A lily is not always in the sunshine; for the greater part of the year it is hidden in the earth. "How they grow"—in the dark, only for a short time are they radiantly beautiful and sweet. . . . We can never be lilies in the garden unless we have spent time as bulbs in the dark, totally ignored. That is how to grow. RTR. 89

GUIDANCE

Supernatural manifestations of guidance are exceptional. The normal way of the Spirit of the God is the way He worked in the life of Jesus Christ. AUG. 43

Affliction and tribulation may destroy all else, but the saint abiding in this secret place of the Most High is untouchable. There is no self-consciousness there, no uncertainty, but only Rest, unfathomable rest in God Himself, not in a vision of God, but in God Himself as a Reality, a living, bright Reality. Walking with God, and talking to Him as friend with friend, knowing that God knows He can do what He likes with us; there are no questions and no perplexities because He knows. Here, in the heart of this way of guidance by Himself, does

God convey to us "the secret of the Lord." CD. VOL. 1, 53

God is not an outward gush of sentiment, not a vague abstraction of impersonal good nature: God is a living, intense Reality, and until this truth is grasped, the puzzles and the questions are more than can be met. But when by the discipline of His Divine guidance, we know Him, and He going with us gives us Rest, then Time and Eternity are merged and lost in that amazing vital relationship. The union is one not of mystic contemplation, but of intense perfection of activity, not the Rest of the placid peace of stagnation, but the Rest of perfect motion. CD. VOL. 1, 56

To be guided by common sense is as foolish as being guided by faith. God is the One Who welds both faith and common sense into one practical personality. NKW. 139

I know it is customary to ridicule certain ways in which some people say God guides them, but I am very chary about ridiculing any methods. For example, it is easy to ridicule this kind of method: 'Lord, direct me to a word, I am just going to shut my eyes and open the Book and put my finger on a passage.' I say it is easy to ridicule it, yet it is absurd to say that God has not led people in that way; He has. Why I mention these facts is to knock certain theories to pieces. You cannot tie God down to a particular line. WG. 14

H

HABITS

Our bodily habits are purely mechanical, and the revolution caused in individual lives by our Lord's salvation is that He enables us to do what He commands us to do, if we will but practice the doing. Habits are built up, not by theory, but by practice. BE. 57

When we begin to work out what God has worked in, we are faced with the problem that this physical body, this mechanism, has been used by habit to obeying another rule called sin; when Jesus Christ delivers us from that rule, He does not give us a new body, He gives us power to break and then re-mould every habit formed while we were under the dominion of sin. BE. 57

Most of the difficulty in forming a special habit is that we will not discipline ourselves. CD. VOL. 2, 30

"The great thing, then, in all education, is to *make our nervous system our ally instead of our enemy*. It is to fund and capitalize our acquisitions, and live at ease upon the interest of the fund. *For this we must make automatic and habitual, as early as possible, as many useful actions as we can*, and guard against the growing into ways that are likely to be disadvantageous to us, as we should guard against the plague. . . . The first (maxim) is that in the acquisition of a new habit, or the leaving off of an old one, we must take care to *launch ourselves with as strong and decided an*

initiative as possible. . . . The second maxim is: *Never suffer an exception to occur till the new habit is securely rooted in your life. . . .* A third maxim may be added to the preceding pair: *Seize the very first possible opportunity to act on every resolution you make, and on every emotional prompting you may experience in the direction of the habit you aspire to gain."* CD. VOL. 2, 30

Enchain your body to habitual obedience. DI. 70

Habit is a mechanical process of which we have ceased to become conscious. The basis of habit is always physical. MFL. 19

Habits are formed in the soul, not in the spirit, and they are formed in the soul by means of the body. MFL. 34

"Our virtues are habits as well as our vices." God does not give us our habits, but He holds us responsible, in proportion, for the habits we form. MFL. 35

We have to work out what God works in, and the way we work it out is by the mechanical process of habit. MFL. 35

The process of habit runs all through physical nature, and our brain is physical. When once we understand the bodily machine with which we have to work out what God works in, we find that our body becomes the greatest ally of our spiritual life. The difference between a sentimental Christian and a sanctified saint is just here. MFL. 39

The sanctified saint is one who has disciplined the body into perfect obedience to the dictates of the Spirit of God, consequently his body does with the greatest of ease whatever God wants him to do. The sentimental type of Christian is the sighing, tear-flowing, beginning-over-again Christian who always has to go to prayer meetings, always has to be stirred up, or to be soothed and put in bandages, because he has never formed the habit of obedience to the Spirit of God. MFL. 39

. . . when we are born again, God does not give us a fully fledged series of holy habits, we have to make those habits. MFL. 40

To refuse to form mental habits is a crime against the way we are made. It is no use praying, 'O Lord, give me mental habits.' God won't; He has made us so that we can make our own mental habits, if we will. MFL. 52

We do not become educated all at once, nor do we form habits all at once; it is done bit by bit, and we have to take ourselves strongly in hand. The one thing that keeps us back from forming habits is laziness. The lazy person in the natural world is always *captious,* and the lazy person spiritually is captious with God, 'I haven't had a decent chance.' Never let the limitation of natural ability come in. We must get to the place where we are not afraid to face our life before God, and then begin to work out deliberately what God has worked in. That is the way the habits which will show themselves in holy and just and unblameable behaviour are formed. MFL. 55

What happens at new birth is that the incoming of a totally new life breaks all the old habits, they are completely dislodged by the "expulsive power of a new affection." Most of us do not realise this and we continue to obey habits when there is no need to. MFL. 77

Never dispute for a second when God speaks; if you debate, you give an opportunity to the old habits to reassert themselves. Launch yourself with as strong an initiative as possible on the line of obedience; it is difficult at first, but immediately you start to obey, you find you can do it. MFL. 77

When in your soul's vision you see clearly what God wants, let me advise you to do something physical immediately. If you accompany a moral or spiritual decision with a physical effort, you give the necessary initiative to form the new habit. A physical exertion is imperative in spiritual transactions, otherwise it is in danger of passing into thin air. When God tells you to do a thing, never wait for a fitting opportunity, *do it now.* You may dream about doing it to further orders, the only thing to do is to launch out at once and make things inevitable, make it impossible to go back on the decision. MFL. 77

Beware of divorcing the physical and the spiritual. Habits are physical, and every command of God has a physical basis. "He that hath ears to hear, let him hear." You cannot hear with your heart if you do not listen with your physical ears. MFL. 78

God does not give us our physical habits or our mental habits; He gives us the power to form any kind of habits we like, and in the spiritual domain we have to form the habit of godly thinking. MFL. 93

The question of forming habits on the basis of the grace of God is a very vital one. God regenerates us and puts us in contact with all His Divine resources, but He connot make us walk according to His will; the practising is ours, not God's. We have to take the initiative and "add to ... faith virtue. ..." To take the initiative means to make a beginning, and each one of us must do it for himself. We have to acquaint ourselves with the way we have to go; and beware of the tendency of asking the way when we know it perfectly well. OBH. 51

We are in danger of forgetting that we cannot do what God does and that God will not do what we can do. We cannot save ourselves or sanctify ourselves; God only can do that; but God does not give us good habits, He does not give us character, He does not make us walk aright; we must do all that. We have to work out what God has worked in. OBH. 52

Many of us lose out spiritually, not because the devil attacks us, but because we are stupidly ignorant of the way God has made us. Remember, the devil did not make the human body; he may have tampered with it, but the human body was created by God, and its constitution after we are saved remains the same as before. For instance, we are not born with a ready-made habit of dressing ourselves; we have to form that habit. Apply it spiritually—when we are born again, God does not give us a fully fledged series of holy habits, we have to make them; and the forming of habits on the basis of God's supernatural work in our souls is the education of our spiritual life.

Many of us refuse to do it; we are lazy and we frustrate the grace of God. OBH. 52

WHEN we are forming a habit we are conscious of it, but in the real Christian life habits do not appear because by practice we do the thing unconsciously. As Christians we have to learn the habit of waiting upon God as He comes to us through the moments, and to see that we do not make common sense our guide; we do until we have seen the Lord. OBH. 63

Watch how God will upset our programmes if we are in danger of making our little Christian habits our god. Whenever we begin to worship our habit of prayer or of Bible reading, God will break up that time. We say—'I cannot do this, I am praying; it is my hour with God.' No, it is our hour with our habit; we pray to a habit of prayer. OBH. 63

As Christians, we have to learn the habit of waiting upon God as He comes to us through the moments, and to see that we do not make common-sense our guide; we do until we have seen the Lord. OBH. 63

If our childlike trust in God is giving place to self-consciousness and self-depreciation, it is a sign that there is something wrong, and the cure for it is to reach the place where every habit is so practised that there is no conscious habit at all. Watch how God will upset our programmes if we are in danger of making our little Christian habits our god. OBH. 63

No one is born with habits, we have to form habits, and the habits we form most easily are those which we form by imitation. When we begin to form a habit we are conscious of it. There are times when we are conscious of becoming virtuous and patient and godly, but that is only a stage; if we stop there we get the strut of the spiritual prig. OBH. 106

God does not make our habits for us or do the practising—God alters our disposition, and we are left to work out the new disposition He has put in, by practice and the forming of habits. OBH. 131

Habits are not transmitted by heredity, only tendencies and qualities; habits are formed by imitation. SA. 109

HAPPINESS

Immorality will produce happiness very quickly—the duration of the happiness is another matter; if you go on doing wrong long enough you will be happy doing wrong and miserable doing right—therefore quit doing right! BE. 14

The end and aim of human life is not happiness, but 'to glorify God and enjoy Him for ever'. Holiness of character, chastity of life, living communion with God—that is the end of a man's life, whether he is happy or not is a matter of moonshine. BE. 14

It is an insult to God and to human nature to have as our ideal a happy life. Happiness is a thing that comes and goes, it can never be an end in itself; holiness, not happiness, is the end of man. BSG. 54

Happiness is not a sign that we are right with God; happiness is a sign of satisfaction, that is all, and the majority of us can be satisfied on too low a level. Jesus Christ disturbs every kind of satisfaction that is less than delight in God. IWP. 109

The sign that we are glorifying God is not that we are happy; happiness is childish, individual and pagan. It is nat-ural for a child to be happy because a child does not face facts, but a Christian who is merely happy is blind. LG. 64

Any number of people are happy without God, because happiness depends on not too profound an understanding of things; 'the god of this world hath blinded their minds'. . . . OPG. 41

'I thought God's purpose was to make me full of happiness and joy.' It is, but it is happiness and joy from God's standpoint, not from ours. PH. 83

The fact that people are happy and peaceful and prosperous is no sign that they are free from the sword of God. If their happiness and peace and well-being and complacency rests on an undelivered life, they will meet the sword before long, and all their peace and rest and joy will be destroyed. PS. 25

Thousands of people are happy without God in this world, but that kind of happiness and peace is on a wrong level. Jesus Christ came to send a sword through every peace that is not based on a personal relationship to Himself. RTR. 60

Happiness means we select only those things out of our circumstances that will keep us happy. It is the great basis of false Christianity. SA. 97

The Bible nowhere speaks about a "happy" Christian; it talks plentifully of joy. Happiness depends on things that happen, and may sometimes be an insult; joyfulness is never touched by external conditions, and a joyful heart is never an insult. SA. 97

Happiness is the characteristic of a child's life, and God condemns us for taking happiness out of a child's life; but we should have done with happiness long ago, we should be men and women facing the stern issues of life, knowing that the grace of God is sufficient for every problem the devil can present. SA. 98

Happiness would be all right if things were reasonable; it would be ideal if there were no self-interest, but everyone of us is cunning enough to take advantage somewhere, and after a while my inclination is to get my happiness at your cost. SA. 98

HATRED

Most of us live our life in the world without ever discovering its hatred, but it is there, and a crisis may suddenly arise and bring it to a head, then we are appalled to find the meaning of Our Lord's words, "And ye shall be hated of all men for My name's sake." BE. 36

I have no business to stir up the hatred of the world through a domineering religious opinionativeness—that has nothing whatever to do with the spirit of Jesus; I am never told to rejoice when men separate me from their company on that account; but when in all modesty I am standing for the honour of Jesus Christ and a crisis arises when the Spirit of God requires that I declare my otherworldliness, then I learn what Jesus meant when He said, men will hate you. BE. 36

Jesus Christ is God manifested in human flesh, and we have to ignore to the point of hatred anything that competes with our relationship to Him. SHH. 49

HEALING

When people come to the Atonement and say—'Now I have deliverance in the Atonement, therefore I have no business to be sick,' they make a fundamental confusion, because there is no case of healing in the Bible that did not come from a direct intervention of the sovereign touch of God. IYA. 85

. . . if it is true that in the Atonement there should be no sickness, it is also true that there should be no death, then we have no business to die! We have no business to have any human limitations, we should be in complete unbroken communion with God, and the people who teach the present resurrection are logically consistent with the folks who say the health of the body depends entirely on our acceptance of the Atonement. IYA. 85

'I want God's life for my body'—at once we are off the track. Our bodies are to be entirely at God's disposal, and not God at our disposal. God does give Divine health, but not in order to show what a wonderful being a divinely healed person is. The life of God has to be followed by us, not utilized; we must not allow the life of God to stagnate in us, or imagine that we are to be put as specimens in a showcase. If God has healed us and keeps us in health, it is not that we might parade it, but that we might follow the life of God for His purposes. LG. 67

The fanatical element in the saint is the element that is devoted to a principle instead of to consistent conduct before God. For instance, I may become a devotee to the doctrine of Divine healing which means I must never be sick, and if I am sick then I say I must have gone wrong. The battle all through is against the absurdity of being consistent to an ideal instead of to God. NKW. 143

If you get off on the line of personal holiness or Divine healing or the Second Coming of Our Lord, and make any of these your end, you are disloyal to Jesus Christ. Supposing the Lord has healed your body and you make Divine healing your end, the dead set of your life is no longer for God but for what you are pleased to call the manifestation of God in your life. Bother your life! 'It can never be God's will that I should be sick.' If it was God's will to bruise His own Son, why should it not be His will to bruise you? The thing that tells is not relevant consistency to an idea of what a saint's life is, but abandonment abjectly to Jesus Christ whether you are well or ill. NKW. 148

The attitude to sickness in the Bible is totally different from the attitude of people who believe in faith-healing. The Bible attitude is not that God sends sickness or that sickness is of the devil, but that sickness is a fact usable by both God and the devil. Never base a principle on your own experience. My personal experience is this: I have never once in my life been sick without being to blame for it. As soon as I turned my mind to asking why the sickness was allowed, I learned a lesson that I have never forgotten, viz. that my physical health depends absolutely on my relationship to God. PS. 77

. . . the Master Physician. When He touches, there is no convalescence. SSY. 88

HEALTH

. . . a bad man whose life is wrong has a hilariously happy time, and a good man whose life is right has a hilarious time.

All in between are more or less diseased and sick, there is something wrong somewhere: the healthy pagan and the healthy saint are the only ones who are hilarious. BP. 78

The Psalmist's first degree of prayer is, "Heal me; for my bones are vexed"; the second degree is, "Heal me; for my soul is also sore vexed," and the third degree is, "Save me for Thy mercies' sake." These are three degrees of perplexity arising from the soul's surroundings: because of pain; because the mental outlook is cloudy, and because God has not said a word. BP. 88

Health is physical peace, but health is not stagnation; health is the perfection of physical activity. Virtue is moral peace, but virtue is not innocence; virtue is the perfection of moral activity. Holiness is spiritual peace, but holiness is not quietness; holiness is the intensest spiritual activity. BSG. 56

. . . if health were a sign that a man is right with God, we should lose all distinction as to what a good character is, for many bad men enjoy good health. GW. 50

One of Satan's greatest delusions is to decoy folks off on to blessings that are merely secondary. We become sidetracked if we make physical health our aim and imagine that because we are children of God we shall always be perfectly well; that there will be great manifestations of God's power, thousands saved, etc. HG. 8

The fact of health and the fact of sickness are there; we have nothing to do with choosing them, they come and go. We have to get on to another platform, the moral platform, and then the spiritual platform, before we can begin to get an explanation of these facts. PS. 77

HEARING

God spoke to Jesus once and the people said it thundered, Jesus did not think it thundered; His ears were trained by the disposition of His soul to know His Father's voice. BP. 74

It is always true that we only hear what we want to hear, and we shout the other sounds down by controversy and dispute. BP. 75

The way to believe it is to listen first. "So then faith cometh by hearing, and hearing by the word of God." OBH. 20

If we are born of the Spirit of God, we do hear it, we hear it more eagerly, more passionately, more longingly than anything else that can be told. OBH. 20

We are invited and commanded by God to believe that we can be made one with Jesus as He is one with God, so that His patience, His holiness, His purity, His gentleness, His prayerfulness are made ours. The way the gift of faith works in us and makes this real is by hearing. OBH. 20

We first hear, and then we begin to trust. It is so simple that most of us miss the way. The way to have faith in the gospel of God's grace, in its deepest profundity as well as in its first working, is by listening to it. OBH. 20

We have to keep our ears trained to detect God's voice, to be continually renewed in the spirit of our mind. If when a crisis comes we instinctively turn to God, we know that the habit of hearkening has been formed. At the beginning there is the noisy clamour of our own misgivings; we are so taken up with what we have heard that we cannot hear any more. We have to hearken to that which we have not listened to before, and to do it we must be insulated on the inside. OBH. 54

We always hear the thing we listen for, and our disposition determines what we listen for. When Jesus Christ alters our disposition, He gives us the power to hear as He hears. PR. 83

HEART

The Bible places in the heart everything that the modern psychologist places in the head. BP. 72

The Bible puts the head in the prominent position, not the central position; the head is the 'finish off,' the manifestation of what the heart is like; the outward expression of the heart, as a tree is the outward expression of the root. This is the relationship between the head and the heart which the Bible reveals. BP. 98

Materialistic scientists say that 'the brain secretes thinking as the liver does bile,' they make the brain the centre of thinking. The Bible makes the heart the centre of thinking, and the brain merely the machinery the heart uses to express itself. This point is very vital in our judgment of men. BP. 98

God never judges men by their brains; He judges them by their hearts. BP. 99

The use of the Bible term 'heart' is best understood by simply saying 'me.' The heart is not merely the seat of the affections, it is the centre of everything. The heart is the central altar, and the body is the outer court. What we offer on the altar of the heart will tell ultimately through the extremities of the body. BP. 99

The heart . . . is the centre of living, the true centre of all vital activities of body and soul and spirit. BP. 99

The Bible always means more than we are apt to mean. The term 'heart' in the Bible means the centre of everything. The human soul has the spirit in and above it and the body by and about it; but the vital centre of all is the heart. When we speak of the heart, figuratively or actually, we mean the mid most part of a person. The Bible teaching differs from that of science in that it makes the heart the soul centre and the spirit centre as well. BP. 99

If we try, as has been tried by psychologists, to take out of the Bible something that agrees with modern science, we shall have to omit many things the Bible says about the heart. According to the Bible the heart is the centre: the centre of physical life, the centre of memory, the centre of damnation and of salvation, the centre of God's working and the centre of the devil's working, the centre from which everything works which moulds the human mechanism. BP. 100

We can develop in the heart life whatever we will; there is no limit to the possible growth and development. If we give ourselves over to meanness and to Satan, there is no end to the growth in devilishness; if we give ourselves over openly to God, there is no end to our development and growth in grace. Our Lord has no fear of the consequences when once the heart is open towards Him. BP. 102

Every characteristic seen in the life of Jesus Christ becomes possible in our lives when once we hand over our hearts to Him to be filled with the Holy Spirit. BP. 104

The heart physically is the centre of the body; the heart sentimentally is the centre of the soul; and the heart spiritually is the centre of the spirit. BP. 107

God deals with the designs of our hearts, either for good or for bad. BP. 109

According to the Bible, thinking exists in the heart, and that is the region with which the Spirit of God deals. We may take it as a general rule that Jesus Christ never answers any questions that spring from a man's head, because the questions which spring from our brains are always borrowed from some book we have read, or from someone we have heard speak; but the questions that spring from our hearts, the real problems that vex us, Jesus Christ answers those. The questions He came to deal with are those that spring from the implicit centre. These problems may be difficult to state in words, but they are the problems Jesus Christ will solve. BP. 125

The heart is the place where God works, and there all conscious unity resides; when once the Spirit of God is in the heart He will bring spirit, soul and body into perfect unity. Other powers can do this beside God, viz., the world, the flesh, and the devil. The world can give a conscious unity to man's heart; so can the flesh and the devil. The man who gives way to sensuality, to worldliness, to devilishness, or to covetousness, is perfectly satisfied without God. God calls that idolatry. BP. 129

The only way to alter the hardened heart is to melt it, and the only power that can melt it is the fire of the Holy Ghost. BP. 140

'Heart' is simply another term for 'personality.' The Bible never speaks of the heart as the seat of the affections. 'Heart' is best understood if we simply say 'me'. MFL. 47

There is only one Being Who can satisfy the last aching abyss of the human heart, and that is the Lord Jesus Christ. MFL. 48

The heart is the altar of which the physical body is the outer court, and whatever is offered on the altar of the heart will tell ultimately through the extremities of the body. "Keep thy heart with all diligence; for out of it are the issues of life." MFL. 113

We have not the remotest conception that what Jesus says about the human heart is true until we come up against something further on in our lives. We are apt to be indignant and say—"I don't believe those things are in my heart," and we refuse the diagnosis of the only Master there is of the human heart. We need never know the plague of our own heart and the terrible possibilities in human life if we will hand ourselves over to Jesus Christ; but if we stand on our own right and wisdom at any second an eruption may occur in our personal lives, and we may discover to our unutterable horror that we can be murderers, etc. SHH. 104

Education cannot deal with the plague of the heart, all our vows cannot touch it; the only Being Who can deal with it is God through a personal relationship to Him, by receiving His Spirit after accepting the diagnosis of Jesus Christ. SHH. 105

Either Jesus Christ must be the supreme Authority on the human heart, or He is not worth listening to. SSM. 27

HEAVEN AND HELL

Hell is the place of angelic condemnation. It has nothing to do primarily with man. God's Book never says that hell was made for man, although it is true that it is the only place for the man who rejects God's salvation. Hell was the result of a distinct condemnation passed by God on celestial beings, and is as eternal as those celestial anarchists. BP. 3

Neither fear of hell nor hope of heaven has anything to do with our personal relationship to Jesus Christ, it is a life hid with Christ in God, stripped of all possessions saving the knowledge of Him. The great lodestar of the life is Jesus Himself, not anything He does for us. MFL. 116

"Heavenly places in Christ Jesus."

That is where God raises us. We do not get there by climbing, by aspiring, by struggling, by consecration, or by vows; God lifts us right straight up out of sin, inability and weakness, lust and disobedience, wrath and self-seeking—lifts us right up out of all this, "up, up to the whiter than snow shine," to the heavenly places where Jesus Christ lived when He was on earth, and where He lives to this hour in the fullness of the plenitude of His power. May God never relieve us from the wonder of it. OBH. 32

". . . reserved in heaven for you." This is a great conception of the New Testament, but it is a conception lost in modern evangelism. We are so much taken up with what God wants us to be here that we have forgotten heaven. PH. 201

The great New Testament conception of heaven is "here-after" without the sin, "new heavens and new earth, wherein dwelleth righteousness"—a conception beyond us. . . . there is an undefiled inheritance awaiting us which has never yet been realised, and that it has in it all we have ever hoped or dreamed or imagined, and a good deal more. PH. 201

Hell is the satisfaction of all sin. PS. 42

Hell is an eternal and an abiding distress to whatever goes into it. Whatever goes into hell can never again be established as a right thing. SHH. 114

The Bible was not written for babes and fools, it was written for men and women who have to face hell's facts in this life as well as heaven's facts. SSM. 39

"Enter ye in at the strait gate." We can only get to heaven through Jesus Christ and by no other way; we can only get to the Father through Jesus Christ, and we can only get into the life of a saint in the same way. SSM. 98

HEREDITY

No man is held responsible by God for having an heredity of sin: what God holds a man responsible for is refusing to let Jesus Christ deliver him from it when he sees that that is what He came to do. BFB. 51

The sins of the fathers are not visited on innocent children, but on children who continue the sins of their fathers. Distinction must be made between punishment and suffering, they are not synonymous terms. A bad man's relation to his children is in God's hand: the child's relation to the badness of his father is in his own hand. Because we see children suffering physically for the sins of their parents, we say they are being punished; they are not, there is no element of punishment in their suffering; there are Divine compensations we know nothing about. The whole subject of heredity and what is transmitted by heredity, if taken out of its Bible setting, can be made the greatest slander against God, as well as the greatest exoneration of the bitterness of a man's spirit. CHI. 73

There is no obstacle, nothing in the past or the present or in his heredity, that can stand in a man's way if he will only make room for Jesus Christ. HGM. 109

HISTORY

According to the Bible, the history of the world is divided into Ages—(1) the pre-Adamic; (2) the Eden; (3) the Antediluvian; (4) the Mosaic; (5) the Church; (6) the Kingdom; and the remarkable thing in the record of the Ages that have been, and that are, and that are going to be, is that each Age ends in apparent disaster . . . This is very unexpected for one would naturally suppose that the Bible would show how successful God had been with the world's Ages, successful, that is, in the way we count success, and because the Bible does not prove this, men's minds revolt and they say that all God's plans have been overthrown by the devil and God has been checkmated, so to speak; or else they say that the Bible view is simply the fancy of a few oriental religious men of genius and is not of any use to us nowadays. CD. VOL. 2, 133

Jesus Christ did not evolve out of history, He came into history from outside history; He is not the best human being the world has ever seen, He is a Being who cannot be accounted for by the human race at all. PH. 78

HOLINESS

The holiness which God demands is impossible unless a man can be re-made from within, and that is what Jesus Christ has undertaken to do. Jesus Christ does not merely save people from hell: "thou shalt call His name JESUS; for it is He that shall save His people from their sins", i.e., make totally new moral men. Jesus Christ came from a holy God to enable men, by the sheer might of His Redemption, to become holy. "Ye shall be holy: for I the Lord your God am holy." BE. 16

Holiness is the characteristic of the man after God's own heart. BE. 16

Try and develop a holy life in private, and you find it cannot be done. Individuals can only live the true life when they are dependent on one another." BE. 29

Immediately you try to develop holiness alone and fix your eyes on your own whiteness, you lose the whole meaning of Christianity. The Holy Spirit makes a man fix his eyes on his Lord and on intense activity for others. BE. 29

Holiness Movements are apt to ignore the human and bank all on the Divine; they tell us that human nature is sinful, forgetting that Jesus Christ took on Him our human nature, and "in Him is no sin". BE. 51

It is much easier to live a holy life than to think on Jesus Christ's lines. BE. 109

There is only one kind of holiness, and that is the holiness of the Lord Jesus. BP. 40

Man's holiness must be progressive. The holiness of Jesus developed through antagonism because He revealed what a holy man should be. BSG. 10

If you are not holy, you will not be tempted to be unholy, because you do not hold holiness. BSG. 29

What Jesus Christ does in new birth is to put in a disposition that transforms morality into holiness. He came to put into the man who knows he needs it His own heredity of holiness; to bring him into a oneness with God which he never had through natural birth. CHI. 22

Practical holiness is the only holiness of any value in this world, and the only kind the Spirit of God will endorse. CHI. 82

Whenever a Holiness Movement raises its head and begins to be conscious of its own holiness, it is liable to become an emissary of the devil, although it started with an emphasis on a neglected truth. DI. 4

If you preach Holiness, or Sanctification, or Divine Healing, or the Second Coming, you are off the track because you de-centralize the Truth. We have to fix our eyes on Jesus Christ, not on what He does. '*I am the Truth.*' DI. 4

There are saints who are being rattled out of holiness by fussy work for God, whereas one five minutes of brooding on God's truth would do more good than all their work of fuss. DI. 8

God's final purpose is holiness, holy men and women, and He restrains none of the forces which go against that purpose. DI. 13

Watch the margins of your mind when you begin to take the view that it doesn't matter whether God is holy or not; it is the beginning of being a traitor to Jesus Christ. DI. 14

It is quite true to say 'I can't live a holy life'; but you can decide to let Jesus make you holy. 'I can't do away with my past'; but you can decide to let Jesus do away with it. DI. 58

If I make personal holiness a cause instead of an effect I become shallow, no matter how profound I seem. It means I am far more concerned about being speckless than about being real; far more concerned about keeping my garments white than about being devoted to Jesus Christ. DI. 58

Jesus Christ can make my disposition as pure as His own. That is the claim of the Gospel. DI. 59

The idea that I grow holy as I go on is foreign to the New Testament. There must have been a place where I was identified with the death of Jesus: "I have been crucified with Christ . . . ;" That is the meaning of sanctification. Then I grow *in* holiness. DI. 59

The ultimate display of Deity is omnipotence, but the essential nature of Deity is holiness. GW. 30

There is a subtle form of carnal pride that is set on *my* holiness; it is unscriptural and morbid and ends in experience rather than in character, in taking myself more and more seriously and God less and less seriously. The cultivation of holiness is impossible without the spiritual concentration which the Holy Spirit enjoins. GW. 143

Jesus Christ came *to make us holy*, not to tell us to be holy: He came to do for us what we could not do for ourselves. HG. 13

We are interested in other men's lives because of a career, a profession, or an ideal we have for them, but God does not seem to care an atom for careers or professions, He comes down with ruthless disregard of all gifts and geniuses and sweeps them on one side; He is interested only in one thing, and that thing was exhibited in the life of our Lord, viz. a balanced holiness before God. HG. 41

The only test of spirituality is holiness, practical, living holiness, and that holiness is impossible unless the Holy Ghost has brought you to your 'last day,' and you can look back and say—'That was the day when I died right out to my right to myself, crucified with Christ.' HG. 109

Until you have stopped trying to be good and being pleased with the evidences of holiness in yourself, you will never open the wicket gate that leads to the more excellent way. IWP. 77

We talk about the difficulty of living a holy life; there is the absolute simple ease of Almighty God in living a holy life because it cost Him so much to make it possible. IYA. 22

The holiness exhibited by the Son of God, and by God's children, is the holiness which expresses itself by means of antagonism. LG. 96

Holiness can only be worked out in and through the din of things as they are. God does not slide holiness into our hearts like a treasure box from heaven and we open the lid and out it comes, holiness works out in us as it worked out in our Lord. LG. 96

. . . Jesus Christ never expected men to be holy; He knew they could not be: *He came to make men holy.* All He asks of men is that they acknowledge they are not right, then He will do all the rest— "Blessed are the poor in spirit." MFL. 91

Personal holiness is never the ground of my acceptance with God; the only ground of acceptance is the Death of the Lord Jesus Christ. NKW. 123

Those of you who are hungering and thirsting after holiness, think what it would mean to you to go out to-night knowing that you may step boldly into the heritage that is yours if you are born of the Spirit, and realise that the perfections of Jesus are yours by His sovereign gift in such a way that you can prove it experimentally! OBH. 15

The Spirit of God Who wrought out that marvellous Life in the Incarnation will baptize us into the very same life, not into a life like it, but into His life until the very holiness of Jesus is gifted to us. It is not something we work out in Him, it is *in Him*, and He manifests it through us while we abide in Him. OBH. 16

The one marvellous secret of a holy life is not in imitating Jesus, but in letting the perfections of Jesus manifest themselves in our mortal flesh. OBH. 19

Abandon in the profound sense is of infinitely more value than personal holiness. Personal holiness brings the attention to bear on my own whiteness, I dare not be indiscreet, or unreserved, I dare not do anything in case I incur a speck. God can't bless that sort of thing, it is as unlike His own character as

could be. The holiness produced through the indwelling of His Son in me is a holiness which is never conscious of itself. There are some people in whom you cannot find a speck and yet they are not abundantly blessed of God, while others make grave indiscretions and get marvellously blessed; the reason being that the former have become devotees of personal holiness, conscientious to a degree; the latter are marked by abandonment to God. Whatever centres attention on anything other than our Lord Himself will always lead astray. The only way to be kept cleansed is by walking in the light, as God is in the light. Only as we walk in that light is the holiness of Jesus Christ not only imputed, but imparted, to us. OPG. 27

There is only one holiness, the holiness of God, and only one sanctification, the sanctification that has its origin in Jesus Christ. "But of Him are ye in Christ Jesus, Who was made unto us . . . sanctification." PH. 41

Jesus Christ's demand is that we be as holy as He is Himself, that we reach the 'whiter than snow-shine' in our conduct, that we are unfathomably pure in heart. PH. 61

Jesus Christ by His death bore away the sin of the world, and by our identification with His death we can be delivered from the heredity of sin and can receive a new heredity, the unsullied holiness of Jesus Christ. We receive this new heredity not by imitation, but by identification, by giving up our right to ourselves to Jesus Christ. PR. 57

. . . we say that the essential nature of God is omnipotence, omnipresence, and omniscience; the New Testament reveals that the essential nature of God is holiness, and that He became the weakest thing in His own creation, viz., a Baby. PR. 130

What is holiness? Transfigured morality blazing with indwelling God. Any other kind of holiness is fictitious and dangerous. One of the dangers of dealing too much with the Higher Christian Life is that it is apt to fizzle off into abstractions. But when we see holiness in the Lord Jesus, we do know what it means, it means an unsullied walk with the feet, unsullied talk with the tongue, unsullied thinking of the mind, unsullied transactions of the bodily organs, un sullied life of the heart, unsullied dreams of the imagination—that is the actual holiness Jesus says He has given them. This is the meaning of sanctification. PR. 135

When the holiness of God is preached, men are convicted of sin; it is not the love of God that first appeals but His holiness. PS. 20

The majority of us have caught on the jargon of holiness without the tremendous panging pain that follows the awakening to holiness. PS. 65

Personal experience bears out the truth that a testimony to holiness produces either rage or ridicule on the part of those who are not holy. PS. 80

You can never make yourself holy by external acts, but, if you are holy, your external acts will be the natural expression of holiness. RTR. 23

The Christian aspect is that God will make a man as holy as He is Himself, and this He has undertaken to do. SA. 29

Jesus Christ's holiness has to do with human life as it is. It is not a mystical, æsthetic thing that cannot work in the ordinary things of life, it is a holiness which "can be achieved with an ordinary diet and a wife and five children." SA. 74

Holiness is the balance between our disposition and the law of God as expressed in Jesus Christ, and it is such a stern thing that the majority of us have either not begun it, or we have begun it and left it alone. SA. 99

Jesus Christ stands for holiness. SA. 100

Any man who knows himself knows that he cannot be holy, therefore if ever he is holy, it will be because God has "shipped" something into him, and he begins to bring forth the fruits of repentance. SA. 121

There is only one type of holiness and that is the holiness of God, and Jesus gives God Almighty as our Example. SSM. 53

Holiness means a perfect balance between our disposition and the laws of God. SSM. 55

His glory was the glory of actual holiness, and that is the glory He says He gives to the saint. The glory of the saint is the glory of actual holiness manifested in actual life here and now. SSY. 99

HOLY SPIRIT

The Holy Ghost makes Jesus Christ both present and real. He is the most real Being on earth, "closer is He than breathing, and nearer than hands and feet". BE. 98

The Holy Spirit alone makes Jesus real, the Holy Spirit alone expounds His Cross, the Holy Spirit alone convicts of sin; the Holy Spirit alone does *in* us what Jesus *did* for us. BE. 99

Immediately the Holy Spirit comes in as life and as light, He will chase through every avenue of our minds; His light will penetrate every recess of our hearts; He will chase His light through every affection of our souls, and make us know what sin is. The Holy Spirit convicts of sin, man does not. BP. 37

The Holy Spirit will take us, spirit, soul and body, and bring us back into communion with God; and if we obey the light He gives, He will lead us into identification with the death of Jesus, until we know experimentally that our old man, my right to myself, is crucified with Him and our human nature is free now to obey the commands of God. BP. 38

We can only discern the spiritual world by the Spirit of God, not by our own spirit; and if we have not received the Spirit of God we shall never discern spiritual things or understand them; we shall move continually in a dark world, and come slowly to the conclusion that the New Testament language is very exaggerated. But when we have received the Spirit of God, we begin to "know the things that are freely given to us of God," and to compare "spiritual things with spiritual," "not in the words which man's wisdom teacheth, but which the Holy Ghost teacheth." BP. 210

We cannot think of a Being Who had no beginning and Who has no end; consequently men without the Spirit of God make a god out of ideas of their own. It is a great moment in our lives when we realize we must be agnostic about God, that we cannot get hold of Him. Then comes the revelation that Jesus Christ will give to us the Holy Spirit, Who will lift us into a new domain and enable us to understand all that He reveals, and to live the life God wants us to live. BP. 213

Man's spirit takes up no room and the Spirit of God takes up no room, they work and interwork. My spirit has no power in itself to lay hold of God; but when the Spirit of God comes into my spirit, He energizes my spirit, then the rest depends upon me. If I do not obey the Spirit of God and bring into the light the wrong things He reveals and let Him deal with them, I shall grieve Him, and may grieve Him away. BP. 214

"God is a Spirit," therefore if we are going to understand God, we must have the Spirit of God. BP. 215

We cannot give ourselves the Holy Spirit; the Holy Spirit is God Almighty's gift if we will simply become poor enough to ask for Him. BP. 220

. . . when the Holy Spirit has come in, there is something we can do and God cannot do, we can obey Him. If we do not obey Him, we shall grieve Him. BP. 220

When the Holy Spirit comes in, unbelief is turned out and the energy of God is put into us, and we are enabled to will and to do of His good pleasure. When the Holy Spirit comes in He sheds abroad the love of God in our hearts, so that we are able to show our fellows the same love that God has shown to us. When the Holy Spirit comes in He makes us as 'light,' and our righteousness will exceed the righteousness of the most moral upright natural man because the supernatural has been made natural in us. BP. 222

The Holy Spirit is identical with God the Father and with God the Son; and being a Person, He must exercise an influence. The more pronounced a person, the more powerful is his influence; but we have to recognize that nowadays the majority of people do not know the Holy Ghost as a Person, they know Him, only as an influence. BP. 223

If the Holy Ghost is indwelling a man or woman, no matter how sweet, how beautiful, how Christ-like they are, the lasting thought you go away with is— What a wonderful Being the Lord Jesus Christ is. BSG. 33

Call the Comforter by the term you think best—Advocate, Helper, Paraclete, the word conveys the indefinable blessedness of His sympathy; an inward, invisible kingdom that causes the saint to sing through every night of sorrow. This Holy Comforter represents the ineffable Motherhood of God. Protestantism has lost for many generations this aspect of the Divine revelation because of its violent antipathy to Mariolatry as practised by the Roman Catholic Church, and it behoves us to remember that Protestantism is not the whole Gospel of God, but an expression of a view of the Gospel of God specially adapted to the crying needs of a particular time. CD. VOL. 1, 44

Beware of telling people they must be worthy to receive the Holy Spirit; you can't be worthy, you must know you are unworthy, then you will ask for the gift—"If ye then, *being evil . . .*" DI. 20

It is extraordinary how things fall off from a man like autumn leaves once he comes to the place where there is no rule but that of the personal domination of the Holy Spirit. DI. 20

The biggest blessing in your life was when you came to the end of trying to be a Christian, the end of reliance on natural devotion, and were willing to come as a pauper and receive the Holy Spirit. The humiliation is that we have to be quite sure we need Him, so many of us are quite sure we don't need Him. DI. 20

The Holy Spirit takes care that we fix our attention on Jesus Christ; then He will look after the presentation given of our Lord through us. DI. 21

The Holy Spirit is concerned only with glorifying Jesus, not with glorifying our human generosities. DI. 21

The deep and engrossing need of those of us who name the Name of Christ is reliance on the Holy Spirit. DI. 21

The salvation of Jesus Christ makes a man's personality intense; very few of us are real until the Holy Spirit gets hold of us. DI. 22

If you are being checked by the Holy Spirit over a wrong thing you are allowing in yourself, beware of only captiously seeing the limitations in other people; you will diverge further away from God if you don't recognize that it is the still small voice of God *to you.* DI. 22

There is nothing so still and gentle as the checks of the Holy Spirit; if they are yielded to, emancipation is the result; but let them be trifled with, and there will come a hardening of the life away from God. Don't 'quench the Spirit'. DI. 22

The inspiration of the Holy Spirit is not an impulse to make me act but to enable me to interpret God's meaning; if I do act on the impulse of the inspiration, it is a mere physical reaction in myself. Impulse is God's knock at my door that He might come in, not for me to open the door and go out. DI. 22

The Holy Spirit does not obliterate a man's personality; He lifts it to its highest use, viz., for the portrayal of the Mind of God. DI. 22

There is one thing we cannot imitate: we cannot imitate being full of the Holy Ghost. DI. 24

The Holy Spirit is the One who regenerates us into the Family to which Jesus Christ belongs, until by the eternal efficacy of the Cross we are made partakers of the Divine nature. DI. 24

The Holy Spirit is not a substitute for Jesus. The Holy Spirit is all that Jesus was, made real in personal experience *now*. DI. 24

The mark of the Holy Spirit in a man's life is that he has gone to his own funeral and the thought of himself never enters. DI. 24

The Holy Spirit works in no other way than to glorify Jesus Christ. HGM. 10

The most rarely recognized aspect of the Holy Spirit's work is that He causes us to do honour to Our Lord. HGM. 21

The Holy Ghost is the One who honours Jesus, and therein lies the essential necessity of receiving Him. HGM. 21

The human spirit uninspired by the Holy Spirit only honours Jesus if He *does* things. It is easier to dishonour Jesus than we are apt to think because He never insists on being honoured. HGM. 21

The Spirit of God must have a deep indignation at the preaching of holiness that is not the holiness of Jesus. The holiness of Jesus is the most humble thing on earth. HGM. 128

Beware of being in bondage to yourself or to other people. Oppression and depression never come from the Spirit of God. He never oppresses, He convicts and comforts. HGM. 145

God does not withhold the best, He cannot give it until we are ready to receive it. Receive the Holy Spirit and let your reason be lifted out of images and out of the good, and instantly you will be lifted into the best. IWP. 77

. . . our conscious life, though only a tiny bit of our personality, is to be regarded by us as a shrine of the Holy Ghost. The Holy Ghost will look after the unconscious part we do not know, we must see we guard the conscious part, for which we are responsible, as a shrine of the Holy Ghost. If we recognise this as we should, we shall be careful to keep our body undefiled for Him. IYA. 107

There are many to-day who are sincere, but they are not real; they are not hypocrites, but perfectly honest and earnest and desirous of fulfilling what Jesus wants of them, but they *really* cannot do it, the reason being that they have not received the Holy Spirit Who will make them real. LG. 109

The Holy Spirit has been given; Jesus has been glorified; the waiting depends upon our fitness, not upon God's providence. The reception of the Holy Ghost depends entirely upon moral preparation. I must abide in the light which the Holy Ghost sheds and be obedient to the word of God; then when the power of

God comes upon such obedience there will be the manifestation of a strong family likeness to Jesus. LG. 120

The Holy Spirit is absolutely honest, He indicates the things that are right and the things that are wrong. LG. 121

We are apt to imagine that God will only work according to precedent. The Holy Ghost is world-wide. God says that He will pour out His spirit 'upon all flesh'. LG. 128

The Spirit of God is always the spirit of liberty; the spirit that is not of God is the spirit of bondage, the spirit of oppression and depression. The Spirit of God convicts vividly and tensely, but He is always the Spirit of liberty. God Who made the birds never made bird-cages; it is men who make bird-cages, and after a while we become cramped and can do nothing but chirp and stand on one leg. When we get out into God's great free life, we discover that that is the way God means us to live "the glorious liberty of the children of God." MFL. 92

Our great need is to ask for and receive the Holy Ghost in simple faith in the marvellous Atonement of Jesus Christ, and He will turn us into passionate lovers of the Lord. It is this passion for Christ worked out in us that makes us witnesses to Jesus wherever we are, men and women in whom He delights, upon whom He can look down with approval; men and women whom He can put in the shadow or the sun; men and women whom He can put upon their beds or on their feet; men and women whom He can send anywhere He chooses. PH. 33

The Holy Spirit is honest, and we know intuitively whether we have or have not been identified with the death of Jesus, whether we have or have not given over our self-will to the holy will of God. PH. 160

When we ask God for the Holy Spirit, we receive the very nature of God, *Holy Spirit*. PR. 13

The Spirit of God brings upset and conviction, He throws light on what is dark, He searches the recesses of the disposition; consequently the preaching of the Gospel, while it awakens an intense craving, awakens an equally intense resentment. PR. 14

The Holy Ghost witnesses only to the Son of God, and not according to our fleshly estimates of things, and if we try and estimate Jesus Christ according to the flesh, we shall find there is no reality in it. PR. 53

The great need for men and women is to receive the Holy Spirit. Our creeds teach us to believe in the Holy Spirit; the New Testament says we must *receive* Him. PR. 112

If we honestly ask God to baptise us with the Holy Ghost and fire, anything that happens is His answer, and some appalling things happen. PR. 125

Our Lord did not tell us to ask for peace or for joy or for life, He told us to ask for the Holy Spirit, and when we ask, the honour of Jesus Christ is at stake. PR. 133

When we receive the Holy Ghost He turns us into passionate followers of Jesus Christ. Then out of our lives will flow those rivers of living water that heal and bless, and we spend and suffer and endure in patience all because of One, and One only. RTR. 25

The Holy Ghost destroys my personal private life and turns it into a thoroughfare for God. RTR. 42

God does not give us the Holy Spirit until we come to the place of seeing that we cannot do without Him. SA. 38

When the Holy Spirit comes in He is unmistakable in the direction of His work, He goes direct to the thing that keeps us from believing in Jesus Christ. The work of the Holy Spirit is to make us realize the meaning of the Redemption. As long as we believe it on the outside it does not upset our complacency, but we don't want to be perturbed on the inside. SHL. 59

No man can receive the Holy Spirit who is not convinced he is a pauper spiritually. SSM. 16

If we are children of God, the simple law of our nature is the Holy Ghost; His one set purpose is the glorification of Jesus, and He pays no attention to our secular or our religious notions. SSY. 112

The Holy Ghost is the One Who expounds the nature of Jesus to us. When the Holy Ghost comes in, He does infinitely more than deliver us from sin, He makes us one with our Lord. SSY. 171

There is only one Being Who understands us all and that is the Holy Spirit, and He understands the Lord Jesus Christ too, and if you keep the avenues of your soul open to Him and get your messages from Him and see that you allow nothing to obscure Him, you will find He will locate the people. For every new message you give, God will give you human beings who have been convicted by it, and you will have to deal with them, whether you like it or not; and you will have not only to deal with them, but you will have to take them on your heart before God. God will make you work for the cure of the souls He has wounded by your message. If the wounding has come along His line, the line of the faithful proclamation of His message, He will let you see Him healing that soul through you as a worker, as you rely on the Holy Spirit. WG. 27

HOLY SPIRIT BAPTISM

When we are baptized with the Holy Ghost self is effaced in a glory of sacrifice for Jesus and we become His witnesses. Self-conscious devotion is gone, self-conscious service is killed, and one thing only remains, Jesus Christ first, second, and third. BSG. 41

The way you will want the baptism of the Holy Ghost and fire is when you begin to see the Lord Jesus; when you see Him, the great heart-hunger, the great longing of the life will be, 'I want to be like Him'. But remember, you must come to Him; it is His prerogative to baptize with the Holy Ghost. It is not a blessing we gain by faith, not a blessing we merge into by devotion and fasting, it is the supernaturally natural result of coming to Jesus as the true Baptizer. GW. 22

People come piously together and ask God to baptize them with the Holy Ghost, but they forget that the first thing the Holy Ghost does is to illuminate the Cross of Christ. HGM. 22

When a man experiences salvation the note of testimony is what Jesus has done for him; when he is baptized with the Holy Ghost he becomes a witness, which means much more than a testifier to blessings received. HGM. 23

The baptism with the Holy Ghost is Jesus putting the final seal on His work in you, His seal on your regenerated and entirely sanctified soul, and is your inauguration into service for Him. The Holy Spirit always works through human instrumentality, and there is never any possibility of pride when the Holy Spirit uses us. We are empowered into union with Christ by the Holy Ghost. HGM. 23

When we are baptized with the Holy Ghost we are no longer isolated believers but part of the Mystical Body of Christ. Beware of attempting to live a holy life alone, it is impossible. HGM. 25

The baptism with the Holy Ghost is not only a personal experience, it is an experience which makes individual Christians one in the Lord. The only way saints can meet together as one is through the baptism of the Holy Ghost, not through external organizations. The end of all divisions in work for God is when He changes fever into white-heated fervour. Oh, the foolish fever there is these days! Organizing this, organizing that; a fever of intense activity for God. HGM. 26

The baptism of the Holy Ghost does not mean signs and wonders, but something remarkably other—a life transfigured by the indwelling of the Holy Spirit and the realization of the Redemption in personal experience. HGM. 29

Historically, the baptism of the Holy Ghost added nothing to the apostles' doctrine, it made them the incarnation of what they preached. The great idea is not that we are at work for God, but that He is at work in us; not that we are devoted to a cause and doing aggressive work for God, but that He is working

out a strong family likeness to His Son in us. HGM. 29

If we want to be baptized with the Holy Ghost that we may be of use, it is all up; or because we want peace and joy and deliverance from sin, it is all up. "He shall baptize you with the Holy Ghost," not for anything for ourselves at all, but that we may be witnesses unto Him. God will never answer the prayer to be baptized with the Holy Ghost for any other reason than to make us witnesses to Jesus. HGM. 30

The baptism of the Holy Ghost does not mean that we are put into some great and successful venture for God, but that we are a satisfaction to Jesus wherever we are placed. It is not a question of service done, but that our living relationship to Him is a witness that satisfies Him. HGM. 38

We are baptized with the Holy Ghost not *for* anything at all, but entirely, as Our Lord puts it, to be His witnesses, those with whom He can do exactly what He likes. HGM. 130

If we seek the baptism of the Holy Ghost in order that God may make us great servants of His, we shall never receive anything. God baptizes us with the Holy Ghost that He may be All in all. IWP. 17

The baptism of the Holy Ghost is not an experience apart from Christ: it is the evidence of the ascended Christ. It is not the baptism of the Holy Ghost that changes men, but the power of the ascended Christ coming into men's lives by the Holy Ghost that changes them. LG. 132

The witness of the Holy Spirit is that we realise with growing amazement Who

Jesus is to us personally, our Lord and Master. The baptism of the Holy Ghost makes us witnesses to Jesus, not wonder-workers. The witness is not to what Jesus does, but to what He is. OBH. 88

The Holy Spirit's influence and power were at work before Pentecost, though He was not here. It is not the baptism of the Holy Ghost that changes men, but the power of the Ascended Christ coming into men's lives by the Holy Ghost that changes men. The baptism of the Holy Ghost is the evidence of the Ascended Christ. The Holy Ghost works along the line of the Redemption of our Lord, and along that line only. The mighty power of the Holy Ghost brings back to God the experiences of saved men and women, and ulimately, if one may put it so, will bring back to God the experiences of a totally redeemed world, a new heaven and a new earth. PH. 31

If we are perplexed over the question of sanctification, or about the baptism of the Holy Ghost, we ourselves are the reason why we are bothered. PR. 125

HOME

A home that does not acknowledge Jesus Christ as the Head will become exclusive on the line of its own affinities; related to Jesus Christ, the home becomes a centre for all the benedictions of motherhood and sonhood to be expressed to everyone—'an open house for the universe.' PH. 37

HONESTY

Men are kept away from Jesus Christ by a sense of honesty as much as by dishonesty. SA. 83

"Honesty is the best policy"; but immediately you are honest for that reason, you cease to be an honest man. SHH, 29

The test of elemental honesty is the way a man behaves himself in grief and in joy. SHH. 95

HOPE

Jesus Christ did not preach a gospel of hope: He came to re-organise humanity from the inside through a tremendous tragedy in His own life called the Cross, and through that Cross every member of the human race can be reinstated in God's favour and enter into a conscious inheritance of the Atonement. BSG. 64

Hope without faith loses itself in vague speculation, but the hope of the saints transfigured by faith grows not faint, but endures "as seeing Him Who is invisible." CD. VOL. 2, 152

The hope of the saint is the expectation and certainty of human nature transfigured by faith. Let it be borne in mind that hope not transfigured by faith dies. CD. VOL. 2, 152

The character produced by the Patience of Hope is one that exhibits the expulsive power of a new affection. CD. VOL. 2, 153

The hope of the saint gives the true value to the things seen and temporal—in fact the real enjoyment of things seen and temporal is alone possible to the saint because he sees them in their true relationship to God, and the sickening emptiness of the worldly-minded who grasp the things seen and temporal as though they were eternal, is unknown to him. CD. VOL. 2, 153

The patience of hope does not turn men and women into monks and nuns, it gives men and women the right use of this world from another world's standpoint. CD. VOL. 2, 153

When we meet extra goodness we feel amazingly hopeful about everybody, and when we meet extra badness we feel exactly the opposite; but Jesus "knew what was in man," He knew exactly what human beings were like and what they needed; and He saw in them something no one else ever saw—hope for the most degraded. Jesus had a tremendous hopefulness about man. CHI. 96

The only hope for a man lies not in giving him an example of how to behave, but in the preaching of Jesus Christ as the Saviour from *sin*. The heart of every man gets hope when he hears that. DI. 64

If your hopes are being disappointed just now it means that they are being purified. There is nothing noble the human mind has ever hoped for or dreamed of that will not be fulfilled. Don't jump to conclusions too quickly; many things lie unsolved, and the biggest test of all is that God looks as if He were totally indifferent.

Remain spiritually tenacious. GW. 136

Some people believe in an omnipotence with no character, they are shut up in a destiny of hopelessness; Jesus Christ can open the door of release and let them right out. There is no door that man or devil has closed but Jesus Christ can open it; but remember, there is the other side, the door He closes no man can open. IWP. 128

HUMANITY

In many sections of the Christian community to-day Enthusiasm for Humanity is the main characteristic, but it gives a sudden alteration to this point of view when we consider the life of our Lord Jesus Christ, and notice that *His* first obedience was to the will of His Father, not to the needs of Humanity. It is a difficult matter to adjust the relationship of these two callings, but the delicate adjustment is brought about by the Spirit of God, for the Spirit and the Word of God ever put first things first, and the first thing is love to God and obedience to God, and the second, service to humanity. CD. VOL. 2, 140

Every temptation to exalt the human, human experiences, human interests and blessings, will fall short; the only thing that prospers in God's hands in His own word. GW. 94

Jesus Christ is a source of deep offense to the educated trained mind of to-day that does not want Him in any other way than as a Comrade. Many do not want to be devoted to Him, but only to the cause He started. If I am only devoted to the cause of humanity, I will be soon exhausted and come to the point where my love will falter, but if I love Jesus Christ I will serve humanity, though men and women treat me like a door-mat. PH. 146

When men depart from the Bible they call humanity 'God' in differing terms; the use of the term 'God' means nothing to them, God is simply the name given to the general tendencies which further men's interests. This spirit is honeycombing everything, we find it coming into the way we talk of Christian experience; there is creeping in the idea that God and Jesus Christ and the Holy

Ghost are simply meant to bless us, to further our interests. When we come to the New Testament we find exactly the opposite idea, that by regeneration we are brought into such harmony and union with God that we realize with great joy that we are meant to serve His interests. PS. 72

The present error is that humanity utilizes Christianity; if Jesus Christ does not coincide with our line of things, we toss Him overboard; Humanity is on the throne. SA. 114

Jesus Christ mirrors what the human race will be like on the basis of Redemption, a perfect oneness between God and man. SA. 116

HUMAN NATURE

Human nature is earthly, it is sordid, but it is not bad, the thing that makes it bad is sin. BE. 52

There is only one kind of human nature, and that is the human nature of us all, and Jesus Christ by means of His identification with our human nature can give us the disposition that He had. We have to see to it that we habitually work out that disposition through our eyes and ears and tongue, through all the organs of our body and in every detail of our life. BP. 40

When a man is saved his human nature is not altered; human nature is marred by sin, but it is not bad. Deliverance from sin does not mean deliverance from human nature. By regeneration a man is perfectly adjusted to God, now he is required to do a man's bit, viz.: to take his human nature and make it serve the new disposition. CHI. 41

Whether we are six years old or sixty, our human nature is thousands of years old. PR. 76

HUMILITY

There is nothing more awful than conscious humility, it is the most Satanic type of pride. BP. 187

Jesus Christ presented humility as a description of what we shall be unconsciously when we have become rightly related to God and are rightly centred in Jesus Christ. BP. 187

Humility is the exhibition of the Spirit of Jesus Christ, and is the touchstone of saintliness. MFL. 102

It is easier to be a fanatic than a faithful soul, because there is something amazingly humbling, particularly to our religious conceit, in being loyal to God. NKW. 144

Humility is the one stamp of a saint. Beware of the complacency of superiority when God's grace has done anything for you. RTR. 9

Humility is not an ideal, it is the unconscious result of the life being rightly related to God. RTR. 21

The great characteristic of the saint is humility. SSM. 80

HYPOCRISY

Beware of hypocrisy with God, especially if you are in no danger of hypocrisy among men. DI. 45

Jesus Christ taught hypocrisy to His disciples! "But thou, when thou fastest, anoint thy head, and wash thy face, that thou be not seen of men to fast." Don't say you are fasting, or that you spent the night in prayer, wash your face; and never let your dearest friend know what you put yourself through. PH. 57

We can always see sin in another because we are sinners. The reason we see hypocrisy and fraud and unreality in others is because they are all in our own hearts. SSM. 80

I

IDEALS

The great tendency to-day is that we are looking for another teacher. The world is sick of teachers and of ideals, the point is, have we ever lived up to any of our ideals? It is not more ideals we want, but the power to live up to what we know we ought to and don't. It is shallowness, not ability, that makes people say we want more teaching and higher ideals—model Sunday School classes, model Bible classes; it is all model. 'Do this and don't do that,' but where is it being carried out? Jesus Christ does not add one burden to the lives of men; He imparts the power to live up to what we know we ought, that is the meaning of His salvation. HG. 13

If one can put it reverently, unless God Almighty can become concrete and actual, He is nothing to me but a mental abstraction, because an ideal has no power unless it can be realized. SA. 59

The only way in which ideals can be made actual is by a personal relationship to God through Jesus Christ. SHH. 104

IDOLATRY

Whenever we take what God has done and put it in the place of Himself, we instantly become idolaters. NKW. 144

IMAGINATION

It takes a long time to get us out of imagining that unless people see as we do they must be wrong. AUG. 60

There is a domain of our nature which we as Christians do not cultivate much, viz., the domain of the imagination. Almost the only way we use our imagination is in crossing bridges before we come to them. The religion of Jesus embraces every part of our make-up, the intellectual part, the emotional part, no part must be allowed to atrophy, all must be welded into one by the Holy Spirit. DI. 32

Undisciplined imagination is the greatest disturber not only of growth in grace, but of spiritual sanity. RTR. 62

IMITATION

God does not expect us to *imitate* Jesus Christ: He expects us to allow the life of Jesus to be manifested in our mortal flesh. AUG. 14

The book entitled "Imitation of Christ" by Thomas à Kempis is exquisitely beautiful, but fundamentally twisted, because Our Lord's own message of regeneration is ignored. Many a one who has started the imitation of Christ has had to abandon it as hopeless because a strain is put on human nature that human nature cannot begin to live up to. To have attitudes of life without the life itself is a fraud; to have the life itself imitating the best Pattern of that life is normal and right. AUG. 63

The life of Jesus Christ is made ours not by imitation, but by means of His death on Calvary and by our reception of His Spirit. BE. 107

"He shall glorify *Me*," said Jesus. The Holy Spirit does not glorify Christ-likeness, because Christ-likeness can be imitated; He glorifies Christ. It is impossible to imitate Jesus Christ. HGM. 21

We cannot live as Jesus lived by trying to imitate Him. IWP. 21

Emulation and imitation both centre around whatever is our ideal. When once we see Jesus, it is good-bye to all ideals; we cannot have them back again, nor do we want them back again if we are true to Him. We have to keep the one Lodestar, the Lord Jesus Christ, in front and be absorbingly taken up with Him; consequently we have to put ourselves through discipline and fast from every other type of emulation. MFL. 72

Sanctification means the impartation to us and through us of the Lord Jesus Christ, His patience, His purity, His holiness. It is not that Jesus Christ enables us to imitate Him; not that the power of God is in us and we try our best and fail, and try again; but that the very virtues of Jesus Christ are manifested in our mortal flesh. OBH. 39

All the qualities of a godly life are characteristic of the life of God; you cannot imitate the life of God unless you have it, then the imitation is not conscious, but the unconscious manifestation of the real thing. OPG. 29

The life of Jesus is to be made ours, not by our imitation, not by our climbing,

but by means of His Death. It is not admiration for holiness, nor aspirations after holiness, but *attainment* of holiness, and this is ours from God, not from any ritual of imitation. PH. 5

Sanctification is an impartation, a gift, not an imitation. Sanctification means "Christ formed in you." Jesus gives us the life inherent in Himself. PH. 226

We cannot get into the life of Jesus by imitation, by trying to do the right thing, because something in us will not do it. We can only enter in by identification with His death. PR. 25

Many of us are imitators of other people; we do Christian work because someone has asked us to do it. We must receive our ministry, which is to testify the gospel of the grace of God, from Jesus Christ Himself, not from other Christians. PR. 56

We talk about imitating Jesus, but isn't it highly absurd! Before we have taken three steps, we come across lust, pride envy, jealousy, hatred, malice, anger—things that never were in Him, and we get disheartened and say there is nothing in it. If Jesus Christ came to *teach* the human race only, He had better have stayed away. But if we know Him first as Saviour by being born again, we know that He did not come to teach merely: He came to *make* us what He teaches we should be; He came to *make* us sons of God. PR. 81

IMPULSE

If you take every impression as a call of the Spirit of God, you will end in hallucinations. BP. 51

Every impulse must wed itself to the express statements of the Bible, otherwise they will lead astray. DI. 7

INCARNATION

In the Incarnation we see the amalgam of the Divine and the human. Pure gold cannot be used as coin, it is too soft; in order to make gold serviceable for use it must be mixed with an alloy. The pure gold of the Divine is of no use in human affairs; there must be an alloy, and the alloy does not stand for sin, but for that which makes the Divine serviceable for use. God Almighty is nothing but a mental abstraction to me unless He can become actual, and the revelation of the New Testament is that God did become actual: "the Word was made flesh". Jesus Christ was not pure Divine, He was unique: Divine and human. BE. 51

God may be a mere mental abstraction; He may be spoken of in terms of culture or poetry or philosophy, but He has not the slightest meaning for us until He becomes incarnate. BE. 104

By the sheer force of the tremendous integrity of His Incarnation, Jesus Christ hewed a way straight through sin and death and hell right back to God, more than conqueror over all. BP. 29

The whole purpose of the Incarnation is the Redemption, viz., to overcome the disasters of the fall and produce a being more noble than the original Adam. BP. 34

Jesus Christ became Incarnate for one purpose, to make a way back to God that man might stand before Him as he was created to do, the friend and lover of God Himself. BSG. 14

Jesus Christ was God Incarnate for one purpose, not to reveal God to us, that is simply one of the outcomes of the Incarnation; the one great purpose of His coming was to bring back the whole human race into oneness with God. BSG. 46

. . . our Lord Incarnate distinctly subjected Himself to limitations. CD. VOL. 2, 147

. . . Jesus Christ is the Worthy One not because He was God Incarnate, but because He was God Incarnate on the human plane. CHI. 119

It takes God Incarnate to wash feet properly. It takes God Incarnate to do anything properly. GW. 9

The great revelation the Bible gives of God is the opposite of what we are apt to imagine Him to be, it is a revelation not of the majestic power of God, but of the fact that God was 'manifested in the flesh'; that God became Incarnate as a Baby in the Person of His Son. That is the last reach of Self-limitation. GW. 30

We may talk about God as the Almighty, the All-powerful, but He means nothing to us unless He has become incarnated and touched human life where we touch it; and the revelation of Redemption is that God's Thought did express itself in Jesus Christ, that God became manifest on the plane on which we live. HGM. 95

The purpose of the Incarnation was not to reveal the beauty and nobility of human nature, but in order to remove sin from human nature. MFL. 104

In the Incarnation the Eternal God was so majestically small that He was not detected, the world never saw Him. NKW. 98

The tremendous revelation of Christianity is not the Fatherhood of God, but the Babyhood of God—God became the weakest thing in His own creation, and in flesh and blood He levered it back to where it was intended to be. No one helped Him; it was done absolutely by God manifest in human flesh. God has undertaken not only to repair the damage, but in Jesus Christ the human race is put in a better condition than when it was originally designed. It is necessary to understand these things if you are to be able to battle for your faith. SA. 27

The first great moral effect of Jesus Christ's coming into the world is that He saves His people from their sins; not simply that He saves them from hell and puts them right for heaven; that is the finding of a Protestant evangel, not the New Testament view, and is only one phase of salvation. SA. 69

The doctrine of the Incarnation means that God became the weakest thing in His own creation, a Baby. SA. 69

The great purpose of Jesus Christ's coming is that He might put man on a line where sin in him can be destroyed. SA. 69

Jesus Christ is God-Man. God in Essence cannot come anywhere near us. Almighty God does not matter to me, He is in the clouds. To be of any use to me, He must come down to the domain in which I live; and I do not live in the clouds but on the earth. The doctrine of the Incarnation is that God did come down into our domain. The Wisdom of God, the Word of God, the exact expression of God, was manifest in the flesh. That is the great doctrine of the New Testament—dust and Deity made one. The pure gold of Deity is of no use to us unless it is amalgamated in the right alloy, viz. the pure Divine working on the basis of the pure human: God and humanity one, as in Our Lord Jesus Christ. There is only one God to the Christian, and His name is Jesus Christ, and in Him we see mirrored what the human race will be like on the basis of Redemption—a perfect oneness between God and man. Jesus Christ has the power of reproducing Himself by regeneration, the power of introducing into us His own heredity, so that dust and Deity again become one. SHH. 9

An Almighty, Incomprehensible, Incognoscible Being does not amount to anything to me. It is when God becomes Incarnate that we see the right amalgam, dust and Deity made one, human flesh presenced with Divinity. That is the meaning of the Incarnation, and Jesus Christ claims He can do it for any one of us. Man cannot be pure Deity and he cannot be pure dust; he has to have the right alloy—dust and Deity, made one by drudgery, and this produces the type of life with the right balance. SHH. 98

INDEPENDENCE

Whenever God touches sin it is independence that is touched and that awakens resentment in the human heart. Independence must be blasted clean out, there must be no such thing left, only freedom, which is very different. Freedom is the ability not to insist on my rights, but to see that God gets His. DI. 62

Independence is not strength but unrealised weakness, and is the very essence of sin. There was no independence in our Lord, the great characteristic of His life was submission to His Father. MFL. 72

INDIVIDUALITY

We talk about 'the struggling mass of humanity'—there is no such thing, the mass is made up of separate individuals. The danger of thinking of people in the mass is that you forget they are human beings, each one an absolutely solitary life. BE. 18

INDIVIDUALITY is a smaller term than Personality. We speak of an individual animal, an individual man, an individual thing. An individual man is one by himself, he takes up so much space, requires so many cubic feet of air, etc. PERSONALITY is infinitely more. Possibly the best illustration we can use is that of a lamp. A lamp unlighted will illustrate individuality; a lighted lamp will illustrate personality. The lighted lamp takes up no more room, but the light permeates far and wide; so the influence of personality goes far beyond that of individuality. "Ye are the light of the world," said our Lord. Individually we do not take up much room, but our influence is far beyond our calculation. When we use the term 'personality,' we use the biggest mental conception we have, that is why we call God a Person, because the word 'person' has the biggest import we know. We do not call God an individual; we call God a Person. He may be a great deal more, but at least He must be that. It is necessary to remember this when the personality of God is denied and He is taken to be a tendency. If God is only a tendency, He is much less than we are. Our personality is always too big for us. BP. 151

The thing that makes me feel I am different from 'the common herd' never came from God: I am not different. Remember, the same stuff that makes the criminal makes the saint. DI. 63

Individuality is the characteristic of the natural man; personality is the characteristic of the spiritual man. KNW. 101

INFLUENCE

The people who influence us are those who have stood unconsciously for the right thing, they are like the stars and the lilies, and the joy of God flows through them all the time. HGM. 49

The only influence that is to tell in a servant of God is God. Let people think what they like about you, but be careful that the last thought they get is God. IWP. 31

We are all so made that we can yield to an influence that is brought to bear upon us, and if we keep ourselves long enough under the right influences, slowly and surely we shall find that we can form habits that will develop us along the line of those influences. MFL. 36

The radiating influence from one person rightly related to God is incalculable; he may not say much, but you feel different, the pressure has gone, you are in contact with one who is on a different plane. PH. 217

It is the most natural thing to be like the person you live with most, therefore live most with Jesus Christ; be absorbingly taken up with Him. RTR. 75

A river touches places of which its source knows nothing, and Jesus says if we have received of His fullness, however small the visible measure of our lives, out of us will flow the rivers that will bless to the uttermost parts of the earth. We have nothing to do with the out-flow—"This is the work of God that ye *believe...*" God rarely allows a soul to see how great a blessing he is. RTR. 91

The people who influence us are not those who set out to do it, they are prigs; but the folk who have a real relationship to God and who never bother whether they are being of use; these are a continual assistance. SHH. 39

The thing that influences us most is not the thing we give most time to, but the thing that springs from our own personal relationship, that is the prime motive that dominates us. SSM. 108

INIQUITY

Beware of iniquity, which means conjuring yourself out of the straight; finding out reasons why you did not do what you know you should have done. The term "iniquity" is used only of the people of God. To "shed just blood" refers to more than actual murder. The Bible never deals with proportionate sin; according to the Bible an impure thought is as bad as adultery; a covetous thought is as bad as a theft. It takes a long education in the things of God before we believe that is true. CHI. 71

If we do not know the tremendous depths of possible iniquity in our hearts, it is because we have never been scrutinized by the Holy Ghost; but let Him turn His searchlight right down to the inmost recesses, and the best of us are shuddering on our faces before God. When the Holy Ghost does scrutinize us (and He will not do it if we do not want Him to, this is the day of our option; a time is coming when He will do it whether we want Him to or not, when we will be only too glad to creep anywhere out of the sight of God whose eyes search as a flame of fire), He reveals not only a depth of possible iniquity

that makes us shudder, but a height of holiness of which we never dreamed. SHL. 49

Iniquity means turning out of the straight. Whenever anything begins to turn you out of the straight, stop and get it put right, no matter what else suffers. If you don't, you will grow in iniquity, and if you grow in iniquity you will call iniquity integrity; sensuality spirituality, and ultimately the devil, God. SHL. 64

INNOCENCE

Innocence means the absence of legal guilt. As long as Adam obeyed God he was in this state of innocence; God placed him in an external setting so that he might transform his innocence into moral character by a series of choices. It was to be a natural progress of development, not from evil to good, but from the natural to the spiritual. BE. 13

No man or woman has any right to be innocent. God demands of men and women that they be pure and virtuous. Innocence is the characteristic of a child, but it is an ignorant and blameworthy thing for a man or woman not to be reconciled to the fact that there is sin. PH. 194

Every child born of natural generation is innocent, but it is the innocence of ignorance. Naturally we are in an impaired state, and when our innocence is turned into knowledge we find to our humiliation how tremendously impaired it is. It is the ignorant innocence of determinedly being without the knowledge of God. It is safer to trust God's revelation than our own innocence. SHL. 63

INSIGHT

Spiritual insight is in accordance with the development of heart-purity. DI. 52

Spiritual insight is not for the purpose of making us realize we are better than other people, but in order that our responsibility might be added to. HG. 12

The insight that relates us to God arises from purity of heart, not from clearness of intellect. MFL. 23

INSPIRATION

Conscious inspiration is mercifully rare or we would make inspiration our god. DI. 51

INTEGRITY

Integrity means unimpaired purity of heart. SSM. 41

Jesus Christ is not teaching ordinary integrity, but supernormal integrity, a likeness to our Father in heaven. SSM. 65

INTELLECT

Jesus Christ lived in the moral domain and, in a sense, the intellect is of no use there. Intellect is not a guide, but an instrument. BFB. 35

If we can know God by means of our intellect, then Jesus Christ's claim to reveal God is a farce, and the Redemption nonsense. BFB. 96

The only reality in life is moral reality, not intellectual or aesthetic. Religion based on intellectualism becomes purely credal, Jesus Christ is not needed in it. The intellect does not get us at Reality, neither do the emotions alone, but conscience does, as soon as it relates

itself to these two. The basis of things is not rational. BFB. 96

Every kind of intellectual excellence is a snare of Satan unless the spirit of the man has been renewed by the incoming of the Spirit of God. A man's intellect may give him noble ideas and power to express them through his soul in language, but it does not give him power to carry them into action. The charge of idolatry is very apt here. BP. 60

Mere intellectuality leads to bloodlessness and passionlessness, to stoicism and unreality. The more merely intellectual a person becomes the more hopelessly useless he is, until he degenerates into a mere criticizing faculty, passing the strangest and wildest verdicts on life, on the Bible, and on our Lord. BP. 103

. . . we cannot penetrate the things of God and understand them by our intelligence; the only way we can understand the things of God is by the Spirit of God. BP. 211

We understand the things of the world by our natural intelligence, and we understand the things of God by "the spirit which is of God." BP. 212

Whenever the Holy Spirit gets us into a corner, He never convinces our intellect; He is busy with the will which expresses itself in our intellect. HG. 107

Intellect is never first in spiritual life. We are not born again by thinking about it, we are born again by the power of God. HGM. 28

Definitions can only be given of things that are perfectly understood and are inferior to the mind that defines them. It is absurd to try and put God into a definition; if I can define God I am greater than God. Intellectual definition is of no use whatever in the spiritual life. HGM. 143

If our intellectual curiosity pushes the barriers further than God has seen fit to open, our moral character will get out of hand and we shall have pain that God cannot bless, suffering from which He cannot protect us. "The way of transgressors is hard." IWP. 126

The intellect only looks for things that are seen and actual, draws its inferences from these and becomes pessimistic and loses heart. PH. 155

Intellect has never changed a man as yet; it may have made him look different, but it will not have altered him. If intellect is the way to get to God, what about the men who have no intellect? There would be whole streaks of man's life and experience to blot out. Or if I can get at God by a fine sense of beauty only what about the men who have no sense of beauty? Some men have a magnificent heredity, while others are practically damned into existence. Rationalism is not the basis; my reason and my intellect are instruments, but there is something deeper about every human life than can be fathomed by intellect. SA. 26

INTERPRETATION

The Holy Spirit never witnesses to a clever interpretation; the exposition the Holy Spirit will witness to is always amazingly and profoundly simple; you feel, 'That certainly is God's truth.' AUG. 62

Beware of interpreters of the Scriptures who take any other context than our Lord Jesus Christ. AUG. 105

Beware of interpreting Scripture in order to make it suit a pre-arranged doctrine of your own. DI. 9

We are never left with a revelation without an interpretation of it. A revelation fact needs a corresponding revelation to interpret it. Just as Jesus Christ is the final revelation of God, so the Bible is the final revelation interpreting Him. Our Lord Jesus Christ (The Word of God) and the Bible (the accompanying revelation) stand or fall together, they can never be separated without fatal results. GW. 34

It is perilously possible to mistake the exposition of the truth for the truth; to run away with the idea that because we are able to expound these things we are living them too. OBH. 34

The delay in interpretation depends on our willingness to obey. Obedience is always the secret of understanding. PH. 219

INTROSPECTION

It is never safe to do much introspection, but it is ruinous to do none. Introspection can never satisfy us, yet introspection is not wrong, it is right, because it is the only way we discover that we need God. It is the introspective power in us that is made alert by conviction of sin. HG. 107

If you examine yourself too much, you unfit yourself for life. There is a stage in life when introspection is necessary, but if it is pushed too far a man becomes abnormally hypersensitive, either in conceit or grovelling. SHH. 98

We are only safe in taking an estimate of ourselves from our Creator, not from our own introspection. But although introspection cannot profoundly satisfy us, we must not conclude that introspection is wrong. Introspection is right, because it is the only way we shall discover that we need God. Introspection without God leads to insanity. The people who have no tendency to introspect are described as 'dead in trespasses and sins', quite happy, quite contented, quite moral, all they want is easily within their own grasp; but they are dead to the world to which Jesus Christ belongs, and it takes His voice and His Spirit to awaken them. SHL. 60

INTUITION

Intuition in the natural world is the power to see things at a glance without reasoning, and the Spirit of God develops that power in the saint. The accuracy of intuitive judgment is in proportion to the moral culture of the one who judges. BE. 40

Keep the intuitive secret life clear and right with God at all costs; never blunt intuition. Whenever a man comes into personal contact with Jesus Christ he knows at once whether he is good or bad; he does not reason it out, he knows it intuitively. BE. 41

Intuition is the power to sense things without reasoning, and is a better guide than what is stated explicitly; but there is something infinitely more satisfactory—the entrance of the Holy Spirit into a man at new birth enabling him to see the Kingdom of God and to enter into it. SSY. 11

ISRAEL

God created them from Abraham to be His servants until through them every nation came to know who Jehovah was. They mistook the election of God's pur-

pose to be the election of God's favouritism, and the story of their distress is due to their determination to use themselves for purposes other than God's. To this day they survive miraculously, the reason for their survival is the purpose of God to be fulfilled through them. OPG. 39

God created a certain nation from the loins of one man, to be His own people; they were not to be like the other nations of the world, but to be the bond slaves of Jehovah until every nation came to know God SHH. 113

God created the people known as Israel for one purpose, to be the servant of Jehovah until through them every nation came to know Who Jehovah was. The nation created for the service of Jehovah failed to fulfil God's predestination for it; then God called out a remnant, and the remnant failed; then out of the remnant came One Who succeeded, the One Whom we know as the Lord Jesus Christ. The Saviour of the world came of this nation. He is called 'the Servant of God' because He expresses exactly the creative purpose of God for the historic people of God. Through that one Man the purpose of God for the individual, for the chosen nation, and for the whole world, is to be fulfilled. It is through Him that we are made 'a royal priesthood'. SSY. 101

There were no nations until after the flood. After the flood the human race was split up into nations, and God called off one stream of the human race in Abraham, and created a nation out of that one man. The Old Testament is not a history of the nations of the world, but the history of that one nation. In secular history Israel is disregarded as being merely a miserable horde of slaves, and justly so from the standpoint of the historian. The nations to which the Bible pays little attention are much finer to read about, but they have no importance in the Redemptive purpose of God. His purpose was the creation of a nation to be His bondslave, that through that nation all the other nations should come to know Him. The idea that Israel was a magnificently developed type of nation is a mistaken one. Israel was a despised, and a despisable nation, continually turning away from God into idolatry; but nothing ever altered the purpose of God for the nation. The despised element is always a noticeable element in the purpose of God. When the Saviour of the world came, He came of that despised nation; He Himself was 'despised and rejected of men,' and in all Christian enterprise there is this same despised element, 'things that are despised hath God chosen.' SSY. 104

God elected a certain nation to be His bondslave, and through that nation a knowledge of His salvation is to come to all the world. The history of that nation is a record of awful idolatry and backsliding, they remained true neither to God's prophets nor to God Himself; but in spite of everything the fulfilment of God's purpose for the nation of His choice is certain. The election of the nation by God was not for the salvation of individuals; the elect nation was to be the instrument of salvation to the whole world. The story of their distress is due entirely to their deliberate determination to use themselves for a purpose other than God's. SSY. 105

J

JESUS CHRIST

In presenting Jesus Christ never present Him as a miraculous Being Who came down from heaven and worked miracles and Who was not related to life as we are; that is not the Gospel Christ. The Gospel Christ is the Being Who came down to earth and lived our life and was possessed of a frame like ours. He became Man in order to show the relationship man was to hold to God, and by His death and resurrection He can put any man into that relationship. Jesus Christ is the last word in human nature. AUG. 44

"We must look upon Christ as a real historic figure, a real man, not a magical prodigy. He shared in the life of limited man, the life of His age and the life of His land. The limitation of His consciousness was no limitation of His moral power but its exercise." AUG. 45

Who is Jesus Christ? God exalted in Christ crucified. AUG. 56

Jesus Christ is not an individual iota of a man; He is the whole of the human race centered before God in one Person, He is God and Man in one. Man is lifted up to God in Christ, and God is brought down to man in Christ. Jesus Christ nowhere said, 'He that hath seen *man* hath seen the Father'; but He did say that God was manifest in human flesh in His own Person that He might become the generating centre for the same manifestation in every human being, and the place of His travail pangs is the incarnation, Calvary, and the Resurrection. AUG. 70

Jesus Christ was not a Being Who became Divine, He was the Godhead Incarnated; He emptied Himself of His glory in becoming Incarnate. Never separate the Incarnation from the Atonement. The Incarnation was not meant to enable God to realize Himself, but that man might realize God and gain readjustment to Him. Jesus Christ became Man for one purpose, that He might put away sin and bring the whole human race back into the oneness of identification. AUG. 70

The character of Jesus Christ is exhibited in the New Testament, and it appeals to us all. He lived His life straight down in the ordinary amalgam of human life, and He claims that the character He manifested is possible for any man if he will come in by the door He provides. AUG. 81

The Christian revelation is not that Jesus Christ represents God to me, but that He *is* God. If Jesus Christ is not God, then we have no God. I am an agnostic; that is why I am a Christian. AUG. 81

Jesus Christ is a Fact; He is the most honourable and the holiest Man, and two things necessarily follow—first, He is the least likely to be deceived about Himself, second, He is least likely to deceive anyone else. AUG. 82

Jesus Christ never asks anyone to define his position or to understand a creed, but—'Who am I to you?' . . . Jesus Christ makes the whole of human destiny depend on a man's relationship to Himself. AUG. 82

We are taken up with interesting details; Jesus Christ was not. His insulation was on the inside, not the outside; His dominating interest was hid with God. His kingdom was on the inside, consequently He took the ordinary social life of His time in a most unobtrusive way. His life externally was oblivious of details, He spent His time with publicans and sinners and did the things that were apparently un-religious. But one thing He never did—He never contaminated His inner kingdom. AUG. 85

The Great Life is to believe that Jesus Christ is not a fraud. AUG. 114

Jesus Christ claims that He can do in human nature what human nature cannot do for itself, viz., "Destroy the works of the devil", remove the wrong heredity and put in the right one. He can satisfy the last aching abyss of the human heart, He can put the key into our hands which will give the solution to every problem that ever stretched before our minds. He can soothe by His pierced hands the wildest sorrow with which Satan or sin or death ever racked humanity. There is nothing for which Jesus Christ is not amply sufficient and over which He cannot make us more than conquerors. BE. 111

On the ground of His absolute, not coercive, authority, every man recognizes sooner or later that Jesus Christ stands easily first. BFB. 90

The writers try to prove that Jesus is not mad according to the standards of this world; but He is mad, absolutely mad, and there is no apology needed for saying it. Either the modern attitude to things must alter, or it must pronounce Jesus Christ mad. BP. 160

Jesus Christ is not a Being with two personalities; He is *Son of God*—the exact expression of Almighty God, and *Son of Man*—the presentation of God's normal Man. BSG. 9

Jesus Christ had a two fold personality: He was Son of God revealing what God is like, and Son of Man revealing what man is to be like. BSG. 77

Jerusalem and Jesus! What a contrast! With what an amazed stare of contempt the personal powers of Jerusalem confronted Jesus, the despised and rejected! Yet He was their Peace for time and eternity, and the things that belonged to their peace were all connected with Him. CD. VOL. 1, 124

In the Name that is above every name we pray that this year may be the year of the First and the Last, the Beginning and the End, Our Lord Jesus Christ. CD. VOL. 1, 142

It is so human and so like us to be attracted by Jesus, to be fascinated by His life; but what a sorrowful revulsion many of us experience when His own words repulse us and blow out the fires of our emotion; and turning away sorrowful, we leave Jesus alone. CD. VOL. 2, 72

Jesus Christ always speaks from the source of things, consequently those who deal only with the surface find Him an offence. CD. VOL. 2, 74

What weakness! Our Lord lived thirty years in Nazareth with His brethren who did not believe on Him; He lived three years of popularity, scandal and hatred; fascinated a dozen illiterate men who at the end of three years all forsook Him and fled; and finally He was taken by the powers that be and crucified outside the city wall. Judged from every standpoint save the standpoint of the Spirit of God, His life was a most manifest expression of weakness, and the idea would be strong to those in the pagan world who thought anything about Him that surely now He and His crazy tale were stamped out.

CD. VOL. 2, 144

Jesus Christ was not a Man who twenty centuries ago lived on this earth for thirty-three years and was crucified; He was God Incarnate, manifested at one point of history. All before looked forward to that point; all since look back to it. The presentation of this fact produces what no other fact in the whole of history ever could produce, viz. : the miracle of God at work in human souls. CHI. 33

The revelation of the Deity of Christ does not come first to a man's intellect, but to his heart and life, and he says with amazement, "Thou art the Christ, the Son of the living God." CHI. 46

There have been great military geniuses, intellectual giants, geniuses of statesmen, but these only exercise influence over a limited number of men; Jesus Christ exercises unlimited sway over all men because He is the altogether Worthy One. CHI. 120

In the days of His flesh Jesus Christ exhibited this Divine paradox of the Lion and the Lamb. He was the Lion in majesty, rebuking the winds and demons:

He was the Lamb in meekness, "who when He was reviled, reviled not again." He was the Lion in power, raising the dead: He was the Lamb in patience—who was "brought as a lamb to the slaughter, and as a sheep before her shearers is dumb, so He openeth not His mouth." He was the Lion in authority, "Ye have heard that it hath been said . . . *but I say unto you . . .*": He was the Lamb in gentleness, "Suffer the little children to come unto Me . . . and He took them up in His arms, put His hand upon them and blessed them."

In our personal lives Jesus Christ proves Himself to be all this—He is the Lamb to expiate our sins, to lift us out of condemnation and plant within us His own heredity of holiness: He is the Lion to rule over us, so that we gladly say, "the government of this life shall be upon His shoulders." And what is true in individual life is to be true also in the universe at large. The time is coming when the Lion of the Tribe of Judah shall reign, and when "the kingdoms of this world shall become the kingdoms of our Lord, and of His Christ." CHI. 121

Never attempt dexterously to show how altogether human Jesus is; allow the facts of Bible revelation to show you the absolute difference between ourselves and Jesus Christ, and because of this difference He is able to lift us up into likeness with Himself, to conform us to His own image. GW. 32

Jesus Christ is not a mere sympathizer, He is a Saviour, and the only One, 'for neither is there any other name under heaven, that is given among men wherein we must be saved.' GW. 72

Jesus Christ is not a sympathizer, neither is He a social reformer, He is unique—the Saviour of the world. The Atonement is God speaking to men in heart-breaking agony and long-suffering patience that they might be reconciled to His way of salvation. GW. 73

The enemies of Christ are triumphant, Christianity is a failure, they say; and the Church of God herself looks on in pain at the shortcomings in her midst. But lo, at length from the very heart of the shadows appears the majestic Figure of Jesus; His countenance is as the sun shineth in His strength, around those wounds in Brow and Side and Hands and Feet—those wounds which shelter countless thousands of broken hearts—are healing rays; in that glorious Figure meets every beauty inconceivable to the imagination of man. GW. 146

The only way to get out of our smiling complacency about salvation and sanctification is to look at Jesus Christ for two minutes and then read Matthew v. 43–48 and see Who He tells us we are to be like, God Almighty, and every piece of smiling spiritual conceit will be knocked out of us for ever, and the one dominant note of the life will be Jesus Christ first, Jesus Christ second, and Jesus Christ third, and our own whiteness nowhere. Never look to your own whiteness; look to Jesus and get power to live as He wants, look away for one second and all goes wrong. HG. 17

We can never take any one virtue and say Jesus Christ was the representative of that virtue; we cannot speak of Jesus Christ being a holy Man or a great Man or a good Man; Jesus Christ cannot be summed up in terms of natural virtues, but only in terms of the supernatural. HG. 42

Never take Jesus Christ as the Representative of God: He *is* God or there is none. If Jesus Christ is not God manifest in the flesh, we know nothing whatever

about God; we are not only agnostic, but hopeless. But if Jesus Christ is what He says He is, then He is God to me. HGM. 38

There is an amazing sanity in Jesus Christ that shakes the foundations of death and hell, no panic, absolute dominant mastery over everything—such a stupendous mastery that He let men take His strength from Him: "He was crucified through weakness," that was the acme of Godlike strength. IWP. 98

Jesus Christ is the last word on God, on sin and death, on heaven and hell; the last word on every problem that human life has to face. IWP. 125

Jesus Christ is not a social reformer; He came to alter us first, and if there is any social reform to be done on earth, we must do it. IYA. 14

Jesus Christ is the love of God incarnated. LG. 68

Imagine Jesus being jaded in the life of God! There was never anything jaded about Him. When we are jaded there is always a reason, and it is either the temper of our mind towards another or towards God. MFL. 83

Jesus Christ stands outside the majority of our lives in the usual run because He deals with the fundamentals; we do not, we deal with the external actuals, and it is only when the external actuals are ploughed into by sorrow or bereavement that we begin to find there is only one Reality—our Lord Jesus Christ, and only one Book that brings light. PH. 151

If men and Satan could only get rid of Jesus Christ, they would never be involved in perplexity, never be upset. Jesus put it very clearly: "If I had not come and spoken unto them, they had not had sin: but now they have no cloke for their sin." The greatest annoyance to Satan and to humanity is Jesus Christ. PS. 72

You cannot work Jesus Christ into any system of thinking. If you could keep Him out, everything could be explained. The world could be explained by evolution, but you cannot fit Jesus Christ into the theory of evolution. Jesus Christ is an annoyance to Satan, a thorn in the side of the world at large, an absolute distress to sin in the individual. If we could crucify Him and stamp Him out, the annoyance would cease. PS. 73

Jesus Christ was born *into* this world, not *from* it. He came into history from the outside of history; He did not evolve out of history. Our Lord's birth was an advent; He did not come from the human race, He came into it from above. Jesus Christ is not the best human being, He is a Being Who cannot be accounted for by the human race at all. He is God Incarnate, not man becoming God, but God coming into human flesh, coming into it from the outside. His Life is the Highest and the Holiest entering in at the lowliest door. Our Lord entered history by the Virgin Mary. PR. 29

Jesus Christ did not come to do anything less than to bear away the sin of the world, that is His vocation as Son of Man. PR. 48

Jesus Christ was not a Being Who became Divine, He was the Godhead Incarnated. PR. 130

God has to rebuke us for our flippant, unthinking familiarity with Jesus Christ; we have forgotten Who He is. RTR. 10

A man is never the same after he has seen Jesus Christ. We are to be judged by our immortal moments. RTR. 19

Jesus Christ is God manifest in the flesh, not a Being with two personalities; He is Son of God (the exact expression of Almighty God) and Son of Man (the presentation of God's normal man). As Son of God He reveals what God is like; as Son of Man He mirrors what the human race will be like on the basis of Redemption—a perfect oneness between God and man. SA. 35

There is only one God to the Christian, and His name is Jesus Christ; any other idea of God is a matter of temperament or of refinement. The Christian is an avowed agnostic; all he knows about God has been accepted through the revelation of Jesus Christ, and to him there is only one name for the God he worships, viz. Jesus Christ. SA. 37

Jesus Christ effaced the God-head in Himself so effectually that men without the Spirit of God despised Him. SA. 50

To-day we have all kinds of Christs in our midst, the Christ of Labour and of Socialism; the Mind-cure Christ and the Christ of Christian Science and of Theosophy; but they are all abstract Christs. The one great sign of Christ is not with them—there are no marks of the Atonement about these Christs. Jesus Christ is the only One with the marks of atonement on Him, the wounded hands and feet, a symbol of the Redeemer Who is to come again. There will be signs and wonders wrought by these other Christs, and great problems may be solved, but the greatest problem of all, the problem of sin, will not be touched. SA. 57

He failed apparently in everything He came to do; all His disciples forsook Him, He was crucified, and yet He talked of His joy. The joy of Our Lord lay in doing what the Father sent Him to do. His purpose was not to succeed, but to fulfil the design of His coming—"For I am come down from heaven not to do Mine own will, but the will of Him that sent me." SHH. 35

The coming of Jesus Christ is not a peaceful thing, it is a disturbing, an overwhelming thing. SHL. 43

If all Jesus Christ came to do was to upset me, make me unfit for my work, upset my friendships and my life, produce disturbance and misery and distress, then I wish He had never come. But that is not all He came to do. He came to lift us up to 'the heavenly places' where He is Himself. The whole claim of the Redemption of Jesus is that He can satisfy the last aching abyss of the human soul, not hereafter only, but here and now. SHL. 45

'It is enough for the disciple that he be as his Master.' At first sight this looks like an enormous honour: to be 'as his Master' is marvellous glory—is it? Look at Jesus as He was when He was here, it was anything but glory. He was easily ignorable, saving to those who knew Him intimately; to the majority of men He was 'as a root out of a dry ground'. For thirty years He was obscure, then for three years He went through popularity, scandal, and hatred; He succeeded in gathering a handful of fishermen as disciples, one of whom betrayed Him, one denied Him, and all forsook Him; and He says, 'It is enough for you to be like that.' The idea of evangelical success,

Church prosperity, civilized manifestation, does not come into it at all. When we fulfil the conditions of spiritual life we become unobtrusively real. SHL. 105

Jesus Christ is the expression of the wisdom of God. SSM. 48

If we have never been hurt by a statement of Jesus, it is questionable whether we have ever really heard Him speak. Jesus Christ has no tenderness whatever towards anything that is ultimately going to ruin a man for the service of God. If the Spirit of God brings to our mind a word of the Lord that hurts, we may be perfectly certain there is something He wants to hurt to death. SSY. 50

If the significance of Christ as the propitiation for sins is limitless, the domain to which His propitiation applies is limitless also. Sinfulness against Christ is as limitless as the propitiation. SSY. 143

Jesus Christ came to do what no human being can do, He came to redeem men, to alter their disposition, to plant in them the Holy Spirit, to make them new creatures. Christianity is not the obliteration of the old, but the transfiguration of the old. Jesus Christ did not come to teach men to be holy: He came to make men holy. His teaching has no meaning for us unless we enter into His life by means of His death. The Cross is the great central point. SSY. 154

Jesus Christ was not a recluse. He did not cut Himself off from society, He was amazingly in and out among the ordinary things of life; but He was disconnected fundamentally from it all. He was not aloof, but He lived in another world. His life was so social that men called Him a glutton and a wine-bibber, a friend of publicans and sinners. His detachments were inside towards God. SSY. 164

Men's minds will always assent that Jesus Christ is right,—why? Because Jesus Christ is Incarnate Reason. There is something in Jesus Christ that appeals to every man, no matter what condition he is in. If once Jesus Christ is brought into contact with a man, let that man seem to us dead and indifferent, destitute of anything like goodness—let him come in contact with Jesus Christ by the Holy Spirit, and you will instantly see that he can grasp something about Him in a way we cannot understand unless we know the Holy Spirit. WG. 24

So many people try to explain things about Jesus Christ, but no worker need ever try to do that. You cannot explain things about Jesus Christ, rely on the Holy Spirit and He will explain Jesus to the soul. WG. 25

People say that it is so hard to bring Jesus Christ and present Him before the lives of men to-day. Of course it is, it is so hard that it is impossible except by the power of the indwelling Holy Ghost. WG. 38

If all Jesus Christ can do is to tell a man he has to cheer up when he is miserable; if all the worker for God can do is to tell a man he has no business to have the 'blues'—I say if that is all Jesus Christ's religion can do, then it is a failure. But the wonder of our Lord Jesus Christ is just this, that you can face Him with any kind of men or women you like, and He can cure them and put them into a right relationship with God. WG. 60

JOY

The Bible talks plentifully about joy, but it nowhere speaks about a 'happy' Christian. Happiness depends on what happens; joy does not. Remember, Jesus Christ had joy, and He prays "that they might have My joy fulfilled in themselves." BP. 115

A man never knows joy until he gets rightly related to God. Satan's claim is that he can make a man satisfied without God, but all he succeeds in doing is to give happiness and pleasure, never joy. BSG. 54

The joy of Jesus was the absolute Self-surrender and Self-sacrifice of Himself to the will of His Father, the joy of doing exactly what the Father sent Him to do. "I delight to do Thy will," and He prays that His disciples may have this joy fulfilled in themselves. BSG. 55

Oh the joy of that life with God and in God and for God! It takes a sharp discipline for many of us to learn that 'my goal is God Himself, not joy, nor peace, nor even blessing, but Himself my God'. GW. 121

If we have no delight in God it is because we are too far away from the childlike relationship to Him. If there is an internal struggle on, get it put right and you will experience delight in Him. HG. 35

Joy is the great note all through the Bible. We have the notion of joy that arises from good spirits or good health, but the miracle of the joy of God has nothing to do with a man's life or his circumstances or the condition he is in. Jesus does not come to a man and say 'Cheer up,' He plants within a man the miracle of the joy of God's own nature. HGM. 48

The stronghold of the Christian faith is *the joy of God,* not *my joy in God.*
HGM. 48

The miracle of the Christian life is that God can give a man joy in the midst of external misery, a joy which gives him power to work until the misery is removed. HGM. 48

Joy is different from happiness, because happiness depends on what happens. There are elements in our circumstances we cannot help, joy is independent of them all. HGM. 48

The joy of Jesus is a miracle, it is not the outcome of my doing things or of my being good, but of my receiving the very nature of God. HGM. 48

A man is only joyful when he fulfils the design of God's creation of him, and that is a joy that can never be quenched.
HGM. 48

We can always know whether we are hearkening to God's voice by whether we have joy or not; if there is no joy, we are not hearkening. HGM. 52

A life of intimacy with God is characterized by joy. You cannot counterfeit joy or peace. What is of value to God is what we *are,* not what we affect to be.
HGM. 52

If Jesus Christ is the life of God and we have to follow Him, we must find out what His joy was. It certainly was not happiness. The joy of the Lord Jesus Christ lay in doing exactly what He came to do. He did not come to save men first of all, He came to do His Father's will. LG. 63

The way God's life manifests itself in joy is in a peace which has no desire for praise. When a man delivers a message which he knows is the message of God, the witness to the fulfilment of the created purpose is given instantly, the peace of God settles down, and the man cares for neither praise nor blame from anyone. That is the joy of the life of God; it is uncrushable life, and there is never life without joy. LG. 65

The joy that a believer can give to God is the purest pleasure God ever allows a saint, and it is very humiliating to realise how little joy we do give Him. PH. 40

The joy of a thing lies in fulfilling the purpose of its creation. Jesus Christ's joy is that He fulfilled the design of His Father's will, and my joy is that I fulfil God's design in calling me, viz., to make me a follower of Him. PH. 146

God has promised to do the thing which, looked at from the basis of our own reason, cannot be done. If a man will commit his 'yesterday' to God, make it irrevocable, and bank in confidence on what Jesus Christ has done, he will know what is meant by spiritual mirth—"Then was our mouth filled with laughter, and our tongue with singing." Very few of us get there because we do not believe Jesus Christ means what He says. PH. 184

The emphasis of the New Testament is on joy, not on happiness. PH. 197

The joy that Jesus gives is the result of our disposiiton being at one with His own disposition. The Spirit of God will fill us to overflowing if we will be careful to keep in the light. We have no business to be weak in God's strength.
PH. 198

The mainspring of a man's action is further in than you can see in his actual life and it accounts for his outlook. When a man has his anchorage in Jesus Christ and knows what is awaiting the human race—that there is a time coming when all things shall be explained fully, it keeps his spirit filled with uncrushable gaiety and joy. PH. 203

Joy is the result of the perfect fulfilment of what a man is created for. Happiness depends on things that happen, and may sometimes be an insult. PR. 55

Joy is neither happiness nor brightness, joy is literally the nature of God in my blood, no matter what happens. PR. 132

The stronghold of the Christian faith is the joy of God, not my joy in God. . . . God reigns and rules and rejoices, and His joy is our strength. RTR. 37

It is a tremendous thing to know that God reigns and rules and rejoices, and that His joy is our strength. The confidence of a Christian is that God is never in the sulks ". . . the Father of lights, with Whom can be no variation, neither shadow that is cast by turning". RTR. 65

If you try to find enjoyment in this order of things, you will end in vexation and disaster. If you try to find enjoyment in knowledge, you only increase your capacity for sorrow and agony and distress. The only way you can find relief and the right interpretation of things as they are is by basing your faith in God, and by remembering that man's chief end is to glorify God and enjoy Him for ever. SHH. 9

The true energy of life lies in being rightly related to God, and only there is true joy found. SHH. 47

Solomon had everything a man could have in life, he had every means of satisfying himself; he tried the beastly line, the sublime line, the æsthetic line, the intellectual line; but, he says, you cannot find your lasting joy in any of them. Joy is only to be found in your relationship to God while you live on this earth, the earth you came from and the earth you return to. SHH. 65

. . . man cannot find the true essential joy of his life anywhere but in his relationship to God. SHH. 105

Joy is not happiness, joy is the result of the perfect fulfilment of the purpose of the life. SSY. 98

JUDGMENT

In every life there is one place where God must have 'elbow room'. We must not pass judgment on others, nor must we make a principle of judging out of our own experience. It is impossible for a man to know the views of Almighty God. BFB. 22

The Bible says that a man knows by the way he is made that certain things are wrong, and as he obeys or disobeys the ordinance of God written in his spirit, he will be judged. BP. 240

The judgments of God are a consuming fire whereby He destroys in order to deliver; the time to be alarmed in life is when all things are undisturbed. CHI. 66

The judgments of God leave scars, and the scars remain until I humbly and joyfully recognize that the judgments are deserved and that God is justified in them. CHI. 70

God never crushes men beneath the fear of judgment without revealing the possibility of victorious virtue. DI. 16

One of the greatest disasters in human life is our wrong standards of judgment, we will judge men by their brains, Jesus never did. Jesus judged men and women by their relationship to His Father, an implicit relationship. HG. 24

Jesus Christ did not come to pronounce judgment, He Himself is the judgment; whenever we come across Him we are judged instantly. HGM. 42

One of the most remarkable things about Jesus Christ is that although He was full of love and gentleness, yet in His presence every one not only felt benefited, but ashamed. It is His presence that judges us; we long to meet Him, and yet we dread to. HGM. 42

It is not simply the things Jesus says to us directly, or what He does in the way of judgment particularly; it is Himself entirely, wherever He comes we are judged. HGM. 43

The judgment that Jesus Christ's presence brings makes us pronounce judgment on ourselves, we feel a sense of shame, or of missing the mark, and we determine never to do that thing again. HGM. 43

There is no vindictiveness in Our Lord's judgments; He passes judgment always out of His personal love. HGM. 46

He is a 'dear dread,' we long to see Him and yet we are afraid to, because we know His presence will bring judgment on the things that are wrong. HGM. 46

The illumination of judgment comes personally when we recognise that the evil and wrong in our sphere of life is there not by accident, but in order that the power of God may come in contact with it as His power has come into us. When we come into contact with objectionable people the first natural impulse of the heart is to ask God to save them because they are a trial to us; He will never do it for that reason. But when we come to see those lives from Jesus Christ's standpoint and realise that He loves them as He loves us, we have a different relationship to them, and God can have His way in their lives in answer to our prayer. MFL. 126

We bring God to the bar of our judgment and say hard things about Him—'Why does God bring thunderclouds and disasters when we want green pastures and still waters?' Bit by bit we find, behind the clouds, the Father's feet; behind the lightning, an abiding day that has no night; behind the thunder a small voice that comforts with a comfort that is unspeakable. PH. 83

God is going to judge us by the light when we have been in living communion with Him, not by what we feel like to-day. God judges us entirely by what we have seen. We are not judged by the fact that we live up to the light of our conscience; we are judged by The Light, Jesus Christ. "I am the light of the world"; and if we do not know Jesus Christ, we are to blame. The only reason we do not know Him is because we have not bothered our heads about Him. PH. 119

It is easy to see the specks and the wrong in others, because we see in others that of which we are guilty ourselves. PH. 121

"This is the judgment," i.e., the critical moment—not the sovereign purpose of God, nor the decree of God, but the critical moment in individual experience—"that the light," Jesus Christ, "is come into the world, and men," individual me, "loved the darkness," their own point of view, their own prejudices and preconceived determinations, "rather than the light." That, says Jesus, is the judgment. PH. 202

The standard for the judgment of Christendom is not the light it has received but the light it ought to have received. PS. 44

The standard for the judgment of Christians is Our Lord. PS. 44

We have judged our fellow men as sinners. If God should judge us like that we would be in hell. God judges us through the marvellous Atonement of Jesus Christ. RTR. 23

There are dark and mysterious and perplexing things in life, but the prevailing authority at the back of all is a righteous authority, and a man does not need to be unduly concerned. When we do find out the judgment of God, we shall be absolutely satisfied with it to the last degree, we won't have another word to say—"that Thou mightest be justified when Thou speakest, and be clear when Thou judgest." SHH. 37

There is no problem, no personal grief, no agony or distress (and God knows there are some fathomless agonies just now—awful injustices and wrongs and evils and nobility all mixed up together) but will have an overwhelming explanation one day. If we will hang in to the fact that God is true and loving and just, every judgment He passes will find us in agreement with it finally. SHH. 38

There is always one fact more in every life of which we know nothing, therefore Jesus says, 'Judge not.' SSM. 79

JUSTICE

We waste our time looking for justice; we have to see that we always give it to others. 'If you are My disciple', Jesus says, 'people won't play you fair; but never mind that, see that you play fair.' HG. 10

Every man knows by the way he is made that there is such a thing as justice, and God forgives on the basis of *His* justice, viz., on the ground of Redemption. HGM. 102

If the mind of man persistently tries to remove the possibility of damnation he destroys the justice of God, destroys his own manhood, and leaves in its place an evolving animal-life to which God is not necessary. OPG. 14

JUSTIFICATION

True justification can only result in sanctification. CHI. 58

The meaning of the Redemption is that God can justify the unjust and remain righteous, and He does it through the Cross of Christ. It is not a thing to reason out, but a thing to have resolute faith in. GW. 45

Justification means two things—first, that God's law is just, and second, that every sinner is unjust; therefore if God is to justify a man He can only do it by vindicating the law, and by destroying the sinner out of him. GW. 85

Beware of justifying yourself when God alone is the justifier. If ever I can justify myself, I make God unjust. If I am right

*Behold, a virgin shall con
they shall call his name Emmanuel, which meu*
Matthew 1:28

and morally based in all I do and say, I do not need a Saviour, and God is not justified in the extravagant waste of sending Jesus Christ to die for me. If God judges me a sinner who needs saving, and I can prove that I am just, I make God unjust. NKW. 91

K

KINGDOM

In this dispensation the emphasis is on the Kingdom within, but in another dispensation there is to be an external manifestation of the Kingdom. To say that the Kingdom is going to be brought in by the earth being swept clean through wars and cataclysms is not true; you cannot introduce the Kingdom in that way, it is impossible. Nothing can bring in the Kingdom saving the Redemption, which works in personal lives through the Cross and in no other way. GW. 54

It may be hard for a rich man to enter into the kingdom of heaven, but it is just as hard for a poor man to seek first the kingdom of God. HG. 23

Whenver Jesus talked about His kingdom the disciples misinterpreted what He said to mean a material kingdom to be established on this earth; but Jesus said, "My kingdom is not of this world: . . . IYA. 23

If we could only find some means of curing everybody of disease, of feeding them and putting them on a good social basis, what a marvellous thing it would be. That is the way we are being told that the kingdom of God is to be established on this earth. 'We do not need any more of this talk about the Atonement, and the shedding of blood; what is needed to-day is to spend ourselves for others.' That is the lure of the wrong road to the kingdom, and we cannot keep out of it if we forget to watch and pray. 'Watch with Me,' said Jesus; 'mine is the only road to the kingdom.' IYA. 24

At the basis of Our Lord's Kingdom is this unaffected loveliness of the commonplace. LG. 37

The idea of a kingdom that is not maintained by might is inconceivable to us, and the 'otherworldly' aspect of Jesus Christ's Kingdom is apt to be forgotten. Jesus Christ's Kingdom is not built on principles that can be discerned naturally, but on 'otherworldliness,' and we must never adapt principles that He did not adapt. OBH. 87

We must realize the frontiers of death, that there is no more chance of our entering the life of God than a mineral has of entering the vegetable kingdom, we can only enter into the Kingdom of God if God will stoop down and lift us up. That is exactly what Jesus Christ promises to do. RTR. 33

This is the day of the humiliation of the saints; in the next dispensation it will be the glorification of the saints, and the Kingdom of God will be outside as well as inside men. SSM. 19

KNOWLEDGE

Never denounce a thing about which you know nothing. AUG. 42

Get at the knowledge of God for yourself, be a continuous learner, and the truth will open on the right hand and on the left until you find there is not a problem in human life that Jesus Christ cannot deal with. AUG. 62

It takes all time and eternity to know God. HGM. 56

It is a great boon to know there are deep things to know. The curse of the majority of spiritual Christians is that they are too cocksure and certain there is nothing more to know than they know. That is spiritual insanity. The more we go on with God the more amazed we are at what there is to find out, until we begin to use the power God gives us to forget earthly things, to be carefully careless about them, but never careless about our relationship to God. IWP. 76

The only way to *know* is to *will* to do His will. MFL. 18

When you know you should do a thing and you do it, immediately you will know more. If you revise where you are stodgy spiritually, you will find it goes back to the point where there was one thing you knew you should do, but you did not do it because there seemed no immediate call to, and now you have no perception, no discernment. Instead of being spiritually self-possessed at the time of crisis, you are spiritually distracted. It is a dangerous thing to refuse to go on knowing. OBH. 119

We learn very few things, because we learn that only to which we give our wits. OBH. 125

L

LAUGHTER

Laughter and weeping are the two intensest forms of human emotion, and these profound wells of human emotion are to be consecrated to God. NKW. 70

The devil is never said to laugh. Laughter that is not the laughter of a heart right with God, a child heart, is terrible; the laughter of sin is as the crackling of burning thorns. NKW. 70

LAW

. . . the moral law is not imperative, because it can be disobeyed and immediate destruction does not follow. And yet the moral law never alters, however much men disobey it; it can be violated, but it never alters. Remember, at the back of all human morality stands God. BE. 7

The moral law ordained by God does not make itself weak to the weak, it does not palliate our shortcomings, it takes no account of our heredity and our infirmities; it demands that we be absolutely moral. Not to recognize this is to be less than alive. BE. 7

God's laws are not watered down to suit anyone; if God did that He would cease to be God. The moral law never alters for the noblest or the weakest; it remains abidingly and eternally the same. BE. 8

The moral law exerts no coercion, neither does it allow any compromise. BE. 8

The inexorable law of God is laid down that I shall be held responsible for the wrong that I do, I shall smart for it and be punished for it, no matter who I am. The Atonement has made provision for what I am not responsible for, viz., the disposition of sin. BP. 157

LIBERTY AND LICENSE

The only liberty a saint has is the liberty not to use his liberty. BE. 25

Licence simply means—'I will not be bound by any laws but my own.' This spirit resents God's law and will not have anything to do with it—'I shall rule my body as I choose, I shall rule my social relationships and my religious life as I like, and I will not allow God or any creed or doctrine to rule me.' That is the way licence begins to work. BP. 136

What is the difference between liberty and licence? Liberty is the ability to perform the law, perfect freedom to fulfil all the demands of the law. To be free from the law means that I am the living law of God, there is no independence of God in my make-up. Licence is rebellion against all law. If my heart does not become the centre of Divine love, it may become the centre of diabolical licence. BP. 136

196

We are not fundamentally free, external circumstances are not in our hands, they are in God's hands, the one thing in which we are free is in our personal relationship to God. CHI. 40

Liberty means ability not to violate the law; licence means personal insistence on doing what I like. DI. 27

Worldly people imagine that the saints must find it difficult to live with so many restrictions, but the bondage is with the world, not with the saints. There is no such thing as freedom in the world, and the higher we go in the social life the more bondage there is. True liberty exists only where the soul has the holy scorn of the Holy Ghost—I will bow my neck to no yoke but the yoke of the Lord Jesus Christ; there is only one law, and that is the law of God. MFL. 127

. . . God allows the human race full liberty, and He allows the spirit of evil, viz. Satan, nearly full liberty also. PS. 68

LIE

A lie is not simply "a terminological incxactitude", a lie is a truth told with bad intent. I may repeat the exact words of someone else and yet tell a lie because I convey a wrong meaning. SHH. 101

A lie is not an inexactitude of speech, a lie is in the motive. I may be actually truthful and an incarnate liar. SSM. 42

LIFE

Our true life is not intellect or morality or bodily eating and drinking; our true life is our relationship to Jesus Christ. If once we recognize that and take care to be identified with Him in the crises of life, God will look after all the rest. If we try to draw out inspiration from elsewhere we will die in the attempt. AUG. 89

No man by nature has the life of the Son of God in him; he has in him the life which God creates in all men, but before he can have in his actual life the life that was in the Son of God, he must be born from above. BE. 42

There are things in life which are irreparable; there is no road back to yesterday. BFB. 16

We are not intended to understand Life. Life makes us what we are, but Life belongs to God. If I can understand a thing and can define it, I am its master. I cannot understand or define Life; I cannot understand or define God; consequently I am master of neither. BFB. 34

Our actual life is a disguise, no one expresses what he really is. BFB. 105

. . . let us face life as it is, not as we feel it ought to be, for it never will be what it ought to be until the kingdom of this world is become the kingdom of our Lord, and of His Christ. CD. VOL. 1, 118

Think of the dignity it gives to a man's life to know that God has put His honour in his keeping. Our lives mean more than we can tell, they mean that we are fulfilling some purpose of God about which we know nothing . . . CHI. 112

The problems of life are only explainable by means of a right relationship to God. CHI. 114

Beware of the people who tell you life is simple. Life is such a mass of complications that no man is safe apart from God. Coming to Jesus does not simplify life, it simplifies my relationship to God. DI. 36

People say they are tired of life; no man was ever tired of life; the truth is that we are tired of being half dead while we are alive. What we need is to be transfigured by the incoming of a great and new life. GW. 69

Experimentally the meaning of life is to attain the excellency of a broken heart, for that alone entails repentance and acceptance, the two great poles of Bible revelation. "The sacrifices of God are a broken spirit"—why, we do not know, but God has made it so. The one thing we are after is to avoid getting broken-hearted. HG. 33

. . . can God do what He likes in your life? Can He help Himself liberally to you? IYA. 44

We have no business to be half-dead spiritually, to hang like clogs on God's plan; we should be filled with a radiant intensity of life, living at the highest pitch all the time without any reaction."I am come that they might have life, and that they might have it more abundantly."

Be being filled with the life Jesus came to give. MFL. 83

Life without conflict is impossible, either in nature or in grace. NKW. 36

The questions that matter in life are remarkably few, and they are all answered by these words "Come unto Me." Not—'Do this' and 'Don't do that,' but 'Come.' "Come unto Me, all ye that labour and are heavy laden." OBH. 101

The basis of human life is tragedy. It is difficult to realise this until one gets through the experiences that are on the surface of life, and we discover we are built with a bigger capacity for pain than for joy, that the undertone of all our life is sorrow, and the great expression and revelation of God in the world is the revelation of the Cross, not of joy. It is one of the things which makes the Bible seem so utterly unreal so long as we are healthy and full of life and spirits. Tragedy is something in which all the forces make for disaster. PH. 150

As soon as we recognise that life is based on tragedy, we won't be too staggered when tragedy emerges, but will learn how to turn to God. PH. 152

We do not enter into the life of God by imitation, or by vows, or by ceremonies, or by Church membership; we enter into it by its entering into us at regeneration. The Cross of Jesus Christ is the gateway into His life. PR. 99

. . . there is only one purpose in our lives, and that is the satisfaction of the Lord Jesus Christ. PS. 46

Jesus Christ can make the weakest man into a Divine dreadnought, fearing nothing. He can plant within him the life that Time cannot touch. RTR. 54

Jesus Christ can put into the man, whose energy has been sapped by sin and wrong until he is all but in hell, a life so strong and full that Satan has to flee whenever he meets him. Jesus Christ can make any life more than conqueror as they draw on His Resurrection life. RTR. 81

God does not give us overcoming life: He gives life to the man who overcomes. In every case of tribulation, from gnats to the cruelty of the sword, we take the step as though there were no God to assist us, and we find He is there. RTR. 81

There will come one day a personal and direct touch from God when every tear and perplexity, every oppression and distress, every suffering and pain, and wrong and injustice will have a complete and ample and overwhelming explanation. SHH, 44

If a man builds his life over a volcano, one day there will come terrific havoc. . . . No wise man will build up his life without knowing what the basis of life is. SHH. 80

No education, no culture, no sociology or government can touch the fathomless rot at the basis of human life in its deepest down storey. We live in the twenty-second storey up, and the tragedies we touch are only personal tragedies; only one in a million comes to understand the havoc that underlies everything. SHH. 103

Life is immensely precarious, haphazard. A Christian does not believe that everything that happens is ordained by God; what he believes is that he has to get hold of God's order no matter what happens in the haphazard. SHH. 130

The natural life is neither moral nor immoral, I make it moral or immoral by my ruling disposition. Jesus teaches that the natural life is meant for sacrifice, we can give it as a gift to God, which is the only way to make it spiritual. SSM. 35

LIFE AND DEATH

We have no more ground for saying that there is eternal life than we have for saying there is eternal death. If Jesus Christ means by 'eternal life,' unending conscious knowledge of God, then eternal death must be never-ending conscious separation from God. The destruction of a soul in Hades, or Hell, is the de-

struction of the last strand of likeness to God. BP. 95

Death is God's delightful way of giving us life. IWP. 80

Jesus does not ask us to die for Him, but to lay down our lives for Him. Our Lord did not sacrifice Himself for death, He sacrificed His *life*, and God wants our life, not our death. OBH. 59

Jesus Christ has destroyed the dominion of death, and He can make us fit to face every problem of life, more than conqueror all along the line. RTR. 54

Within the limits of birth and death I can do as I like; but I cannot make myself un-born, neither can I escape death, those two limits are there. I have nothing to do with placing the limits, but within them I can produce what my disposition chooses. Whether I have a distressful time or a joyful time depends on what I do in between the limits of the durations. SHH. 23

The spell between birth and death is mine, and I along with other human beings make the kind of life I live. SHH. 43

It is a man's personal relationship that tells. When he dies he can take nothing he has done or made in his lifetime with him. The only thing he can take with him is what he *is*. SHH. 65

When death ends the present order, the issue will reveal how you have lived. Only when you live in personal relationship to God does the end explain that you have the right secret of life. SHH. 86

It is in the middle that human choices are made; the beginning and the end remain with God. The decrees of God are birth and death, and in between those limits man makes his own distress or joy. SHH. 87,

It is not within the power of human tongue or archangel's tongue to state what an awful fact death is, and what a still more awful fact life is. But thank God, there is the greatest deliverance conceivable from all that life may bring and from all that death may bring. SHL. 28

LIFE ETERNAL

A great and glorious fact—to believe in Jesus Christ is to receive God, Who is described to the believer as 'eternal life'. Eternal life is not a gift *from* God, but the gift *of* God, that is, God Himself. AUG. 106

We often hear it put as if God gave us a present called 'eternal life'. What Jesus Christ says is, 'he that committeth himself to Me *hath* eternal life', i.e. the life that was characteristic of Himself. AUG. 117

The mortal aspect is strong in the Bible, and the immortal aspect is just as strong. The annihilationists build all their teaching on the mortal aspect; they give proof after proof that because the soul and body are mortal only those who are born again of the Spirit are immortal. The Bible reveals that there is everlasting damnation as well as everlasting life. Nothing can be annihilated. In Scripture the word 'destroy' never means 'annihilate.' In this present bodily aspect the soul is mortal, but in another aspect it is immortal, for God sees the soul in its final connection with spirit in the resurrection. BP. 94

The people who say that eternal damnation is not personal but that eternal life is, put themselves in an untenable position. We know no more about the one than we do about the other, and we know nothing about either saving what the Bible tells us. BP. 95

"The gift *of* God is eternal life"; not the gift *from* God, as if eternal life were a present given by God: it is Himself. CD. VOL. 1, 139

This constitutes eternal life—an increasing knowledge of the unfathomable God and His only begotten Son. This is Eternal Pleasure—to know Him! How far removed it is from our conceptions of rewards and crowns and heaven. The way of a soul walking alone with God, unless we know this same unspeakable fellowship, seems a way overshadowed with sadness and insane with fanaticism. CD. VOL. 2, 119

The parable of the ten virgins reveals that it is fatal from our Lord's standpoint to live this life without preparation for the life to come. That is not the exegesis, it is the obvious underlying principle. HG. 30

Never confound eternal life with immortality. Eternal has reference to the quality of life, not to its duration. Eternal life is the life Jesus exhibited when He was here on earth, with neither time nor eternity in it, because it is the life of God Himself. IWP. 114

"Verily, verily, I say unto you, he that believeth on Me hath everlasting life." The very life that was in Jesus is the life of the soul who believes in Him, because it is created in him by Jesus. This life is only in Jesus Christ, it is not in anyone else, and we cannot get it by obeying or by praying, by vowing or by sacrificing. OBH. 26

"This is life eternal, that they might know Thee." Eternal life is God and God is eternal life; and the meaning of the At-one-ment is that Jesus produces that life in us. By sanctification we enter into the kingdom of perfect oneness with Jesus Christ; everything He is, we are by faith. He is "made unto us wisdom, and righteousness, and sanctification, and redemption", we have nothing apart from Him. OBH. 88

LIGHT

If I walk in the light as God is in the light, sin is not. HG. 117

If we walk in the light, not as holy men are in the light, but as God is in the light, we see behind the show of things—God. IWP. 100

It is better never to have had the light than to refuse to obey it. MFL. 16

How often God's book refers to God as light, to Jesus Christ as light, to the Spirit of God as light, and to the saints as light. By sanctification God places us in the light that He is in, the light in which our Lord Jesus lived His life. "And the life was the light of men." OBH. 39

We are not judged by the light we have, but by the light we have refused to accept. God holds us responsible for what we will not look at. A man is never the same after he has seen Jesus. We are judged by our immortal moments, the moments in which we have seen the light of God. PH. 119

Whenever any light is given you on any fundamental issue and you refuse to set-

tle your soul on it and apprehend it, your doom is sealed along that particular line. PS. 46

"If we walk in the light as He is in the light." Walking in the light means walking according to His standard, which is now ours. RTR. 36

"Ye are the light of the world." We have the idea that we are going to shine in heaven, but we are to shine down here, "in the midst of a crooked and perverse nation." We are to shine as lights in the world in the squalid places, and it cannot be done by putting on a brazen smile, the light must be there all the time. RTR. 84

There are wonderful things about light, but there are terrible things also. When once the light of God's Spirit breaks into a heart and life that has been perfectly happy and peaceful without God, it is hell for that one. 'If I had not come and spoken unto them, they had not had sin.' SSY. 150

LIGHT AND DARKNESS

The condemnation is not that a man is born with an heredity of sin; a man begins to get the seal of condemnation when he sees the Light and prefers the darkness. (*John* iii 19.) BE. 62

"If therefore the light that is in thee be darkness, how great is that darkness!" Darkness is my own point of view; when once I allow the prejudice of my head to shut down the witness of my heart, I make my heart dark. BP. 138

"This is the judgment" (the crisis, the critical moment), "that the light is come into the world, and men loved the darkness rather than the light; for their works were evil." What is light? Jesus says, "I am the light of the world," and He also said, "If therefore the light that is in thee be darkness, how great is that darkness!" Darkness is my own point of view. BP. 157

There is no variableness in God, no "shadow that is cast by turning." We are told that where there is light and substance, there must be shadow; but there is no shadow in God, none whatever. BP. 219

God is a light so bright that the first vision of Himself is dark with excess of light. CD. VOL. 1, 52

The disposition of the natural man, my claim to my right to myself, banks on things of which our Lord makes nothing, e.g., possessions, rights, self-realisation; and if that disposition rules, it will cause the whole body to be full of darkness. Darkness in this connection is our own point of view; light is God's point of view. MFL. 115

God wants to lift us up and poise us in the light that He is in, and that everything that is dark just now will one day be as clear to us as it is to Him. Think of all the things that are dark just now. Jesus said, "There is nothing covered, that shall not be revealed." Things are dark and obscure to us because we are not in a right condition to understand them. Thank God for all that we have understood, for every bit of truth that is so full of light and liberty and wonder that it fills us with joy. Step by step as we walk in that light, and allow the Son of God to meet every circumstance by His virtues, by His power and His presence, we shall understand more and more with a knowledge "which passeth knowledge." OBH. 47

"Let your light so shine before men. . . ." Our light is to shine in the darkness; it is not needed in the light. OBH. 75

We are not called to manifest Jesus in heaven; we have to be the light in the darkness and the squalor of earth. OBH. 82

We all like the twilight in spiritual and moral matters, not the intensity of black and white, not the clear lines of demarcation—saved and unsaved. We prefer things to be hazy, winsome and indefinite, without the clear light. When the light does come difficulty is experienced, for when a man awakens he sees a great many things. We may feel complacent with a background of drab, but to be brought up against the white background of Jesus Christ is an immensely uncomfortable thing. PH. 198

"What I tell you in darkness"—watch where God puts you into darkness, and when you are there, keep your mouth shut. When you are in the dark, listen, and God will give you a very precious message for someone else when you get into the light. RTR. 83

Darkness is my point of view, my right to myself; light is God's point of view. Jesus Christ made the line of demarcation between light and darkness very definite, the danger is lest this division gets blurred. "Men loved darkness rather than light, because their deeds were evil," said Jesus. SSM. 64

LOGIC

Logic is simply a method of working the facts we know; but if we push the logical method to the facts we do not know and try to make God logical and other people logical, we shall find that the experience of life brings us to other conclusions. God sees that we are put to the test in the whole of life. We have to beware of selecting the portions of life only where we imagine we can live as saints and of cutting off any part of life because of the difficulty of being a Christian *there*. OBH. 92

There is no logic for faith or for suffering. The region in which God deals with us is the region of implicit life that cannot be put into words. PH. 76

LOSTNESS

. . . the 'lost' from the Bible standpoint are not doomed. The lost, Jesus Christ is seeking for; the doomed are those who rebel against the seeking Saviour. To Jesus Christ, all men are lost, and the worker who is going to work for the cure of souls must have the same outlook. We have to bear this in mind because workers to-day are not taking the standpoint of the Lord Jesus Christ. WG. 21

. . . if the whole human race—everybody, good, bad and indifferent—is lost, we must have the boundless confidence of Jesus Christ Himself about us, that is, we must know that He can save anybody and everybody. WG. 23

LOVE

Love to be anything at all must be personal; to love without hating is an impossibility, and the stronger and more emphatic the love, the more intense is its obverse, hatred. God loves the world so much that He hates with a perfect hatred the thing that switched men wrong; and Calvary is the measure of His hatred. BE. 32

It is of no use to pray, 'O Lord, for more love! give me love like Thine; I do want

to love Thee better,' if we have not begun at the first place, and that is to choose to receive the Holy Spirit Who will shed abroad the love of God in our hearts. BP. 119

Love for the Lord is not an ethereal, intellectual, dream-like thing; it is the intensest, the most vital, the most passionate love of which the human heart is capable. BP. 169

Our natural heart does not love God; the Holy Ghost is the only Lover of God, and immediately He comes in, He will make our hearts the centre of love for God, the centre of personal, passionate, overwhelming devotion to Jesus Christ. BP. 189

Love never professes; love *confesses*. CD. VOL. 2, 76

The phrase "His own love" is very beautiful; it is God's own peculiar individual love, just as the love of a mother is her own peculiar love, and the love of a father is his own peculiar love. Every different kind of love illustrates some aspect of God's love; but it must not be forgotten that the love of God is His own peculiar love. CD. VOL. 2, 138

The majority of us have an ethereal, unpractical, bloodless abstraction which we call "love for God"; to Jesus love for God meant the most passionate intense love of which a human being is capable. CHL. 75

There is only one Being who loves perfectly, and that is God, yet the New Testament distinctly states that we are to love as God does; so the first step is obvious. If ever we are going to have perfect love in our hearts we must have the very nature of God in us. CHL. 88

When I am possessed by God it is not that He gives me power to love like He does, but that the very nature of God loves through me, just as He put up with the things in me which were not of Him, so He puts up with the things which are not of Him in others through me, and what is manifested is the love of God, the love that suffers long and is kind, the love that does not take account of evil, the love that never fails. GW. 29

The best example of a lover of men is Jesus Christ, and the mainspring of His love for men was His love for God. GW. 39

You cannot prove that God is love if you have not been born from above, because everything around you disproves it. HGM. 97

Love is an indefinable word, and in the Bible it is always used as directly characteristic of God—"God is love." IWP. 10

Love is difficult to define, but the working definition I would like to give is that 'Love is the sovereign preference of my person for another person, embracing everyone and everything in that preference.' LG. 21

Devotion to a Person is the only thing that tells; and no man on earth has the love which Jesus demands, unless it has been imparted to him. We may admire Jesus Christ, we may respect Him and reverence Him; but apart from the Holy Ghost we do not love Him. The only Lover of the Lord Jesus Christ is the Holy Ghost. OBH. 57

The springs of love are in God, not in us. It is absurd to look for the love of God in our natural hearts; the love of God is only there when it has been shed abroad by the Holy Ghost. OBH. 58

God's love for me is inexhaustible, and His love for me is the basis of my love for others. We have to love where we cannot respect and where we must not respect, and this can only be done on the basis of God's love for us. "This is My commandment, That ye love one another, *as I have loved you.*" OBH. 59

The greatest love of a man is his love for his friends; the greatest love of God is His love for His enemies; the highest Christian love is that a man will lay down his life for his Friend, the Lord Jesus Christ—"I have called you friends." OBH. 60

Neither natural love nor Divine love will remain unless it is cultivated. We must form the habit of love until it is the practice of our lives. OBH. 62

The love of God is not mere sentimentality; it is a most practical thing for the saint to love as God loves. The springs of love are in God, not in us. The love of God is only in us when it has been shed abroad in our hearts by the Holy Spirit, and the evidence that it is there is the spontaneous way in which it is manifested. OBH. 117

When the Holy Spirit has shed abroad the love of God in our hearts, then that love requires cultivation. No love on earth will develop without being cultivated. We have to dedicate ourselves to love, which means identifying ourselves with God's interests in other people, and God is interested in some funny people, viz., in you and in me! OBH. 117

Before we can love God we must have the Lover of God in us, viz., the Holy Spirit. OBH. 117

If you love someone you are not blind to his defects but you see the ideal which exactly fits that one. God sees all our crudities and defects, but He also sees the ideal for us; He sees "every man perfect in Christ Jesus", consequently He is infinitely patient. OPG. 45

The Self-expenditure of God for His enemies in the life and death of our Lord Jesus Christ, becomes the great bridge over the gulf of sin whereby human love may cross over and be embraced by the Divine love, and the love that never fails. PH. 27

If human love is always discreet and calculating, never carried beyond itself, it is not of the true nature of love. The characteristic of love is that it is spontaneous, it bursts up in extraordinary ways; it is never premeditated. PH. 140

There is never any risk in love that is "talked". If love is reticent it becomes a secret treasure that enervates. Keep it in the open, have nothing hidden to brood over. RTR. 11

God and love are synonymous. Love is not an attribute of God, it *is* God. Whatever God is, love is. If your conception of love does not agree with justice and judgment, purity and holiness, then your idea of love is wrong. RTR. 34

The springs of love are in God, that means they cannot be found anywhere else. It is absurd for us to try and find the love of God in our hearts naturally, it is not there any more than the life of Jesus Christ is there. Love and life are in God and in Jesus Christ and in the Holy Spirit whom God gives us, not because we merit Him, but according to His own particular graciousness. RTR. 34

"Love never faileth!" What a wonderful phrase that is! but what a still more wonderful thing the reality of that love must be; greater than prophecy—that vast forth-telling of the mind and purpose of God; greater than the practical faith that can remove mountains; greater than philanthropic self-sacrifice; greater than the extraordinary gifts of emotions and ecstacies and all eloquence; and it is this love that is shed abroad in our hearts by the Holy Ghost which is given unto us. RTR. 67

When a man falls in love his personality emerges and he enters into relationship with another personality. Love is not anything for me at all; love is the deliberate giving of myself right out to another, the sovereign preference of my person for another person. The idea, I must have this person for myself, is not love, but lust. Lust counterfeits love in the same way that individuality counterfeits personality. The realization of the Christian self means that Jesus Christ is manifested in my natural life—not Christian sentiment, but *Christian self*. Individuality is not lost, it is transfigured by identification with the Person of Jesus. SHL. 87

No one could have had a more sensitive love in human relationship than Jesus; and yet He says there are times when love to father and mother must be hatred in comparison to our love for Him. SSY. 52

Love is difficult to define, although simple to know; life is difficult to define, although simple to have. SSY. 158

Love cannot be defined. Try and define your love for Jesus Christ, and you will find you cannot do it. Love is the sovereign preference of my person for another person, and Jesus Christ demands that that other person be Himself. That does not mean we have no preference for anyone else, but that Jesus Christ has the sovereign preference; within that sovereign preference come all other loving preferences, down to flowers and animals. The Bible makes no distinction between Divine love and human love, it speaks only of love. SSY. 158

LOYALTY

To be faithful in every circumstance means that we have only one loyalty, and that is to our Lord. Most of us are too devoted to our own ideas of what God wants even to hear His call when it comes. We may be loyal to what we like, but we may find we have been disloyal to God's calling of us by not recognizing Him in either the distress and humiliation or the joy and blessing. The test of loyalty always comes just there. HGM. 131

Loyalty to God and to God's children is the supreme test in the life of a saint. We are never free from disloyalty unless we are actually loyal. PH. 73

Inspired loyalty is not loyalty to my attitude to the truth, but loyalty to The Truth—Jesus Christ. PH. 161

Loyalty to the Master's character means that the missionary believes in his Lord's almightiness on earth as well as in heaven, though every common-sense rational fact should declare loudly that He has no more power than a morning mist. If we are going to be loyal to Jesus Christ's character as it is portrayed in the New Testament, we have a tremen-

dously big task on hand. Loyalty to Jesus is the thing that is stuck at to-day. Folk will be loyal to work, to ideals, to anything, but they are not willing to acknowledge loyalty to Jesus Christ. SSY. 161

Christian workers frequently become intensely impatient of this idea of loyalty to Jesus. Our Lord is dethroned more emphatically by Christian workers than by the world. Loyalty to Jesus is the outcome of the indwelling of the personal Holy Spirit working in us the supernatural Redemption of Christ, and keeping us true to His Name when every common-sense fact gives the lie to it. SSY. 162

LUST

In the Bible, the term 'lust' is used of other things than merely of immorality. It is the spirit of,—'*I must have it at once,* I will have my desire gratified, and I will brook no restraint.' Each temptation of our Lord contains the deification of lust—'You will get the Kingship of the world at once by putting men's needs first; use signs and wonders, and You will get the Kingship of men at once; compromise with evil, judiciously harmonise with natural forces, and You will get the Kingship of men at once.' PR. 69

Love can wait and worship endlessly; lust says—I must have it at once. SHH. 109

The nature of any dominating lust is that it keeps us from arriving at a knowledge of ourselves. SHL. 81

M

MAN

The Bible revelation about man is that man as he is, is not as God made him. BE. 110

. . . God created man in order to counteract the devil. BP. 4

God put man at the head of the Terrestrial Creation. The whole meaning of the creation of the world was to fit and prepare a place for the wonderful being called Man that God had in mind. BP. 5

Man was created out of the earth, and related to the earth, and yet he was created in the image of God, whereby God could prove Himself more than a match for the devil by a creation a little lower than the angels, the order of beings to which Satan belongs. This is, as it were, God's tremendous experiment in the creation of man. BP. 5

God created a unique being, not an angel, and not God Himself; He created man. BP. 5

After the judgment by God on the previous order, God created a new thing, for a totally new being whom no angel had ever seen. This new being, man, stood at the end of the six days' work as a creation of earth, and he stood at the threshold of God's Sabbath Day. BP. 5

Man is the climax of creation. He is on a stage a little lower than the angels, and

God is going to overthrow the devil by this being who is less than angelic. BP. 8

Not only is Man the head and climax of the six days' work, but he is the beginning of, and stands at the threshold of, the Sabbath of God. God's heart is, as it were, absolutely at rest now that He has created man; even in spite of the fact of the fall, and all else, God is absolutely confident that everything will turn out as He said it would. The devil has laughed at God's hope for thousands of years, and has ridiculed and scorned that hope, but God is not upset or alarmed about the final issue; He is certain that man will bruise the serpent's head. This has reference to those who are born again through Jesus Christ's amazing Atonement. BP. 9

The marvel of the creation of man is that he is made "of the earth, earthy." God allowed the enemy to work on this creation of man in a way he cannot work on any other creation, but ultimately God is going to overthrow the rule of His enemy by a being "a little lower than the angels," viz., man. BP. 216

The first and foremost consciousness of Jesus was not the needs of mankind, not the pitiable condition of men, but His relationship to His Father whose Name He had to hallow before all else. BSG. 68

God did not make us in His own image; He made the Federal Head of the race in His image. CHI. 12

207

Man as God created him is a revelation fact, not a fact we get at by our common-sense. We have never seen Man. God *created* the earth and *"formed"* man of the dust of the ground," that is, God did not make man's body by a creative fiat, He deliberately builded it out of the dust of created matter according to a design in the Divine mind. Adam and Jesus Christ both came direct from the hand of God. We are not creations of God, we are pro-created through progenitors, the heredity of the human race is mixed; that accounts for all the perplexities. "And the Lord God formed man of the dust of the ground"—there is nothing the matter with matter; what has gone wrong is the infection of material things by sin, which is not material. Sin is not in matter and material things; if it were, it would be untrue to say that Jesus Christ, who "was made in the likeness of men," was "without sin." CHI. 12

There is a potential hero in every man—and a potential skunk. CHI. 97

. . . what makes Christ's glory is His severity, i.e., His love for God's holy law rather than His love for man: Jesus Christ stood on God's side against man. GW. 85

The whole of creation was designed for man, and God intended man to be master of the life upon the earth, in the air and in the sea; the reason he is not master is because of sin, but he will yet be. HGM. 82

If you want to know the most marvellous thing in the whole of creation, it is not the heavens, the moon and the stars, but—"What is man that Thou art mindful of him? Thou madest him to have dominion over the works of Thy hands." HGM. 82

By creation we are the children of God; we are not the sons and daughters of God by creation; Jesus Christ makes us sons and daughters of God by Regeneration. OBH. 25

God created man a splendid moral being, fitted to rule the earth and air and sea, but he was not to rule himself; God was to be his Master, and man was to turn his natural life into a spiritual life by obedience. PR. 11

Health, Happiness, and Holiness are all divergent views as to what is the main aim of a man's life. SA. 93

God made man a mixture of dust and Deity. SHH. 57

Modern wisdom says that man is a magnificent promise of what he is going to be. If that point of view is right, then there is no need to talk about sin and Redemption, and the Bible is a cunningly devised fable. But the Bible point of view seems to cover most of the facts. SHH. 76

One of the most difficult things to do is to place men. A man who knows men and can place them rightly is worth his weight in gold. SHH. 136

MAN AND WOMAN

. . . the Bible reveals that our Redeemer entered into the world through the woman. Man, as man, had no part whatever in the Redemption of the world; it was "the seed of the woman." BP. 19

God created man, the Federal Head of the human race, in His own image; we are procreated through generations of the human race; Adam was created in the image of God. The male and female together, as they were created, were in the image of God, in perfect union with God. "Adam and Eve" are both needed before the image of God can be perfectly presented. SA. 23

Man, the male being, took the government into his own hands and thereby introduced sin into the human race, and when God spoke He said that the Redeemer should come through the woman. The Mother of Jesus Christ was a virgin. Redemption comes through woman, not through man. SHH. 107

A woman can sink lower than a man because she can rise higher; the woman who has not a right relationship to God may become a she devil, e.g., the attitude of a woman in revenge. The tragedies of human life along this line are appalling. Four things—sex, money, food, and mother earth—make a man a king and a woman a queen, or they make a man a beast and a woman a she devil. SHH. 107

. . . a woman's character comes from the essential relation of her life. If she is essentially related to God, her whole life is a sacrament for God; if not, her life may be a sacrament for the devil. SHH. 108

The one who hauls you nearer to God is your mother or wife or sweetheart; but if your woman is not related to God, then the good Lord deliver you! No man is a match for the iniquity that is feminine when it is out of touch with God. SHH. 108

Any man or woman who falls in love comes right into God's presence, he or she instantly feels religious. Once love—my sovereign preference for another person—is awakened, it always goes direct to God like a homing pigeon. It is not hypocrisy on the part of a lad

when he begins to pray, he cannot help it, his love is the finest lodestar in his life. That is the contrast between love and lust. Love can wait and worship endlessly; lust says—I must have it at once. The thing that can be hellishly wrong can be marvellously right. SHH. 109

A man can neither rise so high nor sink so low as a woman. SHH. 109

MAN, SUPER

All through the New Testament the Spirit of God has foretold that we are going to have the worship of man installed, and it is in our midst to-day. We are being told that Jesus Christ and God are ceasing to be of importance to the modern man, and what we are worshipping more and more now is 'Humanity,' and this is slowly merging into a new phase; all the up-to-date minds are looking towards the manifestation of this "superman," a being much greater than the being we know as man . . . BP. 7

He is to be the darling of every religion; there is to be a consolidation of religions, and of races and of everything on the face of the earth, a great socialism. The ethical standard of the 'superman' claims to be higher than Jesus Christ's standard. The tendency is noticeable already in the objection of some people to Jesus Christ's teaching, such as 'Thou shalt love thy neighbour as thyself'; they say, 'That is selfish, you must love your neighbour and not think of yourself.' The doctrine of the superman is absolute sinless perfection. We are going to evolve a being, they say, who has reached the place where he cannot be tempted. This is all an emanation from Satan. BP. 8

Nietzsche declares that the basis of things is tragic, and that the way out is by the merciless Superman; the Bible reveals that the basis of things is tragic, and that the way out is by Redemption. SHH. 5

MARIOLATRY

In Protestant theology and in the Protestant outlook we have suffered much from our opposition to the Roman Catholic Church on this one point, viz. intense antipathy to Mariolatry, and we have lost the meaning of the woman side of the revelation of God. BP. 19

The Virgin Mary is not only unique as the mother of our Lord, but she stands as the type of what we must expect if we are going to be those whom our Lord calls *"My brother, and sister, and mother."* CD. VOL. 1, 144

What happened to Mary, the mother of our Lord, historically in the conception of the Son of God has its counterpart in what takes place in every born-again soul. Mary represents the natural individual life which must be sacrificed in order that it may be transfigured into an expression of the real life of the Son of God. GW. 64

MARRIAGE

Marriage is one of the mountain peaks on which God's thunder blasts souls to hell, or on which His light transfigures human lives in the eternal heavens. SSM. 38

MARTYRDOM

Because men and women devote themselves to martyrdom for a cause, they think they have struck the profoundest secret of religion; whereas they have but exhibited the heroic spirit that is in all human beings, and have not begun to touch the great fundamental secret of spiritual Christianity, which is wholehearted, absolute consecration of myself to Jesus, not to His cause, not to His 'league of pity,' but to Himself personally. PH. 18

Jesus did not die the death of a martyr: He died the death not of a good man, but the death due to a bad man, with the vicarious pain of Almighty God at His heart. That pain is unfathomable to us, but we get an insight into it in the cry upon the Cross, "My God, my God, why hast Thou forsaken Me?" PH. 137

If Jesus Christ was only a martyr, the New Testament teaching is stupid. SA. 35

MASTERSHIP

Men who are their own masters are masters of nothing else. A man may feel he ought to be master of the life in the sea and air and earth, but he can only be master on the line God designed he should, viz., that he recognised God's dominion over him. CHI. 13

We use the phrase 'Master,' but we use it in a more or less pious way, we do not intend to make Him Master practically; we are much more familiar with the idea that Jesus is our Saviour, our Sanctifier, anything that puts Him in the relationship of a supernatural Comrade. We advocate anything that Jesus does, but we do not advocate Him. IYA. 18

The most remarkable thing about the mastership of Jesus Christ is that He never insists on being Master. We often feel that if only He would insist, we would obey Him. Obedience to Jesus

Christ is essential, but never compulsory; He will never take means to make me obey Him. Jesus Christ will always make up for my deficiencies, He always forgives my disobedience; but if I am going to be a disciple, it is essential for me to obey Him. In the early stages we have the notion that the Christian life is one of freedom, and so it is; but freedom for one thing only—freedom to obey our Master. PH. 108

The conception of mastership which we get from our natural life is totally different from the mastership of Jesus Christ, because He never insists on our obedience. He simply says, "If ye love Me, ye will keep My commandments." That is the end of it. If I do not keep His commandments, He does not come and tell me I have done the wrong thing, I know it, there is no getting away from it. PH. 109

At the beginning of the human race the conception was that Adam was to be master over everything but himself. He was to have dominion over the life on the earth and in the air and in the sea, but he was not to have dominion over himself, God was to have dominion over him. The temptation came on this line—'Disobey, and you will become as God.' Man took dominion over himself and thereby lost his lordship over everything else. According to the Bible, the disposition of sin is my claim to my right to myself. PH. 110

The wonderful thing about our Lord is that He will not master us. He becomes the dust under our feet. He becomes less than the breath we breathe. He becomes Someone we can jeer at and utilise, Someone we can do anything we like with; yet all the time He is Master. We can crucify Him, we can spit on Him, we can slander Him, we can ignore Him,

we can hurt Him; yet He is Master. PH. 111

The conception of mastership that we get from human life is totally different from the mastership of Jesus. If I have the idea that I am being mastered by Jesus, then I am far from being in the relationship to Himself He wants me to be in, a relationship where He is easily Master without my conscious knowledge of it, all I am aware of is that I am His to obey. SSY. 86

To have a master and to be mastered are not the same thing, but diametrically opposed. If I have the idea that I am being mastered, it is a sure proof that I have no master. If I feel I am in subjection to someone, then I may be sure that that someone is not the one I love. To have a master means to have one who is closer than a friend, one whom I know knows me better than I know myself, one who has fathomed the remotest abyss of my heart and satisfied it, one who brings me the secure sense that he has met and solved every perplexity of my mind—that, and nothing less, is to have a master. SSY. 86

'Master' and 'Lord' have very little place in our spiritual vocabulary; we prefer the words 'Saviour' and 'Sanctifier' and 'Healer'. In other words, we know very little about love as Jesus revealed it. It is seen in the way we use the word 'obey'. Our use of the word implies the submission of an inferior to a superior; obedience in Our Lord's use of the word is the relationship of equals, a son and father. SSY. 88

MATURITY

God never destroys the work of His own hands, He removes what would pervert it, that is all. Maturity is the stage where the whole life has been brought under the control of God. CHI. 85

The upward look of a mature Christian is not to the mountains, but to the God who made the mountains. It is the maintained set of the highest powers of a man—not star-gazing till he stumbles, but the upward gaze deliberately set towards God. He has got through the "choppy waters" of his elementary spiritual experience and now he is set on God. "I have set the Lord always before me"—but you have to fight for it. CHI. 85

MEDITATION

A great many delightful people mistake meditation for prayer; meditation often accompanies prayer, but it is not prayer, it is simply the power of the natural heart to get to the middle of things. Prayer is asking, whereby God puts processes to work and creates things which are not in existence until we ask. It is not that God withholds, but He has so constituted things on the ground of Redemption that they cannot be given until we ask. BP. 112

Prayer is definite talk to God, around which God puts an atmosphere, and we get answers back. Meditation has a reflex action; men without an ounce of the Spirit of God in them can meditate, but that is not prayer. BP. 112

Meditation is not being like a pebble in a brook, allowing the waters of thought to flow over us; that is reverie. Meditation is the most intense spiritual act, it brings every part of body and mind into harness. MFL. 65

An hour, or half an hour, of daily attention to and meditation on our own spiritual life is the secret of progress. MFL. 65

MEEKNESS

Our Lord said that He was 'meek and lowly in heart', yet meekness is not the striking feature in the Temple when He drove out those that sold and bought in the temple, and overthrew the tables of the moneychangers. Our Lord was meek towards His Father's dispensations for Him, but not necessarily meek towards men when His Father's honour was at stake. BFB. 13

MEMORY

Forgetting with us is a defect; forgetting with God is an attribute. BP. 123

If one wants a touchstone for the depth of true spiritual Christianity, one will surely find it in this matter of the memory of sin. CHI. 122

Never live on memories. Do not remember in your testimony what you once were; let the word of God be always living and active in you, and give the best you have every time and all the time. OBH. 66

A worker should never tell people to forget the past; preachers of the 'gospel of temperament' do that. If we forget the past we will be hard and obtuse. If we are hard, we are of no use to God; and unless we know the Cross of Christ as the power which takes the stinging stain out of memory and transforms it, we are of no use to others. PH. 69

Unless a worker has had the experience of the grace of God transforming the stain of memory into a personal experience of salvation, there will be a weak-kneed-ness and a feeble-handed-ness about him that will hinder God's message. PH. 70

If there is no sense of sin, no stain in memory to be transformed, the trend of the teaching is apt to be the line of higher education and culture and rarely the great line Paul was always on. PH. 70

The first element in the make-up of a worker is that he knows the service of memory, not a memory of things that he can excuse, but a memory out of which God has taken the sting, so that he is in the place where he can become the minister of salvation to others. PH. 70

Every time the Spirit of God puts His finger on some wrong in the past and the tears of the soul commence, it is that He may show the marvel of His salvation. PH. 71

Remember whose you are and whom you serve. Provoke yourself by recollection and your affection for God will increase tenfold, your imagination will not be starved any longer, but will be quick and enthusiastic, and your hope will be inexpressibly bright. RTR. 31

Let memory have its way. It is a minister of God with its rebuke and chastisement and sorrow. God will turn the "might have been" into a wonderful culture for the future. RTR. 45

MERCY

"Blessed are the merciful: for they shall obtain mercy." As soon as we get right with God we are going to meet things that are contrary, we are going to meet un-merciful good people and un-merciful bad people, un-merciful institutions, un-merciful organizations, and we shall have to go through the discipline of being merciful to the merciless. It is much easier to say, 'I won't bother may head with them'; then we shall never know the blessedness of obtain-

ing God's mercy. Over and over again we will come up against things, and in order to get the eternal blessedness Jesus Christ refers to we shall have to go through the unhappiness of doing something that the standards of men will be contemptuous over. HG. 8

MILLENNIUM

In the Millennium we shall have exactly the same power as saints; we are to "meet the Lord in the air." Is that conceivable to you? If it is, it certainly is not conceivable to me. I do not know how I am going to stay up "in the air" with the Lord; but that is no business of mine, all I know is that God's Book reveals that we shall do so. BP. 256

MIND

Continual renewal of mind is the only healthy state for a Christian. Beware of the ban of finality about your present views. BE. 40

The mind that is not produced by obedience to the Holy Spirit in the final issue hates God. DI. 23

The discipline of our mind is the one domain God has put in our keeping. It is impossible to be of any use to God if we are lazy. God won't cure laziness, we have to cure it. DI. 67

Your mind can never be under your control unless you bring it there; there is no gift for control. You may pray till Doomsday but your brain will never concentrate if you don't make it concentrate. DI. 67

Don't insult God by telling Him He forgot to give you any brains when you were born. We all have brains, what we need is *work*. DI. 68

Irritation may be simply the result of not using your brain. Remember, the brain gets exhausted when it is not doing anything. DI. 69

Make your mind sure of what our Lord taught, and then insist and re-insist on it to the best of your ability. DI. 71

A man's mental belief will show sooner or later in his practical living. DI. 79

Keep the powers of your mind going full pace, always maintaining the secret life right with God. DI. 82

Never stop learning. People stagnate, not through backsliding, but because they stop learning and harden into a wrong mental poise. HGM. 145

A humble, ignorant man or woman depending on the mind of God has an explanation for things that the rational man without the Spirit of God never has. IYA. 74

A man has the Spirit of Jesus given to him, but he has not His mind until he forms it. IYA. 74

Never submit to the tyrannous idea that you cannot look after your mind; you can. If a man lets his garden alone it very soon ceases to be a garden; and if a saint lets his mind alone it will soon become a rubbish heap for Satan to make use of. MFL. 49

We cannot form the mind of Christ once for always; we have to form it *always*; that is, all the time and in everything. MFL. 102

. . . the mind of Christ is supernatural, His mind is not a human mind at all. MFL. 102

'My right to myself' is the carnal mind in essence, and we need a clear thinking view of what it means to be delivered from this disposition. It means that just as our personality used to exhibit a ruling disposition identical with the prince of this world, so the same personality can now exhibit an identity with the Lord Jesus Christ. Sanctification means that and nothing less. MFL. 117

The carnal mind is the brother of the devil; he is all right until you bring him in contact with Jesus, but immediately you do he is a chip of the old block, he hates with an intense vehemence everything to do with Jesus Christ and His Spirit. MFL. 117

The Spirit of Christ is given us, but not the mind of Christ. Every man is born with a human spirit, but he forms his own mind by the way his human spirit reacts in the circumstances he is in, and education gives power to a man to express his personal spirit better and better. The Spirit of Christ comes into me by regeneration, then I have to begin to form the mind of Christ, begin to look at things from a different standpoint, viz., the standpoint of Jesus Christ, and to do that I must lose my soul. Soul is not a thing I have got, soul is the way a man's personal spirit manifests itself in his body, the way he reasons about things, the rational expression of his personal spirit. SA. 110

The test Jesus gives is not the truth of our manner but the temper of our mind. Many of us are wonderfully truthful in manner but our temper of mind is rotten in God's sight. The thing Jesus alters is the temper of mind. SSM. 31

Notion your mind with the idea that God is there. If once the mind is notioned on that line, when we are in difficulties it is as easy as breathing to remember, 'Why, my Father knows all about it!' SSM. 84

One way in which Satan comes as an angel of light to Christians to-day is by telling them there is no need to use their minds. We *must* use our minds; we must keep the full power of our intellect ablaze for God on any subject that awakens us in our study of His word, always keeping the secret of the life hid with Christ in God. Think of the sweat and labour and agony of nerve that a scientific student will go through in order to attain his end; then think of the slipshod, lazy way we go into work for God. SSY. 148

MIRACLE

In our modern Christianity there is no miracle; it is— 'You must pray more'; 'you must give up this and that'—anything and everything but the need to be born into a totally new kingdom. BE. 30

The great miracle of the Redemption is that I can receive an absolutely new heredity, viz., Holy Spirit; and when that heredity begins to work out in me, I manifest in my mortal flesh the disposition of the Son of God. BE. 62

When Jesus Christ raised a man from the dead, He simply did suddenly what we all believe implicitly He is going to do by and by. BP. 258

The miracle of the Redemption of Jesus Christ is that He can take the worst and the vilest of men and women and make saints out of them. BSG. 70

When our Lord's miracles are at work in us they always manifest themselves in a chastened life, utterly restrained. CD. VOL. 1, 147

We marvel, not that He performed miracles, but rather that He performed so few. He who could have stormed the citadels of men with mighty battalions of angels, let men spit upon Him and crucify Him. GW. 119

The Carpenter, who offended so many, is the disguised Son of God, full of majestic power and condescension. We marvel, not that He performed miracles, but rather that He performed so few. GW. 119

The way Jesus manifested Himself after the Resurrection is an indication of what we will be like when everything is related to God, we shall do things which seem miracles to us now. HGM. 83

I have no right to ask God for miracles when my next duty stands neglected. RTR. 48

The heredity of the Son of God is planted in me by God, a moral miracle. SA. 108

Our Lord's miracles were cinematograph shows to His disciples of what His Father was always doing. Our Lord never worked a miracle in order to show what He could do; He was not a wonder worker, and when people sought Him on that line, He did nothing. SHH. 123

The miracles of Jesus were an exhibition of the power of God, that is, they were simply mirrors of what God Almighty is doing gradually and everywhere and all the time; but every miracle Jesus performed had a tremendous lesson behind it. It was not merely an exhibition of the power of God, there was always a moral meaning behind for the individual. That is why God does not heal some people. We are apt to confine life to one phase only, the physical:

there are three phases—physical, psychical and spiritual. SHL. 32

Whenever Jesus touched the physical domain a miracle happened in the other phases as well. If a miracle is wrought by any other power in the physical it leaves no corresponding stamp of truth in the other domains of soul and spirit. In this dispensation it is not a question of whether God will sovereignly permit us to be delivered from sin, it is His expressed will that we should be delivered from sin; but when it comes to healing it is not a question of God's will, but of His sovereignty, that is, whether the pre-dispensational efficacy of the Atonement is active on our behalf just now. There is no case of healing in the Bible that did not come from a direct intervention of the sovereign touch of God. We make the mistake of putting an abstract truth deduced from the Word of God in the place of God Himself. When God does not heal it is time we got down to close quarters with God and asked Him why. There is a deep lesson behind; we cannot lay down a general law for everyone, we can only find out the reason by going to God. SHL. 32

MISSIONARY

If we are going to remain true to the Bible's conception of a missionary, we must go back to the source—a missionary is one sent by Jesus Christ as He was sent by the Father. SSY. 74

The special person called to do missionary work is every person who is a member of the Church of Christ. The call does not come to a chosen few, it is to everyone of us. SSY. 78

Whatever line the missionary takes, whether it be medical or educational, he has only one purpose; one great truth has gripped him and sent him forth and holds him, so that he has nothing else on earth to live for but to proclaim the Death of Christ for the remission of sins. SSY. 79

Jesus Christ is the Master of the missionary. SSY. 86

The aim of the missionary is not to win the heathen, not to be useful, but to do God's will. He *does* win the heathen, and he *is* useful, but that is not his aim; his aim is to do the will of his Lord. SSY. 111

The key to the missionary is the absolute sovereignty of the Lord Jesus Christ. SSY. 140

It is easy to forget that the first duty of the missionary is not to uplift the heathen, not to heal the sick, not to civilize savage races, because all that sounds so rational and so human, and it is easy to arouse interest in it and get funds for it. The primary duty of the missionary is to preach 'repentance and remission of sins in his name.' SSY. 142

The key to the missionary message is the limitless significance of Jesus as the propitiation for our sins. SSY. 142

A missionary is one who is soaked in the revelation that Jesus Christ is 'the propitiation for our sins: and not for ours only, but also for the sins of the whole world.' SSY. 143

The key to the missionary message is not the kindness of Jesus; not His going about doing good; not His revealing of the Fatherhood of God; but the remissionary aspect of His life and death. This aspect alone has a limitless significance. SSY. 143

When the Holy Ghost comes in, He brings us into touch with the Lord Jesus Himself, and gives us the key to the missionary message, which is not the proclaiming of any particular view of salvation, but the proclaiming of 'the Lamb of God, which taketh away the sin of the world!' SSY. 144

The key to the missionary message is the proclamation of this gospel of propitiation for the sins of the whole world. We must be careful lest we become too wise for Jesus and say—'Oh but the people will never understand.' We should say—'God knows how to make them understand, therefore we will do what He tells us.' If we have got hold of the truth of God for ourselves, we have to give it out and not try to explain it. It is our explanations of God's truth that befog men. Let the truth come out in all its rugged force and strength, and it will take effect in its own way. SSY. 146

A missionary is one who is wedded to the charter of his Lord and Master. 'I determined not to know anything among you, save Jesus Christ, and him crucified.' It is easier to belong to a coterie and tell what God has done for us, or to become a devotee to Divine healing, or a special type of sanctification. SSY. 148

Too often a missionary is sent first by a denomination, and secondly by Christ. We may talk devoutly about Jesus in our meetings, but He has to take the last place. SSY. 148

The missionary is the incarnation of Holy Ghost light, and when he comes all the things of the night tremble. The night of heathenism is being split up, not by the incoming of civilization, but by the witness of men and women who are true to God. SSY. 151

Unless the life of a missionary is hid with Christ in God before he begins his work, that life will become exclusive and narrow, it will never become the servant of all men, it will never wash the feet of others. Therefore we come back to the first principle—'The heathen shall know that I am the Lord *when I am sanctified in you before their eyes.*' SSY. 155

Thus we end where we began, with Our Lord Jesus Christ. He is the First and the Last, and laying His hands on the missionary, He says—'Fear not, I have the keys.' SSY. 156

The missionary must be a sacramental personality, one through whom the presence of God comes to others. SSY. 165

MISSIONS

The most delicate mission on earth is to win souls for Jesus without deranging their affections and affinities and sympathies by our own personal fascination. PH. 20

Missionary enterprise, to be Christian, must be based on the passion of obedience, not on the pathos of pity. The thing that moves us to-day is pity for the multitude; the thing that makes a missionary is the sight of what Jesus did on the Cross, and to have heard Him say '*Go*'. Jesus Christ pays no attention whatever to our sentiment. In the New Testament the emphasis is not on the needs of men, but on the command of Christ, '*Go ye*'. The only safeguard in Christian work is to go steadily back to first principles. SSY. 48

Missionary enterprise on the line of education, and healing, and social amelioration is magnificent, but it is secondary, and the danger is to give it the first place. The temptation is more subtle to-day than ever it has been, because the countries of the world are being opened up as never before. It sounds so plausible and right to say— Heal the people, teach them, put them in better surroundings, and then evangelize them; but it is fundamentally wrong. The cry 'Civilize first, and then evangelize' has honeycombed itself into missionary work in every land; and it takes the Spirit of God to show where it is in direct opposition to God's line. It is putting men's needs first, and that is the very heart and kernel of the temptation Satan brought to Our Lord. Our Lord's first obedience was not to the needs of men, but to the will of His Father. SSY. 120

'Pray ye therefore the Lord of the harvest'—not pray because we are wrought up over the needs of the heathen, nor pray to procure funds for a society, but *pray to the Lord of the harvest*. It is appalling how little attention we pay to what Our Lord says. 'As the Father *hath sent* me, even so *send* I you'—to put in a sickle, to reap. SSY. 127

The basis of the missionary appeal is the authority of Jesus Christ. Our Lord puts Himself as the supreme sovereign Lord over His disciples. He does not say the heathen will be lost if you do not go, but simply—'This is My commandment to you as My disciples—Go and teach all nations.' SSY. 132

The awakened sense of responsibility to God for the whole world is seen in the rousing up of the Christian community in sympathy towards missionary enterprise. Within recent years missionary organization from the human standpoint has almost reached the limit of perfection. But if all this perfection of

organization does is to make men discover a new sense of responsibility without an emphatic basing of everything on Redemption, it will end in a gigantic failure. SSY. 150

There is no room for the specialist or the crank or the fanatic in missionary work. A fanatic is one who has forgotten he is a human being. Our Lord never sent out cranks and fanatics, He sent out those who were loyal to His domination. He sent out ordinary men and women, plus dominating devotion to Himself by the indwelling Holy Ghost. SSY. 163

MISTAKE

A man who wants to find an explanation of why things are as they are is an intellectual lunatic. There is nothing gained by saying, 'Why should there be sin and sorrow and suffering?' They *are*; it is not for me to find out why God made what I am pleased to consider a mistake; I have to find out what to do in regard to it all. PH. 192

Jesus never takes the trouble to alter mistakes; He knows they will alter themselves. PH. 218

MONEY

The two things around which our Lord centred His most scathing teaching were money and marriage, because they are the two things that make men and women devils or saints. Covetousness is the root of all evil, whether it shows itself in money matters or in any way. HG. 23

Jesus saw in money a much more formidable enemy of the Kingdom of God than we are apt to recognize it to be. Money is one of the touchstones of reality. People say, 'We must lay up for a rainy day.' We must, if we do not know God. How many of us are willing to go the length of Jesus Christ's teaching? Ask yourself, how does the advocacy of insurance agree with the Sermon on the Mount, and you will soon see how un-Christian we are in spite of all our Christian jargon. The more we try to reconcile modern principles of economy with the teachings of Jesus, the more we shall have to disregard Jesus. HG. 42

No man can stand in front of Jesus Christ and say, 'I want to make money.' MFL. 11

. . . if we listen to what our Lord says about money we shall see how we disbelieve Him. We quietly ignore all He says, He is so unpractical, so utterly stupid from the modern standpoint. MFL. 125

In the natural world it is ungovernably bad taste to talk about money. OBH. 86

Money is one of the touchstones in our Lord's teaching. Nowadays we are taken up with our ideas of economy and thrift, and never see that those ideas are not God's ideas. The very nature of God is extravagance. PH. 141

"Money answereth all things." Although money may cover up defects, yet ultimately it may lead to disaster. SHH. 139

"Give to him that asketh thee." Why do we always make this mean money? Our Lord makes no mention of money. The blood of most of us seems to run in gold. The reason we make it mean money is because that is where our heart is. SSM. 46

The Holy Spirit teaches us to fasten our thinking upon God; then when we come to deal with property and money and everything to do with the matters of earth, He reminds us that our real treasure is in heaven. Every effort to persuade myself that my treasure is in heaven is a sure sign that it is not. When my motive has been put right, it will put my thinking right. SSM. 62

What is mammon? The system of civilised life which organises itself without considering God. SSM. 65

MOODS

Moods never go by praying, moods go by kicking. A mood nearly always has its seat in the physical condition, not in the moral, and it is a continual effort to refuse to listen to those moods which arise from a physical condition; we must not submit to them for a second. It is a great thing to have something to neglect in your life; a great thing for your moral character to have something to snub. MFL. 63

It is a great moment when we realize we have the power to trample on certain moods, a tremendous emancipation to get rid of every kind of self-consciousness and heed one thing only: the relationship between God and myself. RTR. 7

Only when God takes a life in hand can there come deliverance from the 'blues,' deliverance from fits of depression, discouragement and all such moods. WG. 64

MORALITY

The natural life is neither good nor bad, moral nor immoral; it is the principle within that makes it good or bad, moral or immoral. BSG. 10

If a man is not holy, he is immoral; it does not matter how good he seems, immorality is at the basis of the whole thing. It may not show itself as immoral physically, but it will show itself as immoral in the sight of God. DI. 27

In the moral realm if you don't do things quickly, you will never do them. Never postpone a moral decision. DI. 28

Second thoughts on moral matters are always deflections. DI. 28

The religion of Jesus is morality transfigured by spirituality; we have to be moral right down to the depths of our motives. DI. 72

A man is largely responsible for the corruption of his actual life; Jesus Christ does not deal with my morality or immorality, but with 'my right to myself'. HGM. 74

Immediately I am lazy in moral matters, I become immoral. Spiritually it is the same. MFL. 74

If you make a moral struggle and gain a moral victory, you will be a benefit to all you come across, whereas if you do not struggle, you act as a moral miasma. PH. 79

Never keep your moral nature sceptical. Never doubt that justice and truth and love and honour are at the back of everything, and that God must be all these or nothing. SA. 29

Every religious sentiment that is not worked out in obedience, carries with it a secret immorality; it is the way human nature is constituted. SA. 71

I am only moral if I have sufficient moral power in me to fight; immediately I fight, I am moral in that particular. SA. 93

Moral truth is never reached by intellect, but only through conscience. SHH. 88

Morality is not something with which we are gifted, we make morality; it is another word for character. SHL. 13

Morality is not only correct conduct on the outside, but correct thinking within where only God can see. SHL. 14

. . . morality is produced by fight, not by dreaming, not by shutting our eyes to facts, but by being made right with God; then we can make our morality exactly after the stamp of Jesus Christ. SHL. 23

MOTIVE

Not one of us has a single motive; the only One Who had a single motive was Jesus Christ, and the miracle of His Redemption is that He can put a single motive into any man. SHH. 42

There are possibilities below the threshold of our life which no one knows but God. We cannot understand ourselves or know the spring of our motives, consequently our examination of ourselves can never be unbiased or unprejudiced. SHL. 60

The one motive of Jesus is to turn men into sons of God, and the one motive of a disciple is to glorify Jesus Christ. SSM. 63

No one has a single motive unless he has been born from above; we have single ambitions, but not single motives. Jesus Christ is the only One with a single motive, and when His Spirit comes into us the first thing He does is to make us men with a single motive, a single eye to the glory of God. SSM. 64

MUSIC

We can judge a nation by its songs. HG. 7

MYSTERY

Mystery there must be, but the remarkable thing about the mysteries which the Bible reveals is that they never contradict human reason, they transcend it. The mysteries of other religions contradict human reason. The miracles which our Lord performed (a miracle simply means the public power of God) transcend human reason, but not one of them contradicts human reason. BP. 258

There are three big mysteries. The Mystery of the Triune God—Father, Son and Holy Ghost; the Mystery of our Lord Jesus Christ, who is both human and Divine, and . . . the mystery that I, a sinner, can be made into the image of Jesus Christ by the great work of His Atonement in my life. OBH. 16

"O the depth of the riches both of the wisdom and the knowledge of God! how unsearchable are His judgments, and His ways past tracing out!" The purpose of mystery is not to tantalise us and make us feel that we cannot comprehend; it is a generous purpose, and meant to assure us that slowly and surely as we can bear it, the full revelation of God will be made clear. PH. 82

MYSTICISM

Mysticism is a natural ingredient in everybody's make-up, whether they call themselves 'atheist,' or 'agnostic,' or 'Christian.' God does not alter the need of our nature, He fulfils the need on a totally different line. We are so mysterious in personality, there are so many forces at work in and about us which we cannot calculate or cope with, that if we refuse to take the guidance of Jesus Christ, we may, and probably shall be, deluded by supernatural forces far greater than ourselves. BP. 177

The great conception to-day is not our being merged into God, but God being merged into us. The Christian line of things is that we are brought into union with God by love, not that we are absorbed into God. Jesus Christ maintains that this is to be brought about on the basis of His Redemption alone. Mysticism says it can be brought about by a higher refinement of nature. SA. 119

No room is allowed either in the Old or New Testament for mysticism pure and simple, because that will mean sooner or later an aloofness from actual life, a kind of contempt expressed or implied by a superior attitude, by occult relationships and finer sensibilities. That attitude is never countenanced in the Bible. SHH. 4

A man who lives a mystical life or an intellectual life frequently has an attitude of lofty contempt towards others. No man has any right to maintain such an attitude towards another human being, watching him as a spectator for purposes of his own, as journalistic copy, or as a religious specimen; if he does he ceases to be a human being by pretending to be more. SHH. 98

N

NATIONS

The standard of judgment for the natural person is conscience; and the standard of judgment for the nations is conscience. BP. 202

Another demand God makes of His children is that they believe not only that He is not bewildered by the confused hubbub of the nations, but that He is the abiding Factor is the hubbub. The Bible conception of the righteousness of God at work in history is that of fire, intense blazing heat, in the flames of which the nations are seen to be tumbling into confusion as well as rising out of it. GW. 45

We talk about a Christian nation—there never has been such a thing. There are Christians in the nations, but not Christian nations. The constitution of nations is the same as that of a human being. LG. 28

According to the Bible, nations as we know them are the outcome of what ought never to have been. Civilisation was founded on murder, and the basis of our civilised life is competition. LG. 29

We each belong to a nation, and each nation imagines that God is an Almighty representative of that nation. If nations are right, which is *the* right one? LG. 29

The idea of nations is man's, not God's. When Our Lord establishes His Kingdom there will be no nations, only the great Kingdom of God. That is why His Kingdom is not built up on civilized life. NKW. 135

Every country in Christendom has had plenty of opportunity of knowing about Christ, and the doom of a soul begins the moment it consciously neglects to know Jesus Christ or consciously rejects Him when He is known. PS. 44

Jesus Christ is the Lord of the harvest. There are no nations whatever in His outlook, no respect of persons with Him; His outlook is *the world*. SSY. 128

NATURE

The story of the earth itself is so full of sublimities that it requires God, not man, to expound it. If a man cannot expound the sublimities of Nature, he need not expect to be able to expound the sublimity of the human soul. BFB. 79

Our Lord taught us to look at such things as grass and trees and birds; grass is not ideal, it is real; flowers are not ideal, they are real; sunrises and sunsets are not ideal, they are real. These things are all round about us, almost pressing themselves into our eyes and ears, and yet we never look at them. MFL. 61

Jesus Christ drew all His illustrations from His Father's handiwork, from sparrows and flowers, things that none of us dream of noticing; we take our illustrations from things that compel attention. When we are born from above the Spirit of God does not give us new ideals, we begin to see how ideal the real is; and as we pay attention to the things near at hand, we find them to be the gate of heaven to our souls. MFL. 61

Beware of blaspheming the Creator by calling the natural sinful. The natural is not sinful, but un-moral and un-spiritual. It is the home of all the vagrant vices and virtues, and must be disciplined with the utmost severity until it learns its true position in the providence of God. RTR. 71

Everything that happens in Nature is continually being obliterated and beginning again. SHH. 6

NEED

One of the greatest revelations is that Jesus does not appear to a man because he deserves it, but out of the generosity of His own heart on the ground of the man's need. Let me recognize I need Him, and He will appear. HGM. 37

A sense of need is one of the greatest benedictions because it keeps our life rightly related to Jesus Christ. IYA. 60

The entrance into the Kingdom of God is always through the moral frontier of need. LG. 112

"Draw nigh to God"—the door is closed, and you suffer from palpitation as you knock. "Cleanse your hands"—knock a bit louder, you begin to discover where you are dirty. "Purify your heart, ye double-minded"—this is more personal and interior still, you are desperately in earnest now, you will do anything. "Be afflicted and mourn and weep"—have you ever been afflicted before God at the state of your inner life?

When you get there, there is no strand of self-pity left, only a heart-breaking affliction and amazement at finding the kind of man you are. "Humble yourselves in the sight of the Lord." It is a humbling thing to knock at God's door, you have to knock with the crucified thief, with the cunning crafty publican, but—"to him that knocketh, *it shall be opened.*" OBH. 96

The simple proclaiming of the gospel of God creates the need for the gospel. Nothing can satisfy the need but that which creates the need. PH. 136

"And I, if I be lifted up from the earth, will draw all men unto Myself." Once let Jesus be lifted up and the Spirit of God creates the need for Him. PH. 136

God loves the man who needs Him. PH. 167

The more complete our sense of need, the more satisfactory is our dependence on God. RTR. 42

Jesus Christ cannot begin to do anything for a man until he knows his need; but immediately he is at his wits' end through sin or limitation or agony and cannot go any further, Jesus Christ says to him, Blessed are you; if you ask God for the Holy Spirit, He will give Him to you. SA. 38

Numbers are used as symbols for great big generalities, and the Book of Revelation takes the number 666 to be the symbol of *humanity sufficient for itself,* it does not need God. The description given is of a great system in which humanity is its own god. SA. 96

NEIGHBOR

If you are going to live for the service of your fellow-men, you will certainly be pierced through with many sorrows, for you will meet with more base ingratitude from your fellow-men than you would from a dog. You will meet with unkindness and 'two-facedness,' and if your motive is love for your fellow-men, you will be exhausted in the battle of life. But if the mainspring of your service is love for God, no ingratitude, no sin, no devil, no angel, can hinder you from serving your fellowmen, no matter how they treat you. You can love your neighbour as yourself, not from pity, but from the true centring of yourself in God. BP. 181

If my heart is right with God, every human being is my neighbour. CHI. 78

A false religion makes me hyper-conscientious—'I must not do this, or that'; the one lodestar in the religion of Jesus is personal passionate devotion to Him, and oneness with His interests in other lives. Identify yourself with Jesus Christ's interests in others, and life takes on a romantic risk. DI. 37

The only way I can love my neighbour as myself is by having the love of God shed abroad in my heart, then I can love others with that same love. GW. 40

God has given us a precious gift in that looking at other Christians we see not them but the Lord. If you see only where others are *not* the Lord, it is you who are wrong, not they; you have lost the bloom of spirit which keeps you in touch with Jesus Christ. If I cannot see God in others, it is because He is not in me. If I get on my moral high horse and say it is they who are wrong, I become that last of all spiritual iniquities, a suspicious person, a spiritual devil dressed up as a Christian. NKW. 81

The humour of God is sometimes tragic; He engineers across our path the kind of people who exhibit to us our own characteristics—not very flattering, is it? OPG. 46

Whenever you touch your own true interests, others are involved at once. No man can gain a moral or spiritual victory without gaining an interest in other men. PH. 80

If there is the tiniest grudge in your mind against any one, from that second, your spiritual penetration into the knowledge of God stops. RTR. 21

God continually introduces us to people for whom we have no affinity, and unless we are worshipping God, the most natural thing to do is to treat them heartlessly, to give them a text like the jab of a spear, or leave them with a rapped-out counsel of God and go. A heartless Christian must be a terrible grief to God. RTR. 45

"If we walk in the light" God will give us communion with people for whom we have no natural affinity. RTR. 45

The measure of our growth in grace is our attitude towards other people. SSM. 89

Our Lord does not ask us to die for Him, but to identify ourselves with His interests in other people—not identify *Him* with *our* interests in other people. 'Feed my sheep,' see that they get nourished in their knowledge of Me. SSY. 160

NEUTRALITY

There is no such thing as being neutral, we are either children of God or of the devil; we either love or we hate; the twilight is torn away ruthlessly. HGM. 39

Neutrality in religion is always cowardice—'I don't want to take sides.' God turns the cowardice of a desired neutrality into terror. HGM. 39

NEW BIRTH

. . . the only evidence of new birth is not merely that a man lives a different life, but that the basis of that different life is repentance. BE. 38

The new birth will bring us to the place where spirit, soul and body are identified with Christ, sanctified here and now and preserved in that condition, not by intuitions now, not by sudden impulses and marvellous workings of the new life within, but by a conscious, superior, moral integrity, transfigured through and through by our union with God through the Atonement. BP. 27

What takes place at new birth is an 'explosion' on the inside (a literal explosion, not a theoretical one) that opens all the doors which have been closed and life becomes larger, there is the incoming of a totally new point of view. BSG. 62

It is an abiding truth that when we are born of the Holy Ghost, instantly the life becomes impaired from every merely natural standpoint. CD. VOL. 1, 145

This new life impedes us in our natural outlook and ways until we get these rightly related by 'putting on the new man,' until the Son of God is formed in us and both the natural and the holy are the same. CD. VOL. 1, 146

It is the 'preaching of the cross' that produces the crisis we call New Birth. We are in danger of preaching the new birth instead of proclaiming that which produces the new birth, viz., the preaching of Jesus Christ, and Him crucified. GW. 17

The creation performed by God is what the Apostle Paul calls it—a *new* creation; it is not the bringing out of something already there, but the creating of something which was never there before, an entirely new creation, as unlike anything born in a man by nature as Jesus Christ is unlike anything produced by the human race throughout its history. GW. 63

"If any man is in Christ there is a new creation," everything becomes amazingly simple, not easy, but simple with the simplicity of God. HGM. 73

New birth refers not only to a man's eternal salvation, but to his being of value to God in this order of things; it means infinitely more than being delivered from sin and from hell. The gift of the essential nature of God is made efficacious in us by the entering in of the Holy Spirit; He imparts to us the quickening life of the Son of God, and we are lifted into the domain where Jesus lives. LG. 114

Every man has need of new birth. LG. 116

The conception of new birth in the New Testament is not a conception of something that springs out of us, but of something that enters into us. Just as our Lord came into human history from without, so He must come into us from without. Our new birth is the birth of the life of the Son of God into our old human nature, and our human nature has to be transfigured by the indwelling life of the Son of God. LG. 116

When God re-creates us in Christ Jesus He does not patch us up; He makes us *"a new creation."* MFL. 102

Deliverance from sin is only part of the meaning of being born from above, the reason it is so important to us is because we are sinners; but the meaning of new birth from God's side is that a man is brought into the viewpoint of His Son. PH. 60

In new birth God does three impossible things, impossible, that is, from the rational standpoint. The first is to make a man's past as though it had never been; the second, to make a man all over again, and the third, to make a man as certain of God as God is of Himself. New birth does not mean merely salvation from hell, but something more radical, something which tells in a man's actual life. PH. 183

The meaning of New Birth is that we know God by a vital relationship, not only by our intellect. PR. 28

Our human nature is just the same after new birth as before, but the mainspring is different. Before new birth we sin because we cannot help it; after new birth we need not sin. PR. 35

The new birth is not the working of a natural law. The necessity for being born again is indicative of a huge tragedy. Sin has made the new birth necessary; it was not in the original design of God. New birth does not refer simply to a man's eternal salvation, but to his being of value to God in this order of things. PR. 38

When we are born from above the realization dawns that we are built for God, not for ourselves, 'He hath made me.' We are brought, by means of new birth, into the individual realization of God's great purpose for the human race, and all our small, miserable, parochial notions disappear. SSY. 103

NORMALCY

The normal 'Me,' from the Scriptural standpoint, is not the average man. 'Normal' means regular, exact, perpendicular, everything according to rule. 'Abnormal' means irregular, away from the perpendicular; and 'super-normal' means that which goes beyond regular experience, not contradicting it, but transcending it. Our Lord represents the 'super-normal.' Through the salvation of Jesus Christ we partake of the normal, regular, upright; apart from His salvation we are abnormal. BP. 165

Our Lord represents the normal man, not the average man, but the man according to God's norm. His life was not cut up into compartments, one part sacred and another secular, it was not in any way a mutilated life. Jesus Christ was concentrated on one line, viz., the will of His Father, in every detail of His life. That is the normal standard for each of us, and the miracle of the Gospel is that He can put us into the condition where we can grow into the same image. CHI. 51

Our Lord lived His life not in order to show how good He was, but to give us the normal standard for our lives. CHI. 51

O

OBEDIENCE

Spiritually, we are built not to command, but to obey. Always beware of the tendency to want to have things explained; you may take it as an invariable law that when you demand an explanation in connection with a moral problem it means you are evading obedience. BE. 12

Obey the Spirit of God and the word of God, and it will be as clear as a sunbeam what you have to do; it is an attitude of will towards God, an absolute abandon, a glad sacrifice of the soul in unconditional surrender. BE. 89

No one can tell us where the shadow of the Almighty is, we have to find it out for ourselves. When by obedience we have discovered where it is, we must abide there—"there shall no evil befall thee, neither shall any plague come nigh thy dwelling." That is the life that is more than conqueror because the joy of the Lord has become its strength, and that soul is on the way to entering ultimately into the joy of the Lord. BSG. 59

Obedience to God will mean that some time or other you enter into desolation . . . CHI. 69

It is not our power to love God that enables us to obey, but the presence of the very love of God in our heart which makes it so easy to obey Him that we don't even know we are obeying. As you recall to your mind the touchings of the love of God in your life—they are always few—you will never find it impossible to do anything He asks. CHI. 89

If I am going to know who Jesus is, I must obey Him. The majority of us don't know Jesus because we have not the remotest intention of obeying Him. DI. 4

There are some questions God cannot answer until you have been brought by obedience to be able to stand the answer. Be prepared to suspend your judgment until you have heard God's answer for yourself. DI. 13

How long it takes for all the powers in a Christian to be at one depends on one thing only, viz., obedience. DI. 31

The virtue of our Redemption comes to us through the obedience of the Son of God—"though He were a Son, yet learned He obedience by the things which He suffered . . ." Our view of obedience has become so distorted through sin that we cannot understand how it could be said of Jesus that He 'learned' obedience; He was the only One of whom it could be said, because He was "without sin." He did not learn obedience in order *to be* a Son: He came *as* Son to redeem mankind. DI. 55

Weighing the *pros and cons* for and against a statement of Jesus Christ's means that for the time being I refuse to obey Him. DI. 71

We get the life of God all at once, but we do not learn to obey all at once; we only learn to obey by the discipline of life. HG. 38

The curious thing about Our Lord is that He never insists on our obedience. HGM. 130

In order to be able to wield the sword of the Spirit, which is the Word of God, we must obey, and it takes the courageous heart to obey. IYA. 35

The term 'obey' would be better expressed by the word 'use.' For instance, a scientist, strictly speaking, 'uses' the laws of nature; that is, he more than obeys them, he causes them to fulfil their destiny in his work. That is exactly what happens in the saint's life, he 'uses' the commands of the Lord and they fulfil God's destiny in his life. MFL. 54

Jesus Christ's first obedience was to the will of His Father, and our first obedience is to be to Him. The thing that detects where we live spiritually is the word 'obey.' The natural heart of man hates the word, and that hatred is the essence of the disposition that will not let Jesus Christ rule. MFL. 114

In the spiritual domain nothing is explained until we obey, and then it is not so much an explanation as an instant discernment. NKW. 17

Right feeling is produced by obedience, never vice versa. NKW. 39

There are things God tells us to do without any light or illumination other than just the word of His command, and if we do not obey it is because we are independently strong enough to wriggle out of obeying. NKW. 57

God never accepts us because we obey; He can only accept us on the ground of sacrifice, which cost death. Therefore our approach to God can never be on the ground of our merit—that I am being bound by Another; that is the effect of the sacrifice of Christ in me. NKW. 123

The spirit of obedience gives more joy to God than anything else on earth. NKW. 126

We read some things in the Bible three hundred and sixty-five times and they mean nothing to us, then all of a sudden we see what they mean, because in some particular we have obeyed God, and instantly His character is revealed. NKW. 128

Obedience is the means whereby we show the earnestness of our desire to do God's will. OBH. 22

We have to stop hesitating and take the first step; and the first step is to stop hesitating! "How long halt ye between two opinions?" There are times when we wish that God would kick us right over the line and *make* us do the thing; but the remarkable thing about God's patience is that He waits until we stop hesitating. Some of us hesitate so long that we become like spiritual storks; we look elegant only as long as we stand on one leg; when we stand on two we look very ungraceful. OBH. 52

If God tells us to do something and we hesitate over obeying, we endanger our standing in grace. OBH. 53

'Obedience of the heart is the heart of obedience.' Whenever we obey, the delight of the supernatural grace of God meets our obedience instantly. Absolute Deity is on our side at once every time we obey, so that natural obedience and the grace of God coincide. OBH. 112

The only cure for obstinacy is to be blown up by dynamite, and the dynamite is obedience to the Holy Spirit. OBH. 129

In order to maintain friendship and loyalty to Christ, be much more careful of your moral and vital relationship to Him than any other thing, even obedience. Sometimes there is nothing to obey, the only thing to do is to maintain your vital connection with Jesus Christ, to see that nothing interferes with your relationship to Him. Only at occasional times do we have to obey; when a crisis arises we have to find out what God's will is, but the greater part of our life is not conscious obedience, but this maintained relationship. PH. 22

It is the glory of God to conceal His teaching in obedience: we only know as we obey. "If any man willeth to do His will, he shall know of the teaching . . ." It is only by way of obedience that we understand the teaching of God. PH. 82

There is only one golden rule for spiritual discernment, and that is obedience. We learn more by five minutes' obedience than by ten years' study. PR. 22

God never takes away our power to disobey; if He did, our obedience would be of no value, for we should cease to be morally responsible. PR. 35

When we are born from above and the Son of God is formed in us, it is not the passing of the years that matures His life in us, but our obedience. PR. 39

It is not obedience when a man does a thing because he cannot help it, but

when a man is made a son of God by Redemption, he has the free power to disobey, therefore the power to obey. If we have no power to disobey, we have no power to obey. Our obedience would be of no value at all if the power to sin were taken away. PR. 89

Jesus Christ's life must work through our flesh, and that is where we have to obey. So many go into raptures over God's supernatural salvation, over the wonderful fact that God saves us by His sovereign grace (and we cannot do that too much), but they forget that now He expects us to get ourselves into trim to obey Him. PR. 123

Divine silence is the ultimate destiny of the man who refuses to come to the light and obey it. PS. 46

The possibility of disobedience in a child of God makes his obedience of amazing value. PS. 50

The one who is not a child of God is the slave of the wrong disposition, he has not the power to obey; immediately God delivers him from the wrong disposition, he is free to obey, and consequently free to disobey, and it is this that makes temptation possible. PS. 50

My personal life may be crowded with small, petty incidents altogether unnoticeable and mean, but if I obey Jesus Christ in the haphazard circumstances, they become pinholes through which I see the face of God and when I stand face to face with God I shall discover that through my obedience thousands were blessed. RTR. 28

Whenever God's will is in the ascendant all compulsion is gone. When we choose deliberately to obey Him, then with all His almighty power He will tax the remotest star and the last grain of sand to assist us. RTR. 29

"If God so clothe the grass of the field . . . how much more . . ." Jesus says that if we obey the life God has given us, He will look after all the other things. Has Jesus Christ told us a lie? If we are not experiencing the "much more" it is because we are not obeying the life God has given us; we are taken up with confusing considerations. RTR. 30

Obedience to Jesus Christ is essential, but never compulsory. In the early stages we have the notion that the Christian life is one of freedom, and so it is, but freedom for one thing only—freedom to obey our Master. RTR. 35

In order to be able to wield the Sword of the Spirit, which is the Word of God, we must obey, and it takes a courageous heart to obey. RTR. 44

Never take your obedience as the reason God blesses you; obedience is the outcome of being rightly related to God. RTR. 64

Don't put prayer and obedience in the place of the Cross of Christ—"Because I have obeyed, Christ will do this, or that": He won't. The only way we are saved and sanctified is by the free grace of God. RTR. 72

Never try to explain God until you have obeyed Him. The only bit of God we understand is the bit we have obeyed. RTR. 75

If I am going to find out a thing scientifically, I must find it out by curiosity; but if I want to find out anything on the moral line, I can only do it by obedience. SA. 71

Moral insight is gained only by obedience. The second I disobey in personal bodily chastity, I hinder everyone with whom I come in contact; if in moral integrity I disobey for one second, I hinder everyone; and if as a Christian I disobey in spiritual integrity, others will suffer too. SA. 90

Moral problems are only solved by obedience. We cannot see what we see until we see it. Intellectually things can be worked out, but morally the solution is only reached by obedience. One step in obedience is worth years of study, and will take us into the centre of God's will for us. SA. 112

In Christian experience what stands in the way of my obedience to God is not the cost to me, but the cost to my father and mother and others. SHH. 84

The essential element in moral life is obedience and submission. If you want spiritual truth, obey the highest standard you know. SHH. 88

One of the great secrets of life is that obedience is the key to spiritual life as curiosity is the key to intellectual life. In the spiritual domain curiosity is not only of no use but is a direct hindrance. When once a man learns that spiritual knowledge can only be gained by obedience, the emancipation of his nature is incalculable. SHH. 123

The only way to find out things in the moral universe is by obedience. SHL. 62

The great cure for infidelity is obedience to the Spirit of God. SSM. 72

If for one whole day, quietly and determinedly, we were to give ourselves up to the ownership of Jesus and to obeying His orders, we should be amazed at its close to realize all He had packed into that one day. SSY. 129

OFFENSE

It is a serious thing to be offended with Jesus; it means stagnation of character. Jesus Christ can never save an offended man, because the man who is offended with Jesus shuts up his nature against Him; he will not see in Him, the Son of God, his Savior; he will not hear His words of life. GW. 117

God has so constituted human nature that the man who *will not*, ultimately *cannot*, but every man who is willing to come to Jesus and is not offended in Him, is saved and receives forgiveness. GW. 117

Jesus offends men because He lays emphasis on the unseen life, because He speaks of motives rather than of actions; He reveals men to themselves, and because that revelation means hopelessness they turn away from Him who is their only hope. He offended men because He taught that they were lost and could only be saved through Him—'For the Son of Man is come to seek and to save that which was lost.' Finally, He offended men because His own life was blameless, and His very presence disturbed their low-level contentment and happiness. GW. 118

Jesus offended many; His own home-folk were the first to be offended. GW. 118

OLD AGE

There is a marvellous rejuvenescence when once you let God have His way. If you are feeling very old, then get born again and do more at it. PR. 47

. . . a description of Old Age in its frailty: The keepers of the house (arms) and the strong men (legs) are weak and trembling; the grinders cease (teeth) and the windows are darkened (eyesight dimmed), the doors shut (ears are deaf), the grinding low (slow and tedious mastication), the easily startled nerves, and the loss of voice, the inability to climb, and the fear of highway traffic; the whitened hair like the almond tree in blossom, when any work seems a burden, and the failing natural desire, all portray the old man nearing the end of his earthly journey. SHH. 151

OPINION

The great lodestar of our life is—'I believe in Jesus Christ, and in everything on which I form an opinion I make room for Him and find out His attitude.' AUG. 116

You often find people in the world are more desirable, easier to get on with, than people in the Kingdom. There is frequently a stubbornness, a self-opinionativeness, in Christians not exhibited by people in the world. DI. 29

Jesus said, "Go and make disciples", not converts to your opinions. RTR. 47

OPTIMISM/PESSIMISM

The man who thinks must be pessimistic; thinking can never produce optimism. BFB. 12

Optimism is either a matter of accepted revelation or of temperament; to think unimpeded and remain optimistic is not possible. Let a man face facts as they really are, and pessimism is the only possible conclusion. BFB. 16

There is a passion of pessimism at the heart of human life and there is no 'plaster' for it; you cannot say, 'Cheer up, look on the bright side'; there is no bright side to look on. There is only one cure and that is God Himself, and God comes to a man in the form of Jesus Christ. Through Jesus Christ's Redemption the way is opened back to yesterday, out of the blunders and blackness and baffling into a perfect simplicity of relationship to God. BFB. 19

. . . no sane man who thinks and who is not a Christian can be optimistic. Optimism, apart from a man's belief and his acceptance of Christianity, may be healthy-minded, but it is blinded; when he faces the facts of life as they are, uncoloured by his temperament, despair is the only possible ending for him. BFB. 25

Everything man has ever done is constantly being obliterated; everything a man fights for and lives for passes; he has so many years to live and then it is finished. This is neither fiction nor dumps. In true thinking of things as they are, there is always a bedrock of unmitigated sadness. Optimism is either religious or temperamental. No man who thinks and faces life as it actually is, can be other than pessimistic. There is no way out unless he finds it by his religious faith or is blinded by his temperament. SHH. 5

The reason most of us are not pessimistic is either that we are religious or we have a temperament that is optimistic. The basis of life is tragic, and the only way out is by a personal relationship to God on the ground of Redemption. SHH. 14

To look at life as it is, and to think of it as it is, must make a man a pessimist. If we are not pessimistic, it is either because we are generally thickheaded and do not think, or because we have temperaments that are optimistic. If we face things as they are, we shall find that true optimism comes from a source other than temperament. SHH. 43

ORGANIZATION

Whenever a religious community begins to get organized it ceases to 'draw its breath in the fear of the Lord'; the old way of talking is kept up, but the life is not there, and men who used to be keen on proclaiming the Gospel are keen now only on the success of the organization. BE. 46

Overmuch organization in Christian work is always in danger of killing God-born originality; it keeps us conservative, makes our hands feeble. A false artificial flow of progress swamps true devotion to Jesus. DI. 36

P

PAGAN

The only way you can live your life pleasantly is by being either a pagan or a saint; only by refusing to think about things as they are can we remain indifferent. BFB. 18

The natural pagan, a man whose word is as good as his bond, a moral and upright man, is more delightful to meet than the Christian who has enough of the Spirit of God to spoil his sin but not enough to deliver him from it. PH. 168

The healthy pagan and the healthy saint are the ones described in God's Book as hilarious; all in between are diseased and more or less sick. SHL. 46

PAIN

We are born again by pain, not necessarily pain to ourselves any more than our natural birth means pain to us. We are born into the realm where our Lord lives by pain to God, and the pain of God is exhibited on Calvary. PH. 151

We have to learn to take up pain and weave it into the fabric of our lives. PH. 154

Nothing is born without pain, and a man cannot be born into the Kingdom of God without pain. He must have his conscience and his mind readjusted, and this will mean pain. PR. 15

In personal life and in natural life God's order is reached through pain, and never in any other way. Why it should be so is another matter, but that it is so is obvious. SHH. 59

PASSION

The Bible indicates that we overcome the world not by passionlessness, not by the patience of exhaustion, but by passion, the passion of an intense and all-consuming love for God. This is the characteristic in a born again soul—opposition to every sinful passionateness. BP. 59

Passionateness means something that carries everything before it. The prince of this world is intense, and the Spirit of God is intense. BP. 59

The one love in the Bible is that of the Father and the Son; the one passion in the Bible is the passion of Jesus to bring men into the relationship of sons to the Father, and the one great passion of the saint is that the life of the Lord Jesus might be manifested in his mortal flesh. GW. 115

Passion is usually taken to mean something from which human nature suffers; in reality it stands for endurance and high enthusiasm, a radiant intensity of life, life at the highest pitch all the time without any reaction. PH. 196

Sects produce a passion for souls, the Holy Spirit produces a passion for

Christ. The great dominating passion all through the New Testament is for our Lord Jesus Christ. SSM. 59

PAST/PRESENT/FUTURE

There is no other time than *now* with God, no past and no future. GW. 105

Don't be disturbed to-day by thoughts about to-morrow, leave to-morrow alone, and bank in confidence on God's organisation of what you do not see. Yesterday is past, there is no road back to it, to-morrow is not; live in the immediate present, and yours is the life of a child. SHH. 30

It is of no use to pray for the old days; stand square where you are and make the present better than any past has been. SHH. 90

Remain true to God, and remember that certain things are irreparable. There is no road back to yesterday, it is only God on the basis of Redemption Who can get back to yesterday. Logic and reason have to do with things based on space and time, but they cannot push beyond space and time. SHH. 97

PATIENCE

Patience is the result of well-centred strength. To 'wait on the Lord,' and to 'rest in the Lord,' is an indication of a healthy, holy faith, while impatience is an indication of an un-healthy, un-holy unbelief. CD. VOL. 2, 131

The patience of God and the patience of our Lord is working to one grand Divine event, and our Lord knows, as He did in the days of His flesh, how all His saints are straitened till it be accomplished. CD. VOL. 2, 148

There is no patience equal to the patience of God. CHI. 55

God takes the saints like a bow which He stretches and at a certain point says, 'I can't stand any more,' but God does not heed, He goes on stretching because He is aiming at His mark, not ours, and the patience of the saints is that they 'hang in' until God lets the arrow fly. GW. 136

Patience is the result of well-centred strength; it takes the strength of Almighty God to keep a man patient. LG. 96

When we first become rightly related to God we have the idea that we have to talk to everyone, until we get one or two well deserved snubs; then our Lord takes us aside and teaches us His way of dealing with them. How impatient we are in dealing with others! Our attitude implies that we think God is asleep. When we begin to reason and work in God's way, He reminds us first of all how long it took Him to get us where we are, and we realise His amazing patience and we learn to come on other lives from above. As we learn to rely on the Spirit of God He gives us the resourcefulness of Jesus. MFL. 126

The majority of us know nothing about waiting, we don't wait, we endure. Waiting means that we go on in the perfect certainty of God's goodness—no dumps or fear. The attitude of the human heart towards God Who promises should be to give Him credit for being as honest as He ought to be, and then to go on in the actual life as if no promise had been made. That is faithful waiting. NKW. 98

Jesus Christ does not give us power to work up a patience like His own. *His* patience is manifested if we will let His life dwell in us. OBH. 14

Our Lord was never impatient. He simply planted seed thoughts in the disciples' minds and surrounded them with the atmosphere of His own life. We get impatient and take men by the scruff of the neck and say: "You must believe this and that." You cannot make a man see moral truth by persuading his intellect. RTR. 86

All through the Bible, emphasis is laid steadily on patience. A man's patience is tested by three things—God, himself, and other people. An apt illustration is that of a bow and arrow in the hand of an archer. God is not aiming at what we are, nor is He asking our permisson. He has us in His hands for His own purpose, and He strains to the last limit; then when He lets fly, the arrow goes straight to His goal. "Acquire your soul with patience." Don't get impatient with yourself. SHH. 87

PEACE

The peace of sins forgiven, the peace of a conscience at rest with God, is not the peace that Jesus imparts. Those are the immediate results of believing and obeying Him, but it is His own peace He gives, and He never had any sins to be forgiven or an outraged conscience to appease. CD. VOL. 1, 150

The source of peace is God, not myself; it never is my peace but always His, and if once He withdraws, it is not there. CD. VOL. 1, 152

Nothing else is in the least like His peace. It is the peace of God, which passeth all understanding. CD. VOL. 1, 152

The peace of Jesus is not a cherished piece of property that I possess; it is a direct impartation from Him, and my enjoying His peace depends on my recognising this. CD. VOL. 1, 153

We talk glibly about Jesus being 'the Prince of Peace', but when He comes into the world that is peaceably ruled by Satan, He comes to send a sword, not peace. GW. 101

The peace of this world can never be the peace of God. The peace of physical health, of mental healthy-mindedness, of prosperous circumstances, of civilization—not one of these is peace of God, but the outcome of the souls of men being garrisoned by the prince of this world. HG. 8

"Pray for the peace of the city" because it will be better for us as saints if the city is in peace. HG. 15

Immediately a man comes to see what Jesus Christ demands, his peace of mind is upset. PH. 61

"I came not to cast peace, but a sword." Immediately the Holy Spirit brings you face to face with a presentation of truth which you never saw before, your peace is gone, and instead there is the sword of conviction. PH. 61

The coming of Jesus Christ is not a peaceful thing; it is overwhelming and frantically disturbing, because the first thing He does is to destroy every peace that is not based on a personal relationship to Himself. SA. 85

"Men of good taste are averse to the teaching of Jesus Christ," because if He is right, they are wrong. Take up any attitude of Jesus Christ's and let it work, and the first thing that happens is that the old order and the old peace go. You cannot get back peace on the same level. If once you have allowed Jesus Christ to upset the equilibrium, holiness is the inevitable result, or no peace for ever. SA. 99

PENTECOST

Pentecost has made God spiritual to us. Jesus Christ was God Incarnate; Pentecost is God come in the Spirit. BE. 100

The dispensation of Pentecost is not confined to the Jews, not confined to Christendom, it is confined nowhere, it is absolutely universal, the sweep and sway and majesty of the power of the Holy Ghost is at work in every crook and cranny of the universe. BE. 101

The message of Pentecost is an emphasis, not on the Holy Ghost, but on the Risen and Ascended Christ. DI. 21

The Holy Ghost came into this world on the Day of Pentecost, and He has been here ever since. HGM. 21

Pentecost stands for something unrepeatable in the history of the world, viz., the personal descent of the Paraclete. HGM. 21

PERFECTION

Size yourself up with a good sense of humour—'*me*, perfect!' That is what Jesus Christ has undertaken to do. DI. 72

We are to be perfect as our Father in heaven is perfect, not by struggle and effort, but by the impartation of that which is Perfect. IWP. 9

The Bible reveals that "that which is perfect" is a Being. God is the only Perfect Being; no human being is perfect apart from God. IWP. 9

When faced with difficulties, we do not try to brace ourselves up by prayer to meet them, but by the power of the grace of God we let the perfections of Jesus Christ be manifested in us. OBH. 14

God always ignores the present perfection for the ultimate perfection. PH. 83

The sinless-perfection heresy says that when we are saved we cannot sin; that is a devil's lie. When we are saved by God's grace, God puts into us the possibility of not sinning, and our character from that moment is of value to God. SSM. 104

Anything less than the desire to be perfect in a profession or calling is humbug, and so in religion. Beware of quibbling over the word 'perfection'. It does not refer to the full consummation of a man's powers, it simply means perfect fitness for doing the will of God; a perfect adjustment to God until all the powers are perfectly fitted to do His will. SSY. 55

PERSECUTION

People are not persecuted for living a holy life, it is the confession of Jesus that brings the persecution. There is a great deal of social work done to-day that does not confess Jesus, although people may praise Him to further orders; and if you confess Him there, you will find the ostracism He mentions: 'Keep your religion out; don't bring your jargon of sanctification here.' You must take it there, and when you do, the opposition will be tremendous. The reason for the opposition is that men have vested interests which philanthropy and kindness to humanity do not touch, but which the Spirit of Jesus testified to by human lips does touch, and indignation is awakened against the one who dares to carry the cross for his Lord there. AUG. 52

There is a saying of Bacon's to the effect that if prosperity is the blessing of the Old Testament, adversity is the blessing of the New; and the apostle Paul says that "all that will live godly in Christ Jesus shall suffer persecution." BFB. 22

Many of us are persecuted because we have crochety notions of our own, but the mark of a disciple is suffering "For My sake." HG. 10

Try and work your home life or your business life according to the rule of Jesus Christ and you will find that what He said is true, you will be put out of court as a fool, and we don't like to be thought fools. That is the persecution that many a man and woman has to go through if they are true to Jesus Christ, a continual semi-cultured sneering ridicule; nothing can stand that but absolute devotion to Jesus Christ, a creed will never stand it. Christianity is other-worldliness in the midst of this-worldliness. HG. 10

Jesus Christ not only warned that persecution would come, He went further and said that it was profitable to go through persecution. *'Blessed are ye, when men shall . . . persecute you.'* The way the world treats me is the exhibition of my inner disposition. 'Whosoever maketh himself a friend of the world is the enemy of God.' SHL. 16

PERSONALITY

The only One who knows the mysterious, unfathomable depths of our personality is God; we have to deal with the practical part, and see that we have faith in God with regard to the mysterious part while we obey Him in the practical domain. BE. 59

. . . an island may be easily explored, yet how amazed we are when we realize that it is the top of a mountain, whose greater part is hidden under the waves of the sea and goes sheer down to deeper depths than we can fathom. The little island represents our conscious personality. The part of ourselves of which we are conscious is a very tiny part, there is a greater part underneath about which we know nothing; consequently there are upheavals from beneath that we cannot account for. We cannot grasp ourselves at all. We begin by thinking we can, but we have to come to the Bible standpoint that no one knows himself; the only One Who knows him is God. BP. 150

Personality means that peculiar, incalculable being that is meant when you speak of 'you' as distinct from everybody else. People say, 'Oh, I cannot understand myself'; of course you can't! 'Nobody else understands me'; of course they don't! There is only one Being Who understands us, and that is our Creator. BP. 151

The personality of man is his inmost nature; it is distinct from spirit, soul and body, and yet embraces all; it is the innermost centre of man's spirit, soul and body. BP. 152

The personality of a man apart from the Spirit of God becomes enslaved to the desires of the flesh. The marvel of the life of God in a man is that he never need be dominated by anything other than spirit—"Walk in the Spirit, and ye shall not fulfil the lust of the flesh." CHI. 41

Jesus Christ emancipates personality, and He makes individuality pronounced; but it is personality absolutely free from my right to myself, free from identity with any other personality, manifesting a strong family likeness to Jesus, and the transfiguring element is love to Himself. CHI. 50

Individuality can never become a sacrament, it is only personality that can become a sacrament through oneness with Jesus Christ. DI. 28

When I am baptized with the Holy Ghost my personality is lifted up to its right place, viz., into perfect union with God so that I love Him without hindrance. DI. 33

Nothing can hinder God's purpose in a personal life but the person himself. DI. 33

The Bible reveals that in a man's personality there is a bias that makes him choose not the proposition of godliness, but the proposition of ungodliness. This bias is not a matter of man's deliberate choice, it is in his personality when he is born. MFL. 29

God does not search a man without he knows it, and it is a marvellous moment in a man's life when he is explored by the Spirit of God. The great mystic work of the Holy Spirit is in the dim regions of a man's personality where he cannot go. God Himself is the explorer of man's will, and this is how He searches us. MFL. 44

The first great psychological law to be grasped is that the brain and the body are pure mechanisms, there is nothing spiritual about them; they are the machines we use to express our personality. MFL. 51

The men and women who lift and inspire us are those who struggle for self, not for self-assertiveness, that is a sign of weakness, but for the development of personality. There are some people in whose company you cannot have a mean thought without being instantly rebuked. PH. 79

Whenever the Holy Spirit sees a chance to glorify Jesus Christ, He will take your whole personality and simply make it blaze and glow with personal passionate devotion to the Lord Jesus. SSM. 17

PHILOSOPHY

We have not to bring God into our system of philosophy, but to found our philosophy on God. The source and support of all abiding exposition is a man's personal relationship to God. If we base our philosophy on reason, we shall produce a false philosophy; but if we base it on faith in God, we can begin to expound life rightly. Actual conditions come into account, but underneath lies the Redemption. BFB. 102

If you read a book by a philosopher about life it looks as simple as can be, no complications or difficulties; but when you are flung out "into the soup," you find that your simple line of explanation won't work at all. Just when you thought you had found the secret, you find you are off the line. SHH. 124

PIETY

There is no room in the New Testament for sickly piety, but room only for the robust, vigorous, open-air life that Jesus lived—*in* the world but not *of* it, the whole life guided and transfigured by God. Beware of the piety that is not stamped by the life of God, but by the type of a religious experience. Be absolutely and fiercely godly in your life, but never be pious. A 'pi' person does not take God seriously, he only takes himself seriously, the one tremendous worship of his life is his experience. AUG. 15

The dangerous tendency of to-day is not so much the anti-religious tendency as the pietistic tendency, that by prayer and consecration, by giving up things and devoting ourselves to God, He will recognize us. We can never get to God in that way . . . BE. 61

Pious talk paralyses the power to live piously, the energy of the life goes into the talk—sanctimonious instead of sanctified. Unless your mind is free from jealousy, envy, spite, your pious words only increase your hypocrisy. DI. 60

Beware of the piety that has no presupposition of the Atonement, it is no use for anything but leading a sequestered life; it is useless to God and a nuisance to man. We have to base resolutely in unshaken faith on the complete and perfect Atonement of Jesus Christ. OBH. 110

Beware of the piety that denies the natural life, it is a fraud. We can all shine in the sun, but Jesus wants us to shine where there is no sun, where it is dark with the press of practical things. OBH. 112

PITY

When God is weaning a soul from creatures, from Christian experience, from teachers and friends, then is the time that the devil begins the advocacy of self-pity. IWP. 15

No sin is worse than self-pity because it puts self-interest on the throne; it "makes the bastard self seem in the right"; it obliterates God and opens the mouth to spit out murmurings against God; and the life becomes impoverished and mean, there is nothing lovely or generous about it. OBH. 87

If we indulge in the luxury of misery, we become isolated in the conception of our own sufferings; God's riches are banished and self-pity, the deeply entrenched essence of Satanhood, is enthroned in the soul. OBH. 87

There is no self-pity left in the heart that has been bound up and succoured by the Lord Jesus Christ. OBH. 89

POLITICS

In politics also it is difficult to steer a course; there is a complication of forces to be dealt with which most of us know nothing about. We have no affinity for this kind of thing, and it is easy to ignore the condition of the men who have to live there, and to pass condemnation on them. SHH. 115

POSSESSIONS

Our Lord Jesus Christ became poor for our sakes not as an example, but to give us the unerring secret of His religion. Professional Christianity is a religion of possessions that are devoted to God; the religion of Jesus Christ is a religion of personal relationship to God, and has nothing whatever to do with possessions. The disciple is rich not in possessions, but in personal identity. AUG. 24

All that a man possesses is at times not in the hand of God, but in the hand of the adversary, because God has never withdrawn that authority from Satan. BFB. 11

When Jesus Christ talked about discipleship He indicated that a disciple must be detached from property and possessions, for if a man's life is in what he possesses, when disaster comes to his possessions, his life goes too. BFB. 11

There are times when a man's intimate personal possessions are under Satan's domination. BFB. 13

The sense of property is connected, not with the lasting element of our personality, but with that which has to do with sin; it is the sense of property that makes me want to gratify myself. Jesus Christ had no sense of property, there was never any attempt to gratify Himself by possessing things for Himself— 'the Son of man hath not where to lay His head.' GW. 28

The thing that leads me wrong always and every time is what I am persuaded I possess. The thing that is mine is the thing I have with the power to give it. All that I want to possess without the power to give, is of the nature of sin. GW. 28

God has no possessions, consequently I cannot rob God of anything, but I rob myself of God every time I stick to what I possess. Immediately I abandon to God I get that which possesses me but has no possessions with it, there is nothing to keep. Being possessed by God means an untrammelled human life. GW. 28

God seems careless of His children from the standpoint of Time; when we get to the Eternal side of God's Providence we find He does not estimate a man by what he possesses; the only thing He is after is union with Himself, and He will obliterate all our possessions until He leaves only Himself. GW. 28

As long as I have something from God which I possess, I have not got God. God gives us possessions in order to draw us to Himself, and when we get God we are no longer conscious of our possessions, but conscious only of God. What possesses me in a yielded life to God is God Himself. GW. 28

When the Holy Spirit begins to try and break into the house of our possessions in order to grant us the real life of God, we look on Him as a robber, as a disturber of our peace, because when He comes He reveals the things which are not of God and must go; and they are the things which constituted our life before He came in, our golden affections were carefully nested in them. The thing that hurts shows where we live. GW. 29

The realization that my strength is always a hindrance to God's supply of life is a great eye-opener. A man who has genius is apt to rely on his genius rather than on God. A man who has money is apt to rely on money instead of God. So many of us trust in what we have got in the way of possessions instead of entirely in God. GW. 69

Many of us suppress our sense of property, we don't starve it, we suppress it. Undress yourself morally before God of everything that might be a possession until you are a mere conscious human being, and then give God that. That is where the battle is fought—in the domain of the will before God, it is not fought in external things at all. GW. 78

Jesus Christ taught that any one who possesses property of any nature has got to go through a baptism of bereavement in connection with it before he can be His disciple. HG. 8

240

The craze nowadays for those of us who have no property is to take the liberty of hauling to pieces those who have; but Jesus Christ turns it round the other way—'Do you possess *anything*, any property of pride, any sense of goodness, any virture, any gift? Then you will have to go through intolerable bereavement before you can ever be My disciple.' Intellectually that is inconceivable; spiritually it is clear to everyone who is rightly related to the Lord. HG. 8

The thing about our Lord and His teaching which puts Him immeasurably away from us nowadays is that He is opposed to all possessions, not only of money and property, but any kind of possession. That is the thing that makes Him such a deep-rooted enemy to the modern attitude to things. HG. 23

The religion of Jesus Christ is a religion of personal relationship to God and has nothing to do with possessions. MFL. 113

A sense of possessions is sufficient to render us spiritually dense because what we possess often possesses us. MFL. 113

Every possession produces an appetite that clings. NKW. 33

A sense of possession is sufficient to render us spiritually dense. Watch the havoc the winds of God play with possessions. RTR. 11

If your treasure is in gold or in land or the possessions of earth, that is where your heart will be, and when wars and rumours of wars arise, your heart will fail you for fear. SHH. 62

The sense of possession is a snare to true spiritual life. SHH. 63

If you have many possessions, it will ruin your trust and make you suspect everyone, and the better type of life is ruined. SHH. 64

The sense of property and of insurance is one of the greatest hindrances to development in the spiritual life. You cannot lay up for a rainy day if you are trusting Jesus Christ. SSM. 73

Jesus Christ does not claim any of our possessions. One of the most subtle errors is that God wants our possessions. He does not; they are not of any use to Him. He does not want my property, He wants myself. SSY. 60

It is because people live in the things they possess instead of in their relationship to God, that God at times seems to be cruel. SSY. 103

POSSIBLE/IMPOSSIBLE

It is 'impossible' for God to be born into human flesh; but Jesus was. It is 'impossible' for a dead man to rise again; but Jesus rose. It is 'impossible' for a man, even if he rose from the dead, to ascend into heaven; but Jesus did. When we reach the limit of what our common sense tells us can be done, then the word comes—"With God all things are possible." The limit of the possible means that God has a word of impossibility which He will perform in us if we have faith. PH. 126

POVERTY

We have grown literally afraid of being poor. We despise anyone who elects to be poor in order to simplify and save his inner life. If he does not join the general scramble, and pant with the money-making street, we deem him spiritless and lacking in ambition. We have lost the power of imagining what the ancient idealization of poverty could have meant—the liberation from material attachments, the unbribed soul, the manlier indifference, the paying our way by what we are or do, and not by what we have; the right to fling away our life at any moment irresponsibly, the more athletic trim, in short, the moral fighting shape. CD. VOL. 2, 77

The knowledge of my poverty brings me to the frontier where Jesus Christ works, as long as a man is sufficient for himself, God can do nothing for him. CHI. 22

The sign that Jesus Christ has come to us is the sense of our inner unworthiness. GW. 127

The thing in which I am blessed is my poverty. If I know I have no strength of will, no nobility of disposition, then, says Jesus, 'Blessed are you,' because it is through that poverty that I enter into the Kingdom of Heaven. I cannot enter the Kingdom of Heaven as a good man or woman; I can only enter the Kingdom of Heaven as a complete pauper. LG. 37

The bedrock in Jesus Christ's kingdom is poverty, not possession; weakness, not strength of will; infirmity of character, not goodness; a sense of absolute poverty, not decisions for Christ. 'Blessed are the poor in spirit.' LG. 114

God comes in where my helplessness begins, that is the bedrock of entering the kingdom of heaven. "Blessed are the poor in spirit." RTR. 26

Today we are so afraid of poverty that we never dream of doing anything that might involve us in being poor. SHH. 143

The scare of poverty will knock the spiritual backbone out of us unless we have the relationship to God that holds. It is easy to fling away what you have, child's play to sell all you have got and have nothing left, the easiest piece of impulse, nothing heroic in it; the thing that is difficult is to remain detached from what you have so that when it goes you do not notice it. That is only possible by the power of the love of God in Christ Jesus. SHL. 103

POWER

The power that can make a man either a compeer of the Lord or a compeer of the devil is the most terrible power of the soul. BP. 59

Man's personal powers are apt to be looked at as a marvellous promise of what he is going to be; the Bible looks at man as a ruin of what he was designed to be. CHI. 13

The One who made the world and who upholds all things by the word of His power, is the One who keeps His saints. GW. 44

We have a great deal more power than we know, and as we do the overcoming we find He is there all the time until it becomes the habit of our life. HGM. 30

The wonder is not that Jesus showed His marvellous power, but that He did not show it. He continually covered it up. IWP. 109

Physical power is nothing before moral power. A frail simple girl can overcome a brute who has the strength of an ox by moral superiority. IWP. 109

God will never have more power than He has now; if He could have, He would cease to be God. NKW. 55

Can God keep me from stumbling this second? Yes. Can He keep me from sin this second? Yes. Well, that is the whole of life. You cannot live more than a second at a time. If God can keep you blameless this second, He can do it the next. No wonder Jesus Christ said "Let not your heart be troubled!" We do get troubled when we do not remember the amazing power of God. RTR. 87

PRAISE

"All Thy works shall praise Thee." In the ear of God everything He created makes exquisite music, and man joined in the pæan of praise until he fell, then there came in the frantic discord of sin. The realization of Redemption brings man by way of the minor note of repentance back into tune with praise again. AUG. 10

To shout 'Hallelujah' is humbug unless it is genuine. Jesus never tells you to shout 'Hallelujah': He says—'Do as I have done to you.' GW. 96

If we only praise when we feel like praising, it is simply an undisciplined expression, but if we deliberately go over the neck of our disinclination and offer the sacrifice of praise, we are emancipated by our very statements. PH. 208

In the matter of praise, when we are not sure of having done well we always like to find out what people think; when we are certain we have done well, we do not care an atom whether folk praise us or not. SSM. 41

We never want praise if we have done perfectly what we ought to do; we only want praise if we are not sure whether we have done well. Jesus did not want praise; He did not need it, and He says 'that my joy may be in you.' SSY. 98

PRAYER

In our praying we draw on our memories, on our past experiences, on our present desires. We only learn to draw on the grace of God by pureness, by knowledge, by long-suffering. AUG. 125

The time a Christian gives to prayer and communion with God is not meant for his natural life, but meant to nourish the life of the Son of God in him. God engineers the circumstances of His saints in order that the Spirit may use them as the praying-house of the Son of God. If you are spiritual the Holy Spirit is offering up prayers in your bodily temple that you know nothing about, it is the Spirit making intercession in you. BE. 46

The essential meaning of prayer is that it nourishes the life of the Son of God in me and enables Him to manifest Himself in my mortal flesh. BE. 46

Certain things can only be dealt with by ignoring them; if you face them you increase their power. It is absurd to say, Pray about them; when once a thing is seen to be wrong, don't pray about it, it fixes the mind on it; never for a second brood on it, destroy it by neglect. BE. 47

Most of us mouth diction before God; we do not pray; we say in prayer what we ought to say, not what is actually natural to us to say. It may sound very interesting and noble, but it is not our own, it is mere sounding brass and clanging cymbals, there is no reality in it. BFB. 42

It takes a tremendous amount of reiteration on God's part before we understand what prayer is. We do not pray at all until we are at our wits' end. BFB. 75

The most beautiful prayers are prayers that are rites, but they are apt to be mere repetition, and not of the nature of Reality. There is no sting in them, no tremendous grip of a man face to face with things. There is no way out by rites or by religious beliefs, but only, as Jesus Christ indicates, by prayer. BFB. 75

When a man is at his wits' end it is not a cowardly thing to pray, it is the only way he can get in touch with Reality. 'O that I knew where I could get in touch with the Reality that explains things!' There is only one way, and that is the way of prayer. BFB. 75

There is nothing to be valued more highly than to have people praying for us; God links up His power in answer to their prayers. BFB. 76

Jesus Christ did not say, 'Ask what you like, and it shall be done unto you', but 'ask what you *will*, ask when your will is in, the thing that is a real problem to you', and God has pledged His honour that you will get the answer every time. BFB. 77

We do not ask, we worry, whereas one minute in prayer will put God's decree at work, viz., that He answers prayer on the ground of Redemption. BFB. 77

We have not the remotest conception of what is done by our prayers, nor have we the right to try and examine and understand it; all we know is that Jesus Christ laid all stress on prayer. "And greater works than these shall he do; because I go unto My Father. And whatsoever ye

shall ask in My name, that will I do." BP. 159

The revelation of our spiritual standing is what we ask in prayer; sometimes what we ask is an insult to God; we ask with our eyes on the possibilities or on ourselves, not on Jesus Christ. BSG. 58

Do not say, 'If I only had so and so;' you have not got so and so; but you can, if you will, select a place where you are actually. We can always do what we want to do if we want to do it sufficiently keenly. Do it now, "*enter into thy closet;*" and remember, it is a place selected to pray in, not to make little addresses in, or for any other purpose than to pray in, never forget that. CD. VOL. 1, 33

Prayer seems suitable for old men and women and sentimental young people, but for all others it is apt to be looked upon as a religious weakness. CD. VOL. 1, 116

When the veil is lifted we shall find that the seemly conduct of prayer wrought the things of God in men. Let us keep awake and readjust ourselves to our Lord's counsel. He counsels His children to keep alert, to be pure, to yield to no temptation to panic, to false emotion, to illegitimate gain, or to a cowardly sense of futility. We can never be where we are not, we are just where we are; let us keep alert and pray just there for His sake. Then our Lord says we shall be accounted worthy to escape all these things that shall come to pass, and to stand before the Son of Man—stand, not lie, nor grovel, nor cry, but stand upright, in the full integrity of Christian manhood and womanhood before the Son of Man. CD. VOL. 1, 117

. . . our Lord prayed because He was concentrated on God; that is, He did not worship prayer. CD. VOL. 2, 9

. . . in the New Testament, and in the life of our Lord, prayer is not so much an acquired culture as the implicit nature of the spiritual life itself. Outside the New Testament prayer is apt to be presented as something entirely acquired, something placed in the position of a meritorious decoration for valiant service in piety. CD. VOL. 2, 12

. . . the position we are apt to give to prayer is too consciously an attainment of communion, and thus it is presented out of all proportion, so that in times of spiritual declension we are inclined to place the need of prayer instead of penitent approach to God in the forefront. CD. VOL. 2, 12

Prayer does not bring us into contact with the rationality of human existence but into accordance with eternal Reality. The great Reality of Redemption, and Redemption is the platform of prayer. CD. VOL. 2, 14

Prayer is the evidence that I am spiritually concentrated on God, when to forethink is but to pray about everything, and to live in actual conditions is to be thankful in anything. CD. VOL. 2, 15

Prayer is not to be used as the petted privilege of a spoiled child seeking for ideal conditions in which to indulge his spiritual propensities *ad lib.*, the purpose of prayer is the maintenance of fitness in an ideal relationship with God amid conditions which ought not to be merely ideal but really actual. Actualities are not here to be idealized, but to be realized, while by prayer we lay hold on God and He unites us into His consciousness. CD. VOL. 2, 16

The purpose of prayer is to reveal the presence of God equally present all the time in every condition. CD. VOL. 2, 16

In regard to prayer, we are apt to be apologetic and apathetic, complex and confused; yet what a splendid audacity a childlike child has! and that is what our Lord taught us to have. CD. VOL. 2, 17

You very earnestly and solemnly tax your resources to be a praying person; people call at your house but cannot see you because it is your time for prayer. You perhaps have not noticed before that you always take care to tell those to whom it matters how early you rise in the morning to pray, how many all nights of prayer you spend; you have great zealousness in proclaiming your protracted meetings. This is all pious play-acting. Jesus says, 'Don't do it.' CD. VOL. 2, 18

Our Lord did not say it was wrong to pray in the corners of the street, but He did say it was wrong to have the motive to be *"seen of men."* CD. VOL. 2, 18

It is not wrong to pray in the early morning, but it is wrong to have the motive that it should be known. CD. VOL. 2, 18

Avoid every tendency away from the simplicity of relationship to God in Christ Jesus, and then prayer will be as the breath of the lungs in a healthy body. CD. VOL. 2, 19

When we ask 'grace before meat' let us remember that it is not to be a mere pious custom, but a real reception of the idea of Jesus that God enables us to receive our daily bread from Him. CD. VOL. 2, 25

To pray strenuously needs careful cultivation. We have to learn the most natural methods of expressing ourselves to our Father. CD. VOL. 2, 35

. . . a most beneficial exercise in secret prayer before the Father, is to write things down so that I see exactly what I think and want to say. Only those who have tried these ways know the ineffable benefit of such strenuous times in secret. CD. VOL. 2, 36

It is comparatively easy to think or say apt things about private prayer, but it is not so easy to say things about public prayer, the reason probably being that few of us are willing to carry the cross of public prayer, or at least if we do, we repeat aloud to a large extent our own private concerns, which are much better told in secret and alone. It is easier too to evade self-consciousness in private prayer; emancipation from self-consciousness is like a deliverance from a terrible sickness, and one gets rather alarmed at the slightest symptom of it again. Probably this is the reason why many Christians, who ought to be the strength and safeguard of a public prayer meeting in a community of Christians, are not so; they keep silent and just one or two have merely the gift of devotional language are allowed to dominate the prayer meeting; and the mid-week prayer meeting is given up and becomes the mid-week service. We must remember that there is a sacrifice of prayer as well as a sacrifice of praise. CD. VOL. 2, 39

Prayer is simple, as simple as a child making known its wants to its parents; prayer is stupid, because it is not according to common sense; it is certain that God does things in answer to prayer, and this, common sense naturally says, is ridiculous; prayer is supernatural because it relies entirely on God. CD. VOL. 2, 43

Prayer to the natural man who has not been born from above is so simple, so stupid, and so supernatural as to be at once 'taboo.' CD. VOL. 2, 43

Prayer is the outcome of our apprehension of the nature of God, and the means whereby we assimilate more and more of His mind. CD. VOL. 2, 46

If we interpret God's designs by our desires, we will say He gave us a scorpion when we asked an egg, and a serpent when we asked a fish, and a stone when we asked for bread. But our Lord indicates that such thinking and speaking is too hasty, it is not born of faith or reliance on God. *"Everyone that asketh receiveth."* CD. VOL. 2, 48

The battle of prayer is against two things in the earthlies: wandering thoughts, and lack of intimacy with God's character as revealed in His word. Neither can be cured at once, but they can be cured by discipline. CD. VOL. 2, 49

. . . when wandering thoughts come in in prayer, don't ask God to forgive you, but stop having them. It is not a bit of use to ask God to keep out wandering thoughts, you must keep them out. CD. VOL. 2, 50

Prayer is not logical, it is a mysterious moral working of the Holy Spirit. CD. VOL. 2, 51

We lean to our own understanding, or we bank on service and do away with prayer, and consequently by succeeding in the external we fail in the eternal, because in the eternal we succeed only by prevailing prayer. CD. VOL. 2, 57

The prayer of the feeblest saint on earth who lives in the Spirit and keeps right with God is a terror to Satan. The very powers of darkness are paralysed by prayer; no spiritualistic séance can succeed in the presence of a humble praying saint. No wonder Satan tries to keep our minds fussy in active work till we cannot think in prayer. CD. VOL. 2, 59

It is a vital necessity for Christians to think along the lines on which they pray. The philosophy of prayer is that prayer is *the* work. CD. VOL. 2, 60

Remember, you have to ask things which are in keeping with the God whom Jesus Christ reveals. DI. 39

'Asking' in prayer is at once the test of three things—simplicity, stupidity, and certainty of God. DI. 39

Prayer means that I come in contact with an Almighty Christ, and almighty results happen along the lines He laid down. DI. 39

The Bible knows nothing about a gift of prayer, the only prayer the Bible talks about is the prayer that is able to bring down something from God to men. DI. 40

The illustrations of prayer our Lord uses are on the line of importunity, a steady, persistent, uninterrupted habit of prayer. DI. 40

God puts us in circumstances where He can answer the prayer of His Son and the prayer of the Holy Ghost. DI. 40

Prayer is the vital breath of the Christian; not the thing that makes him alive, but the evidence that he *is* alive. DI. 40

If your crowd knows you as a man or woman of prayer, they have a right to expect from you a nobler type of conduct than from others. DI. 41

If I pray that someone else may be, or do, something which I am not, and don't intend to do, my praying is paralysed. DI. 41

When you put God first you will get your times of prayer easily because God can entrust them to the soul who won't use them in an irrational way and give an occasion to the enemy to enter in. DI. 41

See that you do not use the trick of prayer to cover up what you know you ought to do. DI. 42

The prayer of the saints is never self-important, but always God-important. DI. 42

Learn to be vicarious in public prayer. Allow two rivers to come through you: the river of God, and the river of human interests. Beware of the danger of preaching in prayer, of being doctrinal. DI. 48

—tell God what you know He knows in order that you may get to know it as He does. GW. 20

New Testament praying is getting hold of a personal God through the opening up of a channel whereby God can deal directly with those for whom we pray. Such prayer humbles the soul always, and gives the life the benediction of being rightly related to God. GW. 51

We have to pray with our eyes on God, not on the difficulties. GW. 99

Prayer is God's ordained way, the insignificant way of prayer. GW. 99

There is always a suitable place to pray, to lift up your eyes to God; there is no need to get to a place of prayer, pray wherever you are. HG. 22

We discern spiritual truth not by intellectual curiosity or research, but by entreating the favour of the Lord, that is, by prayer and by no other way, not even by obedience, because obedience is apt to have an idea of merit. HGM. 71

Prayer is not only to be about big things, but talking to God about everything— "Let your requests be made known." HGM. 72

It is easy to create a false emotion in prayer, nothing easier than to work ourselves up until we imagine we are really concerned about a thing when we are not because it has never been brought to our mind by the Holy Spirit. That kind of prayer is not natural, we let our emotions carry us away. HGM. 72

God brings His marvels to pass in lives by means of prayer, and the prayers of the saints are part of God's programme. HGM. 78

God allows the prayers of the saints, those who have entered into an understanding of His mind and purpose, to be brought to Him. HGM. 78

The whole idea of the prayers of the saints is that God's holiness, God's purpose, and God's wise ways may be brought about irrespective of who comes or goes. HGM. 79

The prayers of the saints either enable or disable God in the performance of His wonders. The majority of us in praying for the will of God to be done say, 'In God's good time', meaning 'in my bad time'; consequently there is no silence in

heaven produced by or prayers, no results, no performance. HGM. 79

Inarticulate prayer, the impulsive prayer that looks so futile, is the great thing God heeds more than anything else because it is along the line of His programme. HGM. 80

A prayer offered by the humblest and most obscure saint on the ground of the Redemption of Jesus Christ demands the complete attention of God and the performance of His programme. HGM. 80

Specific times and places and communion with God go together. It is by no haphazard chance that in every age men have risen early to pray. The first thing that marks decline in spiritual life is our relationship to the early morning. HGM. 87

If you have ever prayed in the dawn you will ask yourself why you were so foolish as not to do it always: it is difficult to get into communion with God in the midst of the hurly-burley of the day. HGM. 87

We heard it said that we shall suffer if we do not pray; I question it. What will suffer if we do not pray is the life of God in us; but when we do pray and devote the dawns to God His nature in us develops, there is less self-realization and more Christ-realization. HGM. 88

The more you know the less intelligently you pray because you forget to believe that God can alter the difficulties. HGM. 128

We generally look upon prayer as a means of getting things for ourselves, whereas the Bible idea of prayer is that God's holiness and God's purpose and God's wise order may be brought about, irrespective of who comes or who goes. Our ordinary views of prayer are not found in the New Testament. IYA. 10

Prayer is the way the life of God is nourished. Our Lord nourished the life of God in Him by prayer; He was continually in contact with His Father. IYA. 10

Prayer is other than meditation; it is that which develops the life of God in us. IYA. 10

If we look on prayer as a means of developing ourselves, there is nothing in it at all, nor do we find that idea of prayer in the Bible. IYA. 10

Jesus says we are to pray in His name, i.e., in His nature, and His nature is shed abroad in our hearts by the Holy Ghost when we are born from above. IYA. 11

Prayer . . . is not to be used as the petted privilege of a spoiled child seeking for ideal conditions in which to indulge his spiritual propensities *ad lib.*; the purpose of prayer is to reveal the Presence of God, equally present at all times and in every condition. IYA. 11

I question whether the people who continually ask for prayer meetings know the first element of prayer. It is often an abortion of religious hysterics, a disease of the nerves taking a spiritual twist. IYA. 11

It is not so true that "Prayer changes things" as that prayer changes *me*, and then I change things; consequently we must not ask God to do what He has created us to do. IYA. 14

When you pray, *things* remain the same, but *you* begin to be different. IYA. 14

Prayer is not a question of altering things externally, but of working wonders in a man's disposition. IYA. 14

God has so constituted things that prayer on the basis of Redemption alters the way a man looks at things. IYA. 14

The good of praying is that it gets us to know God and enables God to perform His order through us, no matter what His permissive will may be. IYA. 15

If prayer is not easy, we are wrong; if prayer is an effort, we are out of it. IYA. 17

There is only one kind of person who can really pray, and that is the childlike saint, the simple, stupid, supernatural child of God; I do mean 'stupid.' Immediately you try to explain why God answers prayer on the ground of reason, it is nonsense; God answers prayer on the ground of Redemption and no other ground. IYA. 17

. . . our prayers are heard, not because we are in earnest, not because we suffer, but because Jesus suffered. IYA. 17

It is because our Lord Jesus Christ went through the depths of agony to the last ebb in the Garden of Gethsemane, because He went through Calvary, that we have "boldness to enter into the holy place." IYA. 17

. . . what makes prayer easy is not our wits or our understanding, but the tremendous agony of God in Redemption. A thing is worth just what it costs. Prayer is not what it costs us, but what it cost God to enable us to pray. It cost God so much that a little child can pray. It cost God Almighty so much that anyone can pray. But it is time those of us who name His Name knew the secret of the cost, and the secret is here, "My soul is exceeding sorrowful, even unto death." IYA. 22

The tendency nowadays is to worship prayer, stress is put on nights of prayer and the difficulty and cost of prayer. It is not prayer that is strenuous, but the overcoming of our own laziness. If we make the basis of prayer our effort and agony and nights of prayer, we mistake the basis of prayer. The basis of prayer is not what it costs us, but what it costs God to enable us to pray. IYA. 30

We have the idea that prayer is for special times, but we have to put on the armour of God for the continual practice of prayer, so that any struggling onslaught of the powers of darkness cannot touch the position of prayer. IYA. 31

When we pray easily it is because Satan is completely defeated in his onslaughts; when we pray difficultly it is because Satan is gaining a victory. We have not been continuously practising, we have not been facing things courageously, we have not been taking our orders from our Lord. Our Lord did not say, 'Go' or 'Do'; He said, "Watch and pray." IYA. 31

If we struggle in prayer it is because the enemy is gaining ground. If prayer is simple to us, it is because we have the victory. There is no such thing as a holiday for the beating of your heart. If there is, the grave comes next. And there is no such thing as a moral or spiritual holiday. IYA. 32

If we are struggling in prayer it is because the wiles of the enemy are getting the upper hand, and we must look for the cause of it in the lack of discipline in ourselves. IYA. 33

The only way to keep right is to watch and pray. Prayer on any other basis than

that on which it is placed in the New Testament is stupid, and the basis of prayer is not human earnestness, not human need, not the human will, it is Redemption, and its living centre is a personal Holy Ghost. IYA. 35

There is nothing a rationally-minded being can ridicule more easily than prayer. "Praying always"—the unutterable simplicity of it! No panic, no flurry, always at leisure from ourselves on the inside. IYA. 36

. . . the prayers in the Old Testament have to do with an earthly people in an earthly setting; the prayers in the New Testament have to do with a heavenly state of mind in a heavenly people while on this earth. IYA. 39

The 'asking and receiving' prayer is elementary, it is the part of prayer we can understand, but it is not necessarily praying in the Holy Ghost. IYA. 59

The whole meaning of prayer is that we may know God. IYA. 59

When we pray in the Holy Ghost we are released from our petitions. IYA. 59

Praying in the Holy Ghost means the power given to us by God to maintain a simple relationship to Jesus Christ, and it is most difficult to realise this simple relationship in the matter of prayer. IYA. 59

Prayer is not an exercise, it is the life. IYA. 60

When we learn to pray in the Holy Ghost, we find there are some things for which we cannot pray, there is a sense of restraint. Never push and say, 'I know it is God's will and I am going to stick to it.' Beware, remember what is recorded of the children of Israel: "He gave them their request; but sent leanness into their soul." IYA. 60

Let the Spirit of God teach you what He is driving at and learn not to grieve Him. If we are abiding in Jesus Christ we shall ask what He wants us to ask, whether we are conscious of doing so or not. IYA. 61

When we pray relying on the Holy Ghost, He will always bring us back to this one point, that we are not heard because we are in earnest, or because we need to be heard, or because we will perish if we are not heard; we are heard only on the ground of the Atonement of our Lord. IYA. 61

The Holy Ghost will continually interpret to us that the only ground of our approach to God is *"by the blood of Jesus,"* and by no other way. As we learn the spiritual culture of praying in the Holy Ghost, we shall find that the common-sense circumstances God puts us in, and the common-sense people His providence places us amongst, are used by Him to enable us to realise that the one fundamental thing in prayer is the atoning work of Jesus Christ. IYA. 61

So many of us limit our praying because we are not reckless in our confidence in God. In the eyes of those who do not know God, it is madness to trust Him, but when we pray in the Holy Ghost we begin to realise the resources of God, that He is our perfect heavenly Father, and we are His children. IYA. 62

If the Holy Spirit is having His way in us, He will charge the atmosphere round about us. There are things that have to be cleared away by the Holy Ghost. Never fight; stand and wrestle. Wrestling is not fighting, it is closing with the antagonist on your own ground, and maintaining a steady, all-embracing 'stand' and 'with-

stand.' How many of us succumb to flesh and blood circumstances—'I did not sleep well'; or, 'I have indigestion'; or, 'I did not do quite the right thing there.' Never allow any of these things to be the reason to yourself why you are not prevailing in prayer. There are hundreds of people with impaired bodies who know what it is to pray in the Holy Ghost. IYA. 63

In work for God never look at flesh and blood causes; meet every arrangement for the day in the power of the Holy Ghost. It makes no difference what your work is, or what your circumstances are; if you are praying in the Holy Ghost, He will produce an atmosphere round about you, and all these things will redound to the glory of God. IYA. 63

Inarticulate prayer, the impulsive prayer that looks so futile, is the thing God always heeds. The habit of ejaculatory prayer ought to be the persistent habit of each one of us. IYA. 63

We think of prayer as a preparation for work, or a calm after having done work, whereas prayer is the essential work. It is the supreme activity of everything that is noblest in our personality. IYA. 83

There is a real danger of worshipping prayer instead of praying because we worship. It is easy to do it if once we lose sight of our Lord and the emphasis is put not on His command, but on the thing which He commands. IYA. 93

Prayer is simple, prayer is supernatural, and to anyone not related to our Lord Jesus Christ, prayer is apt to look stupid. IYA. 93

Not only is prayer the work, but prayer is the way whereby fruit abides. Our Lord puts prayer as the means to fruit-producing and fruit-abiding work; but remember, it is prayer based on His agony, not on our agony. IYA. 94

The reason prayer is so important is, first of all, because our Lord told us that prayer on the ground of His Redemption is the most mighty factor He has put into our hands, and second, because of the personal presence of the Holy Ghost in the day in which we live. IYA. 96

We realise that we are energised by the Holy Spirit for prayer, we know what it is to pray in the atmosphere and the presence of the Holy Spirit; but we do not so often realise that the Holy Spirit Himself prays in us with prayers that we cannot utter. IYA. 99

Some of the qualities of God must be merged into us before our prayers can be fit for His acceptance. IYA. 101

The sinner out of heart with self is nearest God in prayer. IYA. 103

When we draw on the human side of our experience only, our prayers become amazingly flippant and familiar, and we ourselves become amazingly hard and metallic; but if along with the human element we rely on the Holy Spirit, we shall find that our prayers become more and more inarticulate; and when they are inarticulate, reverence grows deeper and deeper, and undue familiarity has the effect of a sudden blow on the face. IYA. 106

Ask yourself how much time you have taken up asking God that you may not do the things you do. He will never answer, you have simply not to do them. Every time God speaks, there is something we must obey. We should do well to revise what we pray about. Some of the things we pray about are as absurd as if we prayed, 'O Lord, take me out of this room,' and then refused to go. MFL. 40

One of our greatest needs is to have a place where we deliberately attend; that is the real meaning of prayer. "Enter into thy closet, and when thou hast shut thy door, pray to thy Father which is in secret." MFL. 59

Our prayers for God's help are often nothing but incarnate laziness, and God has to say, "Speak no more unto Me of this matter. Get thee up . . ." MFL. 73

The majority of us are unable to fix our thoughts in prayer, we lie all abroad before God and do not rouse ourselves up to lay hold of Him, consequently we have wandering thoughts continually. God will not bring every thought and imagination into captivity; we have to do it, and that is the test of spiritual concentration. MFL. 79

The inattentive, slovenly way we drift into the presence of God is an indication that we are not bothering to think about Him. Whenever our Lord spoke of prayer, He said, "*ask.*" It is impossible to ask if you do not concentrate. MFL. 80

Prayer is not an emotion, not a sincere desire; prayer is the most stupendous effort of the will. "Let your requests be made known unto God. And the peace of God, which passeth all understanding, shall guard your hearts and your thoughts in Christ Jesus," the poising power of the peace of God will enable you to steer your course in the mix-up of ordinary life. MFL. 95

Prayer is the supreme activity of all that is noblest in our personality, and the essential nature of prayer is faith. NKW. 79

Unless you are a saint, your praying is pious humbug; but if you are a saint, you soon realize that you discover the Divine by energetically doing the human, provided you are maintaining a personal relationship to God. NKW. 143

In prayer have we learned the wonderful power of that phrase ". . . boldness to enter into the holiest by the blood of Jesus?" It means that we can talk to God as Jesus Christ did, but only through the right of His Atonement. We must never allow the idea that because we have been obedient, because our need is great, because we long for it, therefore God will hear us. There is only one way into the holiest, and that is by the blood of Jesus. OBH. 45

Nothing is more difficult than to ask. We long, and desire, and crave, and suffer, but not until we are at the extreme limit will we *ask*. A sense of unreality makes us ask. We cannot bring ourselves up against spiritual reality when we like—all at once the staggering realization dawns that we are destitute of the Holy Spirit, ignorant of all that the Lord Jesus stands for. The first result of being brought up against reality is this realization of poverty, of the lack of wisdom, lack of the Holy Spirit, lack of power, lack of a grip of God. "If any of you lack wisdom, let him ask of God . . .", but be sure you do lack wisdom. OBH. 93

Prayer is not a question of altering things externally, but of working wonders in a man's disposition. OBH. 116

Our Lord's teaching about prayer is so amazingly simple but at the same time so amazingly profound that we are apt to miss His meaning. The danger is to water down what Jesus says about prayer and make it mean something more common sense; if it were only common sense, it was not worth His while to say it. The things Jesus says about prayer are supernatural revelations. OBH. 116

Never *say* you will pray about a thing; *pray about it.* OBH. 116

One great effect of prayer is that it enables the soul to command the body. By obedience I make my body submissive to my soul, but prayer puts my soul in command of my body. OBH. 116

If God sees that my spiritual life will be furthered by giving the things for which I ask, then He will give them, but that is not the end of prayer. The end of prayer is that I come to know God Himself. OBH. 116

The meaning of prayer is that we recognize we are in the relationship of a child to his father. "Your heavenly Father knoweth what things ye have need of, before ye ask Him." OBH. 122

Prayer in distress dredges the soul. It is a good thing to keep a note of the things you prayed about when you were in distress. We remain ignorant of ourselves because we do not keep a spiritual autobiography. OPG. 58

Beware of having plans in your petitions before God; they are the most faithful source of misgiving. If you pray along the line of your plans misgivings are sure to come, and if the misgivings are not heeded you will pervert God's purpose in the very thing which was begun at His bidding. OPG. 59

". . . Ask whatsoever ye will," i.e. not what you like, but ask that which your personal life is in. There is very little that our personal life is in when we pray, we spell out platitudes before God and call it prayer, but it is not prayer at all. PH. 163

Jesus has pledged His honour that everything I ask with the blood of my life in, I shall have. No false emotion is necessary, we have not to conjure up petitions, they well up. PH. 163

The 'greater works' are done by prayer because prayer is the exercise of the essential character of the life of God in us. PH. 163

Prayer is not meant to develop us naturally, it is meant to give the life of the Son of God in us a chance to develop that the natural order may be transfigured into the spiritual. PH. 163

Our true character comes out in the way we pray. PH. 167

It is rarely the big compellings of God that get hold of us in our prayers, instead we tell God what He should do, we tell Him that men are being lost and that He ought to save them. This is a terrific charge against God, it means that He must be asleep. PH. 179

'But I don't feel that God is my Father': Jesus said, 'Say it'—"*say*, Our Father," and you will suddenly discover that He is. The safeguard against moral imprisonment is prayer. Don't pray according to your moods, but resolutely launch out on God, say "Our Father," and before you know where you are, you are in a larger room. PH. 210

Every time we pray our horizon is altered, our attitude to things is altered, not sometimes but every time, and the amazing thing is that we don't pray more. PH. 215

Prayer is a complete emancipation, it keeps us on the spiritual plane. PH. 215

Prayer with us often becomes merely a way of patronising God. PR. 74

Our Lord's view of prayer is that it represents the highest reach possible to a man or woman when rightly related to God, perfectly obedient in every particular, and in perfect communion with Him. PR. 74

. . . no man has time to pray, he has to take time from other things that are valuable in order to understand how necessary time for prayer is. The things that act like thorns and stings in our personal lives will go instantly we pray; we won't feel the smart any more, because we have got God's point of view about them. PR. 97

Prayer means that we get into union with God's view of other people. Our devotion as saints is to identify ourselves with God's interests in other lives. God pays no attention to our personal affinities; He expects us to identify ourselves and *His* interests in others. PR. 97

When you have been touched by the Holy Spirit and have received His quickening, note what you evade in prayer. There is nothing that will detect spiritual rottenness quicker than to *ask*, i.e., with the will. We shall find we have to stop asking a number of things, and this will simplify prayer. PR. 125

Do not ask others to pray for you; our Lord says, 'Pray yourself, *ask*.' PR. 126

Interest is natural, attention must be by effort. One of the great needs of the Christian life is to have a place where we deliberately attend to realities. That is the real meaning of prayer. RTR. 14

The secret of our inefficiency for God is that we do not believe what He tells us about prayer. Prayer is not rational but Redemptive. Little books of prayer are full of "buts". The New Testament says that God will answer prayer every time. The point is not—"will you believe?", but "will I, who know Jesus Christ, believe on your behalf?" RTR. 20

When we lean to our own understanding we do away with prayer and bank all on service. Consequently by succeeding in the external we fail in the eternal. In the eternal we succeed only by prevailing prayer. RTR. 24

The habit of ejaculatory prayer ought to be the persistent habit of each one of us. RTR. 44

Prayer imparts the power to walk and not faint. RTR. 50

Mental wool-gathering can be stopped immediately the will is roused. Prayer is an effort of will, and the great battle in prayer is the overcoming of mental wool-gathering. We put things down to our own inability to concentrate. "My soul, wait thou only upon God", i.e. pull yourself together and be silent unto God. RTR. 66

Prayer is often a temptation to bank on a miracle of God instead of on a moral issue, i.e., it is much easier to ask God to do my work than it is to do it myself. Until we are disciplined properly, we will always be inclined to bank on God's miracles and refuse to do the moral thing ourselves. It is our job, and it will never be done unless we do it. SA. 90

Prayer alters a man on the inside, alters his mind and his attitude to things. The point of praying is not that we get things from God, but that we learn by prayer to detect the difference between God's order and God's permissive will. God's order

is—no pain, no sickness, no devil, no war, no sin: His permissive will is all these things, the "soup" we are in just now. What a man needs to do is to get hold of God's order in the kingdom on the inside, and then he will begin to see how to handle the riddle of the universe on the outside. SHH. 19

We are all agnostic about God, about the Spirit of God, and prayer. It is nonsense to call prayer reasonable; it is the most super-reasonable thing there is. SHH. 97

Prayer, says Jesus, is to be looked at in the same way as philanthropy, viz., your eyes on God, not on men. Watch your motive before God; have no other motive in prayer than to know Him. The statements of Jesus about prayer which are so familiar to us are revolutionary. Call a halt one moment and ask yourself—'Why do I pray? What is my motive? Is it because I have a personal secret relationship to God known to no one but myself?' SSM. 58

. . . get a place for prayer where no one imagines that that is what you are doing, shut the door and talk to God in secret. SSM. 58

It is impossible to live the life of a disciple without definite times of secret prayer. You will find that the place to enter in is in your business, as you walk along the streets, in the ordinary ways of life, when no one dreams you are praying, and the reward comes openly, a revival here, a blessing there. SSM. 58

Prayer is not getting things from God, that is a most initial stage; prayer is getting into perfect communion with God; I tell Him what I know He knows in order that I may get to know it as He does. SSM. 59

Prayer is not only asking, it is an attitude of heart that produces an atmosphere in which asking is perfectly natural, and Jesus says, "every one that asketh receiveth." SSM. 84

When we pray on the fundamental basis of the Redemption, our prayers are made efficacious by the personal presence of the Holy Ghost Who makes real *in* us what Jesus did *for* us. SSY. 24

Prayer is the miracle of Redemption at work in us, which will produce the miracle of Redemption in the lives of others. SSY. 126

Jesus Christ says—*Pray*. It looks stupid; but when we labour at prayer results happen all the time from His standpoint, because God creates something in answer to, and by means of prayer, that was not in existence before. SSY. 130

'*Labour.*' It is the one thing we will not do. We will take open-air meetings, we will preach—but labour at prayer! There is nothing thrilling about a labouring man's work, but it is the labouring man who makes the conceptions of the genius possible; and it is the labouring saint who makes the conceptions of His Master possible. SSY. 130

We have to live depending on Jesus Christ's wisdom, not on our own. He is the Master, and the problem is His, not ours. We have to use the key He gives us, the key of prayer. Our Lord puts the key into our hands, and we have to learn to pray under His direction. That is the simplicity which He says His Father will bless. SSY. 131

Prayer is the answer to every problem there is. SSY. 131

PRAYER, ANSWERS

God has based the Christian life on Redemption, and as we pray on this basis God's honour is at stake to answer prayer. BFB. 109

Our Lord never referred to unanswered prayer; He taught that prayers were always answered, "*For every one that asketh receiveth.*" (Luke xi. 10.) He ever implied that prayers were answered rightly because of the Heavenly Father's wisdom, "*Your Father knoweth what things ye have need of, before ye ask Him.*" CD. VOL. 2, 17

Our prayers should be in accordance with the nature of God, therefore the answers are not in accordance with our nature but with His. We are apt to forget this and to say without thinking that God does not answer prayer; but He always answers prayer, and when we are in close communion with Him we know that we have not been misled. CD. VOL. 2, 45

Our Lord does not attempt to answer our questions on our level, He lifts us up to His level and allows us to make no excuse for not continuing in prayer. CD. VOL. 2, 49

The answers to prayer never come by introspection but always as a surprise. We don't hear God because we are so full of noisy introspective requests. DI. 40

According to the New Testament, prayer is God's answer to our poverty, not a power we exercise to obtain an answer. DI. 41

The greatest answer to prayer is that I am brought into a perfect understanding with God, and that alters my view of actual things. DI. 41

God does not give faith to answer to prayer: He reveals Himself in answer to prayer, and faith is exercised spontaneously. DI. 42

It is one thing to cry to God and another thing to hear Him answer. We don't give God time to answer. We come in a great fuss and panic, but when all that is taken out of our hearts and we are silent before God, the quiet certainty comes— 'I know God has heard me.' HG. 9

In the New Testament 'name' frequently stands for 'nature'. When we pray 'in the Name of Jesus' the answers are in accordance with His nature, and if we think our prayers are unanswered it is because we are not interpreting the answer along this line. HGM. 95

Our Lord in His teaching regarding prayer never once referred to unanswered prayer; He said God always answers prayer. If our prayers are in the name of Jesus, i.e., in accordance with His nature, the answers will not be in accordance with our nature, but with His. We are apt to forget this, and to say without thinking that God does not always answer prayer. He does every time, and when we are in close communion with Him, we realise that we have not been misled. IYA. 12

God answers prayer on the ground of Redemption and on no other ground. IYA. 17

Never make the blunder of trying to forecast the way God is going to answer your prayer. IYA. 39

God's silences are His answers. If we only take as answers those that are visible to our senses, we are in a very elementary condition of grace. IYA. 48

It is quite true God does not answer some prayers because they are wrong, but that is so obvious that it does not need a revelation from God to understand it. God wants us to stop understanding in the way we have understood and get into the place He wants us to get into, i.e., He wants us to know how to rely on Him. IYA. 48

It will be a wonderful moment for some of us when we stand before God and find that the prayers we clamoured for in early days and imagined were never answered, have been answered in the most amazing way, and that God's silence has been the sign of the answer. If we always want to be able to point to something and say, 'This is the way God answered my prayer,' God cannot trust us yet with His silence. IYA. 49

Some prayers are followed by silence because they are wrong, others because they are bigger than we can understand. IYA. 49

If it has been a prayer to know God better, a prayer for the baptism of the Holy Ghost, a prayer for the interpretation and understanding of God's word, it is a prayer in accordance with God's will. You say, 'But He has not answered.' He has, He is so near to you that His silence is the answer. His silence is big with terrific meaning that you cannot understand yet, but presently you will. IYA. 50

Remember that Jesus Christ's silences are always signs that He knows we can stand a bigger revelation than we think we can. If He gives you the exact answer, He cannot trust you yet. IYA. 51

One wonderful thing about God's stillness in connection with your prayers is that He makes you still, makes you perfectly confident, the contagion of Jesus

Christ's stillness gets into you—'I know He has heard me'—and His silence is the proof He has heard. IYA. 51

. . . if we are spiritual and can interpret His silence, we always get the trust in God that knows prayers are answered every time, not sometimes. The manifestation of the answer in place and time is a mere matter of God's sovereignty. Be earnest and eager on the line of praying. IYA. 51

Because Jesus Christ keeps silence it does not mean that He is displeased, but exactly the opposite, He is bringing us into the great run of His purpose, and the answer will be an amazing revelation. No wonder our Lord said, ". . . greater works than these shall he do; . . . And whatsoever ye shall ask in My name, that will I do." That is what prayer means, not that God may bless us. IYA. 52

As long as we have the idea only that God will bless us in answer to prayer, He will do it, but He will never give us the grace of a silence. If He is taking us into the understanding that prayer is for the glorifying of His Father, He will give us the first sign of His intimacy—silence. The devil calls it unanswered prayer. IYA. 52

God does not exist to answer our prayers, but by our prayers we come to discern the mind of God, and that is declared in John xvii, "That they may be one, even as We are one." IYA. 55

The efficacy of the atoning work of Christ is the one thing that the Holy Ghost works into our understanding, and as He interprets the meaning of that work to us we shall never bank on our own earnestness, or on our sense of need, nor shall we ever have the idea

that God does not answer, we shall be so restfully certain that He always does. IYA. 61

"Your Father knoweth what things ye have need of, before ye ask Him." Then why pray? To get to know your Father. It is not sufficient for us to say, 'Oh yes, God is love,' we have to know He is love, we have to struggle through until we do see He is love and justice, then our prayer is answered. IYA. 87

Our understanding of God is the answer to prayer; getting things from God is God's indulgence of us. When God stops giving us things, He brings us into the place where we can begin to understand Him. As long as we get from God everything we ask for, we never forget to know Him, we look upon Him as a blessing-machine that has nothing to do with God's character or with our characters. IYA. 87

It does sound unreasonable to say that God will do things in answer to prayer, yet our Lord said that He would. Our Lord bases everything on prayer, then the key to all our work as Christians is, "Pray ye therefore." IYA. 93

If we are abiding in Jesus and His words are abiding in us, then Jesus says God will answer our prayers. OBH. 122

Whenever the insistence is on the point that God answers prayer, we are off the track. The meaning of prayer is that we get hold of God, not of the answer. RTR. 31

God never answers prayer to prove His own might. RTR. 53

We impoverish God in our minds when we say there must be answers to our prayers on the material plane; the biggest answers to our prayers are in the realm of the unseen. RTR. 63

It is far more rare to find a sincere soul than one might suppose. No one but a fool or a sincere soul would ever pray this prayer—'Search me, O God, search me right out to the remotest depths, to the innermost recesses of my thoughts and imaginations; scrutinize me through and through until I know that Thou dost know me utterly, that I may be saved from my own ways and brought into Thy way.' Any soul who prays that prayer will be answered. SHL. 46

We are ill-taught if we look for results only in the earthlies when we pray. A praying saint performs far more havoc among the unseen forces of darkness than we have the slightest notion of. SHL. 55

If you are right with God and God delays the manifested answer to your prayer, don't misjudge Him, don't think of Him as an unkind friend, or an unnatural father, or an unjust judge, but keep at it, your prayer will certainly be answered, for "every one that asketh receiveth." SSM. 59

'Pray because you have a Father, not because it quietens you, and give Him time to answer.' SSM. 59

We pray pious blether, our will is not in it, and then we say God does not answer; we never *asked* Him for anything. Asking means that our wills are in what we ask. SSM. 85

You are born into this world and will probably never know to whose prayers your life is the answer. SSY. 15

Our lives are the answers not only to the prayers of other people, but to the prayer the Holy Spirit is making for us, and to the prayer of Our Lord Himself. SSY. 15

How God works in answer to prayer is a mystery that logic cannot penetrate, but that He does work in answer to prayer is gloriously true. SSY. 24

God's 'nothings' are His most positive answers. We have to stay on God and wait. Never try to help God to fulfil His word. SSY. 28

Prayer to us is not practical, it is stupid, and until we do see that prayer is stupid, that is, stupid from the ordinary natural common-sense point of view, we will never pray. 'It is absurd to think that God is going to alter things in answer to prayer!' But that is what Jesus says He will do. It sounds stupid, but it is a stupidity based on His Redemption. The reason that our prayers are not answered is that we are not stupid enough to believe what Jesus says. It is a child, and only a child who has prayer answered; a wise and prudent man does not. SSY. 125

PRAYER, INTERCESSORY

In Regeneration God works below the threshold of our consciousness; all we are conscious of is a sudden burst up into our conscious life, but as to when God begins to work no one can tell. This emphasizes the importance of intercessory prayer. A mother, a husband, or a wife, or a Christian worker, praying for another soul has a clear indication that God has answered their prayer; outwardly the one prayed for is just the same, there is no difference in his conduct, but the prayer is answered. The work is unconscious as yet, but at any second it may burst forth into conscious life. We cannot calculate where God begins to work any more than we can say when it is going to become conscious; that is why we have to pray in reliance on the Holy Spirit. BP. 158

If we only look for results in the earthlies when we pray, we are ill-taught. A praying saint performs far more havoc amongst the unseen forces of darkness than we have the slightest notion of. "The effectual fervent prayer of a righteous man availeth much in its working." BP. 159

Pray for your friends, and God will turn your captivity also. The emancipation comes as you intercede for them; it is not a mere reaction, it is the way God works. BFB. 109

Our importunity must be intercessory, and the whole power of our intercession lies in the certainty that prayer will be answered. CD. VOL. 2, 50

We take for granted that prayer is preparation for work, whereas prayer is *the* work, and we scarcely believe what the Bible reveals, viz. that through intercessory prayer God creates on the ground of the Redemption; it is His chosen way of working. CD. VOL. 2, 57

Intercessory prayer is part of the sovereign purpose of God. If there were no saints praying for us, our lives would be infinitely balder than they are, consequently the responsibility of those who never intercede and who are withholding blessing from other lives is truly appalling. CD. VOL. 2, 57

Intercessory prayer for one who is sinning prevails, God says so. The will of the man prayed for does not come into question at all, he is connected with God by prayer, and prayer on the basis of

the Redemption sets the connection working and God gives life. CD. VOL. 2, 58

Jesus Christ carries on intercession for us in heaven; the Holy Ghost carries on intercession in us on earth; and we the saints have to carry on intercession for all men. CD. VOL. 2, 60

If I am a Christian, I am not set on saving my own skin, but on seeing that the salvation of God comes through me to others, and the great way is by intercession. DI. 39

The reason for intercession is not that God *answers* prayer, but that God tells us to pray. DI. 40

Intercession does not develop the one who intercedes, it blesses the lives of those for whom he intercedes. The reason so few of us intercede is because we don't understand this. DI. 41

By intercessory prayer we can hold off Satan from other lives and give the Holy Ghost a chance with them. No wonder Jesus put such tremendous emphasis on prayer! DI. 41

Beware lest activity in proclaiming the Truth should mean a cunning avoidance of spiritual concentration in intercession. DI. 42

The meaning of prayer is that I bring power to bear upon another soul that is weak enough to yield and strong enough to resist; hence the need for strenuous intercessory prayer. DI. 42

Never try to make people agree with your point of view, begin the ministry of intercession. The only Being worth agreeing with is the Lord Jesus Christ. DI. 42

Intercessory prayer is the test of our loyalty. GW. 61

God expects us to be intercessors, not dogmatic fault-finders, but vicarious intercessors, until other lives come up to the same standard. HG. 12

The prominent people for God are marked for the wiles of the devil, and we must pray for them all the time; God gives us every now and again an alarming exhibition of what happens if we don't. IYA. 36

When we pray for others the Spirit of God works in the unconscious domain of their being that we know nothing about, and the one we are praying for knows nothing about, but after the passing of time the conscious life of the one prayed for begins to show signs of unrest and disquiet. We may have spoken until we are worn out, but have never come anywhere near, and we have given up in despair. But if we have been praying, we find on meeting them one day that there is the beginning of a softening in an enquiry and a desire to know something. It is that kind of intercession that does most damage to Satan's kingdom. It is so slight, so feeble in its initial stages that if reason is not wedded to the light of the Holy Spirit, we will never obey it, and yet it is that kind of intercession that the New Testament places most emphasis on, though it has so little to show for it. It seems stupid to think that we can pray and all that will happen, but remember to Whom we pray, we pray to a God Who understands the unconscious depths of a personality about which we know nothing, and He has told us to pray. The great Master of the human heart said, "Greater works than these shall he do. . . . And whatsoever ye shall ask in My name, that will I do." IYA. 94

There is only one field of service that has no snares, and that is the field of intercession. All other fields have the glorious but risky snare of publicity; prayer has not. IYA. 96

It is a mistake to interpret prayer on the natural instead of on the spiritual line, to say that because prayer brings us peace and joy and makes us feel better, therefore it is a Divine thing. This is the mere accident or effect of prayer, there is no real God-given revelation in it. This is the God-given revelation: that when we are born again of the Spirit of God and indwelt by the Holy Spirit, He intercedes for us with a tenderness and an understanding akin to the Lord Jesus Christ and akin to God, that is, He expresses the unutterable for us. IYA. 103

. . . your intercessions can never be mine, and my intercessions can never be yours, but the Holy Ghost makes intercession in our particular editions, without which intercession someone will be impoverished. Let us remember the depth and height and solemnity of our calling as saints. IYA. 109

The greatest barrier to intercession is that we take ourselves so seriously, and come to the conclusion that God is reserved with us; He is not. God has to ignore things we take so seriously until our relationship to Him is exactly that of a child. MFL. 83

It is an insult to sink before God and say 'Thy will be done' when there has been no intercession. That is the prayer of impertinent unbelief—There is no use in praying, God does whatever He chooses. The saying of 'Thy will be done' is born of the most intimate relationship to God whereby I talk to Him freely. NKW. 79

Repetition in intercessory importunity is not bargaining, but the joyous insistence of prayer. NKW. 79

The cure of uncertainty is a new note of intercessory prayer. The reason for perplexity in meeting the actual occurrences of life is because we are losing face-to-face contact with Jesus Christ through His Cross. We must get back to the place where we are concerned only about facing our own inner souls with Jesus Christ Who searches us right down to the inmost recesses. PH. 88

Intercession leaves you neither time nor inclination to pray for your own "sad sweet self". The thought of yourself is not kept out because it is not there to keep out, you are completely and entirely identifed with God's interest in other lives. RTR. 29

Quit praying about yourself, and be spent in vicarious intercession as the bondslave of Jesus. SSY. 24

Our part in intercessory prayer is not to enter into the agony of intercession, but to utilize the common-sense circumstances God has placed us in, and the common-sense people He has put us amongst by His providence, to bring them before God's throne and give the Holy Spirit a chance to intercede for them. That is how God is going to sweep the whole world with His saints. SSY. 25

PREACHER

The majority of orthodox ministers are hopelessly useless, and the unorthodox seem to be the only ones who are used. We need men and women saturated with the truth of God who can re-state the old truth in terms that appeal to our day. AUG. 17

The one calling of a New Testament preacher is to uncover sin and reveal Jesus Christ as Saviour, consequently he cannot be poetical, he has to be surgical. We are not sent to give beautiful discourses which make people say, 'What a lovely conception that is,' but to unearth the devil and his works in human souls. AUG. 20

As a preacher never have as your ideal the desire to be an orator or a beautiful speaker; if you do, you will not be of the slightest use. AUG. 20

A preacher must remember that his calling is different from every other calling in life; his personality has to be submerged in his message. An orator has to work *with* men and enthuse them; a New Testament preacher has to come *upon* men with a message they resent and will not listen to at first. AUG. 38

The only safety for the preacher is to face his soul not with his people, or even with his message, but to face his soul with his Saviour all the time. AUG. 46

The test of an instructor in the Christian Church is that he is able to build me up in my intimacy with Jesus Christ, not that he gives me new ideas, but I come away feeling I know a bit more about Jesus Christ. AUG. 83

To-day the preacher is tested, not by the building up of saints but on the ground of his personality. AUG. 83

. . . be perfectly clear and emphatic with regard to your preaching of God's truth, but amazingly kind in your treatment of people. Some of us have a hard, metallic, way of dealing with people which never has the stamp of the Holy Ghost on it. The word of God is "sharper than any two-edged sword", but when you deal with people, deal with them in kindness; remember yourself, that you are where you are by the grace of God. Don't make God's word what it is not. AUG. 126

The preacher is there not by right of his personality or oratorical powers, but by right of the message he proclaims. BE. 52

An orator rouses human nature to do what it is asleep over: the New Testament preacher has to move men to do what they are dead-set against doing, viz., giving up the right to themselves to Jesus Christ; consequently the preaching of the Gospels awakens a terrific longing, but an equally intense resentment. BE. 52

The danger of pseudo-evangelism is that it makes the preacher a 'superior person', not that he is necessarily a prig, but the attitude is produced by the way he has been taught. BFB. 23

If you are called to preach, God will put you through mills you never dreamed of. To testify for God is absolutely essential, but never open your mouth as a preacher unless you are called of God. If you are, it is a "woe is unto me if I preach not," not a delight. BSG. 17

The world is cursed with holiness preachers who have never trembled under awesome Sinai, or lain prostrate in shame before Calvary and had the vile ownership of themselves strangled to death in the rare air heights of Pentecost. Testify to what the Lord has done for you, but at the peril of being cast away as reprobate silver, presume to preach or teach what you have not bought by suffering. Out on the disastrous shallowness that teaches and preaches *experiences*! CD. VOL. 2, 70

The true holiness preacher is one whose experience has led him to know that he is charged with the oracles of God, and, backed by Jehovah, an awful woe is on him if he preaches not the Gospel. CD. VOL. 2, 70

It does not impair the inspiration of the Gospel to have it preached by a bad man, but the influence of the preacher, worthy or unworthy, apart altogether from his preaching, has a tremendous effect. If I know a man to be a bad man the sinister influence of his personality neutralises altogether the effect of God's message through him to me; but let me be quite sure that my intuition springs from my relationship to God and not from human suspicion. CHI. 103

If a man is called to preach the Gospel, God will crush him till the light of the eye, the power of the life, the ambition of the heart, is all riveted on Himself. That is not done easily. It is not a question of saintliness, it has to do with the Call of God. DI. 11

The preacher must be part of his message, he must be incorporated in it. That is what the baptism of the Holy Ghost did for the disciples. When the Holy Ghost came at Pentecost He made these men living epistles of the teaching of Jesus, not human gramophones recording the facts of His life. DI. 43

The preacher's duty is not to convict men of sin, or to make them realize how bad they are, but to bring them into contact with God until it is easy for them to believe in Him. DI. 43

God's denunciation will fall on us if in our preaching we tell people they must be holy and we ourselves are not holy. If we are not working out in our private life the messages we are handing out, we will deepen the condemnation of our own souls as messengers of God. DI. 44

The life of a preacher speaks louder than his words. DI. 44

A clever exposition is never right because the Spirit of God is not clever. Beware of cleverness, it is the great cause of hypocrisy in a preacher. DI. 45

Penetration attracts hearers to God; ingenuity attracts to the preacher. Dexterity is always an indication of shallowness. DI. 45

If you are standing for the truth of God you are sure to experience reproach, and if you open your mouth to vindicate yourself you will lose what you were on the point of gaining. Let the ignominy and the shame come, be "weak in Him". DI. 45

The determination to be a fool if necessary is the golden rule for a preacher. DI. 45

Beware of being disappointed with yourself in delivery; ignore the record of your nerves. DI. 48

If any man's preaching does not make me brace myself up and watch my feet and my ways, one of two things is the reason—either the preacher is unreal, or I hate being better. DI. 49

The great thing is not to hunt for texts, but to live in the big comprehensive truths of the Bible and texts will hunt you. DI. 50

Never get a studied form; prepare yourself mentally, morally, and spiritually and you need never fear. DI. 50

As a student of the Word of God, keep your mind and heart busy with the great truths concerning God, the Lord Jesus Christ, the Holy Spirit, the Atonement, sin, suffering, etc. DI. 50

To talk about 'getting a message', is a mistake. It is preparation of myself that is required more than of my message. DI. 50

"The heart of the righteous studieth to answer." To give your congregation extemporaneous thinking, i.e., thinking without study, is an insult—ponderous 'nothings'. The preacher should give his congregation the result of strenuous thinking in un-studied, extemporaneous speech. DI. 50

Beware of detaching yourself from your theme in order to heed the way you present it. Never be afraid of expressing what is really *you*. DI. 51

The work we do in preparation is meant to get our minds into such order that they are at the service of God for His inspiration. DI. 51

The burning heart while Jesus talks with us and opens up the Scriptures to us is a blessed experience, but the burning heart will die down to ashes unless we keep perennially right with God. DI. 51

Always check private delight in preparation. Close your preparation with prayer and leave it with God till wanted. DI. 51

The speaker without notes must have two things entirely at his command—the Bible and his mother-tongue. DI. 52

In order to expound a passage, live in it well beforehand. DI. 52

If you are called to preach, God will put you through 'mills' that are not meant for you personally, He is making you suitable bread to nourish other lives. It is after sanctification you are put through these things. DI. 60

'My word . . . shall not return to Me void,'—that is the perennial, unbreakable hope of the preacher; he knows the power of the word of God and he builds his confidence nowhere else but in God. GW. 49

God's word is as a seed. The 'seed-thought' idea is one that preachers and evangelists need to remember. We imagine we have to plough the field, sow the seed, reap the grain, bind it into sheaves, put it through the threshing machine, make the bread—all in one discourse. GW. 94

The preachers and teachers who have not taken on them the yoke of Christ are always inclined to exalt natural good, natural virtues, natural nobility and heroism; the consequence is Jesus Christ pales more and more into the background until He becomes "as a root out of a dry ground." IWP. 99

Our Lord did not say 'that you may preach the right thing.' It is an easy business to preach, an appallingly easy thing to tell other people what to do; it is another thing to have God's message turned into a boomerang—'You have been teaching these people that they should be full of peace and joy, but what about yourself? Are *you* full of peace and joy?' The truthful witness is the one who lets his light shine in works which exhibit the disposition of Jesus; one who *lives* the truth as well as preaches it. LG. 46

The test of a preacher or teacher is that as we listen to him we are built up in our faith in Jesus Christ and in our intimacy with Him; otherwise he is not a gift from God. To-day we are apt to test the preacher on the ground of his personality and not by his building up of the saints. LG. 130

If we as preachers or teachers are rightly related to God in obedience, God is continually pouring through us. When we stop obeying Him, everything becomes as hard and dry as a ditch in mid-summer. When we are placed in a position by God and we keep rightly related to Him, He will see to the supply. MFL. 128

It is of immense value to know what the Cross of Christ can do for me, but that does not constitute a preacher: a preacher is constituted by the fact that he has seen God's heart revealed in the Cross of Christ, and says—'I am determined henceforth to preach nothing but Jesus Christ, and Him crucified,' not—'myself crucified with Christ,' that is a mere experience; but—'the one Figure I am determined to present is Jesus Christ, and Him crucified.' PH. 72

If a preacher uses his position to further his own ends, he is heading for disaster. There are many devoted to causes, but few devoted to Jesus Christ. If I am devoted to a particular cause only, when that cause fails I fail too. PH. 145

A preacher has no business to stir up emotions without giving his hearers some issue of will on which to transact. PH. 210

. . . there are times when a preacher if he is eloquent or poetical must fast from his own conceptions of things until he has accepted the appointment of God for his life. PR. 58

The majority of present day preachers understand only the blessings that come to us from the Cross, they are apt to be devoted to certain doctrines which flow from the Cross. Paul preached one thing only: the crucified Christ, "Who of God is made unto us wisdom, and righteousness, and sanctification, and redemption". RTR. 87

Man cannot order the seasons or make the seed to grow; and as preachers and teachers we are powerless to make saints. SHL. 113

God honours His word no matter who preaches it. SSM. 103

We are apt to have the idea that a man called to the ministry is called to be a different kind of being from other men. According to Jesus Christ, he is called to be the 'doormat' of other men; he is their spiritual leader, but never their superior. SSY. 22

Preparation is not something suddenly accomplished, but a process steadily maintained. It is easy to imagine that we get to a settled state of experience where we are complete and ready; but in work for God it is always preparation *and preparation.* Moral preparation comes before intellectual preparation, because moral integrity is of more practical value than any amount of mental insight. SSY. 40

. . . beware of the snare of putting anything first in your mind but Jesus Christ. If you put the needs of your people first, there is something between you and the power of God. WG. 27

PREACHING

The great passion in much of the preaching of to-day is to secure an audience. As workers for God our object is never to secure our audience, but to secure that the Gospel is presented to men. Never presume to preach unless you are mastered by the motive born of the Holy Ghost: "For I determined not to know any thing among you, save Jesus Christ, and Him crucified." AUG. 32

. . . preaching is God's ordained method of saving the world. AUG. 36

Don't's and Do's about Texts

Don't be Clever.
Don't be Controversial.
Don't be Conceited.
Do be Careful.
Do be Consecrated.
Do be Concentrated. AUG. 41

In preaching the Gospel remember that salvation is the great thought of God, not an experience. AUG. 47

The reason some of us have no power in our preaching, no sense of awe, is that we have no passion for God, but only a passion for Humanity. The one thing we have to do is to exhibit Jesus Christ crucified, to lift Him up all the time. AUG. 56

The great sterling test in preaching is that it brings everyone to judgment; the Spirit of God locates each one. AUG. 58

. . . it is not the tones of a man's speech or the passion of a man's personality, it is the pleading power of the Holy Ghost coming through him. AUG. 126

If I prefer to preach my philosophy I prevent God creating His miracles, but when I am simple enough to preach the Cross, God performs His miracles every time. BE. 55

Preaching from prejudice is dangerous, it makes a man dogmatic and certain that he is right. BFB. 22

If you have the Spirit of God in you, the preaching of the Cross is according to the wisdom of God: if you have not the Spirit of God in you, the preaching of Christ crucified is foolishness. BP. 264

We are nowhere told to preach salvation, or sanctification, or Divine healing; we are told to lift up Jesus, who is the Redeemer, and He will produce His redemptive results in the souls of men. If I preach only the effects of the Redemption, describe in persuasive speech what God has done for me, nothing will happen. It is only when I am humble enough, and stupid enough, to preach the Cross that the miracle of God takes place. The "preaching of the Cross" creates that which enables a man to believe in God, because the Cross *is* the manifestation of the Redemption. The Cross "condemns men to salvation." The "foolishness of preaching" is the way God has chosen to make the Redemption efficacious in human lives. You can't *persuade* a man to believe in God; belief in God is not an act of the intellect, it is a moral creation produced by the interaction of God's Spirit and my spirit in willing obedience; intellect comes in afterwards to explain what has happened. In preaching the Cross we use our intellect, not to prove that Jesus died, but to present the fact of His death. CHL. 35

To preach the Jesus of the Gospels at the expense of the Christ of the Epistles is a false thing, such a false thing that it is antichrist to the very core, because it is a blow direct at what Jesus said the Holy Spirit would do, viz.: expound Him to the disciples, and "through their word" to innumerable lives to the end of Time. CHL. 37

If you stand true as a disciple of Jesus He will make your preaching the kind of message that is incarnate as well as oral. DI. 43

To preach the Gospel makes *you* a sacrament; but if the Word of God has not become incorporated into you, your preaching is 'a clanging cymbal', it has never cost you anything, never taken you through repentance and heartbreak. DI. 43

Live in the reality of the Truth when you preach it. DI. 44

Impressive preaching is rarely Gospel-preaching: Gospel-preaching is based on the great mystery of belief in the Atonement, which belief is created in others, not by my impressiveness, but by the insistent conviction of the Holy Spirit. DI. 45

There is far more wrought by the Word of God than we will ever understand, and if I substitute anything for it, fine thinking, eloquent speech, the devil's victory is enormous, but I am of no more use than a puff of wind. DI. 45

We have to preach something which to the wisdom of this world is foolishness. If the wisdom of this world is right, then God is foolish; if God is wise, the wisdom of this world is foolishness. Where we go wrong is when we apologize for God. DI. 45

Never assume anything that has not been made yours by faith and the experience of life; it is presumptuous to do so. On the other hand, be ready to pay the price of 'foolishness' in proclaiming to others what is really yours. DI. 46

People only want the kind of preaching which does not declare the demands of a holy God. 'Tell us that God is loving, not that He is holy, and that He demands we should be holy'. The problem is not with the gross sinners, but with the intellectual, cultured, religious-to-the-last-degree people. DI. 46

All the winsome preaching of the Gospel is an insult to the Cross of Christ. What is needed is the probe of the Spirit of God straight down to a man's conscience till his whole nature shouts at him, 'That is right, and *you* are wrong.' DI. 46

Beware as of the devil of good taste being your standard in presenting the truth of God. DI. 47

When you preach, you speak for God, and from God to the people; in prayer, you talk to God for the people, and your proper place is among the people as one of them. It is to be a vicarious relation, not the flinging of theology at their heads from the pulpit. DI. 48

People say, 'Do preach the simple Gospel', if they mean by 'the simple Gospel' the thing we have always heard, the thing that keeps us sound asleep, then the sooner God sends a thrust through our stagnant minds the better. DI. 49

A joyous, humble belief in your message will compel attention. DI. 49

Extemporaneous speech is not extemporaneous thinking, but speech that has

been so studied that you are possessed unconsciously with what you are saying. DI. 50

When you speak, abandon yourself in confidence; don't try to recall fine points in preparation. DI. 51

To develop your expression in public you must do a vast amount of writing in private. Write out your problems before God. Go direct to Him about everything. DI. 51

In impromptu speaking, begin naturally, and the secret of beginning naturally is to forget you are religious. Many wear a crushing religious garb. DI. 51

Learn to fast over your subject in private; do the mechanical work and trust God for the inspirational in delivery. DI. 52

Get moved by your message, and it will move others in a corresponding way. DI. 52

The great thing about the Gospel is that it should be preached. Never get distressed over not seeing immediate results. No prophet of the Old Testament, or apostle of the New (or saint of the present day), ever fully understood the import of what he said or did, hence to work for immediate results is to make myself a director of the Holy Ghost. DI. 54

Don't preach salvation; don't preach holiness; don't preach the baptism of the Holy Ghost; preach Jesus Christ and everything else will take its right place. GW. 48

. . . no individual and no community is ever the same after listening to the word of God, it profoundly alters life. The force and power of a word of God will work and work, and bring forth fruit after many days. Hence the necessity of revising much of what we preach and what we say in meetings. GW. 94

Our duty is to sow the word, see that it is the word of God we preach, and not 'huckster' it with other things, and God says it will prosper in the thing whereto He sends it. GW. 94

We are so anxious about the word, so anxious about the people who have accepted the word; we need not be, if we have preached what is a word of God it is not our business to apply it, the Holy Spirit will apply it. GW. 94

Never have the idea that you are going to persuade men to believe in God; you can persuade them of His standard. You have to force an issue of will; but remember, along with your faithful preaching comes a thing you cannot intellectually state, the working of the Spirit of God. GW. 109

The great condemnation of much of our modern preaching is that it conveys no sense of the desperate tragedy of conviction of sin. When once the real touch of conviction of sin comes, it is hell on earth—there is no other word for it. HG. 98

In evangelical work it is not preaching holiness, or sanctification, or bodily healing, it is preaching Christ Jesus, "I, if I be lifted up, will draw all men unto Me." IWP. 78

If I preach a particularly searching discourse and never give the people a chance to act according to their inspired instincts at the time, their blood is on my head before God. If I make the issue clear and give them the opportunity to act, I clear my soul from their blood, whether they answer or not. The devil's counterfeit for this is wanting to see how many people we can get out to the penitent form. As preachers and teachers we have to bring people to the point of doing something. MFL. 15

We may see no result in our congregation, but if we have presented the truth and anyone has seen it for one second, he can never be the same again, a new element has come into his life. It is essential to remember this and not to estimate the success of preaching by immediate results. MFL. 20

If we preach anything other than "Jesus Christ, and Him crucified," we make our doctrines God, and ourselves the judge of others. MFL. 91

It is one thing to thrill an audience with fine rhetoric, or by a magnetic personality, but the New Testament order of preaching is that of John the Baptist— "He must increase, but I must decrease." PH. 135

It seems so remote from actual things to say that the preaching of the Cross conveys the Presence of God, but God has chosen to save in this way. "It was God's good pleasure through the foolishness of the preaching to save them that believe," because behind the preaching of the Gospel is the creative Redemption of God at work in the souls of men. That is the miracle of God. If you can tell how a corn of wheat put into the ground will bring forth what it never was before, you can also tell how the Word of God put into a man's soul will bring forth what was not there before—a new life. The same God is the Author of both. PH. 136

Jesus did not say—'Go out and spread propaganda,' but "Feed My sheep." They are not our sheep, but His. PH. 160

When we preach Christ, it is not His birth that we preach, but His Cross, and we bring ourselves face to face with the wonder and the power of His resurrection life. PR. 81

Be as stern and unflinching as God Almighty in your preaching, but as tender and gentle as a sinner saved by grace should be when you deal with a human soul. PS. 81

A man can never be the same again, I don't care who he is, after having heard Jesus Christ preached. He may say he pays no attention to it; he may appear to have forgotten all about it, but he is never quite the same, and at any moment truths may spring up into his consciousness that will destroy all his peace and happiness. RTR. 77

To terrorise a man into believing in God is never the work of God, but the work of human expediency. If we want to convince a congregation of a certain thing, we may use terror to frighten them into it; but never say that is God's way, it is our way. If we do not get conversions one way, then we preach hell fire and produce terror; we don't care what we preach as long as we dominate. To call that God's method is a travesty of the character of God. The methods God uses are indicated in Jesus Christ, and He never terrorised anyone. SHH. 29

Preaching is worthy in God's sight when it costs something, when we are really living out what we preach. The truth of God is to be presented in such a way that it produces saints. SHL. 121

Never water down the word of God to the understanding of your people. WG. 78

PREDESTINATION

The great doctrines of predestination and election are secondary matters, they are attempts at definition, but if we take sides with the theological method we will damn men who differ from us without a minute's hesitation. BFB. 56

We must be careful not to confuse the predestination of God by making His election include every individual; or to have the idea that because God elected a certain nation through whom His salvation was to come, therefore every individual of that nation is elected to salvation. The history of the elect nation disproves this, but it does not alter God's purpose for the nation. Individuals of the elect nation have to be saved in the same way as individuals of nations that have not been elected. Election refers to the unchangeable purpose of God, not to the salvation of individuals. SSY. 106

Each individual has to choose which line of predestination he will take— God's line or the devil's line. Individual position is determined by individual choice, but that is neither here nor there in connection with God's purpose for the human race. Individuals enter into the realization of the creative purpose of God for the human race by being born again of the Spirit; but we must not make the predestination of God for the race to include every individual, any more than God's predestination for the elect nation included every individual. SSY. 106

270

PRE-EXISTENCE

In the creation of man the Bible reveals that his body was created first, not his soul. The body existed before the soul in creation; so we cannot trace the history or the destiny of the human soul before the creation of the human race. BP. 86

God deliberately said what was in His mind before He created man—"Let us make man in our image," after our likeness—the pre-existence of man in the mind of God. BP. 86

Life can only come from pre-existing life: I must get the life of God from the One who has it. BE. 42

PREJUDICE

Prejudice means a judgment passed without sufficiently weighing the evidence. We are all prejudiced, and we can only see along the line of our prejudices. BFB. 22

Until the Holy Spirit comes in we see only along the line of our prejudices; when we let the Holy Spirit come in, He will blow away the lines of our prejudices with His dynamic power, and we can begin to 'go' in God's light. DI. 138

It is perilously possible to credit God with all our mean little prejudices even after we are sanctified. DI. 60

'God is no respecter of persons.' Christianity cuts out a man's personal prejudices. LG. 127

Wherever you find a prejudice in yourself, take it to Jesus Christ. Our Lord is the only standard for prejudice, as He is the only standard for sin. MFL. 123

Instead of God being on the side of our prejudices, He deliberately wipes them out by ignoring them. God mortifies our prejudices, runs clean athwart them by His providence. God has no respect for anything we bring Him, He is after one thing only, and that is our unconditional surrender to Him. OBH. 97

PRESENT

The purpose of God in calling us is not something in the future, but this very minute—'Now is the accepted time,' always *now*; God's training is for now, not presently. The ultimate issue will be manifested presently, but we have nothing to do with the afterwards of obedience. We get wrong when we think of the afterwards, the purpose of God is our obedience. GW. 37

We have to be transformed by the renewing of our mind, that we may 'prove what is the will of God, even the thing which is good and acceptable and perfect,' not the thing that is going to be acceptable, but which is good and acceptable and perfect *now*. If we have a further end in view we do not pay sufficient attention to the immediate minute; when we know that obedience is the end, then every moment is the most precious. GW. 38

"I have been crucified with Christ . . . and that life which I now live in the flesh . . ." The word "now" is very annoying, if only Paul had said 'hereafter'—'this is the kind of life I am going to live after I am dead and in heaven; down here I am compassed about with infirmities and am a miserable sinner.' But he did not, he said "*now*," "that life which I now live in the flesh" . . . i.e., the life men could see. ". . . I live in faith, the faith which is in the Son of God." PH. 157

PRETENCE

The modern Pharisee is the one who pretends to be the publican—'Oh, I would never call myself a saint!' Exaggerated self-depreciation and exaggerated conceit are both diseased. DI. 30

The life of God has no pretence, and when His life is in you, you do not pretend to feel sweet, you *are* sweet. OPG. 29

It is appallingly easy to pretend. If once our eyes are off Jesus Christ, pious pretence is sure to follow. SSM. 99

PRIDE

God alters our estimates, and we shall find that God gives us a deeper horror of carnality that ever we had of immortality; a deeper horror of the pride which lives clean amongst men but lifts itself against God, than of any other thing. Pride is the central citadel of independence of God. BP. 114

When once a man really sees himself as the Lord Jesus Christ sees him, it is not the abominable social sins of the flesh that shock him, it is the awful nature of the pride of his own heart against the Lord Jesus Christ—the shame, the horror, the desperate conviction that comes when we realise ourselves in the light of Jesus Christ as the Spirit of God reveals Him to us. That is the true gift of repentance and the real meaning of it.

CD. VOL. 1, 130

It is easy to be shocked at immorality, but how much education in the school of Christ, how much reliance on the Holy Spirit, does it take to bring us to the place where we are shocked at pride against God? That sensitivity is lacking today. CHI. 99

Self-complacency and spiritual pride are always the beginning of degeneration. When I begin to be satisfied with where I am spiritually, instantly I begin to degenerate. DI. 31

There is no pride equal to spiritual pride, and no obstinacy equal to spiritual obstinacy, because they are nearest to the throne of God, and are most like the devil. DI. 31

'Show me what to do and I'll do it'—you won't. It is easy to knock down one type of pride and erect another. DI. 31

The only reason I can't get to God is pride, no matter how humble I seem. DI. 31

There is something in human pride that can stand big troubles, but we need the supernatural grace and power of God to stand by us in the little things. OBH. 108

According to the Bible, self-seeking did not begin on earth, it began in heaven and was turned out of heaven because it was unworthy to live there, and it will never get back again. OBH. 115

When a man comes to Jesus it is not sin that is in the way, but self-realisation, pride, his claim to himself. 'I must realise myself, I must be educated and trained, I must do the things that will help me to develop myself.' Self-realisation is anti-Christian. All this is vigorous paganism, it is not Christianity. PH. 132

Pride, disdain for the people you talk to, will shut your mouth quicker than anything. When you speak, see that behind your voice is the life of God. RTR. 15

The essence of sin is self-realisation, my prideful right to myself. The disposition that ought to rule is God's right to me, i.e., Christ-realisation. SHH. 50

PROFESSION

The majority of us "hang on" to Jesus Christ, we are thankful for the massive gift of salvation, but we don't do anything towards working it out. That is the difficult bit, and the bit the majority of us fail in, because we have not been taught that that is what we have to do, consequently there is a gap between our religious profession and our actual practical living. To put it down to human frailty is a wiggle, there is only one word for it, and that is "humbug." CHI. 63

In my actual life I live below the belief which I profess. We can do nothing towards our salvation, but we can work out what God works in and the emphasis all through the New Testament is that God gives us sufficient energy to do it if we will. CHI. 63

We can slay a grousing mood by stating what we believe, and we are emancipated into a higher level of life immediately; but the "say so" must come before the emancipation is ours. PH. 208

Many of us are on the verge of a spiritual vision the realisation of which never becomes ours because we will not open our mouths to "say so." We have to "say so" before we 'feel so.' PH. 208

In the matter of human love it is a great emancipaton to have it expressed; there may be intuitions of the love, but the realisation of it is not ours until it is expressed. PH. 209

If I will not confess with my mouth what I believe in my heart, that particular phase of believing will never be mine actually. PH. 209

PROFUNDITY

Beware of posing as a profound person; God became a Baby. NKW. 69

PROGRAM

The disciple has no programme, only a distinguished passion of devotion to his Lord. AUG. 109

To-day we hold conferences and conventions and give reports and make our programmes. None of these things were in the life of Jesus, and yet every minute of His life He realized that He was fulfilling the purpose of His Father. HG. 27

Beware of making God an item, even the principal item, in your programme. God's ways are curiously abrupt with programmes, He seems to delight in breaking them up. OPG. 59

If you are a saint God will continually upset your programme, and if you are wedded to your programme you will become that most obnoxious creature under heaven, an irritable saint. RTR. 10

God's order comes in the haphazard, and never according to our scheming and planning. God takes a great delight in breaking up our programmes. RTR. 48

PROMISE

No one can fulfil a promise but the one who made it. NKW. 97

The word of a natural man is his bond; the word of a saint binds God. It is a question of relationship to God all through. NKW. 111

The promises of God are of no use to me until by obedience I understand the nature of God. NKW. 128

PROSPERITY

A man's idea of prosperity is according to where his hopes are founded—on God or on a hearsay God, on the living God, or on ideas of God. CD. VOL. 2, 120

We blunder when we try to make out that the prosperity referred to in the Old Testament is intended for us in this dispensation. Plainly that prosperity has never yet been fulfilled in the history of the world; it is going to be fulfilled, but it does not refer to this dispensation, which is the dispensation of the humiliation of the saints, not of their glorification. HG. 8

In times of prosperity we are apt to forget God, we imagine it does not matter whether we recognize Him or not. As long as we are comfortably clothed and fed and looked after, our civilization becomes an elaborate means of ignoring God. HG. 15

PUNISHMENT

The question of eternal punishment is a fearful one, but let no one say that Jesus Christ did not say anything about it, He did. He said it in language we cannot begin to understand, and the least thing we can do is to be reverent with what we do not understand. BP. 260

We talk on the moral and spiritual line as if God were punishing us, but He is not, it is because of the way God has constructed man's nature that "the way of transgressors is hard." MFL. 37

PURITY

The purity God demands is impossible unless we can be re-made from within, and that is what Jesus Christ undertakes to do through the Atonement. BE. 10

He will keep your heart so pure that you would tremble with amazement if you knew how pure the Atonement of the Lord Jesus can make the vilest human heart, if we will but keep in the light, as God is in the light. BP. 124

Jesus Christ claims that He can take a man or woman who is fouled in the springs of their nature by heredity and make them as pure as He is Himself. HG. 60

"Blessed are the pure in heart," literally, 'Blessed are the God in heart,' i.e. in whom the nature of God is. HG. 115

Prudery is the outcome of obedience to a principle; whereas, according to Our Lord, purity is the outcome of an implicit relationship. If we look upon purity as the outcome of the obedience to a particular standard, we produce the opposite of what Our Lord intends. He said, "Except . . . ye become *as little children* . . ." LG. 41

The possibility of being impure means that there is some value to Jesus Christ in our being pure. God gives us His supernatural life, but we have to keep entirely free from the world with a purity which is of value to God; we have to grow in purity. LG. 72

"If we walk in the light as He is in the light . . . the blood of Jesus Christ His Son cleanseth us from all sin." That is cleansing not from conscious sin only but from infinitely more, it is cleansing

to the depths of crystalline purity so that God Himself can see nothing impure. That is the work of the Lord Jesus Christ; to make His work anything less would be blasphemous. LG. 142

Purity of heart, not subtlety of intellect, is the place of understanding. The Spirit of God alone understands the things of God, let Him indwell, and slowly and surely the great revelation facts of the Atonement begin to be comprehended. The Mind of God as revealed in the Incarnation becomes slowly and surely the mind of the spiritual Christian. MFL. 26

Purity is not innocence, it is much more. Purity means stainlessness, an unblemishedness that has stood the test. Purity is learned in private, never in public. Jesus Christ demands purity of mind and imagination, chastity of bodily and mental habits. The only men and women it is safe to trust are those who have been tried and have stood the test; purity is the outcome of conflict, not of necessity. MFL. 88

Beware of insulting God by being a pious prude instead of a pure person. NKW. 67

What do we mean by "pure in heart"? We mean nothing less and nothing else than what the Son of God was and is. When God raises us up into the heavenly places He imparts to us the very purity that is Jesus Christ's. That is what the sanctified life means—the undisturbable range of His peace, the unshakable, indefatigable power of His strength, and the unfathomable, crystalline purity of His holiness. There is plenty of room in the heavenly places to grow into the realisation of the unfathomable depths of the purity of Christ's heart. OBH. 36

The wonder of a pure heart is that it is as pure as Jesus Christ's heart. Sanctification does not mean that a purity like Jesus Christ's is gifted to us, but that *His* purity is gifted to us. OBH. 37

By no prayer, by no self-sacrifice, by no devotion, and by no climbing can any man attain to that "Blessed are the pure in heart," which Jesus Christ says is essential to seeing God. PH. 5

The purity of Christ is not a winsome thing, it hurts perilously everything that is not pure. "For our God is a consuming fire." PH. 75

Purity is something that has been tested and tried, and triumphed; innocence has always to be shielded. SHL. 48

There is no human being on earth with an innocence which is not based on ignorance, and if we have come to the stage of life we are now in with the belief that innocence and purity are the same thing, it is because we have paid no attention to what Jesus Christ said. SHL. 48

Purity is difficult to define; it is best thought of as a state of heart just like the heart of our Lord Jesus Christ. SSM. 26

Purity is not a question of doing things rightly, but of the doer on the inside being right. SSM. 26

Purity is not innocence; innocence is the characteristic of a child, and although, profoundly speaking, a child is not pure, yet his innocence presents us with all that we understand by purity. Innocence in a child's life is a beautiful thing, but men and women ought not to be innocent, they ought to be tested and tried and pure. SSM. 26

No man is born pure: purity is the outcome of conflict. The pure man is not the man who has never been tried, but the man who knows what evil is and has overcome it. SSM. 26

Jesus Christ has undertaken by His Redemption to put in me a heart that is so pure that God can see nothing to censure in it. SSM. 27

Jesus Christ demands that the heart of a disciple be fathomlessly pure, and unless He can give me His disposition, His teaching is tantalising. If all He came to do was to mock me by telling me to be what I know I never can be, I can afford to ignore Him, but if He can give me His own disposition of holiness, then I begin to see how I can lay my account with purity. SSM. 27

Our natural idea of purity is that it means according obedience to certain laws and regulations, but that is apt to be prudery. There is nothing prudish in the Bible. The Bible insists on purity, not prudery. SSM. 33

Q

QUARRELING

No one damns like an theologian, nor is any quarrel so bitter as a religious quarrel. BFB. 54

R

READING

Keep yourself full with reading. Reading gives you a vocabulary. DI. 52

Don't read to remember, read to realize. DI. 52

The things we listen to and read ought to be beyond our comprehension, they go into our minds like seed thoughts, and slowly and surely bring forth fruit. This is good counsel for boys and girls in their teens. SHH. 66

REALITY

No one preaches more earnestly, talks more earnestly, than we do, we are absolutely sincere, but we are not real because we have never acted when the opportunity occurred along the line Jesus Christ wants us to. The thing the world is sick of to-day is sincerity that is not real. BE. 59

If Reality is not to be found in God, then God is not found anywhere. BFB. 36

I can never find Reality by looking within; the only way I can get at Reality is by dumping myself outside myself on to Someone else, viz.: God, immediately I do I am brought in touch with Reality. CHI. 29

I cannot get at Reality by my intellect or by emotion, but only by my conscience bringing me in touch with the Redemption. When the Holy Spirit gets hold of

my conscience He convicts me of unreality, and when I respond to God I come in touch with Reality and experience a sense of wonder—"That He should have done this for me!" CHI. 30

Jesus Christ riddles us from all unreality. What He did shocks all affectation, pious fraud, religious pretence, sanctimoniousness, and religiosity always. GW. 96

By Reality we mean that all the hidden powers of our life are in perfect harmony with themselves and in perfect harmony with God. None of us are real in the full sense of the word; we become real bit by bit as we obey the Spirit of God. It is not a question of sham and reality or of hypocrisy and reality, but of sincerity being transformed into reality. It is possible to be perfectly real to ourselves but not real to God, that is not reality. It is possible to be perfectly real to ourselves and real to other people, but not real in our relationship to God; that is not reality. The only reality is being in harmony with ourselves and other people and God. That is the one great reality towards which God is working, and towards which we are working as we obey Him. PS. 32

The people who are sincere without being real are not hypocrites, they are perfectly earnest and honest, and desirous of fulfilling what Jesus wants, but they really cannot do it, the reason being that they have not received the

One Who makes them real, viz., the Holy Spirit. SSM. 32

Jesus Christ makes us real, not merely sincere. SSM. 32

REASON

To "believe also" in Jesus means that we submit our intelligence to Him as He submitted His intelligence to His Father. This does not mean that we do not exercise our reason, but it does mean that we exercise it in submission to Reason Incarnate. AUG. 105

According to rationalism there is no need to be born again—'develop the best in yourself'. That was God's original design for the human race, viz., that man should take part in his own development by a series of moral choices whereby he would transfigure the natural into the spiritual; but sin entered and there came an hiatus, a break, and man's development is not now based on the rational progression God designed, but on the Redemption, which deals with the tragedy caused by sin. BE. 53

Rationalism fundamentally is rotten. The boldness of rationalism is not in what it does, but in the way it criticizes. The basis of things is not rational, it is tragic; there is something wrong at the heart of life that reason cannot account for. BE. 53

Reason is our guide among the facts of life, but it does not give us the explanation of them. Sin, suffering, and the Book of God all bring a man to the realization that there is something wrong at the basis of life, and it cannot be put right by his reason. Our Lord always dealt with the 'basement' of life, i.e., with the real problem; if we only deal

with 'the upper storey' we do not realize the need of the Redemption. BFB. 17

When a so-called rationalist points out sin and iniquity and disease and death, and says, 'How does God answer that?' you have always a fathomless answer—the Cross of Christ. DI. 12

The way the serpent beguiled Eve through his subtlety was by enticing her away from personal faith in God to depend on her reason alone. GW. 108

Men must reason according to their god, and the god of to-day is common sense; that is why Jesus Christ's teaching is ruled out of court. HG. 42

If I believe in God I pray on the ground of Redemption and things happen; it is not reasonable, it is Redemptive. Where reason says 'There is a mountain, it is impossible', I do not argue and say 'I believe God can remove it', I do not even see the mountain; I simply set my face unto the Lord God and make my prayer, and the mountain ceases to be. HGM. 71

A man's reasoning is based on something more than reason, there is always an incalculable element. MFL. 11

A child of faith must never limit the promise of God by what seems good to him, but must give to the power of God the preference over his own reason. God never contradicts reason. He transcends it always. NKW. 75

We cannot enter into the kingdom of heaven head first. PH. 185

We would never know that our spirit was wrong unless Jesus rebuked it, because it is so emphatically right according to our reason. The one thing to mark is the effect on our conscience—does my spirit bear the mark of native self-assertiveness or of disciplined self-conquest? RTR. 16

The great fundamental point of view in the Bible is neither rationalism nor common sense. Either it is a revelation, or it is unmitigated blether. The basis of life is not mathematical or rational; if it were we could calculate our ends, and make absolutely sure of certain things on clear, rational, logical lines. We have to take into account the fact that there is an incalculable element in every child and in every man. There is always "one fact more," and we get at it by agony. SA. 20

The basis of things is not rational, but tragic. Reason is our guide among facts as they are, but reason cannot account for things being as they are. This does not mean that a man is not to use his reason; reason is the biggest gift he has. The rationalist says that everything in between birth and death is discernible by human reason; but the actual experience of life is that things do not run in a reasonable way, there are irrational elements to be reckoned with. SHH. 3

Reason and logic and intellect have to do with the time between birth and death, but they can give no explanation of before birth or after death. All we infer of either is speculation; it may be interesting but it is apt to blind us to true facts. SHH. 39

The rationalist demands an explanation of everything. The reason I won't have anything to do with God is because I cannot define Him. If I can define God, I am greater than the God I define. SHH. 144

Our Lord never talks on the basis of reason. He talks on the basis of Redemp-

tion. What is nonsense rationally is Redemptive Reality. SSY. 164

REBELLION

The Bible looks upon the human race as it is as the result of a mutiny against God; consequently you find in the Bible something you find in no other book or conception. The modern view of man is—What a marvellous promise of what he is going to be! The Bible looks at man and sees the ruin of what he once was. In the Bible everything is based on the fact that there is something wrong at the basis of things. BE. 33

The diabolical nature of sin is that it hates God, it is not *at* enmity against God; it *is* enmity. GW. 83

The Bible looks on sin, not as a disease, but as red-handed rebellion against the domination of the Creator. The essence of sin is—'I won't allow anybody to "boss" me saving myself', and it may manifest itself in a morally good man as well as in a morally bad man. Sin has not to do with morality or immorality, it has to do with my claim to my right to myself, a deliberate and emphatic independence of God, though I veneer it over with Christian phraseology. OPG. 7

I have to recognise that sin is a fact, not a defect; it is red-handed mutiny against God, and acquaintance with the grief of it means that unless I withstand it to the death, it will withstand me to the death. PH. 189

Sin is not weakness, it is not a disease; it is red-handed rebellion against God, and the magnitude of that rebellion is expressed by Calvary. RTR. 62

When a man is fed up with a certain line of things, he revolts and goes to the opposite extreme. To-day tyranny and oppression have eaten into men's sense of justice, and they have revolted and gone to the other extreme. SHH. 40

REDEMPTION

The Redemption means a great deal more than my personal salvation and yours, that is a mere outcome; pseudoevangelism is apt to make it the great thing. The great thing according to the New Testament is not that the Redemption touches *me*, but that it avails for the whole human race. BE. 65

If there is no tragedy at the back of human life, no gap between God and man, then the Redemption of Jesus Christ is 'much ado about nothing'. BFB. 16

The New Testament never says that Jesus Christ came primarily to teach men: it says that He came to reveal that He has put the basis of human life on Redemption, that is, He has made it possible for any and every man to be born into the Kingdom where He lives. BFB. 19

If Redemption is not the basis of human life, and prayer man's only resource, then we have 'followed cunningly devised fables'. BFB. 33

In the Redemption, it was not God the Son paying a price to God the Father: it was God the Father, God the Son, and God the Holy Ghost surrendering this marvellous Being, the Lord Jesus Christ, for one definite purpose. Never separate the Incarnation from the Atonement. The Incarnation is for the sake of the Atonement. In dealing with the Incarnation, we are dealing with a revelation fact, not with a speculation. BP. 33

Redemption is not going to be finished: it is finished. Believing does not make a man redeemed; believing enables him to realize that he is redeemed. BSG. 53

Men are not *going* to be redeemed; they *are* redeemed. "It is finished." It was not the salvation of individual men and women like you and me that was finished: the whole human race was put on the basis of Redemption. CHI. 8

The Redemption is not only for mankind, it is for the universe, for the material earth; everything that sin and the devil have touched and marred has been completely redeemed by Jesus Christ. There is a day coming when the redemption will be actually manifested, when there will be "a new heaven and a new earth," with a new humanity upon it. CHI. 9

If you look upon Jesus Christ from the common-sense standpoint you will never discern who He is; but if you look upon Him as God "manifested in the flesh" for the purpose of putting the whole human race back to where God designed it to be, you get the meaning of Redemption. The great marvellous revelation of Redemption is that it atones for everyone; men are "condemned to salvation." CHI. 11

The difficulty of believing in the Redemption in the sense of assimilating it is that it demands renunciation. I have to give up my right to myself in complete surrender to my Lord before what I celebrate becomes a reality. There is always the danger of celebrating what Jesus Christ has done and forgetting the need on our part of moral surrender to Him; if we evade the surrender we become the more intense in celebrating what He has done. CHI. 125

The great thing about the Redemption is that it deals with *sin*, i.e., my claim to my right to myself, not primarily with man's sins. It is one of the most flattering things to go and rescue the degraded, one of the social passions of mankind, but not necessarily the most Christian: it is quite another thing to tell men who are among the best of men that what Jesus Christ asks of them is that they give up the right to themselves to Him. DI. 54

The danger is to preach a subjective theology, something that wells up on the inside. The Gospel of the New Testament is based on the absoluteness of the Redemption. DI. 54

Unless we have faith in the Redemption, all our activities are fussy impertinences which tell God He is doing nothing. HG. 95

Jesus Christ is not working out the Redemption, it is complete; we are working it out, and beginning to realize it by obedience. HG. 95

When a man has been profoundly moved in his spirit by the experience of Redemption, then out of him flow rivers of living water. HG. 96

If the Redemption of Christ cannot go deeper down than hell, it is not redemption at all. HG. 98

When the Redemption is effective in me, I am a delight to God, not to myself. I am not meant for myself, I am meant for God. HG. 120

The fact of Redemption amounts to nothing in my actual life unless I get awakened to a sense of need. It is a matter of moonshine to me whether Jesus Christ lived or died until I come up against things—either sin in myself or something that ploughs deeply into me, then I find I have got beyond anything I know, and that is where the revelation of Jesus Christ comes in; if I will commit myself to Him, I am saved, saved into the perfect light and liberty of God on the ground of Redemption. HGM. 64

The majority of us know nothing about the Redemption or forgiveness until we are enmeshed by the personal problem—something happens which stabs us wide awake and we get our indifferent hide pierced; we come up against things and our conscience begins to be roused. HGM. 101

Redemption means that Jesus Christ can give me His own disposition, and all the standards He gives are based on that disposition. *Jesus Christ's teaching is for the life He puts in.* LG. 125

Everything that sin and Satan have touched and blighted, God has redeemed; Redemption is complete. We are not working *for* the redemption of the world, we are working *on* the Redemption, which is a very different thing. OBH. 61

God is a holy God, and the marvel of the Redemption is that God the Holy One puts into me, the unholy one, a new disposition, the disposition of His Son. PH. 65

Redemption is the basis of things, it is God's 'bit'; we have to live our actual life on that basis. We are apt to get a conception of the Redemption that enables us to 'hang in' to Jesus mentally and do nothing else. This seems the natural outcome of the way Redemption has too often been presented. PH. 157

Redemption makes a man right for heaven, but there is much more in it than that. New birth has to do with being of value to God in this present order of things. PR. 15

Redemption is absolutely finished and complete, but its reference to individual men is a question of their individual action. PR. 50

The Son of God alone can redeem, and because He was the Son of God, He became Man that He might bring man back to God. PR. 52

Jesus Christ came to redeem us; to put us right with God; to deliver us from the power of death; to reveal God the Father; and when we receive the Holy Spirit He will make experimentally real in us all that Jesus Christ came to do. PR. 112

Redemption does not only mean personal salvation and the redemption of our body, it means the absolute and complete redemption of the whole material earth in every iota, and not only the earth, but the whole material universe. PR. 134

Everything that sin and Satan have ruined is going to be reconstructed and readjusted through the marvellous Redemption of our Lord Jesus Christ. PS. 75

Through the Redemption, God undertakes to deal with a man's past, and He does it in two ways: by forgiving him, and by making the past a wonderful culture for the future. RTR. 40

The great need is not to *do* things, but to *believe* things. The Redemption of Christ is not an experience, it is the great act of God which He has performed through Christ, and I have to build my faith upon it. RTR. 41

Nothing that happens can upset God or the almighty reality of Redemption. RTR. 51

The whole claim of the Redemption of Jesus is that He can satisfy the last aching abyss of the human soul, not only hereafter, but here and now. RTR. 60

The greatest note of triumph that ever sounded in the ears of a startled universe was that sounded on the Cross of Christ—"It is finished". That is the last word in the Redemption of man. RTR. 82

No man can redeem the world; God has done it; Redemption is complete. That is a revelation, not something we get at by thinking; and unless we grant that Redemption is the basis of human life, we will come up against problems for which we can find no way out. SA. 14

Redemption is a moral thing, Jesus Christ does not merely save from hell; "He shall save his people from their sins," i.e., make totally new moral men. Jesus Christ did not come to give us pretty ideas of God, or sympathy with ourselves; He came from a holy God to enable men, by the sheer power of His Redemption, to become holy. SA. 18

Redemption is not a thing we are consciously experiencing, it is a revelation given by the Christian religion of the basis of human life, and it takes some thinking about. SA. 22

Men may not feel the need of Redemption, but that does not mean it is not there. The Christian revelation is the revelation of why Redemption was necessary. God's standard is to make of man the counterpart of Himself; man has to be brought into perfect communion with God. SA. 22

Redemption does not amount to anything to a man until he meets an agony; until that time he may have been indifferent; but knock the bottom board out of his wits, bring him to the limit of his moral life, produce the supreme suffering worthy of the name of agony, and he will begin to realize that there is more in Redemption than he had ever dreamed, and it is at that phase that he is prepared to hear Jesus Christ say, "Come unto Me." Our Lord said, "I did not come to call the man who is all right; I came to call the man who is at his wits' end, the man who has reached the moral frontier." SA. 28

Redemption cost God everything, and that is the reason why salvation is so easy for us. SA. 31

As long as we have our morality well within our own grasp, to talk about Jesus Christ and His Redemption is "much ado about nothing;" but when a man's thick hide is pierced, or he comes to his wits' end and enters the confines of an agony, he is apt to find that there is a great deal from which he has been shut away, and in his condition of suffering he discovers there is more in the Cross of Christ than intellectually he had thought possible. SA. 66

God never laid the sin of the human race on anybody but Himself, and in Redemption He has dealt with the disposition of sin. SA. 105

If the human race apart from Jesus Christ is all right, then the Redemption of Jesus Christ is a useless waste. SA. 120

God has put the whole human race on the basis of Redemption. A man cannot redeem himself; Redemption is absolutely finished and complete; its reference to individual men is a question of their individual action. SA. 121

No man can redeem his own soul, or give himself a new heredity; that is the work of the sovereign grace of God. Man has nothing to do with Redemption, it is God's "bit"; but God cannot give a man a good character, that is not God's business, nor is it an inevitable thing. God will give us what we cannot give ourselves, a totally new heredity. SHH. 94

An understanding of Redemption is not necessary to salvation any more than an understanding of life is necessary before we can be born into it. SSM. 49

The point of spiritual honour in my life as a saint is the realization that I am a debtor to every man on the face of the earth because of the Redemption of the Lord Jesus Christ. SSY. 21

When I realize what Jesus Christ has done for me, then I am a debtor to every human being until they know Him too, not for their sake, not because they will otherwise be lost, but because of Jesus Christ's Redemption. SSY. 23

We have to beware of becoming the advocate of a certain view of the limitless. The Redemption avails for everyone— 'The Lamb of God which taketh away the sin of the world!' not the sin of those who belong to any particular country, but the sin *of the world*. The words are worthy only of Almighty God's wisdom, not of man's. SSY. 145

The only final thing in the world is the Redemption of Jesus Christ. SSY. 145

REGENERATION

Regeneration does not resolve a human being into imbecility, it lifts him powerfully into oneness with God in Christ Jesus. BE. 11

Beware of making conversion synonymous with regeneration. Conversion is simply the effort of a roused human being; the sign of regeneration is that a man has *received* something. BE. 38

Reformation is a good thing, but like every other good thing it is the enemy of the best. Regeneration means filling the heart with something positive, viz., the Holy Spirit. CHI. 26

People say, 'Oh yes, the Sermon on the Mount is very beautiful, our ideals must be better than we can attain, we shall drift into the Lord's ideals in time somehow or other'; but Jesus says we won't, we will miss them. "The manifold forms of failure exhibited in actual experience" is ignored by other ethical teachers. They say it is never too late to mend—it is; that you can start again—you cannot; that you can make the past as though it had never been—it is impossible; that anyway you can put yourself in such a condition that what you have done need not count—you cannot, and our Lord is the only One who recognizes these things. We think because we fail and forget it, therefore it is overlooked by God—it is not. Jesus Christ's standard remains, and the entrance into His kingdom and into a totally new life is by Regeneration, and in no other way. HG. 20

In regeneration, a man's personal spirit is energized by the Holy Spirit, and the Son of God is formed in him. LG. 113

God alters the thing that matters. MFL. 97

By regeneration the Son of God is formed in me and He has the same setting in my life as He had when on earth. PH. 35

The heredity of the Son of God is put into me at regeneration, a life neither time nor death can touch. RTR. 64

RELATIONSHIP

Jesus Christ restores the three aspects of a man's personal life to their pristine vigour: we come into real, definite communion with God through Jesus Christ; we come to a right relationship with our fellow-men and with the world outside, and we come to a right relationship with ourselves, we become God-centred instead of self-centred. BP. 200

God created everything that was created; God created the being who became Satan and He created the being who became the sinner. But sin is not a creation; sin is the outcome of a wrong relationship set up between two of God's creations. From the very beginning God holds Himself responsible for the possibility of sin. BP. 228

We have to take pains to make ourselves what God has taken pains to make us. You can take a horse to the trough, but you can't make him drink; you can send your child to school, but you can't make him study; and God can put a saint into a right relationship with Himself, but He cannot make him work out that relationship, the saint must do that himself. CHI. 57

The culture of the Christian life is to learn to be carefully careless over everything saving our relationship to God. It is not sin that keeps us from going on spiritually, but "the cares of the world," "the lusts of other things" that crowd out any consideration of God. CHI. 109

It is possible to be first in suffering for the Truth and in reputation for saintliness, and last in the judgment of the great Searcher of hearts. The whole question is one of heart-relationship to Jesus. DI. 35

Every human relationship is put by Jesus on an eternal basis, otherwise the relationships born from the centre of what we call natural love end with this life, there is nothing more to them; but when they are rooted in the nature of God they are as eternal as God Himself. GW. 40

Never allow anything to fuss your relationship to Jesus Christ, neither Christian work, nor Christian blessing, nor Christian anything. Jesus Christ first, second and third; and God Himself by the great indwelling power of the Spirit within will meet the strenuous effort on your part, and slowly and surely you will form the mind of Christ and become one with Him as He was one with the Father. The practical test is—'Is Jesus Christ being manifested in my bodily life?' MFL. 119

. . . human nature possesses an incurable suspicion of God. Its origin is explained in the Bible; two great primal creatures of God, the angel who became Satan, and Adam, negotiated a relationship which God never sanctioned. That was how sin was introduced into the world. PS. 13

Thank God for every one who has learned that the dearest friend on earth is a mere shadow compared with Jesus Christ. There must be a dominant, personal, passionate devotion to Him, and only then are all other relationships right. SSH. 65

RELIGION

If my religion is based on my right to myself, that spells 'Satan' in my soul; I may be right-living, but I am anti-God. 'If you are going to be My disciple,' Jesus says, 'you must give up your right to yourself.' BE. 63

We are not to worship reminiscences; this is the characteristic of all other religions, saving the Bible religion. The Bible religion is one of eternal progress, an intense and militant going on. CD. VOL. 1, 25

The citadel of true religion is personal relationship to God, let come what will. CHI. 111

'What has my religion done for me I could not do for myself?' That is a question every man is forced to ask. Religion ostensibly is faith in Someone, or a form of belief in some power, I would be the poorer if I did not have, and I should be able to state in what way I would be poorer. DI. 37

If my religion is not based on a personal history with Jesus it becomes something I suffer from, not a joyous thing, but something that keeps me from doing what I want to do. DI. 38

Never have an exercise of religion that blots God clean out. DI 47

This attitude is spreading amongst us to-day amazingly, people are enchanted with the truth, sympathetic with the truth of God, but remaining in sin. 'Repentance' is not in their vocabulary, only regret; there is no confession of sin, only admitting. Religion is turned into education, and the Christian life is made to mean a happy life instead of a new life. GW. 91

Religion is never intellectual, it is always passionate and emotional; but the curious thing is that it is religion that leads to emotion, not emotion to religion. If religion does not make for passion and emotion, it is not the true kind. When you realize that you are saved, that God has forgiven your sins, given you the Holy Spirit, I defy you not to be carried away with emotion. Religion which makes for logic and reason is not religion, but to try to make religion out of emotion is to take a false step. HG. 33

The religion of Jesus Christ is not a religion of ethical truth, but of Redemption. HG. 96

Many of us are supernaturally solemn about our religion because it is not real. Immediately our religion becomes real, it is possible to have humour in connection with it. PH. 217

We carry our religion as if it were a headache, there is neither joy nor power nor inspiration in it, none of the grandeur of the unsearchable riches of Christ about it, none of the passion of hilarious confidence in God. PH. 223

The curse of much modern religion is that it makes us so desperately interested in ourselves, so overweeningly concerned about our own whiteness. PR. 44

Unless our salvation works out through our finger tips and everywhere else, there is nothing to it, it is religious humbug. PR. 101

It is easy to turn our religious life into a cathedral for beautiful memories, but there are feet to be washed, hard flints to be walked over, people to be fed. Very few of us go there, but that is the way The Son of God went. RTR. 8

If our faith or our religion does not help us in the conditions we are in, we have either a further struggle to go through, or we had better abandon that faith and religion. SA. 80

The stupendous difference between the religion of Jesus Christ and every other religion under heaven is that His religion is one which brings help to the bottom of hell, not a religion that can deal only with what is fine and pure. SA. 119

If a man cannot prove his religion in the valley, it is not worth anything. SHH. 18

Don't be fanatically religious and don't be irreverently blatant. Remember that the two extremes have to be held in the right balance. If your religion does not make you a better man, it is a rotten religion. The test of true religion is when it touches these four things— food, money, sex and mother earth. These things are the test of a right sane life with God, and the religion that ignores them or abuses them is not right. SHH. 99

Religion is a matter of taste, a matter in which a man's religious life and his actual life do not necessarily agree. In spiritual life that could never be; spiritual life means the real life, and it is significant that whenever Jesus talks about discipleship He speaks of it in actual terms. SHL. 105

Jesus Christ did not come to found religion, nor did He come to found civilisation, they were both here before He came; He came to make us spiritually real in every domain. In Jesus Christ there was nothing secular and sacred, it was all real, and He makes His disciples like Himself. SSM. 49

The main idea in the region of religion is, Your eyes on God, not on men. SSM. 56

Unless your religion will go to the lowest and the worst and the most desperate case you know of, your religon is of no use. There are a great many forms of belief which cannot begin to touch the worst of mankind, they can only deal with cultured minds and hearts. Jesus Christ's religion goes down to the lowest of the low as well as up to the highest of the high, and to all in between. The marvel of Jesus Christ is that He takes facts as they are. He Himself is the answer to every problem of heart and mind and life. WG. 39

There are only two religions that accept gloom as a fact (I mean by gloom, sin, anguish and misery, the things that make people feel that life is not worth living), viz., Buddhism and Christianity. Every other religion ignores it. WG. 63

REPENTANCE

Repentance is the blood of sanctification, the exhibition of a real gift of God; not only am I sorry for my sin, that is human, but in the sorrow for sin God slips in something else—the power never to do the thing again. BE. 64

The only repentant man is the holy man, and the only holy man is the one who has been made so by the marvel of the Atonement. BE. 117

Because a man has altered his life it does not necessarily mean that he has repented. A man may have lived a bad life and suddenly stop being bad, not because he has repented, but because he is like an exhausted volcano. The fact that he has become good is no sign of his having become a Christian. BFB. 103

Repentance means that I estimate exactly what I am in God's sight and I am sorry for it, and on the basis of the Redemption I become the opposite. BFB. 103

The only repentant man is the holy man, i.e., the one who becomes the opposite of what he was because something has entered into him. Any man who knows himself knows that he cannot be holy, therefore if he does become holy, it is because God has 'shipped' something into him; he is now 'presenced with Divinity,' and can begin to bring forth 'fruits meet for repentance'. BFB. 103

Jesus Christ's claim is that He can put a new disposition, His own disposition, Holy Spirit, into any man, and it will be manifested in all that he does. But the disposition of the Son of God can only enter my life by the way of repentance. BFB. 104

Strictly speaking, repentance is a gift of God. No man can repent when he chooses. A man can be remorseful when he chooses, but remorse is a lesser thing than repentance. Repentance means that I show my sorrow for the wrong thing by becoming the opposite. BFB. 108

Repentance to be true must issue in holiness, or it is not New Testament repentance. Repentance means not only sorrow and distress for the wrong done, but the acceptance of the Atonement of

Jesus which will make me what I have never been—holy. BSG. 26

Never mistake remorse for repentance; remorse simply puts a man in hell while he is on earth, it carries no remedial quality with it at all, nothing that betters a man. An unawakened sinner knows no remorse, but immediately a man recognizes his sin he experiences the pain of being gnawed by a sense of guilt, for which punishment would be a heaven of relief, but no punishment can touch it. CHI. 23

Remorse is not the recognition that I am detected by somebody else, I can defy that; remorse comes when intellectually and morally, I recognize my own guilt. It is a desperate thing for me to realize that I am a sneak, that I am sensual and proud, that is my sin finding *me* out. CHI. 24

That a man stops being bad and becomes good may have nothing to do with salvation; the only one sign that a man is saved is repentance. CHI. 25

Repentance is the experimental side of Redemption and is altogether different from remorse or reformation. "Repentance" is a New Testament word and cannot be applied outside the New Testament. We all experience remorse, disgust with ourselves over the wrong we have done when we are found out by it, but the rarest miracle of God's grace is the sorrow that puts an end for ever to the thing for which I am sorry. Repentance involves the receiving of a totally new disposition so that I never do the wrong thing again. CHI. 26

The essence of repentance is that it destroys the lust of self-vindication; wherever that lust resides the repentance is not true. CHI. 27

Repentance brings us to the place where we are willing to receive any punishment under heaven so long as the law we have broken is justified. That is repentance, and I think I am right in saying that very few of us know anything at all about it. We have the idea nowadays that God is so loving and gentle and kind that all we need do is to say we feel sorry for the wrong we have done and we will try to be better. That is not repentance; Repentance means that I am remade on a plane which justifies God in forgiving me. CHI. 27

The last delusion God delivers us from is the idea that we don't deserve what we get. Once we see ourselves under the canopy of God's overflowing mercy we are dissolved in wonder, love and praise. That is the meaning of repentance, which is the greatest gift God ever gives a man. CHI. 70

Holiness is based on repentance, and the holy man is the most humble man you can meet. My realization of God can be measured by my humility. CHI. 70

Salvation from sin is frequently confounded with deliverance from sins. A man can deliver himself from sins without any special work of God's grace. The bedrock of New Testament salvation is repentance, and repentance is based on relationship to a Person. DI. 65

Self-knowledge is the first condition of repentance. HG. 35

Watch Jesus Christ whenever there is the tiniest sign of repentance, He is the incarnation of forgiving and forgetting, and He says that is God's nature. HG. 35

The only truly repentant man is the holy man, he has been made holy through the incoming of God by his willing reception of Him. HG. 102

The realization of the nature of God's love produces in me the convulsions of repentance, and repentance fully worked out means holiness, a radical adjustment of the life. HG. 105

Repentance means that we recognize the need for forgiveness—'hands up, I know it.' HGM. 101

The deepest repentance is not in the sinner but in the saint. Repentance means not only sorrow for sin, but it involves the possession of a new disposition that will never do the thing again. OBH. 71

To *admit* instead of *confess* is to trample the blood of the Son of God under foot, but immediately we allow the Holy Spirit to give us the gift of repentance, the shed blood of Christ will purge our conscience from dead works and send us into heart-spending service for God with a passionate devotion. OBH. 71

The 'repenting' of God in individual cases means that God remains true to His purpose and must mean my condemnation, and my condemnation causes Him grief and agony. It is not that God won't overlook wrong, it is that He cannot, His very love forbids it. OPG. 16

The new life will manifest itself in conscious repentance and unconscious holiness, never the other way about. The bedrock of Christianity is repentance. If ever you cease to know the virtue of repentance, you are in darkness. RTR. 51

The bed-rock of Christianity is repentance. SA. 121

Repentance means that I estimate exactly what I am in God's sight, and I am sorry for it, and on the basis of Redemption I become the opposite. SA. 121

The disposition of the Son of God can only enter my life by the road of repentance. SA. 121

Repentance is not a reaction, remorse is. Remorse is—I will never do the thing again. Repentance is that I deliberately become the opposite to what I have been. SHH. 53

REPUTATION

What we stand up for proves what our character is like. If we stand up for our reputation it is a sign it needs standing up for! God never stands up for His saints, they do not need it. The devil tells lies about men, but no slander on earth can alter a man's character. BP. 114

God has staked His reputation on the work of Jesus Christ in the souls of the men and women whom He has saved and sanctified. DI. 59

We are only what we are in the dark; all the rest is reputation. What God looks at is what we are in the dark—the imaginations of our minds; the thoughts of our heart; the habits of our bodies; these are the things that mark us in God's sight. LG. 73

Reputation is what other people think of you; "character is what you are in the dark," where no one sees but yourself. SHH. 78

It is possible to blast a man's reputation by raising your shoulders; but you can never blast a man's character. Character is what a man is; reputation is what other people think he is. SHH. 134

RESPONSIBILITY

. . . anything that relieves us from the individual responsibility of being personally related to God is corrupt. BE. 14

There are many things in life that look like irresponsible blunders, but the Bible reveals that God has taken the responsibility for these things, and that Jesus Christ has bridged the gap which sin made between God and man; the proof that He has done so is the Cross. God accepts the responsibility for sin, and on the basis of the Redemption men find their personal way out and an explanation. BFB. 18

Through the identification of Jesus Christ with sin we can be brought back again into perfect harmony with God; but God does not take away our responsibility; He puts upon us a new responsibility. BP. 39

Individual responsibility for others without becoming an amateur providence, is one of the accomplishments of the Holy Spirit in a saint. DI. 86

God never holds a woman responsible in the same way as He does a man. NKW. 50

I alone am responsible for the wrong I do. NKW. 52

Our human nature is meant for the Son of God to manifest Himself in, and this brings us to the margin of our responsibility. OBH. 73

The Redemption of the human race does not necessarily mean the salvation of every individual. Redemption is of universal application, but human responsibility is not done away with. Jesus Christ states emphatically that there are possibilities of eternal damnation for the man who positively neglects or positively rejects His Redemption. PR. 79

We are in danger of forgetting that we cannot do what God does, and that God will not do what we can do. We cannot save ourselves nor sanctify ourselves, God does that; and God will not give us good habits, He will not give us character, He will not make us walk aright. We have to do all that ourselves, we have to work out the salvation God has worked in. RTR. 90

God holds *me* responsible if I refuse to let Him deliver me from sin. SA. 14

REST

What a man wants is somewhere to rest his mind and heart, and the only place to rest in is God, and the only way to come to God is by prayer. BFB. 77

There is only one point of rest, and that is in the Lord, not in our experiences. We are never told to rest in the experience of salvation or of sanctification or in anything saving the Lord Himself. PS. 30

RESURRECTION

Our Lord never speaks of the resurrection of spirit; the spirit does not need resurrecting; He speaks of a resurrection body for glorification and a resurrection body for damnation. BP. 260

We know what the resurrection body for glorification will be like: it will be like "His glorious body"; but all we know about the resurrection of the bad is that Jesus Christ (Who ought to know what

He is talking about) says that there will be a resurrection to damnation. BP. 260

The only way in which bitter tears can be evaded is either by a man's shallowness, or by his coming into a totally new relation to the Lord Jesus Christ through His Resurrection. PH. 123

The dust shall return to the earth, but resurrection means the restoration of the full-orbed life of a man. SHH. 152

REVELATION

Be sceptical of any revelation that has not got as its source the simplicity by means of which a "babe" can enter in, and which a "fool" can express. CHI. 53

If we eliminate the supernatural purpose of Jesus Christ's coming, viz., to deliver us from sin, we become traitors to God's revelation. DI. 66

We look to God to manifest Himself to His children: God manifests Himself *in* His children, consequently the manifestation is seen by others, not by us. GW. 25

If some of us are ever going to see God we shall have to go one step outside our particular relationship to things, religious or otherwise, and step into the revelation that Jesus Christ is our Lord and Master as well as our Saviour. HGM. 79

God never tell us what He is going to do, He reveals Who He is. NKW. 122

REVERENCE

Reverence and solemnity are not the same. Solemnity is often nothing more than a religious dress on a worldly spirit. Solemnity which does not spring from reverence towards God is of no use whatever. OBH. 97

REVIVAL

Always distinguish between yielding to the Spirit and receiving the Spirit. When the Spirit is at work in a time of mighty revival it is very difficult not to yield to the Spirit, but it is quite another thing to receive Him. If we yield to the power of the Spirit in a time of revival we may feel amazingly blessed, but if we do not receive the Spirit we are left decidedly worse and not better. BE. 95

To-day we are trying to work up a religious revival while God has visited the world in a moral revival, and the majority of us have not begun to recognize it. The characteristics that are manifested when God is at work are self-effacement, self-suppression, abandonment to something or someone other than myself. BFB. 23

Over and over again during times of revival and great religious awakening workers are presented with this puzzle, that people do unquestionably make restitution—men who stole pay up like sheep, with no notion why they do it, and if the worker is not well taught he will mistake this for the work of the Holy Spirit and a sign that they are born again, when the fact is that the truth has been so clearly put that it caused their nature to react towards reformation. The thing to do with people in that condition is to get them to *receive* something from God. CHI. 26

If there is to be another Revival it will be through the readjustment of those of us on the inside who call ourselves Christians. DI. 29

Some of us are rushing on at such a headlong pace in Christian work, wanting to vindicate God in a great Revival, but if God gave a revival we would be the first to forget Him and swing off on some false fire. DI. 47

Brood on what Jesus Christ came to do, and then in the full possession of your mind, not in the excitement of a revival moment, nor in the enthusiasm of a great spiritual ecstasy, but in the calm quiet knowledge of what you are doing, say—'My life to Thee, my King, I humbly dedicate'. GW. 114

There are places of revival to which the people of God take pilgrimages and spend hours and days and weeks there, trying to get a jaded life back again into communion with God, trying to revive by meditation and the power of association what can never be made alive apart from the living presence of God Himself. God is not confined to places, and where He once blessed, He may not bless again, it depends on the motive in seeking it. GW. 120

There is an idea in regard to a revival that the thing is done suddenly, by a magic pill. Some things in a man's life are done suddenly, but there is always the price to pay afterwards; he has to set his face to it. GW. 140

What is needed to-day is not so much a revival as a resurgent form of awakening, the incoming of the tremendous life of God in a new form. PH. 87

A revival adds nothing, it simply brings back what had been lost and is a confession of failure. The effects of a revival may be deplorable. "Oh that we had the ancient days of simplicity and sunshine"—days of adversity and humbug! Things are bad and difficult now, but not a tithe as difficult as they used to be. It is of no use to pray for the old days; stand square where you are and make the present better than any past has been. Base all on your relationship to God and go forward, and presently you will find that what is emerging is infinitely better than the past ever was. The present excels the past because we have the wealth of the past to go on. SHH. 90

RIGHT AND WRONG

To say that if I am persuaded a thing is wrong I won't do it, is not true. The mutiny of human nature is that it will do it whether it is wrong or not. DI. 26

There is no such thing as a *wrong* wrong, only a *right* that has gone wrong. Every error had its start in a truth, else it would have no power. DI. 28

If you remain true to your relationship to Jesus Christ the things that are either right or wrong are never the problem; it is the things that are right but which would impair what He wants you to be that are the problem. DI. 35

If I am a child of God, distress will lead me to Him for direction. The distress comes not because I have done wrong, it is part of the inevitable result of not being at home in the world, of being in contact with those who reason and live from a different standpoint. HG. 8

Depravity must be taken to mean much more than going wrong, it means rather to be so established in the wrong that the result is a real pleasure in it. OPG. 14

RIGHTEOUSNESS

Every man who comes to Jesus Christ has to go through the ordeal of condemnation, he has to have his beauty "consume away like a moth," and his righteousness drop from him "as filthy rags" when he stands face to face with God. CD. VOL. 1, 158

Imputed righteousness must never be made to mean that God puts the robe of His righteousness over our moral wrong, like a snow-drift over a rubbish heap; that He pretends we are all right when we are not. The revelation is that "Christ Jesus is made unto us, righteousness"; it is the distinct impartation of the very life of Jesus on the ground of the Atonement, enabling me to walk in the light as God is in the light, and as long as I remain in the light God sees only the perfections of His Son. We are "accepted in the Beloved." CHI. 81

The righteousness of God must be the foundation of our life as Christians. It is easy to talk about God's righteousness and His justice, but too often we banish the revelation of His character into the limbo of the abstract; we accept His righteousness as a theological doctrine, but we do not believe it practically. GW. 44

The greatest demand God makes of us is to believe that He is righteous when everything that happens goes against that faith. GW. 44

If I try to be right, it is a sure sign I am wrong; the only way to be right is by stopping the humbug of trying to be and remaining steadfast in faith in Jesus Christ. 'He that *doeth* righteousness is righteous, even as He is righteous.' GW. 46

Righteousness cannot be imitated. If I abide in Jesus, His righteousness is done through me. Nowadays the tendency is to switch away from abiding in Christ; it is—'Do this', and 'Do that'. You can-not do anything at all that does not become, in the rugged language of Isaiah, 'as filthy rags', no matter how right it looks, if it is divorced from abiding in Christ. Haul yourself up a hundred times a day till you learn to abide. GW. 46

The majority of us know nothing whatever about the righteousness that is gifted to us in Jesus Christ, we are still trying to bring human nature up to a pitch it cannot reach, because there is something wrong with human nature. The old Puritanism which we are apt to ridicule did the same service for men that Pharisaism did for Saul, and that Roman Catholicism did for Luther; but nowadays we have no 'iron' in us anywhere; we have no idea of righteousness, we do not care whether we are righteous or not. We have not only lost Jesus Christ's idea of righteousness, but we laugh at the Bible idea of righteousness; our god is the conventional righteousness of the society to which we belong. HG. 12

Righteousness must never be made to mean less than a guiltless position in the presence of justice and right. God justifies me by my supernatural faith in Him, but it is my just walk that proves Him just in saving me; if I do not walk in the life of faith, I am a slander to God. NKW. 46

"Except your righteousness shall exceed"—not be different from but "exceed" that is, we have to be all they are and infinitely more! We have to be right in our external behaviour, but we have to be as right, and "righter" in our internal behaviour. We have to be right in our words and actions but we have to be right in our thoughts and feelings. RTR. 59

All our righteousness is "as filthy rags" unless it is the blazing holiness of Jesus in us uniting us with Him until we see nothing but Jesus first, Jesus second, and Jesus third. SSM. 54

RIGHTS

Any fool can insist on his rights, and any devil will see that he gets them; but the Sermon on the Mount means that the only right the saint will insist on is the right to give up his rights. HGM. 130

Equal duties, not equal rights, is the keynote of the spiritual world; equal rights is the clamour of the natural world. The protest of power through grace, if we are following Jesus, is that we no longer insist on our rights, we see that we fulfil our duty. IWP. 110

The Holy Ghost gives us the power to forgo our rights. MFL. 37

The characteristic of a Christian is that he has the right not to insist on his rights. That will mean that I refuse to do certain things because they would cause my brother to stumble. MFL. 37

The only right a Christian has is the right to give up his rights. PR. 103

The reward for doing right is not that I get an insurance ticket for heaven, but that I do the right because it is right. SHH. 119

The only right a Christian has is the right not to insist upon his rights. Every time I insist upon my rights I hurt the Son of God. SSM. 45

RITUAL

If rites and ceremonies are put as a road to perfection they will become the path away from it. To put prayer, devotion, obedience, consecration, or any experience, as the means of sanctification is the proof that we are on the wrong line. PH. 86

There is a use for ritual in a man's religious life. Because a thing is necessary at one time of life, it does not follow that it is necessary all through. There may be times when ritual is a good thing and other times when it is not. Bear in mind that in the Hebrew religion there is an insistence on ecclesiasticism and ritual. In the New Testament that is finished with; but Ezekiel prophesies that the true worship of God will yet be established on earth as it has never yet been, and there will be ritual then to an extraordinary degree. SHH. 52

In the history of the salvation of a man's soul it may be better for him to worship in a whitewashed building, with a bare rugged simplicity of service; but while it is true that man may go through forms and ceremonies and be a downright hypocritical humbug, it is also true that he may despise ritual and be as big a humbug. SHH. 52

When a man is in a right relationship to God ritual is an assistance; the place of worship and the atmosphere are both conducive to worship. We are apt to ignore that ritual is essential in a full-orbed religious life, that there is a rectitude in worship only brought about by the right use of ritual. . . . when Jesus Christ taught His disciples to pray, He gave them a form of prayer which He knew would be repeated through the Christian centuries. SHH. 52

S

SACRIFICE

Jesus makes us saints in order that we may sacrifice our saintship to Him, and it is this sacrifice which keeps us one with our Lord. AUG. 109

We talk about the sacrifice of the Son of God and forget that it was the sacrifice of God Himself. "*God was in Christ* reconciling the world unto Himself." BSG. 47

The real burnt-offering God requires is 'a living sacrifice', the giving back to God the best He has given me that it might be His and mine for ever. GW. 65

Sacrifice in the Bible means that we give to God the best we have; it is the finest form of worship. Sacrifice is not giving up things, but giving to God with joy the best we have. LG. 148

We have a natural life to be sacrificed and thereby turned into a spiritual life. The meaning of sacrifice is giving the best we have to God, denying it to ourselves, that He may make it an eternal possession of His and ours. OBH. 115

Sacrifice means giving up something that we mind giving up. We talk of giving up our possessions; none of them are ours to give up. "A man's life consisteth not in the abundance of the things which he possesseth." Our Lord tells us to give up the one thing that is going to hurt badly, viz., our right to ourselves. PH. 57

The characteristic of your life if you are devoted to Jesus, is that you lay down your life for Him, not die for Him, but lay down your life for Him. PH. 80

God does not ask us to give up things for the sake of giving them up; He asks us to sacrifice them, to give back to Him the best He has given us in order that it may belong to Him and us for ever. Sacrifice is the source of spiritual discipleship. PH. 133

Our notion of sacrifice is the wringing out of us something we don't want to give up, full of pain and agony and distress. The Bible idea of sacrifice is that I give as a love-gift the very best thing I have. RTR. 26

SAINT

In the Christian life the saint is ever young; amazingly and boisterously young, certain that everything is all right. AUG. 90

To be a saint, a walking, talking, living, practical epistle of what God Almighty can do through the Atonement of the Lord Jesus Christ—one in identity with the faith of Jesus, one in identity with the love of Jesus, one in identity with the Spirit of Jesus until we are so one in Him that the high-priestly prayer not only begins to be answered, but is clearly manifest in its answering—"that they may be one, even as We are one." AUG. 112

A saint is not an ethereal creature too refined for life on this earth; a saint is a mixture of the Divine and the human that can stand anything. BE. 52

The truly godly person is one who is entirely sanctified, and he or she is never sanctimonious, but absolutely natural. The characteristic of a saint is freedom from anything in the nature of self-consciousness. BE. 83

According to consistent argument, the New Testament saint should be leagues ahead of the Old Testament saint, but in reality no character in the New Testament is superior to those in the Old Testament. The revelation of Redemption given through our Lord Jesus Christ is retrospective in our day; in the Old Testament it is prospective. BFB. 31

A saint is not a human being who is trying to be good, trying by effort and prayer and longing and obedience to attain as many saintly characteristics as possible; a saint is a being who has been re-created. "If any man is in Christ, he is a new creation." BP. 218

A saint is a creature of vast possibilities, knit into shape by the ruling personality of God. CD. VOL. 1, 9

The New Testament idea of a saint is not a cloistered sentiment gathering around the head of an individual like a halo of glory, but a holy character reacting on life in deeds of holiness.
CD. VOL. 1, 80

The soul of the sanctified saint is *en rapport* with God, he has no responsibility, he is 'without carefulness' because his Father cares, God's predestinations are that soul's voluntary choosings. The pre-eminent mystery in this thought is the mystery of the nature of Love: the saint knows, with a knowledge 'which passeth knowledge'. This truth is never discerned by the powerful in intellect, but only by the pure in heart.
CD. VOL. 1, 84

The production of a saint is the grandest thing earth can give to Heaven. A saint is not a person with a saintly character: a saint *is* a saintly character. Character, not ecstatic moods, is the stuff of saintliness. A saint is a living epistle written by the finger of God, known and read of all men. CD. VOL. 1, 99

The vocation of a saint is to be in the thick of it "for Thy sake." Whenever Jesus Christ refers to discipleship or to suffering, it is always, "for My sake." The deep relationship of a saint is a personal one, and the reason a saint can be radiant is that he has lost interest in his own individuality and has become absolutely devoted to the Person of the Lord Jesus Christ. CD. VOL. 1, 156

An artist is never consciously artistic, and a saint is never consciously a praying one. A saint endeavours consciously and strenuously to master the technical means of expressing God's life in himself. CD. VOL. 2, 13

The true child of God is such from an inward principle of life from which the life is ordered by implicit loving devotion, as natural as breathing, and as spontaneous as the life of a little child.
CD. VOL. 2, 80

The characteristic of the saint is not so much the renunciation of the things seen and temporal as the perfect certainty that these things are but the shows of reality. CD. VOL. 2, 153

A saint is never horror-stricken because although he knows that what our Lord says about the human heart is true, he knows also of a Saviour who can save to the uttermost. CHI. 71

If we put a saint or a good man as the standard, we blind ourselves to ourselves, personal vanity makes us do it; there is no room for personal vanity when the standard is seen to be God Himself. DI. 32

The mark of the saint is the good right things he has the privilege of not doing. There are a hundred and one right and good things which, if you are a disciple of Jesus, you must avoid as you would the devil although there is no devil in them. DI. 35

The Lord can never make a saint out of a good man, He can only make a saint out of three classes of people—the godless man, the weak man, and the sinful man, and no one else, and the marvel of the Gospel of God's grace is that Jesus Christ can make us naturally what He wants us to be. HG. 32

As saints we are called to go through the heroism of what we believe, not of stating what we believe, but of standing by it when the facts are dead against God. HGM. 80

. . . nothing clings to us more closely than trying to live up to the ideas we have got from saintly people. We have nothing to do with saintly people, we have only to do with 'looking to Jesus.' HGM. 144

There is only one lodestar to the saint, the Lord Jesus Christ. LG. 73

The saint is at home anywhere on Mother Earth; he dare be no longer parochial or denominational; he belongs to no particular crowd, he belongs to Jesus Christ. LG. 131

A saint is a sacramental personality, one through whom the presence of God comes to others. LG. 131

A saint's life is in the hands of God as a bow and arrow in the hands of an archer. God is aiming at something the saint cannot see; He stretches and strains, and every now and again the saint says: 'I cannot stand any more.' But God does not heed; He goes on stretching until His purpose is in sight, then He lets fly. We are here for God's designs, not for our own. LG. 132

We have to learn that this is the dispensation of the humiliation of the saints. The Christian Church has blundered by not recognizing this. In another dispensation the manifestation of the saints will take place, but in this dispensation we are to be disciples of Jesus Christ, not following our own convictions but remaining true to Him. LG. 132

A saint is a bundle of specially qualified reactions. For every possible circumstance in life there is a line of behaviour marked out in advance for us; it is not stated in black and white, we have to be so familiar with God's Book that when we come to a crisis the Spirit of God brings back to our memory the things we had read but never understood, and we see what we should do. God is making characters, not mechanisms. MFL. 56

A saint is not an angel and never will be; a saint is the flesh and blood theatre in which the decrees of God are carried to successful issues. All of which means that God demands of us the doing of common things while we abide in Him. NKW. 43

Just as the stars are poised by God Almighty, so the Apostle says the great power of the Father lifts the saints into the light that He and His Son are in, and poises them there, as eternally established as the stars. OBH. 46

The dominant thing about a saint is not self-realisation, but the Lord Himself; consequently a saint can always be ignored because to the majority of eyes our Lord is no more noticeable in the life of a saint than He was to men in the days of His flesh. But when a crisis comes the saint is the one to whom men turn; and the life which seemed colourless is seen to be the white light of God. OBH. 65

To say "Oh I'm no saint; I can't stand the folks who testify that they are sanctified" is acceptable with men; they will say it is true humility to talk in that way. But say this before God, and though it may sound humble, it is blasphemy because it means God cannot make me a saint. OBH. 80

The reason I am not a saint is either that I do not want to be a saint or I do not believe God can make me one. OBH. 103

. . . the only standard for judging the saint is Jesus Christ, not saintly qualities. OPG. 29

A strong saintly character is not the production of human breeding or culture, it is the manufacture of God. PH. 4

A sanctified saint is at leisure from himself and his own affairs, confident that God is bringing all things out well. PH. 41

. . . a saint is a piece of rugged human stuff re-made by the Atonement into oneness with God by the power of the Holy Ghost. PH. 87

As saints we are responsible for one thing only, viz., to maintain our conception right in relationship to God; this is the whole secret of the devotional life of a saint. The right conception is not Christian duty or service to men, but keeping Jesus as Master. PH. 110

God expects us to maintain in our individual lives the honour of a saint. It is up to us to live the life of a saint in order to show our gratitude to God for His amazing salvation, a salvation which cost us nothing but which cost God everything. PH. 157

We have not sufficiently emphasised the fact that we have to live as saints, and that in our lives the honour at stake is not our personal honour, but the honour of Jesus Christ. PH. 160

The attitude of a saint is that he is related to God through Jesus Christ, consequently the spring of his life is other than the world sees. PH. 163

If the saint is paying attention to the Source, Jesus Christ, out of him and unconsciously to him are flowing the rivers of living water wherever he goes. Men are either getting better or worse because of us. PR. 44

Jesus Christ was absolutely interested in God, and the saint is to be a simple, unaffected, natural human being indwelt by the Spirit of God. PR. 44

. . . the curse of the saint is his goodness! PS. 22

If God were to remove from us as saints the possibility of disobedience there would be no value in our obedience, it would be a mechanical business. PS. 50

The one dominant note of the life of a saint is first of all sympathy with God and God's ideas, not with human beings. PS. 81

There was nothing secular in our Lord's life and in the saint the sacred and the secular must be all His, the one must express the other. I have to turn consciously from the shallow to the profound, there is something radically wrong, not in the shallow, but in the profound. RTR. 19

A saint is one who, on the basis of the Redemption of Jesus Christ, has had the centre of his life radically altered, and has deliberately given up his right to himself. This is the point where the moral issue comes, the frontier whereby we get in contact with God. SA. 39

A saint does not mean a man who has not enough sin to be bad, but a man who has received from Jesus Christ a new heredity that turns him into another man. SA. 50

God made His own Son to be sin that He might make the sinner a saint. SA. 120

The saints who satisfy the heart of Jesus are the imperial people of God for ever, nothing deflects them, they are superconquerors, and in the future they will be side by side with Jesus. 'He that overcometh, I will give to him to sit down with Me in My throne, even as I also overcame, and sat down with My Father, in His throne.' SHL. 123

When a man is born from above, he does not need to pretend to be a saint, he cannot help being one. SSM. 30

We do not need the grace of God to stand crises; human nature and our pride will do it. We can buck up and face the music of a crisis magnificently, but it does require the supernatural grace of God to live twenty-four hours of the day as a saint, to go through drudgery as a saint, to go through poverty as a saint, to go through an ordinary, unobtrusive, ignored existence as a saint, unnoted and unnoticeable. SSY. 69

SALT

Savourless salt is a most cursed influence in the physical world, and a saint who has lost his saintliness is a pestilential influence in the spiritual world. PS. 51

"Ye are the salt of the earth." Some modern teachers seem to think our Lord said 'Ye are the *sugar* of the earth,' meaning that gentleness and winsomeness without curative-ness is the ideal of the Christian. SSM. 19

. . . a Christian is salt, and salt is the most concentrated thing known. Salt preserves wholesomeness and prevents decay. It is a disadvantage to be salt Think of the action of salt on a wound, and you will realise this. If you get salt into a wound, it hurts, and when God's children are amongst those who are 'raw' towards God, their presence hurts. The man who is wrong with God is like an open wound, and when 'salt' gets in it causes annoyance and distress and he is spiteful and bitter. The disciples of Jesus in the present dispensation preserve society from corruption; the 'salt' causes excessive irritation which spells persecution for the saint. SSM. 19

SALVATION

The conscious ring of our life is a mere phase, Jesus Christ did not die and rise again to save that only; the whole personality of man is included. BP. 159

We have to beware of estimating Jesus Christ's salvation by our experience of it. Our experience is a mere indication in the conscious life of an almighty salvation that goes far beyond anything we ever can experience. BP. 159

Nowhere does the Bible say that God holds man responsible for having the disposition of sin; but what God does hold man responsible for is refusing to let Him deliver him from that heredity the moment he sees and understands that that is what Jesus Christ came to do. BP. 228

The Bible does not only teach the way of salvation, but the way of spiritual sanity. BP. 240

We are saved and sanctified for God, not to be specimens in His showroom, but for God to do with us even as He did with Jesus, make us broken bread and poured-out wine as He chooses. BSG. 27

Salvation means that if a man will turn—and every man has the power to turn, if it is only a look towards the Cross, he has the power for that—if a man will but turn, he will find that Jesus is able to deliver him not only from the snare of the wrong disposition within him, but from the power of evil and wrong outside him. CHI. 97

When a man experiences salvation it is not his belief that saves him; teaching goes wrong when it puts a man's belief as the ground of his salvation. Salvation is God's 'bit' entirely. DI. 54

Salvation is a free gift through the Redemption; positions in the Kingdom are not gifts, but attainments. DI. 55

A charge made against some methods of evangelism is that self-interest is made the basis of the whole thing: salvation is looked upon as a kind of insurance scheme whereby I am delivered from punishment and put right for heaven. But let a man experience *deliverance from sin*, and his rejoicing is not in his own interests, but that he is thereby enabled to be of use to God and his fellow men. DI. 55

Salvation is based on the *revelation* fact that God has redeemed the world from the possibility of condemnation on account of sin. The *experience* of salvation means that a man can be regenerated, can have the disposition of the Son of God put into him, viz., the Holy Spirit. DI. 56

No man can be saved by praying, by believing, by obeying, or by consecration; salvation is a free gift of God's almighty grace. We have the sneaking idea that we earn things and get into God's favour by what we do—by our praying, by our repentance: the only way we get into God's favour is by the sheer gift of His grace. GW. 11

We are apt to have the idea that salvation is a kind of watertight compartment and if we enter in all our liberty will be destroyed. That is not our Lord's conception; He says he 'shall go in and go out'. GW. 110

Many of us are saved by the skin of our teeth, we are comfortably settled for heaven, that is all we care for, now we can make a pile on earth. HG. 39

It is impossible to locate the 'soul-saving' idea in the New Testament. The glory of the Lord's disciples is not the saving of souls; but the 'soul of salvation' expressed in personal lives. It is God's work to save souls. HGM. 28

We are busy praying that our particular phase of things may succeed, that men's souls may be saved; but what is meant by 'a saved soul' is frequently determined by our doctrine of salvation and not by a personal relationship to Jesus Christ. HGM. 78

If we get taken up with salvation or with holiness or Divine healing instead of with Jesus Christ, we will be disillusioned. HGM. 110

When once you let the God of peace grip you by salvation and squeeze the suspicion out of you till you are quiet before Him, the believing attitude is born, there is no more suspicion, you are in moral agreement with God about everything He wants to do. IYA. 70

If there is one point where we say 'I won't' then we shall never know His salvation. LG. 143

When once a man has been awakened from sin to salvation, the only propositions that are alive to his will are the propositions of God. There is an insatiable inquiry after God's commands, and to every command there is a desire to act in obedience. MFL. 30

The amazing thing about the salvation of our Lord is that He brings us into contact with the reality that is, until we are just like children, continually seeing the wonder and beauty of things around us. MFL. 60

The salvation of Jesus is not a Divine anticipation, it is an absolute fact. People talk about the magnificent ideals that are yet to be; but the marvel of being born from above is that the reality is infinitely more wonderful than all we have imagined. MFL. 60

The reality of the salvation of Jesus Christ is that He makes us pay attention to realities, not appearances. MFL. 61

There is a difference between the way we try to appreciate the things of God and the way in which the Spirit of God teaches. We begin by trying to get fundamental conceptions of the creation and the world; why the devil is allowed; why sin exists. When the Spirit of God comes in He does not begin by expounding any of these subjects. He begins by giving us a dose of the plague of our own heart; He begins where our vital interests lie—in the salvation of our souls. MFL. 98

In one aspect Jesus Christ became identified with the weakest thing in His own creation, a Baby; in another aspect He went to the depths of a bad man's hell, consequently from the babe to the vilest criminal Jesus Christ's substitution tells for salvation, nothing can prevail against Him. MFL. 106

One of the dangers of present-day teaching is that it makes us turn our eyes off Jesus Christ on to ourselves, off the Source of our salvation on to salvation itself. The effect of that is a morbid, hypersensitive life, totally unlike our Lord's life, it has not the passion of abandon that characterised Him. MFL. 108

Salvation is sudden, but the working of it out in our lives is never sudden. It is moment by moment, here a little and there a little. God educates us down to the scruple. MFL. 120

In the matter of salvation it is God's honour that is at stake, not our honour. NKW. 64

We cannot do anything for our salvation, but we must do something to manifest it; we must work it out. OBH. 81

"Work out your own salvation. . . ." We have not to work out that which tells for our salvation, but to work out in the expression of our lives the salvation which God has worked in. What does my tongue say? What things do my ears like to listen to? What kind of bodily associates do I like to be with? OBH. 131

Salvation is not an edict of God; salvation is something wrought out on the human plane through God becoming Man. OPG. 24

Salvation is so wonderful, so full of ease and power, because of what it cost Jesus Christ. PH. 88

There is a difference between being saved and being a disciple. Some of us are saved, "yet so as through fire." We are grateful to God for saving us from sin, but we are of no use to Him in so far as our actual life is concerned. We are not spiritual disciples. PH. 132

The purpose of salvation and sanctification is that we may be made broken bread and poured out wine for others as Jesus Christ was made broken bread and poured out wine for us. When we recognise God's purpose we hand ourselves back to God to do what He likes with. He may put me in the front of things, or He may put me on the shelf if He wants

to. I separate the holy thing God has created to the Holy God. PH. 193

If you are religious, beware lest you are keener on the plan of salvation than on the Saviour. PH. 230

The centre of salvation is the Cross of Jesus Christ, and why it is so easy to obtain salvation is because it cost God so much; and why it is so difficult to experience salvation is because human conceit will not accept, nor believe, nor have anything to do with unmerited salvation. PR. 107

Salvation means the incoming into human nature of the great characteristics that belong to God, and there is no salvation that is not supernatural. PR. 121

Salvation is always supernatural. The Holy Ghost brings me into union with God by dealing with that which broke the union. It is dangerous to preach a persuasive gospel, to try and persuade men to believe in Jesus Christ with the idea that if they do, He will develop them along the natural line. PR. 122

Jesus Christ can take anyone, no matter who he is, and presence him with His wonderful Divine salvation. PR. 123

We may not only be supernaturally saved, we may be supernaturally sanctified. PR. 128

The purpose of the sword is to destroy everything that hinders a man being delivered. The first thing in salvation is the element of destruction, and it is this that men object to. PS. 24

If you have a passion for souls it is because your salvation has made such a practical change in you that you would part with your right hand to get every man there too. RTR. 16

Unless we are damnable, we are not worth saving. If we cannot go to the devil, we cannot go to God. The measure of the depth to which a man can fall is the height to which he can rise. Virtue is the outcome of conflict, not of necessity. SHH. 101

If you have been making a great profession in your religious life but begin to find that the Holy Spirit is scrutinizing you, let His searchlight go straight down, and He will not only search you, He will put everything right that is wrong; He will make the past as though it had never been; He will 'restore the years the cankerworm hath eaten'; He will 'blot out the handwriting of ordinances that is against you'; He will put His Spirit within you and cause you to walk in His ways; He will make you pure in the deepest recesses of your personality. Thank God, Jesus Christ's salvation is a flesh-and-blood reality! SHL. 51

Thank God for the amazing security of His salvation! It keeps us not only in conscious life but from dangers of which we know nothing, unseen and hidden dangers, subtle and desperate. SHL. 61

Salvation means not only a pure heart, an enlightened mind, a spirit right with God, but that the whole man is comprehended in the manifestation of the marvellous power and grace of God, body, soul, and spirit are brought into fascinating captivity to the Lord Jesus Christ. SSM. 88

The salvation of God not only saves a man from hell, but alters his actual life. SSM. 92

Salvation is of universal application, but human responsibility is not done away with. SSY. 106

SANCTIFICATION

Sanctification means not only that we are delivered from sin, but that we start on a life of stern discipline. It is not a question of praying but of performing, of deliberately disciplining ourselves. BE. 48

Sanctification is not a question of being delivered from hell, but of identifying myself with the death of Christ. BE. 69

We are made part of the mystical Body of Christ by sanctification. BP. 40

In the Bible the experiences of salvation and sanctification are never separated as we separate them; they are separable in experience, but when God's Book speaks of being "in Christ" it is always in terms of entire sanctification. BP. 71

When we are sanctified we do not get something like a landslide of holiness from heaven; we are introduced into a relationship of one-ness with God, and as Our Lord met antagonistic forces and overcame them, so must we. The life Jesus lived is the type of our life after sanctification. We are apt to make sanctification the end; it is only the beginning. Our holiness as saints consists in the exclusive dedication to God of all our powers. BSG. 37

When we are sanctified, our spiritual education goes along the same lines—the deliberate sacrifice to God of the self God has sanctified; the determined subordination of our intelligence to God, and the determined submission of our will to God. What a glorious opportunity there is for Jesus Christ in our lives! BSG. 38

The fullest meaning of sanctification is that Jesus Christ is 'made unto us sanctification,' that is, He creates in us what He is Himself. BSG. 55

Sanctification begins at regeneration, and goes on to a second great crisis, when God, upon an uttermost abandonment in consecration, bestows His gracious work of entire sanctification. The point of entire sanctification is reached not by the passing of the years but by obedience to the heavenly vision and through spiritual discipline. CS. VOL. 2, 84

There is no difficulty in getting sanctified if my will and affections have at their heart the earnest desire for God's glory. CHI. 54

If I am willing for God to strangle in me the thing that makes me everlastingly hanker after my own point of view, my own interests, my own whiteness—if I am willing for all that to be put to death, then "the God of peace will sanctify me wholly." CHI. 54

Sanctification means a radical and absolute identification with Jesus until the springs of His life are the springs of my life. "Faithful is He that calleth you, who also will do it." CHI. 54

The way we are to overcome the world, the flesh and the devil is by the force of our love for God regulating all our passions until every force of body, soul and spirit is devoted to this first great duty. This is the one sign of sanctification in a life; any experience of sanctification which is less than that has something diseased about it. CHI. 76

Notice where God puts His disapproval on human experiences, it is when we begin to adhere to our conception of what sanctification is, and forget that sanctification itself has to be sanctified. CHI. 95

After sanctification it is difficult to state what your aim in life is, because God has taken you up into His purposes. CHI. 95

People talk a lot about their "experience" of sanctification and too often there is nothing in it, it doesn't work out in the bodily life or in the mind, it is simply a doctrine . . . CHI. 104

Beware of preaching Sanctification without knowing Jesus; we are saved and sanctified in order that we might know Him. DI. 58

If we are to be of any use to God in facing present-day problems we must be prepared to run the sanctification-metaphysic for all it is worth. DI. 59

The test of sanctification is not our talk about holiness and singing pious hymns; but, what are we like where no one sees us? with those who know us best? DI. 60

If I exalt Sanctification, I preach people into despair; but if I lift up Jesus Christ, people learn the way to be made holy. DI. 60

It is a great snare to think that when you are sanctified you cannot make mistakes; you can make mistakes so irreparably terrible that the only safeguard is to 'walk in the light, as God is in the light.' DI. 60

When you come under the searchlight of God after sanctification, you realize much more keenly what sin is than ever you could have done before. DI. 60

Never try to build sanctification on an unconfessed sin, on a duty left undone; confess the wrong, do what you ought to have done, then God will clear away all the hyper-conscientious rubbish. DI. 61

You can always test the worth of your sanctification. If there is the slightest trace of self-conscious superiority about it, it has never touched the fringe of the garment of Christ. DI. 61

The deliverances of God are not what the saint delights in, but in the fact that *God* delivered him; not in the fact that he is sanctified, but that *God* sanctified him; the whole attention of the mind is on God. DI. 61

The sanctification of the Bible never fixes you on the fact that you are delivered from sin: it fixes you on the One who *is* Sanctification. Sanctification is not something Jesus Christ gives me, it is Himself in me. GW. 48

The value to God of one man or woman right out in supreme sanctification is incalculable. GW. 126

To imagine that Jesus Christ came to save and sanctify *me* is heresy: He came to save and sanctify me *into Himself.* HGM. 130

. . . we are not sanctified for our sakes, but for God's sake. IWP. 16

An unconditional 'give up' is the condition of sanctification, not claiming something for ourselves. IWP. 17

. . . the one purpose of sanctification is that Jesus might be "marvelled at in all them that believe." IWP. 54

To coin a phrase, Jesus Christ 'sanctified His sanctification,' that is, He determinedly sacrificed His holy Self to His Father. Jesus Christ separated, or sanctified, Himself by sacrificing His holy Self to the will of His Father; He sanctified His intelligence by submitting His intelligence to the word of His Father, and He sanctified His will by submitting His will to the will of His Father. As the sanctified children of God we need to bear in mind that after the experience of sanctification we have to separate our holiness to God. We are not made holy for ourselves, but for God, there is to be no insubordination about us. IYA. 66

Are we prepared for what sanctification will cost? It will cost an intense narrowing of all our interests on earth, and an immense broadening of our interest in God. IYA. 67

Some people pray and long and yearn for the experience of sanctification, but never get anywhere near it; others enter in with a sudden marvellous realisation. Sanctification is an instantaneous, continuous work of grace; how long the approach to it takes depends upon ourselves, and that leads some to say sanctification is not instantaneous. The reason why some do not enter in is because they have never allowed their minds to realise what sanctification means. IYA. 67

. . . sanctification means an intense concentration on God's point of view— every power of spirit, soul and body chained and kept for God's purpose only. IYA. 67

America has a phrase—'Pray through.' What we have to 'pray through' is all our petulant struggling after sanctification, all the inveterate suspicion in our hearts that God cannot sanctify us.

When we are rid of all that and are right before God, then God lets us see how He alone does the work. IYA. 70

If we are to be sanctified, it must be by the God of peace Himself. The power that makes the life of the saint does not come from our efforts at all, it comes from the heart of the God of peace. IYA. 70

Sanctification covers not only the narrow region where we begin the spiritual life, but the whole rational man, sanctified wholly in imagination and reasoning power. IYA. 74

Sanctification is an instantaneous, continuous work of God; immediately we are related rightly to God it is manifested instanter in spirit, soul and body. The reason the Church as a whole does not believe it is because they will not soak in the massive truths of God, consequently every now and again in the history of the Church, God has had to raise up some servant of His to emphasise afresh this intense, vivid sanctification of the whole spirit, the whole soul, and the whole body, preserved blameless unto the coming of our Lord Jesus Christ. IYA. 75

Sanctification means that God keeps my whole spirit and soul and body undeserving of censure in His sight. LG. 138

To say that the doctrine of sanctification is unnatural is not true, it is based on the way God has made us. MFL. 72

We are sanctified for one purpose only, that we might sanctify our sanctification and give it to God. MFL. 108

If we want to know Jesus Christ's idea of a saint and to find out what holiness

means, we must not only read pamphlets about sanctification, we must face ourselves with Jesus Christ, and as we do so He will make us face ourselves with God. MFL. 110

Sanctification is not *once for all*, but *once for always*. Sanctification is an instantaneous, continuous work of grace. If we think of sanctification as an experience once for all, there is an element of finality about it; we begin the hop, skip and jump testimony, 'Bless God, I am saved and sanctified,' and from that second we begin to get *'scantified'*. MFL. 117

Sanctification means we have the glorious opportunity of proving daily, hourly, momentarily, this identity with Jesus Christ, and the life bears an unmistakable likeness to Him. MFL. 117

Sanctification means the perfection of Jesus Christ manifesting itself in actual experience. NKW. 42

Sanctification is not something Our Lord does in me; sanctification is *Himself* in me. 'Of Him are ye in Christ Jesus, who is made unto us . . . sanctification.' NKW. 96

We have the idea that sanctification means deliverance from sin only; it means much more, it means that we start on a life of discipline such as nine out of every ten of us will have nothing to do with. NKW. 102

Sanctification is not the end of Redemption, it is the gateway to the purpose of God. NKW. 133

I believe there are numbers of Christians who have laid themselves on one side, as it were, and come to the conclusion that sanctification is not meant for them; the reason being that they have tried to work sanctification out in their own way instead of in God's way, and have failed.

There are others who by strange penances, fastings and prayers, and afflictions to their bodies are trying to work out sanctification. They, too, have tried to penetrate the mystery in a way other than God's appointed way.

Are you trying to work out sanctification in any of these ways? You know that salvation is a sovereign work of grace, but, you say, sanctification is worked out by degrees. God grant that the Spirit of God may put His quiet check on you, and enable you to understand the first great lesson in the mystery of sanctification which is *"Christ Jesus, who of God is made unto us . . . sanctification."* OBH. 13

Sanctification does not put us into the place that Adam was in and require us to fulfil the will of God as He makes it known to us; sanctification is something infinitely more than that. In Jesus Christ is perfect holiness, perfect patience, perfect love, perfect power over all the power of the enemy, perfect power over everything that is not of God, and sanctification means that all that is ours in Him. OBH. 13

Sanctification is Christ formed in us; not the Christ-life, but Christ Himself. In Jesus Christ is the perfection of everything, and the mystery of sanctification is that we may have in Jesus Christ, not the start of holiness, but the holiness of Jesus Christ. All the perfections of Jesus Christ are at our disposal if we have been initiated into the mystery of sanctification. OBH. 14

Sanctification does not mean that the Lord gives us the ability to produce by a slow, steady process a holiness like His; it is *His* holiness in us. OBH. 14

So many have the idea that in sanctification we draw from Jesus the power to be holy. We draw from Jesus the holiness that was manifested in Him, and He manifests it in us. This is the mystery of sanctification. OBH. 14

The Spirit of God conveys to the initiated, to those who are born again, what a marvellous thing sanctification is. The perfections of Jesus—ours by the sheer gift of God. God does not give us power to imitate Him: He gives us His very Self. OBH. 16

The mystery of sanctification is that the perfections of Jesus Christ are imparted to us, not gradually, but instantly, when by faith we enter into the realisation that Christ is made unto us sanctification. Sanctification does not mean anything less than the holiness of Jesus Christ being made ours manifestly, and faith is the instrument given us to use in order to work out this unspeakable mystery in our lives. There are two 'means'; the Gospel of the Grace of God, and faith, which enables the life and liberty and power and marvel of the holiness of Jesus Christ to be wrought out in us. OBH. 19

It is no use looking for sanctification through prayer or obedience; sanctification must be the direct gift of God by means of this instrument of faith, not a half-hearted faith, but the most earnest, intense, and personal faith. OBH. 21

It is *His* wonderful life that is imparted to us in sanctification, and it is imparted by faith. It will never be imparted as long as we cling to the idea that we can get it by obedience, by doing this and that. We have to come back to one thing, faith alone, and after having been put right with God by sanctification, it is still a life of faith all through. Those who are in the experience of sanctification know that it means that the holiness of Jesus is imparted as a sovereign gift of God's grace. We cannot earn it, we cannot pray it down, but, thank God, we can take it by faith, "through faith in His blood." OBH. 21

Satan tries to come in and make the saint disbelieve that sanctification is only by faith in God; he comes in with his 'cinematograph show' and says, 'You must have this and you must do that.' The Spirit of God keeps us steadily to one line—faith in Jesus, and the trial of our faith, until the perfections of Jesus Christ are lived over again in our lives. OBH. 21

Those of you who have never had this experience of sanctification, think! The perfections of Jesus Christ made yours entirely! The Lord showing His love, His purity, His holiness through you! "I live, yet not I, but Christ liveth in me." OBH. 22

. . . the idea of sanctification is not that God gives us a new spirit of life, and then puts Jesus Christ in front of us as a copy and says, 'Do your best and I will help you'; but that God imparts to us the perfections of Jesus Christ. By the perfections of Jesus we do not mean His attributes as Son of God. What is imparted to us is the holiness of Jesus, not a principle of life that enables us to imitate Him, but *the holiness of Jesus* as it met life in Him. OBH. 24

Sanctification means that we are taken into a mystical union which language cannot define. It is Jesus Christ's holiness that is granted to us, not something pumped up by prayer and obedience and discipline, but something created in us by Jesus Christ. OBH. 27

Sanctification is the impartation to us of the holy qualities of Jesus Christ. It is His patience, His love, His holiness, His faith, His purity, His godliness that are manifested in and through every sanctified soul. The presentation that God by sanctification plants within us His Spirit, and then setting Jesus Christ before us says—'There is your Example, follow Him and I will help you, but you must do your best to follow Him and do what He did,' is an error. It is not true to experience, and, thank God, it is not true to the wonderful Gospel of the grace of God. The mystery of sanctification is *"Christ in you, the hope of glory."* "That which hath been made was life in Him," that is, Jesus Christ can create in us the image of God even as it was in Himself. OBH. 31

What the heart of Jesus wanted most was God's glory, and sanctification means that that same desire is imparted to us. OBH. 35

The sanctified soul realises with growing amazement what we are trying feebly to put into words, that all these things are ours if we are willing for God to realise His claim in us. "All things are your's . . . and ye are Christ's; and Christ is God's." OBH. 37

By sanctification we enter into the kingdom of perfect oneness with Jesus Christ; everything He is, we are by faith. OBH. 88

We speak about testifying to the experience of sanctification; what we really testify to is not an *experience* of sanctification but to a revelation granted us by God of what sanctification is: the *expe-*

rience of sanctification is the rest of life from that moment. OBH. 125

A sanctified saint remains perfectly confident in God, because sanctification is not something the Lord gives me, sanctification is *Himself in me*. PH. 41

The Lord Jesus Christ is the beginning, the middle and the end. Many are willing to accept sanctification, but they do not want the One Who is sanctification. PH. 45

. . . when I think I can define what sanctification is, I have done something God refuses to do. Books about sanctification are much clearer than the Bible. The Bible is uncommonly confusing, so is human life. There is only one thing that is simple, and that is our relationship to Jesus Christ. PH. 87

We do not experience sanctification for any purpose other than God's purpose. PH. 225

. . . after the work of sanctification, when the life of a saint really begins, God lifts His hand off and lets the world, the flesh, and the devil do their worst, for He is assured that "greater is He that is in you, than he that is in the world." PR. 75

Before sanctification we know nothing, we are simply put in the place of knowing; that is, we are led *up* to the Cross; in sanctification we are led *through* the Cross—for what purpose? For a life of outpouring service to God. PS. 17

After sanctification the characteristic of the life is clear—Jesus Christ first, Jesus Christ second and Jesus Christ third, all that the Lord wants; the life goes on with a flood of intense energy, adoration unspeakable. PS. 37

In the first experience of sanctification we lose altogether the consciousness of our own identity, we are absorbed in God; but that is not the final place, it is merely the introduction to a totally new life. We lose our natural identity and consciously gain the identity that Jesus had, and it is when God begins to deal with sanctified souls on that line that darkness sometimes comes and the strange misunderstanding of God's ways. PS. 37

Sanctification is the gateway to real union with God, which is life unutterable. PS. 47

Sanctification means intense concentration on God's point of view. It means every power of body, soul and spirit chained and kept for God's purpose only. RTR. 31

Sanctification is the work of Christ in me, the sign that I am no longer independent, but completely dependent upon Him. SHL. 88

SANITY/INSANITY

Sanity in ordinary human life is maintained by a right correspondence with outer facts, and sanity in Christian life is produced by the correspondence with the facts revealed by our Lord Jesus Christ. CD. VOL. 2, 95

. . . this is a day of intolerant inquisitiveness, people will not wait for the slow, steady, majestic way of the Son of God, they enter in by this door and that, and the consequence is moral, spiritual and physical insanity. IWP. 124

SARCASM

If a weak man is presented with facts he cannot understand, he invariably turns to sarcasm. BFB. 54

Sarcasm is the weapon of the weak man; the word literally means to tear flesh from the bone. BFB. 54

SATAN

According to the Bible, man is responsible for the introduction of Satan: Satan is the result of a communication set up between man and the devil. BFB. 8

One of the most cunning travesties is to represent Satan as the instigator of external sins. The satanically-managed man is moral, upright, proud and individual; he is absolutely self-governed and has no need of God. BFB. 8

Satan counterfeits the Holy Spirit. BFB. 8

Satan's sneer is the counterpart of the devil's sneer in Genesis iii.; there, the devil's object is to sneer about God to man; here, Satan's object is to sneer about man to God, he is 'the accuser of the brethren'. BFB. 9

Satan's aim is to make a man believe that God is cruel and that things are all wrong; but when a man strikes deepest in agony and turns deliberately to the God manifested in Jesus Christ, he will find Him to be the answer to all his problems. BFB. 19

Satan is to be humiliated by man, by the Spirit of God in man through the wonderful regeneration of Jesus Christ. BP. 8

After the fall, God cursed this beautiful creature into the serpent, to feed on dust and to crawl. The serpent in the physical domain is a picture of Satan in the spiritual domain. BP. 18

The pretensions of Satan are clear. He is the god of this world and he will not allow relationship to the true God. Satan's attitude is that of a pretender to the throne, he claims it as his right. Wherever and whenever the rule of God is recognized by man, Satan proceeds to instil the tendency of mutiny and rebellion and lawlessness. BP. 20

Satan's pretension is that he is equal with God. His perversion is two-fold: he tries to pervert what God says to us, and also to pervert God's mind about us. BP. 22

Satan is an awful being, he is able to deceive us on the right hand and on the left, and the first beginnings of his deceptions are along the lines of self-pity. Self-pity, self-conceit, and self-sympathy will make us accept slanders against God. BP. 22

Satanic anarchy is conscious and determined opposition to God. Wherever God's rule is made known, Satan will put himself alongside and oppose it. Satan's sin is at the summit of all sins; man's sin is at the foundation of all sins, and there is all the difference in the world between them. BP. 24

Satan's sin is conscious, emphatic, and immortal rebellion against God; he has no fear, no veneration, and no respect for God's rule. Whenever God's law is stated, that is sufficient, Satan will break it, and his whole purpose is to get man to do the same. Satanic anarchy is a conscious, tremendous thing. BP. 24

Men are responsible for doing wrong things, and they do wrong things because of the wrong disposition in them. The moral cunning of our nature makes us blame Satan when we know perfectly well we should blame ourselves; the true blame for sins lies in the wrong disposition in us. In all probability Satan is as much upset as the Holy Ghost is when men fall into external sin, but for a different reason. When men go into external sin and upset their lives, Satan knows perfectly well that they will want another Ruler, a Saviour and Deliverer; as long as Satan can keep men in peace and unity and harmony apart from God, he will do so. BP. 24

Satan's sin is dethroning God. BP. 24

Satan uses the problems of this life to slander God's character; he tries to make us think that all the calamities and miseries and wrongs spring from God. BP. 134

Our Lord continually saw things and beings we do not see. He talked about 'Satan' and 'demons' and 'angels.' We don't see Satan or demons or angels, but Jesus Christ unquestionably did, and He sees their influence upon us. BP. 156

Satan is the prince of this world, and during this dispensation he has power to give authority to those who will yield to him and compromise. We are here to stand true to God, not to attack men. No prophet ever lived by his message; immediately he tries to, he must accommodate his message to the standards of the people. BSG. 33

Satan's primary concern is to sneer against God, he is after disconcerting God, putting God in a corner, so to speak, where He will have to take action along Satan's proposed lines. CHI. 110

Satan does not come as "an angel of light" to anybody but a saint. DI. 19

The only soul Satan cannot touch is the soul whose spiritual life and rational life and physical life is hid with Christ in God; that soul is absolutely secure. IWP. 35

Satan does not come on the line of tempting us to sin, but on the line of making us shift our point of view, and only the Spirit of God can detect this as a temptation of the devil. LG. 153

Satan's great aim is to deflect us from the centre. He will allow us to be devoted 'to death' to any cause, any enterprise, to anything but the Lord Jesus. PH. 17

Satan is to be overcome and conquered by human beings. That is why God became Incarnate. It is in the Incarnation that Satan is overcome. PR. 62

Satan tried to put Jesus Christ on the way to becoming King of the world and Saviour of men in a way other than that pre-determined by God. PR. 63

Self-realisation is the essential principle of his government. PR. 105

The sin of Satan is revealed only dimly, but the dim outline indicates that it was the summit of all sin, full, free, conscious, spiritual sin; he was not entrapped into it, he was not ensnared into it, he sinned with the full clear understanding of what he was doing. PS. 11

Satan guards the main body of his purpose; neither Eve nor Adam had the slightest notion who he was; he was as far removed in his first snare from his real body of intent as could possibly be. PS. 11

Satan had the possibility of disobedience and when the temptation producing the dilemma came, he inclined to rebellion against God. PS. 54

Satan is never represented in the Bible as being guilty of sins, of doing wrong things; he is *a wrong being*. PS. 59

Satan has no power to dispossess God of me. RTR. 50

For a thing to be Satanic does not mean that it is abominable and immoral; the Satanically-managed man is absolutely self-governed and has no need of God. SHL. 42

The Bible holds man responsible for the introduction of Satan. Satan is the representative of the devil, and the devil is the adversary of God in the rule of man. When our Lord came face to face with Satan He dealt with him as representing the attitude man takes up in organizing his life apart from any consideration of God. SHL. 42

SATISFACTION

The man or woman who does not know God demands an infinite satisfaction from other human beings which they cannot give, and in the case of the man, he becomes tyrannical and cruel. It springs from this one thing, the human heart must have satisfaction, but there is only one Being Who can satisfy the last abyss of the human heart, and that is the Lord Jesus Christ. SHH. 49

SAVIOUR

We shall not think of our Lord as a Saviour if we look at Him in the light of our own minds, because no natural man imagines he needs to be saved. PH. 124

Jesus Christ is the sternest and the gentlest of Saviours. SSM. 28

SCIENCE

If the Bible agreed with modern science, in about fifty years both would be out of date. All scientific findings have at one time been modern. Science is simply man's attempt to explain what he knows. BP. 224

The Bible reveals that the force behind everything is the great Spirit of God. A great change has come over what is called material science, and scientists are coming back to the Bible point of view, viz., that at the back of everything is spirit; that the material world holds itself in existence by spirit. In the early days when men tried to explain the material world, they said that it was made up of atoms; then they found that those atoms could be split up, and the split-up elements were called molecules; then they found that the molecules could be split up, and that the split-up molecules were made of electrons; then they discovered that the electron itself is like a solar system. BP. 224

SECRETS

Our Lord never pried into His Father's secrets, neither will the saint. Some have made the blunder of trying to wrest God's secrets from Him. OBH. 37

SELF

The phrase 'Self-mastery' is profoundly wrong although practically correct. Profoundly, a man can never be master of what he does not understand, therefore the only master of a man is not himself, or another man, but God. 'Self-mastery' is correct if it means carrying out the edicts of God in myself. DI. 30

"I lay down My life," said Jesus; "*I lay it down of Myself.*" If you are sanctified, you will do the same. It has nothing to do with 'Deeper Death to Self', it has to do with the glorious fact that I have a self, a personality, that I can sacrifice with glad alacrity to Jesus every day I live. DI. 61

God is the only One who has the right to myself and when I love Him with all my heart and soul and mind and strength, self in its essence is realized. GW. 40

Self is not to be absorbed into God, it is to be centred in God. GW. 40

So many of us get depressed about ourselves, but when we get to the point where we are not only sick of ourselves, but sick to death, then we shall understand what the Atonement of the Lord Jesus Christ means. It will mean that we come to Him without the slightest pretence, without any hypocrisy, and say, 'Lord, if You can make anything of me, do it,' and He will do it. HG. 32

We have no business to bring in that abomination of the lower regions that makes us think too little of ourselves; to think too little of ourselves is simply the obverse side of conceit. If I am a disciple of Jesus, He is my Master, I am looking to Him, and the thought of self never enters. IWP. 111

By heeding the reality of God's grace within us we are never bothered again by the fact that we do not understand ourselves, or that other people do not understand us. If anyone understood me, he would be my god. The only Being Who understands me is the Being Who made me and Who redeems me, and He will never expound me to myself; He will only bring me to the place of reality, viz., into contact with Himself, and the heart is at leisure from itself for ever afterwards. MFL. 63

I have determinedly to take no one seriously but God, and the first person I have to leave severely alone as being the greatest fraud I have ever known is myself. NKW. 61

Everyone has to begin with this struggle for self, and striving to enter in at the strait gate is a picture of the struggle. Anything that does not enter in at the strait gate, e.g., selfishness, self-interest, self-indulgence, ends in destruction. The struggle to enter in, no matter with what it may be in connection, braces us morally. Self-indulgence is a refusal to struggle, a refusal to make ourselves fit. PH. 79

We cannot receive ourselves in success, we lose our heads; we cannot receive ourselves in monotony, we grouse; the only way we can find ourselves is in the fires of sorrow. Why it should be so I do not know, but that it is so is true not only in Scripture, but in human life. PH. 192

God engineers our circumstances and He brings across our paths some extraordinary people, viz., embodiments of ourselves in so many forms, and it is part of the humour of the situation that we recognize ourselves. RTR. 57

The first thing to do in examining the power that dominates me is to take hold of the unwelcome fact that I am responsible for being thus dominated because I have yielded. If I am a slave to myself, I am to blame for it because at a point, away back, I yielded myself to myself.

Likewise, if I obey God, I do so because I have yielded myself to Him. RTR. 83

Most of us have no ear for anything but ourselves, anything that is not 'me' we cannot hear. SSY. 10

SELFISHNESS

Selfishness means that which gives me pleasure without considering Jesus Christ's interests. Talk about self-ishness on its bad side, and you will have everyone's sympathy; but talk about selfishness from Jesus Christ's standpoint and you will arouse the interest of very few and the antipathy of a great many. BP. 192

Struggle to gain the mastery over self-ishness, and you will be a tremendous assistance; but if you don't overcome the tendency to spiritual sluggishness and self-indulgence, you are a hindrance to all around you. PH. 79

One of the most deeply ingrained forms of selfishness in human nature is that of misery. The isolation of misery is far more proud than any other form of conceit. SHH. 125

SELF-KNOWLEDGE

We only know ourselves as God searches us. 'God knows me' is different from 'God is omniscient'; the latter is a mere theological statement; the former is a child of God's most precious possession—'O Lord, Thou hast searched *me*, and known *me.*' BE. 85

As long as we are flippant and stupid and shallow and think that we know our-selves, we shall never give ourselves over to Jesus Christ; but when once we become conscious that we are infinitely more than we can fathom, and infini-

tely greater in possibility either for good or bad than we can know, we shall be only too glad to hand ourselves over to Him. BP. 258

It is well to remember that our examina-tion of ourselves can never be unbiased or unprejudiced, so that we are only safe in taking the estimate of ourselves from our Creator instead of from our own in-trospection, whether conceited or de-pressed. DI. 30

Jesus Christ revealed that men were evil, and that He came that He might plant in them the very nature that was in Himself. He cannot, however, begin to do this until a man recognizes him-self as Jesus sees him. HG. 43

To be found out by yourself is a terrible thing. OPG. 52

SELF-REALIZATION

Self-realization is a modern phrase—'Be moral, be religious, be upright in order that you may realize yourself.' Nothing blinds the mind to the claims of Jesus Christ more effectually than a good, clean-living, upright life based on self-realization. The issue with us to-day is not with external sins, but with the ideal of self-realization, because Jesus Christ reveals that that ideal will divide clean asunder from Him. If we are going to be His disciples our ideal must be *Christ*-realization. AUG. 96

The relationship set up between Adam and the devil was self-realization, not immorality and vice, but, my claim to my right to myself, whether it is man-ifested in clean living or unclean living is a matter of indifference; sin is the fun-damental relationship underneath. BE. 62

Self-realization and God cannot live together. BE. 64

Self . . . is not to be annihilated, but to be rightly centered in God. *Self*-realization has to be turned into *Christ*-realization. Our Lord never taught "Deeper death to self"; He taught death right out to my right to myself, to self-realization. He taught that the principal purpose of our creation is "to glorify God and to enjoy Him forever"; that the sum total of my self is to be consciously centred in God. BP. 183

When we realize what Jesus means when He says, 'If you would be My disciple, give up your right to yourself to Me,' we begin to understand that "the carnal mind is enmity against God." 'I will not give up my right to myself; I will serve God as I choose.' Jesus Christ came to remove this disposition of self-realization. BSG. 10

There is nothing more highly esteemed among men than self-realisation, but it is the one thing of which Jesus Christ is the enemy because its central citadel is independence of God. CHI. 17

The reason self-interest is detected in us is because there are whole tracts of our nature that have never been fused by the Spirit of God into one central purpose. DI. 31

The true import of love is the surrender of my self, I go out of myself in order to live in and for God. To be indwelt by the Spirit of Jesus means I am willing to quit my own abode from the self-interested standpoint and live only in and for God. It is not the surrender to a conqueror, but the surrender of love, a sovereign preference for God. I surrender myself— not because it is bad, self is the best thing I have got, and I give it to God;

then self-realization is lost in God-realization. GW. 41

There is nothing more highly esteemed among men than self-realization, but Jesus says that "that which is highly esteemed among men is abomination in the sight of God". HGM. 74

Jesus Christ did not say, 'He that believeth on Me, in himself shall realise the blessing of the fulness of God,' but 'out of him shall escape everything he has received.' Our Lord always preaches anti-self-realisation; He is not after developing a man at all, He is after making a man exactly like Himself, and the measure of the Son of God is self-expenditure. PH. 127

Nothing blinds the mind to the claims of Jesus Christ more effectually than a good, clean-living, upright life based on self-realisation. For a thing to be Satanic does not mean that it is abominable and immoral. The satanically managed man is moral, upright, proud, and individual; he is absolutely self-governed and has no need of God. PR. 105

Self-realization naturally cares nothing about God, it does not care whether Jesus lived or died or did anything at all. For ourselves we live and for ourselves we die; that is self-realization that leads to death and despair; it is absolutely and radically opposed to Christ-realization. PS. 35

SELF, RIGHT TO

The term self-denial has come to mean giving up things; the denial Jesus speaks of is a denial right out to my right to myself, a clean sweep of all the decks to the mastership of Jesus. AUG. 53

What is the best God has given you? Your right to yourself. 'Now,' He says, 'sacrifice that to Me.' If you do, He will make it yours and His for ever. If you do not, it will spell death to you. AUG. 88

'If any man will come after Me,' said Jesus, 'the condition is that he must leave something behind,' viz. his right to himself. Is Jesus Christ worth it, or am I one of those who accept His salvation but thoroughly object to giving up my right to myself to Him? AUG. 97

He is not teaching us to deny one part of ourselves in order to benefit another part of ourselves, which is what self-denial has come to mean. The full force of our Lord's words is—'let him deny his right to himself; let him give up his right to himself to Me.' AUG. 97

Jesus Christ is always unyielding on one point, viz., that I must give up my right to myself to Him. BE. 48

As long as my right to myself remains, I respect it in you, you respect it in me, and the devil respects it in the whole crowd, and amalgamates humanity under one tremendous rule which aims at blotting the one true God off His throne. BE. 115

Redemption is easy to experience because it cost God everything, and if I am going to be regenerated it is going to cost me something. I have to give up my right to myself. BFB. 76

The approaches to Jesus are innumerable; the result of coming to Him can be only one—the dethroning of my right to myself, or I stop short somewhere. DI. 34

Jesus Christ is always unyielding to my claim to my right to myself. DI. 35

My right to myself is not merely something I claim, but something that continually makes me insist on my own way. DI. 62

There is only one crisis and the majority of us have never been through it, we are brought up to it, and kick back every time, until God by His engineering brings us right to the one issue, 'Deny for ever your right to yourself'. It is a stubborn detachment, yielding bit by bit, not because the character is noble, but because it is despicably proud. GW. 42

"I don't mind being saved from hell and receiving the Holy Spirit, but it is too much to expect me to give up my right to myself to Jesus Christ, to give up my manhood, my womanhood, all my ambitions." HG. 99

. . . the meaning of sacrifice is the deliberate giving of the best I have to God that He may make it His and mine for ever: if I cling to it, I lose it, and so does God. HGM. 75

Wherever Christian experience is proving unsatisfactory it is because the Holy Spirit is still battling around this one point, my right to myself, and until that is deliberately given over by me to Jesus Christ I will never have the relationship to Him He asks for. HGM. 140

We do not object to being delivered from sin, but we do not intend to give up the right to ourselves; it is this point that is baulked. Jesus will never make us give up our right to ourselves; we must do it of our own deliberate choice. LG. 123

No one has any right to give up the right to himself or to herself to anyone but God Almighty, and devotion to a cause, no matter how noble or how beautiful, nowhere touches the profundity of this lesson. PH. 16

It is no longer my claim to my right to myself that rules my personal life—I am not dead, but the old disposition of my right to myself has gone, it is Jesus Christ's right to me that rules me now, "and that life which I now live in the flesh" I live from that centre. PH. 163

It is not only that we give up our right to ourselves to Jesus Christ, but that determinedly we relate ourselves to life so that we may be appealed to only by the things that appeal to Him, and do in the world only the things with which He is associated. PR. 102

We are apt to imagine that the cross we have to carry means the ordinary troubles and trials of life, but we must have these whether we are Christians or not. Neither is our cross suffering for conscience' sake. Our cross is something that comes only with the peculiar relationship of a disciple to Jesus Christ; it is the evidence that we have denied our right to ourselves. PR. 102

The right to ourselves is the only thing we have to give to God. We cannot give our natural possessions, because they have been given to us. If we had not our right to ourselves by God's creation of us, we should have nothing to give, and consequently could not be held responsible. PR. 102

How many of us are of any worth to Jesus Christ? Our attitude is rather that we are much obliged to God for saving us, but the idea of giving up our chances to realise ourselves in life is too extravagantly extreme. Some of us will take all God has to give us while we take good care not to give Him anything back. PR. 103

Naturally, a man regards his right to himself as the finest thing he has, yet it is the last bridge that prevents Jesus Christ having His way in that life. RTR. 38

It is one of the most flattering things to go and rescue the degraded, one of the social passions of mankind, but it is not the most Christian. It is quite another thing to proclaim to men who are among the best, that *they* have to give up their right to themselves to Jesus Christ. RTR. 78

Any fool will give up wrongdoing and the devil, if he knows how to do it; but it takes a man in love with Jesus Christ to give up the best he has for Him. Jesus Christ does not demand that I give up the wrong, but the right, the best I have for Him, viz., my right to myself. SA. 112

SENSUALITY

Sensualities are not gross only, they can be very refined. DI. 24

Sensuality is not sin, it is the way my body works in connexion with external circumstances whereby I begin to satisfy myself. Sensuality will work in a man who is delivered from sin by Jesus Christ as well as in a man who is not. I do not care what your experience may be as a Christian, you may be trapped by sensuality at any time. SA. 70

With regard to sensuality, that is my business; I have to mortify it, and if I don't, it will never be mortified. If I take any part of my natural life and use it to satisfy myself, that is sensuality. SA. 70

Sensuality is that which gratifies my particular senses, it is the working of my body in connection with external circumstances whereby I begin to satisfy myself. Sensuality may be unutterably disgusting or it may be amazingly refined, but it is based on the wrong thing and has to go; it can have nothing to do with the temple of God, i.e., with man as God created him. SHL. 71

SERMON ON THE MOUNT

People will listen more readily to an exposition of the Sermon on the Mount than they will to the meaning of the Cross; but they forget that to preach the Sermon on the Mount apart from the Cross is to preach an impossibility. BE. 66

The Sermon on the Mount is quite unlike the Ten Commandments in the sense of its being absolutely unworkable unless Jesus Christ can remake us. SSM. 21

Talk about the Sermon on the Mount being an ideal! Why, it rends a man with despair—the very thing Jesus means it to do, for when once we realise that we cannot love our enemies, we cannot bless them that curse us, we cannot come anywhere near the standard revealed in the Sermon on the Mount, then we are in a condition to receive from God the disposition that will enable us to love our enemies, to pray for those that despitefully use us, to do good to those that hate us. SSM. 52

Put into practice any of the teaching of the Sermon on the Mount and you will be treated with amusement at first; then if you persist, the world will get annoyed and will detest you. SSM. 65

SERVANT

A servant is one who, recognising God's *sovereign will*, leaps to do that will of his own *free choice*. CD. VOL. 1, 30

A servant of God is one who has given up for ever *his right to himself,* and is bound to his Lord as His slave. CD. VOL. 1, 30

'A servant of God'—the meaning of this phrase is largely lost to-day. The phrase that suits our modern mood better is, 'a servant of men.' Our watch-cry to-day is, 'The greatest good for the greatest number.' The watch-cry of the servant of God is, 'The greatest obedience to my Lord.' CD. VOL. 1, 31

The great motive and inspiration of service is not that God has saved and sanctified me, or healed me; all that is a fact, but the great motive of service is the realization that every bit of my life that is of value I owe to the Redemption; therefore I am a bondslave of Jesus. SSY. 23

SERVICE

Jesus our Lord says we must pay attention to the Source—belief in Him, and He will look after the outflow. He has promised that there shall be 'rivers of living water', but we must not look at the outflow, nor rejoice in successful service. AUG. 106

May God save us from Christian service which is nothing more than the reaction of a disappointed, crushed heart, seeking surcease from sorrow in social service. Christian service is the vital, unconscious result of the life of a believer in Jesus. AUG. 107

Our Lord was thirty years preparing for three years' service. The modern stamp is three hours of preparation for thirty years of service. CD. VOL. 2, 68

When you are consciously being used as broken bread and poured-out wine you are interested in your own martyrdom, it is consciously costing you something; when you are laid on the altar of the Cross all consciousness of self is gone, all consciousness of what you are doing for God, or of what God is doing through you, is gone. It is no longer possible to talk about "my experience of sanctification"; you are brought to the place where you understand what is meant by our Lord's words, "Ye shall be My witnesses." Wherever a saint goes, everything he or she does becomes a sacrament in God's hands, unconsciously to himself. You never find a saint being consciously used by God; He uses some casual thing you never thought about, which is the surest evidence that you have got beyond the stage of conscious sanctification, you are beyond all consciousness because God is taking you up into His consciousness; you are His, and life becomes the natural simple life of a child. To be everlastingly on the look-out to do some work for God means I want to evade sacramental service—"I want to do what I want to do." Maintain the attitude of a child towards God and He will do what He likes with you. If God puts you on the shelf it is in order to season you. If He is pleased to put you in limited circumstances so that you cannot go out into the highways of service, then enter into sacramental service. Once you enter that service, you can enter no other. CHI. 93

The design for God's service is that He can use the saint as His hands or His feet. Jesus taught that spiritually we should "grow as the lilies," bringing out the life that God blesses. CHI. 95

Our service is to be a living sacrifice of devotion to Jesus, the secret of which is identity with Him in suffering, in death, and in resurrection. DI. 35

I have no business in God's service if I have any personal reserve, I am to be broken bread and poured-out wine in His hands. DI. 47

We are saved and sanctified not for service, but to be absolutely Jesus Christ's, the consuming passion of the life is for Him. DI. 61

Christian service is not our work; loyalty to Jesus is our work. DI. 85

Whenever success is made the motive of service infidelity to our Lord is the inevitable result. DI. 85

Nothing hoodwinks us more quickly than the idea that we are serving God. DI. 88

The greatest service we can render God is to fulfil our spiritual destiny. It is the despised crowd God is counting on, insignificant but holy. GW. 126

The reason some of us are so tepid spiritually is that we do not realize that God has done anything for us. Many people are at work for God, not because they appreciate His salvation, but because they think they should be doing something for other people. Our Lord never called anyone to work for Him because they realize a need, but only on the basis that He has done something for them. The only basis on which to work for God is an esteemed appreciation of His deliverance, that is, our personal history with God is so poignant that it constitutes our devotion to Him. HG. 26

Social service that is not based on the Cross of Christ is the cultured blasphemy of civilized life against God, because it denies that God has done anything, and puts human effort as the only way whereby the world will be redeemed. HG. 100

Thank God for seeing Jesus transfigured, and for the almightiness of the visions He does give, but remember that the vision is to be made real in actual circumstances; the glory is to be manifested in earthen vessels. It has to be exhibited through finger-tips, through eyes and hands and feet; everywhere where Jesus exhibited it. IYA. 27

There is only one service that has no snares, and that is prayer. Preaching has snares to the natural heart; so has public service. Prayer has no snare because it is based on the Redemption of the Lord Jesus Christ made efficacious all the time by the Holy Spirit. IYA. 36

God does not expect us to work *for* Him, but to work *with* Him. IYA. 56

. . . 'passion for souls,' the great craze for successful service. Our Lord told the disciples not to rejoice in successful service, but to rejoice because they were rightly related to Him. LG. 38

The only way we can serve God is by having "no confidence in the flesh." PH. 69

If you are devoted to the cause of humanity, you will soon be exhausted and have your heart broken by ingratitude, but if the mainspring of your service is love for Jesus, you can serve men although they treat you as a door-mat.

Never look for justice in this world, but never cease to give it. PH. 80

With us, Christian service is something we do; with Jesus Christ it is not what we *do for* Him, but what we *are to* Him that He calls service. Our Lord always puts the matter of discipleship on the basis of devotion not to a belief or a creed, but to Himself. There is no argument about it, and no compulsion, simply—'If you would be My disciple, you must be devoted to Me.' PH. 144

There are men and women who ought to be princes and princesses with God but they are away on God's left, they may even be sanctified, but they are left at a particular stage because they chose to be left; instead of obeying the heavenly vision, the natural judicious decisions of an average Christian life have been preferred. It has nothing to do with salvation, but with lost opportunities in service for God. PS. 46

Looking for opportunities to serve God is an impertinence; every time and all the time is our opportunity of serving God. RTR. 52

The idea is not that we do work for God, but that we are so loyal to Him that He can do His work through us—"I reckon on you for extreme service, with no complaining on your part and no explanation on Mine." God wants to use us as He used His own Son. RTR. 92

God never uses in His service those who are sentimentally devoted to Him; He uses only those who are holy within in heart and holy without in practice. SHL. 120

Whether our work is a success or a failure has nothing to do with us. Our call is not to successful service, but to faithfulness. SSY. 123

Any work for God that has less than a passion for Jesus Christ as its motive will end in crushing heartbreak and discouragement. SSY. 161

SHALLOWNESS

A religious view which causes a man to deal only with the shallow side has the ban of finality about it. BFB. 47

It is the shallow things that put us wrong much more quickly than the big things. OPG. 57

To be shallow is not a sign of being wicked, nor is shallowness a sign that there are no depths; the ocean has a shore. The shallow amenities of life, eating, drinking, walking, talking are all ordained by God. These are the things in which our Lord lived. He lived in them as the Son of God, and He said that "the disciple is not above his Master". RTR. 28

Common sense is all very well in the shallow things, but it can never be made the basis of life, it is marked by timidities. We may say wise and subtle things, but if we bank on common sense and rationalism we shall be too timid to do anything. SHH. 143

Go to the house of mourning and see your friend dead, and it will alter your attitude to things; don't be shallow. There is a place for the shallow, however, as well as the profound. One of the greatest defects in Christianity is that it is not shallow enough, in this respect it knows a great deal better than Jesus Christ. It is religious enough, supernormally moral, but not able to eat, drink and be merry. Jesus Christ made the shallow and the profound, the give and the take, one. The art of shallow conversation is one that is rarely learned. It is a great gift as well as a real ministration to be able to say *nothing* cleverly. It is an insult to be everlastingly introducing subjects that make people think on the deepest lines. It takes all the essence of Christianity to be shallow properly. SSH. 81

SHOW BUSINESS

Beware of the 'show business'—'I want to be baptized with the Holy Ghost so that I may do wonderful works'. God never allows anyone to do wonderful works: *He* does them, and the baptism of the Holy Ghost prevents my seeing them in order to glory in them. DI. 23

The abominable 'show business' is creeping into the very ranks of the saved and sanctified—'We must get the crowds.' We must not; we must keep true to the Cross; let folks come and go as they will, let movements come and go, let ourselves be swept along or not, the one main thing is—true to the yoke of Christ, His Cross. IWP. 103

This is the age of humiliation for the saints, just as it was the age of humiliation for Our Lord when He was on earth; we cannot stand the humiliation unless we are His disciples, we want to get into the 'show business,' we want to be successful, to be recognized and known; we want to compromise and put things right and get to an understanding. IWP. 125

There is a risk in discipleship because God never shields us from the world, the flesh and the devil. Christianity is character, not a 'show-business.' IYA. 57

We are not here to be specimens of what God can do, but to have our life so hid with Christ in God that our Lord's words will be true of us, that men beholding our good works will glorify our Father in heaven. There was no 'show business' in the life of the Son of God, and there is to be no 'show business' in the life of the saint. MFL. 108

There is no snare or danger of infatuation or pride or the 'show business' in prayer. Prayer is a hidden, obscure ministry which brings forth fruit that glorifies the Father. OBH. 123

We have no right to call on God to do supernatural wonders. The temptation of the Church is to go into the 'show business.' When God is working the miracle of His grace in us it is always manifested in a chastened life, utterly restrained. PH. 36

Whenever Jesus got down to His truth, the crowds left Him. To-day the craze is for crowds. SSY. 37

The 'show business', which is so incorporated into our view of Christian work to-day, has caused us to drift far from Our Lord's conception of discipleship. It is instilled in us to think that we have to do exceptional things for God; we have not. We have to be exceptional in ordinary things, to be holy in mean streets, among mean people, surrounded by sordid sinners. SSY. 69

SIGHT

Our eyes record to the brain what they look at, but our disposition makes our eyes look at what it wants them to look at, and they will soon pay no attention to anything else. When the disposition is right, the eyes, literally the body, may be placed wherever you like and the disposition will guard what it records. This is not a figure of speech; it is a literal experience. God does alter the desire to look at the things we used to look at; and we find our eyes are guarded because He has altered the disposition of our soul life. BP. 73

The disposition of my soul determines what I see, and the disposition of my soul determines what I hear. BP. 75

We *see* for the first time when we do not look. We see actual things, and we say that we see them, but we never really see them until we see God; when we see God, everything becomes different. It is not the external things that are different, but a different disposition looks through the same eyes as the result of the internal surgery that has taken place. We see God, and then we see things actually as we never saw them before. NKW. 54

The way to keep our sight fit is by looking at the things which are not seen, and external things become a glorious chance of enabling us to concentrate on the invisible things. Once we realise that God's order comes to us in the passing moments, then nothing is unimportant. Every disagreeable thing is a new way of bringing us to realise the wonderful manifestation of the Son of God in that particular. OBH. 77

If I see better than I act on, I am sealing my soul with damnation. SA. 36

One of the first things Jesus Christ does is to open a man's eyes and he sees things as they are. Until then he is not satisfied with the seeing of his eyes, he wants more, anything that is hidden he must drag to the light, and the wandering of desire is the burning waste of a man's life until he finds God. His heart lusts, his mind lusts, his eyes lust, everything in him lusts until he is related to God. It is the demand for an infinite satisfaction and it ends in the perdition of a man's life. SHH. 74

The great emancipation in the salvation of God is that it gives a man the sight of his eyes, and he sees for the first time the handiwork of God in a daisy. SHH. 75

SIMPLICITY

The marvel of the grace of God is that He can take the strands of evil and twistedness out of a man's mind and imagination and make him simple towards God. Restoration through the Redemption of Jesus Christ makes a man simple, and simplicity always shows itself in action. There is nothing simple in the human soul or in human life. The only simple thing is the relationship of the soul to Jesus Christ, that is why the Apostle Paul says, 'I fear, lest by any means, . . . your minds should be corrupted from the simpliciy that is in Christ.' SHL. 65

SIN

God made His own Son to be sin that He might make the sinner a saint. The Bible reveals all through that Jesus Christ bore the sin of the world by *identification*, not by sympathy. He deliberately took upon Himself and bore in His own Person the whole massed sin of the human race, and by so doing He rehabilitated the human race, that is, put it back to where God designed it to be, and anyone can enter into union with God on the ground of what Our Lord did on the Cross. AUG. 71

There is always a twist about everyone of us until we get the dominating inspiration of the Spirit of God. It makes

us condemn the sins we are not inclined to while we make any amount of excuses for those we have a mind to, and they may be ten times worse. AUG. 88

Sin is not measured by a creed or a constitution or a society, but by a Person. AUG. 106

Sin is the outcome of a relationship set up between man and the devil whereby man becomes 'boss' over himself, his own god. BE. 52

Sin is not wrong doing, it is wrong being, independence of God; God has undertaken the responsibility for its removal on the ground of the Redemption. BE. 62

God never lays the sin of the human race on anyone saving Himself; the revelation is not that God punished Jesus Christ for our sins, but that *"Him who knew no sin, He made to be sin on our behalf . . ."* BE. 62

Sin has to be cleansed, *sins* must be forgiven; the Redemption of Jesus Christ deals with *sin*. BE. 63

. . . in the Cross God "condemned *sin* in the flesh", not *sins*. Sins I look after; sin God looks after. The Redemption deals with sin. BE. 68

Knowledge of what sin is is in inverse ratio to its presence; only as sin goes do you realize what it is; when it is present you do not realize what it is because the nature of sin is that it destroys the capacity to know you sin. BE. 78

If we have light views about sin we are not students in the school of Christ. The fact of sin is the secret of Jesus Christ's Cross; its removal is the secret of His risen and ascended life. BE. 114

. . . God so radically, so gloriously, and so comprehensively copes with sin in the Atonement that He is more than master of it, and that a practical experience of this can take place in the life of anyone who will enter into identification with what Jesus Christ did on the Cross. BE. 117

The disposition of sin that rules our human nature is not suppressed by the Atonement, not sat on, not cabined and confined, it is removed. BE. 117

Sin is not man's problem, but God's. God has taken the problem of sin into His own hands and solved it, and the proof that He has is the Cross of Calvary. The Cross is the Cross of God. BFB. 102

'No crime has ever been committed that every human being is not capable of committing.' BP. 104

Satan's sin is at the summit of all sins; our sin is at the base of all sins. If sin has not reached its awful height in us, it may do so unless we let God alter the springs of our heart. BP. 117

There is no such thing as God overlooking sin. That is where people make a great mistake with regard to love; they say, 'God is love and of course He will forgive sin': God is holy love and He *cannot* forgive sin. Jesus Christ did not come to forgive sin; He came to save us from our sins. The salvation of Jesus Christ removes the 'sinner' out of my heart and plants in the 'saint.' That is the marvellous work of God's grace. BP. 135

The Bible says that "sin entered into the world by one man," but sin is not an act on my part at all. Sin is a disposition, and I am in no way responsible for having the disposition of sin; but I am responsible for not allowing God to deliver me from the disposition of sin when once I see that that is what Jesus Christ came to do. BP 157

Sin puts man's self altogether out of centre, and he becomes ec-centric. BP. 182

Sin is not a creation, it is a relationship. The essential nature of sin is my claim to my right to myself. BSG. 10

Sin interrupted the normal development of man, and it required another Man to take up the story where it was broken off and complete it, without the sin. BSG. 13

We are delivered from sin that we might actually live as saints amongst men who treat us as we once treated our Heavenly Father. CD. VOL. 2, 28

Sin is a revelation fact, not a common-sense fact. No natural man is ever bothered about sin; it is the saint, not the sinner, who knows what sin is. If you confound *sin* with *sins*, you belittle the Redemption, make it "much ado about nothing." It is nonsense to talk about the need of Redemption to enable a man to stop committing sins—his own will power enables him to do that, a decent education will prevent him from breaking out into sinful acts, but to deny that there is *an heredity of sin* running straight through the human race, aims a blasphemous blow at the Redemption. The only word that expresses the enormity of sin is "Calvary." CHI. 16

The essence of sin is my claim to my right to myself, it goes deeper down than all the sins that ever were committed. Sin can't be forgiven because it is not an act; you can only be forgiven for the sins you commit, not for an heredity. CHI. 18

To say that what God condemned in the Cross was social sins is not true; what God condemns in the Cross is *sin*, which is away further down than any moral quirks. CHI. 108

The sin that shocks God is the thing which is highly esteemed among men— self-realization, pride, my right to myself. CHI. 123

Certain forms of sin shock us far more than they shock God. The sin that shocks God, the sin that broke His heart on Calvary, is not the sin that shocks us. CHI. 123

Am I becoming more and more in love with God as a holy God, or with the conception of an amiable Being who says, 'Oh well, sin doesn't matter much'? DI. 14

The guilt abroad to-day can never be dealt with by pressing a social ethic or a moral order, or by an enfolding sympathy for man, while pooh-poohing the demands of a holy God. DI. 27

Our Lord did not scathe sin; He came to save from it. DI. 63

Our Lord never sympathized with sin; He came to "proclaim liberty to the captives", a very different thing. We have to see that we don't preach a theology of sympathy, but the theology of a Saviour from sin. DI. 64

The life of the Holy Spirit in a saint is fierce and violent against any tendency to sin. DI. 64

The attitude of Jesus towards *sin* is to be our attitude towards *sins*. DI. 64

Sin is reality; sins are actuality. DI. 65

Measure your growth in grace by your sensitiveness to sin. DI. 65

On the threshold of the Christian life people talk a lot about sin, but there is no realization of what sin is, all that is seen is the effects of sin. DI. 65

It was not social crimes, but the great primal sin of independence of God, that brought the Son of God to Calvary. DI. 66

The sin which has come down to us from Adam is not an act, but an hereditary disposition; the Bible nowhere says that a man is held responsible for having inherited a disposition in which he had no choice: the Redemption deals with sin. GW. 83

If you have never realized the impossibility of God dealing with sin on any other ground than that of the Redemption, you are living in a fool's paradise rationally. GW. 83

Sin has nothing to do with circumstances or with temptation on the outside, it has to do with the bias on the inside; it is an opposing principle and has nothing to do with human nature as God constituted it. GW. 83

We would fly from sin in terror if we knew its nature, but it presents itself as a most desirable thing. GW. 83

Sin in me is a disposition of self-sufficiency which connects me with the body of sin; the connection is not in my human nature, but in my claim to my right to myself, which is the essence of sin—I'll do what I like. GW. 84

The final issue in every life is—God must kill sin in me, or sin will kill God out of me. GW. 85

It is blasphemy to make little of sin. GW. 85

Knowledge of what sin is is evidence that I am delivered from it; ignorance of what sin on the inside is is evidence that I have never been touched by the Atonement. Knowledge of what sin is is in inverse ratio to its presence. GW. 87

. . . it is perilously easy to have amazing sympathy with God's truth and remain in sin. GW. 91

Sin is the independence of human nature which God created turning against God. Holiness is this same independence turning against sin. HG. 35

Sins are wrong acts; sin is an independence that will not bow its neck to God, that defies God and all He presents, that will not go to the excellency of a broken heart. HG. 35

The sense of sin is in inverse ratio to its presence, that is, the higher up and the deeper down we are saved, the more pangingly terrible is our conviction of sin. The holiest person is not the one who is not conscious of sin, but the one who is most conscious of what sin is. HG. 45

The one who talked most about sin was our Lord Jesus Christ. We are apt to run off with the idea that a man in order to be saved from sin must have lived a vile life himself; but the One who has an understanding of the awful horror of sin is the spotlessly holy Christ, Who "knew no sin." The lower down we get into the experience of sin, the less conviction of sin we have. When we are re-

generated and lifted into the light, we begin to know what sin means. HG. 45

Sin destroys the capacity of knowing what sin is. It is when we have been delivered from sin that we begin to realize by the pure light of the Holy Ghost what sin is. HG. 45

Sin is not measured by a standard of moral rectitude and uprightness, but by my relationship to Jesus Christ. The point is, am I morally convinced that the only sin there is in the sight of the Holy Ghost, is disbelief in Jesus? HG. 108

The nature of sin is that it destroys the possibility of knowing that you sin. Sin ceases when I am in the light as God is in the light, and in no other way. HGM. 132

Sin enough and you will soon be unconscious of sin. HGM. 132

This is the principle of sin. Anything in spiritual life or in sensual life that makes us draw our life from anything less than God is of the essence of sin. IWP. 20

The true characteristic of sin is seen when we compare ourselves with Jesus Christ. We may feel quite happy and contented as long as we compare ourselves with other people, because we are all pretty much the same; but when we stand before Jesus Christ we realise what He meant when He said, "If I had not come . . . they had not had sin: . . . but now they have no cloke for their sin." MFL. 122

Transgression is nearly always an unconscious act, there is no conscious determination to do wrong; sin is never an unconscious act. We blunder when we refuse to discern between these two. NKW. 28

Because a man who has lived in sin stops sinning, it is no sign that he is born from above. NKW. 59

The history of Sodom reveals that sin is the beginning of the most appalling corruption. Always distinguish between what we are apt to call sin and what the Bible calls sin. The Bible does not call the corruption of Sodom sin; sin is a disposition, not a deed; the corruption of Sodom is the criminal result of sin. NKW. 81

Sin is a step *aside*; being born of the Spirit of God is a step *inside*, and sanctification is being built into all the perfect character of Jesus Christ *by a gift*. OBH. 13

Sin dwells in human nature, but it has no right there, it does not belong to human nature as God created it. OBH. 111

Sin is a monarch ruling on the outside, demanding obedience on the inside. We can add nothing to the Atonement, we can do nothing for our deliverance, but we must manifest that we are delivered from sin. If you obey in this matter of deliverance, you will realize that there is no bondage in the Atonement. OBH. 111

Our Lord never taught us to deny sin: sin must be destroyed, not denied. Nothing sinful can ever be good. OBH. 115

Sin does not belong to human nature as God designed it, it is abnormal, therefore to speak of sin being 'eradicated', rooted up, is nonsense, it never was planted in. OPG. 4

The diabolical nature of sin is that it hates God, because when I am face to face with the holiness of God I know there is no escape, consequently there is nothing the natural heart of man hates like a holy God. OPG. 8

If God overlooked one sin in me, He would cease to be God. OPG. 16

If God were to say of any sin, 'Oh well, he didn't mean it, I will let it go', that would be a change in God's purpose. OPG. 16

If you indulge in practices which the Holy Spirit condemns, or in imaginations you have no business to indulge in, the appalling lash of ruined sanctity is that 'my sins finds *me* out'. 'If I could only fling the whole thing overboard!'— but you cannot. God has made the way of transgressors hell on earth. The first mark of degeneration is to deem a wrong state permissible, and then propose it as a condition of sanctity. OPG. 48

We are easily roused over things that hurt us; we are scandalised at immortality because it upsets us. There is something infinitely more vital than the horror roused by social crimes, and that is the horror of God's Son at sin. PH. 36

External sins are to a large extent the accident of upbringing, but when the Spirit of God comes in and probes to the depths and reveals the disposition of sin, we begin to understand what salvation is. God cannot take anything from the sinner but his solid sin, otherwise salvation would have no meaning for him. PH. 55

Sin has made a gap between God and the human race, and consequently when we try to explain our lives on the line of logic or reason, we find things don't work out that way. PH. 150

The climax of sin is that it crucified Jesus Christ. PH. 188

When we begin our life we do not reconcile ourselves to the fact of sin; we take a rational view of life and say that a man by looking after his own instincts, educating himself, controlling the ape and the tiger in him, can produce that life which will slowly evolve into the life of God. But as we go on we find there is something that we have not taken into consideration, viz., sin, and it upsets all our calculations. Sin has made the basis of things not rational, but wild. PH. 188

If sin rules in me, the life of God will be killed in me; if God rules in me, sin will be killed in me. There is no possible ultimate but that. PH. 189

In our mental outlook we have to reconcile ourselves to the fact that sin is the only explanation as to why Jesus Christ came, the only explanation of the grief and the sorrow that there is in life. There may be a great deal that is pathetic in a man's condition, but there is also a lot that is bad and wrong. There is the downright spiteful thing, as wrong as wrong can be, without a strand of good in it, in you and in me and in other people by nature, and we have to reconcile ourselves to the fact that there *is* sin. That does not mean that we compromise with sin, it means that we face the fact that it is there. PH. 189

Unless we recognise the fact of sin, there is something that will laugh and spit in the face of every ideal we have. Unless we reconcile ourselves to the fact that there will come a time when the power of darkness will have its own way, and that by God's permission, we

will compromise with that power when its hour comes. If we refuse to take the fact of sin into our calculation, refuse to agree that a base impulse runs through men, that there is such a thing as vice and self-seeking, when our hour of darkness strikes, instead of being acquainted with sin and the grief of it, we will compromise straight away and say there is no use battling against it. PH. 190

The man who accepts salvation from Jesus Christ recognises the fact of sin, he does not ignore it. Thereafter he will not demand too much of human beings. PH. 190

Always beware of a friendship, or of a religion, or of a personal estimate of things that does not reconcile itself to the fact of sin; that is the way all the disasters in human friendships and in human loves begin, and where the compromises start. PH. 193

Sin is not in having a body and a nature that needs to be sacrificed; sin is in refusing to sacrifice them at the call of God. PR. 11

Sin is not a creation; sin is the outcome of a relationship which God never ordained, a relationship set up between the man God created and the being God created who became the devil. PR. 11

Sin is a disposition which rules the body, and regeneration means not only that we need not obey the disposition of sin, but that we can be absolutely delivered from it. PR. 12

Sin dwells in human nature . . . it is an abnormal thing, it has no right there, it does not belong to human nature as God designed it. Sin has come into human nature and perverted and twisted it. PR. 16

In the Bible it is never, Should a Christian sin? The Bible puts it emphatically: *A Christian must not sin.* PR. 34

The one thing that will enable us to stop sinning is the experience of new birth, i.e., entire sanctification. PR. 35

When we are born into the new realm the life of God is born in us, and the life of God in us cannot sin. That does not mean that we *cannot* sin; it means that if we obey the life of God in us, we *need not* sin. PR. 35

By regeneration God puts in us the power not to sin. PR. 35

The revelation in the Bible is not that Jesus Christ was punished for our *sins*; but that He took on Him the *sin* of the human race and put it away—an infinitely profounder revelation. PR. 49

Intellectually, we are inclined to ignore sin. The one element in man that does not ignore sin is conscience. The Holy Spirit deals with conscience first, not with intellect or emotions. When the Holy Spirit gets hold of a man and convicts him of sin, he instantly gets to despair, for he recognises that the holiness of Jesus Christ is the only thing that can ever stand before God, and he knows there is no chance for him. PR. 122

Only when we are driven to extremes do we realize that the Bible is the only Book that gives us any indication of the true nature of sin, and where it came from. PS. 10

Sin is that factor in human nature which has a supernatural originator who stands next to God in power. PS. 11

To sin alone is never possible. PS. 12

If we are only living on the surface of things the Bible line will appear stupid, but if we have had a dose of 'the plague of our own heart,' and realize what God has delivered us from, we know much too much ever to accept man's definition of sin, we know that there is no other explanation than the Bible one, and nothing but pity is awakened when we hear people trying to explain sin apart from the Bible. PS. 15

If I refuse to let God destroy my sin, there is only one possible result—I must be destroyed with my sin. PS. 25

The light of the Lord's presence convicts of sin. PS. 25

Sin is never imputed unless it is conscious. PS. 25

Sin has got to be satisfied, or else strangled to death by a supernatural power. PS. 42

To walk in the light, as God is in the light, is the one condition of being kept cleansed from all sin. PS. 43

Sin is a disposition of self-love that obeys every temptation to its own lordship. Sin is literally self-centred rule, a disposition that rules the life apart from God. PS. 56

The sense of sin is in proportion to the sense of holiness. PS. 64

If you want to know what sin is, don't ask the convicted sinner, ask the saint, the one who has been awakened to the holiness of God through the Atonement; he is the one who can begin to tell you what sin is. PS. 65

Sin in its beginning is simply being without God. PS. 71

Whenever you come in contact with the great destructive sins in other lives, be reverent with what you don't understand. There are facts in each life you know nothing about and God says: "Leave him to Me". RTR. 74

A good way to measure our spiritual life is to ask ourselves—What is it that produces the greatest perturbation in me? Is it the sins of men against men, or is it the sins of spiritual pride against God? RTR. 80

Sin is a thing we are born with, and we cannot touch sin; God touches sin in Redemption. SA. 105

Other religions deal with sins; the Bible alone deals with sin. SA. 116

The revelation is not that Jesus Christ was punished for our sins, but that He was made *to be sin*. "Him who knew no sin" was made to be sin, that by His identification with it and removal of it, we might become what He was. SA. 120

The revelation is not that Jesus Christ took on Him our fleshly sins—a man stands or falls by his own silly weaknesses—but that He took on Him *the heredity of sin*. SA. 120

God Himself became sin, and removed sin; no man can touch that. SA. 120

God Almighty took the problem of the sin of the world on His own shoulders, and it made Him stoop; He rehabilitated the whole human race; that is, He put the human race back to where He designed it to be, and any one of us in our actual conditions can enter into union with God on the ground of Jesus Christ's Redemption. SA. 121

Sin is not measured by a creed or social order: sin is measured by a Person, Jesus Christ. SHL. 59

The characteristic of sin is independence of God—'I can look after myself; I know exactly how far to go.' SHL. 64

Jesus Christ never tolerated sin for one moment, and when His nature is having its way in us the same intolerance is shown. SHL. 65

Deliverance from sin is not deliverance from conscious sin only, it is deliverance from sin in God's sight, and He can see down into a region I know nothing about. SSM. 28

Jesus Christ went through identification with sin, and put away sin on the Cross, so that every man on earth might be freed from sin by the right of His Atonement. God made His own Son to be sin that He might make the sinner a saint—'that we might become the righteousness of God in him.' SSY. 144

SINNERS

. . . if you are not delivered from any particular element of sin, the reason is either you don't believe God can deliver you or you don't want Him to. Immediately you want Him to deliver you, the power of God is yours and it is done, not presently, but now, and the manifestation is wonderful. Let a man give up the right to himself to Jesus Christ, and the efficacy of His Redemption works out instanter. BE. 69

God can never save human pride. Jesus Christ has no mercy whatever when it comes to conviction of sin. He has an amazing concern for the sinner, but no pity for sin. CHI. 98

Beware of attempting to diagnose sin unless you have the inner pang that you are one of the worst of sinners. DI. 62

". . . Christ Jesus came into the world to save sinners." What is a sinner? Everyone who is not one with Jesus as He is one with God. DI. 63

Many a man gets to the place where he will call himself a sinner, but he does not so readily come to the place where he says, "*Against Thee, Thee only, have I sinned . . .*" DI. 65

Sin is a positive thing, it is the enthronement of human independence, because man's pride must worship itself. GW. 83

Jesus Christ came to save sinners; He did not say so, He said, 'I came to call *sinners to repentance*'. GW. 85

The effect of being justified by God's grace is that He begins to entrust us with the realization of what sin is. It is the saint who knows what sin is; it is the man who has been identified with the death of Jesus who begins to get the first inkling of what sin is, because the only Being who knows what sin is, is not the sinner, but God. GW. 86

The only One who knows what the elemental human heart is like, is not the sinner, but Jesus Christ. It takes the last reach of the Atonement—the revelation of the perfections of Jesus as He is 'made unto us sanctification', to make us know what sin is, because sin is what He faced on Calvary. GW. 86

The real attitude of sin in the heart towards God is that of being without God; it is pride, the worship of myself, that is the great atheistic fact in human life. GW. 90

When men go into external sins and upset their life, Satan knows perfectly well that they will want a Saviour, and as long as he can keep men in peace and unity and harmony apart from God, he will do it. GW. 100

We have come to the conclusion nowadays that a man must be a conscious sinner before Jesus Christ can do anything for him. The early disciples were not attracted to Jesus because they wanted to be saved from sin; they had no conception that they needed saving. They were attracted to Him by a dominating sincerity, by sentiments other than those which we say make men come to Jesus. There was nothing theological in their following, no consciousness of passing from death unto life, no knowledge of what Jesus meant when He talked about His Cross. It was on the plane where all was natural, although mysterious and wonderful. LG. 102

"Come unto Me," says Jesus, and by coming to Him your actual life will be brought into accordance with the reality revealed in Jesus. You will actually cease from sin and from sorrow, and actually find the song of the Lord begin; you will actually find that He has transformed you, the sinner, into a saint. But if you want this actual experience, you must come to Jesus. Our Lord makes Himself the touchstone. OBH. 101

Personal contact with Jesus alters everything. He meets our sins, our sorrows, and our difficulties with the one word— 'Come.' OBH. 102

This is the greatest revelation that ever struck the human life, viz., that God loves the sinner. God so loved the world when it was sinful that He sent His Son to die for it. Our Lord has no illusions about any of us. He sees every man and woman as the descendants of Adam who sinned, and with capacities in our hearts of which we have no idea. PH. 54

We preach to men as if they were conscious of being dying sinners; they are not, they are having a good time, and our talk about being born again is from a domain of which they know nothing. The natural man does not want to be born again. PR. 11

To say that 'God loves the sinner, but hates his sin' sounds all right, but it is a dangerous statement, because it means that God is far too loving ever to punish the sinner. PS. 25

SIN, CONVICTION OF

Pseudo-evangelism makes an enormous blunder when it insists on conviction of sin as the first step to Jesus Christ. When we have come to the place of seeing Jesus Christ, then He can trust us with the facing of sin. BFB. 28

Jesus Christ takes the man who has been broken on the wheel by conviction of sin and rendered plastic by the Holy Spirit, and re-moulds him and makes him a vessel fit for God's glory. BP. 183

What our Lord Jesus Christ wants us to present to Him is not our goodness, or our honesty, or our endeavour, but our real solid sin, that is all He can take. "For He hath made Him to be sin for us, Who knew no sin." And what does He give in exchange for our solid sin? Great solid righteousness—"that we might be made the righteousness of God in Him"; but we must relinquish all pretence of being anything, we must relinquish in every way all claim to being worthy of God's consideration. That is the meaning of conviction of sin. CD. VOL. 1, 129

. . . it requires the Holy Ghost to convict a man of sin; any man knows that immorality is wrong, his conscience tells him it is; but it takes the Holy Ghost to convince a man that the thing he most highly esteems, viz.: his own self-government, is "an abomination in the sight of God." CHI. 17

Some men are driven to God by appalling conviction of sins, but conviction of sins is not conviction of *sin*. Conviction of sin never comes as an elementary experience. If you try to convict a man of sin to begin with you draw him to a plan of salvation, but not to Jesus Christ. CHI. 17

May the conviction of God come with swift and stern rebuke upon any one who is remembering the past of another, and deliberately choosing to forget his restoration through God's grace. When a servant of God meets these sins in others, let him be reverent with what he does not understand and leave God to deal with them. CHI. 123

It is not our business to convict men of sin, the Holy Ghost alone convicts of sin, our duty is to lift up the One who sets free from sin. It is not a question of something being curbed, or counteracted, or sat on, it is a radical alteration on the inside, then I have to assimilate that alteration so that it is manifested in the practical relationships of my life. DI. 64

When conviction of sin by the Holy Spirit comes it gives us an understanding of the deeps of our personality we are otherwise not conscious of. DI. 64

A great many people are delighted to hear about the life of Jesus, its holiness and sublimity, but when the Holy Ghost begins to convict them of sin, they resent it, and resent it deeply. DI. 65

Conviction of sin in the beginning is child's play compared with the conviction the Holy Ghost brings to a mature saint. DI. 65

Humiliation by conviction of sin is rare to-day. You can never be humiliated by another human being after the conviction of sin the Holy Ghost gives. DI. 65

It is of the mercy of God that no man is convicted of *sin* before he is born again; we are convicted of *sins* in order to be born again, then the indwelling Holy Spirit convicts us of sin. If God gave us conviction of sin apart from a knowledge of His Redemption, we would be driven insane. When conviction of what sin is in the sight of God comes home to me, language cannot support the strain of the verbal expression of its enormity; the only word that expresses it is 'Calvary'. If I see sin apart from the Cross, suicide seems the only fool's way out. GW. 84

Beware of attempting to deal with sin apart from a complete reliance on the Redemption, and when you see men sinning, remember, your heart should be filled with compassion, because if you have ever had the slightest dose of conviction of sin yourself, you will know what awaits them when the recognition of sin comes home. GW. 85

It is the shallowest nonsense that makes people say, 'God will forgive us because He is love'; once we are convicted of sin we never talk like that again. GW. 86

We don't take Jesus Christ's way, our first aim is to convict people of sin; Jesus Christ's aim was to get at them where they lived. HGM. 33

. . . when a man gets convicted of sin (which is the most direct way of knowing that at the basis of life there is a problem too big for him to solve), he knows that God dare not forgive him; if He did, then man has a bigger sense of justice than God. HGM. 100

Never try to prevent a soul feeling real disgust at what he is like in God's sight. The first thing the Holy Spirit does when He comes in is to convict, not to comfort, because He has to let us know what we are like in God's sight; and then He brings the revelation that God will fill us with His own nature if we will let Him. OBH. 58

To experience conviction of sin is not a cause for misgiving, but an occasion for understanding the impossible thing God has done in the Redemption. OPG. 51

When we experience misgiving because we have sinned there is never any ambiguity as to its cause, the Holy Spirit brings conviction home like a lightning flash. OPG. 57

By conviction of sin a man is probed wide awake and made to realise that he needs to be regenerated; when he gets there, Jesus says—'Blessed are you.' PH. 61

If once the moral equilibrium has been upset by conviction of sin, holiness is the only result or no peace for ever. PH. 61

The awful nature of the conviction of sin that the Holy Spirit brings makes us realize that God cannot, dare not, must not forgive sin; if God forgave sin without atoning for it our sense of justice would be greater than His. PS. 20

Conviction of sin makes a man's beauty "to consume away like a moth." SA. 95

Sin is a thing that puts a man's self out of centre altogether, making it ex-centric; and when the Spirit of God convicts him, the man knows he is wrongly related to God, to his own body, and to everything around him, and he is in a state of abject misery. The health of the body is upset, the balance pushed right out, by conviction of sin. SA. 95

SIN, ORIGINAL

Original sin is doing without God. A noticeable feature in the conduct of Adam and Eve is that when God turned them out of the garden, they did not rebel. The characteristic of sin in man is fear and shame. Sin in man is doing without God, but it is not rebellion against God in its first stages. BP. 20

Original sin is 'doing without God'. That phrase covers sin in its beginning in human consciousness and its final analysis in the sight of God. DI. 63

SLANDER

God never vindicates Himself, He deliberately stands aside and lets all sorts of slanders heap on Him, yet He is not in any hurry. BFB. 29

If Satan in his malice and cunning can slander God to His own children, he will do it because that is his whole aim. GW. 98

Absolute devastation awaits the soul that allows suspicion to creep in. Suspi-

cion of God is like a gap in a dyke, the flood rushes through, nothing can stop it. The first thing you will do is to accept slanders against God. PS. 13

SLEEP

If I take time from sleep, God's punishment rests on me; or if I take time in sleep when I should be working, He punishes me. Sloth is as bad as being a fussy workman in God's sight. We have no business to be distracted. HG. 38

Sleep is God's celestial nurse who croons away our consciousness, and God deals with the unconscious life of the soul in places where only He and His angels have charge. As you retire to rest, give your soul and God a time together, and commit your life to God with a conscious peace for the hours of sleep, and deep and profound developments will go on in spirit, soul and body by the kind creating hand of our God. HG. 39

The sleep of a labouring man is sweet, it recreates him. The Bible indicates that sleep is not meant only for the recuperation of a man's body, but that there is a tremendous furtherance of spiritual and moral life during sleep. SHH. 63

SLOTH

Spiritual sloth must be the greatest grief to the Holy Ghost. Sloth has always a moral reason, not a physical one; the self-indulgent nature must be slothful. DI. 52

Slovenliness is an insult to the Holy Ghost. Our Lord is scrupulous in His saving of us, surely we can be scrupulous in the conduct of His temple, our bodies and our bodily connections. That will mean God's greatness coming down into our human setting, and we see to it that we do everything in keeping with the greatness of God. NKW. 137

SOCIAL REFORM

The introduction of socialism into the history of civilization is the next thing to be manifested, everything else has been tried, and socialism will end as every other human attempt has ended, in proving that man cannot establish himself in unity with God and ignore Jesus Christ, either in individual or in national life. HGM. 96

Social reform is part of the work of ordinary honourable humanity and a Christian does it because his worship is for the Son of God, not because he sees it is the most sensible thing to do. The first great duty of the Christian is not to the needs of his fellow-men, but to the will of his Saviour. PR. 65

Jesus Christ is not a social reformer; He came to alter *us* first, and if any social reform is to be done on earth, we will have to do it. PR. 65

The vision of Socialism is magnificent; there are benedictions and blessings for mankind on the line of Socialism which have never been yet; but if once the root is cut from Redemption, it will be one of the most frantic forms of despotic tyranny the human race has ever known. SA. 97

SOLITUDE

Beware of isolation; beware of the idea that you have to develop a holy life alone. It is impossible to develop a holy life alone, you will develop into an oddity and a peculiarism, into something utterly unlike what God wants you to be. The only way to develop spiritually is to go into the society of God's own children, and you will soon find how God alters your set. God does not contradict our social instincts. BP. 174

From the Bible standpoint, whenever a man gets alone, it is always in order to fit him for society. Getting alone with God is such a dangerous business that God rarely allows it unless it means that we come into closer contact with people afterwards. It is contact with one another that keeps us full-orbed and well-balanced, not only naturally but spiritually. BP. 175

Solitude with God repairs the damage done by the fret and noise and clamour of the world. CD. VOL. 2, 66

SONSHIP

We are not made sons of God by magic; we are saved in the great supernatural sense by the sovereign work of God's grace, but sonship is a different matter. I have to become a son of God by deliberate discernment and understanding and chastisement, not by spiritual necromancy, imagining I can ascend to heaven in leaps and bounds. The 'short cut' would make men mechanisms, not sons, with no discernment of God. If God did not shield His only Begotten Son from any of the requirements of sonship ("Though He was a Son, yet learned obedience by the things which He suffered"), He will not shield us from all the requirements of being His sons and daughters by adoption. PH. 101

There is only one beloved Son of God; we are sons of God through His Redemption. PR. 52

SORROW

One of the greatest emancipators of personal life is sorrow. BFB. 109

There are crushing, unspeakable sorrows in this world. To any man with his eyes open, life is certainly not worth living apart from Jesus Christ. If it is worth living, it is because he is blind. HGM. 49

Tears are not going to be wiped away by our receiving pettings from God; the revelation is that through the marvel of the Redemption God is going to make it impossible for there to be any more crying or sorrow, all will be as satisfactory as God Himself. HGM. 84

It is a farce to make nothing of death; the natural expressions of the heart are not suppressed, but tempered and transfigured. It is no part of faith to affect insensibility to sorrow, that is stoical humbug. In certain stages of religious experience we have the idea that we must not show sorrow when we are sorrowful. That idea is an enemy to the Spirit of Jesus Christ, because it leads to heartlessness and hypocrisy. Not to sorrow is not even human, it is diabolical. The Spirit of God hallows sorrow. NKW. 134

"And God shall wipe away every tear from their eyes." Unless God wipes away our tears, they will always return. The day to which our Lord rose is a day in which tears are not done away with, but transfigured—a day that has no twilight, nor evening nor night. This does not mean that no more tears will be shed, but that they will never be shed again in the way they were before. We do not know what will take the place of tears, but a life in which there is no equivalent to tears would be intolerable to the imagination. PH. 122

People say there ought to be no sorrow; but the fact remains that there *is* sorrow, there is not one family just now without its sorrow, and we have to learn to receive ourselves in its fires. If we try to evade sorrow and refuse to lay our account with it, we are foolish, for sorrow is one of the biggest facts in life, and there is no use saying it ought not to be, it is. It is ridiculous to say things ought not to be when they are. PH. 191

. . . sorrow does not necessarily make a man better; sorrow burns up a great amount of unnecessary shallowness, it gives me my self, or it destroys me. If a man becomes acquainted with sorrow, the gift it presents him with is his self. PH. 192

You always know the person who has been through the fires of sorrow and has received himself; you never smell the fire on him, and you are certain you can go to him when you are in trouble. It is not the man with the signs of sorrow on him who is helpful, but the one who has gone through the fires and received himself; he is delivered from the small side of himself, and has ample leisure for others. The one who has not been through the fires of sorrow has no time for you and is inclined to be contemptuous and impatient. If I have received myself in the fire of sorrow, then I am good stuff for other people in the same condition. PH. 194

A sunset or a sunrise may thrill you for half a minute, so may beautiful music or a song, but the sudden aftermath is a terrific, and almost eternal sadness. SHH. 6

The most delightful saint is the one who has been chastened through great sorrows. SHL. 97

SOUL

The term 'soul' generally, is used in three distinct ways. First, as applied to men and animals alike as distinct from all other creations; second, the more particular use of the word as applied to men distinguished from animals; and third, as applied to one man as distinct from another. BP. 44

The Bible nowhere says that God has a soul; the only way in which the soul of God is referred to is prophetically in anticipation of the Incarnation. Angels are never spoken of as having souls, because soul has reference to this order of creation and angels belong to another order. Our Lord emphatically had a soul, but of God and of angels the term 'soul' is not used. The term 'soul' is never applied to plants. A plant has life, but the Bible never speaks of it as having soul. BP. 44

Nothing can enter the soul but through the senses, God enters into the soul through the senses. BP. 51

In the life of Jesus Christ there was no division into secular and sacred, but with us when this power begins to be realized it always manifests itself in a line of cleavage. There are certain things we won't do; certain things we won't look at; certain things we won't eat; certain hours we won't sleep. It is not wrong, it is the Spirit of God in a soul beginning to utilize the powers of the soul for God; and as the soul goes on it comes to a full-orbed condition, where it manifests itself as in the life of the Lord Jesus and all is sacred. BP. 61

The Bible nowhere says the soul sleeps; it says that the body sleeps but never the personality; the moment after death, unhindered consciousness is the state. BP. 94

The human soul is so mysterious that in the moment of a great tragedy men get face to face with things they never gave heed to before, and in the moment of death it is extraordinary what takes place in the human heart towards God. CD. VOL. 1, 110

'Soul' refers to the way a personal spirit reasons and thinks in a human body. We talk about a man exhibiting 'soul' in singing or in painting, that is, he is expressing his personal spirit. HGM. 74

Soul is "me," my personal spirit, manifesting itself in my body, my way of estimating things. OBH. 77

Soul is the expression of my personal spirit in my body, the way I reason and think and act, and Jesus taught that a man must lose his soul in order to gain it; he must lose absolutely his own way of reasoning and looking at things, and begin to estimate from an entirely different standpoint. PH. 64

'Soul' in the Bible nearly always refers to the fleshly nature, it is the only power a man has for expressing his true spirit. PS. 15

The soul . . . is simply the spirit of a man expressing itself. The spirit of a child can rarely express itself, the soul has not become articulate. PS. 15

Beware of believing that the human soul is simple, or that human life is simple. Our relationship to God in Christ is the only simple thing there is. If the devil succeeds in making this relationship complicated, then the human soul and human life will appear to be simple;

whereas in reality they are far too complex for us to touch. SSY. 39

SOUL-WINNING

We are not here to win souls, to do good to others, that is the natural outcome, but it is not our aim, and this is where so many of us cease to be followers. LG. 63

The passion for souls is not a New Testament idea at all, but religious commercialism. LG. 64

Pay attention to the Source, believe in Jesus, and God will look after the outflow. God grant we may let the Holy Ghost work out His passion for souls through us. We have not to imitate Jesus by having a passion for souls like His, but to let the Holy Ghost so identify us with Jesus that His mind is expressed through us as He expressed the mind of God. MFL. 118

In order to catch men for the Lord Jesus Christ, you must love Jesus Christ absolutely, beyond all others. You must have a consuming passion of love, then He will flow through you in a passion of love and yearning and draw men to Himself. WG. 88

SPIRITUALISM

"For we wrestle not against flesh and blood, but against principalities, against powers, against the rulers of the darkness of this world, against spiritual wickedness in high places." This inference is a great guide in regard to Spiritualism. Spiritualism, according to the Bible, is not a trick; it is a fact. Man can communicate with beings of a different order from his own, and can put himself into a state of subjectivity in which angels can appear. BP. 13

Spiritualism is the great crime; it pushes down God's barriers and brings us into contact with forces we cannot control. BP. 53

Theosophy lends itself largely to speculation, and all theosophic and occult speculations are ultimately dangerous to the mental, moral and spiritual balance. Speculate if you care to, but never teach any speculation as a revelation from the Bible. BP. 83

Telepathy is one enticing way in which the speculation of transmigration and pre-existence is introduced to our minds. Telepathy means being able to discern someone else's thought by my own. This opens up the line of auto-suggestion. If one man can suggest thoughts to another man, then Satan can do the same, and the consciousness of auto-suggestion on the human side opens the mind to it diabolically. Telepathy is mentioned because all these occult things come down to our lives in seemingly harmless phases. For instance, spiritualism comes by way of palmistry, reading fortunes in tea-cups or in cards, by planchette, and so on, and people say there is no harm in any of these things. There is all the harm and the 'backing up' of the devil in them. Nothing awakens curiosity more quickly than reading fortunes in tea-cups or by cards. The same is true of all theosophic speculations, they come right down to our lives on the line of things which is wrongly called 'psychology' and awaken an insatiable curiosity. BP. 83

In religious meetings it is the impressionable people who are the dangerous people. When you get that type of nature to deal with, pray as you never prayed, watch as you never watched, and travail in communion as you never travailed in communion, because the soul that is inclined to be a medium between any supernatural forces and himself will nearly always be caught up by the supernatural forces belonging to Satan instead of by God. Insanity is a fact, demon possession is a fact, and mediumship is a fact. The Bible says regarding the false Christs, ". . . if it were possible, they shall deceive the very elect." BP. 162

A spiritualistic medium commits the greatest psychical crime in the world, that is, the greatest crime against the soul. Drunkenness and debauchery are child's play compared with spiritualism. BP. 162

New Theology, Christian Science and Theosophy all teach that God created the Being called His Son in order to realize Himself. They say, in effect, that the term 'Son of God' means not only our Lord Jesus Christ, but the whole creation of man. God is All, and the creation of man was in order to help God to realize Himself. The practical outcome of this line of thinking is to make men say, 'It is absurd to talk about sin and the fall; sin is merely a defect, and to talk about the need of an atonement is nonsense.' The Bible nowhere says that God created the world in order to realize Himself. The Bible reveals that God was absolutely Self-sufficient, and that the manifestation of the Son of God was for another purpose altogether, viz., for the solution of the gigantic problem caused by sin. BP. 215

Spiritualism is more than trickery; it has hold of powers that are not characterized by the holy integrity of Jesus. LG. 122

There is such a thing as being haunted on the inside of the life. It begins when a man tampers with the borders of spiritualism and communicates with supernatural powers; he opens the unconscious part of his personality to all kinds of powers he cannot control. The only cure is to fear God, to be rightly related to God, and these fears and hauntings will go. "Put on the whole armour of God." When a man is related to God through Jesus Christ, God protects not only the conscious life but the unconscious life as well. SHH. 56

According to the Bible, spiritualism is not a trick, it is a fact. Man can communicate with beings of a different order from his own; he can put himself into a state of subjectivity in which spirits can appear. A medium commits the great crime psychically because he gives himself over to a force the nature of which he does not know. He does great violence to his own rectitude and tampers with the balance of his sanity by putting himself into league with powers the character of which he does not know. Mediumship, whereby unseen spirits talk to men and women, will destroy the basis of moral sanity because it introduces a man into domains he had better leave alone. SHL. 55

There are people in whom the walls between the seen and unseen are exceedingly thin and they are constantly being tortured; the salvation of Jesus Christ can save them from it all. SHL. 56

SPIRITUALITY

We can estimate our life on the spiritual line by our dominant interest. How do we know what is our dominant interest? It is not the thing that occupies most time. The dominating interest is a peculiarly personal one, viz. the thing that is really fundamentally ours in a crisis. In sorrow or joy we reveal our dominating interest. AUG. 85

We have entirely divorced tasting and smelling, seeing and hearing and touching, from spiritual conditions, because the majority of Christian workers have never been trained in what the Bible has to say about ourselves. It can be proved over and over again, not only in personal experience, but all through God's Book, that He does alter the taste, not merely mental tastes, but physical tastes, the taste for food and drink; but there is something far more practical even than that, the blessing of God on our soul life gives us an added sensitiveness of soul akin to taste or to sight or hearing. BP. 75

We have no business to be half-dead spiritually, to hang like clogs on God's plan; we have no business to be sickly, unless it is a preparatory stage for something better, or God is nursing us through some spiritual illness: but if it is the main characteristic of the life, there is something wrong somewhere. BP. 79

Our Lord distinctly taught His disciples that if they were going to live the spiritual life, they must barter the natural for it; that is, they must forgo the natural life. We mean by the 'natural' life, the ordinary, sensible, healthy, worldly-minded life. The highest love is not natural to the human heart. BP. 133

There are not three stages in spiritual life—worship, waiting and work. Some of us go in jumps like spiritual frogs, we jump from worship to waiting, and from waiting to work. God's idea is that the three should go together. They were always together in the life of our Lord. RTR. 24

Buck up and face the music, get related to things. It is a great thing to see physical pluck, and greater still to see moral pluck, but the greatest to see of all is spiritual pluck, to see a man who will stand true to the integrity of Jesus Christ no matter what he is going through. RTR. 67

Spirituality is not a sweet tendency towards piety in people who have not enough life in them to be bad; spirituality is the possession of the life of God which is masculine in its strength, and He will make spiritual the most corrupt, twisted, sin-stained life if He be obeyed. SSM. 36

STOICISM

Stoicism has come so much into the idea of the Christian life that we imagine the stoic is the best type of Christian; but just where stoicism seems most like Christianity it is most adverse. A stoic overcomes the world by passionlessness, by eviscerating all personal interest out of life until he is a mere submissive recording machine. Christianity overcomes the world by passion, not by passionlessness. PH. 196

STRENGTH AND WEAKNESS

The Cross, the climax of our Lord's earthly life, is likewise an exhibition of the weakness of God. CD. VOL. 2, 146

To be weak in God's strength is a crime. GW. 14

The great marvel of Jesus was that He was voluntarily weak. "He was crucified through weakness." IWP. 110

All God's commands are enablings, therefore it is a crime to be weak in His strength. NKW. 57

The Bible characters never fell on their weak points but on their strong ones; unguarded strength is double weakness. It is in the after-part of the day spiritually that we have to be alert. This does not mean that you are to be morbidly introspective, looking forward with dread, but that you keep alert; don't forecast where the temptation will come. PH. 47

When we try to reserve our strength it works out in weariness. Spend to the hilt all we have got and God's recreating power is greater than all the expended power. RTR. 25

"Be strong *in* the Lord",—we much prefer to be strong *for* the Lord. The only way to be strong *in* the Lord is to be "weak in Him". RTR. 62

No power on earth or in hell can conquer the Spirit of God in human spirit, it is an inner unconquerableness. If you have the whine in you kick it out ruthlessly. It is a positive crime to be weak in God's strength. RTR. 65

SUCCESS AND FAILURE

Jesus Christ distinctly recognizes that we have to succeed, and He indicates the kind of success we must have. The advantage with which we are to end is that we become preserving salt and shining lights; not losing our savour but preserving health, and not covering our light with a bushel but letting it shine. BP. 173

Beware of succumbing to failure as inevitable; make it the stepping-stone to success. DI. 68

Never put your dream of success as God's purpose for you; His purpose may be exactly the opposite. GW. 36

We have nothing whatever to do with what men call success or failure. If God's command is clear; and the constraint of His Spirit is clear, we have nothing to do with the result of our obedience. GW. 36

God's purpose for you is that you depend upon Him and His power *now*; that you see Him walking on the waves—no shore in sight, no success, just the absolute certainty that it is all right because you see Him. GW. 37

Every denomination or missionary enterprise departs from its true spiritual power when it becomes a successful organization, because the advocates of the denomination or of the missionary enterprise after a while have to see first of all to the establishment and success of their organization, while the thing which made them what they are has gone like a corn of wheat into the ground and died. HGM. 68

Look at the history of every vigorous movement born spontaneously of the Holy Ghost, there comes a time when its true spiritual power dies, and it dies in correspondence to the success of the organization. HGM. 68

It is the 'broken-bread' aspect which produces the faithfulness that God looks upon as success; not the fact of the harvest, but that the harvest is being turned into nutritious bread. HGM. 68

We are not called to be successful in accordance with ordinary standards, but in accordance with a corn of wheat falling into the ground and dying, becoming in that way what it never could be if it were to abide alone. HGM. 68

The estimate of success has come imperceptibly into Christian enterprise and we say we must go in for winning souls; but we cannot win souls if we cut ourselves off from the source, and the source is belief in Jesus Christ. Immediately we look to the outflow, i.e., the results, we are in danger of becoming specialists of certain aspects of truth, of banking on certain things, either terror or emotionalism or sensational presentations—anything rather than remaining confident that "He must reign." HGM. 68

Every temptation of the devil is full of the most amazing wisdom and the understanding of every problem that ever stretched before men's view. Satan's kingdom is based on wisdom, along the lines he advocates lies success, and men recognize this. Jesus Christ is not on the line of success but on the spiritual line, the holy, practical line and no other. LG. 155

One of the biggest snares is the idea that God is sure to lead us to success. NKW. 13

We are not called to success but to faithfulness. OBH. 82

If we believe on Jesus Christ it is not what we gain but what He pours through us that counts. It is not that God makes us beautifully rounded grapes, but that He squeezes the sweetness out of us. We cannot measure our lives by spiritual success, but only by what God pours through us, and we cannot measure that at all. PH. 127

God called Jesus Christ to unmitigated disaster; Jesus Christ called His disciples to come and see Him put to death; He led every one of those disciples to the place where their hearts broke. The whole thing was an absolute failure from every standpoint but God's, and yet the thing that was the biggest failure

from man's standpoint was the ultimate triumph from God's, because God's purpose was not man's. PH. 181

Sum up the life of Jesus Christ by any other standard than God's, and it is an anticlimax of failure. "It is required in stewards, that a man be found faithful"—not successful. SHH. 96

If a man wants success and a good time in the actual condition of things as they are, let him keep away from Jesus Christ, let him ignore His claims and the heroism of His holiness, there is no commercial value in it. In the final wind up it is the man who has stuck true to God and damned the consequences who will come out the best; whether he has made the best or the worst of himself in this life is another matter. SHH. 119

If you are going to succeed in anything in this world, you must concentrate on it, practice it, and the same is true spiritually. SSM. 63

SUFFERING

When we talk about suffering we are apt to think only of bodily pain, or of suffering because we have given up something for God, which is paltry nonsense. AUG. 28

Why there should be suffering we do not know; but we have to remain loyal to the character of God as revealed by Jesus Christ in the face of it. BE. 93

Real suffering comes when a man's statement of his belief in God is divorced from his personal relationship to God. The statement of belief is secondary, it is never the fundamental thing. It is always well to note the things in life that your explanations do not cover. BFB. 17

There is suffering before which you cannot say a word; you cannot preach 'the gospel of temperament'; all you can do is to remain dumb and leave room for God to come in as He likes. BFB. 24

Suffering is the touchstone of saintliness, just as temptation is, and suffering wrongfully will always reveal the ruling disposition because it takes us unawares. BSG. 44

We miss the mark when we think on the aesthetic line and take Our Lord as a specimen of a highly strung, superbly fine nature, suffering from contact with coarse natures; we are talking nonsense if we put His suffering there. He never paid the remotest attention to that kind of suffering, nor is there any allusion made to it in the New Testament. His suffering is not the suffering of a man of refined sensibilities among brutes, of a holy character among unholy characters; His suffering is in a totally different domain and along a different line from anything from which we suffer, it is the suffering of a Saviour. BSG. 46

. . . to be able to explain suffering is the clearest indication of never having suffered. Sin, suffering, and sanctification are not problems of the mind, but facts of life—mysteries that awaken all other mysteries until the heart rests in God, and waiting patiently knows *"He doeth all things well."* CD. VOL. 1, 61

To 'suffer as a Christian' is not to be marked peculiar because of your views, or because you will not bend to conventionality; these things are not Christian, but ordinary human traits from which all men suffer irrespective of creed or religion or no religion. To 'suffer as a Christian' is to suffer because there is an essential difference between you and the world which rouses the contempt of the world, and the disgust and hatred of the spirit that is in the world. To 'suffer as a Christian' is to have no answer when the world's satire is turned on you, as it was turned on Jesus Christ when He hung upon the cross, when they turned His words into jest and jeer; they will do the same to you. He gave no answer, neither can you. CD. VOL. 1, 68

Suffering is the heritage of the bad, of the penitent, and of the Son of God. Each one ends in the cross. The bad thief is crucified, the penitent thief is crucified, and the Son of God is crucified. By these signs we know the widespread heritage of suffering. CD. VOL. 1, 77

Suffering is grand when the heart is right with God. But for the night *"the moon and the stars, which Thou hast ordained"*, would never be seen. And so God giveth to His own *"the treasures of darkness"*. CD. VOL. 1, 85

Oh, the sublimity of the sufferings of the sanctified! Suffering according to the will of God, not so much for personal perfecting as to enable God to express His ideas in the life. CD. VOL. 1, 89

To suffer from the hatred of men, to be separated from their company, to be reproached of men, to be considered as having an evil name, is not necessarily to have fellowship with His sufferings. We only have fellowship with Him if we suffer *"for the Son of man's sake"*. To suffer martyrdom, to lose your life, to leave father and mother, houses and lands, is not to have fellowship with His sufferings unless it is done because of Him and for His sake. CD. VOL. 1, 92

Let it be said with reverence, even with bated breath, and in the atmosphere of the deepest humility, that suffering 'according to the will of God' raises us to a freedom and felicity in the Highest that baffles all language to express. As ever, the only sufficient language is the language of Scripture. CD. VOL. 1, 96

. . . the saint knows not why he suffers as he does, yet he comprehends with a knowledge that passeth knowledge that all is well. CD. VOL. 2, 105

When we understand that the saints are the rich glory of Jesus Christ's inheritance, we have added light on the mystery of the suffering of the saints. CD. VOL. 2, 105

The Bible makes little of physical suffering. The modern mind looks on suffering and pain as an unmitigated curse; the Bible puts something akin to purifying in connection with suffering, e.g., "for he that hath suffered in the flesh hath ceased from sin". CHI. 111

There is suffering that is preventable, but there is an inevitable suffering that is essentially God's will for us. GW. 129

The picture of God in the Bible is of One who suffers, and when the mask is torn off life and we see all its profound and vast misery, the suffering, sorrowing God is the only One who does not mock us. 'He was despised, and rejected of men; a man of sorrows, and acquainted with grief.' GW. 129

The sufferings of the sanctified are caused by growing into the idea of the will of God. God did not spare His own Son, and He does not spare His sanctified ones from the requirements of saintship. A child is a perfect specimen of the genus *homo*, so is a man. The child as it develops, suffers; it is a false mercy that spares a child any requirements of its nature to complete the full

stature of manhood, and it is a false mercy that spares the sanctified child of God any of the requirements of its nature to complete 'the measure of the stature of the fulness of Christ.' GW. 130

Suffering was inevitable to our Lord before God could make His Saviourhood a fact; He 'learned obedience by the things which He suffered.' Jesus Christ is not our Example, He is the Captain of our salvation; His position is unique. We do not suffer in order that we may become saviours; we suffer in order to enable God to fulfil His idea of saintship in us. GW. 130

If you are suffering, it is intensely difficult to look up. HG. 18

It is strange that God should make it that "through the shadow of an agony cometh Redemption"; strange that God's Son should be made perfect through suffering; strange that suffering should be one of the golden pathways for God's children. HG. 25

. . . the great characteristic of the life of a child of God is the power to suffer, and through that suffering the natural is transformed into the spiritual. IWP. 109

Talk to a saint about suffering and he looks at you in amazement—'Suffering? Where does it come in?' It comes in on God's side along the line of interpretation; on the side of the saint it is an overwhelming delight in God; not delight in suffering, but if God's will should lead through suffering, there is delight in His will. MFL. 127

There is no suffering to equal the suffering of self-love arising from independent individuality which refuses to submit either to God or to its nobler self. NKW. 103

We all know people who have been made much meaner and more irritable and more intolerable to live with by suffering: it is not right to say that all suffering perfects. It only perfects one type of person—the one who accepts the call of God in Christ Jesus. PH. 153

It is obvious nonsense to say that suffering makes saints, it makes some people devils. PH. 153

The finest men and women suffer, and the devil uses their sufferings to slander God. God is after one thing—bringing many sons to glory, and He does not care what it costs us, any more than He cared what it cost Him. PR. 113

The folk who are most actively beneficent to you are those who are being crushed with suffering that would send you staggering. RTR. 12

The world, the flesh and the devil will put imaginary grief in your way just when Jesus Christ is wanting you to enter into fellowship with His sufferings. RTR. 24

The way of approach to the holy ground of God is nearly always through suffering; we are not always in the natural mood for it, but when we have been ploughed into by suffering or sorrow, we are able to approach the moral frontiers where God works. SA. 15

Agony means severe suffering in which something dies—either the base thing, or the good. No man is the same after an agony; he is either better or worse, and the agony of a man's experience is nearly always the first thing that opens his mind to understand the need of Redemption worked out by Jesus Christ. SA. 23

Very few of us know anything about suffering for Christ's sake. A man who knows nothing about Christ will suffer for conscience or conviction's sake. To suffer for Christ's sake is to suffer because of being personally related to Him. SHH. 83

Suffering, and the inevitable result of suffering, is the only way some of us can learn, and if we are shielded God will ultimately take the one who interferes by the scruff of the neck and remove him. The fingers that caress a child may also hurt its flesh; it is the power of love that makes them hurt. SHH. 96

In the suffering there is a compensation which cannot be got at in any other way. It is not seen from the outside because the compensation cannot be articulately stated. SHH. 97

You rarely hear a man who has been through the real agony of suffering who says he disbelieves in God; it is the one who watches others going through suffering who says he disbelieves in God. SHH. 97

In this dispensation it is the patient long-suffering of God that is being manifested. God allows men to say what they like and do what they like. SHH. 118

. . . God is long-suffering, and He is giving us ample opportunity to try whatever line we like both in individual and national life. If God were to end this dispensation now, the human race would have a right to say, You should have waited, there is a type of thing You never let us try.

God is leaving us to prove to the hilt that it cannot be done in any other way than Jesus Christ's way, or the human race would not be satisfied. SHH. 118

God does not prevent physical suffering because it is of less moment than what He is after. 'And fear not them which kill the body, but are not able to kill the soul.' SHL. 102

When God is putting His saints through the experience of the millstones, we are apt to want to interfere. Hands off! No saint dare interfere in the discipline of the suffering of another saint. God brings these things into our lives for the production of the bread that is to feed the world. SHL. 118

To choose suffering is a disease; but to choose God's will even though it means suffering is to suffer as Jesus did—'*according to the will of God*'. SHL. 121

In the Bible it is never the idealizing of the sufferer that is brought out, but the glorifying of God. God always serves Himself out of the saint's personal experience of suffering. SHL. 121

The sufferings of Job were not in order to perfect him. The explanation of Job's sufferings was that God and Satan had made a battleground of his soul, and the honour of God was at stake. SSH. 2

SURRENDER

We sentimentally believe, and believe, and believe, and nothing happens. We pray "Lord, increase our faith", and we try to pump up the faith, but it does not come. What is wrong? The moral surrender has not taken place. AUG. 112

No one is ever united with the Lord Jesus Christ until he is willing to relinquish all of the life he held before. This does not only mean relinquishing sin, it means relinquishing the whole way of looking at things. To be born from above

of the Spirit of God means that we must let go before we lay hold. CD. VOL. 1, 129

There are many people who believe in Jesus Christ but they have not relinquished anything, consequently they have not received anything; there is still the realisation of a life that has not been relinquished. CD. VOL. 1, 129

There is no bigger word and no word made more shallow than 'surrender.' To say 'I surrender all' may be blethering sentiment, or it may be the deep passionate utterance of the life. HG. 103

Belief in the Redemption is difficult because it needs surrender first. I never can believe until I have surrendered myself to God. HG. 106

... take an absolute plunge into the love of God, and when you are there you will be amazed at your foolishness for not getting there before. IWP. 48

When we stay our feeble efforts,
    And from struggling cease,
Unconditional surrender
    Brings us God's own peace. IYA. 71

Our Lord habitually submitted His will to His Father, that is, He engineered nothing but left room for God. The modern trend is dead against this submission; we do engineer, and engineer with all the sanctified ingenuity we have, and when God suddenly bursts in in an expected way, we are taken unawares. It is easier to engineer things than determinedly to submit all our powers to God. We say we must do all we can: Jesus says we must let God do all He can. MFL. 109

God nowhere tells us to give up things for the sake of giving them up; He tells us to give them up for the sake of the only thing worth having, viz. life with Himself. NKW. 124

If we want something conscious from God, it means there is a reserve; the will has not been surrendered; immediately we do surrender, the tidal wave of the love of God carries us straight into all the fulness of God. OBH. 86

Submission does not mean that I submit to the power of God because I must. A stoic submits without passion, that is slavery; a saint sees God's will and submits to it with a passionate love, and in his daily life exhibits his love to God to Whom he has submitted. PH. 56

We are so happy, so sure and so satisfied, that we have lost altogether the note of surrender which marked the life of Jesus. PH. 88

Spiritual reality is what is wanted. 'I surrender all'—and you feel as if you did, that is the awkward thing. The point is whether, as God engineers your circumstances, you find that you really have surrendered. Immediately you do surrender, you are made so much one with your Lord that the thought of what it cost never enters any more. PR. 104

The tendency is strong to say—"O God won't be so stern as to expect me to give up that!" *but He will;* "He won't expect me to walk in the light so that I have nothing to hide", *but He will;* "He won't expect me to draw on His grace for everything" *but He will.* RTR. 3

By surrendering ourselves to quiet communion with God, by resting for a while from all our thinking and acting and serving, by leaving all things for once in our Heavenly Father's hands, secret wounds are healed, gathering unbelief is

dispelled, and displaced armour refixed. RTR. 81

One of the dangers of modern evangelism is that it lays too much emphasis on decision for Christ instead of on surrender to Jesus Christ. SHH. 55

There is only one Being to Whom we must yield, and that is the Lord Jesus Christ. Be sure that it is Jesus Christ to whom you yield, then the whole nature is safeguarded for ever. SHL. 56

SYMBOLISM

A symbol represents a spiritual truth by means of images or properties of natural things. A symbol must not be taken as an allegory, an allegory is simply a figurative discourse with a meaning other than that contained in literal words. A symbol is sealed until the right spirit is given for its understanding, and God's symbols are undetected unless His Spirit is in His child to enable him to understand. What did the cloudy pillar by day or the fiery pillar by night signify to the hordes in the desert? Nothing more than the mystery of ever-varying cloud forms. To the children of God, they meant the manifested guidance of God. How a man interprets God's symbols reveals what manner of man he is. CD. VOL. 1, 24

A perilous time ensues for the individual and for the religious world whenever God shifts His symbols. Obedience to the voice of the Spirit within, the Word of God without, and the suffering of the tribulation around, enable the child of God to hear God's voice and recognise His changing symbols. This discipline of Divine guidance by symbols is a serious, momentous discipline, and God never leaves His children alone in such times, for,

> ". . . behind the dim unknown Standeth God within the shadows, Keeping watch upon His own." CD. VOL. 1, 25

SYMPATHY

Never sympathize with a soul whose case makes you come to the conclusion that God is hard. God is tenderer than anyone we can conceive of, and if a man cannot get through to him it is because there is a secret thing he does not intend to give up. AUG. 21

Beware of saying that Jesus took on the sin of the human race by sympathy. It is being said nowadays that Jesus had such a profound sympathy for the human race, He was such a pure noble character and realized so keenly the shame and horror of sin, that He took our sin on Himself by sympathy. All through the Bible it is revealed that Our Lord bore the sin of the world by *identification*, not by sympathy. BSG. 26

If our human sympathy with the one who is suffering under the hand of God is justified, then God is cruel. CHI. 68

If we pour out sympathy upon one who is bereaved, all we do is to make that one more submissive to his grief. The unique thing about Jesus is that He comes to sorrowing men as a complete Saviour from all sorrow. PH. 123

Never sympathize with a soul who cannot get through to God on Jesus Christ's lines. The Lord is never hard nor cruel, He is the essence of tender compassion and gentleness. The reason any soul cannot get through is that there is something in him that won't budge; immediately it does, Jesus Christ's marvellous life will have its way. PS. 53

T

TEACHING

Our Lord's teaching does not mean anything to a man until it does, and then it means everything. DI. 71

Our Lord did not come to this earth to *teach* men to be holy: He came to *make* men holy, and His teaching is applicable only on the basis of experimental Redemption. DI. 71

If you are a teacher sent from God your worth in God's sight is estimated by the way you enable people to see Jesus. IWP. 112

If a teacher fascinates with his doctrine, his teaching never came from God. The teacher sent from God is the one who clears the way to Jesus and keeps it clear; souls forget altogether about him because the vision of Jesus is the only abiding result. When people are attracted to Jesus Christ through you, see always that you stay on God all the time, and their hearts and affections will never stop at you. IWP. 112

The enervation that has crippled many a church, many a Sunday School class and Bible class, is that the pastor or teacher has won people to himself, and the result when they leave is enervating sentimentality. The true man or woman of God never leaves that behind, every remembrance of them makes you want to serve God all the more. IWP. 112

If once you get the thought, 'It is my winsome way of putting it, my presentation of the truth that attracts'—the only name for that is the ugly name of thief, stealing the hearts of the sheep of God who do not know why they stop at you. Keep the mind stayed on God, and I defy anyone's heart to stop at you, it will always go on to God. IWP. 112

. . . the spheres God brings us into are not meant to teach us something but to *make* us something. LG. 52

Our Lord's teaching is so simple that the natural mind pays no attention to it, it is only moral perplexity that heeds. For instance, Our Lord said: "Ask, and it shall be given you." These words have no meaning for us if we are wearing any kind of ecclesiastical 'blinkers,' and are refusing to see what we do not wish to see. OBH. 92

The dissolving of the Person of Jesus by analysis is prevalent because men refuse to know Him after the Spirit, they will only know Him after the reasoning of their own minds. The test of any teaching is its estimate of Jesus Christ. The teaching may sound wonderful and beautiful, but watch lest it have at its centre the dethroning of Jesus Christ. PR. 76

Our Lord is not the great Teacher of the world, He is the Saviour of the world and the Teacher of those who believe in Him, which is a radically different matter. RTR. 44

TEMPTATION

Jesus Christ was tempted, and so shall we be tempted when we are rightly related to God. BP. 191

Temptation is no temptation at all if it is clearly to evil. BSG. 30

The temptation which beset Our Lord with such fascination and power is the very temptation which is besetting the modern Christian—'Heal bodies, cast out devils, feed the poor, and men will crown You King.' The temptation is more powerful to-day than ever it has been in the history of the Church, to put mens' needs first, not God; to spell God in the term 'humanity'; to make God an *etcetera* for blessing humanity. BSG. 31

We have to get rid of the idea that because Jesus was God He could not be tempted. Almighty God cannot be tempted, but in Jesus Christ we deal with God as man, a unique Being—God-Man. CHI. 56

Temptation overcome is the transfiguration of the natural into the spiritual and the establishment of conscious affinity with the purest and best. CHI. 57

God Almighty was never "tempted in all points like as we are," Jesus Christ was. God Almighty knows all that Jesus Christ knows; but, if I may say it reverently, *God in Christ* knows more, because *God in Christ* "suffered being tempted," and therefore He is "able to succour them that are tempted." CHI. 99

Our deadliest temptations are not so much those that destroy Christian belief as those that corrupt and destroy the Christian temper. DI. 5

To be raised above temptation belongs to God only. DI. 76

Satan does not tempt to gross sins, the one thing he tempts to is putting myself as master instead of God. DI. 76

How are we to face the tempter? By prayer? No. With the Word of God? No. Face the tempter with Jesus Christ, and He will apply the word of God to you, and the temptation will cease. DI. 76

Jesus was tempted of the devil, perhaps you are also, but no one guesses it. There is never any comrade for your soul when you are tempted. IYA. 56

We are apt to imagine that our Lord was only tempted once and that then His temptations were over. His temptations went on from the first moment of His conscious life to the last, because His holiness was not the holiness of Almighty God, but the holiness of man, which can only progress by means of the things that go against it. LG. 152

The temptations of Jesus continued all His earthly life, and they will continue all the time of His life in us. LG. 154

Temptations do not come in fits and starts, they abide all the time, and to continue with Jesus in them is the way the holiness of our life is going to be to the glory of God. LG. 157

Temptations in the life of faith are not accidents, each temptation is part of a plan, a step in the progress of faith. NKW. 117

The temptations of Jesus are not those of a Man as man, but the temptations of GOD as Man. "Wherefore it behoved Him in all things to be made like unto His brethren." PH. 35

Jesus Christ's temptations and ours move in different spheres until we become His brethren by being born from above. PH. 35

The agony Jesus went through in the Temptation was surely because He had the vision of the long way and saw the suffering it would entail on men through all the ages if He took His Father's way. He knew it in a way we cannot conceive. His sensitiveness is beyond anything we can imagine. PH. 99

Temptation is the testing by an alien power of the possessions held by a personality in order that a higher and nobler character may come out of the test. PR. 60

Temptation is a suggested short cut to the realisation of the highest at which we aim. PR. 60

Temptation is not sin; we are bound to meet it if we are men. Not to be tempted would be to be beneath contempt. PR. 60

We are apt to imagine that when we are saved and sanctified we are delivered from temptation; we are not, we are loosened into it. Before we are born again, we are not free enough to be tempted, neither morally nor spiritually. Immediately we are born into the Kingdom of God, we get our first introduction into what God calls temptation, viz., the temptations of His Son. PR. 61

The records of our Lord's temptations are given not that we might fathom Him, but that we might know what to expect when we are regenerated. When we are born again of the Spirit of God and enter into fellowship with Jesus Christ, then the temptations of our Lord are applicable to us. PR. 61

Jesus Christ was not born with a heredity of sin; He was not tempted in all points as ordinary men are, but tempted like His brethren, those who have been born from above by the Spirit of God and placed in the Kingdom of God by supernatural regeneration. PR. 61

The devil does not tempt us to do wrong things; he tries to make us lose what God has put into us by regeneration, the possibility of being of value to God. When we are born from above the central citadel of the devil's attack is the same in us as it was in our Lord—viz., to do God's will in our own way. PR. 63

In His temptation our Lord does not stand as an individual Man; He stands as the whole human race vested in one Personality, and every one of us when regenerated can find his place and fellowship in those temptations. PR. 64

Temptation yielded to is lust deified. PR. 69

The practical test for us when we have been through a season of temptation is whether we have a finer and deeper affinity for the highest. PR. 70

Temptation must come, and we do not know what it is until we meet it. When we do meet it, we must not debate with God, but stand absolutely true to Him no matter what it costs us personally, and we will find that the onslaught will leave us with higher and purer affinities than before. PR. 70

God does not keep us from temptation, He succours us in the midst of it. PR. 71

Temptation is not something we may escape; it is essential to the full-orbed life of a son of God. PR. 71

We have to beware lest we think we are tempted as no one else is tempted. What we go through is the common inheritance of the race, not something no one ever went through before. It is most humiliating to be taken off our pedestal of suffering and made to realise that thousands of others are going through the same thing as we are going through. PR. 71

We have the notion at first that when we are saved and sanctified by God's supernatural grace, He does not require us to do anything, but it is only then that He begins to require anything of us. God did not shield His own Son; not only did He not shield Him, but He allowed Him to be driven into the wilderness to be tempted of the devil. After the baptism of Jesus and the descent of the Holy Ghost upon Him, God took His sheltering hand off Him, as it were, and let the devil do his worst. PR. 75

The tendencies that make temptation possible are inherent in man as God created him, Adam and Our Lord Jesus Christ being witnesses; and we have to bear in mind that regeneration does not remove those tendencies but rather increases them. The possibility of temptation reaches its height in Jesus Christ. PS. 47

Temptation is not sin; temptation must always be possible for our sonship to be of worth to God. It would be no credit for God to bring mechanical slaves to glory—"for it became Him . . . in bringing many *sons* unto glory"—not slaves, not useless channels, but vigorous, alert, wide-awake men and women, with all their powers and faculties devoted absolutely to God. PS. 50

Temptation trains innocence into character or else into corruption. There are some temptations, however, by which we have no business to be tempted any longer; we should be on a higher plane dealing with other temptations. We may have our morality well within our own grasp and be comparatively free from temptation, but as soon as we are regenerated by the Spirit of God we begin to understand the force of spiritual temptations of which we were unconscious before. PS. 54

The sign that you have gone through temptation rightly is that you retain your affinity with the highest. PS. 56

The records of the temptation of Jesus are the records of how God as man is tempted, not of how man is tempted as man. PS. 57

The devil does not need to bother about the majority of us; we have enough lust on the inside to keep us in sin, but when once a man is born from above, the temptations alter instantly, and he realizes where the temptation is aimed, viz. at the disposition. PS. 58

Impeccable—liable not to sin. The idea that because Jesus Christ was without sin therefore He could not be tempted, has become woven into religious belief. If that were so, the record of His temptation is a mere farce. Could Jesus Christ be tempted? Undoubtedly He could, because temptation and sin are not the same thing. SHH. 100

TESTIMONY

Every Christian must testify, testimony is the nature of the life; but for preaching there must be the agonizing grip of God's hand. AUG. 8

Testimony frequently stops short because the armour of righteousness is not on the right hand and on the left. Keep drawing on the grace of God, then there will be the power of the proclaimed testimony. AUG. 127

You cannot draw on the grace of God for testimony if these three things are not there—the word of God, the power of God, and the consciousness that you are walking in the integrity of that testimony in private, if they are there, then there is an unfaltering certainty. AUG. 127

The first motive of testimony is not for the sake of other people but for our own sake, we realize that we have no one but God to stand by us. Always give your testimony in the presence of God, and ever remember God's honour is at stake. AUG. 127

Am I trying to live up to a testimony, or am I abiding in the Truth? DI. 77

It is easier to stand true to a testimony mildewed with age, because it has a dogmatic ring about it that people agree with, than to talk from your last moment of contact with God. DI. 77

To say a thing is the sure way to begin to believe it. That is why it is so necessary to testify to what Jesus Christ has done for you. DI. 77

It is never our testimony that keeps our experience right: our experience makes us testify. DI. 77

Never give an educated testimony, i.e., something you have taught yourself to say; wait till the elemental moves in you. DI. 78

Be prepared to be unreserved in personal testimony; but remember, personal testimony must never be lowered into personal biography. DI. 78

If my testimony makes anyone wish to emulate me, it is a mistaken testimony, it is not a witness to Jesus. DI. 78

The Holy Spirit will only witness to a testimony when Jesus Christ is exalted higher than the testimony. DI. 78

How few of us do speak! When we talk to a soul, we talk like a tract! GW. 48

If you have been saved from sin, say so; if you have been sanctified by God's grace, say so. Don't substitute some other refinement in its place. By using other words you are not testifying to God, but compromising with the atmosphere of those to whom you are talking. HG. 96

It is easy to preach, nothing easier, but it is another thing to confess. Confessing means to say with every bit of me that Jesus Christ has come into my flesh. HGM. 98

To say a thing is the sure way to thinking it. That is why it is so necessary to testify to what Jesus Christ has done for us. A testimony gets hold of the mind as it has hold of the heart; but the same thing is true of the opposite, if we say a wrong thing often enough we begin to think it. IWP. 30

It is impossible to go on in our life with God if the element of personal testimony is left out. NKW. 23

To say 'I have got the victory' is a selfish testimony; the testimony of the Spirit of God is that the Victor has got me. NKW. 40

If my testimony is only a thrilling experience, it is nothing but a dead, metallic thing, it kills me and those who listen to me. But when I am in contact with Jesus Christ every testimony of mine will reveal Him. OBH. 80

A witness is not one who is entranced by Jesus, by the revelation He gives, by what He has done; but one who has received the energy Jesus Himself had, and is become a witness that pleases Him, wherever he is placed, whatever he is doing, whether he is known or unknown. The energy in him is the very energy of the Holy Ghost, and the expression of it in life makes a witness that satisfies Jesus Christ. PH. 174

If you cannot express yourself on any subject, struggle 'till you can. You must struggle to get expression experimentally, then there will come a time when that expression will become the very wine of strengthening to someone else. Try to re-state to yourself what you implicitly feel to be God's truth, and you give God a chance to pass it on to someone else through you. RTR. 22

For one man who can introduce another to Jesus Christ by the way he lives and by the atmosphere of his life, there are a thousand who can only talk jargon about Him. Whenever you come across a man or woman who in your time of distress introduces you to Jesus Christ, you know you have struck the best friend you ever had, one who has opened up the way of life to you. SA. 41

Our Lord never tells us to confess anything but Himself, "Whosoever shall confess *ME* before men . . ." SSM. 83

Testimonies to the world on the subjective line are always wrong, they are for saints, for those who are spiritual and who understand; but our testimony to the world is our Lord Himself, confess Him, 'He saved me, He sanctified me, He put me right with God.' SSM. 83

If a thing has its root in the heart of God, it will want to be public, to get out, it must do things in the external and the open, and Jesus not only encouraged this publicity. He insisted upon it. SSM. 102

It is God's law that men cannot hide what they really are. If they are His disciples it will be publicly portrayed. SSM. 102

The word 'confess' means that every particle of our nature says the same thing, not our mouth only, but the very make up of our flesh and blood, confesses that Jesus Christ has come in the flesh. SSY. 72

To be a witness means to live a life of unsullied, uncompromising, and unbribed devotion to Jesus. A true witness is one who lets his light shine in works that exhibit the disposition of Jesus. Our Lord makes the one who is a witness His own possession, He becomes responsible for him. SSY. 171

THEOLOGY

Theology is a great thing, so is a man's creed; but God is greater than either, and the next greatest thing is my relationship to Him. BFB. 24

The theological view ought to be constantly examined; if we put it in the place of God we become invincibly ignorant, that is, we won't accept any other point of view, and the invincible ignorance of fanaticism leads to delusions for which we alone are to blame.

The fundamental things are not the things which can be proved logically in practical life. BFB. 49

We only believe along the line of what we conceive of God, and when things happen contrary to that line, we deny the experience and remain true to our theological method. BFB. 56

Theology is second, not first; in its place it is a handmaid of religion, but it becomes a tyrant if put in the first place. BFB. 56

Theology is the science of religion, an intellectual attempt to systematize the consciousness of God. BFB. 56

Any theology which ignores Jesus Christ as the supreme Authority ceases to be Christian theology. BFB. 90

Many of the theological terms used nowadays have no grip, we talk glibly about sin, and about salvation; but let the truth be presented along the line of a man's deep personal need, and at once it is arresting. DI. 46

We have been taken up with creeds and doctrines, and when a man is hit we do not know what to give him; we have no Jesus Christ, we have only theology. SA. 41

Intellect is the expression of life. In the same way, theology is said to be religion; theology is the instrument of religion. SSY. 158

THOUGHT

You can never become a Christian by thinking, you can only become a Christian by receiving something from God; but you must think after you are a Christian. BE. 50

No thinking will ever make me a Christian; I can only become a Christian through listening to what is preached and accepting salvation as a gift; but I must think after I am a Christian. BE. 53

If we insist that a man must believe the doctrine of the Trinity and the inspiration of the Scriptures before he can be saved, we are putting the cart before the horse. All that is the effect of being a Christian, not the cause of it; and if we put the effect first we produce difficulties because we are putting thinking before life. BFB. 91

In the Bible the heart, and not the brain, is revealed to be the centre of thinking. BP. 97

The Christian method of thinking puts the intellect second, not first; the modern view puts intellect on the throne. God does not sum up a man's worth by his thinking, but by the way he expresses his thinking in actual life, that is, by his character. It is possible for there to be a tremendous divorce between a man's thinking and his practical life; the only thing that tells in the sight of God is a man's character. Beware of putting principles first instead of a Person. Jesus Christ puts personal relationship first—'Be rightly related to Me, then work out your thinking.' BSG. 71

One is made to turn with weary exhaustion from the unthinking, hand to mouth experience of much of the religious literature of the day. To *think* as a Christian is a rare accomplishment, especially as the curious leaven which puts a premium on ignorance works its sluggish way. To speak of Plato to the majority of Christian preachers, particularly holiness preachers, would be to meet not a consciousness of ignorance, but a blatant pride which boasts of knowing nothing outside the Bible, which, in all probability, means knowing nothing inside it either. Christian thinking is a rare and difficult thing; so many seem unaware that the first great commandment according to our Lord is, *"Thou shalt love the Lord thy God . . . with all thy mind . . ."* CD. VOL. 1, 22

As soon as we begin to examine the foundations of our salvation we are up against the thoughts of God, and as Christians we ought to be busy thinking God's thoughts after Him. That is where we fall short; we are delighted with the fact that "once I was this, and now I am that," but simply to have a vivid experience is not sufficient if we are to be at our best for God. It is because of the refusal to think on Christian lines that Satan has come in as angel of light and switched off numbers of God's children in their head, with the result that there is a divorce between heart and head. CHI. 19

The Christian thought is not fatalistic, it is based on the revelation of God given by Jesus Christ. CHI. 47

The majority of us recognise the necessity of receiving the Holy Spirit for living, but we do not sufficiently recognise the need for drawing on the resources of the Holy Spirit for thinking. CHI. 47

Think of the labour and patience of men in the domain of science and then think of our lack of patience in endeavouring to appreciate the Atonement, and you see the need there is for us to be conscientious in our thinking, basing everything on the reality of the Atonement. We prefer to be average Christians, we don't mind it having broken God's heart to save us, but we do object to having a sleepless night while we

learn to say 'Thank you' to God so that the angels can hear us. We need to be staggered out of our shocking indolence. DI. 79

We have no business to limit God's revelations to the bias of the human mind. DI. 79

I can think out a whole system of life, reason it all out well, but it does not necessarily make any difference to my actual life, I may think like an angel and live like a tadpole. DI. 80

Truth is discerned by moral obedience. There are points in our thinking which remain obscure until a crisis arises in personal life where we ought to obey, immediately we obey the intellectual difficulty alters. Whenever we have to obey it is always in something immensely practical. DI. 80

Obedience is the basis of Christian thinking. Never be surprised if there are whole areas of thinking that are not clear, they never will be until you obey. DI. 80

Until you get an answer that satisfies your best moods only, don't stop thinking, keep on querying God. The answers that satisfy you go all over you, like health, or fresh air. DI. 80

With regard to other men's minds, take all you can get, whether those minds are in flesh-and-blood editions or in books, but remember, the best you get from another mind is not that mind's verdict, but its standpoint. Note the writers who provoke you to do your best mentally. DI. 80

Never cease to think until you think things home and they become character. DI. 80

Our thinking is often allowed to be anti-Christian while our feelings are Christian. The way I think will colour my attitude toward my fellow-men. DI. 81

If you have ever done any thinking you don't feel very complacent after it, you get your first touch of pessimism; if you don't, you have never thought clearly and truly. DI. 82

The first thing that goes when you begin to think is your theology. If you stick too long to a theological point of view you become stagnant, without vitality.
DI. 82

Never be distressed at the immediate result of thinking on the deep truths of religion because it will take years of profound familiarity with such truths before you gain an expression sufficient to satisfy you. DI. 82

As you go on with God He will give you thoughts that are a bit too big for you. God will never leave a servant of His with ideas he can easily express, He will always express through him more than he can grasp. DI. 83

It takes a long time to get rid of atheism in thinking. DI. 83

Our right standing is proved by the fact that we can walk; if we are not rightly related to God in our thinking we cannot walk properly. Walk means character. GW. 13

We are saved in only one way, by the supernatural efficacy of the Redemption; but to be saved and never *think* about it is a crime. 'My people doth not consider,' says God; they won't think.
GW. 16

We can never become God's people by thinking, but we must think *as* God's people. It is possible to understand all about the plan of salvation without being personally related to the reality of Redemption. GW. 16

We have to work out, not our redemption, but our human appreciation of our redemption. We owe it to God that we refuse to have rusty brains. GW. 17

People won't go through the labour of thinking, consequently snares get hold of them, and remember, thinking is a tremendous labour. We have to labour to 'bring every thought into captivity to the obedience of Christ'. GW. 104

God's Thought expressed itself not only in the universe which He created, but in a Being called "the Word", whose name to us is 'Jesus Christ'. HGM. 96

It will take all Time and Eternity to experience God's Thought—"And this is life eternal, that they should know Thee . . ."—a continual new wonder. The schooling we are going through just now is to develop us into an understanding of the Thought of God. HGM. 98

The great lack to-day is of people who will *think* along Christian lines; we know a great deal about salvation but we do not go on to explore the 'unsearchable riches of Christ'. We do not know much about giving up the right to ourselves to Jesus Christ, or about the intense patience of 'hanging in' in perfect certainty that what Jesus says is true. LG. 133

. . . we can and we must choose our thinking, and the whole discipline of our mental life is to form the habit of right thinking. It is not done by praying, it is done only by strenuous determination, and it is never easy to begin with. MFL. 36

Never pray about evil thoughts, it will fix them in the mind. 'Quit'—that is the only thing to do with anything that is wrong; to ruthlessly grip it on the threshold of your mind and allow it no more way. MFL. 49

If you have received the Holy Spirit, you will find that you have the power to bring "every thought into captivity to the obedience of Christ." MFL. 49

We are not meant to spend our lives in the domain of intellectual thinking. A Christian's thinking ought never to be in reflection, but in activities. MFL. 51

Thinking is the habit of expressing what moves our spirit. In order to think we must concentrate. Thinking is a purely physical process. No one can tell us how to begin to think, all they can do is to tell us what happens when we do think. In the grey matter of the brain are multitudes of blood-vessels, distributed equally all over the brain, and when we think, the blood gathers to the one part of the brain we are using. This is called concentration. Dissipated thinking means that the blood goes back to the other parts of the brain and wakens up associated ideas. When we focus our will around certain thoughts, the blood converges to that particular part of the brain, and if we can hold our wills fixed there for five minutes, we have done a tremendous thing, we have begun to form the habit of mental concentration. The majority of us allow our brains to wool-gather, we never concentrate on any particular line. Concentration is physical, not spiritual. The brain must be brought into order by concentration, then when the Spirit of God brings a spontaneous illumination of a par-

ticular theme instantly the brain is at the disposal of God. If we have not learned to concentrate, the brain cannot focus itself anywhere, it fusses all round and wool-gathers. No one is responsible for that but ourselves. MFL. 79

The danger in spiritual matters is that we do not *think* godliness; we let ideas and conceptions of godliness lift us up at times, but we do not form the habit of godly thinking. Thinking godliness cannot be done in spurts, it is a steady habitual trend. MFL. 93

A devotee to doctrines does not need to think, but a man who is devoted to Jesus Christ is obliged to think, and to think every day of his life, and he must allow nothing to dissipate his thinking. It is not courage men lack, but concentration on Jesus Christ. We have to get out of our laziness and indifference and excuses, and rouse ourselves up to face the Cross of Christ. PH. 88

As long as the devil can keep us terrified of thinking, he will always limit the work of God in our souls. RTR. 33

We do not think on the basis of Christianity at all. We are taught to think like pagans for six days a week and to reverse the order for one day, consequently in critical moments we think as pagans and our religion is left in the limbo of the inarticulate. Our thinking is based not on Hebrew Wisdom and confidence in God, but on the Wisdom of the Greeks which is removed from practical life, and on that basis we persuade ourselves that if a man knows a thing is wrong he will not do it. That is not true. The plague with me, apart from the grace of God, is that I know what is right, but I'm hanged if I'll do it! What I want to know is, can anyone tell me of a

power that will alter my "want to"?
SHH. 106

TIME

Time is nothing to God. IYA. 50

Remember we have all the time there is. The majority of us waste time and want to encroach on eternity. MFL. 65

The only time you will have is the day after you are dead, and that will be eternity. MFL. 65

We can choke God's word with a yawn; we can hinder the time that should be spent with God by remembering we have other things to do. "I haven't time!" Of course you have time! Take time, strangle some other interests and make time to realize that the centre of power in your life is the Lord Jesus Christ and His Atonement. RTR. 68

There is no space or time with Almighty God. We cannot think beyond the limits of birth and death; if we are to know anything beyond them, it must be by revelation. SHH. 23

TITHING

There are teachers who argue that the Sermon on the Mount supersedes the Ten Commandments, and that, because "we are not under law, but under grace," it does not matter whether we honour our father and mother, whether we covet, *et cetera*. Beware of statements like this: There is no need nowadays to observe giving the tenth either of money or of time; we are in a new dispensation and everything belongs to God. SSM. 21

The giving of the tenth is not a sign that all belongs to God, but a sign that the tenth belongs to God and the rest is ours, and we are held responsible for what we do with it. SSM. 22

TONGUE

The tongue and the brain are under our control, not God's. BP. 126

To bridle the tongue does not mean to hold your tongue, that might mean "If I speak, I would say something!" It means to have the tongue under the control of a disciplined heart; that tongue need never apologize. RTR. 50

. . . the great test of a man's character is his tongue. SHH. 27

The tongue only came to its right place within the lips of the Lord Jesus Christ, because He never spoke from His right to Himself. He Who was the Wisdom of God Incarnate, said "the words that I speak unto you, I speak not of Myself," i.e., from the disposition of my right to Myself, but from My relationship to My Father. We are either too hasty or too slow; either we won't speak at all, or we speak too much, or we speak in the wrong mood. The thing that makes us speak is the lust to vindicate ourselves. SHH. 27

To 'confess' Christ means to say, not only with the tongue, but with every bit of our life, that Jesus has come into our flesh. SSY. 96

Men never suffer because they live a godly life; they suffer for their speech. Humanly speaking, if Our Lord had held His tongue, He would not have been put to death. 'If I had not come *and spoken unto them*, they had not had sin; but now they have no cloke for their sin.' SSY. 107

TRANSFIGURATION

All that transpired in the life of Our Lord after the Transfiguration is altogether vicarious, we are without a guide to it in our own experience. Up to the Transfiguration we can understand His holy life and follow in His steps when we have received the Holy Spirit; after the Transfiguration there is no point of similarity, everything is unfamiliar to us. Jesus Christ has a consciousness about which we know nothing. We have come to the place where He is completing the will of God for the salvation of fallen humanity. BSG. 39

If Jesus Christ had gone to heaven from the Mount of Transfiguration we might have worshipped Him, but we would have had no power to live the kind of life He lived. But Jesus did not come to show us what a holy life was like: He came *to make us holy by means of His death.* BSG. 39

When the Transfiguration took place Our Lord as Son of Man had fulfilled all the requirements of His Father for His earthly life and He was back in the glory which He had with the Father before the world was. BSG. 39

There was only one brilliant moment in the life of Jesus, and that was on the Mount of Transfiguration. We do not know what the glory was which He had with the Father before the world was, but if we stand with Him on the Mount we see what He emptied Himself of. BSG. 43

The Transfiguration was the 'Great Divide' in the life of Our Lord. He stood there in the perfect, spotless holiness of His Manhood; then He turned His back on the glory and came down from the Mount to be identified with sin, that through His death fallen humanity might not only be redeemed, but be enabled to have a conscious entrance into the life He lived. BSG. 49

It is so easy when we see things in vision to start out and do them. We are caught up into the seventh heaven, far above all the grubby things of earth and it is magnificent for a time, but we have got to come down. After the Mount of Transfiguration comes the place where we have to live, viz., the demon-possessed valley. The test of reality is our life in the valley, not that we fly up among the golden peaks of the early morning. IYA. 26

Our Lord had emptied Himself of His glory for the purposes of the Incarnation, and the Transfiguration reveals His glory again. PR. 76

Jesus Christ emptied Himself of His glory a second time; He came down from the Mount of Transfiguration and accomplished His death at Jerusalem . . . PR. 79

From the Transfiguration on, we are dealing not so much with the life our Lord lived as with the way He opened the door for us to enter into His life. PR. 118

TREASURE

Treasure in heaven is the wealth of character that has been earned by standing true to the faith of Jesus, not to the faith in Jesus. HG. 39

Treasure in heaven is faith that has been tried. IWP. 58

Our Lord's counsel is to lay up treasure that never can be touched, and the place where it is laid up cannot be touched. "And made us to sit with Him in the heavenly places, in Christ Jesus". MFL. 112

If our treasure is in heaven we do not need to persuade ourselves that it is, we prove it is by the way we deal with matters of earth. MFL. 113

It is the glory of God to conceal His treasures in embarrassments, i.e., in things that involve us in difficulty. "I will give thee the treasures of darkness." We would never have suspected that treasures were hidden there, and in order to get them we have to go through things that involve us in perplexity. PH. 84

In some lives you can see the treasure, there is a sweetness and beauty about them, "the ornament of a meek and quiet spirit," and you wonder where the winsome power of God came from. It came from the dark places where God revealed His sovereign will in unexpected issues. "Thou hast enlarged me when I was in distress." PH. 85

To make treasure is different from making profit. Treasure is the thing that is esteemed for itself, not for what it brings. The Bible tirades against possession for possession's sake. SHH 62

TRINITY

The essential nature of God the Father, of God the Son and of God the Spirit is the same. The characteristics that marked God the Father in the old dispensation, and that marked God the Son when He lived on this earth, mark God the Holy Ghost in this present dispensation. BE. 100

If we take the doctrine of the Trinity (which is a noble attempt of the mind of man to put into an theological formula the Godhead as revealed in the Bible) and say—'That is God', every other attempt at a statement of the Godhead is met by a sledge-hammer blow of finality. My theology has taken the place of God and I have to say—'That is blasphemy'. BFB. 56

The word 'Trinity' is not a Bible word. Over and over again in the Bible the Triune God is revealed, so that the idea conveyed by the Trinity is thoroughly Scriptural. The following distinctions have existed from all eternity:

The Essence of Godhead *(esse)* usually known as God the Father;

The Existence of Godhead *(existere)* usually known as God the Son;

The Proceeding of Godhead *(procedere)* usually known as God the Holy Ghost. BP. 30

Just as God the Father was rejected and spurned in the Old Testament dispensation, and Jesus Christ the Son was despised and spurned in His dispensation, so God the Holy Ghost is despised (as well as flattered), in this dispensation. BP. 37

. . . the essential nature of one Person of the Trinity is the essential nature of the other Persons of the Trinity. If we understand God the Holy Ghost, we shall understand God the Son and God the Father; therefore the first thing for us to do is to receive the Holy Ghost. BP. 213

Every Christian knows Jesus Christ *as God*, not as the equivalent of God; the call to proclaim Him to others means that I see Him and know Him as God. There is no God that is not Father, Son and Holy Ghost—the Triune aspect of one God, from all Eternity to all Eternity. GW. 30

Our conception of the Trinity is an attempt of the human mind to define how God manifested Himself. HGM. 96

The term 'Trinity' is not a Bible word, but a term that arose in the throes of a great conflict of minds, and is the crystallised attempt to state the Godhead in a word. PR. 130

Things go by threes in the Bible: Father, Son and Holy Ghost; God, Church, converts; husband, wife, children. It is God's order, not man's. Whenever one of the three is missing, there is something wrong. RTR. 59

The doctrine of the Trinity is not a Christian revelation, it is an attempt on the part of the mind of man to expound the Christian revelation, which is that there is only one God to the Christian, and His name is Jesus Christ. SA. 69

TRUST

There are great perplexities in life, but thank God, if we will trust, with the bold, implicit trust of our natural life, in the Son of God, He will bring out His perfect, complete purposes in and through our particular lives.
CD. VOL. 1, 149

If we would learn on the threshold of our life with God to put away as impertinent, and even iniquitous, the debates as to whether or not we will trust God, we would not remain under the delusions we do; we would abandon without the slightest hesitation, cut the shore lines, burn our bridges behind us, and realize that what has happened is the positive miracle of the Redemption at work—we know with a knowledge which passeth knowledge. GW. 8

Whenever I say 'I want to reason this thing out before I can trust', I will never trust. The reasoning out and the perfection of knowledge come after the response to God has been made. GW. 8

It is not our trust that keeps us, but the God in whom we trust who keeps us. We are always in danger of trusting in our trust, believing our belief, having faith in our faith. All these things can be shaken; we have to base our faith on those things which cannot be shaken. HG. 28

Trustfulness is based on confidence in God whose ways I do not understand; if I did, there would be no need for trust. HGM. 52

"Though He slay me, yet will I trust Him." That is the most sublime utterance of faith in the Old Testament. MFL. 87

We have to stake ourselves on the truthfulness of God's character; what He does with us is a matter of indifference. NKW. 64

Beware of trusting in your trust and see that you trust in the Lord, and you will never know you trust Him because you are taken up into His certainty. NKW. 64

We put our trust in God up to a certain point, then we say, 'Now I must do my best.' There are times when there is no human best to be done, when the Divine best must be left to work, and God expects those of us who know Him to be confident in His ability and power. PH. 40

The bravery of God in trusting us! It is a tremendously risky thing to do, it looks as if all the odds were against Him. The majority of us don't bother much about

Him, and yet He deliberately stakes all He has on us, He stands by and lets the world, the flesh and the devil do their worst, confident we will come out all right. PH. 180

There is nothing so secure as the salvation of God; it is as eternal as the mountains, and it is our trust in God that brings us the conscious realization of this. RTR. 58

If a man will resign himself in implicit trust to the Lord Jesus, he will find that He leads the wayfaring soul into the green pastures and beside the still waters, so that even when he goes through the dark valley of the shadow of some staggering episode, he will fear no evil. Nothing in life or death, time or eternity, can stagger a soul from the certainty of the Way, for one moment. RTR. 71

To trust in the Lord is to be foolish enough to know that if we fulfil God's commands, He will look after everything. RTR. 75

If I put my trust in human beings first, I will end in despairing of everyone; I will become bitter, because I have insisted on man being what no man ever can be—absolutely right. Never trust anything but the grace of God in yourself or in anyone else. RTR. 91

There are times when God cannot lift the darkness, but trust Him. Jesus said God will appear at times like an unkind friend, but He is not; He will appear like an unnatural father, but He is not; He will appear like an unjust judge, but He is not. The time will come when everything will be explained. SSM. 84

Never trust the best man or woman you ever met; trust the Lord Jesus only. SSM. 107

TRUTH

The Bible does not reveal all truth, we have to find out scientific truth and common-sense truth for ourselves, but knowledge of the Truth, our Lord Himself, is only possible through the reception of the Holy Spirit. BE. 123

Spiritual truth is discernible only to a pure heart, not to a keen intellect. It is not a question of profundity of intellect, but of purity of heart. BSG. 42

The one great Truth to keep stedfastly before us is the Lord Jesus Christ; He is the Truth. Only the whole truth is The Truth, any part of the truth may become an error. If you have a ray of light on The Truth never call it the whole truth; follow it up and it will lead you to the central Truth, the Lord Jesus Christ. BSG. 69

Truth is not a system, not a constitution, nor even a creed; the Truth is the Lord Jesus Christ Himself, and He is the Truth about the Father just as He is the Way of the Father. CD. VOL. 1, 138

Our tendency is to make truth a logical statement, to make it a principle instead of a Person. Profoundly speaking there are no Christian principles, but the saint by abiding in Christ in the Way of the Fatherhood of God discerns the Truth of God in the passing moments. Confusion arises when we disassociate ourselves from our Lord and try to live up to a standard merely constructed on His word. CD. VOL. 1, 138

Would that men who name the Name of Christ realised that He *is* the Truth, not the proclaimer of it; that He *is* the Gospel, not the preacher of the Gospel; that He *is* the Way of the Fatherhood of God. CD. VOL. 1, 138

Truth is not in a particular statement; Truth is a Person, "I am the Truth." CHI. 46

If a man is talking the truth of God those who listen will meet it again whether they like it or not; if he is not talking God's truth they won't come across it any more. CHI. 48

Truth is a Person, not a proposition; if I pin my faith to a logical creed I will be disloyal to the Lord Jesus. DI. 2

Every partial truth has so much error in it that you can dispute it, but you can't dispute 'truth as it is in Jesus.' DI. 3

You can't unveil Truth when you like; when the unveiling comes, beware. That moment marks your going back or your going on. DI. 3

Truth is of the implicit order, you can't define Truth, and yet every man is so constituted that at times his longing for Truth is insatiable. It is not sufficient to remain with a longing for Truth, because there is something at the basis of things which drives a man to the Truth if he is honest. DI. 3

The test of God's truth is that it fits you exactly; if it does not, question whether it is His truth. DI. 7

No man is ever the same after listening to the truth, he may say he pays no attention to it, he may appear to forget all about it, but at any moment the truth may spring up into his consciousness and destroy all his peace of mind. DI. 44

Beware of making God's truth simpler than He has made it Himself. DI. 49

Much is written about our Lord speaking so simply that anyone could understand, and we forget that while it remains true that the common people heard Him gladly, no one, not even His own disciples, understood Him until after the Resurrection and the coming of the Holy Spirit, the reason being that a pure heart is the essential requirement for being 'of the truth'. GW. 34

With God a thing is never too good to be true; it is too good not to be true. HG. 34

The right attitude to the truth is, 'Lord, Thou knowest'; otherwise we shall find to our cost that what Jesus said about the human heart is true. HGM. 40

Spiritual truth is never discerned by intellect, only by moral obedience. HGM. 78

The Truth is our Lord Himself, consequently any part of the truth may be a lie unless it leads to a relation to *the* Truth. Salvation, sanctification, the Second Coming are all parts of the Truth, but none is the Truth; and they are only parts of the Truth as they are absorbed by the Truth, our Lord Himself. IWP. 10

We are not told to expound the way of salvation, or to teach sanctification, but to lift up Jesus, i.e. to proclaim the truth. IWP. 10

We ought to give much more time than we do—a great deal more time than we do—to brooding on the fundamental truths on which the Spirit of God works the simplicity of our Christian experience. The fundamental truths are—Redemption and the personal presence of the Holy Ghost, and these two are focused in one mighty Personality, the Lord Jesus Christ. IYA. 21

You cannot make a man see moral truth by persuading his intellect. 'When He, the Spirit of truth, is come, He shall guide you into all the truth.' LG. 107

The only way to prove spiritual truth is by experiment. MFL. 19

If for one moment, we have discerned the truth, we can never be the same again; we may ignore it, or forget it, but it will not forget us. Truth once discerned goes down into the subconscious mind, but it will jump up in a most awkward way when we least expect it. MFL. 20

The truth of God is only revealed to us by obedience. MFL. 29

The only way in which a truth can become of vital interest to me is when I am brought into the place where that truth is needed. MFL. 98

Food is not health, and truth is not holiness. Food has to be assimilated by a properly organised system before the result is health, and truth must be assimilated by the child of God before it can be manifested as holiness. We may be looking at the right doctrines and yet not assimilating the truths which the doctrines reveal. Beware of making a doctrinal statement of truth *the* truth—"I am . . . the Truth," said Jesus. Doctrinal statement is our expression of that vital connection with Him. OBH. 79

It takes a long while for us to begin to see that Jesus Christ is The Truth. Truths exist that have no meaning for us until we get into the domain of their power. PH. 102

Jesus does not take men and say—'This is the truth and if you don't believe it you will be damned.' He simply shows us the truth—"I am the Truth," and leaves us alone. PH. 102

We see saints hard and metallic because they have become loyal to a phase of truth, instead of remembering that Jesus does not send His disciples out to advocate certain phases of truth, but to feed His sheep and tend His lambs. The inspired loyalty is to Jesus Himself. PH. 161

It is a great emancipation in a man's life when he learns that spiritual and moral truths can only be gained by obedience, never by intellectual curiosity. All God's revelations are sealed, and they will never be opened by philosophy, or by thinking; whereas the tiniest fragment of obedience will bring a man right through into the secret of God's attitude to things. PH. 219

Truth is not discerned intellectually, it is discerned spiritually. PR. 116

Beware of paddling in the ocean of God's truth, when you should be out in it, swimming. RTR. 42

To understand the tiniest bit of truth about God is to love it with all our heart and soul and mind; all that lies dark and obscure just now, is one day going to be as clear, as radiantly and joyously clear, as the bit we have seen. RTR. 78

If you only take your own ideas, you will never know the truth. The whole truth is the only truth, and the whole truth is Jesus Christ—"I am the Truth". Any bit of truth is an error if taken alone. RTR. 87

Personal relationship brings us to the truth, and it is truth that relates a man personally to God. SHH. 65

Truth is never a matter of intellect first, but of moral obedience. The great secret of intellectual progress is curiosity, but curiosity in moral matters is an abomination. SHH. 88

There is no one in the world more easy to get to than God. Only one thing prevents us from getting there, and that is the refusal to tell ourselves the truth. SHL. 76

If you talk truth that is vital to yourself you will never talk over anyone's head. See that you sow the real seed of the Word of God, and then leave it alone. SHL. 115

A truth may be of no use to you just now, but when the circumstances arise in which that truth is needed, the Holy Spirit will bring it back to your remembrance. SSM. 13

A man may say wonderfully truthful things, but his thinking is what tells. It is possible to say truthful things in a truthful manner and to tell a lie in thinking. SSM. 42

There are some truths that God will not make simple. The only thing God makes plain in the Bible is the way of salvation and sanctification, after that our understanding depends entirely on our walking in the light. SSM. 82

U

UNDERSTANDING

The unexplained things in life are more than the explained. God seems careless as to whether men understand Him or not; He scarcely vindicates His saints to men. CD. VOL. 1, 63

You cannot understand Jesus Christ unless you accept the New Testament revelation of Him, you must be biased for Him before you can understand Him. DI. 2

Half the misery in the world comes because one person demands of another a complete understanding, which is absolutely impossible. MFL. 63

It is of God's infinite mercy that we do not understand what He says until we are in a fit condition. If God came down with His light and power, we should be witless; but our Lord never enthrals us. PH. 113

Understanding comes only by obedience, never by intellect. PH. 219

It is leaning to our own understanding that keeps the bridges behind. SHH. 92

The secret of all spiritual understanding is to walk in the light, not the light of our convictions, or of our theories, but the light of God. SSM. 22

UNITY

. . . the characteristics of man's union with God are faith in God and love for Him. This union was the first thing Satan aimed at in Adam and Eve, and he did it by perverting what God had said. BP. 20

Beware of the craze for unity. It is God's will that all Christians should be one with Him as Jesus Christ is one with Him, but that is a very different thing from the tendency abroad to-day towards a unity on a basis that ignores the Atonement. DI. 56

UNIVERSALISM

"It is finished," and in the Cross of Jesus Christ all men are condemned to salvation. That is very different from what is called Universalism. The redemption is of universal application, but human responsibility is not done away with. Universalism looks like a Christian flower, but it has not its roots in the Christian faith. Jesus Christ is most emphatic on the fact that there are possibilities of eternal damnation for the man who positively neglects or positively rejects His redemption. PH. 202

There is no warrant in the Bible for the modern speculation of a second chance after death. There may be a second chance. There may be numbers of interesting things—but it is not taught in the Bible. The stage between birth and death is the probation stage. SHH. 65

367

Death transforms nothing. Every view of death outside the Bible view concludes that death is a great transformer. The Bible says that death is a confirmer. Instead of death being the introduction to a second chance, it is the confirmation of the first chance. SHH. 142

USEFULNESS

God's main concern is that we are more interested in Him than in work for Him. Once you are rooted and grounded in Christ the greatest thing you can do is to *be*. Don't try and be useful; be yourself and God will use you to further His ends. AUG. 86

Neither usefulness nor duty is God's ultimate purpose, His aim is to bring out the message of the Gospel, and if that can only be done by His 'bruising' me, why shouldn't He? DI. 36

Your dead-set determination to be of use never means half so much as the times you have not been thinking of being used—a casual conversation, an ordinary word, while your life was "hid with Christ in God". DI. 86

Stop the concern of whether you are of any use in the world. "He that believeth in me," said Jesus, "out of him shall flow rivers of living water"; whether we see it or not is a matter of indifference. Heed the Source. HG. 96

It is a great thing to watch with God rather than put God to the trouble of watching me in case I burn myself. We tax the whole arrangement of heaven to watch us, while God wants us to come and watch with Him, to be so identified with Him that we are not causing Him any trouble, but giving Him perfect delight because He can use us now instead of taxing some other servants of heaven to look after us. IYA. 90

The true character of the loveliness that tells for God is always unconscious. Conscious influence is priggish and un-Christian. When we begin to wonder whether we are of any use, we instantly lose the bloom of the touch of the Lord. Jesus says—'He that believeth in Me, out of him shall flow rivers of living water.' If we begin to examine the outflow, we lose touch with the Source. We have to pay attention to the Source and God will look after the outflow. LG. 38

Whenever we think we are of use to God, we hinder Him. We have to form the habit of letting God carry on His work through us without let or hindrance as He did through Jesus, and He will use us in ways He dare not let us see. We have to efface every other thought but that of Jesus Christ. It is not done once for all; we have to be always doing it. MFL. 107

If once you have seen that Jesus Christ is All in all, make the habit of letting Him be All in all. It will mean that you not only have implicit faith that He is All in all, but that you go through the trial of your faith and prove that He is. After sanctification God delights to put us into places where He can make us wealthy. Jesus Christ counts as service not what we do for Him, but what we are to Him, and the inner secret of that is identity with Him in person. *"That I may know Him."* MFL. 107

"Be ye therefore perfect, even as your Father which is in heaven is perfect." When once the truth lays hold of us that we have to be God-like, it is the death-blow for ever to attempting things in our own strength. The reason we do attempt things in our own strength is that we have never had the vision of what Jesus Christ wants us to be. We have to be God-like, not good men and women. There are any number of good men and women who are not Christians. MFL. 110

The only place to prosecute our life in Christ is just where we are, in the din of things, and the only way in which we can prosecute our life in Christ is to remember that it is God Who engineers circumstances, and that the only place where we can be of use to Him is where we are, not where we are not. God is in the obvious things. OBH. 113

If you want to be of use to God, get rightly related to Jesus Christ and He will make you of use unconsciously every minute you live. RTR. 47

Never be deluded into making this statement: "I am here because I am so useful", say rather "I am here because God wants me here". The one lodestar of the saint is God Himself, not estimated usefulness. RTR. 54

God does not do anything with us, only *through* us. RTR. 64

If you want to be of use, get rightly related to Jesus Christ and He will make you of use unconsciously every moment you live; the condition is believing on Him. SSM. 71

We have to learn not only how useless we are, but how marvellously mighty God is. 'Many are called, but few prove the choice ones.' SSY. 31

. . . our Lord speaks about the joy of finding lost things, and . . . there is always this appeal: the Lord wants my eyes to look through; is He looking through them? The Lord wants my brain to think through; is He thinking through it? The Lord wants my hands to work with; is He working with them? The Lord wants my body to live and walk in for one purpose—to go after the lost from His standpoint; am I letting Him walk and live in me? WG. 26

V

VENGEANCE

Vengeance is the most deeply rooted passion in the human soul, and the impersonation of it is the devil. BP. 117

. . . the man who loses his temper quickest is the one who finds it quickest. The man you need to beware of is not the man who flares up, but the man who smoulders, who is vindictive and harbours vengeance. SHH. 136

VICTORY

Wherever you make the Most High your habitation, just there you will have victory. RTR. 50

If you once allow the victory of a wrong thing in you, it is a long way back again to get readjusted. RTR. 52

VIRTUE

"All my fresh springs are in Thee." Notice how God will wither up every other spring you have. He will wither up your natural virtues, He will break up confidence in your natural powers, He will wither up your confidence in brain and spirit and body, until you learn by practical experience that you have no right to draw your life from any source other than the tremendous reservoir of the resurrection life of Jesus Christ. BP. 41

Our Lord never patches up our natural virtues, He replaces the whole man from within, until the new man is shown in the new manners. God does not give new manners; we make our own, but we have to make them out of the new life. BP. 41

Our natural virtues are our deepest inheritance, but when the miracle of new birth is experienced, the first thing that happens is the corruption of those virtues because they can never come anywhere near what God demands. Jesus Christ loved moral beauty, but He never said it would do. The natural virtues are a delight to God because He designed them, they are fine and noble, but behind them is a disposition which may cause a man's morality to go by the board. CHI. 22

Never run away with the idea that Satan is sceptical of all virtue, he knows God too well and human nature too well to have such a shallow scepticism; he is sceptical only of virtue that has not been tried. Faith un-tried is simply a promise and a possibility, which we may cause to fail; tried faith is the pure gold. Faith must be tried, otherwise it is of no worth to God. CHI. 112

The natural virtues in some people are charming and delightful, but let a presentation of truth be given they have not seen before, and there is an exhibition of the most extraordinary resentment, proving that all their piety was purely temperamental, an unexplored inheritance from ancestors. DI. 32

370

To cling to my natural virtues is quite sufficient to obscure the work of God in me. DI. 32

God wants to get us out of the love of virtue and in love with the God of virtue—stripped of all possessions but our knowledge of Him. IWP. 78

Physically, we are healthy according to our power of fight on the inside; morally, we are virtuous according to our moral calibre—virtue is always acquired; and spiritually, if we are drawing on the resurrection life of Jesus, spiritual stamina comes as we learn to 'score off' the things that come against us, and in this way we produce a holy character. LG. 90

It is a deep instruction to watch how natural virtues break down. The Holy Spirit does not patch up our natural virtues, for the simple reason that no natural virtue can come anywhere near Jesus Christ's demands. God does not build up our natural virtues and transfigure them, He totally recreates us on the inside. "And every virtue we possess is His alone." As we bring every bit of our nature into harmony with the new life which God puts in, what will be exhibited in us will be the virtues that were characteristic of the Lord Jesus, not our natural virtues. The supernatural is made natural. The life that God plants in us develops its own virtues, not the virtues of Adam but of Jesus Christ, and Jesus Christ can never be described in terms of the natural virtues. OBH. 98

A virtuous man or a pure woman is a tremendous assistance wherever he or she goes. PH. 80

When the Spirit of God comes into a man the first thing that happens is the corruption of the natural virtues. Natural virtues are remnants of the human race as God designed it; when a man is born again his natural virtues begin to crumble, and he is plunged into perplexity. Natural good has to die in me before the best can come. That is the keynote of spiritual reality. It is not the bad that is the enemy of God, but the good that is not good enough. PH. 101

At the first we have the idea that everything apart from Christ is bad; but there is much in our former life that is fascinating, any amount of paganism that is clear and vigorous, virtues that are good morally. But we have to discover they are not stamped with the right image and superscription, and if we are going to live the life of a saint we must go to the moral death of those things, make a termination of them, turn these good natural things into the spiritual. PH. 159

Natural virtues are beautiful in the sight of Jesus, but He knows as none other could know, that they are not promises of what man is going to be, but remnants, 'trailing clouds of glory,' left in man, and are not of the slightest atom of practical use to him. PS. 69

No man is born virtuous, virtue and purity are the outcome of fight; innocence is natural. Man has to have enough moral muscle in him to fight against the thing that wants to make him immoral; immediately he fights, he becomes virtuous in that particular. It is a difficult thing to fight for virtue. Virtue for a man, purity for a woman, and innocence for a child, is God's order. SA. 78

. . . everything that does not partake of the nature of virtue is the enemy of virtue in me, and it depends on what moral calibre I have as to whether I overcome and produce virtue. SA. 93

Virtue is acquired, and so is purity. Everything that is not virtuous tries to make me immoral. SA. 94

VISION

We are inclined to be ashamed of the vision we get because it marks us out as being different from other people, and we are afraid of being considered 'speckled birds'. The vision will mark you out as different, but if you take your direction from the vision, you will not only make a straight path for yourself but for others also. GW. 133

The vision of the agnostic, the socialist, the imperialist, or the Christian is the same; they all see the thing that is right—a time of peace on earth, a state of goodwill and liberty at present inconceivable. There is nothing wrong with the vision, and there is no difference in the vision, because its source is the Spirit of God. The thing to be criticized is not the vision, but the way in which the vision is to be realized. HGM. 31

The way we get demented, off our balance, is by dreaming of what is yet to be—the Utopian vision of the grand state of society when all men are going to be brothers. It is not the vision that is wrong, it is right, what is wrong is the way men are trying to bring it about, and if they don't look to Jesus Christ they easily get unbalanced. HGM. 84

Soak and soak and soak continually in the one great truth of which you have had a vision; take it to bed with you, sleep with it, rise up in the morning with it, continually bring your imagination into captivity to it, and slowly and surely as the months and years go by

God will make you one of His specialists in that particular truth. God is no respecter of persons. PS. 40

If when a clear emphatic vision of some truth is given you by God, not to your intellect but to your heart, and in spite of it all you decide to take another course, the vision will fade and may never come back. PS. 46

A man with the vision of God is not devoted simply to a cause or a particular issue, but to God Himself. SSY. 170

VOICE

To believe our Lord's consciousness about Himself commits us to accept Him as God's last endless Word. That does not mean that God is not still speaking, but it does mean that He is not saying anything different from "This is My beloved Son: hear Him." AUG. 105

There are voices that are not true to the character of Jesus Christ; the inspiration of these voices is not to glorify Jesus, but to glorify something which He does. Give time to heed the call of God. The voice of God never contradicts the character of God. GW. 134

We maintain our relationship to Jesus by the use of the means which He gives us, viz., His words. Some of us can only hear God in the thunder of revivals or in public worship; we have to learn to listen to God's voice in the ordinary circumstances of life. OBH. 121

To be brought within the zone of God's voice is to be profoundly altered. SSY. 10

VOWING

We make vows which are impossible of fulfilment because no man can remain master of himself always; there comes a time when the human will must yield allegiance to a force greater than itself, it must yield either to God or to the devil. GW. 132

The vices of vowing outweigh the virtues, because vowing is built on a misconception of human nature as it really is. If a man had the power to will pure will it would be different, but he has not. There are certain things a man cannot do, not because he is bad, but because he is not constituted to do them. GW. 132

'Don't vow; because if you make a vow, even in ordinary matters, and do not fulfil it, you are the worse for it.' To make a promise may simply be a way of shirking responsibility. Never pile up promises before men, and certainly not before God. It is better to run the risk of being considered indecisive, better to be uncertain and not promise, than to promise and not fulfil. GW. 132

Make no vows at . . . New Year time, but look to God and bank on the Reality of Jesus Christ. GW. 133

Jesus Christ bases the entrance to His Kingdom not on a man's vowing and making decisions, but on the realization of his inability to decide. Decisions for Christ fail because the bedrock of Christianity is ignored. It is not our vows before God that tell, but coming to God exactly as we are, in all our weakness, and being held and kept by Him. GW. 133

The Old Testament Scriptures always regard the oath as a peculiar sacrament. If you read what the Bible says about vowing you will see how culpably negligent we are in the way we promise. If we do not fulfil a promise, we damage our moral and spiritual life. It is infinitely better to refuse to promise anything, even in the most superficial relationships, than to promise and not perform. Spiritual leakages are accounted for in this way. Always do what you ought to do, but be careful of promising anything, because a promise puts the blood of God on your character. NKW. 110

Always beware of vowing, it is a risky thing. If you promise to do a thing and don't do it, it means the weakening of your moral nature. We are all so glib in the way we promise and don't perform and never realize that it is sapping our moral energy. RTR. 15

W

WAR

War is a conflict of wills, either in individuals or in nations, and just now there is a terrific conflict of wills in nations. If I cannot make my will by diplomacy bear on other people, then the last resort is war, and always will be until Jesus Christ brings in His Kingdom. CD. VOL. 1, 107

As sure as there is will *versus* will, there must be punch *versus* punch. LG. 29

"Is war of the devil or of God?" It is of neither. It is of man, though both God and the devil are behind it. SA. 55

. . . to call war either diabolical or Divine is nonsense; war is human. War is a conflict of wills, not something that can be solved by law or philosophy. If you take what I want, you may talk till all's blue, either I will hit you or you'll hit me. It is no use to arbitrate when you get below into the elemental. In the time between birth and death this conflict of wills will go on until men by their relationship to God receive the disposition of the Son of God, which is holiness. SHH. 28

WAY/TRUTH/LIFE

"*I* am the Way, the Truth, and the Life"—the Way in the waylessness of this wild universe; the Truth amidst all the contending confusions of man's thought and existence; the Life amidst all the living deaths that sap men's characters and their relationships and connections with the highest. BE. 112

Jesus Christ's way exalts everything about us, it exalts our bodies, exalts our flesh and blood relationships, exalts our homes, exalts our social standing, exalts all the inner part of our life, our mind and morals and mysticism, until we have at-one-ment with God in them all. BP. 177

Our Lord said, "*I am the way,*" not the way to any one or anything; He is not a road we leave behind us, He is the Way to the Father in which we abide. He *is* the Way, not He was the Way, and there is not any way of living in the Fatherhood of God except by living in Christ. 'Whoso findeth himself in Christ findeth life.' The Way to the Father is not by the law, nor by obedience, or creed, but Jesus Christ Himself, He is the Way of the Father whereby any and every soul may be in peace, in joy, and in divine courage. . . . CD. VOL. 1, 137

Jesus Christ not only has dominion now, but in the ages to come. God never says to man 'You must'; He says, 'You will ultimately come there.' We may come in the right way or by breaking our neck, but we will come, not by compulsion but by absolute agreement that Jesus Christ alone is The Way. HGM. 96

Men defy, but they cannot frustrate, and in the end they come to see that Jesus Christ's is the only way. IWP. 127

We have to acquaint ourselves with the way we have to go and beware of the tendency of asking the way when we know it perfectly well. OBH. 51

We want to get at truth by 'short cuts'; the wonder is our Lord's amazing patience. He never insists that we take His way; He simply says—"I am the Way." We might as well learn to take His way at the beginning, but we won't, we are determined on our own way. PH. 102

Jesus Christ is not the way to God, not a road we leave behind us, a fingerpost that points in the right direction; He is the way itself. PR. 137

However far we may drift, we must always come back to these words of our Lord: 'I am the way'—not a road that we leave behind us, but the way itself. Jesus Christ is the way *of God*, not a way that leads to God; that is why He says— 'Come unto *me*'; 'abide in *me*'. 'I am the truth', not the truth about God, not a set of principles, but the truth itself. Jesus Christ is the Truth *of God*. 'No man cometh unto the Father, but by me.' We can get to God as Creator in other ways, but no man can come to God as Father in any other way than by Jesus Christ. 'I am the life.' Jesus Christ is the Life *of God* as He is the Way and the Truth of God. Eternal life is not a gift *from* God, it is the gift of *God Himself*. The life imparted to me by Jesus is the life of God. 'He that hath the Son hath the life;' 'I am come that they might have life;' 'And this is life eternal, that they should know thee the only true God.' We have to abide in the *way*; to be incorporated into the *truth*; to be infused by the *life*. SSY. 92

The Master says He is the Way; then abide in Him. He says He is the Truth; then believe in Him. He says He is the Life; then live on Him. SSY. 131

WEALTH

Earthly inheritances are particular possessions of our own, and in taking them we may impoverish others; but the marvellous thing about spiritual wealth is that when we take our part in that, everyone else is blessed; whereas if we refuse to be partakers, we hinder others from entering into the riches of God. OBH. 86

When God is beginning to be satisfied with us, He impoverishes every source of fictitious wealth. After sanctification God will wither up every other spring until we know that all our fresh springs are in Him. He will wither up natural virtues; He will break up all confidence in our own powers until we learn by practical experience that we have no right to draw our life from any other source than the tremendous reservoir of the unsearchable riches of Jesus Christ. OBH. 88

If you turn away from the Source and look at the outflow, at what God is doing through you, the Source will dry up and you will sit down on the outskirts of the entrance and howl—It is dreadfully hard to live the Christian life! Turn round and enter into the kingdom, pay attention to the Source, Our Lord Himself, and you will experience the hilarity of knowing that you see God. Never be surprised at what God does, but be so taken up with Him that He may continue to do surprising things through you. OBH. 89

It is the trial of our faith that makes us wealthy in God's sight. PH. 73

God delights to put me in a place where He can make me wealthy. "Follow Me, and thou shalt have treasure in heaven." RTR. 23

It is the *trial* of your faith that makes you wealthy, and it works in this way: every time you venture out on the life of faith, you will come across something in your actual life which seems to contradict absolutely what your faith in God says you should believe. Go through the trial of faith and lay up your confidence in God, not in your common-sense, and you will gain so much wealth in your heavenly banking account, and the more you go through the trial of faith the wealthier you will become in the heavenly regions, until you go through difficulties smilingly and men wonder where your wealth of trust comes from. SSM. 62

WILL

We have no choice about being born into the world, but to be born again, if we will but come to Jesus and receive His Spirit, is within our own power. This is true all along in the Christian life, you can be renewed in the spirit of your mind when you choose, you can revive your mind on any line you like by sheer force of will. BE. 40

A human soul can withstand the devil successfully, and it can also withstand God successfully. This self-living power is the essence of the human spirit, which is as immortal as God's Spirit and as indestructible; whether the human spirit be good or bad, it is as immortal as God. This power of the soul enables it to put itself on a par with God; this is the very essence of Satan. BP. 58

When the Spirit of God comes into a man, He brings His own generating will power and causes him to will with God, and we have the amazing revelation that the saint's free choices are the pre-determinations of God. That is a most wonderful thing in Christian psychology, viz., that a saint chooses exactly what God pre-determined he should choose. If you have never received the Spirit of God this will be one of the things which is 'foolishness' to you; but if you have received the Spirit and are obeying Him, you find He brings your spirit into complete harmony with God and the sound of your goings and the sound of God's goings are one and the same. BP. 215

The first fundamental characteristic of the mighty nature of God is will; consequently when God's Spirit comes into our spirit, we can will to do what God wants us to do. "For it is God which worketh in you both to will and to do of His good pleasure." BP. 216

Will is not a faculty. We talk of a person having a weak will, or a strong will; that is misleading. 'Will' means the whole nature active, and when we are energized by the Spirit of God, we are enabled to do what we could not do before; that is, we are able to obey God. BP. 217

You will find the supreme crisis in your life is 'will-issues' all the time. *Will* I relinquish? *Will* I abandon? It is not that God won't make us fit, it is that He cannot. CD. VOL. 1, 135

God cannot make us fit to meet Him in the air unless we are willing to let Him. He cannot make us fit as the dwellings of His Son unless we are willing, because He wants sons and daughters. If you are up against a crisis, go through with it, relinquish all, and let Him make you fit for all He requires of you in this day. CD. VOL. 1, 135

Let me stake my all, blindly, as far as feelings are concerned, on the Reality of the Redemption, and before long that Reality will begin to tell in my actual life, which will be the evidence that the transaction has taken place. But there must be the deliberate surrender of will, not a surrender to the persuasive power of a personality, but a deliberate launching forth on God and what He says. Remember, you must urge the will to an issue; you must come to the point where you *will* to believe the Redeemer, and deliberately wash your hands of the consequences. CHI. 29

It is never our wicked heart that is the difficulty, but our obstinate will. DI. 31

"If any man would come after Me, let him deny himself," i.e., 'deny his right to himself'. Jesus never swept men off their feet in ecstasy, He always talked on the line that left a man's will in the ascendant until he saw where he was going. It is impossible for a man to give up his right to himself without knowing he is doing it. DI. 34

Is Jesus Christ absolutely necessary to me? Have I ever shifted the basis of my reasoning on to Incarnate Reason? ever shifted my will on to His will? my right to myself on to His right to me? DI. 35

We are at liberty to stop short at any point, and our Lord will never cast it up at us; but think what we shall feel like when we see Him if all the 'thank you' we gave Him for His unspeakable salvation was an obstinate determination to serve Him in our own way, not His. HG. 11

Be yourself exactly before God, and present your problems, the things you know you have come to your wits' end about. Ask what you *will*, and Jesus

Christ says your prayers will be answered. We can always tell whether our will is in what we ask by the way we live when we are not praying. IYA. 13

"If ye abide in Me, and My words abide in you, ye shall ask what ye *will*," i.e., what your will is in. There is very little our wills are in, consequently it is easy to work up false emotions. IYA. 13

Beware of praising Jesus Christ whilst all the time you cunningly refuse to let the Spirit of God work His salvation efficaciously in your life. Remember, the battle is in the will; whenever we say 'I can't', or whenever we are indifferent, it means 'I won't'. It is better to let Jesus Christ uncover the obstinacy. If there is one point where we say 'I won't' then we shall never know His salvation. LG. 143

Will is the essential element in God's creation of a man. I cannot *give up* my will: I must exercise it. MFL. 9

Will is the whole effort of a man consciously awake with the definite end of unity in view, which means that body, soul and spirit are in absolute harmony. MFL. 29

Will is the very essence of personality, and in the Bible will is always associated with intelligence and knowledge and desire. The will of a saint is not to be spent in dissipation in spiritual luxuries, but in concentration upon God. MFL. 31

God allows ample room for man and the devil to do their worst; He allows the combination of other wills to work out to the last lap of exhaustion so that that way need never be tried again, and men will have to confess, either reluctantly or willingly, that God's purpose was right after all. NKW. 56

We are potentially sons and daughters of God through God's claim upon us in Christ, but we are only sons and daughters of God *in reality* through our will. OBH. 27

It is one thing to realise in speechless wonder, when the heart is attuned to an impulse of worship, what the claim of God is, and another thing to tell God that we want Him to realise His claim in us. OBH. 27

When we are rightly related to God we have uncovered to us for the first time the power of our own wills. Our wills are infirm through sin, but when we are sanctified there is revealed to us the pure pristine will-power with which God created us, and which the Holy Ghost calls into action. Then we have to submit our will to Jesus as He submitted His will to His Father. OBH. 81

We are to have only one aim in life, and that is that the Son of God may be manifested; then all dictation to God will vanish. Our Lord never dictated to His Father, and we are not to dictate to God; we are to submit our wills to Him so that He works through us what He wants. OBH. 83

Will is the essential element in the creation of man; sin is a perverse disposition that has entered into man. The profound thing in man is his will, not sin. OBH. 129

If I am a child of God, I realize not only that God is the source of my will, but that God is *in* me to will. I do not bring an opposed will to God's will, God's will *is* my will, and my natural choices are along the line of His will. Then I begin

to understand that God engineers circumstances for me to do His will in them, not for me to lie down under them and give way to self-pity. OBH. 130

Will is the whole man active, and the whole active power and force of the saint is to be laid at the feet of Jesus Christ. We busy ourselves with work for Him while He waits for all our individual energy to be curbed and submitted to Him that He may re-direct it into the channels He wants. PH. 89

Will is 'me' active, not one bit of me but the whole of me. Self-will is best described as the whole of myself active around my own point of view. PH. 158

If I am going to maintain the honour of a saint, I have deliberately to go to the death of my self-will. PH. 161

We are slandering God if we sympathise with the wilfulness of a person and think how difficult God makes it for him. It is never hard to get to God unless our wilfulness makes it hard. PR. 113

There is a philosophy which says that if a man wills it, he need never die; but he cannot will it! There is a limit to will; no man can will pure will. SHH. 38

Whenever our spiritual life is unsatisfactory it is because we have said to God—"I won't." SHH. 92

Will is the whole man active; there are terrific forces in the will. SSM. 85

WISDOM

The wisdom of God is shown in that Jesus Christ is 'made unto us righteousness, . . .' GW. 45

The Holy Ghost cannot delight in our wisdom; it is the wisdom of God He delights in. IYA. 64

It is never wise to be cocksure. SA. 48

The Wisdom of the Hebrews is based on an accepted belief in God; that is, it does not try to find out whether or not God exists, all its beliefs are based on God, and in the actual whirl of things as they are, all its mental energy is bent on practical living. The Wisdom of the Greeks, which is the wisdom of our day, is speculative; that is, it is concerned with the origin of things, with the riddle of the universe, etc., consequently the best of our wits is not given to practical living. SHH. 1

The amazing simplicity of the nature of God is foolish judged by human wisdom; but 'the foolishness of God is wiser than men'. SSY. 146

WONDER

To lose wonder is to lose the true element of religion. HG. 33

Whenever you give a trite testimony the wonder is gone. The only evidence of salvation or sanctification is that the sense of wonder is developing, not at things as they are, but at the One who made them as they are. HGM. 143

We are too free from wonder nowadays, too easy with the Word of God; we do not use it with the breathless amazement Paul does. Think what sanctification means—*Christ in me; made like Christ; as He is, so are we.* OBH. 28

Spiritually beware of anything that takes the wonder out of life and makes you take a prosaic attitude; when you lose wonder, you lose life. PH. 186

'Now that I am saved and sanctified, God will surely turn the world upside down and prove what a wonderful thing He has done in me—every unsaved soul will be saved, every devil-possessed man delivered, and every sick person healed'! 'You will easily get Your Kingship of men if You will use signs and wonders and stagger men's wits,' said Satan to our Lord, and the same temptation comes to the Church and to individual Christians, His brethren. PR. 67

WORDS

The greatest insult you can offer God is pious talk unless it is backed up by holy actions. BE. 35

The Bible says that words are born in the heart, not in the head. BP. 125

. . . the mainspring of the heart of Jesus Christ was the mainspring of the heart of God the Father, consequently the words Jesus Christ spoke were the exact expression of God's thought. In our Lord the tongue was in its right place; He never spoke from His head, but always from His heart. BP. 126

The words of the Bible express the inner soul; the words we use to-day are nearly all technical, borrowed from somewhere else, and our most modern words do not express the spirit at all, but cunningly cloak it over and give no expression. BP. 246

Words are full of revelation when we do not simply recall or memorize them but receive them. Receive these words from Jesus—'Father,' 'heaven,' 'Hallowed be Thy Name,' 'kingdom,' 'will,' there is all the vocabulary of the Deity and Dominion and Disposition of Almighty God in relation to men in these words. Or take the words—'bread,' 'forgiveness,' 'debts,' 'temptation,' 'deliverance,' 'evil,' in these words the primary psychological colours which portray the perplexing puzzles and problems of personal life, are all spelled out before our Father.

Or, lastly, look at such words as 'power,' 'glory,' for ever, 'Amen,'—in them there sounds the transcendant triumphant truth that all is well, that God reigns and rules and rejoices, and His joy is our strength. CD. VOL. 2, 26

Don't be discouraged if you suffer from physical aphasia, the only cure for it is to go ahead, remembering that nervousness overcome is power. DI. 48

Jesus was killed for His words, He would not have been crucified if He had kept quiet. HG. 35

God never fits His word to suit me; He fits me to suit His word. NKW. 118

To take God at His word may mean expecting God to come up to my standard; whereas true faith does not so much take God at His word as take the word of God as it is, in the face of all difficulties, an act upon it, with no attempt to explain or expound it. NKW. 120

If we are Christians that is where the word of God is—in our hearts. OBH. 68

The word is "not in heaven . . . neither is it beyond the sea . . . but the word is very nigh unto thee, in thy mouth, and in thy heart, that thou mayest do it." (Deuteronomy xxx. 12–13.) If we are Christians that is where the word of God is—in our hearts. OBH. 68

It is not the length of time we give to a thing that matters, but whether the time we give opens the door to the greatest power in our life. The greatest factor in life is that which exerts most power, not the element which takes most time. The five minutes we give to the words of Jesus the first thing in the morning are worth more than all the rest of the day. OBH. 121

The Spirit of God has the habit of taking the words of Jesus out of their scriptural setting and putting them into the setting of our personal lives. OBH. 121

The fanatic hears only the word of God that comes through the Bible. The word of God comes through the history of the world, through the Christian Church, and through Nature. We have to learn to live by every word of God, and it takes time. If we try to listen to all the words of God at once, we become surfeited. PH. 35

The Bible never glorifies our natural conception of things; it does not use the words 'rest' and 'joy' and 'peace' as we use them, and our common-sense interpretation of words must be keyed up to the way God uses them, otherwise we lose the 'humour' of God. PH. 39

Morally and spiritually we live, as it were, in sections, and the door from one section to another is by means of words, and until we say the right word the door will not open. PH. 209

The door into a moral or spiritual emancipation which you wish to enter is a word. Immediately you are prepared to abandon your reserve and say the word, the door opens and in rushes the Godward side of things and you are lifted on to another platform immediately. "Speech maketh a full man." PH. 210

I like to listen to this talk about Jesus Christ, but don't put your finger on the thing that upsets my mind. Why should

I bother with a standard of things that upset me? SA. 95

So the administering of the word is not ministering it where we think it is needed; the word has to be sown in living touch with the Lord of the harvest, sown in touch with Him in solitude and prayer, and He will bring the folks round—black and white, educated and uneducated, rich and poor. They are all there, 'white already to harvest', but most of us are so keen on our own notions that we do not recognize that they are ripe for reaping. If we are in touch with Jesus Christ, He says all the time—This is the moment; this one here, that one there, is ready to be reaped. We say—'Oh, but I want to go and get scores of heathen saved, I do not want to be the means of reaping my brother'; but your brother happens to be the one who is white to harvest. The commission is to teach, to disciple—that is, to administer the word. SSY. 139

WORK

The only way to keep true to God is by a steady persistent refusal to be interested in Christian work and to be interested alone in Jesus Christ. AUG. 64

The appeal made in Christian work nowadays is that we must keep ourselves fit for our work, we must not; we must be in the hands of God for God to do exactly what He likes with us, and that means disentanglement from everything that would hinder His purpose. If you want to remain a full-orbed grape you must keep out of God's hands for He will crush you, wine cannot be had in any other way. The curse in Christian work is that we want to preserve ourselves in God's museum; what God wants is to see where Jesus Christ's men and women are. The saints are always amongst the unofficial crowd, the crowd that is not noticed, and their one dominant note is Jesus Christ. AUG. 66

Notice the disproportion between the modern disease called Christian work and the one characteristic of the fruit of the Spirit. The craze in everyone's blood nowadays is a disease of intemperate work, external activities. AUG. 126

We have to work out what God has worked in, and we have to beware of the snare of blaming God for not doing what we alone can do. BP. 132

Spiritual insight does not so much enable us to understand God as to understand that He is at work in the ordinary things of life, in the ordinary stuff human nature is made of. DI. 15

The work we do for God is made by Him a means till He has got us to the place where we are willing to be purified and made of worth to Himself. DI. 36

The great fever in people's blood to-day is, 'Do something'; 'Be practical'. The great need is for the one who is un-practical enough to get down to the heart of the matter, viz., personal sanctification. Practical work not based on an understanding of what sanctification means is simply beating the air. DI. 59

The curse of much modern Christian work is its determination to preserve itself. DI. 85

Where would you be if God took away all your Christian work? Too often it is our Christian work that is worshipped and not God. DI. 86

It is much easier to do Christian work than to be concentrated on God's point of view. DI. 89

The parable of the talents is our Lord's statement with regard to the danger of leaving undone the work of the lifetime. HG. 30

Have we ever got into the way of letting God work, or are we so amazingly important that we really wonder in our nerves and ways what the Almighty does before we are up in the morning! We are so certain we know what is right, and if we don't always keep at it God cannot get on. IWP. 65

The whole basis of modern Christian work is the great impulsive desire to evade concentration on God. We will work for Him any day rather than let Him work in us. IWP. 66

We slander God by our very eagerness to work for Him without knowing Him. LG. 58

God works in the great incalculable element of our personality; we have to work out what He works in and bring it out into expression in our bodily life. It has not sufficiently entered into us that in our practical life we must do what God says we must do, not try to do it, but *do it*, and the reason we can do it is that it is God Who works in us to will. MFL. 45

The stars do their work without fuss; God does His work without fuss, and saints do their work without fuss. PH. 41

We can never get into touch with God by our own effort; but we must maintain touch with God by our own effort. PR. 123

What are 'dead works'? Everything done apart from God. All prayer, all preaching, all testifying, all kind, sacrificial deeds done apart from God, are dead works that clog the life. PS. 22

It is possible for practical Christian work to be active disobedience to God. We would rather work for God than sit for one moment before Him and let the Spirit riddle us through with His light. RTR. 17

We get the idea that the best thing to do is to hurry over our work in order to get a time alone with God, and when we do get it along that line it is mildewed, not fresh and vigorous, and we feel dissatisfied instead of refreshed. Then sometimes in the midst of our work there suddenly springs up a wonderful well of inner contemplation, which is so full of recreation that we thank God for it, and we don't know how it came. RTR. 22

It is never "Do, do" with the Lord, but "Be, be" and He will "do" *through* you. RTR. 43

It is impossible to get exhausted in work for God; we get exhausted because we try to do God's work in our own way and refuse to do it in dependence on Him. RTR. 74

"Labour". It is the one thing we will not do. We will take open-air meetings, we will preach—but labour at prayer! There is nothing thrilling about a labouring man's work, but it is the labouring man who makes the conceptions of the genius possible; and it is the labouring saint who makes the conceptions of his Master possible. RTR. 77

We are not to ask God to do what He has created us to do, any more than we are to attempt to do what He alone can do. SA. 90

The Bible nowhere teaches us to work for work's sake. That is one of the great bugbears of the anti-Christian movement in the heart of Christianity to-day. It is Work with a capital W in which the worship of Jesus Christ is lost sight of. People will sacrifice themselves endlessly for *the work*. Perspiration is mistaken for inspiration. Our guidance with regard to work is to remember that its value is in what it does for us. SHH. 128

When you deify work, you apostatise from Jesus Christ. In the private spiritual life of many a Christian it is work that has hindered concentration on God. When work is out of its real relation it becomes a means of evading concentration on God. SHH. 129

Thousands of people are 'losing their life' for the sake of a cause; this is perilously wrong because it is so nearly right. Anything that rouses us to act on the line of principles instead of a relationship to a person fosters our natural independence and becomes a barrier to yielding to Jesus Christ. Have we recognized that our body is a temple of the Holy Ghost, or are we jabbering busybodies, so taken up with Christian work that we have no time for the Christ whose work it is, no time for Him in the morning, no time for Him at night, because we are so keen on doing the things that are called by His Name? SHL. 78

We are always in danger of confounding what we can do with what we cannot do. We cannot save ourselves, or sanctify ourselves, or give ourselves the Holy Spirit; only God can do that. Confusion continually occurs when we try to do what God alone can do, and try to persuade ourselves that God will do what we alone can do. SSM. 94

We imagine that God is going to make us walk in the light; God will not; it is we who must walk in the light. God gives us the power to do it, but we have to see that we use the power. God puts the power and the life into us and fills us with His Spirit, but we have to work it out. "Work out your own salvation," says Paul, not, 'work for your salvation,' but '*work it out*'; and as we do, we realise that the noble life of a disciple is gloriously difficult and the difficulty of it rouses us up to overcome, not faint and cave in. It is always necessary to make an effort to be noble. SSM. 95

We deal with the great massive phases of Redemption—that God saves men by sheer grace through the Atonement, but we are apt to forget that it has to be worked out in practical living amongst men. SSH. 95

Salvation is God's 'bit', it is complete, we can add nothing to it; but we have to bend all our powers to work out His salvation. SSM. 96

The danger to-day is to make practical work the driving wheel of our enterprises for God. All the intense social work and aggressive movements of our day are apt to be anti-Christian. They are antagonistic to the sovereignty of the Lord Jesus Christ, because they are based on the conception that human ingenuity is going to bring in the Kingdom of God, and Jesus Christ is made of no account. SSY. 133

WORKER

The first thing a worker has to learn is how to be God's noble man or woman amid a crowd of paltry things. A Christian worker must never make this plea—'If only I were somewhere else!' The only test that a worker is Christ's witness is that he never becomes mean from contact with mean people any more than he becomes sinful from contact with sinful people. AUG. 7

The stamp of the worker gripped by God is that, slowly and surely, one here and another there is being won for God. AUG. 9

To recognize that my Lord counts us faithful removes the last snare of idealizing natural pluck. If we have the idea that we must face the difficulties with pluck, we have never recognized the truth that He has counted us faithful; it is His work in me He is counting worthy, not my work for Him. The truth is we have nothing to fear and nothing to overcome because He is all in all and we are more than conquerors through Him. The recognition of this truth is not flattering to the worker's sense of heroics, but it is amazingly glorifying to the work of Christ. He counts us worthy because He has done everything for us. It is a shameful thing for Christians to talk about 'getting the victory'; by this time the Victor ought to have got us so completely that it is His victory all the time, not ours. AUG. 11

The spiritual life of a worker is literally, 'God manifest in the flesh.' AUG. 15

The Christian worker must be sent; he must not elect to go. AUG. 26

The life God places in the Christian worker is the life of Jesus Christ, which is continually changing spiritual innocence into glorious practical character. AUG. 34

Our confidence is to be based on the fact that it is God who provides the issue in lives; we have to see that we give Him the opportunity of dealing with men by ceasing to be impressive individuals. DI. 84

Be a worker with an equal knowledge of sin, of the human heart, and of God. DI. 84

How many people have you made homesick for God? DI. 85

As a worker, you must know how to link yourself on to the power of God; let the one you are talking to have the best of it for a time, don't try to prove that you are in the right and he is in the wrong. If we battle for a doctrinal position we will see no further spiritually. DI. 86

Never interfere with God's providential dealings with other souls. Be true to God yourself and watch. DI. 86

As workers for God, feed your heart and mind on this truth, that as individuals we are mere iotas in the great purpose of God. Every evangelical 'craze' is an attempt to confine God to our notions, whereas the Holy Spirit constrains us to be what God wants us to be. DI. 86

Never shrink from dealing with any life you are brought up against, but never go unless you are quite sure God wants you to, He will guide. God's permission means there is no shadow of doubt on the horizon of consciousness; when there is, wait. God never guides by fogs or by lightning flashes, He guides naturally. DI. 87

Don't insult God by despising His ordinary ways in your life by saying, 'Those things are beneath me'. God has no special line, anything that is ordinary and human in His line. DI. 87

If my life as a worker is right with God I am not concerned about my public pose—using discreet terms that will impress people; my one concern in public and private is to worship God. DI. 88

When a worker jealously guards his secret life with God the public life will take care of itself. DI. 88

Remember, in estimating other lives there is always one fact more you don't know. You don't know why some men turn to God and others don't, it is hidden in the inscrutable part of a man's nature. DI. 88

If we realize the intense sacredness of a human soul in God's sight we will no longer romp in where angels fear to tread, we will pray and wait. DI. 88

Never talk for the sake of making the other person see you are in the right, talk only that he may see the right, and when he does see it you will be so obliterated that he will forget to say, 'Thank you'. DI. 88

Notice carefully by what you are hurt and see whether it is because you are not being obeyed, or whether it is because the Holy Spirit is not being obeyed. If it is because you are not being obeyed, there is something desperately wrong with you. DI. 88

The last lesson we learn is 'Hands off', that God's hands may be on. DI. 89

As 'workers together with God' we are called upon not to be ignorant of the forces of the day in which we live. God does not alter, the truths of the Bible do not alter, but the problems we have to face do alter. DI. 89

Never give a soul the help God alone should give; hand him right on to God. DI. 89

Keep your mind stayed on God, and I defy anyone's heart to stop at you, it will always go on to God. Our duty is to present God, and never get in the way even in thought. DI. 89

My business as a worker is to see that I am living on the basis of the Atonement in my actual life. DI. 89

The worker whose work tells for God is the one who realizes what God has done in him. GW. 48

When once God's purpose is begun He seems to put His hand on the life and uproot and detach it in every way, and there is darkness and mystery and very often kicking. We can be impertinent to God's providence the moment we choose; there is no punishment, we have simply chosen not to be workers for God in that particular. GW. 125

If I work for God because I know it brings me the good opinion of those whose good opinion I wish to have, I am a Sadducee. HG. 40

The difference between a Christian worker and one who does not know Jesus Christ is just this—that a Christian worker can never meet anyone of whom he can despair. If we do despair of anyone, it is because we have never met Jesus Christ ourselves. HG. 44

The thing that makes our hearts fail is the profound disbelief on the part of Christian workers that God has done anything, and the wearing out of life to do what is already done. All the fuss and energy and work that goes on if we are not believing in Jesus Christ and His Redemption, has not a touch of the almighty power of God about it; it is a panic of unbelief veneered over with Christian phrases. HG. 104

So many of us put prayer and work and consecration in place of the working of God; we make ourselves the workers. God is the Worker, we work out what He works in. IWP. 63

We are not here to do work *for* God, we are here to be workers *with* Him, those through whom He can do His work. NKW. 137

So many of us put prayer and consecration in place of God's work; we make ourselves the workers. God is the Worker, and He is after spirituality. God does nothing other than the profound; we have to do the practical. OBH. 132

If you become a necessity to a soul you have got out of God's order, your great need as a worker is to be a friend of the Bridegroom. Your goodness and purity ought never to attact attention to itself, it ought simply to be a magnet to draw others to Jesus; if it does not draw them to Him it is not holiness of the right order, it is an influence which will awaken inordinate affection and lead souls off into side issues. PH. 21

The saint must become like his Master, utterly unobtrusive. For "we preach not ourselves, but Christ Jesus as Lord; and ourselves as your servants for Jesus' sake." If you are serving men for their sakes you will soon have the heart knocked out of you; but if you are personally and passionately devoted to the Lord Jesus Christ, then you can spend yourselves to the last ebb because your motive is love to the Lord. PH. 134

If we do only what we are inclined to do, some of us would do nothing for ever and ever! There are unemployables in the spiritual domain, spiritually decrepit people, who refuse to do anything unless they are supernaturally inspired.

The proof that we are rightly related to God is that we do our best whether we feel inspired or not. RTR. 79

A great many Christian workers worship their work. The one concern of the workers should be concentration on God, and this will mean that all other margins of life are free with the freedom of a child—a worshipping child, not a wayward child. RTR. 79

It is an interesting study in psychology to watch people who are engaged in drastic social and rescue work and find out whether they are doing it for a surcease from their own troubles, to get relief from a broken heart. In a great many cases the worker wants a plaster for his own life. He takes up slum work, not because it is the great passion of his life, but because he must get something to deliver him from the gnawing pain of his own heart. The people he works amongst are often right when they say he is doing it to save his own soul. SHH. 47

WORLD

When the world comes before us with its fascination and its power, it finds us dead to it, if we have agreed with God on His judgement about sin and the world. AUG. 102

What is the world? The set of people with the ambitions, religious or otherwise, that are not identified with the Lord Jesus Christ. AUG. 102

To love the world as it is is the wrong kind of love, it is that sentiment which is 'the enemy of God', because it means I am the friend of the system of things which does not take God into account. We are to love the world in the way God loves it, and be ready to spend and be spent until the wrong and evil are removed from it. BE. 33

No man is capable of solving the riddle of the universe because the universe is mad, and the only thing that will put it right is not man's reason, but the sagacity of God which is manifested in the Redemption of Jesus Christ. BFB. 38

The world as God originally designed it, was the best of all possible worlds, but it has now become the worst of all possible worlds; in fact, the Bible reveals that it could not be any worse than it is. Individual men who take the wrong line get worse, but the world itself cannot get worse. BFB. 40

The Cross of Calvary and the Redemption have to do with the sins of the world. If God began to punish the nations for their sins there would be no nation left on the face of the earth. BFB. 81

The order and beauty of this world were created by God for man. BP. 5

There ought to be in us a holy scorn whenever it comes to being dictated to by the spirit of the age in which we live. The age in which we live is governed by the prince of this world who hates Jesus Christ. His great doctrine is self-realization. BP. 39

The world means what it says, but it cannot impart. Our Lord imparts what He says, He does not give like the world does. CD. VOL. 1, 152

The world pays no attention to those who tell them how God convicted of sin and how He delivered them; the warnings of God are of no use to sinners until they are convicted of sin and the warnings become applicable to them. CHI. 67

God so loves the world that He hates the wrong in it. CHI. 69

As men and women we have to live in this world, in its misery and sinfulness, and we must do the same if we are disciples. CHI. 127

Beware of the temptation to compromise with the world, to put their interests, their needs, first—'They have kindly become interested in our Christian work, given so much time to it, now let us winsomely draw them in'— they will winsomely draw you away from God. DI. 85

God is not saving the world; it is done, our business is to get men and women to realize it, and we cannot do it unless we realize it ourselves. HG. 104

Jesus Christ does not make monks and nuns, He makes men and women fit for the world as it is. IYA. 56

In the New Testament 'world' means the system of things which has been built on God's earth, the system of religion or of society or of civilization that never takes Jesus Christ into account. Jesus says we are to be the light there. LG. 44

The world is glad of an excuse not to listen to the Gospel message, and the inconsistencies of Christians is made the excuse. LG. 94

Jesus Christ's outward life was densely immersed in the things of the world, yet He was inwardly disconnected; the one irresistible purpose of His life was to do the will of His Father. MFL. 30

Jesus warns the disciple never to be afraid of the contempt of the world when he possesses spiritual discernment. Those who are in the heavenly places see God's counsels in what to the wisdom of the world is arrogant stupidity. OBH. 25

The Holy Spirit severs human connections and makes connections which are universal—a complete union of men and women all over the world in a bond in which there is no snare. God's call is for *the world*; the question of location is a matter of the engineering of God's providence. PH. 38

When the Spirit of God comes into a man, He gives him a world-wide outlook. God has no favourites. PH. 81

The world is that system of things which organises its life without any thought of Jesus Christ. PR. 105

In the New Testament, "world" means the system of things which has been built on God's earth, the system of religion or of society or of civilization that never takes Jesus Christ into account. RTR. 84

The powers that press from the natural world have one tendency, and one only, to deaden all communication with God. SHL. 25

. . . there is a division as high as heaven and as deep as hell between the Christian and the world. "Whosoever therefore will be a friend of the world is the enemy of God." SSM. 64

WORLDLINESS

If a worldling is not a worldling at heart, he is miserable; and if a Christian is not a Christian at heart he carries his Christianity like a headache instead of something worth having, and not being able to get rid of his head, he cannot get rid of his headache. BE. 33

When a worldly person who is happy, moral and upright comes in contact with Jesus Christ, Who came to destroy all that happiness and peace and put it on a different level, he has to be persuaded that Jesus Christ is a Being worthy to do this, and instead of the Gospel being attractive at first, it is the opposite. BP. 80

One of the most misleading statements is that worldlings have not a happy time; they have a thoroughly happy time. The point is that their happiness is on the wrong level, and when they come across Jesus Christ, Who is the enemy of all that happiness, they experience annoyance. BP. 80

The worldling is annoyed at the worker because the worker is always dealing with a crisis that he does not see and does not want to see. No matter what he touches on, the worker always comes back to the claim of God, and the worldling gets annoyed at this. The man of the world analyses the easy parts of life and tells you that these are all quite obvious, all the practical outcomes of life are within his reach; but when the worker begins to touch on God's message he says, 'That is nonsense, you are up in the clouds and unpractical'. That is why the worker's voice is always an annoyance to the worldling. LG. 93

We preach to men as if they were conscious they were dying sinners, they are not; they are having a good time, and our talk about being born from above is in a domain they know nothing of. SHL. 40

Never have the idea that a worldling is unhappy, a worldling is perfectly happy, as thoroughly happy as a Christian. The persons who are unhappy are the worldlings or the Christians if they are not at one with the principle that binds them. SHL. 44

In the midst of the success of worldliness we get an outburst of spiritualism, of supernaturalism, fire called down from heaven by the authority of the devil, and all kinds of signs and wonders whereby people say, 'Lo, here is Christ.' Jesus said, 'The kingdom of God cometh not with observation.' SHL. 96

WORRY

The one great crime on the part of a disciple, according to Jesus Christ, is worry. Whenever we begin to calculate without God we commit sin.
CD. VOL. 1, 110

The clearest evidence that God's grace is at work in our hearts is that we do not get into panics. CD. VOL. 1, 111

The child of God can never think of anything the Heavenly Father will forget; then to worry is spiritual irritability with our Lord. CD. VOL. 2, 15

The secret of Christian quietness is not indifference, but the knowledge that God is my Father, He loves me, I shall never think of anything He will forget, and worry becomes an impossibility. IYA. 14

"In every thing give thanks." Never let anything push you to your wits' end, because you will get worried, and worry makes you self-interested and disturbs the nourishment of the life of God. Give thanks to God that *He* is there, no matter what is happening. IYA. 14

Suppose that God is the God we know Him to be when we are nearest to Him, what an impertinence worry is! LG. 150

When once we realize that we can never think of anything our Father will forget, worry becomes impossible. Beware of getting into a panic. Panic is bad for the natural heart, and it is destructive to the spiritual life. "*Let not* your heart be troubled"—it is a command. OBH. 122

A great point is reached spiritually when we stop worrying God over personal matters or over any matter. God expects of us the one thing that glorifies Him—and that is to remain absolutely confident in Him, remembering what He has said beforehand, and sure that His purposes will be fulfilled. PH. 40

The saint recognises in all the ordinary circumstances of his life the hand of God and the rule of God, and Jesus says we cannot do that unless we are born from above. In the beginning we only discern the rule of God in exceptional things, in crises like a friendship, or marriage, or death, but that is an elementary stage. As we go on we learn to see God's rule in all the ordinary haphazard circumstances of a commonsense life, and to say, 'I shall never think of anything my Heavenly Father will forget, then why should I worry?' Are we irritable and worried? Then do not let us say we are born from above, because if what Jesus says is true, how can we worry? Worry means one of two things—private sin, or the absence of new birth. PR. 33

It is easy to trust in God when we have not to hunt for money, but immediately the penny that is not there looms large, we allow the mosquito of worry to irritate our whole life away from rest in God. RTR. 10

To be continually worrying—"Does God want me to say this or do that?" is to be in an infirm condition. There is no light of the knowledge of the glory of God in that, it means I am a self-conscious spiritual prig. RTR. 18

God cannot trust us with His unsearchable riches if we are not faithful in the least things. "The cares of this world" will make us put the least things as the most important. RTR. 27

Don't be disturbed today by thoughts about tomorrow; leave tomorrow alone, and bank in confidence on God's organizing of what you do not see. RTR. 34

Worry is nothing in the world but personal irritation with God because I cannot see what He is after—only I don't call it that, I talk about "an overwhelming burden of care". RTR. 63

Have you ever noticed what Jesus said would choke the word He puts in? The devil? No, the cares of this world. It is the little worries always. I will not trust where I cannot see, that is where infidelity begins. The only cure for infidelity is obedience to the Spirit. RTR. 90

Put all "supposing" on one side and dwell in the shadow of the Almighty. Deliberately tell God that you will not fret about that thing. All our fret and worry is caused by calculating without God. RTR. 91

WORSHIP

Worship is giving to God the best He has given us, and He makes it His and ours for ever. AUG. 88

Worship is giving the best we have unreservedly to God. IWP. 79

Rush is always wrong; there is plenty of time to worship God. There are not three stages—worship, waiting and work; some of us go in jumps like spiritual frogs, we jump from worship to waiting and from waiting to work. God's idea is that the three should go together; they were always together in the life of Our Lord, He was unhasting and unresting. It is a discipline, we cannot get there all at once. NKW. 19

All natural religion reaches its climax in ritual, in the beauties of aesthetic and sensuous worship. God's altar is discerned only by the Holy Spirit when that Spirit is in a man. PH. 16

The spiritual order of Jesus Christ in my life is that I take what God has given me and give it back to Him; that is the essence of worship. PH. 193

Worship is the love offering of our keen sense of the worth-ship of God. True worship springs from the same source as the missionary himself. To worship God truly is to become a missionary, because our worship is a testimony to Him. It is presenting back to God the best He has given to us, publicly not privately. Every act of worship is a public testimony, and is at once the most personally sacred and the most public act that God demands of His faithful ones. SSY. 149

To worship God 'in the spirit' is not to worship Him sincerely, in the remote part of our nature; but to worship Him by the power of the Spirit He gives to us. SSY. 170

Worship is the tryst of sacramental identification with God; we deliberately give back to God the best He has given us that we may be identified with Him in it. ssy. 171

WRATH

When we speak of the wrath of God we must not picture Him as an angry sultan on the throne of heaven, bringing a lash about people when they do what He does not want. There is no element of personal vindicativeness in God. CHI. 67

The love of God and the wrath of God are obverse sides of the same thing. If we are morally rightly related to God we see His love side, but if we reverse the order and get out of touch with God, we come to a place where we find everything is based on wrath—not that God is angry, like a Moloch, but wrath is inevitable; we cannot get out of it. SHL. 90

Y

YIELDING

The Spirit of God is everywhere, would that men would yield to Him! The reason we do not yield is that in the deep recesses of our hearts we prefer the captaincy of our own lives, we prefer to go our own way and refuse to let God govern. BE. 101

A yielded life to God becomes a doormat for men. He leaves us here to be trampled on. GW. 29

Woe be to you, if, when Jesus has asked us to yield to Him, you refuse; but be sure it is Jesus Christ to Whom you yield, and His demands are tremendous. MFL. 23

"Won't you yield to Jesus? He has done so much for you"—to talk in that way is an insult to God and a crime against human nature. It is the presentation of an overplus of human sentiment smeared over with religious jargon. RTR. 72

YOKE

We ought to be free from the dominion of the prince of this world; only one yoke should be upon our shoulders, the yoke of the Lord Jesus. BP. 39

The Spirit of God in you will not allow you to bow your neck to any yoke but the yoke of the Lord Jesus Christ. When you stand on this platform of God's grace, you see instantly that the bond-age is in the world. The etiquette and standards of the world are an absolute bondage, and those who live in them are abject slaves, and yet the extraordinary thing is that when a worldly person sees anyone emancipated and under the yoke of the Lord Jesus Christ, he says they are in bondage, whereas exactly the opposite is true. BP. 63

Indignation towards every yoke but the yoke of Christ is the only attitude for the saint. PH. 73

"Take My yoke upon you, and learn of Me." It seems amazingly difficult to put on the yoke of Christ, but immediately we do put it on, everything becomes easy. SSM. 97

YOUTH

A young Christian is remarkably full of impulse and delight, because he realizes the salvation of God; but this is the real gaiety of knowing that we may cast all our cares on Him and that He careth for us. This is the greatest indication of our identification with Jesus Christ. AUG. 90

A boy or girl just emerging from the 'teens' is always chaotic; if a young life is normal it is a chunk of chaos; if it is not, there is something wrong, there ought to be the chaotic element. BE. 19

'Don't try to make up for your youth by dogmatism and talk, but see that you walk in such a manner that you are an example to the believers'. No really

392

wise, liberal-minded person ever needs to say, 'Remember how old I am'. BFB. 55

When a young life is trying to express itself, it experiences exquisite suffering; music is run to, theatres are run to, literature is run to—anything to try and get the power to express what is there in longing; and if a life goes on too long on these lines, it will never form a responsible intelligence, but will become most unpractical. The discipline of the machinery of life enables us to get the power to express what is in us. BP. 245

One of the greatest benefits when a young life is trying to express itself is to have something to work at with the hands, to model in wax, to paint, or write, or dig, anything that will give an opportunity of expression. BP. 246

Young life must be in chaos or there is no development possible. DI. 80

The characteristic of young men and women of to-day is an affected tiredness of everything, nothing interests them. MFL. 60

When a young life passes from early childhood into girlhood or boyhood, there is a new birth of the mind, and the boy or girl becomes interested in literature, in poetry, and usually in religion; but that is not spiritual new birth, and has nothing to do with the working of the Spirit of God; it has to do with the ordinary natural development of the life. At this stage great devotion to God and to Christian service may be manifested, and this is apt to be looked on as an evidence of the work of the Spirit of God, whereas it is the mere outcome of

the natural life beginning to unfold itself in the process of development. These things always go together—physical development, an alteration in bodily organs, and mental, moral, and spiritual development. The boy or girl sees more purely and clearly than the man or woman. No man thinks so clearly at any time or is ever so thrilled as he is in his 'teens.' PR. 38

The young man who cannot enjoy himself is no good, he has a sinister attitude to life. The man who can enjoy himself is not pretending to be what he is not. SHH. 147

YOUTH AND AGE

The Hebrews regarded life as complete when it was full of days and riches and honour. Age was looked upon as a sign of favour. Whenever a nation becomes unspiritual, it reverses this order, the demand is not for old age but for youth. This reversal in the modern life of to-day is indicative of apostasy, not of advance. NKW. 149

The mature saint is just like a little child, absolutely simple and joyful and gay. Go on living the life that God would have you live and you will grow younger instead of older. PR. 47

Spiritually we never grow old; through the passing of the years we grow so many years young. The characteristic of the spiritual life is its unageing youth, exactly the opposite of the natural life. PR. 47

Youth is youth and age is age, and we have no business to require the head of age on the shoulders of youth. SHH. 147

Z

ZEAL

The reason you are not so zealous for the glory of God as you used to be, not so keen about the habits of your spiritual life, is because you have imperceptibly begun to surrender morally. PH. 46

Zeal to serve God may be, and very often is, an insistence on God's proving that I am right. RTR. 49

Index